The Constitution Under Siege

The Constitution Under Siege

Presidential Power versus the Rule of Law

Christopher H. Pyle

Richard M. Pious

Carolina Academic Press

Durham, North Carolina

The first edition of this book was published by the Free Press in 1984 as *The President, Congress, and the Constitution.*

Library of Congress Cataloging-in-Publication Data

Pyle, Christopher H.
  The constitution under siege : presidential power versus the rule of law / Christopher H. Pyle and Richard M. Pious.
    p. cm.
  Includes bibliographical references and index.
  ISBN 978-1-59460-877-3 (alk. paper)
  1. Separation of powers--United States. 2. War and emergency powers--United States. 3. Terrorism--Prevention--Law and legislation--United States. 4. Executive power--United States. 5. Constitutional law--United States. I. Pious, Richard M., 1944- II. Title.

  KF4565.P95 2010
  342.73'044--dc22   2010015174

Carolina Academic Press
700 Kent Street
Durham, North Carolina 27701
Telephone (919) 489-7486
Fax (919) 493-5668
www.cap-press.com

Printed in the United States of America

Contents

Preface

For most teachers of American politics and constitutional law, this is a new kind of book, not radically new, but sufficiently different to warrant an explanation of its purposes and format.

Political scientists should find it a useful addition to courses on the presidency, Congress, and the courts. By focusing on the legitimacy of power as well as the conditions of its exercise, these materials should counterbalance a literature that currently emphasizes amoral aspects of political behavior and the policy-making process. This volume can be used either as a core or supplementary text in courses that focus on the Constitution, the presidency, Congress, or American political thought.

This book will also introduce students of politics to the intellectual challenges of the Socratic method of teaching as it is practiced in American law schools. It is not a "reader" of illustrative articles poised in sham debate; it is a collection of cases, materials, notes, questions, and original essays designed to force students to join issue and take sides on some of the most profound controversies of our times.

Teachers of constitutional law at both the undergraduate and graduate levels will find that this book differs in several respects from most casebooks currently in use. First, it abjures the "illustrative case" method of many undergraduate casebooks, in which a single court opinion is put forth as if to represent all that is worth knowing about a constitutional theory of power. Second, unlike many law school casebooks, it does not let the vagaries of litigation determine the classroom agenda. What the courts have said about the Constitution is important and is covered, but it is not always the starting point for analysis. Constitutional interpretation should be more than the matching of cases, the making of deductions, or the connection of intellectual dots into doctrines. It should be an adventure in rethinking the basic premises of our political order. We should study constitutional doctrines not just to bring predictability to what judges do in courtrooms, but to refine the operative political thought of the Republic. Over this enterprise, judges and lawyers can have no monopoly.

Accordingly, this book contains not only the opinions of judges, but the ideas of philosophers, historians, political scientists, and law professors. These are juxtaposed to the assertions of politicians and the pleadings of their legal counsel. The materials span the entire course of American political development, from Magna Carta to the Bush and Obama administrations, but the issues are timeless. By viewing contemporary claims to power in historical perspective, students should come to discover something of their future in the nation's past. They should also come to understand history as more than a story to be appreciated for its own sake. They should see it as a weapon of analysis and persuasion that can be used, and is now being used, for both good and evil ends. So armed, students might even come in time to improve the intellectual and moral quality of American political debate.

Acknowledgments

Christopher Pyle gratefully acknowledges the assistance of Julie Arons Auster, Willa Perlmutter, and Denise Vingiello, who helped with the initial research for this book, and Miriam Musgrave, Katherine Kozub, Anne Chisholm, and Sarah James, who brought the first edition to fruition. He also appreciates the assistance of Ralitsa Donkova, Mickey Rathbun, Joan Davis, and James Gehrt in preparing the second edition.

Richard Pious extends his special thanks to Rose Ho, Miriam Feldblum, Sharon Epstein, and Patricia Dooley for their labors in the labyrinths of the Columbia University libraries.

Both authors thank Professor Jeffrey Tulis, now of the University of Texas, for his excellent suggestions regarding the first edition of this book, and Louis Fisher of the Library of Congress for his outstanding contributions, both scholarly and practically, to the field. The authors are also grateful to their students at Mount Holyoke College, Barnard College, and the Graduate Faculties of Columbia University, on whom these materials were first inflicted.

Finally, the authors acknowledge Charles Livingston Bull, artist of the World War I recruiting poster that was adapted for the cover with the help of Maureen Scanlon.

Permissions

The authors gratefully acknowledge permission to reprint the following materials:

Excerpts from Louis Fisher, *President and Congress*, The Free Press, 1972. Copyright © 1972 by The Free Press, A Division of Macmillan Publishing Co., Inc.

Excerpts from Arthur S. Miller, "The Constitutional Revolution Consolidated: The Rise of the Positive State," *George Washington Law Review* 35:2, December 1966, 172–184. Reprinted with permission of the author.

Edward S. Corwin, "Our Constitutional Revolution," *Pennsylvania Bar Association Quarterly* 19, April 1948, 261–284.

Richard M. Nixon, "The National Security Power," *The New York Times*, May 20, 1977, p. B10. Copyright © 1977 by The New York Times Company.

Excerpts from Clinton L. Rossiter, *Constitutional Dictatorship: Crisis Government in the Modern Democracies*. Copyright 1948, © renewed by Princeton University Press.

Ronald Goldfarb, "The Permanent State of Emergency," *The Washington Post*, January 6, 1974, p. B1. Reprinted with permission of the author.

Excerpts from Barry Goldwater, "Treaty Termination Is a Shared Power," *American Bar Association Journal* 65, February 1979, 198–200.

Excerpts from Edward Kennedy, "Normal Relations with China: Good Law, Good Policy," *Policy Review*, Spring 1979, 126–131.

Introduction

*The United States is, as G. K. Chesterton said, "a nation with the soul of a church."…
The Declaration and the Constitution constitute the holy scripture of the American
civil religion.*

—Samuel P. Huntington,
American Politics (1981)

*It is ironic that a culture which has experienced a centuries-long "melancholy, long-
withdrawing roar" from religious faith can believe so blithely in the continuing reality of citizens organized around a constitutional faith. The "death of
constitutionalism" may be the central event of our time just as the "death of God"
was that of the past century.*

—Sanford Levinson,
"The Constitution in American Civil Religion,"
Supreme Court Review (1979)

A. Focus: The Legitimacy of Claims to Power

This is a book about principles, politics, and power—constitutional principles and
how they affect the power of the president, Congress, and the courts to decide some of
the most momentous issues of our time.

The cases and materials examined here address fundamental questions about the authority of presidents, the armed forces, and intelligence agencies to wage clandestine wars,
detain people without trial, operate secret prisons, suspend habeas corpus, torture prisoners, and assassinate citizens as well as foreigners, in secret and without accountability.
At stake is nothing less than who we are, or wish to be, as a nation.

Contrary to the dominant thrust of most writing about American politics since the
1930s, this book focuses not on the short-term acquisition and exercise of political power,
but on the *legitimacy* of claims to power that would fundamentally alter the constitutional distribution of policy-making authority. It is based on the pedagogically useful,
but increasingly questionable assumption that the United States still has a Constitution
of Limitations as well as a Constitution of Powers despite contrary evidence from the Watergate, Iran-Contra, and Torture scandals.

The book starts with "first principles"—limited government, guaranteed liberties,
separation of powers, checks and balances, popular sovereignty, representative government, and the rule of law—and explores how these principles have fared in the constitutional confrontations among the branches of government since the Puritan Revolution.

The book attempts to show how these principles often clash with one another and how accommodations have evolved among them and between the different branches. The objective is to give students the ability to see the long-term implications of particular distributions of power and authority, discern the tactical uses to which constitutional arguments are often put, and appreciate how easily the politics of fear can debase American government when the rule of law is disregarded.

B. The Justification of Power

The chief business of political science, from Woodrow Wilson's time to our own, has been to *describe* and *explain* the distribution of political power and to answer the question "Who gets (and doesn't get) what, when, why, and how?" In this behavioral analysis of politics there has often been an implicit judgment that the existing allocation is good or bad, usually in terms of some immediate policy objective the political scientist has in mind.

The chief business of political theory, from Plato's time to our own, has been to *justify* and *prescribe* particular allocations of power, usually in terms of some long-term conception of the right and the good. However, since the rise of behavioral political science, the study of political theory has been reduced to the study of a few great thinkers, rather than the analysis of the long-term implications of particular changes in the allocation of power in existing political systems.

Thus, the business of justifying and prescribing changes in the long-term allocation of power has been left chiefly to politicians, lawyers, and judges—professionals poorly trained to do it. Trained or not, these professionals practice political theory, day in and day out. Often the theoretical implications of their arguments and actions are not immediately appreciated. Even when they are, their significance maybe denied for the sake of short-term gains.

Acknowledged or not, there are theoretical dimensions to structural changes in the allocation of power. These dimensions become apparent each time someone contends that a particular allocation is not only useful, but legitimate. Then the proponent is no longer talking just about power; he is talking about authority.

The distinction between raw power and legitimate authority marks the line between most behavioral scientists and constitutional lawyers, between most lawyers and the philosophers of law, and between most politicians and statesmen. However, to talk about legitimate authority presupposes that there are ways to allocate and limit political power that will be conducive, in the long term, to some fundamental values, such as liberty, equality, or justice. It also presupposes that a consensus can be reached regarding these fundamental values. Where people take little interest in history, the comparative study of governments, political theory, or philosophy, finding such a consensus can be difficult.

In the American political system, however, something very much like a consensus regarding the proper allocation of power is continually being formed and re-formed. We refer, of course, to constitutional law. Unlike the public law of most regimes, American constitutional law does not depend upon a consensus of contemporary officials or public opinion. The process by which it is made and the obstacles that prevent its easy alteration require a consensus within the major political coalitions that span decades, if not centuries. To achieve this consensus, the living must not only speak to the living; they must commune with the dead.

The language of this debate is not simply the language of interests; it is also the language of principles. It is the language of justification. The entire system of means and ends cannot be altered overnight, so the debate is rarely between one comprehensive philosophy and another. Rather, it is many smaller debates among many partial philosophies, most of which have been debated before under historical circumstances that were both similar and different. The records of those debates are much more than the writings of interesting thinkers; they are often law. As such, they are difficult to ignore.

Most difficult to ignore is an unambiguous provision of the Constitution, the supreme law of the land. But unambiguous provisions in that document are relatively rare. Most of the constitutional provisions purporting to grant, allocate, or limit authority are open to interpretation. Thus it becomes important to decide which methods of reading the Constitution are legitimate. When the provisions are ambiguous, some resort to the underlying rationale—the political theory of the Constitution—becomes both necessary and proper. This can be done in a variety of ways, running the gamut from the strictest to the loosest mode of construction. What follows is a brief inventory of the principal modes of constitutional interpretation—modes which can be separated for analytical purposes but which, in "real life," almost always appear in combination.[1]

1. Textual analysis. Textual analysis focuses on the meaning of the Constitution's words and phrases. Chief Justice Marshall was a master of this technique, using "commonsense" synonyms to transform ambiguous passages into great doctrines of law. If "common sense" fails to produce the "plain meaning" of a clause, resort may be made to dictionaries or other writings (especially law treatises) to determine what the words "must" have meant to the ratifiers or to educated men of their day. Thus, to understand the powers of the president as "commander in chief," a textualist might seek to determine how the British and colonial forces used that term in the seventeenth and eighteenth centuries.

When a document is young, textual analysis can be used as Marshall used it, to greatly expand its scope and force. However, as interpretations accumulate, this technique is more likely to be employed, particularly by legal positivists and the proponents of judicial self-restraint, to produce a narrow, restrictive meaning, or to divert attention away from other provisions of the Constitution that might undermine the interpretation sought.

2. Contextual analysis. Textual analysis, therefore, is usually answered with, or supplemented by, a contextual analysis that reads particular clauses in the context of the larger document, the theories alleged to be implicit in it, or the objectives its framers "must" have sought to achieve. Thus, a contextualist would insist that the president's powers as "commander in chief" cannot be understood without reference to the Constitution's larger scheme for allocating power over the declaration and making of war, the arming of forces, and the control of expenditures.

3. Framers' intent. Another, related form of analysis is to attempt to plumb the meaning of a clause by a search for the "intent" of those who drafted, voted for, or ratified the provision. This is commonly done by searching the records of the Constitutional Convention, the state ratifying conventions, and contemporary expositions, such as *The Federalist Papers*. Intent can also be inferred from the evils the framers (or the preceding generation of revolutionaries) sought to remedy or the values and theories they inherited or espoused. A practitioner of this approach to constitutional analysis would interpret the commander-in-chief clause in light of the founders' revulsion against the English

---

1. For an extended and still classic exposition on how to read a constitution, see Joseph Story, *Commentaries on the Constitution of the United States* (5th ed., 1905), Chap. 5, 304–49.

system of executive warmaking, particularly as expressed by Hamilton's assertion in *The Federalist Papers* that the commander in chief was not intended to be anything more than "first general" and "first admiral."

Determination of the collective intent of fifty-five delegates to the Constitutional Convention (or hundreds of delegates to the state ratifying conventions) rarely can be done with anything approaching statistical certainty. Evidence of framers' intent, therefore, has its greatest force when it demonstrates which ideas the founders rejected and why, or when it reveals persuasive arguments for reading an idea into the document or keeping it there.

4. Precedent and synthesis. Because the Constitution is part of a legal system in which consistency is achieved by following the doctrine of *stare decisis* (adhering to the rationale of previous decisions), prior judicial interpretations of the document have great force. Lower court judges, in particular, are under a powerful obligation to carry out the reasoning of the Supreme Court, even when they consider it mistaken. Supreme Court justices, on the other hand, are not so strictly bound. The cases they get are the ones for which no hard-and-fast precedent exists, or in which a choice can be made between several conflicting lines of cases. In these situations, the justices are often forced to look behind the language of prior opinions for the unarticulated premises and, by examining them, come up with a rearticulation of the governing principle. Constitutional interpretation is therefore not simply an exercise in making deductions from major premises; it is a continual effort to refine those premises and the political theory they contain.

This effort can focus narrowly, and rather mechanically, on a few clear-cut precedents and the factual situations they contain, or it can range more broadly in search of a "neutral principle" that will "solve" all past, current, and imaginable cognate cases. Proponents of the "neutral principle" approach argue that it is the only "legitimate" one, on the grounds that the doctrines it produces are likely to offer the most intellectual satisfaction, be the most intellectually defensible, and therefore be the most lasting.

5. Constitutional policy making. Finally, for lack of a better term, there is an approach— or a range of approaches—that can be called constitutional policy making, not because the foregoing techniques do not involve policy making, but because they are further removed from the standard techniques of non-constitutional legal analysis. They are less closely tied to text, dictionaries, treatises, and precedent, and hence are more obviously innovative. They start from Chief Justice John Marshall's premise that "it is a *constitution* we are expounding."[2] Constitutions, particularly short ones like ours, are not meant to be so narrowly construed that they become frozen in time, susceptible to change only through the difficult amendment process. The framers themselves, it is frequently said, intended and invited broad judicial interpretation by using such ambiguous language in the first place. Faced with imprecise terms like "commander in chief," "executive power," and "war," judges have no choice—unless they abstain from decision—but to go beyond the document for help.

Whether their interpretations are deemed legitimate, therefore, often depends on judgments regarding the scope of this search for outside assistance. Despite protestations to the contrary, most constitutional interpreters concede that the Constitution should be read with a view toward "making the venture succeed." Their disagreement, which can be substantial, is over the nature and objectives of that constitutional venture. Proponents of "natural rights," for example, argue that the nature of the venture is best stated

---

2. *McCulloch v. Maryland*, 170 U.S. (4 Wheat) 316, 407 (1819).

in the Declaration of Independence and the priority it places on liberty. Others stress the importance of a "common defense," on the theory that "the Constitution is not a suicide pact" and that all governments have a "natural right" of self-preservation. Accordingly, where some find "inherent rights" and "inherent limitations" on government, others find "inherent powers" to act in ways that may limit liberty.

There is also controversy over the way in which judges attempt to make the venture succeed. To some "minimalists," like Justice Ruth Bader Ginsberg, it is important for judges to go slowly, deciding difficult questions on a case-by-case basis, and resisting the temptation to announce broad principles. Critics have called this "ad hoc" utilitarianism, full of expediency and devoid of principle. Others have attempted, in the manner of Immanuel Kant, to articulate certain "categorical imperatives"—unchanging universal principles against which all governmental conduct can be measured with great certainty. Practitioners of this approach are often called absolutists and are accused of elevating a few moral principles (such as freedom of expression) over all other values, including national survival. Finally, there is a wide variety of policy-oriented balancers who seek to find a middle ground by rearticulating doctrines over and over again. For lack of a better term, most of these adaptors can be characterized as rule utilitarians.

There is also great controversy over which values the judges should keep uppermost in their minds. Many people believe that legal systems must be judged, like political systems, by the policies and practices produced. They are likely to take an activist approach to constitutional interpretation. Others see the court's role primarily as procedural, and judge the legitimacy of what it does primarily in terms of how well it protects guaranteed liberties, particularly those of underrepresented people, while allowing most issues, including issues of economics, war, and diplomacy, to be worked out largely through the normal processes of partisan politics. Still others try, in different ways, to judge the legitimacy of constitutional interpretations in terms of both the ends of government and the means of adjudication.

6. Abstention. Finally, judges have one other way to affect the struggle for political power, and that is by deciding not to decide. Judges have many ways to duck constitutional cases. They can find that the party raising the claim lacks legal "standing" to do so, that the case is not ripe for adjudication, or has been rendered moot by the passage of time or the concessions of officials. Or judges can declare the issue non-justiciable on the ground that it raises a "political question" that is not for judges to decide.

Decisions not to decide are not without political consequence. Technically, they do not alter legal doctrine; as a practical matter, they give a green light to public officials to go on doing what they have been doing, even if they violate obvious principles of law and justice. The legitimacy of these abstentions is thus also part of the legitimacy debate.

Each of the foregoing approaches to giving meaning to the Constitution, and hence to defining the operative political theory of the Republic, has been used extensively, usually in combination with others. Enthusiasm for certain approaches over others often has less to do with their intrinsic merits than with the substantive outcomes they are likely to produce.

No abstract formula has ever been devised that will predict which line of justification is most likely to produce the most "legitimate" constitutional interpretation. The very concept of legitimacy is itself ambiguous. To philosophers and jurisprudes (the philosophers of law), legitimacy connotes a form of intellectual respectability. To most lawyers and judges, however, it is enough that an interpretation is consistent with precedent and with the forms and processes of law. To most political scientists (for whom democracy, judicial independence, or social stability are supreme values), the important thing is that the interpretation (and the interpreters) are politically acceptable (or tolerable) to the dominant political groups in the society.

However, persons with a strong sense of justice and decency are likely to demand more. Indeed, they may care less for intellectual respectability, form, and process, or popularity, than they care that a particular outcome will actually enhance the enjoyment of a particular value they prize, such as liberty, equality, political participation, or the accountability of officials.

Each concept of legitimacy has merit. Most judgments about the legitimacy of a particular constitutional interpretation are amalgams of several. Consistent application of these tests of legitimacy is rare, and in the long run probably impossible. In nearly everyone's calculus, some values outweigh others and some ends are important enough to justify less than perfect means. Also, what may be a legitimate form of constitutional exigesis for working out the powers of contending branches of government, between which political power continually ebbs and flows, may be inappropriate to the task of defining a fundamental right of individuals.

Thus, to decide what constitutes a legitimate exercise of power by any branch of government is not an easy task. However, it is an obligation of citizenship that we evade at our peril. What John Marshall said of judges applies equally to us all: "With whatever doubts, with whatever difficulties.... we must decide.... Questions may occur which we would gladly avoid; but we cannot avoid them. All we can do is, to exercise our best judgment, and conscientiously to perform our duty."[3]

C. A Note on Studying Cases

This book, like most casebooks, is designed for Socratic-method teaching. This method, derived from dialogues attributed to the ancient Greek philosopher Socrates, presupposes that one mark of a truly intelligent person is the ability to ask incisive questions. Accordingly, Socratic-method teachers do little lecturing and much questioning. Often, students' questions are answered with still more questions, because the primary objective of the classroom dialogue is not to produce the "right" answer but to develop defensible modes of inquiry. The questions are based on cases and materials that have been selected and arranged so as to bring out the clash of ideas, interests, and values and to encourage students to find their own answers and their own modes of inquiry by continually questioning not only the logic of the writings, but the assumptions implicit in those writings.

The "case method" of teaching issues of law and politics relies heavily on collections of judicial opinions—usually by appellate courts. There is no one best way to get the most out of cases, but the following advice may help. It involves three steps: briefing, syndicating, and synthesizing.

Briefing. "Briefing" is the process of preparing summaries of specific cases. (The term "brief" also refers to the written argument that a lawyer submits to a court, usually prior to oral argument.) Student briefs can be extensive or short, depending on the nature of the case involved and the depth of classroom and course analysis. A comprehensive stu-

---

3. *Cohens v. Virginia*, 19 U.S. (6 Wheat.) 264, 404 (1821).

dent brief should contain the following elements: (1) title, (2) facts, (3) issues, (4) decisions, (5) reasoning, (6) separate opinions, (7) analysis.

The title of the case tells who is opposing whom. The name of the party who started the litigation in that particular court usually appears first. Since the losers often take their cases to a higher court, this can get confusing. A few definitions may help: *Plaintiffs* sue *defendants* in civil suits in trial courts. The *state* (or the United States) prosecutes *defendants* in criminal cases in trial courts. The losing party may ask a higher (appellate) court to review his case on the ground that the trial court judge made a mistake in interpreting or applying the law. If the law gives the loser a right to higher court review, his lawyers will *appeal*. If not, they may ask the higher court to issue a writ of *certiorari* (literally "call up the record" from the court below). Under the certiorari procedure, the appellate courts have discretion to pick and choose which requests for review they will grant. These two procedures, *appeals* and *petitions* for *certiorari*, are sometimes loosely referred to as "appeals" because they both involve review by an appellate court.

A person who seeks a writ of certiorari is known as a *petitioner.* The person who must respond to that petition (the winner of the case below), is called the *respondent.*

A person who files a formal appeal because the jurisdictional statute gives persons in his situation a right to appeal is known as an *appellant.* His opponent is an *appellee.*

Next to, or right below, the title of a case is the citation that tells you where to find the case in the reports of each court. For example, the decisions of the U.S. Supreme Court are published in a series of volumes known as the *United States Reports.* The abbreviation for this set of reports is "U.S." The volume number is listed before the abbreviation; the page on which the report begins follows and is, in turn, followed by the date on which the opinion was handed down by the court. Ancient sets of Supreme Court reports are named after the court reporters who compiled them. Thus the famous case of *Marbury v. Madison is* often cited as 1 Cranch 137 (1803).

A good brief will contain a *fact* section, which summarizes both the facts and the law involved in the case. It will tell the nature of the litigation, who sued whom, based on what occurrences, and what happened in the courts below. Often the facts are conveniently summarized at the beginning of the court's opinion. In other instances, they will be scattered throughout the opinion. Sometimes the best recital of the facts will be found in a dissenting or concurring opinion. Note: judges are not beyond seeing only those facts they want to see. This becomes critically important when students try to reconcile apparently inconsistent cases, because how a judge chooses to characterize and "edit" the facts will often determine which way he will vote and, as a result, which rule of law he will choose to apply.

The *issues* or questions of law raised by the peculiar facts of each case are often stated explicitly by the court. However, students should be alert for the occasional judge who misstates the questions raised in the court below or by the parties on appeal. Misstating the issues is a common strategy of judges who do not wish to make a certain decision, or who wish to make a decision they do not have to make.

Constitutional cases frequently involve multiple issues, some of interest only to litigants and lawyers, others of broader significance to citizens and officials. Very often the issues of law will turn on the meaning of a provision of the Constitution, a law, or a judicial doctrine. That provision or phrase must be captured verbatim in the student's restatement of the issue. It should be set off with quotation marks and underlined. Key words should be capitalized as well. This will help when the time comes to try to reconcile a string of apparently conflicting cases. When noting the issues, the student should try to phrase them in terms of questions that can be answered with a precise yes or no. The quickest way for a student to appear "stupid" in the eyes of a Socratic-method class is to tell the professor that "the issue in the case was whether the official's conduct was unconstitutional." The intelligent response is to say, "The issue was whether the official's conduct [describe it] or the enactment of a specific provision of a law [quote it] violated a specific clause of the Constitution [quote it]." If the issue is phrased precisely, the *decision* will be a succinct yes or no.

The *holding* of a case is the issue answered in a declarative sentence. There are narrow procedural holdings ("case reversed and remanded to the court below") and broader substantive holdings that deal with the application or interpretation of the Constitution, laws, or judicial doctrines. Holdings should be distinguished from *dicta,* which are statements of what the judge thinks the law is but which are not legally binding on other courts under the doctrine of *stare decisis* because they are not logically necessary to justify the decision reached.

The *reasoning* of a judicial opinion is the chain of major and minor premises that led to the decision. Grossly simplified, it will consist of a statement of what the applicable law is, followed by a characterization of what the official did or failed to do, followed by a conclusion that the law was, or was not, violated. This is often the least interesting aspect of the opinion. The most interesting aspect is often how the judge came to the conclusion that the law is what he or she says it is. Much of the reasoning in constitutional law consists of reshaping the major premises by interpretations that manipulate constitutional text, framers' intent, history, and the opinions of experts in light of perceived exigencies.

Concurring and dissenting opinions should be subjected to the same sort of searching analysis. Awareness of how individual justices have voted and reasoned also is essential to understanding the larger philosophical debates of the court and to anticipating how individual judges will vote in future cases.

The analysis section of a brief should evaluate the significance of the case, its relationship to other cases, its place in history, its impact on litigants, government, or society, what it illustrates about the court, its members, its decision-making processes, and anything else that seems pertinent given the objectives of the course. It should also include attempts to answer the note questions that follow the case in the casebook. Here the implicit assumptions and values of the justices should be probed, the "rightness" of the decision debated, and its logic reconsidered. The appropriate frame of mind for a student of judicial opinions is disputatiousness.

Syndicating. Students who content themselves with briefing cases soon get lost in the forest. One way out is to form a "syndicate" or study group to discuss the cases, to puzzle out the note questions, and to try to anticipate the line of questioning the professor will pursue in class. Meeting after class to go over what was discussed (and hinted at by the professor) can often be more valuable than meeting before class, but meeting times should be kept short to prevent extraneous discussion.

Synthesizing. The law is not always a seamless web of syllogisms, but treating it as if it were is often the surest way to find its flaws and to expose the "politics" that went into its making. A "synthesis" is a summary of related cases that captures the key elements of each case, shows how they relate to other cases, and shows how those relationships may contribute to a better picture of what the prevailing legal doctrine is, or, at least, what the debate over the law is, at any given moment.

The process of synthesizing (or attempting to synthesize) the legal principles employed to decide like cases in order to produce a reliable statement of ruling law is the most important process in legal reasoning. Cases are classified, categorized, compared, contrasted, and distinguished for many reasons. Sometimes the objective is to enhance precision in the interpretation of a specific provision of law. Other times the purpose is to highlight inconsistencies, to uncover implicit assumptions about facts or values, or to predict how judges will rule in the future. Still other times it is to reveal how politics and law influence each other and how culture and language influence both.

The Constitution
Under Siege

Chapter One

First Principles

"It is at all times necessary, and more particularly so during the progress of a revolution and until right ideas confirm themselves by habit, that we frequently refresh our patriotism by reference to first principles."

—Thomas Paine, *Dissertation on First Principles of Government* (1795)

"The Constitution contains no theories, it is as practical a document as Magna Carta...."

—Woodrow Wilson, *Constitutional Government in the United States* (1908)

"In framing a government which is to be administered by men over men, the great difficulty lies in this: you must first enable the government to control the governed; and in the next place oblige it to control itself. A dependence on the people is, no doubt, the primary control on the government; but experience has taught mankind the necessity of auxiliary precautions."

—James Madison, *The Federalist* No. 51 (1788)

"The probabilities of power do not derive from the literary theory of the Constitution."

—Richard E. Neustadt, *Presidential Power* (1960)

A. Introduction

When the text of the Constitution is ambiguous, recourse must be had to the ideas underlying the text: ideas inferrable from the document as a whole, from the intent of the framers, and from the political thought imputable to the framers or to their document. Where the political thought of the framers cannot be ascertained, recourse may be had to precedent (past judicial decisions), to pragmatic syntheses of legal doctrine drawn from precedents and imagined cognate cases, to general political theory, and even to the hypotheses and data of the social sciences.

All of these ideas may be referred to, in Tom Paine's words, as "first principles." To most traditionalists, the term refers to those principles which came first historically. To reformers (e.g., Progressives, New Deal liberals, civil rights advocates, and civil libertarians), the Constitution is organic, not static, and "first principles" are all principles deemed fundamental to the political order as it has evolved, and as they believe it ought to evolve.

3

Of course, to contrast these views sharply is to imply that there is more conflict than consensus when, in practice, the opposite is true. Most constitutional conservatives share Edmund Burke's disposition to innovate cautiously, and most constitutional reformers seek to conserve and to learn from the past even as they innovate. Thus constitutional reinterpretation in the United States follows the ancient pattern of the common law, under which old rules of decision have been adapted to new circumstances by artful restatements that maintain continuity—or the appearance of continuity—while permitting gradual change.

In reality, most disputes over the meaning of the Constitution have been over the rate and direction of reinterpretation, rather than over the legitimacy of the courts as authoritative reinterpreters of the law. This is not always how it seems, because much of the debate has been presented as if the central issue were the proper role of the courts and the legitimacy of judicial review. However, most charges of judicial usurpation have been more tactical than principled. Prior to 1937, it was the reformers (the Progressives and the New Deal liberals) who denied the legitimacy of judicial review because they disliked judicial interpretations of the Constitution that hampered federal regulation of the economy. Since 1937, it has been the self-styled conservatives who have attacked the legitimacy of judicial review in opposition to court rulings forbidding segregation, expanding the rights of minorities and defendants, ordering the reapportionment of legislatures and the integration of schools, restricting the military and intelligence agencies, and permitting abortions. At no time, however, has there ever been substantial support for the proposition that all constitutional change must proceed by way of the amendment process.

This book is about the legitimacy of contending claims to authority advanced on behalf of the president and Congress. This opening chapter is about those "first principles" that have governed, or that people believe should govern, the allocation of authority. And, because the unusual political stability of the United States has permitted those principles to evolve gradually, the chapter can proceed historically from seventeenth-century British thought about limited government, guaranteed liberties, and separation of powers, through eighteenth-century American thought about "checks and balances," to twentieth-century legal positivism and behavioralist political science, which argue that it is the effective exercise of power in a pluralistic democracy, rather than the force of so-called first principles, that determines the legitimacy of claims of authority today.

B. The Ancient Rights of Englishmen

Magna Carta
(1215)

38. Henceforth no bailiff shall put anyone on trial by his own unsupported allegation, without bringing credible witnesses to the charge.

39. No free man shall be taken or imprisoned or disseised or outlawed or exiled or in any way ruined, nor will we go or send against him, except by the lawful judgment of his peers or by the law of the land.

40. To no one will we sell, to no one will we deny or delay right or justice.

King John at the signing of the Magna Carta

41. [Foreign merchants] found in our land at the outbreak of war ... shall be detained without damage to their persons or goods, until we or our chief justiciar know how the merchants of our land are treated in the enemy country; and if ours are safe there, the others shall be safe in our land....

45. We will not [appoint] justices, constables, sheriffs or bailiffs who do not know the law of the land and mean to observe it well....

63. Wherefore we wish and firmly command that the English church shall be free, and the men in our realm shall have and hold all the aforesaid liberties, rights and concessions well and peacefully, freely and quietly, fully and completely for them and their heirs and our heirs in all things and places for ever, as is aforesaid.

.... Given under our hand in the meadow which is called Runnymede, between Windsor and Staines on the fifteenth day of June in the seventeenth year of our reign.

—John Rex

The barons who extracted Magna Carta (the Great Charter) from King John viewed it as a restatement of English law. The king's supporters denounced it as an intrusion upon royal prerogatives. Still others saw it as an attempt to secure feudal privileges on behalf of the nobility. Not until the Puritans revolted against the Stuart kings in the seventeenth century and the American colonies achieved independence in the eighteenth century, did Magna Carta come to be viewed as a charter of liberties for all the people. Today a copy of the Great Charter is displayed in the National Archives alongside the Constitution and the Declaration of Independence.

Petition of Right
(1628)

The Petition of Right, submitted to Charles I in 1628 by law reformers in Parliament, was, like the American Declaration of Independence, a list of grievances against monarchial rule. Among other things, the predominantly Puritan Parliament protested:

- taxation without representation,
- the detention, without charges or trial, of prominent persons for failure to pay a special Ship Tax that Parliament had not authorized,
- the housing of soldiers and sailors in private homes to prevent a possible uprising, and
- the imposition of martial law, with trials before military commissions in circumvention of the common law courts.

Charles I refused to grant the Puritans' Petition of Right, declaring that "for none of the house of commons, joint or separate, … have any power either to make or declare a law without my consent."

In 1640, Puritans in Parliament defied this assertion by abolishing the secret court of Star Chamber, which had authorized the torture of the king's critics, and enacting the Habeas Corpus Act, which reasserted the right of prisoners to challenge their detention without trial in a court of law. Civil war broke out in 1642. Parliament put an army into the field. The monarchy was overthrown and in 1649 Charles I was beheaded. Parliament adopted a republican form of government, but it degenerated into a military dictatorship under Oliver Cromwell. In 1660, Charles II was invited to return from exile and govern "in concert" with Parliament. He was succeeded by his brother, James II, whose autocratic ways (and closet Catholicism) led to Parliament's "Glorious Revolution" of 1688.

English Declaration of Rights
(1689)

Following the defeat of King James II at the Battle of the Boyne in Ireland, Parliament invited William and Mary, prince and princess of Orange, to assume the throne, under the condition that they accede to an "Act Declaring the Rights and Liberties of the Subject and Settling the Succession to the Crown." Like the American Declaration of Independence (1776), the British declaration of 1689, which William and Mary were required to sign, began with a list of grievances against the king, and then asserted the following "ancient rights and liberties:"

- That the pretended power of suspending the laws or the execution of laws by regal authority without consent of Parliament is illegal;
- That the pretended power of dispensing with laws or the execution of laws by regal authority, as it has been assumed and exercised of late, is illegal; …
- That levying money for or to the use of the Crown by pretence of prerogative, without grant of Parliament, for longer time, or in other manner than the same is or shall be granted, is illegal;
- That the raising or keeping of a standing army, within the kingdom in time of peace, unless it be with the consent of Parliament, is against the law;

- That the subjects which are Protestants may have arms for their defense suitable to their conditions and as allowed by law;

- That elections of members of Parliament ought to be free;

- That the freedom of speech and debates or proceedings in Parliament ought not to be impeached or questioned in any court or place out of Parliament;

- That excessive bail ought not to be required, nor excessive fines imposed, nor cruel and unusual punishment inflicted;

- That jurors ought to be duly impaneled and returned, and jurors which pass upon men in trials for high treason ought to be freeholders;

- That all grants and promises of fines and forfeitures of particular persons before conviction are illegal and void;

- And that for redress of all grievances, and for the amending, strengthening and preserving of the laws, Parliaments ought to be held frequently....

Upon which their said Majesties [William and Mary] did accept the crown and royal dignity of the kingdoms of England, France and Ireland, and the dominions thereunto belonging, according to the resolution and desire of the said Lords and Commons contained in said declaration.

Notes and Questions

1. *The suspension and dispensation powers.* Note that the first two provisions in this declaration rendered illegal the assertion by Stuart kings that they could suspend the laws, and thereby rule by decree (martial law), or dispense with the enforcement of specific laws, much as Presidents George W. Bush and Barack Obama did when they refused to enforce the laws against torture against CIA agents. Note too that this declaration, like the Puritans' unsuccessful Petition of Right, stressed limited government as the primary means for assuring rights and liberties, and defined individual rightsholders as "persons," not "citizens" (with the exception of the right to bear arms, which was limited to Protestants). The American Constitution originally stressed limited government too, while the Bill of Rights (ratified in 1791) affirmed the rights of "persons" and "the people," and not just the rights of "citizens" or "Protestants."

C. The British Theory of Separation of Powers

John Locke,
The Separation of Powers
(1690)

The American colonists derived their thinking about politics from many sources: Puritan church covenants, the charters of colonial trading corporations, and the English common law. They were also deeply influenced by the two civil wars that disrupted both England and the colonies: the Puritan Revolution of 1640–1649 and the so-called Glorious Revolution of 1688. Out of these events, in which voluntary associations played an unprecedented role, came a number of political beliefs that have characterized American political thought ever since. By the end of the seventeenth century, most colonists be-

John Locke

lieved that political leadership gained its authority not from God, through the lords temporal and spiritual, but through an implicit contractual relationship between the rulers and the ruled made in the eyes of God. The Puritans, through their incessant political and religious organizing, transformed the subjects of the king into citizens who came to believe that governments are not only instituted among men, but derive their just powers from the consent of the governed.

These propositions were central to the American Revolution. During that conflict, however, Americans relied on the political thought of the English Whigs, who had triumphed in the Revolution of 1688, for the idea of parliamentary, or legislative, independence from the Crown, and even dominance over the king, through a variety of constitutional arrangements including parliamentary control over the king's revenues. Many writers advanced theoretical justifications for the political arrangements that permitted William and Mary to assume the throne in 1689 as invited guests of Parliament, but none has become more prominent over the years than John Locke, whose theory of separated institutions is excerpted here:

150. In all Cases, whilst the Government subsists, the *Legislative is the Supream Power*. For what can give Laws to another, must needs be superiour to him: and since the Legislative is no otherwise Legislative of the Society, but by the right it has to make Laws for all the parts and for every Member of the Society, prescribing Rules to their actions, and giving power of Execution, where they are transgressed, the *Legislative* must needs be the *Supream*, and all other Powers in any Members or parts of the Society, derived from and subordinate to it....

153. But because the Laws, that are at once, and in a short time made, have a constant and lasting force, and need a *perpetual Execution*, or an attendance thereunto: Therefore 'tis necessary there should be a *Power always in being*, which

should see to the *Execution* of the Laws that are made, and remain in force. And thus the *Legislative* and *Executive Power* come often to be separated. When the *Legislative* hath put the *Execution* of the Laws they make into other hands, they have a power still to resume it out of those hands, when they find cause, and to punish for any mal-administration against the Laws. The same holds also in regard of the *Federative Power*, that and the Executive being both *Ministerial and subordinate to the Legislative*, which as has been shew'd in a Constituted Commonwealth, is the Supream.

[Locke defined the "federative power" as follows.]

145. There is another *Power* in every Commonwealth, which one may call natural, because it is that which answers to the Power every Man naturally had before he entered into Society. For though in a Commonwealth the Members of it are distinct Persons still in reference to one another, and as such are governed by the Laws of the Society; yet in reference to the rest of Mankind, they make one Body, which is, as every Member of it before was, still in the State of Nature with the rest of Mankind. Hence it is, that the Controversies that happen between any Man of the Society with those that are out of it, are managed by the publick; and an injury done to a Member of their Body, engages the whole in the reparation of it. So that under this Consideration, the whole Community is one Body in the State of Nature, in respect of all other States or Persons out of its Community.

146. This therefore contains the Power of War and Peace, Leagues and Alliances, and all the Transactions, with all Persons and Communities without the Commonwealth, and may be called *Federative*, if any one pleases. So the thing be understood, I am indifferent as to the Name.

Two Treatises of Government (1690; Laslett ed., 1960), Second Treatise, sections 150, 153, 145, 146.

Notes and Questions

1. *Sovereignty.* John Locke, the philosopher of the Whig Revolution of 1688, espoused the theory of parliamentary sovereignty as a justification for that revolt against the Crown. In the wake of that revolution, Parliament stripped the monarchy of most of its prerogative powers. American colonists applauded these developments, and by the end of the seventeenth century their assemblies attempted to treat royal governors as executors of the laws they passed, rather than as the representatives of a sovereign monarch. This caused great strain between colonists and the British government.

2. *Parliamentary independence.* During the eighteenth century Parliament found its dominance over the Crown (a euphemism for the king and his council of parliamentary leaders) undermined by royal bribes and patronage. American colonists, chafing under the authority of royal governors and other officials, embraced the Whig doctrine of separation of powers, believing that the imbalance between the relative powers of Crown and Parliament in Britain accounted for many of their troubles. They also believed that colonial assemblies should be superior to the royal governors, whose salaries they paid.

3. *Separation of powers.* While Parliament found it difficult to retain its independence against the Crown, the judiciary was more successful. By the 1760s British judges had secured lifetime appointments on good behavior, and their separation from the crown as an independent branch of government was increasingly recognized. In 1748 the French commentator Baron de Montesquieu published *The Spirit of the Laws*, an analysis of the

British "constitution," in which he perceived separate executive, legislative, and judicial powers. To the extent he thought the legislature in England was independent of the domination of the Crown he was mistaken. However, his endorsement of that idea was not lost on Americans.

4. *Popular sovereignty.* The notion that governments derive their legitimacy ("just powers") from the consent of the governed is traditionally associated with Locke, but he also spoke of legislative sovereignty. What happens to the consent of the governed if the legislature is deemed to be supreme not only over the executive, but over the people as well?

In the late 1770s the American colonists knew they were revolting against Parliament as well as the king, but they were also revolting in favor of their own legislatures. This caused some conceptual confusion, but with the invention of written constitutions and constitutional conventions (especially in Massachusetts), the Whig theory of legislative supremacy gave way to the idea that the people were sovereign and that all officials, in all branches of government, are their servants and govern with powers delegated to them by the people.

5. *The federative power.* Is Locke's theory of a "federative power" consistent with the theory of parliamentary supremacy? Which branch, the legislative or executive, would necessarily exercise the federative power? Why?

William Blackstone,
The Balanced Constitution
(1765)

William Blackstone completed his magisterial *Commentaries on the Laws of England* between 1755 and 1765. By 1771 over a thousand sets of this treatise had been exported to the American colonies. They quickly became a standard reference work on both sides of the Atlantic for college students and practicing lawyers. Blackstone was a Tory, but he greatly admired the political theory of the Whigs' Glorious Revolution of 1688. Ignoring the gains in power that the Crown had achieved in his own lifetime through bribery and the sale of places in government, Blackstone described British public law as if it had created and maintained a well-balanced structure of power. The radical Whigs who organized the American Revolution understood the disparity between Blackstone's "constitution" and the actual system of power in England, but they found Blackstone's writings useful both as a standard by which to judge George III to be a tyrant and as a guide to creating their own state governments during the revolution.

In the following passage Blackstone presents the idea of separation of powers as he understood it.

> And herein indeed consists the true excellence of the English government, that all parts of it form a mutual check upon each other. In the legislature, the people are a check upon the nobility, and the nobility a check upon the people, by the mutual privilege of rejecting what the other has resolved: while the king is a check upon both, which preserves the executive power from encroachments. And this very executive power is again checked and kept within bounds by the two houses, through the privilege they have of inquiring into, impeaching and punishing the conduct (not indeed of the king, which would destroy his constitutional independence; but, which is more beneficial to the public) of his evil and pernicious counsellors.... Like three distinct powers in mechanics, they jointly impel the machine of government in a direction different from what either, acting by itself, would have done; but at the same time in a direction par-

taking of each, and formed out of all; a direction which constitutes the true line of the liberty and happiness of the community.

Commentaries on the Laws of England (1765–1769; University of Chicago ed. 1979), I, 150–51.

Notes and Questions

1. *Representation.* When Blackstone claimed that the House of Commons represents the people, he did not mean that the members of that body should be viewed as delegates charged with looking out for the parochial interests of their districts. Rather, he saw them as "re-pre-senting" the entire people of England and acting in the best interests of the Realm. This theory of "virtual representation," made famous by Edmund Burke, was used to justify the failure to reapportion the boroughs of England from the reign of Elizabeth I to the Second Reform Bill of 1867. It was also used to justify the Crown's refusal to allow colonists to send representatives to Parliament. By this failure to reapportion boroughs to reflect demographic changes, and by a slow expansion of the suffrage, aristocrats, large landowners, and rural gentry were able to dominate the House of Commons until the late nineteenth century.

2. *The mixed constitution.* Since ancient times, political theorists have advanced the idea of a mixed constitution in which separate institutions would represent different so-cial classes. As Blackstone's idea of the balanced constitution suggests, the Whig theory of separation of the powers of Parliament from the powers of the Crown served to pro-vide enchanced representation for the lower social classes of Great Britain. But was this class-based theory easily transferred to the American colonies? Louis Hartz addresses this question in *The Liberal Tradition in America* (1955). Some of the founders of the Amer-ican republic did make use of the idea of "mixed government." John Adams, in his *De-fence of the Constitutions of the Government of the United States of America* (1786), argued that the separation of legislatures from executives and the separation of legislatures into upper and lower houses gave different social classes representation and allowed them to check each other in ways that would prevent the rise of class-based political parties, which might subvert the system of checks and balances through corruption. Early in the Con-stitutional Convention of 1787, James Madison proposed a senate that would have rep-resented the more affluent and better-educated class of Americans—what he and his friends liked to think of as the "natural aristocracy." See Robert Dahl, *Pluralist Democracy in the United States* (1967), 113–14. Did this desire to balance social classes off against each other actually come to be expressed in the Constitution? If not, why not?

D. From Separation of Powers to Checks and Balances

James Otis,
Checks and Balances
(1764)

James Otis was a fiery Boston lawyer who championed the American cause against Britain during the 1760s and 1770s. In 1761 he resigned his position as the king's advo-cate general in Massachusetts to represent Boston merchants opposed to the writs of as-

James Otis, flanked by Hercules and Athena, on the frontispiece of a 1770 edition of *Bickerstaff's Almanac.*

sistance (credentials, really) that permitted customs officers to conduct warrantless searches for evidence of smuggling. Otis also tutored the young John Adams in law and politics and wrote a pamphlet on *The Rights of the British Colonies* (1764). A portion of the pamphlet follows.

> Let no Man think I am about to … advocate for *despotism,* because I affirm that government is founded on the necessity of our natures; and that an original supreme Sovereign, absolute, and uncontroulable, *earthly* power *must* exist in and preside over every society; from whose final decisions there can be no appeal but directly to Heaven. It is therefore *originally* and *ultimately* in the people. I say supreme absolute power is *originally* and *ultimately* in the people; and they never did in fact *freely,* nor can they *rightfully* make an absolute, unlimited renunciation of this divine right. It is ever in the nature of the thing given in *trust,* and on a condition, the performance of which no mortal can dispence with; namely, that the person or persons on whom the sovereignty is confer'd by the people, shall *incessantly consult their* good. Tyranny of all kinds is to be abhor'd, whether it be in the hands of one, or of the few, or of the many….
>
> The *end* of government being the *good* of mankind, points out its great duties: It is above all things to provide for the security, the quiet, and happy enjoyment

of life, liberty, and property. There is no one act which a government can have a *right to make, that does not tend to the advancement of the security, tranquility and prosperity of the people....*

The form of government is by *nature* and by *right* so far left to the *individuals* of each society, that they may alter it from a simple democracy or government of all over all, to any other form they please....

The same law of nature and of reason is equally obligatory on a *democracy,* an *aristocracy,* and a *monarchy.* Whenever the administrators, in any of those forms, deviate from truth, justice and equity, they verge towards tyranny, and are to be opposed; and if they prove incorrigible, they will be *deposed* by the people, if the people are not rendered too abject....

See here the grandeur of the British constitution! See the wisdom of our ancestors! The supreme *legislative,* and the supreme *executive,* are a perpetual check and balance to each other. If the supreme executive errs, it is informed by the supreme legislative in parliament: If the supreme legislative errs, it is informed by the supreme executive in the King's courts of law. Here, the King appears, as represented by his judges, in the highest lustre and majesty, as supreme executor of the commonwealth; and he never shines brighter, but on his Throne, at the head of the supreme legislative. This is government! This, is a constitution! to preserve which, either from foreign or domestic foes, has cost oceans of blood and treasure in every age; and the blood and the treasure have upon the whole been well spent.

The Rights of the British Colonies Asserted and Proved (1764; University of Missouri Studies, 1929), vol. 4, 52–55, 79.

Notes and Questions

1. *The British constitution.* In *The Writs of Assistance Case* against the blue-coated customs officers, Otis argued boldly that an act of Parliament "against the constitution is void."[1] To what "constitution" was he referring? Previous acts of Parliament that Parliament could repeal? Judicial interpretations of acts of Parliament and the common law, that Parliament could override? Or a body of political principles more fundamental than, and theoretically antecedent to, the transient acts of contemporary officials? If the last, how does one go about "finding" the British constitution?

2. *Sovereignty.* According to Otis, where is "sovereignty" located? How is this sovereignty to be enforced: by revolution alone, as Locke implied, or also by litigation enforcing the people's constitution?

3. *Supremacy.* In Otis's view of the British political system, who is truly "supreme"? He describes both the legislature and the executive as supreme and the people as sovereign, places the king at the head of the legislature, and refers to the courts as the king's courts. Yet in the Writs of Assistance Case, he asserted that the king's courts had the authority, indeed the duty, to refuse to enforce an act of the king's Parliament on the ground that it violated a form of law called the "constitution." Was Otis mad (as some claim he was), or was there method in his madness? Was Otis simply a believer in legislative independence from executive domination, or was he laying the groundwork for a much

---

1. *Legal Papers of John Adams,* 2 (Wroth and Zobel ed., 1965), 139, 144.

broader theory of government, with difference branches and levels, among which elements of "sovereignty" may be divided, so that multiple legal authorities will perpetually check and balance each other?

4. *Montesquieu's theory of separation of powers.* It is often said that Americans learned about separation of powers chiefly from Baron de Montesquieu's *The Spirit of Laws* (1748). Montesquieu wrote:

> The political liberty of the subject is a tranquility of mind, arising from the opinion each person has of his safety. In order to have this liberty it is requisite the government be so constituted as one man need not be afraid of another.
>
> When the legislative and executive powers are united in the same person, or in the same body of magistracy, there can be then no liberty; because apprehensions may arise, lest the same monarch or senate should enact tyrannical laws, to execute them in a tyrannical manner....
>
> If the prince were to have a share in the legislature by the power of enacting, liberty would be lost. But as it is necessary he should have a share in the legislative for the support of his own prerogative, this share must consist in the power of refusing.[2]

Did Otis go so far as to say that liberty would be lost if the prince were to have a role in the making (or rejection) of legislation? Did the authors of the Constitution adopt Montesquieu's view? Otis and Montesquieu agree that the power of judging must be separate from the legislative and executive powers, but Montesquieu did not believe in an independent profession of judges enforcing a body of legal precedent, interpreted with a liberal dose of "right reason." The baron despised judges and would have turned the business of judging over to ad hoc juries of laymen. See generally Fisher, *President and Congress* (1972), appendix and works cited therein.

Thomas Paine,
A Criticism of Mixed Government
(1776)

Central to British thinking about separation of powers was a deep veneration of the monarchy, an attitude that Tom Paine did much to destroy in the colonies with his extraordinarily popular pamphlet, *Common Sense* (1776):

> Some writers have so confounded society with government, as to leave little or no distinction between them; whereas they are not only different, but have different origins. Society is produced by our wants, and government by our wickedness....
>
> Society in every state is a blessing, but Government, even in its best state, is but a necessary evil; in its worst state an intolerable one....
>
> I draw my idea of the form of government from a principle in nature which no art can overturn, viz. that the more simple any thing is, the less liable it is to be disordered, and the easier repaired when disordered; and with this maxim in view I offer a few remarks on the so much boasted constitution of England. That it was noble, for the dark and slavish times in which it was erected, is granted. When the world was overrun with tyranny the least remove therefrom was a glo-

---

2. *The Spirit of Laws* (1748; Carrithers ed., 1977), chap. 3, pars. 3, 4, 53.

Thomas Paine

rious rescue. But that it is imperfect, subject to convulsions, and incapable of producing what it seems to promise, is easily demonstrated....

I know it is difficult to get over local or long standing prejudices, yet if we will suffer ourselves to examine the component parts of the English constitution, we shall find them to be the base remains of two ancient tyrannies, compounded with some new Republican materials.

First.—The remains of Monarchical tyranny in the person of the King.

Secondly.—The remains of Aristocratical tyranny in the persons of the Peers.

Thirdly.—The new Republican materials, in the persons of the Commons, on whose virtue depends the freedom of England.

The two first, by being hereditary, are independent of the People; wherefore in a *constitutional sense* they contribute nothing towards the freedom of the State....

To say that the constitution of England is a union of three powers, reciprocally *checking* each other, is farcical; either the words have no meaning, or they are flat contradictions.

To say that the Commons is a check upon the King, presupposes two things.

First.—That the King is not to be trusted without being looked after; or in other words, that a thirst for absolute power is the natural disease of monarchy.

Secondly.—That the Commons, by being appointed for that purpose, are either wiser or more worthy of confidence than the Crown.

But as the same constitution which gives the Commons a power to check the King by withholding the supplies, gives afterwards the King a power to check the Commons, by empowering him to reject their other bills; it again supposes that the King is wiser than those whom it has already supposed to be wiser than him. A mere absurdity!

There is something exceedingly ridiculous in the composition of Monarchy; it first excludes a man from the means of information, yet empowers him to act in cases where the highest judgment is required. The state of a king shuts him from the World, yet the business of a king requires him to know it thoroughly; wherefore the different parts, by unnaturally opposing and destroying each other, prove the whole character to be absurd and useless....

That the crown is this overbearing part in the English constitution needs not be mentioned, and that it derives its whole consequence merely from being the giver of places and pensions is self-evident; wherefore, though we have been wise enough to shut and lock a door against absolute Monarchy, we at the same time have been foolish enough to put the Crown in possession of the key.

The prejudice of Englishmen, in favour of their own government, by King, Lords and Commons, arises as much or more from national pride than reason. Individuals are undoubtedly safer in England than in some other countries: but the will of the king is as much the law of the land in Britain as in France, with this difference, that instead of proceeding directly from his mouth, it is handed to the people under the formidable shape of an act of parliament. For the fate of Charles the First [beheaded in 1649] hath only made kings more subtle—not more just.

Wherefore, laying aside all national pride and prejudice in favour of modes and forms, the plain truth is that *it is wholly owing to the constitution of the people, and not to the constitution of the government* that the crown is not as oppressive in England as in Turkey....

The nearer any government approaches to a Republic, the less business there is for a King. It is somewhat difficult to find a proper name for the government of England. Sir William Meredith calls it a Republic; but in its present state it is unworthy of the name, because the corrupt influence of the Crown, by having all the places [patronage jobs] in its disposal, hath so effectually swallowed up the power, and eaten out the virtue of the House of Commons (the Republican part in the constitution) that the government of England is nearly as monarchical as that of France or Spain. Men fall out with names without understanding them. For 'tis the Republican and not the Monarchical part of the constitution of England which Englishmen glory in, viz. the liberty of choosing an House of Commons from out of their own body—and it is easy to see that when Republican virtues fail, slavery ensues. Why is the constitution of England sickly, but because monarchy hath poisoned the Republic; the Crown hath engrossed the Commons.

In England a King hath little more to do than to make war and give away places; which, in plain terms, is to impoverish the nation and set it together by the ears. A pretty business indeed for a man to be allowed eight hundred thousand sterling a year for, and worshipped into the bargain! Of more worth is one honest man to society, and in the sight of God, than all the crowned ruffians that ever lived.

Common Sense (1776), in *The Writings of Thomas Paine* (Conway ed., 1894), 1, 67–84.

Notes and Questions

1. *Insularity.* Paine justified parliamentary supremacy over the king on the theory that the House of Commons is bound to be wiser because elections make it better informed and less insulated from the people and "the World." Are elected officials necessarily wiser, better informed, or less insulated than nonelected officials? For the argument that even elected presidents of the United States can become insulated from reality, see George Reedy, *Twilight of the Presidency* (1970). Is Paine's argument about relative wisdom of brances or the people one that Locke, Blackstone, or Montesquieu would have endorsed?

2. *Thirst for power.* Paine also argues that the power of Commons to check the Crown is justified because kings have a "thirst for absolute power." Are executives the only officials with a thirst for power?

The Declaration of Independence and the Idea of Tyranny

(1776)

The Declaration of Independence is always remembered for its purple prose about the inalienable rights of man and the right of the people to overthrow governments that are destructive of these rights. But is that the only political theory to be found in the Declaration? Consider the following grievances for what they may reveal about the attitudes of the American revolutionaries about the separation of powers.

[The King] has called together legislative bodies at places unusual, uncomfortable, and distant from the depository of their Public Records, for the sole purpose of fatiguing them into compliance with his measures.

He has dissolved Representative Houses repeatedly, for opposing with manly firmness his invasions on the rights of the people.

He has refused for a long time, after such dissolutions, to cause others to be elected; whereby the Legislative Powers, incapable of Annihilation, have returned to the People at large for their exercise; the State remaining in the meantime exposed to all the dangers of invasion from without, and convulsions within....

He has obstructed the Administration of justice, by refusing his Assent to Laws for establishing judiciary Powers. He has made judges dependent on his Will alone, for the tenure of their offices, and the amount and payment of their salaries.

Separation of Powers in the Early State Constitutions

(1776–1784)

During the Revolution, the American colonies transformed themselves into states under written constitutions that provided for strong legislatures and weak governors. Several of the state constitutions expressly provided for a separation of powers.

The Constitution of North Carolina, 1776:

Article IV. That the legislative, executive, and supreme judicial powers of government, ought to be forever separate and distinct from each other.

The Constitution of Maryland, 1776:

> Article VI. That the legislative, executive, and judicial powers of government, ought to be forever separate and distinct from each other.

The Constitution of Massachusetts, 1780:

> Article XXX. In the government of this commonwealth, the legislative department shall never exercise the executive and judicial powers, or either of them; the executive shall never exercise the legislative and judicial powers, or either of them; the judicial shall never exercise the legislative and executive powers, or either of them; to the end that it may be a government of laws and not of men.

The Constitution of New Hampshire, 1784:

> Article XXXVII. In the government of this state, the three essential powers thereof, to wit, the legislative, executive and judicial, ought to be kept as separate from and independent of each other, as the nature of a free government will admit, or as is consistent with that chain of connection that binds the whole fabric of the constitution in one indissoluble bond of union and amity.

> William F. Swindler, ed., *Sources and Documents of the United States Constitutions* (1975), 7, 40 (NC.), 4, 373 (Md.), 5, 96 (Mass.), 6, 347 (N.H.).

Notes and Questions

1. *The meaning of "separation of powers."* What did the references to "separation of powers" mean in these state constitutions? Did they mean that there are certain functions of government which are, by their very nature, legislative rather than executive, or judicial rather than executive or legislative? Can clear lines be drawn between legislative and executive functions? Must all adjudicatory functions necessarily be allocated to the court system, provided due process is guaranteed? Or did "separation of powers" simply denote the separation of institutions and thus confirm Parliament's fight for independence, the judiciary's fight for life tenure upon good behavior, and the disgust of American revolutionaries with the Crown's bribery of legislators, the sale of "places" (positions in government), and grants of hereditary privileges and immunities?

James Madison, *The Partial Separation of Powers*
(1788)

The new Constitution was submitted to state conventions for ratification in 1788. During the ratification debates in New York, a series of newspaper articles written by James Madison, Alexander Hamilton, and John Jay, later collected into what is today known as *The Federalist Papers,* provided a spirited explication of the new Constitution.

In *The Federalist* No. 47, Madison developed his conception of how the system of separation of powers could be successfully maintained.

> … The accumulation of all powers legislative, executive and judiciary in the same hands, whether of one, a few or many, and whether hereditary, self appointed, or elective, may justly be pronounced the very definition of tyranny. Were the federal constitution therefore really chargeable with this accumulation of power or with a mixture of powers having a dangerous tendency to such an accumulation, no further arguments would be necessary to inspire a universal

reprobation of the system. I persuade myself however, … that the charge cannot be supported, and that the maxim on which it relies has been totally misconceived and misapplied. In order to form correct ideas on this important subject, it will be proper to investigate the sense in which the preservation of liberty requires that the three great departments of power should be separate and distinct.

The oracle who is always consulted and cited on this subject, is the celebrated Montesquieu. If he be not the author of this invaluable precept in the science of politics, he has the merit at least of displaying, and recommending it most effectually to the attention of mankind. Let us endeavour in the first place to ascertain his meaning on this point.…

On the slightest view of the British constitution we must perceive, that the legislative, executive and judiciary departments are by no means totally separate and distinct from each other. The executive magistrate forms an integral part of the legislative authority. He alone has the prerogative of making treaties with foreign sovereigns, which when made have, under certain limitations, the force of legislative acts. All the members of the judiciary department are appointed by him; can be removed by him on the address of the two Houses of Parliament, and form, when he pleases to consult them, one of his constitutional councils. One branch of the legislative department forms also, a great constitutional council to the executive chief; as on another hand, it is the sole depositary of judicial power in cases of impeachment, and is invested with the supreme appellate jurisdiction, in all other cases. The judges again are so far connected with the legislative department, as often to attend and participate in its deliberations, though not admitted to a legislative vote.

From these facts by which Montesquieu was guided it may clearly be inferred, that in saying "there can be no liberty where the legislative and executive powers are united in the same person, or body of magistrates," or "if the power of judging be not separated from the legislative and executive powers," he did not mean that these departments ought to have no *partial agency* in, or no *controul* over the acts of each other. His meaning, as his own words import, and still more conclusively as illustrated by the example in his eye, can amount to no more than this, that where the *whole* power of one department is exercised by the same hands which possess the *whole* power of another department, the fundamental principles of a free constitution are subverted. This would have been the case in the constitution examined by him, if the King who is the sole executive magistrate, had possessed also the complete legislative power, or the supreme administration of justice; or if the entire legislative body, had possessed the supreme judiciary, or the supreme executive authority. This however is not among the vices of that constitution. The magistrate in whom the whole executive power resides cannot of himself make a law, though he can put a negative on every law, nor administer justice in person, though he has the appointment of those who do administer it. The judges can exercise no executive prerogative, though they are shoots from the executive stock, nor any legislative function, though they may be advised with by the legislative councils. The entire legislature, can perform no judiciary act, though by the joint act of two of its branches, the judges may be removed from their offices; and though one of its branches is possessed of the judicial power in the last resort. The entire legislature again can exercise no executive prerogative, though one of its branches constitutes the supreme executive magistracy; and another, on the impeachment of a third, can try and condemn all the subordinate officers in the executive department.

The reasons on which Montesquieu grounds his maxim are a further demonstration of his meaning. "When the legislative and executive powers are united in the same person or body," says he, "there can be no liberty, because apprehensions may arise lest *the same* monarch or senate should *enact* tyrannical laws, to *execute them* in a tyrannical manner." Again "Were the power of judging joined with the legislative, the life and liberty of the subject would be exposed to arbitrary controul, for *the judge* would then be *the legislator*. Were it joined to the executive power, *the judge* might behave with all the violence of an oppressor. "Some of these reasons are more fully explained in other passages; but briefly stated as they are here, they sufficiently establish the meaning which we have put on this celebrated maxim of this celebrated author.

If we look into the constitutions of the several states we find that notwithstanding the emphatical, and in some instances, the unqualified terms in which this axiom has been laid down, there is not a single instance in which the several departments of power have been kept absolutely separate and distinct.

The Federalist Papers (1788; Cooke ed., 1961), 324–27.

In *The Federalist* No. 51, Madison continued:

In order to lay a due foundation for that separate and distinct exercise of the different powers of government, which to a certain extent is admitted on all hands to be essential to the preservation of liberty, it is evident that each department should have a will of its own; and consequently should be so constituted that the members of each should have as little agency as possible in the appointment of the members of the others....

It is equally evident that the members of each department should be as little dependent as possible on those of the others for the emoluments annexed to their offices. Were the executive magistrate, or the judges, not independent of the legislature in this particular, their independence in every other would be merely nominal.

But the great security against a gradual concentration of the several powers in the same department consists in giving to those who administer each department the necessary constitutional means and personal motives to resist encroachments of the others. The provision for defense must in this, as in all other cases, be made commensurate to the danger of attack. Ambition must be made to counteract ambition. The interest of the man must be connected with the constitutional rights of the place. It may be a reflection on human nature that such devices should be necessary to control the abuses of government. But what is government itself but the greatest of all reflections on human nature? If men were angels, no government would be necessary. If angels were to govern men, neither external nor internal controls on government would be necessary. In framing a government which is to be administered by men over men, the great difficulty lies in this: you must first enable the government to control the governed; and in the next place oblige it to control itself. A dependence on the people is, no doubt, the primary control on the government; but experience has taught mankind the necessity of auxiliary precautions....

But it is not possible to give to each department an equal power of self-defense. In republican government, the legislative authority necessarily predominates.

The remedy for this inconveniency is to divide the legislature into different branches; and to render them, by different modes of election and different principles of action, as little connected with each other as the nature of their common functions and their common dependence on the society will admit. It may even be necessary to guard against dangerous encroachments by still further precautions. As the weight of the legislative authority requires that it should be thus divided, the weakness of the executive may require, on the other hand, that it should be fortified. An absolute negative on the legislature appears, at first view, to be the natural defense with which the executive magistrate should be armed. But perhaps it would be neither altogether safe nor alone sufficient. On ordinary occasions it might not be exerted with the requisite firmness, and on extraordinary occasions it might be perfidiously abused. May not this defect of an absolute negative be supplied by some qualified connection between this weaker department and the weaker branch of the stronger department, by which the latter may be led to support the constitutional rights of the former, without being too much detached from the rights of its own department?

The Federalist Papers (Cooke ed., 1961), 348–50.

Notes and Questions

1. *Framers' intent.* The Federalist Papers originated as a series of newspaper articles written to persuade New Yorkers to ratify the proposed federal Constitution. In time they have come to be treated by many scholars and judges as synonymous with the intent of the framers. Is it legitimate to infer the intentions of fifty-five delegates to the Philadelphia Convention from the writings of three campaigners for ratification a year later in New York? If so, why? If not, what kind of evidence of framers' intent should be acceptable? Individual quotations or syntheses of multiple views? For a good example of the latter, see Gordon S. Wood, *The Creation of the American Republic, 1776–1787* (1969).

2. *Practicalities.* Why, according to Madison, won't separation of powers work? How does he define that term? Is the concept of "checks and balances" more supportive of what users of the term "separation of powers" sought to attain? What is it about the label "separation of powers" that make Madison reject it? Most constitutional texts and most judges continue to use the term "separation of powers." Should they?

3. *Textual analysis.* Compare Articles I and II of the Constitution to the following opinions of Justices Miller and Sutherland. Are the justices correct in their interpretations of the constitutional scheme for allocating powers among the branches?

MR. JUSTICE MILLER:

It is ... essential to the successful working of this system [of separation of powers] that the persons entrusted with power in any one of these branches shall not be permitted to encroach upon the powers confided to the others, but that each shall by the law of its creation be limited to the exercise of the powers appropriate to its own department and no other. To these general propositions there are in the Constitution ... some important exceptions [citing the veto power, senatorial consent to appointments, and the impeachment power]. In the main, however, ... the powers confided by the Constitution to one of these departments cannot be exercised by another. [*Kilbourn v. Thompson*, 103 U.S. 168, 191 (1882)].

MR. JUSTICE SUTHERLAND:

It may be stated…, as a general rule inherent in the American constitutional system, that, unless otherwise expressly provided or incidental to the powers conferred, the legislature cannot exercise either executive or judicial power; the executive cannot exercise either legislative or judicial power; the judiciary cannot exercise either executive or legislative power. The existence in the various constitutions of occasional provisions expressly giving to one of the departments powers which by their nature otherwise would fall within the general scope of the authority of another department emphasizes, rather than casts doubt upon, the generally inviolate character of this basic rule. [*Springer v. Philippine Islands*, 277 U.S. 189, 201–202 (1928)]

Compare Richard E. Neustadt, *Presidential Power* (1960; 1980 ed.), 26:

The constitutional convention of 1787 is supposed to have created a government of "separated powers." It did nothing of the sort. Rather, it created a government of separated institutions *sharing* powers.

Louis Fisher,
The Principle of Separated Powers
(1972)

There is a tension between limited and efficient government. Allow government to become weak and popular dissatisfaction may tempt a strongman to overthrow it. Permit too much energy in government and authoritarian administrators may subvert democratic principles.

In the following selection, political scientist Louis Fisher examines how the Constitutional Convention dealt with the need for both efficient government and separated institutions capable of checking each other.

Students are often taught that powers are separated as a means of preserving liberties; yet it is equally true that too much stress on separation can *destroy* liberties. The historic antagonism in France between executive and legislature, characterized by an oscillation between administrative and representative forms of government, is a classic example of the danger of extreme separation. The constitutions of 1791 and 1848 represented the most ambitious attempts in France to establish a pure separation of powers. The consequence, in the first case, was the Committee of Public Safety, the Directory, and the reign of Napoleon Bonaparte, while the second experiment led to Louis Napoleon, reaction, and the Second Empire….

It was just this kind of political fragmentation and paralysis of power that the framers of the American Constitution wanted to avoid. Justice Story explained that the framers accepted a separation of power, but "endeavored to prove that a rigid adherence to it in all cases would be subversive of the efficiency of the government, and result in the destruction of the public liberties."…

It is curious that we still identify the framers with a doctrinaire view of separated powers, instead of placing our emphasis on the practical considerations that gave rise to three branches. I would not go so far as to claim that the framers' search for administrative efficiency, and their adoption of a separate executive for that purpose, represents the whole truth. Still, it is at least half the truth, and since this side of the story receives so little attention it should be told.

The Articles of Confederation (1777) did not provide for a national executive. There was a President of Congress, but he was merely a presiding officer, without executive power. Thus the Continental Congress had to handle both legislative and executive duties. Congress first delegated administrative responsibilities to a number of committees. That failed to work, and so did the subsequent system of boards staffed by men outside Congress. When departments run by single executives were finally established, in 1781, it was not until delays and makeshift arrangements had imperiled the war effort....

Instead of setting up a separate executive body, the Articles of Confederation authorized ... Congress to appoint "such other committees and civil officers as may be necessary for managing the general affairs of the United States."...

A rapid proliferation of committees prevented members of Congress from carrying out their deliberative functions. John Adams was kept busy from four in the morning until ten at night, serving, by his own count, on close to ninety recorded committees, as well as on a great number of others that were unrecorded. The appearance of literally hundreds of committees was in part a reflection of factional struggles within Congress. When members failed to gain dominance over one committee, they were often successful in setting up special committees which they could control. Matters having to do with foreign affairs, for instance, were sometimes referred to special committees. The Committee for Foreign Affairs was periodically reduced to the status of an investigating body, or "a mere burial vault for questions which the parent body did not care to face."

As a compromise between the committee system and a single executive, Congress tried to relieve delegates of managerial details by establishing boards composed of men from outside Congress....

The introduction of outside personnel helped relieve legislators of some committee work, but it did not noticeably improve the efficiency and dispatch of the war effort. A new Board of War and Ordnance was reconstituted to include members of Congress. Financial administration was divided between a Board of Treasury and the Committee of Finance. When mistakes by the boards occurred, or when the work proceeded at too slow a pace, no single party could be held responsible. Moreover, the boards could not execute legislative business unless Congress disciplined its own activities and expedited matters. There is ample evidence that much of the time saved by delegating matters to the boards was subsequently lost in trifling debate....

Not until 1781 did Congress take the next step in efficient administration: the appointment of single officers. In the meantime, power fell into the hands of the more energetic and able public officials.

... Early in 1779, American representatives in Europe were instructed to obtain copies of the "arrangements and forms of conducting the business of the treasury, war office, marine, and other offices of government" in France or Great Britain, and in any other kingdoms and republics to which they were accredited.

On February 7 [1781] Congress adopted a resolution for the creation of three new executive officers: the Superintendent of Finance, the Secretary of War, and the Secretary of Marine. The office of Attorney General was created on February 16 to prosecute all suits on behalf of the United States and to advise Congress on all legal matters submitted to him. This separation of power—the result of a painfully slow evolution of executive departments—stands as a victory not for abstract doctrine but for *force majeure*. In a striking phrase, Francis Wharton [a writer of legal treatises, eds.] said that the Constitution "did not make this distribution of power. It would be more proper to say that this distribution of power made the Constitution of the United States."

Having taken five years to establish executive departments, Congress let several months go by before choosing their Secretaries. Robert Morris, unanimously elected Superintendent of Finance on February 20, refused to take the post unless Congress strengthened it according to his instructions. The chairman of the committee formed to study these demands confessed anxiety at this increase in executive power, but no alternative seemed possible: "Those Powers, or similar ones, must be vested in some one Person, in Order to extricate our Affairs from the Confusion in which they are at present involved. The Board of Treasury only make bad, worse. To go in the present Train is *absolutely impossible*. A *total Stagnation* must soon take Place, and Ruin cannot be far off. Were our Affairs in a State of *Beginning*, Powers so extensive would not be necessary; but perplexed, deranged and clogged with Abuses and Mismanagements as they are at present, it really appears to me that less Powers would be altogether unavailing." The committee agreed to Morris' terms and he accepted the position....

Ironically, just at the point when Congress had finally consented to appoint single executives, changing events undermined their positions of responsibility. The surrender of Cornwallis in the fall of 1781, and the subsequent initiation of negotiations for peace, removed the chief incentive for stronger national powers and more vigorous executives. Since no external enemy existed to push power to the center, the centrifugal pull of state sovereignty reasserted itself....

... The framers [of the federal Constitution] had had the good fortune to watch state governments function over a ten-year period. They saw that paper barriers in the state constitutions were not sufficient to prevent legislatures from usurping executive and judicial powers. They also came to appreciate the administrative bottlenecks in the Continental Congress. Faced with the extremes of an artificial and unreliable separation of powers at the state level, and no separation at all at the national level, the framers offered a subtle formulation: there had to be an overlapping of powers so as to guarantee the continued separation of the departments.

That is not to say that Madison and the other leading figures possessed a clear conception of the separation doctrine. On the contrary, no other principle gave them such trouble. The concept seemed to defy definition, since the problems for which the framers were seeking structural remedies were constantly changing.

According to textbooks, speeches on the floor of Congress, and even Supreme Court decisions, the framers held executive power in distrust. Justice Black, for instance, in striking down President Truman's seizure of the steel mills in 1952, declared that "The Founders of this Nation entrusted the lawmaking power to the Congress alone in both good and bad times. It would do no good to recall the historical events, the fears of power and the hopes for freedom that lay behind their choice."

This suggests an antagonistic relationship between executive power and individual liberties, yet one does not find such attitudes in the writings of John Adams, Madison, Jefferson, Jay, and others, at least not before 1789. True, the attitude did prevail during the colonial period, when it was automatically assumed that the public interest was enhanced whenever the legislature gained new power from the royal governor, and such distrust of the executive persisted for a few years after independence. But an accumulation of legislative abuses on the state level, combined with a demonstration of legislative incompetence on the national, had created by this time a new outlook toward executive power [on the part of Constitution's proponents]....

In the months prior to the Philadelphia Convention, Madison itemized for Jefferson the essential elements of the new national government, including a reorganization to provide for separate branches. Madison's interest in three branches was drawn more from administrative necessities than from the writings of Montesquieu. Congress had mismanaged its power under the confederation, he told Jefferson, while administrative responsibilities under the new government would be even more demanding....

The Virginia Plan, presented to the Convention on May 29, 1787, provided for three branches but made no reference to "separate and distinct" or to any other formulation of the separation doctrine. In fact, the executive was to be chosen by the legislature and joined with the judiciary so as to form a council of revision. Late in July, the Convention adopted a resolution explicitly affirming the separation doctrine, stating that the three national departments were to be kept distinct and independent, except in specified cases. However, the version presented to the Convention on August 6 by the Committee of Detail omitted the separation clause, and the Constitution was adopted in September without reference to it.

On the relationship between Congress and the President, Madison reminded the delegates that experience had proved "a tendency in our governments to throw all power into the Legislative vortex. The Executives of the States are in general little more than Cyphers; the legislatures omnipotent." The separation set up in the state constitutions had turned out to be a matter of mere parchment barriers, which were incapable of preventing legislatures from drawing other branches into their orbit. The principal anxiety in 1787 was not over executive power, the threat of a dictator, or the emergence of a George III at home, even if some delegates did warn that a single executive would be the "foetus of monarchy." The people of America, James Wilson said in rebuttal, did not oppose the British King "but the parliament—the opposition was not agt. an Unity but a corrupt multitude."

The chief and overriding fear for Wilson was that the "natural operation of the Legislature will be to swallow up the Executive." Gouverneur Morris maintained that the "Legislature will continually seek to aggrandize & perpetuate themselves," while John Mercer of Maryland took it as an axiom that careful construction of the Constitution could obviate "legislative usurpation and oppression."

The veto represented one means of self-defense for the federal executive. Some of the Antifederalists, taking the doctrine of separated powers in its most rigid form, considered the executive veto an encroachment of legislative powers. One critic of the Constitution called it "a political error of the greatest magnitude, to allow the executive power a negative, or in fact any kind of control over the proceedings of the legislature."

Delegates at Philadelphia did more than accept the executive veto as a necessary check on legislative ambitions; they also proposed that it be shared with the judiciary. To those delegates who denounced this as a patent violation of the separation doctrine, Wilson replied that the executive and judiciary should share the negative, for "they cannot otherwise preserve their importance against the legislature." Madison agreed, urging that the judiciary be introduced in "the business of Legislation — they will protect their Department, and uniting [with] the Executive render their Check or negative more respectable."

Later, when the proposal for joint revisionary power was still under consideration, Madison argued that a blending of the two departments would operate as an "auxiliary precaution" in preserving a lasting and durable separation. That line of reasoning must have baffled those who adhered to strict separation, but Madison preferred to assure separation in practice by deviating from it in theory whenever necessary. Merely to declare a separation of powers, he said, was not sufficient, since experience demonstrated the need for introducing "a balance of powers and interests, as will guarantee the provisions on paper."

After the convention had adjourned, Madison confided to Jefferson that the boundaries between the executive, legislative, and judicial powers, "though in general so strongly marked in themselves, consist in many instances of mere shades of difference." He set out in the Federalist Papers to contrast the overlapping of powers in the Constitution with the abstract and impracticable partitioning of powers advocated by some of the Antifederalists.

… "How is the executive?" cried one delegate at the Virginia ratifying convention. "Contrary to the opinion of all the best writers, blended with the legislative. We have asked for bread, and they have given us a stone." The Constitution was attacked at the North Carolina ratifying convention for violating the maxim whereby the three branches "ought to be forever separate and distinct from each other." Overlapping of departments also provoked criticism in Pennsylvania. Opponents of the Constitution maintained that the Senate's judicial power in impeachment, as well as the executive's legislative power in making treaties, constituted an "undue and dangerous mixture of the powers of government." A lengthy quotation from Montesquieu was introduced to demonstrate the dependence of freedom and liberty on a separation of powers.

These three states insisted that a separation clause be added to the national bill of rights. Virginia's recommendations in June 1788 included the clause: "legislative, executive, and judiciary powers of Government should be separate and distinct," while Pennsylvania and North Carolina offered their own versions of a separation clause. Congress compiled a tentative list of restrictions on the national government, among which was the following: "The powers delegated by this constitution are appropriated to the departments to which they are respectively distributed: so that the legislative department shall never exercise the powers vested in the executive or judicial nor the executive exercise the powers vested in the legislative or judicial, nor the judicial exercise the powers vested in the legislative or executive departments."

Surprisingly, Madison supported that clause, but this does not mean that he had suddenly embraced the notion of pure separation. What he feared was that additional blending, resulting from encroachment, would benefit the legislature and weaken the executive. In the House debates in 1789, he opposed Senate participation in the removal power because that might reduce Presidential power to a "mere vapor." The unity and responsibility of the executive, he said, were intended to secure liberty and the public welfare. Join the president with the Senate in the removal power, and the executive becomes a "two-headed monster," deprived of responsibility.

So concerned was Madison about the independence of the executive branch that he began to use the kind of abstract phrases he had earlier rejected. For now he was to say, "if there is a principle in our constitution, indeed in any free constitution, more sacred than another, it is that which separates the legislative, executive, and judicial powers." However, from the context of this remark, we know that Madison was presenting separation of powers not in its rigid form, but was using it rather for the explicit purpose of opposing legislative participation in the designation of officers. Once again he expresses his concern for the independence of the executive branch: "The Legislature creates the office, defines the powers, limits its duration, and annexes a compensation. This done, the legislative power ceases. They ought to have nothing to do with designating the man to fill the office. That I conceive to be of an executive nature."

These debates in the House help explain Madison's support for the separation clause in the bill of rights. The Senate journal, unfortunately, tells us very little about the discussion on that clause. It was among seventeen constitutional amendments sent to the Senate. The members struck it from the list of proposed amendments on September 7, 1789. A substitute amendment (to make the three departments "separate and distinct," and to assure that the legislative and executive departments would be restrained from oppression by "feeling and participating the public burdens" through regular elections) was also voted down. Three members of the House, Madison among them, met with the Senate in conference to reconcile their different lists of amendments. In the days that followed, the list of seventeen was cut to twelve. Among the deleted amendments was the separation clause.

It is widely argued that the separation doctrine, while not explicitly stated in the Constitution, is nevertheless implied. Perhaps so, but that does not take us a step closer to understanding exactly what is implied or to what degree the departments must remain separate. Similar questions are raised when one states that the framers believed in a separation of power. No doubt they did, but for what purpose? With what objective in mind?

[I]t seems fair to say that the framers shared a desire for greater administrative efficiency and more reliable governmental machinery. Direct experience with state government and the Continental Congress convinced them of the need for a separate executive and interdepartmental checks. Chief among their concerns was the need to protect against legislative usurpations and to preserve the independence of the executive and judicial branches. Those were the dominant thoughts behind the separation of powers, not the doctrine of Montesquieu, fear of executive power, or a basic distrust of government. If the framers had wanted weak government, they could have had that with the Articles of Confederation.

Had the separation clause been accepted by Congress and ratified by the states, its primary effect would have been a warning against departmental encroachments. It would not have affected the blending of departments and powers already sanctioned by the Constitution, nor would it have prohibited the delegation of legislative powers to the President. Congress was no more capable in 1789 of administering the nation's business than it had been during the previous decade.

The complexities of national growth, the need for economic regulation, and new international responsibilities all provided fresh incentives for granting new powers to the executive branch.

President and Congress (1972), chap. 1, passim.

Notes and Questions

1. *The constitutional text.* There is no better source for the intent of the framers than the language of the Constitution they wrote. Reread Articles I, II, and III and then consider the following questions.

(a) Article I says, "All legislative Powers herein granted shall be vested in a Congress of the United States, which shall consist of a Senate and a House of Representatives." Is this really what Article I does? Does the president play a role in the legislative process? Is Congress limited to making laws? Does the president have a monopoly on foreign policy?

(b) Article II says, "The executive Power shall be vested in a President of the United States of America." Is this really what Article II does? Is the president granted complete control over civil and military officers? See Article I, Section 8, clause 18. Is it significant that Article II does not limit the president to those "powers herein granted," as Article I limits Congress?

(c) Article III says, "The Judicial Power of the United States shall be vested in one supreme court, and in such inferior Courts as the Congress may from time to time ordain and establish." Are the Congress and president denied any authority over who the judges are, what values they bring to their work, or what opportunities they have to interpret the Constitution? Is the judiciary deprived of all opportunity to affect the legislative and executive processes? To affect the enforceability of what Congress or the president might do?

2. *The viability of "separation of powers" as a concept.* How would you characterize the evolution of separation of powers talk during the seventeenth and eighteenth centuries? What had happened to that concept by 1789? Is the term adequate to describe what the Constitution did, or what the framers intended it to do? If not, what term better characterizes the Constitution's scheme for allocating power? On the evolution of separation of powers thought in the seventeenth and eighteenth centuries, see Stanley N. Katz, "The Origins of American Constitutional Thought," *Perspectives in American History,* 3 (1969), 474–90, and works reviewed therein.

3. *Separation of powers versus checks and balances.* Compare the terms "separation of powers" and "checks and balances." Which is more likely to imply that each branch of government was meant to be autonomous, fully equipped with its own authority, and not subject to domination by another branch? Which is more likely to imply that the Constitution was meant to allocate certain functions, including the making of laws, the enforcement of law, and the interpretation of law, to specified officials on the theory that they know best how to exercise those functions? Which term is the most mechanistic, suggesting that the Constitution is no more flexible than a clock? Which suggests that the Constitution is susceptible to evolution like a living organism? Which term comes closest to the framers' intent—if that can be inferred from what you have read of *The Federalist Papers?*

4. *Functions versus processes.* Which is the more accurate description of the Constitution of 1789: that it allocates certain functions to different officials, on the theory that they know best how to exercise those functions, or that it sets up certain processes for

policy making which permit different officials, with different constituencies, priorities, and modes of thinking, to interact with each other in the making of public policy over time, on the theory that the policies they produce are more likely, in the long run, to reflect a broader range of constitutional values than any other system? For a sophisticated analysis of the distinction between function and process, see Vile, *Constitutionalism and the Separation of Powers* (1967).

5. *Mechanical versus political modes of analysis.* Historians and political scientists throughout the Western world are in general agreement that the men who wrote the U.S. Constitution were unusual in their political acumen and statesmanship. Assuming that is true, must we assume that the document they wrote is so brilliant in its conception that it can be adhered to for centuries without significant change, like some great master blueprint? Did the framers regard it as a finished work of art, beyond improvement? Or is it more realistic to view the Constitution as the result of a political process, not unlike the political processes of our own time, involving accommodations and compromises among a variety of powerful interests, groups, regions, and values, negotiated by fallible men groping through their own uncertainties to devise a system of government more efficient (and yet still safe from tyranny) than the one they had experienced under the Articles of Confederation?

6. *Checks versus balances.* The term "check" connotes a mechanistic approach to the distribution of power, but does the existence of certain checks—such as the presidential veto, senatorial refusals to consent to appointments or treaties, or judicial review—guarantee that these powers will be used or, if used, that their exercise will be sufficient to ensure the objectives of those who use them? The constitutional system of checks does give certain political actors distinct advantages, but does it fully determine their relative influence within the system at any given time? What does determine the relative balances of political power within the system at any given moment, or over time? As a matter of historic record, has the constitutional scheme ensured an unchangeable balance of power among the branches or among other power centers in the American political system during the past two centuries? Does the Constitution specify where leadership on any particular issue must come from? Does it assume that the legislative or executive or judicial processes are to control policy making in any given area? Are the branches required to come into agreement if they expect to get anything substantial accomplished? Is any one branch likely to prevail over the determined opposition of the other two branches? Under what circumstances is one branch likely to aggrandize power at the expense of another branch?

Arthur F. Bentley,
Separated Institutions and the Routes to Power
(1908)

Arthur Bentley was one of the founders of the modern science of politics. His 1908 classic, *The Process of Government*, dispelled many of the illusions common to American government textbooks of his day. He focused not on abstract doctrines of political philosophy and constitutional law, but on the activities of individuals and groups in the real world of political action. Like Woodrow Wilson, Bentley championed the behavioral approach to studying American politics.

In the following selection Bentley explores one of the effects of a system of separated institutions: the way in which it provides an efficient accommodation to changing electoral and group pressures and provides for a stable yet evolving and adaptable political system.

... If group interests tend in a certain direction, and are checked in their course through Congress, they will find their way through the presidency. If the group interests take permanently a form which makes Congress an inadequate agency for them, then the presidency will consolidate its power. If, on the other hand, the shifting of the interests or the change in Congress makes the latter agency adequate, then the presidency's power will readjust accordingly....

... Do certain interests block the legislature? Then the executive may be set free. And vice versa. Meanwhile there is a process through the courts checking both. Instead of conditions corresponding to class domination, we have in our organization of the interests conditions corresponding to the breaking down of set classes, and a technique which helps to keep free the avenues of group approach. We do not have by any means the most free avenues of approach. Looking at a section of our history a decade or two long, one may easily be tempted to say we have a government which tends to favor class dominance. But despite some tremendously strong underlying group interests, we have nevertheless frequent evidences of the giving away of the fortifications of one set of groups at the assault of another, and the freeing of the executive from class domination. We have avenues of approach through the government such that the class tendency can only advance to a certain degree before being overwhelmed, and that degree one which probably falls far short, except in most exceptional temporary cases, of the degree in which a resort to violence as the only effective technique becomes necessary.

... If the executive yields to a group organization gathering force from without, before the legislature yields, it will gain in power as compared to the legislature, until the legislature yields in its turn. Its gain in power will seem a menace merely to those who are immediately hurt by it, never to those who benefit by it....

We may put it thus: that if the group interests work out a fair and satisfying adjustment through the legislature, then the executive sinks in prominence; that when the adjustment is not perfected in the legislature, then the executive arises in strength to do the work; that the judiciary ... bears in these points a relation to the executive somewhat similar to that which the legislature bears, similar, that is, in quality, if not in quantity; that the growth of executive discretion is therefore a phase of the group process; that it cannot be understood in any other way, and that no judgment concerning it will maintain itself except through the group process and by the test of the group process.

The Process of Government (1908), 351–59.

Notes and Questions

1. *Political stabilizers.* Bentley, like most political scientists of the pluralist (or group politics) persuasion, was much impressed by the Constitution's mechanisms for ensuring political stability. One of these mechanisms is what space scientists call "systems redundancy": if one system fails, a backup system takes over. A similar principle is "load sharing": if the president is preoccupied with international affairs, a greater role in domestic leadership can be assumed by Congress, the states, or the municipalities. Thus the political system is protected against crippling breakdowns, overloads, or revolution.

2. *The public interest.* But is stability the only objective of systems design in politics? According to Bentley and his followers, whose interests are served by these safeguards? Does

a political order that serves the dominant groups well necessarily serve other interests and values well too? Are all groups in American politics equally well organized, financed, and led? Are all values central to the constitutional scheme adequately represented by interest groups? In a system dominated by the competition of interest groups, how is the public interest defined? Should all aspects of the public interest be defined in this manner, e.g., foreign policy, military policy, weapons procurement, delegation of powers, civil rights and liberties?

E. The Rise of Positive Government and Presidential Initiative

Woodrow Wilson,
The Constitution Contains No Theories
(1908)

Woodrow Wilson was one of the founders of modern political science and one of the first to reject the syllogistic, deductive approach to constitutional interpretation favored by nineteenth-century judges. Wilson taught at Princeton University before embarking on the political career that carried him to the White House.

The makers of the Constitution seem to have thought of the President as what the stricter Whig theorists wished the king to be: only the legal executive, the presiding and guiding authority in the application of law and the execution of policy. His veto upon legislation was only his "check" on Congress.... He was

Woodrow Wilson

empowered to prevent bad laws, but he was not to be given an opportunity to make good ones. As a matter of fact he has become very much more. He has become the leader of his party and the guide of the nation in political purpose, and therefore in legal action. The constitutional structure of the government has hampered and limited his action in these significant roles, but it has not prevented it....

... Greatly as the practice and influence of Presidents has varied, there can be no mistaking the fact that we have grown more and more inclined from generation to generation to look to the President as the unifying force in our complex system, the leader both of his party and of the nation. To do so is not inconsistent with the actual provisions of the Constitution; it is only inconsistent with a very mechanical theory of its meaning and intention. The Constitution contains no theories. It is as practical a document as Magna Carta.... What is it that a nominating convention wants in the man it is to present to the country for its suffrages? A man who will be and who will seem to the country in some sort an embodiment of the character and purpose it wishes its government to have—a man who understands his own day and the needs of the country, and who has the personality and the initiative to enforce his views both upon the people and upon Congress....

As legal executive, his constitutional aspect, the President cannot be thought of alone. He cannot execute laws. Their actual daily execution must be taken care of by the several executive departments and by the now innumerable body of federal officials throughout the country. In respect of the strictly executive duties of his office the President may be said to administer the Presidency in conjunction with the members of his Cabinet, like the chairman of a commission. He is even of necessity much less active in the actual carrying out of the law than are his colleagues and advisers. It is therefore becoming more and more true, as the business of the government becomes more and more complex and extended, that the President is becoming more and more a political and less and less an executive officer. His executive powers are in commission, while his political powers more and more center and accumulate upon him and are in their very nature personal and inalienable.... There is no national party choice except that of President. No one else represents the people as a whole, exercising a national choice; and inasmuch as his strictly executive duties are in fact subordinated, so far at any rate as all detail is concerned, the President represents not so much the party's governing efficiency as its controlling ideals and principles. He is not so much part of its organization as its vital link of connection with the thinking nation. He can dominate his party by being spokesman for the real sentiment and purpose of the country, by giving direction to opinion, by giving the country at once the information and the statements of policy which will enable it to form its judgments alike of parties and of men.

For he is also the political leader of the nation, or has it in his choice to be. The nation as a whole has chosen him, and is conscious that it has no other political spokesman. His is the only national voice in affairs. Let him once win the admiration and confidence of the country, and no other single force can withstand him, no combination of forces will easily overpower him. His position takes the imagination of the country. He is the representative of no constituency, but of the whole people. When he speaks in his true character, he speaks for no special interest. If he rightly interpret the national thought and boldly insist upon it, he is irresistible; and the country never feels the zest of action so much as when its President is of such insight and caliber. Its instinct is for unified action, and it craves a single leader. It is for this reason that it will often prefer to choose a man rather than a party. A President whom it trusts can not only lead it, but form it to his own views.... He may be both the leader of his party and the leader of the nation, or he may be one or the other. If he lead the nation, his party can hardly resist him. His office is anything he has the sagacity and force to make it.

The Constitution of the United States is not a mere lawyers' document: it is a vehicle of life, and its spirit is always the spirit of the age. Its prescriptions are clear and we know what they are; a written document makes lawyers of us all, and our duty as citizens should make us conscientious lawyers, reading the text of the Constitution without subtlety or sophistication; but life is always your last and most authoritative critic.

Some of our Presidents have deliberately held themselves off from using the full power they might legitimately have used, because of conscientious scruples, because they were more theorists than statesmen. They have held the strict literary theory of the Constitution, the Whig theory, the Newtonian theory, and have acted as if they thought that Pennsylvania Avenue should have been even longer than it is; that there should be no intimate communication of any kind between the Capitol and the White House; that the President as a man was no more at liberty to lead the houses of Congress by persuasion than he was at liberty as President to dominate them by authority — supposing that he had, what he has not, authority enough to dominate them. But the makers of the Constitution were not enacting Whig theory, they were not making laws with the expectation that, not the laws themselves, but their opinions, known by future historians to lie back of them, should govern the constitutional action of the country. They were statesmen, not pedants, and their laws are sufficient to keep us to the paths they set us upon. The President is at liberty, both in law and conscience, to be as big a man as he can. His capacity will set the limit; and if Congress be overborne by him, it will be no fault of the makers of the Constitution — it will be from no lack of constitutional powers on its part, but only because the President has the nation behind him, and Congress has not. He has no means of compelling Congress except through public opinion....

One of the greatest of the President's powers I have not yet spoken of at all: his control, which is very absolute, of the foreign relations of the nation. The initiative in foreign affairs, which the President possesses without any restriction whatever, is virtually the power to control them absolutely. The President cannot conclude a treaty with a foreign power without the consent of the Senate, but he may guide every step of diplomacy, and to guide diplomacy is to determine what treaties must be made, if the faith and prestige of the government are to be maintained. He need disclose no step of negotiation until it is complete, and when in any critical matter it is completed the government is virtually committed. Whatever its disinclination, the Senate may feel itself committed also.... The President can never again be the mere domestic figure he has been throughout so large a part of our history. The nation has risen to the first rank in power and resources. The other nations of the world look askance upon her, half in envy, half in fear, and wonder with a deep anxiety what she will do with her vast strength....

Our President must always, henceforth, be one of the great powers of the world, whether he act greatly and wisely or not, and the best statesmen we can produce will be needed to fill the office of Secretary of State. We have but begun to see the presidential office in this light; but it is the light which will more and more beat upon it, and more and more determine its character and its effect upon the politics of the nation. We can never hide our President again as a mere domestic officer. We can never again see him the mere executive he was in the [eighteen] thirties and forties. He must stand always at the front of our affairs, and the office will be as big and as influential as the man who occupies it.

How is it possible to sum up the duties and influence of such an office in such a system in comprehensive terms which will cover all its changeful aspects? In the view of the makers of the Constitution the President was to be the legal executive; perhaps the leader of the nation; certainly not the leader of the party, at any rate while in office. But by the operation of forces inherent in the very nature of government he has become all three, and by inevitable consequence the most heavily burdened officer in the world.

Constitutional Government in the United States (1908), 54–81.

Notes and Questions

1. *Whig theory.* Wilson refers to the Whig, or "literary," theory of the Constitution. The Whigs to whom he refers were members of an American political party formed in the 1830s in reaction to the strong presidency of Andrew Jackson. These Whigs, like their British and colonial ancestors, believed that executive powers should be narrowly construed, and that legislatures should be supreme over executives. To ensure legislative dominance they argued that presidents should serve for only one term, abstain from influencing members of Congress, and follow the lead of legislative party leaders. Is Wilson correct to suggest that Madison and the Federalists who drafted the Constitution were not strict Whig theorists?

2. *Constitutional theory.* Is it true, as Wilson asserts, that neither Constitution nor Magna Carta contains any theories? What consequences might result from that view? Ought federal officials to be free to do whatever the Constitution does not expressly forbid? If one reads the Constitution "without subtlety or sophistication" as Wilson urges, which branch of government is most likely to gain power? Would President Wilson endorse Professor Wilson's approach?

3. *The foreign-affairs power.* Does the Constitution grant to the president a "very absolute" control over foreign relations? Does the power to initiate foreign relations, expressly granted by the Constitution, also imply "the power to control them absolutely"? Which theory does Wilson advance in the realm of foreign affairs, separation of powers or checks and balances?

Arthur S. Miller,
The Rise of the Positive State
(1966)

In this selection, a distinguished law professor considers the implications of the "Constitutional Revolution" of the late 1930s, when both judges and Americans generally came to view the Constitution less as a source of limitations than as a source of affirmative powers.

In the long constitutional history of the United States, a very few landmarks stand out with particular clarity. One surely is *Marbury v. Madison....* Another is the Civil War, an episode which settled in blood that this nation is truly a union and which settled in law that *raison d'etat* is an operative principle of the American constitutional order. When that war was followed by the anti-slavery amendments, a new constitutional order was ushered in, the contours of which are still being traced in judicial and other official decisions. A third is the rise and fall of "economic due process" in the fifty years before 1937, a period in which the Supreme Court became "the first authoritative faculty of political economy in the world's history." Finally, there is the rise of "positive" government—the Positive State—during the past three decades, epitomized by enactment of the Employment Act of 1946....

The Positive State is a shorthand label for the express acceptance by the federal government—and thus by the American people—of an affirmative responsibility for economic well-being. It involves a societal undertaking and duty to create and maintain economic growth, employment opportunities, and general access to the basic necessities of life. The notion of a constitutional duty upon government itself represents a new departure. Exemplified in a broad range of programs, federal and state, it is the American version of the "welfare state."

The Positive State received its charter not by constitutional amendment but by statute: the Employment Act of 1946, surely one of the most important congressional acts in American constitutional history.

With the pronouncement of its preamble, which made constitutional law as surely as it is created by amendment and, more importantly, by the Supreme Court, came the culmination of the "New Deal" and of the "constitutional revolution" of the 1930's; the act capped a series of statutes, upheld by the Supreme Court beginning in the watershed year of 1937, under which affirmative government sprang, Minerva-like, from the brow of Congress. The "negative, night watchman state" died and was quietly buried, the final obsequies coming in 1953 when the first Republican administration after the birth of the Positive State not only failed to reject it but in fact contributed to its growth....

In a series of legitimizing decisions beginning with *Nebbia v. New York* and the *Gold Clause Cases*, the Supreme Court gave constitutional blessing to the Positive State. The change was so complete that by 1946, when the Employment Act became law, no challenge to its validity could be or was made. The consequences of this new posture of government are still in a process of evolutionary development, but enough is known to enable us to trace their contours.

Most fundamental, perhaps, is the change in the economic sphere from a Constitution of limitations to one of powers; or as Edward S. Corwin put it, "a Constitution of powers in a secular state." The American charter of government was drafted by men who feared despotism and fragmented political power to avoid it. Its core principle was that the national government was to be limited to those powers specifically delegated to it. Even when the Supreme Court rewrote the Constitution in 1819 to add the concept of implied powers, the general posture was still one of limitation; the apotheosis of this concept came in the judicial attempt to establish a laissez-faire government in the late 19th and early 20th centuries.

The notion of limitation, viewed retrospectively, has yielded in the past three decades to the idea that the government has the power, even duty, to take action. This transition was not quite so abrupt as it appeared, for the coming of affirmative government in the post-1937 period can only be understood as part of a process grounded on the principle that government in the United States has always been as strong (or positive) as conditions demanded. Chief Justice Hughes expressed the new concept aptly in *West Coast Hotel v. Parrish*: "[T]he liberty safeguarded [by the Fourteenth Amendment] is liberty in a social organization which *requires* the protection of law against the evils which menace the health, safety, morals and welfare of the people." With these words, the Chief Justice gave constitutional sanction to the concept within a decade enacted into law in the Employment Act. His next sentence is one of the most pregnant statements in constitutional history: *Liberty under the Constitution is … necessarily subject to the restraints of due process, and regulation which is reasonable in relation to its subject and is adopted in the interests of the community is due process.*

With that utterance the nature of liberty under the Constitution was changed; the Positive State received its constitutional underpinnings. The Court expressly recognized that liberty could be infringed by forces other than government and that to counteract them government intervention may be required. Due process became not only liberty against government, but a concept to be used by government to justify restraining the liberty of some in the interests of the "community." …

The second noteworthy feature of the Positive State is the advent of a system of "economic planning" by federal government.

The American system of planning is noncoercive; it is "facilitative." Government persuades rather than commands. Basic reliance upon the private character of business enterprise is accomplished by an insistence that certain decisions of corporate managers and trade union leaders be taken "in the public interest." As such, the American system falls far short of the almost completely directed economies of Communist China and the USSR, and even short of the system of "indicative programming" employed by such nations as France.…

Third in this listing of the contours of the Positive State is the change which has occurred and which is continuing to take place in the constitutional framework of government, principally in the doctrines of federalism and the separation of powers. Economic planning may well be "the DDT of federalism." Any large-scale planning by government generates a need for unified and perhaps uniform economic policies throughout the nation. That need runs counter to the diversity inherent in federalism; it is also contrary to the fragmentation of power within the national government itself, and leads toward centralization of official power. Moreover, of at least tangential interest are the trend toward centralization of governmental power within the executive branch itself and the trend toward "multinationalism." …

The alteration in American federalism from the "dual" system established in 1787 to the "cooperative" system of the Positive State is an indisputable fact, although it may be deplored by some and political leaders may plump for "creative" federalism. The political, economic, and technological imperatives of the modern era do not now, and probably never again will, permit that diversity which is the glory and *raison d'être* of federalism. The formal structure of American government may remain, for a political organization has a way of surviving, like a vermiform appendix, long after it has ceased to function, but the substance and the content will be elsewhere. The *important* decisions of government today are made in Washington, even though administration may be and often is in state capitals, county seats, and cities.

As with federalism, so too has the separation of powers in the national government given way to centralization of power. The Positive State is the "administrative state" and the locus of power within the national government, if it can be located at all, is within the executive.…

The judiciary also has a changed function with the coming of the Positive State. At one time the ultimate decision-maker in economic policy matters, the Supreme Court now has been reduced to interpretation of statutes and review of administrative actions. While this does not leave the High Bench without power, nonetheless its decisions can be (and have been) reviewed by the avowedly political branches of government.… A consequence is that one of the considerations of the judicial process in administrative law matters must be the possibility of legislative reversal of a Court decision.…

The fourth item in this listing of the contours of the Positive State concerns both the nature of law and the role of the judiciary: the "politicization" of law and the legal process.

The externalization of standards which Holmes asserted was the hallmark of the growth of a legal system is being lost in the onslaught of an all-pervasive system of public law. Public law, that is, the nebulous standards under which executive—administrative action is ostensibly canalized under the Supreme Court statement of the meaning of the Constitution, is a marriage of "politics" and "external command," of necessarily forward-looking policy-making conducted within the pre-existing limits of known law. But the ideal of a "government of laws and not of men" has never been met; the Positive State is "emphatically a government of men and not of laws."

However much administrators and executive officials may use the terminology of law and justify their actions by using legal opinions, probing beneath the surface shows that law is used for policy ends; it is readily apparent that law and the legal process have been politicized. That conclusion is the lesson to be drawn from the statement by Judge Henry J. Friendly "that the basic deficiency, which underlies and accounts for the most serious troubles of the agencies, is the failure to 'make law' within the broad confines of the agencies' characters.…" His point was that much of the "justified dissatisfaction" with administration is the failure of administrators and others "to develop standards sufficiently definite to permit decisions to be fairly predictable and the reasons for them to be understood.…"

Judge Friendly was talking principally of the regulatory commissions. If his analysis is valid, then the commissions, too, are involved in a system of politicized law. The description is even more apt for other organs of the public administration which make more important public-policy decisions without the semblance of procedural due process through which the commissions ostensibly operate—those which set monetary and fiscal policy, to take but one example. Here again is public law of great importance, created and administered outside the framework of the judiciary and without reference to those procedural safeguards imbedded in the concept of due process. Here, in short, is politicized law. It is difficult to see how government could otherwise operate given the number and complexity of tasks which face it today. Law in the Positive State is being redefined; no longer does it fit the neat classifications of the premodern era—if indeed it ever did.…

Fifth and last in this listing of prominent features of the Positive State is a trend toward the progressive blurring of what purportedly is public and what supposedly is private. In many respects this is a corollary of the fourth characteristic, discussed above, about the symbiotic relationship between government and governed in the American polity—particularly when the governed is made up of those in the pluralistic power centers. The development may be seen in several places, including the reciprocal participation by business leaders in government decisions and by government officials in business decisions; the dependency of large segments of the business community upon government for their existence; and the close reciprocating interactions between the professions and government.... Through these and similar relationships, bound together at times by the legal instrument of contract, a radically new posture is evolving in the position of government and the individuals, natural and artificial, who make up American society.

The consequences of this process go far beyond the progressive blurring of the line between public and private. To take just one for illustration: The development has had great significance for the nature of American private law. Property is changing from the ownership of "things" to ownership of "rights"—often made up of government largess. Wealth largely consists of promises, whether from government in the form of largess, corporations in the form of stock, insurance companies in the form of annuities, or from pension funds.... In essence, the change in private law is from a system based on individualistic notions to one which, haltingly and imperfectly, reflects the organizational basis of society and the position of the individual in that society.

The bureaucratization of American society, a consequence of the organizational revolution which has taken place since the Civil War, is itself a development of constitutional importance. Not the individual, but the organization, predominates in this nation, particularly in economic matters. The individual *qua* individual is diminishing in importance; what significance he has derives from his membership in a group (or several groups). The "autonomous man," is becoming an exceedingly rare phenomenon....

35 *Geo. Wash. L. Rev.* 172–84 (1966).

Notes and Questions

1. *Raison d'état.* Did the Civil War, or the so-called Constitutional Revolution of 1937, establish *raison d'état* as "an operative principle of the American constitutional order"? How should one go about ascertaining the operative principles of the constitutional order?

2. *Death of the negative state.* Has the negative state, in the sense of a constitution of limitations, died? What does it take to kill a constitutional principle?

3. *The nature of liberty.* When Chief Justice Hughes wrote that "Liberty under the Constitution is ... necessarily ... subject to ... regulation which is reasonable," was he saying anything new? Did the pre-1937 court decisions proclaiming a "liberty of contract" and a freedom from certain economic regulations deny the legitimacy of economic regulations that served the common good? See, e.g., *Lochner v. New York*, 198 U.S. 45 (1905). Or did the constitutional revolution of the 1930s simply consist of a change in public and court perceptions of what should be the proper balance between the liberty of individuals (and corporations) and the demands that a community might appropriately make on individuals (and corporations) under changing economic and geopolitical conditions?

4. *The nature of the public good.* Theodore Lowi has argued that the most significant development of the 1930s was the rise of "interest group liberalism," the belief that competition among organized interests, not just in the legislative halls but in the bureaucratic corridors, is essentially democratic, and that the public interest consists of nothing more than the sum total of specialized, organized interests.[3] Is the proliferation of highly organized, well-financed interest groups, and the extension of their political activity into the precincts of bureaucracy, a net gain for democracy, or for the principles of republican government? Should the public interest be viewed as nothing more than the balance of the political weights that organized interests can throw on the political scales? If so, can viable distinctions continue to be drawn between rights and interests, between what is private and what is public, or between law and politics?

5. *Role of the Supreme Court.* Has the rise of administrative lawmaking reduced the Supreme Court to "interpretation of statutes and review of administrative actions"? Has the Court's authority to enforce constitutional limitations been curbed in any way?

6. *Delegation of policy making to administrators.* Does the delegation by Congress and the president of extensive policy-making authority to administrators mean that the United States has ceased to be a government of laws? Are not all governments a mixture of law and discretion? What, if anything, is wrong with the current balance between law and discretion in the federal government? Again, consider Lowi, who argues that the rise of the positive state, the proliferation of certain organized interests at the expense of others, and the decline of normative concepts of the public interest have turned over much of the law-making function to unelected officials and have turned the idea of law as a body of morally defensible principles into law as the amoral outcome of processes in which the most effectively organized interests predominate.

Edward S. Corwin,
Total War and the Constitution
(1948)

Wilson's New Freedom, Roosevelt's New Deal, the two world wars, and the cold war led many Americans to look to the presidency for decisive leadership. Most political scientists of the post-World War II generation promoted constitutional theories calculated to ensure a strong presidency little encumbered by checks and balances. The glory of the New Deal, they asserted, was that it reduced conflict in society by transforming issues of principle into issues of interests, which could then be negotiated safely in the amoral market of group politics. In their view, constitutional law and theory were largely irrelevant to the explication of American politics. They focused instead on the clash of interest groups, the behavior of bureaucrats, and the processes of decision making.

The term "Whig," once synonymous with prevention of executive tyranny through checks and balances, became a term of derision applied by some political scientists to constitutionalists like Professor Edward S. Corwin of Princeton, who worried openly about the "high-flying prerogatives" that Franklin Roosevelt and his successors were asserting. He feared that the founders' Constitution of Limitations" was rapidly being supplanted by a "Constitution of Powers," and the the presidency was becoming all sail an no anchor.

In the following speech, Corwin discussed some of the implications that the New Deal and the Second World War had for the principle of constitutionally limited powers, the

---

3. *The End of Liberalism* (2d ed., 1980), ch. 3.

system of checks and balances, the rule of law, the preservation of individual rights, and the role of the courts in enforcing constitutional principles.

War today [circa 1948] is a very different affair. In World War II the whole of our American society was regimented. Labor was regimented, industry and agriculture were regimented, even talent was regimented for use in propaganda work; and so on and so forth. War today is, in the functional sense, *total war*, in that it brings into operation all of the forces of the society that is involved.... But technical progress and the necessity of maintaining at the front the vast forces which are the product of conscription, those two facts simply mean that war while it is waging absorbs all the energies of society, which means in turn that a tremendous strain is placed on governmental powers and so on the Constitution itself.

What then, has been the effect of war on the idea that this is a government of enumerated [and therefore limited] powers? In a word, the effect has been to water this idea down very decidedly....

But, you may ask, what difference does it make whether ours is a government of *enumerated* powers or a government of *plenary* powers in the waging of war? It makes just this difference, that under the doctrine of enumerated powers you must go to the Constitution to find a special warrant for the things that are necessary to be done, but that under the doctrine of a plenary *inherent* war power, you resort to the Constitution only to find out if there is definite language which *forbids* the things necessary to be done. The doctrine of inherent powers, in other words, *makes constitutionally available all of the resident forces of the United States as a national community in the waging of war*. It makes all of the resources of the nation constitutionally available.

We now turn to the proposition that the legislature cannot delegate its powers. That was cast overboard for purposes of war as early as World War I. The Congress of the United States was suddenly confronted with the problem of adapting legislative power to the exigencies of war, a vast new range of subject matter that had never before been brought within the national government's orbit, and at the same time to give its legislation affecting this enlarged subject matter a form which would render it easily responsive to the ever-changing requirements of a naturally fluid war situation. How could that be done? There was only one way and that was to say to the President, you may do this, you may do that and the other thing, and to lay down only a minimum of restraints upon the exercise of these broad powers....

We come now to our third doctrine; that this is a government of laws and not of men. It was the Civil War which brought about the demise of that doctrine so far as war is concerned. [L]et me show you into what extraordinary courses Mr. Lincoln was driven in sustaining his policy.

During this period of ten weeks he enrolled the state militias in a huge volunteer army to serve for ninety days; created a volunteer army of forty thousand men to serve for three years; added twenty-three thousand men to the regular army; eighteen thousand men to the navy; paid out two million dollars from unappropriated funds in the Treasury; closed the Post Office to "treasonable correspondence"; subjected passengers to and from foreign countries to new passport regulations; suspended the writ of habeas corpus in certain localities; caused the arrest and military detention of persons who were "represented to him as being engaged in treasonable practices"—and all this, except for the call to the state militias, without any statutory authorization.

In his message of July 4, Lincoln informed Congress of most of the things he had done. He didn't tell them quite all. He didn't tell them about the two million dollars until after the thing was smoked out in May of the following year, when he had to admit he had done that too....

But to get to the point. Some of these things were ratified by Congress, some were not. Some of them, indeed, had had their intended effect before Congress met. What conclusion is forced upon us? It is obvious that many of these acts assert for the President for the first time in our history *an initiative of indefinite scope in meeting the domestic aspects of a war emergency*; and in meeting them, by what was virtually an exercise of *legislative* power.

And, in World War I, Mr. Wilson imitated Lincoln to some, although not to a great, extent....

In World War II you get a great expansion of this quasi-legislative power of the President, one that is simply amazing when you come to study it in detail.... [T]ake the Board of Economic Warfare, the National Housing Agency, the National War Labor Board, the Office of Censorship, the Office of Civilian Defense, the Office of Defense Transportation, the Office of Facts and Figures, the Office of War Information, the War Production Board, which superseded the earlier Office of Production Management, the War Manpower Commission, and later on the Economic Stabilization Board, all these and many others I could recite were created by the President simply by virtue of power which he claimed as Commander-in-Chief.

One result of the creation of these agencies was this: the President conferred upon them certain powers, some of which he had from statute; some of which he claimed as "Commander-in-Chief in wartime." But in either case the agencies themselves rested on no statutory foundation....

I turn now to *the effect of war on private rights*. I think perhaps the best illustration of the effect of war on private rights is the growth of the use of military conscription. To begin with, when the Constitution was framed Congress was authorized to provide for the calling of the militia into the service of the United States to enforce the laws, to suppress insurrection and repel invasion. The clause of the Constitution bestowing this power reflects the old common law, and indeed legislation from the time of Edward III, when the King of England was conceded to have the power to call the militia out from the counties for the purpose of repelling invasion. Otherwise the militia could be required to serve only within the country's borders.

The first suggestion of conscription in this country for the raising of a national army was made by James Monroe when he was President Madison's Secretary of State during the War of 1812. Daniel Webster, then a member of the House of Representatives, made a most savage attack on the measure, calling it a "dance of blood" and a "gamble with death" and the House of Representatives failed to act till the end of the war made it unnecessary to do so. During the Civil War you get a draft to suppress "insurrection," that at least was the theory of the federal government. So you see the draft was still kept within the categories of repelling invasion, suppressing insurrection, and enforcement of the laws.

During World War I, of course, we had the Selective Service Act under which an army was raised to serve abroad....

Next we have in the act of September, 1940, the first *peacetime* draft, and there was assurance given that these men would not serve abroad, but when war came fifteen months later that clause of the act was quickly repealed. But the final step was President Roosevelt's surprise message of February 5, 1944, in which he asked for a conscription of labor, a suggestion which did not get to first base in Congress.

[I]t is a lesson of our constitutional history that a power claimed successfully on the justification of war emergency may come later to be assimilated to the normal peacetime powers of government. This happened in respect to the power of the national government to give its paper notes the legal tender quality; and I am not at all certain that some, if not most, of the measures put into operation over industry and labor by the government during World War II may not be justified under certain New Deal cases as regulations of commerce. It is, in short, impossible to say yet to what extent World War II has remade the Constitution not only for war, but for peace as well.

But I have dwelt too long on these details, I am afraid. I come now to my second main point. What you have here, in consequence of all these developments, is a tremendous increase in the powers of the national government. These additional powers of the *national government* are, moreover, all brought to focus and application upon the situations for which they were devised *by the President*—in other words, *the aggrandizement of the national government has meant the aggrandizement of the presidential office.*

Is there any change in the structural constitution indicated or demanded by this tremendous flow of power into the national government and through it into the hands of the President? That is the question to which I wish now to address myself briefly.

Of course, we want two things: an efficient government, a government that is capable of acting on serious matters before it is too late; we also, however, wish to preserve some of our constitutional liberties. What, then, can we do ...?

Can we establish ... a relationship between the President and Congress that will, on the one hand, *support* the President, and on the other hand *control* him?

19 *Pa. Bar Assn. Q.* 261–84 (1948).

Notes and Questions

1. *Lessons of history.* Corwin argues that "it is a lesson of our constitutional history that a power claimed successfully on the justification of war emergency may come later to be assimilated to the normal peacetime powers of government." Is that true of the broad war powers that Lincoln claimed during the Civil War? Did the broad warmaking authority delegated by Congress to Wilson during World War I survive that conflict? Is it possible that the New Deal's sweeping delegations of economic powers to the president owe anything to the delegation of emergency economic powers during World War I?

2. *Commerce power.* Do you agree with Corwin that many of the economic regulations put into effect during World War II could be justified under the broad interpretation of the power to regulate interstate and foreign commerce adopted by the Supreme Court in response to the economic emergency of the 1930s? Does the recogniton of emergency

powers in one context encourage their recognition in other contexts? Has there been, in effect, a merger of commerce and war powers during the 1970s and 1980s as the term "national security" has come to replace "war powers" in the political lexicon, and as the CIA and military have become more deeply involved in the struggle to control or manipulate petroleum, food, and other "strategic commodities"?

Richard E. Neustadt,
The Power to Persuade
(1960)

Since Plato, political scientists have dreamed of counseling princes, while princes have generally ignored political scientists. One exception was President John F. Kennedy, who heartily endorsed Professor Neustadt's book *Presidential Power*. Neustadt explained how presidents may best use their resources, skill, will, and reputations to amass influence over Congress, the bureaucracy, the press, and the public. Presidential power, according to Neustadt, is not a question of legitimate authority. It is the power to persuade and as such is legitimate to the extent that it is acceptable to the electorate and to the Washington community. Checks and balances, in his view, is merely a "literary theory" of the Constitution. The checks that really matter are those of the hour and the day. Thus, in a subsequent comment on the Cuban missile crisis, Neustadt could accept, with equanimity, the prospect that debate within the executive branch could replace Congress as the means of limiting error and abuse.[4] Later he was forced to confess: "Nixon proved me wrong."[5] Nixon, in ordering the Cambodian incursion, did not consult his inner circle, Congress, or anyone else. He went to see the movie *Patton* instead.

Consider the assumptions implicit in the following passage from Neustadt's book, which became required reading in nearly all courses on the American presidency for more than 40 years.

> In the American political system the President sits in a unique seat and works within a unique frame of reference. The things he personally has to do are no respecters of the lines between "civil" and "military," or "foreign" and "domestic," or "legislative" and "executive," or "administrative" and "political." At his desk—and there alone—distinctions of these sorts lose their last shred of meaning. The expectations centered in his person converge upon no other individual; nobody else feels pressure from all of *his* constituencies; no one else takes pressure in the consciousness that *he* has been elected "by the Nation." Besides, nobody but the President lives day by day with *his* responsibility in an atomic age amidst cold war. And he alone can claim unquestionable right to everybody's information on the mysteries of that age and that war. His place and frame of reference are unique....
>
> The things a President must think about if he would build his influence are not unlike those bearing on the viability of public policy. The correspondence may be inexact, but it is close. The man who thinks about the one can hardly help contributing to the other. A President who senses what his influence is made of and who means to guard his future will approach his present actions with an eye to the reactions of constituents in Washington and out.... And because the President's own frame of reference is at once so all-encompassing and so political, what he sees as a balance for himself is likely to be close to what is viable in terms of

---

4. "Afterword" in Kennedy, *Thirteen Days* (1971), 118–19.
5. *Presidential Power* (1980 ed.), 173.

public policy. Viability requires three ingredients. First is a purpose that moves with the grain of history, a direction consonant with coming needs. Second is an operation that proves manageable to the men who must administer it, acceptable to those who must support it, tolerable to those who must put up with it, in Washington and out. Timing can be crucial for support and acquiescence; proper timing is the third ingredient. The President who sees his power stakes sees something very much like the ingredients that make for viability in policy....

The contributions that a President can make to government are indispensable. Assuming that he knows what power is and wants it, those contributions cannot help but be forthcoming in some measure as by-products of his search for personal influence. In a relative but real sense one can say of a President what Eisenhower's first Secretary of Defense once said of General Motors: what is good for the country is good for the President, and *vice versa*. There is no guarantee, of course, that every President will keep an eye on what is "good" for him; his sense of power and of purpose and the source of his self-confidence may turn his head away. If so, his "contributions" could be lethargy not energy, or policy that moves against, not with, the grain of history.

Presidential Power (1960), 183–85.

Notes and Questions

1. *Power stakes.* Two lines of argument flow from Neustadt's analysis of presidential power. The first is a simple proposition: what the president wants is best for the country and should be adopted. The second line of argument is somewhat more complicated. The president, confronted by demands from electoral and interest group constituencies, operating within the formal constraints of the systems of separated powers and checks and balances, must calculate what he can achieve through his powers of persuasion and influence. This calculation, made by a president conscious of all the constraints placed upon him by the formal structure of government as well as by the informal constraints of the party system, leads him to make decisions that are closer to what is politically viable than what is constitutionally permissible.

2. *Viability versus legitimacy.* Is a viable policy necessarily a legitimate one? By Neustadt's standards, would the policies of Hitler and Mussolini have been "viable"? Is what is good for the country always what is good for a particular president's career? Is what is good for a president's career necessarily good for the country? If so, do we need a Constitution to limit presidential power or put checks upon it? What is "the grain of history"? Is that a reliable, useful, or moral standard against which to judge the performance of a politician? Or is it more likely to be used to justify whatever actions are taken by the president?

Arthur M. Schlesinger, Jr.,
The Imperial Presidency
(1973)

Reviewing post-World War II developments in light of the Nixon presidency, historian Arthur M. Schlesinger, Jr., wrote:

The assumption of [war-making] power was gradual and usually under the demand or pretext of emergency. It was as much a matter of congressional abdication as of presidential usurpation. As it took place, there dwindled away checks, both written and unwritten, that had long held the presidency under control. The written checks were in the Constitution. The unwritten checks were in the forces and institutions a President once had to take into practical account before he made decisions of war and peace—the cabinet and the executive branch itself, the Congress, the judiciary, the press, public opinion at home and the opinion of the world. By the early 1970s the American President had become on issues of war and peace the most absolute monarch (with the possible exception of Mao Tse-tung of China) among the great powers of the world.

The Imperial Presidency (Boston: Houghton Mifflin, 1973), ix.

Chapter Two

Emergency Powers

"*Nonsense! Nonsense!*" *snorted Tasbrough.* "*That couldn't happen here in America, not possibly! We're a country of freedom.*"

— Sinclair Lewis, *It Can't Happen Here* (1935)

"*We're faced with an unprecedented problem. Not only are revolutionary terrorists finding it easier to infiltrate the bureaucracy, but we're getting more people in government who feel they should be ruled by a sense of conscience.*"

— Robert Mardian, assistant attorney general, (1972)

A. Introduction

In the American political system, most debates over the proper ends of governmental policy soon come to involve disputes over the appropriate means for achieving those ends.

Today we take the American presidency for granted as an appropriate means for achieving constitutionally permissible ends, but that has not always been true. The Articles of Confederation and Perpetual Union, adopted in 1781, made no mention of an executive branch. As Louis Fisher indicated in the preceding chapter, the United States was governed for several years by committees of Congress and by commissioners appointed by Congress. The Constitution was a victory for Federalists who sought a stronger executive apparatus.

The question is: How strong? If the intent of the framers has any relevance to the modern legitimacy debate, we must have some sense of what the founders sought to achieve and avoid.

Clearly a monarchy was out of the question. A monarchy would require an established church and a titled nobility, neither of which existed in the United States. The radicals, debtors, and others who insisted on weak state and national executives would have none of the ceremonial extravagance of a hereditary ruling class. Neither, for that matter, would Yankee merchants or southern planters. The men of property in America intended to make their fortunes in commerce, finance, land speculation, and agriculture. They would not support a return to feudal monopolies and privileges, or to mercantile regulations. They wanted a stronger national government, one that could enforce international trade agreements and clear away state obstacles to free trade among the states. But they were not agreed on what form the executive of this strengthened national government should take, from what sources his powers should derive, who should hold him accountable and how, or where, the initiative should be located.

Three alternatives were proposed. Those least enthusiastic about strengthening the national government at the expense of state legislatures argued that the executive should be no more than a ministry for carrying out the will of the legislature, which should be considered supreme and perhaps sovereign. This was the model that Locke and the seventeenth-century English Whigs had advocated, and it was the popular form of government at both the state and national level during and immediately after the Revolution.

Second, those most concerned with strengthening the national government looked to the British model, not for its hereditary ruling class, established church, or feudal land laws, but for some of its executive prerogatives. At least initially, their number included George Washington, who knew the difficulties of dealing with an all powerful Congress in matters of war and diplomacy, Robert Morris, who knew the problems of executive finance, and Alexander Hamilton, who, although he was an officer in the Revolution, believed that the British system was still "the best in the world." Hamilton worked closely with Gouverneur Morris (his partner in chartering the Bank of New York) and James Wilson (counsel for the Bank of North America).

The third alternative, as yet untried nationally anywhere in the world, was a system of checks and balances among separated institutions, grounded in different constituencies, but sharing particular powers of government. This quickly became the compromise model, with the result that all subsequent debates have become debates over the relative authority of the branches within this general scheme.

To say this, however, is to leave many issues unresolved. The terms "checks and balances" and "separation of powers" do not appear in the Constitution. Checks and balances is the general pattern, but there is plenty of room for debate over the particulars. For example, the opening lines of Articles I and II can be read to prescribe a very Whiggish separation of functions, while the presidential pardon power can be seen as the continuation of a royal prerogative. The enumeration of powers to each branch can be read narrowly, as limitations, or broadly, as mandates. Silences also can be pregnant. Article I, in which the powers of Congress are enumerated, contains a "necessary and proper" clause, but Article II, which describes the powers of the president, does not. And finally, what was adopted can be interpreted in light of proposals that were rejected, such as a strict separation of powers provision, and the kinds of experiences the framers preferred not to repeat.

When a president claims the authority to make a decision concerning domestic policy or national security without congressional authorization and free from judicial scrutiny, he asserts, in effect, that the power to govern is his exclusive *prerogative*. Until the administration of President George W. Bush, however, presidents rarely went that far. They asserted the power to act unless and until Congress acted, or they acted under claims of exclusive authority when, in fact, Congress has already given them some, or all, of the authority they claimed. In some emergencies, presidents completely ignored existing law and hoped for subsequent ratification by Congress. Each of these claims of authority, and its potential limits, will be examined in this chapter.

Among historians, "great" presidents are usually those who interpreted their powers expansively to deal with some great crisis, such as the Civil War or World War II. The focus of most historians is on great leadership, but the implication of their writing is "all's well that ends well." Or, more precisely, all assertions of presidential power that end well are, *ipso facto*, legitimate. This chapter will examine that assumption.

In the normal course of events, a president will decide to do something, and lawyers in the White House, the Justice Department, and the State Department will scurry around to find legal arguments to justify the claims of authority implicit in the president's decision. Later, political scientists and historians will attempt to square the assertion of authority with theories of politics that seem indigenous to the American political order.

The chief problem for the president's lawyers is that the Constitution is ambiguous. For example, does the opening sentence of Article II — "The Executive Power shall be vested in a President of the United States" — confer any powers on the president, or does it simply designate the president as the person who shall exercise whatever executive powers Congress may choose to confer upon him? If the Constitution, and not the Congress, gives to the president his "Executive Power," what is that power? What, if any, are its limits, and may Congress limit or abolish it? Can one find constitutional authority for the modern presidency without granting independent potency to this provision? If not, then to what body of political thought does one turn for its definition and limitation?

The chief problem for lawyers, political scientists, and historians is that the underlying body of political thought to which they might turn is also ambiguous. Thus, the first sentence of Article II can be read in light of the concept of separation of powers to support a "strong" presidency, or in light of the concept of checks and balances to support a limited, or at least limitable, presidency. Broad presidential authority can also be seen as more democratic and legitimate than the narrow veto power of obstructionist committees of Congress. On the other hand, the exercise of the congressional power to obstruct can be seen as democratic in that it carries out the will of the "People" who ordained and established the Constitution.

The chief problem for students and citizens is that most of the writing about presidential claims to unilateral authority is highly tactical: each side seems plausible, and what is left out, or presumed, is often more important than what is argued. This was as true about "tories," who sought a "strong" executive, as it was about "whigs," who preferred a limited, and limitable, presidency. Close attention must be paid to the criteria of legitimacy presumed by each advocate. Readers must decide for themselves how much weight should be given to historical or legal precedents, whether the *dicta* of judges (statements not necessary to the decision) should be treated as authoritative, whether certain cases should be confined to their peculiar facts or reasoned from expansively, and whether the relevant cases or past practices establish a pattern of political thought that meets the requirements of legitimacy and practicality on which good government ultimately depends.

B. Early Thinking about Executive Power

John Locke,
Of Prerogative
(1690)

159. Where the Legislative and Executive Power are in distinct hands, (as they are in all moderated Monarchies, and well-framed Governments) there the good of the Society requires that several things should be left to the discretion of him, that has the Executive Power. For the Legislators not being able to foresee, and provide, by Laws, for all, that may be useful to the Community, the Executor of the Laws, having the power in his hands, has by the common Law of Nature, a right to make use of it, for the good of the Society, in many Cases, where the municipal Law has given no direction, till the Legislative can conveniently be Assembled to provide for it. Many things there are which the Law can by no

means provide for, and those must necessarily be left to the discretion of him, that has the Executive Power in his hands, to be ordered by him, as the publick good and advantage shall require: nay 'tis fit that the Laws themselves should in some Cases give way to the Executive Power, or rather to this Fundamental Law of Nature and Government, *viz.* That as much as may be, all the Members of the Society are to be *preserved*. For since many accidents may happen, wherein a strict and rigid observation of the Laws may do harm; (as not to pull down an innocent Man's House to stop the Fire, when the next to it is burning) and a Man may come sometimes within the reach of the Law, which makes no distinction of Persons, by an action, that may deserve reward and pardon; 'tis fit, the Ruler should have a Power, in many Cases, to mitigate the severity of the Law, and pardon some Offenders: For the *end of Government* being the *preservation of all*, as much as may be, even the guilty are to be spared, where it can prove no prejudice to the innocent.

160. This Power to act according to discretion, for the publick good, without the prescription of the Law, and sometimes even against it, is that which is called *Prerogative*. For since in some Governments the Lawmaking Power is not always in being, and is usually too numerous, and so too slow, for the dispatch requisite to Execution: and because also it is impossible to foresee, and so by laws to provide for, all Accidents and Necessities, that may concern the publick; or to make such Laws, as will do no harm, if they are Executed with an inflexible rigour, on all occasions, and upon all Persons, that may come in their way, therefore there is a latitude left to the Executive power, to do many things of choice, which the Laws do not prescribe.

161. This power whilst employed for the benefit of the Community, and suitably to the trust and ends of the Government, is *undoubted Prerogative*, and never is questioned. For the People are very seldom, or never scrupulous, or nice in the point: they are far from examining *Prerogative*, whilst it is in any tolerable degree imploy'd for the use it was meant; that is, for the good of the People, and not manifestly against it. But if there comes to be a *question* between the Executive Power and the People, *about* a thing claimed as a *Prerogative*; the tendency of the exercise of such *Prerogative* to the good or hurt of the People, will easily decide that Question....

163. And therefore they have a very wrong Notion of Government, who say, that the People have *incroach'd upon the Prerogative*, when they have got any part of it to be defined by positive Laws. For in so doing, they have not pulled from the Prince any thing, that of right belong'd to him, but only declared, that that Power which they indefinitely left in his, or his Ancestors, hands, to be exercised for their good, was not a thing, which they intended him, when he used it otherwise. For the end of government being the good of the Community, whatsoever alterations are made in it, tending to that end, cannot be an *incroachment* upon any body: since no body in Government can have a right tending to any other end. And those only are *incroachments* which prejudice or hinder the publick good. Those who say otherwise, speak as if the Prince had a distinct and separate Interest from the good of the Community, and was not made for it, the Root and Source, from which spring almost all those Evils, and Disorders, which happen in Kingly Governments. And indeed if that be so, the People under his Government are not a Society of Rational Creatures entered into a Community for their mutual good; they are not such as have set Rulers over themselves, to

guard, and promote that good; but are to be looked on as an Herd of inferiour Creatures, under the Dominion of a Master who keeps them, and works them for his own Pleasure or Profit. If men were so void of Reason, and brutish as to enter into Society upon such Terms, *Prerogative* might indeed be, what some Men would have it, an Arbitrary Power to do things hurtful to the People....

168. The old Question will be asked in this matter of *Prerogative*, But *who shall be Judge* when this Power is made a right use of? I Answer: Between an Executive Power in being, with such a Prerogative, and a Legislative that depends upon his will for their convening, there can be no *Judge on Earth*: As there can be none, between the Legislative, and the People, should either the Executive, or the Legislative, when they have got the Power in their hands, design, or go about to enslave, or destroy them. The People have no other remedy in this, as in all other cases where they have no judge on Earth, but to *appeal to Heaven.* For the Rulers, in such attempts, exercising a Power the People never put into their hands (who can never be supposed to consent, that anybody should rule over them for their harm) do that, which they have not a right to do. And where the Body of the People, or any single Man, is deprived of their Right, or is under the Exercise of a power without right, and have no Appeal on Earth, there they have a liberty to appeal to Heaven, whenever they judge the Cause of sufficient moment. And therefore, tho' the *People* cannot be *Judge*, so as to have by the Constitution of that Society any Superior power, to determine and give effective Sentence in the case; yet they have, by a Law antecedent and paramount to all positive Laws of men, reserv'd that ultimate Determination to themselves, which belongs to all Mankind, where there lies no Appeal on Earth, *viz.* to judge whether they have just Cause to make their Appeal to Heaven. And this Judgment they cannot part with, it being out of a Man's power so to submit himself to another, as to give him a liberty to destroy him; God and Nature never allowing a Man so to abandon himself, as to neglect his own preservation: And since he cannot take away his own Life, neither can he give another power to take it. Nor let any one think, this lays a perpetual foundation for Disorder: for this operates not, till the Inconvenience is so great, that the Majority feel it, and are weary of it, and find a necessity to have it amended. But this the Executive Power, or wise Princes, never need come in the danger of: And 'tis the thing of all others, they have most need to avoid, as of all others the most perilous.

Two Treatises of Government (1690; Laslett ed., 1960), Second Treatise, sections 159–61, 163, 168.

Notes and Questions

1. *Who shall judge?* Under the U.S. Constitution, who will typically be called upon to judge whether the president has exceeded his lawful powers? When Locke says that the people have no recourse against executives who act against the "publick good" except to "appeal to heaven," what is he really saying?

2. *Emergency powers.* Reread the Constitution. Did the founders take Locke's advice and provide for extraconstitutional rule in emergencies? What emergency powers are provided for in the Constitution? As a matter of constitutional interpretation, what conclusion should be drawn when some powers are listed, but others of the same nature are not, although they were well known at the time? Does the president's oath requiring him to "preserve, protect, and defend" the Constitution provide him with unlimited emer-

gency powers, independent of the requirement that "he shall take Care that the Laws be faithfully executed"? Compare Schlesinger, Jr., *The Imperial Presidency* (1974), 19–21, with Pious, *The American Presidency* (1979), 45.

3. *Pardon power.* May a president, like George W. Bush or Barack Obama, "pre-pardon" CIA agents to shield them from prosecution for war crimes? May a president properly pardon his predecessor for any and all crimes he *may have* committed while in office, as President Gerald Ford pardoned Richard M. Nixon? Or should the pardon power have to follow specific convictions, or admissions to specific crimes? Recall the "dispensing power" that the Stuart kings asserted, and that was renounced when William and Mary signed the Declaration of Rights in 1689. If presidents may unilaterally relieve their subordinates of any duty to obey the criminal law, what is left of the constitutional system of checks and balances, individual rights, or the rule of law?

Prerogative Powers in the Seventeenth and Eighteenth Centuries

The founders of the American Republic learned much about the art of limiting government from the puritans and whigs of seventeenth-century England. At the beginning of that century, England was the last stronghold of the medieval doctrine: "To princes belong government; to private persons, property."[1] By the end of the century, this adage of Seneca no longer applied. The doctrine of royal sovereignty had been gutted. Sovereignty was euphemistically said to vest in "the Crown," which consisted of the king or queen "in Parliament" or, more precisely, the dominant party in Parliament, which selected the king's ministers and who governed in his name.

The first two Stuart kings James I (reigned 1603–1625) and Charles I (reigned 1625–1649) based their claims to sovereign status on the laws of God (divine right) and the law of nations. Their theory of royal sovereignty was broad enough to imply that all government was the king's prerogative and that all law, including the law of private property, could be brushed aside for "reasons of state." However, in practice, even the Stuart kings conceded the legitimacy of the common law and agreed that most ordinary affairs of state should proceed according to law and precedent. In effect, they accepted Francis Bacon's distinction between "disputable" and "indisputable" prerogatives. Disputable prerogatives, Bacon argued, could be questioned in the courts (and Parliament in those days was a court as well as an incipient legislature). Indisputable prerogatives were absolute. Like the so-called political questions of American constitutional law, courts lacked jurisdiction to question them. Indeed, all persons lacked jurisdiction to question them, for to doubt their exercise openly was to risk prosecution for treason.

It would be difficult to compile a complete list of those prerogatives which the Stuart kings regarded as absolute. Among the most important were the powers to lay imposts on imports, to levy taxes without the consent of Parliament in times of fiscal emergency, to imprison persons without charges or trial for "reasons of state," to exempt government agents from the obligation to obey certain laws, and to suspend the application of entire laws. Others included the power to call subjects to arms in case of invasion, to pull down houses to stop fires or plague, to seize property or crops to supply armies in wartime, to pardon criminals, and to declare martial law.

---

1. Charles McIlwain, *The Growth of Political Thought in the West* (1932), 394.

Sir Edward Coke (left), England's chief justice in the early 1600s, challenged James I (right) and his claim to unlimited power. According to Coke, even the king was "under the law." James removed Coke from the bench in 1616, but could not stem the hostility of Puritan lawyers towards his claims of absolute and indefeasible prerogative.

The battle against these claims of absolute, unreviewable power was led by lawyers like Sir Edward Coke (pronounced "Cook") who allied themselves with Parliament and the Puritan cause. Their strategy was to transform gradually all absolute prerogatives into ordinary ones, which in the language of the law meant that they could be disputed and, therefore, subject to legislative limitations and judicial modifications. One of the earliest, most audacious, assertions of this theory took place on a Sunday in 1612, when King James took offense at the asserted independence of his judges and raged: "Then I am to be *under* the law—which it is treason to affirm." Chief Justice Coke replied: "Thus wrote Bracton, 'The King ought not to be under any man, but he is under God and the Law.'"[2] Of course, Coke was being disingenuous, because the judges claimed the authority to "discover" what the law was. Coke lost that debate and was removed from the bench in 1616, but the idea itself could not be stopped. It can be found, for example, in James Otis' argument in the famous *Writs of Assistance Case, supra,* Chapter 1.

The Puritans and their lawyers also argued, as Locke would later, that whatever absolute prerogatives the king did possess could only be exercised for the public good (*salus populi*). This concept, which had medieval roots, eventually became the political justification for the Puritans' exercise of their "right" of revolution, or what Locke meant by an "appeal to heaven."

England underwent two civil wars during the seventeenth century: the Puritan Revolution of 1641–1651 (sometimes divided into three wars) and the so-called Glorious Revolution of 1688. As a result of these parliamentary revolts against unpopular kings, subsequent monarchs became the invited guests of Parliament. Parliamentary approval of all taxes and imposts was established, and arbitrary arrests without charges or bail

---

2. 12 Coke 65, 18 *Eng. Hist. Rev.* 664–75. Campbell, *Lives of the Chief Justices,* 1 (1849), 272.

were ended by legislation (1640 and 1679) guaranteeing the writ of habeas corpus. The continental doctrine of "reasons of state" was largely abandoned, and executive claims of unreviewable authority became reviewable in Parliament, although not always in the courts.[3]

By the mid-eighteenth century, the doctrine of royal prerogative had shrunk in both fact and theory to a relatively narrow doctrine of emergency powers subject to subsequent review by Parliament. One of the emergency prerogatives to survive the rise of Parliament was the greatest of them all, the power to declare martial law (i.e., martial rule) as a means of suppressing insurrection and disorders. However, the exercise of this prerogative by the royal governor of Massachusetts in 1776 ignited the American Revolution.

C. The Debate in the Political Arena

The Neutrality Debate of 1793

Like so much of the Constitution, the meaning of Article II had to be worked out in practice. Its brevity and ambiguity were due not only to the humid heat of the summer in which it was drafted, but also to the confidence that the delegates placed in George Washington, the man they presumed would be their first president. The first major test of Washington's judgment came in 1793 and involved the question of who would decide the new nation's foreign policy toward the British and French, then at war. Pro-British Americans, represented by Alexander Hamilton, advocated a policy of strict neutrality. Pro-French Americans, led by Thomas Jefferson and James Madison, urged "benevolent neutrality," which would keep the country out of direct hostilities, but would permit Frenchmen like Citizen Genêt to raise money and troops in the United States and outfit privateers (privately owned warships) to raid British shipping. Washington issued a Proclamation of Neutrality which favored the pro-British position and by his action triggered an intense constitutional debate. Did he have the authority to proclaim neutrality? Hamilton, under the pen name Pacificus, argued that he did. Madison, writing as Helvidius, insisted that Congress, too, had a role to play in the decision. The opening letters of their debate were published in the *Gazette of the United States*, a Philadelphia newspaper, and are reproduced here, beginning with Hamilton's.

Alexander Hamilton,
Pacificus, Letter No. 1
(June 29, 1793)

It will not be disputed that the management of the affairs of this country with foreign nations is confided to the Government of the UStates.

It can as little be disputed, that a Proclamation of Neutrality, where a Nation is at liberty to keep out of a War in which other Nations are engaged and means so to do, is a *usual* and a *proper* measure....

---

3. For the theory and practice of prerogative powers in the seventeenth century, see generally Francis Wormuth, *The Royal Prerogative, 1603–1649* (1939).

Alexander Hamilton

The inquiry then is—what department of the Government of the UStates is the prop[er] one to make a declaration of Neutrality in the cases in which the engagements [of] the Nation permit and its interests require such a declaration?

A correct and well informed mind will discern at once that it can belong neit[her] to the Legislative nor Judicial Department and of course must belong to the Executive.

The Legislative Department is not the *organ* of intercourse between the UStates and foreign Nations. It is charged neither with *making* nor *interpreting* Treaties. It is therefore not naturally that Organ of the Government which is to pronounce the existing condition of the Nation, with regard to foreign Powers, or to admonish the Citizens of their obligations and duties as founded upon that condition of things. Still less is it charged with enforcing the execution and observance of obligations and those duties.

It is equally obvious that the act in question is foreign to the Judiciary Department of the Government. The province of that Department is to decide litigations in particular cases. It is indeed charged with the interpretation of treaties; but it exercises this function only in the litigated cases; that is where contending parties bring before it a specific controversy. It has no concern with pronouncing upon the external political relations of Treaties between Government and Government. This position is too plain to need being insisted upon.

It must then of necessity belong to the Executive Department to exercise the function in Question—when a proper case for the exercise of it occurs.

It appears to be connected with that department in various capacities, as the *organ* of intercourse between the Nation and foreign Nations—as the interpreter of the National Treaties in those cases in which the Judiciary is not competent, that is in the cases between Government and Government—as that Power, which is charged with the Execution of the Laws, of which Treaties form a part—as that Power which is charged with the command and application of the Public Force....

The second Article of the Constitution of the UStates, section 1st, establishes this general Proposition, That "The Executive Power shall be vested in a President of the United States of America."

The same article in a succeeding Section proceeds to designate particular cases of Executive Power. It declares among other things that the President shall be Commander in Chief of the army and navy of the UStates, and of the Militia of the several states when called into the actual service of the UStates, that he shall have power by and with the advice of the senate to make treaties; that it shall be his duty to receive ambassadors and other public Ministers and to take care that the laws be faithfully executed.... Because the difficulty of a complete and perfect specification of all the cases of Executive authority would naturally dictate the use of general terms—and would render it improbable that a specification of certain particulars was designed as a substitute for those terms, when antecedently used. The different mode of expression employed in the constitution in regard to the two powers the Legislative and the Executive serves to confirm this inference. In the article which grants the legislative powers of the Governt. the expressions are—"*All Legislative powers herein granted shall be vested in a Congress of the UStates;*" in that which grants the Executive Power the expressions are, as already quoted "The Executive Po(wer) shall be vested in a President of the UStates of America."

The enumeration ought rather therefore to be considered as intended by way of greater caution, to specify and regulate the principal articles implied in the definition of Executive Power; leaving the rest to flow from the general grant of that power, interpreted in conformity to other parts (of) the constitution and to the principles of free government.

The general doctrine then of our constitution is that the Executive Power of the Nation is vested in the President; subject only to the *exceptions* and *qualifications* which are expressed in the instrument....

With these exceptions the *Executive Power* of the Union is completely lodged in the President. This mode of construing the Constitution has indeed been recognized by Congress in formal acts, upon full consideration and debate. The power of removal from office is an important instance....

If the Legislature have a right to make war on the one hand—it is on the other the duty of the Executive to preserve Peace till war is declared; and in fulfilling that duty, it must necessarily possess a right of judging what is the nature of the obligations which the treaties of the Country impose on the Government; and when in pursuance of this right it has concluded that there is nothing in them inconsistent with a *state* of neutrality, it becomes both its province and its duty to enforce the laws incident to that state of the Nation. The Executive is charged with the execution of all laws, the laws of Nations as well as the Municipal law, which recognises and adopts those laws. It is consequently bound, by faithfully executing the laws of neutrality, when that is the state of the Nation, to avoid giving a cause of war to foreign Powers.... The Legislature is free to perform its own duties according to its own sense of them—though the Executive in the exercise of its constitutional powers, may establish an antecedent state of things which ought to weigh in the legislative decisions. From the division of the Executive Power there results, in reference to it, a *concurrent* authority, in the distributed cases....

It deserves to be remarked, that as the participation of the senate in the making of Treaties and the power of the Legislature to declare war are exceptions out of the general "Executive Power" vested in the President, they are to be construed strictly—and ought to be extended no further than is essential to their execution.

While therefore the Legislature can alone declare war, can alone actually transfer the nation from a state of Peace to a state of War—it belongs to the "Executive Power," to do whatever else the laws of Nations cooperating with the Treaties of the Country enjoin, in the intercourse of the UStates with foreign Powers.

The President is the constitutional Executor of the laws. Our Treaties and the laws of Nations form a part of the law of the land. He who is to execute the laws must first judge for himself of their meaning. In order to the observance of that conduct, which the laws of nations combined with our treaties prescribed to this country, in reference to the present War in Europe, it was necessary for the President to judge for himself whether there was any thing in our treaties incompatible with an adherence to neutrality. Having judged that there was not, he had a right, and if in his opinion the interests of the Nation required it, it was his duty, as Executor of the laws, to proclaim the neutrality of the Nation, to exhort all persons to observe it, and to warn them of the penalties which would attend its non observance.

Works of Alexander Hamilton, 7 (Hamilton ed., 1851), 76–85.

James Madison,
Helvidius, Letter No. 1
(August–September, 1793)

Outraged by Hamilton's argument in favor of implied powers, Jefferson wrote to Madison: "For God's sake, my dear Sir, take up your pen, select the most striking heresies, and cut him to pieces in the face of the public."[4] The first of Madison's five letters follows.

If we consult, for a moment, the nature and operation of the two powers to declare war and to make treaties, it will be impossible not to see, that they can never fall within a proper definition of executive powers. The natural province of the executive magistrate is to execute laws, as that of the legislature is to make laws. All his acts, therefore, properly executive, must presuppose the existence of the laws to be executed. A treaty is not an execution of laws: it does not presuppose the existence of laws. It is, on the contrary, to have itself the force of a *law*, and to be carried into *execution*, like all *other laws*, by the *executive magistrate*. To say then that the power of making treaties, which are confessedly laws, belongs naturally to the department which is to execute laws, is to say, that the

4. Jefferson, *Writings*, VI (Ford ed., 1892–1899), 338.

James Madison

executive department naturally includes a legislative power. In theory this is an absurdity—in practice a tyranny.

The power to declare war is subject to similar reasoning. A declaration that there shall be war, is not an execution of laws: it does not suppose pre-existing laws to be executed: it is not, in any respect, an act merely executive. It is, on the contrary, one of the most deliberate acts that can be performed; and when performed, has the effect of *repealing* all the *laws* operating in a state of peace, so far as they are inconsistent with a state of war; and of *enacting*, as a *rule for the executive, a new code* adapted to the relation between the society and its foreign enemy. In like manner, a conclusion of peace *annuls* all the *laws* peculiar to a state of war, and *revives* the general *laws* incident to a state of peace....

From this view of the subject it must be evident, that although the executive may be a convenient organ of preliminary communications with foreign governments, on the subjects of treaty or war; and the proper agent for carrying into execution the final determinations of the competent authority; yet it can have no pretensions, from the nature of the powers in question compared with the nature of the executive trust, to that essential agency which gives validity to such determinations.

It must be further evident, that if these powers be not in their nature purely legislative, they partake so much more of that, than of any other quality, that under a constitution leaving them to result to their most natural department, the legislature would be without a rival in its claim.

Another important inference to be noted is, that the powers of making war and treaty being substantially of a legislative, not an executive nature, the rule of interpreting exceptions strictly must narrow, instead of enlarging, executive pretensions on those subjects....

Let us examine:

In the general distribution of powers, we find that of declaring war expressly vested in the congress, where every other legislative power is declared to be vested; and without any of other qualification than what is common to every other legislative act. The constitutional idea of this power would seem then clearly to be, that it is of a legislative and not an executive nature....

The power of treaties is vested jointly in the president and in the senate, which is a branch of the legislature. From this arrangement merely, there can be no inference that would necessarily exclude the power from the executive class: since the senate is joined with the president in another power, that of appointing to offices, which, as far as relates to executive offices at least, is considered as of an executive nature. Yet on the other hand, there are sufficient indications that the power of treaties is regarded by the constitution as materially different from mere executive power, and as having more affinity to the legislative than to the executive character.

One circumstance indicating this, is the constitutional regulation under which the senate give their consent in the case of treaties. In all other cases, the consent of the body is expressed by a majority of voices. In this particular case, a concurrence of two-thirds at least is made necessary, as a substitute or compensation for the other branch of the legislature, which, on certain occasions, could not be conveniently a party to the transaction.

But the conclusive circumstance is, that treaties, when formed according to the constitutional mode, are confessedly to have force and operation of *laws*, and are to be a rule for the courts in controversies between man and man, as much as any *other laws*. They are even emphatically declared by the constitution to be "the supreme law of the land." ...

"The president shall be commander in chief of the army and navy of the United States, and of the militia when called into the actual service of the United States."

There can be no relation worth examining between this power and the general power of making treaties. And instead of being analogous to the power of declaring war, it affords a striking illustration of the incompatibility of the two powers in the same hands. Those who are to *conduct a war* cannot in the nature of things, be proper or safe judges, whether a *war ought* to be *commenced, continued, or concluded*. They are barred from the latter functions by a great principle in free government, analogous to that which separates the sword from the purse, or the power of executing from the power of enacting laws....

"He shall take care that the laws shall be faithfully executed, and shall commission all officers of the United States." To see the laws faithfully executed constitutes the essence of the executive authority. But what relation has it to the power of making treaties and war, that is, of determining what the *laws shall be* with regard to other nations? No other certainly than what subsists between the powers of executing and enacting laws; no other, consequently, than what forbids a coalition of the powers in the same department....

Thus it appears that by whatever standard we try this doctrine, it must be condemned as no less vicious in theory than it would be dangerous in practice. It is countenanced neither by the writers on law; nor by the nature of the powers themselves; nor by any general arrangements, or particular expressions, or plausible analogies, to be found in the constitution.

Whence then can the writer have borrowed it?

There is but one answer to this question.

The power of making treaties and the power of declaring war, are *royal prerogatives* in the *British government,* and are accordingly treated as *executive prerogatives* by British commentators.

Madison, *Writings,* 1 (Hunt ed., 1906), 611–21.

Notes and Questions

1. *Construing silences in the Constitution.* Hamilton and Madison agree that a neutrality proclamation is a diplomatic power, but they disagree over which branch that power should be assigned to in the absence of explicit constitutional language. How does Hamilton assign the power to the president? Why would his method of construing silences lead to a vast expansion of presidential power in other areas? Why would Madison's approach to silences lead to greater authority for Congress and an executive with limited powers? Which interpretation of the Constitution has come to prevail?

2. *The executive power.* Madison argues that "the natural province of the executive magistrate is to execute laws, as that of the legislature is to make laws. All his acts, therefore, properly executed, must presuppose the existence of laws to be executed." Would Hamilton agree? What does Hamilton mean by referring to executive power as a "general grant"? What limits on this general grant does Hamilton recognize? These issues will be considered in Section D of this chapter, "Claims to Inherent Executive Power and the Supreme Court."

3. *Tyranny.* Why does Madison argue that to assign diplomatic powers to the president, with only such exceptions as are explicitly provided for in the Constitution, would result in a "tyranny"?

Thomas Jefferson,
The Constitutionality of the Louisiana Purchase
(1803)

Few presidents have been more Whiggish than Thomas Jefferson about limitations on governmental authority, yet when Napoleon offered to sell the entire Louisiana Territory to the United States for a mere $15 million, Jefferson was faced with an offer he could not refuse. In the following letter to John C. Breckenridge, dated August 12, 1803, Jefferson set forth his constitutional misgivings and how they might best be resolved.

This treaty must of course be laid before both Houses, because both have important functions to exercise respecting it. They, I presume, will see their duty to their country in ratifying & paying for it, so as to secure a good which would otherwise probably be never again in their power. But I suppose they must then appeal to *the nation* for an additional article to the Constitution, approving & confirming an act which the nation had not previously authorized. The constitution has made no provision for our holding foreign territory, still less for incorporating foreign nations into our Union. The Executive in seizing the fugitive occurrence which so much advances the good of their country, have done an act beyond the Constitution. The Legislature in casting behind them meta-

Thomas Jefferson

physical subtleties, and risking themselves like faithful servants, must ratify & pay for it, and throw themselves on their country for doing for them unauthorized what we know they would have done for themselves had they been in a situation to do it. It is the case of a guardian, investing the money of his ward in purchasing an important adjacent territory; & saying to him when of age, I did this for your good; I pretend to no right to bind you: you may disavow me, and I must get out of the scrape as I can: I thought it my duty to risk myself for you. But we shall not be disavowed by the nation, and their act of indemnity will confirm & not weaken the Constitution, by more strongly marking out its lines.…

Writings, VIII (Ford ed., 1892–1899), 244.

Notes and Questions

1. *Prerogative powers?* Jefferson's purchase of Louisiana has been cited by many, including President Truman and Chief Justice Vinson, as an example of unilateral presidential initiative in a moment of great urgency. Was it? Consider the following words of Arthur Schlesinger, Jr., "Congress set up a clamor for Louisiana, confirmed the envoys who negotiated the purchase, appropriated the funds for the purchase, ratified the treaty consummating the purchase and passed bills authorizing the President to receive the purchase and to establish government and law in the newly acquired territory."[5]

2. *Whose power?* Were Jefferson's doubts about the powers of the president, independent of Congress, or about the powers of the new national government as a whole?

3. *Second thoughts.* Six days later, when Jefferson learned that the treaty might face defeat in Congress, he wrote again to Breckenridge: "A letter received yesterday shows that

---

5. *The Imperial Presidency* (1973), 35.

nothing must be said on that subject [the possible unconstitutionality of the purchase] which may give a pretext for retracting [the treaty]; but that we should do sub silentio what shall be found necessary. Be so good therefore as to consider that part of my letter as confidential."[6] In a letter to the attorney general dated August 30, 1803, Jefferson was even more blunt: "The less said about any constitutional difficulty, the better; it will be desirable for Congress to do what is necessary, *in silence*. I find but one opinion as to the necessity of shutting up the country for some time."[7]

Thomas Jefferson,
The Higher Law of Necessity

Jefferson's Whiggery, like that of most presidents, continued to decline with experience. Consider the following letter, written in 1810, after he had purchased Louisiana, unilaterally spent unappropriated funds to restock military arsenals after the British seized the frigate *Chesapeake* to remove alleged British seamen from it, and after Aaron Burr, Jefferson's former vice president, was tried for plotting a private military expedition with the suspected purpose of separating a portion of the American Southwest from the United States.

SIR, — ... The question you propose, whether circumstances do not sometimes occur, which make it a duty in officers of high trust, to assume authorities beyond the law, is easy of solution in principle, but sometimes embarrassing in practice. A strict observance of the written laws is doubtless *one* of the high duties of a good citizen, but it is not the *highest*. The laws of necessity, of self-preservation, of saving our country when in danger, are of higher obligation. To lose our country by a scrupulous adherence to written law, would be to lose the law itself, with life, liberty, property and all those who are enjoying them with us; thus absurdly sacrificing the end to the means.

[T]o exemplify the principle, I will state an hypothetical case. Suppose it had been made known to the Executive of the Union in the autumn of 1805, that we might have the Floridas for a reasonable sum, that that sum had not indeed been so appropriated by law, but that Congress were to meet within three weeks, and might appropriate it on the first or second day of their session. Ought he, for so great an advantage to his country, to have risked himself by transcending the law and making the purchase? The public advantage offered, in this supposed case, was indeed immense; but a reverence for law, and the probability that the advantage might still be *legally* accomplished by a delay of only three weeks, were powerful reasons against hazarding the act. But suppose it [was] foreseen that a John Randolph would find means to protract the proceeding on it by Congress, until the ensuing spring, by which time new circumstances would change the mind of the other party. Ought the Executive, in that case, and with that foreknowledge, to have secured the good to his country, and to have trusted to their justice for the transgression of the law? I think he ought, and that the act would have been approved.

After the affair of the *Chesapeake*, we thought war a very possible result. Our magazines were ill provided with some necessary articles, nor had any appropriations been made for their purchase. We ventured, however, to provide them, and to place our country in safety; and stating the case to Congress, they sanctioned the act.

---

6. Writings, VIII (Ford ed., 1892–1899), 244–45.
7. Ibid., 246.

To proceed to the conspiracy of Burr, and particularly to General Wilkinson's situation in New Orleans. In judging this case, we are bound to consider the state of the information, correct and incorrect, which he then possessed. He expected Burr and his band from above, a British fleet from below, and he knew there was a formidable conspiracy within the city. Under these circumstances, was he justifiable, 1st, in seizing notorious conspirators? On this there can be but two opinions; one, of the guilty and their accomplices; the other, that of all honest men. 2d. In sending them to the seat of government, when the written law gave them a right to trial in the territory? The danger of their rescue, of their continuing their machinations, the tardiness and weakness of the law, apathy of the judges, active patronage of the whole tribe of lawyers, unknown disposition of the juries, an hourly expectation of the enemy, salvation of the city, and of the Union itself, which would have been convulsed to its centre, had that conspiracy succeeded; all these constituted a law of necessity and self-preservation, and rendered the *salus populi* supreme over the written law. The officer who is called to act on this superior ground, does indeed risk himself on the justice of the controlling powers of the constitution, and his station makes it his duty to incur that risk. But those controlling powers, and his fellow citizens generally, are bound to judge according to the circumstances under which he acted. They are not to transfer the information of this place or moment to the time and place of his action; but to put themselves into his situation....

From these examples and principles you may see what I think on the questions proposed. They do not go to the case of persons charged with petty duties, where consequences are trifling, and time allowed for a legal course, nor to authorize them to take such cases out of the written law. In these, the example of overleaping the law is of greater evil than a strict adherence to its imperfect provisions. It is incumbent on those only who accept of great charges, to risk themselves on great occasions, when the safety of the nation, or some of its very high interests are at stake. An officer is bound to obey orders; yet he would be a bad one who should do it in cases for which they were not intended, and which involved the most important consequences. The line of discrimination between cases may be difficult; but the good officer is bound to draw it at his own peril, and throw himself on the justice of his country and the rectitude of his motives.

Letter to John V. Colvin, Sept. 10, 1810, *Writings*, IX (Ford ed., 1892–1899), 279–80.

Notes and Questions

1. *Ratification.* In the first two examples that Jefferson cites—the purchase of territory and the expenditure of unappropriated funds in anticipation of immediate military hostilities—was he asserting a unilateral presidential power? Were the actions he cited irreversible?

2. *Due process of law.* It is a well-established principle of Anglo-American jurisprudence that criminal defendants have a right to be tried by a court close to the site of their alleged crime. Territorial law gave the Burr conspirators a right to be tried within the territory, but Jefferson's administration transported them to Richmond, Virginia, where they could be tried with less chance of being rescued. Do you agree with Jefferson's assertion that this sort of emergency would justify ignoring laws establishing a fundamen-

tal, individual right? Do you agree with Congress and President Obama that the trial of those charged with the attacks of September 11, 2001, can take place at Guantanamo Bay, Cuba, rather than New York City or Washington, D.C., where the crimes occurred, and in military rather than civilian courts?

3. *Prerogative power.* Is Jefferson in this letter advancing a version of Locke's extra-constitutional prerogative, or is he taking an expansive view of the president's constitutional powers? Which modern presidents might cite Jefferson's "law of necessity" in defense of their assertions of extraconstitutional power?

4. *Legitimacy.* Is it sufficient to argue that constitutional violations are permissible so long as the violator admits the violation and "throws himself on the justice of the country"? Who metes out that justice? Congress? The electorate? If so, what of last-term presidents? Under Jefferson's theory, would the president be able to suspend application of the Bill of Rights? Compare with Locke, section B, this chapter, on the recourse of the people to heaven.

Abraham Lincoln,
The Preservation of the Union
(1864)

During the Civil War, President Lincoln unilaterally issued a proclamation purporting to emancipate all slaves within the rebellious states. His justification for this abrogation of private property rights follows.

[M]y oath to preserve the constitution to the best of my ability, imposed upon me the duty of preserving, by every indispensable means, that government—

Abraham Lincoln

that nation—of which that constitution was the organic law. Was it possible to lose the nation, and yet preserve the constitution? By general law life *and* limb must be protected; yet often a limb must be amputated to save a life; but a life is never wisely given to save a limb. I felt that measures, otherwise unconstitutional, might become lawful, by becoming indispensable to the preservation of the constitution, through the preservation of the nation. Right or wrong, I assumed this ground, and now avow it. I could not feel that, to the best of my ability, I had even tried to preserve the constitution, if, to save slavery, or any minor matter, I should permit the wreck of government, country, and Constitution all together. When, early in the war, Gen. Fremont attempted military emancipation, I forbade it, because I did not then think it an indispensable necessity. When a little later, Gen. Cameron, then Secretary of War, suggested the arming of the blacks, I objected, because I did not yet think it an indispensable necessity. When, still later, Gen. Hunter attempted military emancipation, I again forbade it, because I did not yet think the indispensable necessity had come. When, in March, and May, and July 1862 I made earnest, and successive appeals to the border states to favor compensated emancipation, I believed the indispensable necessity for military emancipation, and arming the blacks would come, unless averted by that measure. They declined the proposition; and I was, in my best judgment, driven to the alternative of either surrendering the Union, and with it, the Constitution, or of laying strong hand upon the colored element. I chose the latter. In choosing it, I hoped for greater gain than loss; but of this, I was not entirely confident. More than a year of trial now shows no loss by it in our foreign relations, none in our home popular sentiment, none in our white military force,—no loss by it any how or any where. On the contrary, it shows a gain of quite a hundred and thirty thousand soldiers, seamen, and laborers. These are palpable facts, about which, as facts, there can be no cavilling. We have the men, and we could not have had them without the measure.

Letter to Albert C. Hodges, Apr. 4, 1864, *Collected Works*, VII (Basler ed., 1953–55), 281–82.

Notes and Questions

1. *Source of the power.* Does Lincoln assert the same sort of extra-constitutional prerogative advanced by Locke and Jefferson, or does he claim that his authority is derived from the Constitution? How does he derive the authority he claims?

2. *Property rights.* When Lincoln took office, the most authoritative interpretation of the federal government's authority to curb slavery was to be found in *Dred Scott v. Sandford*, 60 U.S. (19 How.) 393 (1857). In that decision, the Supreme Court concluded that the Missouri Compromise (forbidding slavery in certain new states) was unconstitutional because an act of Congress that deprived "a citizen of his … property merely because he … brought his property [a slave] into a particular territory of the United States … could hardly be dignified with the name of due process of law" (Ibid., 450). In the Court's view, property rights were, under the Constitution's theory of federalism, to be decided by the states. By what authority, then, could Lincoln issue a proclamation purporting to abrogate the property rights of southern slaveholders? Does the power of military commanders to seize property in war zones when needed for military purposes—the so-called forage power—authorize the president as commander in chief to free southern slaves, or simply to use them and return them to their lawful

owners when his military need for them is over? If emancipation was a legitimate war measure, then under both the Fifth Amendment's taking clause and international law the United States was bound to compensate the slaveowners (all of whom were still considered American citizens) for their losses. Of course, no compensation was ever offered.

3. *Congressional authority to free slaves.* Did Congress have constitutional authority to abrogate the property rights of slaveowners? If so, under what provision of the Constitution? In *Dred Scott v. Sandford*, the Court concluded that Congress could not do so under its power to naturalize aliens. Did any provision of the Constitution prior to the ratification of the Thirteenth and Fourteenth Amendments authorize Congress to enforce the federal Bill of Rights (or other federally defined rights) against the states and their laws? Like Lincoln (see his First Inaugural Address), Congress did not consider itself bound by the *Dred Scott* decision. In 1861 it passed a Consfiscation Act purporting to free all slaves put to hostile use by the Confederate forces. It also passed an act freeing slaves who crossed over to Union lines, and a law emancipating slave soldiers who enlisted in the Union Army after escaping from their secessionist owners. Were these laws "necessary and proper" to the exercise of Congress's power to "support Armies" or to "suppress Insurrections"?

Abraham Lincoln,
On Suspension of the Writ of Habeas Corpus
(1861)

Since 1215, if not earlier, it has been unlawful for the executive to arrest persons and imprison them without trial. Persons so imprisoned have the right, through their attorneys, to go into court and seek a writ of habeas corpus. The writ is a court order directing the jailer to justify the prisoner's incarceration. If the executive does not charge the prisoner with a crime and commence proceedings against him, the jailer will be ordered by the court to release the prisoner.

Article I, Section 9, of the Constitution provides that "the Privilege of the Writ of Habeas Corpus shall not be suspended, unless when in Cases of Rebellion or Invasion the public Safety may require it." During the Civil War, President Lincoln authorized his military commanders to seize approximately 17,000 civilians suspected of sympathizing with the South and to hold them in military prisons without trial for months, and even years. Many of those arrested were seized far from the war zones. In the following message to Congress, Lincoln justified his assumption of this power:

> Soon after the first call for militia, it was considered a duty to authorize the Commanding General, in proper cases, according to his discretion, to suspend the privilege of the writ of habeas corpus; or, in other words, to arrest, and detain, without resort to the ordinary processes and forms of law, such individuals as he might deem dangerous to the public safety. This authority has purposely been exercised but very sparingly. Nevertheless, the legality and propriety of what has been done under it, are questioned and the attention of the country has been called to the proposition that one who is sworn to "take care that the laws be faithfully executed," should not himself violate them. Of course some consideration was given to the questions of power, and propriety, before this matter was acted upon. The whole of the laws which were required to be faithfully executed, were being resisted, and failing of execution, in nearly one-third of the States. Must they be allowed to finally fail of execution, even had it been per-

fectly clear, that by the use of the means necessary to their execution, some single law, made in such extreme tenderness of the citizen's liberty, that practically, it relieves more of the guilty than of the innocent, should, to a very limited extent, be violated? To state the question more directly, are all the laws, *but one*, to go unexecuted, and the government itself go to pieces, lest that one be violated? Even in such a case, would not the official oath be broken, if the government should be overthrown, when it was believed that disregarding the single law, would tend to preserve it? But it was not believed that this question was presented. It was not believed that any law was violated. The provision of the Constitution that "The privilege of the writ of habeas corpus, shall not be suspended unless when, in cases of rebellion or invasion, the public safety may require it," is equivalent to a provision—is a provision—that such privilege may be suspended when, in cases of rebellion, or invasion, the public safety *does* require it. It was decided that we have a case of rebellion, and that the public safety does require the qualified suspension of the privilege of the writ which was authorized to be made. Now it is insisted that Congress, and not the Executive, is vested with this power. But the Constitution itself, is silent as to which, or who, is to exercise the power; and as the provision was plainly made for a dangerous emergency, it cannot be believed the framers of the instrument intended, that in every case, the danger should run its course, until Congress could be called together; the very assembling of which might be prevented, as was intended in this case, by the rebellion.

Message to Congress, July 4, 1861, *Collected Works*, IV (Basler ed., 1953–55), 429–30.

Notes and Questions

1. *Whose power?* Is the Constitution silent on which branch of government may suspend the privilege of the writ in times of rebellion? Does the location of the provision allowing for emergency suspensions in Article I rather than Article II provide an answer? If the president's power to suspend the privilege does not come from Article I, where does it come from? The power to see to it that the laws are faithfully executed? His oath of office? Was Lincoln asserting an absolute prerogative, or just a temporary prerogative until Congress could be convened?

2. *Limits on the power.* May the president legitimately direct the military jailers to ignore writs of habeas corpus issued by civilian judges, or do the courts, even in times of rebellion and invasion, retain the authority to scrutinize the factual basis for the claim that an emergency exists? May Congress instruct the military to ignore judicial writs if the president cannot? See *Ex parte Milligan*, in Section D of this chapter.

Theodore Roosevelt, *The Stewardship Theory*
(1913)

The nineteenth century was, with the exceptions of Lincoln and perhaps Jackson, the century of the legislature. The twentieth century, almost without exception, has been the century of the executive. The turning point came in the 1890s with the Progressive movement, the Spanish-American War, and the emergence of the United States as an industrial power. The administrations of Theodore Roosevelt (1901–1908) mark the shift to a

Theodore Roosevelt

more activist conception of the presidency, in peace as well as war. In his *Autobiography*, Roosevelt argued:

> The most important factor in getting the right spirit in my Administration, next to the insistence upon courage, honesty, and a genuine democracy of desire to serve the plain people, was my insistence upon the theory that the executive power was limited only by specific restrictions and prohibitions appearing in the Constitution or imposed by the Congress under its constitutional powers.
>
> My view was that every executive officer, and above all every executive officer in high position, was a steward of the people bound actively and affirmatively to do all he could for the people, and not to content himself with the negative merit of keeping his talents undamaged in a napkin. I declined to adopt the view that what was imperatively necessary for the nation could not be done by the President unless he could find some specific authorization to do it. My belief was that it was not only his right but his duty to do anything that the needs of the nation demanded, unless such action was forbidden by the Constitution or by the laws. Under this interpretation of executive power I did and caused to be done many things not previously done by the President and the heads of the departments. I did not usurp power, but I did greatly broaden the use of executive power. In other words, I acted for the public welfare, I acted for the common well being of all our people, whenever and in whatever manner was necessary, unless prevented by direct constitutional or legislative prohibition.
>
> The course I followed, of regarding the Executive as subject only to the people, and, under the Constitution, bound to serve the people affirmatively in cases where the Constitution does not explicitly forbid him to render the service, was substantially the course followed by both Andrew Jackson and

Abraham Lincoln. Other honorable and well-meaning presidents, such as James Buchanan, took the opposite and, as it seems to me, narrowly legalistic view that the president is the servant of Congress rather than of the people, and can do nothing, no matter how necessary it be to act, unless the Constitution explicitly commands the action. Most able lawyers who are past middle age take this view, and so do large numbers of well meaning, respectable citizens.

The Autobiography of Theodore Roosevelt (1913; Andrews ed., 1958), 197–98.

Notes and Questions

1. *Nature of the power.* Is Roosevelt's president a "steward" for all occasions, or only in emergencies? Are the powers of his steward absolute, or are they subject to legislative or judicial restraint?

2. *Scope of the power.* Compare Roosevelt's justification for taking an expansive view of the executive power with Hamilton's views expressed as "Pacificus." How does Roosevelt's approach differ from Hamilton's with regard to legitimizing expansive executive power? Is Roosevelt arguing that the executive powers clause contains an implicit "general welfare" clause, authorizing the president to do anything necessary as the steward of the people to promote their welfare? Does Roosevelt concede any limits to his powers as steward besides those expressly prohibited by the Constitution? Does Article I grant as much power to Congress? Compare Roosevelt's stewardship theory to Locke's theory of emergency prerogative, *supra,* this chapter. Which conception is broader?

William Howard Taft, *Our Chief Magistrate and His Powers*
(1916)

William Howard Taft was Theodore Roosevelt's choice for president, but the approaches taken by the two men to exercising presidential power contrasted sharply. Roosevelt used the metaphor of the responsible "steward," but he really saw the president as holding what lawyers call a general power of attorney—legal authority to do anything necessary for the good of the client. His theory of presidential authority thus had a good deal in common with medieval theories of princely power, although Roosevelt would have been loath to admit it. Moreover, his theory of presidential power turned out to be much less aggressive in practice. He used his office as a "bully pulpit," but corporations were not hampered significantly by his antitrust efforts, and not a single American soldier died from hostile fire during his administration.

Taft, who later became chief justice of the Supreme Court, saw himself more in the tradition of an old-fashioned magistrate—an executive official with judicial functions whose primary function was to settle disputes among contending interests in society. Ironically, Taft's antitrust policy won more victories against corporations than Roosevelt's and, at Taft's direction, U.S. Marines invaded Nicaragua and began an occupation that lasted twenty years.

> The true view of the Executive functions is, as I conceive it, that the President can exercise no power which cannot be fairly and reasonably traced to some specific grant of power or justly implied and included within such express grant as proper and necessary to its exercise. Such specific grant must be either in the federal Constitution or in an act of Congress passed in pursuance thereof. There

William Howard Taft

is no undefined residuum of power which he can exercise because it seems to him to be in the public interest, and there is nothing in the *Neagle* case and its definition of a law of the United States, or in other precedents, warranting such an inference. The grants of Executive power are necessarily in general terms in order not to embarrass the Executive within the field of action plainly marked for him, but his jurisdiction must be justified and vindicated by affirmative constitutional or statutory provision, or it does not exist.

… We have had Presidents who felt the public pulse with accuracy, who played their parts upon the political stage with histrionic genius and commanded the people almost as if they were an army and the President their Commander in Chief. Yet in all these cases, the good sense of the people has ultimately prevailed and no danger has been done to our political structure and the reign of law has continued. In such times when the Executive power seems to be all prevailing, there have always been men in this free and intelligent people of ours who, apparently courting political humiliation and disaster, have registered protest against this undue Executive domination and this use of the Executive power and popular support to perpetuate itself.

The Constitution does give the President wide discretion and great power, and it ought to do so. It calls from him activity and energy to see that within his proper sphere he does what his great responsibilities and opportunities require. He is no figurehead, and it is entirely proper that an energetic and active clear-sighted people, who, when they have work to do, wish it done well, should be willing to rely upon their judgment in selecting their Chief Agent, and having selected him, should entrust to him all the power needed to carry out their governmental purpose, great as it may be.

Our Chief Magistrate and His Powers (1916), 139, 156–57.

Notes and Questions

1. *Scope of the power.* The foregoing statements by Roosevelt and Taft are frequently presented by political scientists and historians as representing substantially different theories of presidential authority. Do they? How, if at all, do they differ, from each other and from the arguments of Pacificus and Helvidius? Is the difference between these twentieth-century presidents one of leadership style only, or does it have a constitutional dimension? A comparison of the two views appears in Fisher, *President and Congress* (1972), 33–37.

Franklin D. Roosevelt,
"Stewardship Theory" in World War II
(1942)

Perhaps the most aggressive assertion of the "stewardship theory" came during the dark days of World War II, when President Franklin D. Roosevelt demanded that Congress forthwith repeal a provision of the Emergency Price Control Act which he believed was impeding the war effort.

What is needed … is an overall stabilization of prices, salaries, wages, and profits. That is necessary to the continued production of planes and tanks and ships and guns at the present constantly increasing rate.

We cannot hold the actual cost of food and clothing down to approximately the present level beyond October 1, [1942]. No one can give any assurances that the cost of living can be held down after that date.

Therefore, I ask the Congress to pass legislation under which the President would be specifically authorized to stabilize the cost of living, including the price

Franklin D. Roosevelt

of all farm commodities. The purpose should be to hold farm prices at parity, or at levels of a recent date, whichever is higher.

I ask the Congress to take this action by the first of October. Inaction on your part by that date will leave me with an inescapable responsibility to the people of this country to see to it that the war effort is no longer imperiled by threat of economic chaos.

In the event that the Congress should fail to act, and act adequately, I shall accept the responsibility, and I will act.

At the same time that farm prices are stabilized, wages can and will be stabilized also. This I will do.

The President has the powers, under the Constitution and under congressional acts, to take measures necessary to avert a disaster which would interfere with the winning of the war.

I have given the most thoughtful consideration to meeting this issue without further reference to the Congress. I have determined, however, on this vital matter to consult with the Congress.

There may be those who will say that, if the situation is as grave as I have stated it to be, I should use my powers and act now. I can only say that I have approached this problem from every angle, and that I have decided that the course of conduct which I am following in this case is consistent with my sense of responsibility as President in time of war, and with my deep and unalterable devotion to the processes of democracy.

The responsibilities of the President in wartime to protect the Nation are very grave. This total war, with our fighting fronts all over the world, makes the use of Executive power far more essential than in any previous war.

If we were invaded, the people of this country would expect the President to use any and all means to repel the invader.

The Revolution and the War between the States were fought on our own soil, but today this war will be won or lost on other continents and remote seas.

I cannot tell what powers may have to be exercised in order to win this war.

The American people can be sure that I will use my powers with a full sense of my responsibility to the Constitution and to my country. The American people can also be sure that I shall not hesitate to use every power vested in me to accomplish the defeat of our enemies in any part of the world where our own safety demands such defeat.

When the war is won, the powers under which I act automatically revert to the people—to whom they belong.

88 *Cong. Rec.* 7044 (Sept. 7, 1942).

Notes and Questions

1. *Source of the authority.* What is the source of the authority that Roosevelt claimed he could exercise if Congress did not repeal the law: the Constitution or the legislation? If there were acts of Congress authorizing the president to ignore the Price Control Act, as he suggests, did he need to claim a constitutional power to ignore the act? Did Roo-

sevelt allege that the statute was unconstitutional and that he could disregard it for that reason?

2. *Scope of the theory.* Is the "stewardship theory" asserted here the same as the theory advanced by Theodore Roosevelt, *supra,* this chapter? If not, how does it differ?

3. *Prerogative government.* Is the claim asserted here distinguishable from the "Lockean prerogative," *supra,* this chapter? Did Roosevelt strengthen his claim by promising that "when the war is won, the powers under which I act automatically revert to the people—to whom they belong"? Which theory of representation is implicit in Roosevelt's threat: the idea that the people are *re-presented* in Congress, or that the sovereignty the people possess is *embodied* in the executive?

Richard M. Nixon,
The National Security Power
(1977)

President Richard M. Nixon's name will forever be associated with the "Watergate" scandal, which began in June 1972, when a team of former CIA operatives were caught burglarizing the offices of the Democratic National Committee in the Watergate apartment complex in Washington, D.C. Later it was discovered that the same team, operating out of the White House, had burglarized the offices of Dr. Daniel Ellsberg's psychatrist, hoping to find information that could be used politically to discredit Ellsberg, a critic of the Vietnam War. However, what historians now refer to as the Watergate era actually began in January 1970, when it was disclosed that Army intelligence had 1,500 plainclothes agents spying on the anti-war and civil rights movements. The disclosures led to the first congressional hearings into the misconduct of secret agencies, led by Senator

Richard Nixon

Sam J. Ervin, Jr. (D-N.C.), who later went on to investigate President Nixon's role in the Watergate scandal. Ervin's investigations were soon followed by House and Senate investigations into the domestic surveillance activities not only of Army intelligence, but the National Security Agency, the FBI, and the CIA.

Among other things, the Senate Select Committee on Intelligence, headed by Senator Frank Church (D-Idaho), learned that during the summer of 1970 President Nixon had signed the "Huston Plan," a secret order directing the CIA, the FBI, military intelligence, and other federal intelligence agencies to engage in burglaries and other illegal surveillance activities against politically active persons who were not suspected of violating the criminal law. Authorization of these activities, which the order admitted were criminal, prompted one of the articles of impeachment returned against the president in 1974, and led to his resignation from office.

In the following 1977 interview with David Frost, a television talk-show host (for which Frost paid Nixon $600,000), the former president explained his theory of presidential powers in matters involving "national security."

> Frost: So what, in a sense, you're saying is that there are certain situations, and the Huston Plan or that part of it was one of them, where the President can decide that it's in the best interests of the nation or something, and do something illegal.
>
> Nixon: Well, when the President does it, that means it is not illegal.
>
> Frost: By definition.
>
> Nixon: Exactly. Exactly. If the President, for example, approves something because of national security, or in this case because of a threat to internal peace and order of significant magnitude, then the President's decision in that instance is one that enables those who carry it out, to carry it out without violating a law. Otherwise they're in an impossible position.
>
> Frost: So, that in other words, really you were saying in that answer, really, between the burglary and murder, again, there's no subtle way to say that there was murder of a dissenter in this country because I don't know any evidence to that effect at all. But, the point is: just the dividing line, is that in fact, the dividing line is the President's judgment?
>
> Nixon: Yes, and the dividing line and, just so that one does not get the impression that a President can run amok in this country and get away with it, we have to have in mind that a President has to come up before the electorate. We also have to have in mind, for example, that as far as the C.I.A.'s covert operations are concerned, as far as the F.B.I.'s covert operations are concerned, through the years, they have been disclosed on a very, very limited basis to trusted members of Congress. I don't know whether it can be done today or not.
>
> ... I couldn't care less about the punk [antiwar dissenter]. I wanted to discredit that kind of activity which was despicable and damaging to the national interest.
>
> Frost: Pulling some of our discussions together, as it were; speaking of the Presidency and in an interrogatory filed with the Church committee, you stated, quote, "It's quite obvious that there are certain inherently government activities, which, if undertaken by the sovereign in protection of the interests of the nation's security are lawful, but which if undertaken by private persons, are not."

What at root, did you have in mind there?

Nixon: Well, what I, at root I had in mind I think was perhaps much better stated by Lincoln during the War Between the States. Lincoln said, and I think I can remember the quote almost exactly, he said, "Actions which otherwise would be unconstitutional, could become lawful if undertaken for the purpose of preserving the Constitution and the Nation."

Now that's the kind of action I'm referring to. Of course in Lincoln's case it was the survival of the Union in war time, it's the defense of the nation and, who knows, perhaps the survival of the nation.

Frost: But there was no comparison, was there, between the situation you faced and the situation Lincoln faced, for instance?

Nixon: This nation was torn apart in an ideological way by the war in Vietnam as much as the Civil War tore apart the nation when Lincoln was President. Now it's true that we didn't have the North and South—

Frost: But when you said, as you said when we were talking about the Huston plan, you know, "If the President orders it, that makes it legal," as it were. Is the President in that sense—is there anything in the Constitution or the Bill of Rights that suggests the President is that far of a sovereign, that far above the law?

Nixon: No, there isn't. There's nothing specific that the Constitution contemplates in that respect. I haven't read every word, every jot and every title, but I do know this: that it has been, however, argued that as far as a President is concerned, that in war time, a President does have certain extraordinary powers which would make acts that would otherwise be unlawful, lawful if undertaken for the purpose of preserving the nation and the Constitution, which is essential for the rights we're all talking about.

New York Times, May 20, 1977, B-10.

Notes and Questions

1. *Faithful execution.* Article II requires the president to "take care that the laws be faithfully executed." Did Nixon see this constitutional provision as limiting the president's discretion in any way? If the president may define what is legal or illegal, what remains of the doctrines of separation of powers, checks and balances, or, for that matter, the Bill of Rights or habeas corpus?

2. *Plebiscitary presidency.* Nixon mentioned the electorate as the only check against a president's running amok. Arthur Schlesinger, Jr., compared this to Napoleon II's theory of a "plebiscitary presidency"—an elected dictatorship for a fixed term.[8] Is Nixon's theory broader or narrower than the stewardship theory advanced by Theodore Roosevelt quoted earlier in this section?

3. *Emergency powers.* Nixon noted that Abraham Lincoln claimed the authority to act in certain circumstances in apparent violation of the law. Under what circumstances did Lincoln, or Jefferson, or Locke, justify an executive power to ignore certain laws? Did any of the circumstances they had in mind compare to the surveillance (and harassment) of law-abiding civil rights and anti-war protesters?

---

8. *The Imperial Presidency* (1973), 254.

4. *Additional assertions.* The foregoing statement presents Nixon's general theory of presidential prerogatives. For specific assertions by his counsel, and judicial responses to those assertions, see *Nixon v. Sirica*, 487 F. 2d 700 (1973); *United States v. Nixon*, 418 U.S. 683 (1974); and *Kissinger v. Halperin*, 425 U.S. 713 (1981). Note also that William H. Rehnquist, then head of the Office of Legal Counsel in the Department of Justice, defended the Army's domestic spying in 1971 as an instance of "modified martial law" in time of war. Nixon went on to appoint Rehnquist to the Supreme Court.

5. *An alternative theory of "national security."* In 1983, Richard V. Allen, former national security adviser to President Ronald Reagan, articulated an alternative theory of the national-security powers concept: "In the 1980's, 'national security' is in itself an all-encompassing term too often narrowly construed as having to do only with foreign policy and defense matters. In reality, it must include virtually every facet of international activity, including (but not limited to) foreign affairs, defense, intelligence, research and development policy, outer space, international economic and trade policy, monetary policy and reaching deeply even into the domains of the Departments of Commerce and Agriculture. In a word, 'national security' must reflect the Presidential perspective, of which diplomacy is but a single component."[9] If Allen is correct, can any distinctions be maintained between the allocations of authority prescribed by the Constitution, or do the commerce power, the power to raise and support armies, the power to receive ambassadors, and so forth all merge into an aggregate and undistinguished mass of presidential powers?

6. *The Iran-Contra affair.* Allen's sweeping theory of presidential power was embraced by the Reagan administration, which then secretly sold U.S. arms to Iran, which it called a terrorist nation, and used the profits to fund a secret guerilla war by former elements of the Nicaraguan national guard against the leftist Sandinista regime. That controversy will be discussed in Chapter 4.

7. *John Yoo's Constitution.* In response to the attacks of September 11, 2001, the administration of President George W. Bush went beyond Richard Nixon to assert unlimited powers to initiate warfare and conduct covert operations anywhere on earth without notice to, or authorization from, Congress, so long as it was trying to "keep Americans safe" from terrorists. Among other things, the Bush administration asserted unilateral executive power to imprison approximately 5,000 resident aliens for over three months without charges or trial, detain suspected terrorists (including American citizens) in military prisons indefinitely without trial, torture and abuse prisoners in Afghanistan, Iraq, Cuba (at the U.S. naval base on Guantánamo Bay) and in secret CIA prisons in at least eight foreign countries. The administration also claimed the power to intercept the telephone, FAX, and e-mail communications of millions of American citizens, secretly and without court orders, in violation of the criminal provisions of the Foreign Intelligence Surveillance Act of 1978.

The impetus for these sweeping claims of executive power came from the office of Vice President Dick Cheney. They were more fully developed by John Yoo, a mid-level attorney in the Justice Department's Office of Legal Counsel, in a series of secret legal memoranda written between 2001 and 2003. According to Yoo, the president could, as commander in chief, secretly authorize the interrogation of alleged terrorists under torture, despite treaties and statutes to the contrary, and secretly order warrantless wiretapping of American citizens in disregard of both the Fourth Amendment and the Foreign Intelligence Sur-

---

9. *New York Times*, Jan. 25, 1983, A 22.

veillance Act. Yoo also argued that the president could, as an exercise of his war powers in a perpetual war against terrorism, use the U.S. military to arrest and detain suspected terrorists and their supporters within the United States, and that such activities would not violate the Posse Comitatus Act, which makes it a crime for the president or anyone else to use the military for law enforcement purposes. According to Yoo, the framers of the Constitution intended to confer these powers on the president without limitation. Some of the secret memoranda can be found in Greenberg and Dratel, eds., *The Torture Papers* (2005). See also John Yoo, *The Powers of War and Peace: The Constitution and Foreign Affairs After 9/11* (2005); Richard M. Pious, *The War on Terrorism and the Rule of Law* (2006); and Christopher H. Pyle, *Getting Away with Torture: Secret Government, War Crimes, and the Rule of Law* (2009). The Bush administration's claims to unlimited executive power will be examined later in this chapter, and in Chapters 4 and 5.

D. Claims to Inherent Executive Power and the Supreme Court

As the foregoing excerpts from the political debate indicate, presidents, and those who speak for them, frequently assert the existence of executive powers not expressly stated in the Constitution. These claims come in a variety of verbal cloaks. For example, some presidents say simply that the powers they assert are *inherent* in the nature of the government, as deduced either from constitutional theory or from the nature of governments generally. Others find the powers they allege to be *implied* by the Constitution or what the framers said that they intended. Some claim that certain executive powers may be *inferred*, on the theory that ambiguous constitutional phrases must be read in a way that will permit the governmental venture to succeed. Still others assert that the powers they claim are *incidental* to certain express authorizations, just as Congress has authority to take all action "necessary and proper" to the carrying out of its enumerated powers.

In addition, some presidents lay claim to that *residuum* of sovereign powers left over when all of the express, implied, inferred, and incidental powers are subtracted from the sum total of powers inherent in the nature of the federal government as a member of the family of nations. The term *residual* has also been used to refer to the broad range of discretionary powers that a president must exercise to carry out the intent of legislation or take necessary and appropriate action when the legislature is not in session.

Sometimes presidents will concede that while no particular provision of Article II grants them authority, authority nonetheless may be deduced from the *aggregate* of all their powers. Last but not least, presidents lay claim to a variety of emergency powers, on the theory that the Constitution must be read so as to permit the government, or the country, to survive.

In common parlance, these diverse claims have come to be referred to as "inherent powers," by which is meant nothing more than that they are alleged powers not expressly granted by the Constitution or delegated to the president by Congress. However, it is important to be more precise. When a nonexpress power is asserted, it is necessary to ask: Is the president claiming a power derived from the Constitution, however broadly, or is he asserting a Lockean-style prerogative to take admittedly extraconstitutional action in an emergency? Is he claiming a power to act in the absence of legislation forbidding him to act, or does he allege that Congress lacks any constitutional authority to limit, channel, or block his initiatives? Does he claim a plenary power for himself, or does he concede that other provisions of the Constitution, including the Bill of Rights, might properly be invoked in the courts to constrain him? Does he view the people, and their "sovereignty," as *re-presented* in the Congress, or does he claim that they are *embodied* in the executive?

The cases that follow are frequently cited as proof that the Supreme Court has, or has not, recognized some sort of inherent executive powers. In reading them, consider not only the questions posed above, but whether the cases acknowledge a power inherent in the executive, as opposed to another branch (or branches), or recognize a delegation of power from Congress, rather than one derived from the Constitution. Consider also whether the broad powers the Court has recognized are for emergency or routine use. Finally, if inherent powers have been acknowledged by the Court in certain circumstances, what is the precedential value of those decisions? When, if ever, is a president "bound" by a court decision? Would such a case be decided the same way again, or is the outcome best attributed to historical conditions and political pressures, and therefore, to paraphrase Justice Frankfurter, "best consigned to history?"

Ex parte Milligan
71 U.S. (4 Wall.) 2 (1866)

No president has ever violated private constitutional rights more flagrantly, or for better motives, than Abraham Lincoln. Pursuant to his orders, private homes were searched without judicial warrants, men were imprisoned without trial, and writs of habeas corpus ordering their release were ignored. The process was so casual that Secretary of State Seward could boast that whenever he wanted someone arrested, all he had to do was ring a little bell on his desk.

Lambdin P. Milligan was a civilian with strong southern sympathies. He was arrested on order of the general in charge of the military district of Indiana and convicted by a military commission of conspiracy to organize an insurrection behind Union lines. While under sentence to be hanged, Milligan sought a writ of habeas corpus on the grounds that his imprisonment and sentence were the product of violations of his constitutional right to a trial by a civilian jury.

MR. JUSTICE DAVIS delivered the opinion of the Court.

The importance of the main question presented by this record cannot be overstated; for it involves the very framework of the government and the fundamental principles of American liberty.

During the late wicked Rebellion, the temper of the times did not allow that calmness in deliberation and discussion so necessary to a correct conclusion of a purely judicial question. *Then*, considerations of safety were mingled with the exercise of power; and feelings and interests prevailed which are happily terminated. *Now* that the public safety is assured, this question, as well as all others, can be discussed and decided without passion or the admixture of any element not required to form a legal judgment. We approach the investigation of this case, fully sensible of the magnitude of the inquiry and the necessity of full and cautious deliberation....

The controlling question in the case is this: Upon the *facts* stated in Milligan's petition, and the exhibits filed, had the military commission mentioned in it *jurisdiction*, legally, to try and sentence him? Milligan, not a resident of one of the rebellious states, or a prisoner of war, but a citizen of Indiana for twenty years past, and never in the military or naval service, is, while at his home, arrested by the military power of the United States, imprisoned, and, on certain criminal charges preferred against him, tried, convicted, and sentenced to be hanged by a military commission, organized under the direction of the military commander of the military district of Indiana. Had this tribunal the *legal* power and authority to try and punish this man?

No graver question was ever considered by this court, nor one which more nearly concerns the rights of the whole people; for it is the birthright of every American citizen when charged with crime, to be tried and punished according to law.... Time has proven the discernment of our ancestors;.... Those great and good men foresaw that troublous times would arise, when rulers and people would become restive under restraint, and seek by sharp and decisive measures to accomplish ends deemed just and proper; and that the principles of constitutional liberty would be in peril, unless established by irrepealable law. The history of the world had taught them that what was done in the past might be attempted in the future. The Constitution of the United States is a law for rulers and people, equally in war and in peace, and covers with the shield of its protection all classes of men, at all times, and under all circumstances. No doctrine, involving more pernicious consequences, was ever invented by the wit of man than that any of its provisions can be suspended during any of the great exigencies of government. Such a doctrine leads directly to anarchy or despotism, but the theory of necessity on which it is based is false; for the government, within the Constitution, has all the powers granted to it, which are necessary to preserve its existence; as has been happily proved by the result of the great effort to throw off its just authority.

Have any of the rights guaranteed by the Constitution been violated in the case of Milligan? and if so, what are they?

Every trial involves the exercise of judicial power; and from what source did the military commission that tried him derive their authority? Certainly no part of the judicial power of the country was conferred on them; because the Constitution expressly vests it "in one supreme court and such inferior courts as the Congress may from time to time ordain and establish," and it is not pretended that the commission was a court ordained and established by Congress. They cannot justify on the mandate of the President; because he is controlled by law, and has his appropriate sphere of duty, which is to execute, not to make, the laws; and there is "no unwritten criminal code to which resort can be had as a source of jurisdiction."

But it is said that the jurisdiction is complete under the "laws and usages of war."

It can serve no useful purpose to inquire what those laws and usages are, whence they originated, where found, and on whom they operate; they can never be applied to citizens in states which have upheld the authority of the government, and where the courts are open and their process unobstructed. This court has judicial knowledge that in Indiana the Federal authority was always unopposed, and its courts always open to hear criminal accusations and redress grievances; and no usage of war could sanction a military trial there for any offence whatever of a citizen in civil life, in nowise connected with the military service. Congress could grant no such power; and to the honor of our national legislature be it said, it has never been provoked by the state of the country even to attempt its exercise. One of the plainest constitutional provisions was, therefore, infringed when Milligan was tried by a court not ordained and established by Congress, and not composed of judges appointed during good behavior....

Another guarantee of freedom was broken when Milligan was denied a trial by jury.... If ideas can be expressed in words, and language has any meaning, *this right*— one of the most valuable in a free country—is preserved to everyone accused of crime who is not attached to the army, or navy, or militia in actual service....

The discipline necessary to the efficiency of the army and navy, required other and swifter modes of trial than are furnished by the common law courts; and, in pursuance of the power conferred by the Constitution, Congress has declared the kinds of trial, and the manner in which they shall be conducted, for offences committed while the party is in the military or naval service.... *All other persons,* citizens of states where the courts are open, if charged with crime, are guaranteed the inestimable privilege of trial by jury....

It is claimed that martial law covers with its broad mantle the proceedings of this military commission. The proposition is this; that in a time of war the commander of an armed force (if in his opinion the exigencies of the country demand it, and of which he is to judge), has the power, within the lines of his military district, to suspend all civil rights and their remedies, and subject citizens as well as soldiers to the rule of *his will*; and in the exercise of his lawful authority cannot be restrained, except by his superior officer or the President of the United States.

If this position is sound to the extent claimed, then when war exists, foreign or domestic, and the country is subdivided into military departments for mere convenience, the commander of one of them can, if he chooses, within his limits, on the plea of necessity, with the approval of the Executive, substitute military force for and to the exclusion of the laws, and punish all persons, as he thinks right and proper, without fixed or certain rules.

The statement of this proposition shows its importance; for, if true, republican government is a failure, and there is an end of liberty regulated by law. Martial law, established on such a basis, destroys every guarantee of the Constitution, and effectually renders the "military independent of and superior to the civil power"—the attempt to do which by the King of Great Britain was deemed by our fathers such an offence, that they assigned it to the world as one of the causes which impelled them to declare their independence. Civil liberty and this kind of martial law cannot endure together; the antagonism is irreconcilable; and, in the conflict, one or the other must perish.

This nation, as experience has proved, cannot always remain at peace, and has no right to expect that it will always have wise and humane rulers, sincerely attached to the principles of the Constitution. Wicked men, ambitious of power, with hatred of liberty and contempt of law, may fill the place once occupied by Washington and Lincoln; and if this right is conceded, and the calamities of war again befall us, the dangers to human liberty are frightful to contemplate. If our fathers had failed to provide for just such a contingency, they would have been false to the trust reposed in them. They knew—the history of the world told them—the nation they were founding, be its existence short or long, would be involved in war; how often or how long continued, human foresight could not tell; and that unlimited power, wherever lodged at such a time, was especially hazardous to freemen. For this, and other equally weighty reasons, they secured the inheritance they had fought to maintain, by incorporating in a written constitution the safeguards which time had proved were essential to its preservation. Not one of these safeguards can the President, or Congress, or the judiciary disturb, except the one concerning the writ of habeas corpus.

It is essential to the safety of every government that, in a great crisis, like the one we have just passed through, there should be a power somewhere of suspending the writ of habeas corpus.

In the emergency of the times, an immediate public investigation according to law may not be possible; and yet, the peril to the country maybe too imminent to suffer such persons to go at large. Unquestionably, there is then an exigency which demands that the government, if it should see fit in the exercise of a proper discretion to make arrests, should not be required to produce the persons arrested in answer to a writ of habeas corpus. The Constitution goes no further. It does not say after a writ of habeas corpus is denied a citizen, that he shall be tried otherwise than by the course of the common law; if it had intended this result, it was easy by the use of direct words to have accomplished it. The illustrious men who framed that instrument ... limited the suspension to one great right, and left the rest to remain forever inviolable. But, it is insisted that the safety of the country in time of war demands that this broad claim for martial law shall be sustained. If this were true, it could be well said that a country, preserved at the sacrifice of all the cardinal principles of liberty, is not worth the cost of preservation. Happily, it is not so.

It will be borne in mind that this is not a question of the power to proclaim martial law, when war exists in a community and the courts and civil authorities are overthrown. Nor is it a question what rule a military commander, at the head of his army, can impose on states in rebellion to cripple their resources and quell the insurrection. The jurisdiction claimed is much more extensive. The necessities of the service, during the late Rebellion, required that the loyal states should be placed within the limits of certain military districts and commanders appointed in them; and, it is urged, that this, in a military sense, constituted them the theatre of military operations: and, as in this case, Indiana had been and was again threatened with invasion by the enemy, the occasion was furnished to establish martial law.

The conclusion does not follow from the premises. If armies were collected in Indiana, they were to be employed in another locality, where the laws were obstructed and the national authority disputed. On *her* soil there was no hostile foot; if once invaded, that invasion was at an end, and with it all pretext for martial law. Martial law cannot arise from a *threatened* invasion. The necessity must be actual and present: the invasion real, such as effectually closes the courts and deposes the civil administration.

It is difficult to see how the *safety* of the country required martial law in Indiana. If any of her citizens were plotting treason, the power of arrest could secure them, until the government was prepared for their trial, when the courts were open and ready to try them. It was as easy to protect witnesses before a civil as a military tribunal; and as there could be no wish to convict, except on sufficient legal evidence, surely an ordained and established court was better able to judge of this than a military tribunal composed of gentlemen not trained to the profession of the law.

It follows, from what has been said on this subject, that there are occasions when martial rule can be properly applied. If, in foreign invasion or civil war, the courts are actually closed, and it is impossible to administer criminal justice according to law, *then,* on the theatre of active military operations, where war really prevails, there is a necessity to furnish a substitute for the civil authority, thus overthrown, to preserve the safety of the army and society; and as no power is left but the military, it is allowed to govern by martial rule until the laws can have their free course. As necessity creates the rule, so it limits its duration; for, if this government is continued *after* the courts are reinstated, it is a gross usurpation of power. Martial rule can never exist where the courts are open, and in the proper and unobstructed exercise of their jurisdiction. It is also confined to the locality of actual war....

We are not without precedents in English and American history illustrating our views of this question; but it is hardly necessary to make particular reference to them.

From the first year of the reign of Edward the Third, when the Parliament of England reversed the attainder of the Earl of Lancaster, because he could have been tried by the courts of the realm, and declared, "that in time of peace no man ought to be adjudged to death for treason or any other offence without being arraigned and held to answer; and that regularly when the king's courts are open it is a time of peace in judgment of law," down to the present day, martial law, as claimed in this case, has been condemned by all respectable English jurists as contrary to the fundamental laws of the land, and subversive of the liberty of the subject....

So sensitive were our Revolutionary fathers on this subject, although Boston was almost in a state of siege, when General Gage issued his proclamation of martial law, they spoke of it as an "attempt to supersede the course of the common law, and instead thereof to publish and order the use of martial law." The Virginia Assembly, also, denounced a similar measure on the part of Governor Dunmore "as an assumed power, which the king himself cannot exercise; because it annuls the law of the land and introduces the most execrable of all systems, martial law."

In some parts of the country, during the war of 1812, our officers made arbitrary arrests and, by military tribunals, tried citizens who were not in the military service. These arrests and trials, when brought to the notice of the courts, were uniformly condemned as illegal....

The two remaining questions in this case must be answered in the affirmative. The suspension of the privilege of the writ of habeas corpus does not suspend the writ itself. The writ issues as a matter of course; and on the return made to it the court decides whether the party applying is denied the right of proceeding any further with it.

If the military trial of Milligan was contrary to law, then he was entitled, on the facts stated in his petition, to be discharged from custody by the terms of the act of Congress of March 3d, 1863....

But it is insisted that Milligan was a prisoner of war, and, therefore, excluded from the privileges of the statute. We are not without precedents in English and American history illustrating our views of this question; but it is hardly necessary to make particular reference to them. It is not easy to see how he can be treated as a prisoner of war, when he lived in Indiana for the past twenty years, was arrested there, and had not been, during the late troubles, a resident of any of the states in rebellion. If in Indiana he conspired with bad men to assist the enemy, he is punishable for it in the courts of Indiana; but, when tried for the offence, he cannot plead the rights of war; for he was not engaged in legal acts of hostility against the government, and only such persons, when captured, are prisoners of war. If he cannot enjoy the immunities attaching to the character of a prisoner of war, how can he be subject to their pains and penalties?

The Chief Justice [CHASE] delivered the following opinion.

Four members of the court, concurring with their brethren in the order heretofore made in this cause, but unable to concur in some important particulars ... think it their duty to make a separate statement of their views....

We do not doubt that the Circuit Court for the District of Indiana had jurisdiction of the petition of Milligan for the writ of habeas corpus.... [I]t is equally clear that he was entitled to the discharge prayed for....

But the [majority] opinion ... asserts not only that the military commission held in Indiana was not authorized by Congress, but that it was not in the power of Congress to authorize it; from which it may be thought to follow that Congress has no power to indemnify the officers who composed the commission against liability in civil courts for acting as members of it. We cannot agree to this.

We agree in the proposition that no department of the government of the United States—neither President, nor Congress, nor the Courts—possesses any power not given by the Constitution.

We assent, fully, to all that is said, in the opinion, of the inestimable value of the trial by jury, and of the other constitutional safeguards of civil liberty. And we concur, also, in what is said of the writ of habeas corpus, and of its suspension, with two reservations: (1.) That, in our judgment, when the writ is suspended, the Executive is authorized to arrest as well as to detain; and (2.) that there are cases in which, the privilege of the writ being suspended, trial and punishment by military commission, in states where civil courts are open, may be authorized by Congress, as well as arrest and detention.

We think that Congress had power, though not exercised, to authorize the military commission which was held in Indiana....

Congress has power to raise and support armies; to provide and maintain a navy; to make rules for the government and regulation of the land and naval forces; and to provide for governing such part of the militia as may be in the service of the United States....

It is not denied that the power to make rules for the government of the army and navy is a power to provide for trial and punishment by military courts without a jury. It has been so understood and exercised from the adoption of the Constitution to the present time.

Nor, in our judgment, does the fifth, or any other amendment, abridge that power. "Cases arising in the land and naval forces, or in the militia in actual service in time of war or public danger," are expressly excepted from the fifth amendment, "that no person shall be held to answer for a capital or otherwise infamous crime, unless on a presentment or indictment of a grand jury," and it is admitted that the exception applies to the other amendments as well as to the fifth.

... Congress is but the agent of the nation, and does not the security of individuals against the abuse of this, as of every other power, depend on the intelligence and virtue of the people, on their zeal for public and private liberty, upon official responsibility secured by law, and upon the frequency of elections, rather than upon doubtful constructions of legislative powers?...

Congress has the power not only to raise and support and govern armies but to declare war. It has, therefore, the power to provide by law for carrying on war. This power necessarily extends to all legislation essential to the prosecution of war with vigor and success, except such as interferes with the command of the forces and the conduct of campaigns. That power and duty belong to the President as commander-in-chief. Both these powers are derived from the Constitution, but neither is defined by that instrument. Their extent must be determined by their nature, and by the principles of our institutions....

We cannot doubt that, in such a time of public danger, Congress had power, under the Constitution, to provide for the organization of a military commission, and for trial by that commission of persons engaged in this conspiracy. The fact that the Federal courts were open was regarded by Congress as a sufficient reason for not exercising the power; but that fact could not deprive Congress of the right to exercise it. Those courts might be open and undisturbed in the execution of their functions, and yet wholly incompetent to avert threatened danger, or to punish, with adequate promptitude and certainty, the guilty conspirators.

In Indiana, the judges and officers of the courts were loyal to the government. But it might have been otherwise. In times of rebellion and civil war it may often happen, indeed, that judges and marshals will be in active sympathy with the rebels, and courts their most efficient allies. We have confined ourselves to the question of power. It was for Congress to determine the question of expediency. And Congress did determine it....

We have thus far said little of martial law, nor do we propose to say much. What we have already said sufficiently indicates our opinion that there is no law for the government of the citizens, the armies or the navy of the United States, within American jurisdiction, which is not contained in or derived from the Constitution....

There are under the Constitution three kinds of military jurisdiction: one to be exercised both in peace and war; another to be exercised in time of foreign war without the boundaries of the United States, or in time of rebellion and civil war within states or districts occupied by rebels treated as belligerents; and a third to be exercised in time of invasion or insurrection within the limits of the United States, or during rebellion within the limits of states maintaining adhesion to the National Government, when the public danger requires its exercise. The first of these may be called jurisdiction under MILITARY LAW, and is found in acts of Congress prescribing rules and articles of war, or otherwise providing for the government of the national forces; the second may be distinguished as MILITARY GOVERNMENT, superseding, as far as may be deemed expedient, the local law, and exercised by the military Commander under the direction of the President, with the express or implied sanction of Congress; while the third may be denominated MARTIAL LAW PROPER, and is called into action by Congress, or temporarily, when the action of Congress cannot be invited, and in the case of justifying or excusing peril, by the President, in times of insurrection or invasion, or of civil or foreign war, within districts or localities where ordinary law no longer adequately secures public safety, and private right.

We think that the power of Congress, in such times and in such localities, to authorize trials for crimes against the security and safety of the national forces, may be derived from its constitutional authority to raise and support armies and to declare war, if not from its constitutional authority to provide for governing the national forces.

We have no apprehension that this power, under our American system of government, in which all official authority is derived from the people, and exercised under direct responsibility to the people, is more likely to be abused than the power to regulate commerce, or the power to borrow money. And we are unwilling to give our assent by silence to expressions of opinion which seem to be calculated, though not intended, to cripple the constitutional powers of the government, and to augment the public dangers in times of invasion and rebellion....

MR. JUSTICE WAYNE, MR. JUSTICE SWAYNE, and MR. JUSTICE MILLER concur with me in these views.

Notes and Questions

1. *Whose power?* Is this case about an asserted presidential prerogative, or is it about the kind of authority that Congress may constitutionally delegate to the president? Should the courts defer to Congress's or the executive's judgment that military necessity requires suspension of habeas relief?

2. *Martial law proper.* Is the distinction drawn by Chief Justice Chase between "military government" and "martial law proper" clear? The emergency power which the chief justice defines as "martial law proper" was considered to be an absolute royal prerogative prior to the American Revolution, subject only to Parliament's control of the purse strings. Do you think it likely that the framers intended to give the president the same prerogative to declare martial law, subject only to a subsequent law denying him funds, which would have to be passed by two-thirds majorities of both Houses in order to override his veto? Does the Court, or the chief justice, clearly state the conditions under which presidents may declare martial law (and forcibly close courthouses or otherwise seize all governmental powers) without prior legislative authority? In time of war, who defines the "war zones"? Are these definitions beyond judicial review? Are they entitled to judicial deference?

3. *Ex parte Merryman.* Lamdin Milligan was not the first to challenge the detention without trial of Southern sympathizers. In May 25, 1861, Chief Justice Roger Taney issue a writ of habeas corpus ordering General George Cadwalader, commander of Fort McHenry, to justify his detention of John Merryman, who was suspected of training a secessionist cavalry unit that had helped destroy bridges and telegraph lines to the North in April. Cadwalader refused, claiming that he was "duly authorized by the president ... to suspend the writ of habeas corpus for the public safety." Taney immediately held the general in contempt of court, but the U.S. marshal sent to serve the order was denied admission to the fort. In a subsequent opinion, the Chief Justice declared Lincoln's suspension of the writ unconstitutional, reasoning that if military detention without trial were permitted to continue without legislative authorization, the life, liberty, and property of every citizen would be subject to "the will and pleasure of the army officer." 17 F. Cas. 144 (C.C.D. Md. 1861). Was Taney correct, as a matter of law? As a matter of sound judicial discretion, should he have issued his order and opinion immediately, or given Congress, which was not in session, time to ratify Lincoln's order, possibly by referring the question to the full Supreme Court?

Years later, one of Lincoln's bodyguards claimed, in an unpublished memoir, that the president was so angered by Taney's ruling that he issued a warrant, quickly rescinded, for the justice's arrest. Whether this is true or not, Lincoln did order the military to place a prominent District of Columbia judge, William Matthew Merrick, under house arrest for a similar habeas decision. The president also directed Secretary of State Seward to withhold the judge's salary.

4. *Civil damages or injunctions.* Milligan subsequently sued the general who had ordered his arrest for unlawful imprisonment. The jury ruled in Milligan's favor, but he was awarded only nominal damages.

5. *Congressionally authorized commissions?* Could congressional legislation establishing military commissions to try civilians cure the constitutional defects discussed by Justice Davis in *Milligan*? Would the assertion of such a power be beyond judicial review?

Court-stripping. In the First Reconstruction Act of 1867, Congress provided for military government in the South and for military commissions of the very sort that the Court in *Milligan* had declared that the president could not create. To protect itself from another *Milligan* decision, Congress stripped the Supreme Court of jurisdiction to hear appeals in cases involving writs of habeas corpus. The Supreme Court agreed that this denial of its jurisdiction was within the power of Congress to make exceptions to the appellate jurisdiction of the Supreme Court (Article III), and military governors continued to deprive civilians of their right to trial by jury. *Ex parte McCardle*, 74 U.S. (7 Wall.) 506 (1869).

Was the Court right to uphold this jurisdiction stripping law? In a pending case? In future cases? Is there a constitutional right to an appeal before the Supreme Court? Could requests for writs still be heard and granted by lower courts? Suppose that the Congress had stripped all federal courts of jurisdiction to issue writs of habeas corpus. Would there still be courts to which petitioners could repair? In the Reconstruction South? Elsewhere? Would state courts be likely to issue writs of habeas corpus to federal jailers? Would those writs be enforceable? At what point, if ever, would the denial of an effective remedy to a violation of a constitutional right constitute a legislative violation of the Fifth Amendment right not to be denied liberty without due process of law?

6. *Injunctive relief.* The first attack on the constitutionality of the Reconstruction Acts occurred when the State of Mississippi sued to enjoin their enforcement by the president. In *Mississippi v. Johnson*, 71 U.S. (4 Wall.) 475 (1867), the Supreme Court ruled that it lacked the power to issue such an order against the president. The State of Georgia brought a similar action against the secretary of war. It was dismissed on the ground that it raised a nonjusticiable "political question." *Georgia v. Stanton*, 73 U.S. (6 Wall.) 50 (1868). If money damages for illegal imprisonment can be levied against a general, why not an injunction against the secretary of war or the president in advance? Compare *United States v. Nixon*, 418 U.S. 683 (1974) (declaratory judgment), and *National Treasury Employees' Union v. Nixon*, 492 F. 2d 587 (1974).

In re Neagle
135 U.S. 1. (1890)

For most of the nineteenth century, primacy in law enforcement was concededly a state responsibility, and local sheriffs and constables believed that they had the authority to arrest U.S. marshals for shooting people in the course of enforcing the fugitive slave laws in the North, the laws imposing reconstruction on the South after the Civil War, and federal laws against illegal distilleries (moonshining). Congress sometimes granted federal agents limited immunity from state prosecution when arrested in the course of enforcing specific federal laws, but at the time the *Neagle* case arose in 1889 had never expressly authorized the president to appoint U.S. marshals to protected federal judges from persons who threatened to do them harm.

David Neagle, a U.S. marshal, was appointed to protect Supreme Court Justice Stephen J. Field from David and Sarah Terry, two former litigants who had threatened Field's life for a ruling he had made against them in a previous circuit court case. When David Terry assaulted the justice in a railroad dining room, Neagle found it necessary to shoot him, after which the U.S. marshal was arrested by a state constable and charged with murder under state law.

The federal circuit court ordered state authorities to release Neagle on the grounds that the killing was, in the words of the federal habeas corpus statute, "an act done in pursuance of a law of the United States." That was the issue before the Supreme Court: Did the president have constitutional or statutory authority to appoint Neagle to guard the justice?

MR. JUSTICE MILLER delivered the opinion of the court....

We have no doubt that Mr. Justice Field when attacked by Terry was engaged in the discharge of his duties as Circuit Justice of the Ninth Circuit, and was entitled to all the protection under those circumstances which the law could give him.

It is urged, however, that there exists no statute authorizing any such protection as that which Neagle was instructed to give judge Field in the present case, and indeed no protection whatever against a vindictive or malicious assault growing out of the faithful discharge of his official duties; and that the language of section 753 of the Revised Statutes, that the party seeking the benefit of the writ of habeas corpus must in this connection show that he is "in custody for an act done or omitted in pursuance of a law of the United States," makes it necessary that upon this occasion it should be shown that the act for which Neagle is imprisoned was done by virtue of an act of Congress. It is not supposed that any special act of Congress exists which authorizes the marshals or deputy marshals of the United States in express terms to accompany the judges of the Supreme Court through their circuits, and act as a body-guard to them, to defend them against malicious assaults against their persons. But we are of opinion that this view of the statute is an unwarranted restriction of the meaning of a law designed to extend in a liberal manner the benefit of the writ of habeas corpus to persons imprisoned for the performance of their duty. And we are satisfied that if it was the duty of Neagle, under the circumstances, a duty which could only arise under the laws of the United States, to defend Mr. Justice Field from a murderous attack upon him, he brings himself within the meaning of the section we have recited. This view of the subject is confirmed by the alternative provision, that he must be in custody "for an act done or omitted in pursuance of a law of the United States or of an order, process, or decree of a court or judge thereof, or is in custody in violation of the Constitution or of a law or treaty of the United States."

In the view we take of the Constitution of the United States, any obligation fairly and properly inferrable from that instrument, or any duty of the marshal to be derived from the general scope of his duties under the laws of the United States, is "a law" within the meaning of this phrase. It would be a great reproach to the system of government of the United States, declared to be within its sphere sovereign and supreme, if there is to be found within the domain of its powers no means of protecting the judges, in the conscientious and faithful discharge of their duties, from the malice and hatred of those upon whom their judgments may operate unfavorably....

The Constitution, section 3, Article 2, declares that the President "shall take care that the laws be faithfully executed." Is this duty limited to the enforcement of acts of Congress or of treaties of the United States according to their *express terms,* or does it include the rights, duties and obligations growing out of the Constitution itself, our international relations, and all the protection implied by the nature of the government under the Constitution?

So, if the President or the Postmaster General is advised that the mails of the United States, possibly carrying treasure, are liable to be robbed and the mail carriers assaulted and murdered in any particular region of country, who can doubt the authority of the President or of one of the executive departments under him to make an order for the protection of the mail and of the persons and lives of its carriers, by doing exactly what was done in the case of Mr. Justice Field, namely, providing a sufficient guard, whether it be by soldiers of the army or by marshals of the United States, with a *posse comitatus* properly armed and equipped, to secure the safe performance of the duty of carrying the mail wherever it may be intended to go?...

We cannot doubt the power of the President to take measures for the protection of a judge of one of the courts of the United States, who, while in the discharge of the duties of his office, is threatened with a personal attack which may probably result in his death, and we think it clear that where this protection is to be afforded through the civil power, the Department of justice is the proper one to set in motion the necessary means of protection....

But there is positive law investing the marshals and their deputies with powers which not only justify what Marshal Neagle did in this matter, but which imposed it upon him as a duty. In chapter fourteen of the Revised Statutes of the United States, which is devoted to the appointment and duties of the district attorneys, marshals, and clerks of the courts of the United States, section 788 declares:

"The marshals and their deputies shall have, in each State, the same powers, in executing the laws of the United States, as the sheriffs and their deputies in such State may have, by law, in executing the laws thereof."

If, therefore, a sheriff of the State of California was authorized to do in regard to the laws of California what Neagle did, that is, if he was authorized to keep the peace, to protect a judge from assault and murder, then Neagle was authorized to do the same thing in reference to the laws of the United States.

Section 4176 of the Political Code of California reads as follows:

"The sheriff must:

"First. Preserve the peace.

"Second. Arrest and take before the nearest magistrate for examination all persons who attempt to commit or have committed a public offence.

"Third. Prevent and suppress all affrays, breaches of the peace, riots and insurrections, which may come to his knowledge...."

That there is a peace of the United States; that a man assaulting a judge of the United States while in the discharge of his duties violates that peace; that in such case the marshal of the United States stands in the same relation to the peace of the United States which the sheriff of the county does to the peace of the State of California; are questions too clear to need argument to prove them. That it would be the duty of a sheriff, if one had been present at this assault by Terry upon judge Field, to prevent this breach of the peace, to prevent this assault, to prevent the murder which was contemplated by it, cannot be doubted. And if, in performing this duty, it became necessary for the protection of judge Field, or of himself, to kill Terry, in a case where, like this, it was evidently a question of the choice of who should be killed, the assailant and violator of the law and disturber of the peace, or the unoffending man who was in his power, there can be no question of the authority of the sheriff to have killed Terry. So the marshal of the United States, charged with the duty of protecting and guarding the judge of the United States court against this special assault upon his person and his life, being present at the critical moment, when prompt action was necessary, found it to be his duty, a duty which he had no liberty to refuse to perform, to take the steps which resulted in Terry's death. This duty was imposed on him by the section of the Revised Statutes which we have recited, in connection with the powers conferred by the State of California upon its peace officers, which become, by this statute, in proper cases, transferred as duties to the marshals of the United States....

We therefore affirm the judgment of the Circuit Court authorizing his discharge from the custody of the sheriff of San Joaquin County.

MR. JUSTICE LAMAR (with whom concurred MR. CHIEF JUSTICE FULLER) dissenting.

[W]e agree, taking the facts of the case as they are shown by the record, that the personal protection of Mr. Justice Field, as a private citizen, even to the death of Terry, was not only the right, but was also the duty of Neagle and of any other bystander. And we maintain that for the exercise of that right or duty he is answerable to the courts of the State of California, and to them alone. But we deny that upon the facts of this record, he, as deputy marshal Neagle, or as private citizen Neagle, had any duty imposed on him by the laws of the United States growing out of the official character of judge Field as a Circuit Justice. We deny that anywhere in this transaction, accepting throughout the appellee's version of the facts, he occupied in law any position other than what would have been occupied by any other person who should have interfered in the same manner, in any other assault of the same character, between any two other persons in that room. In short, we think that there was nothing whatever in fact of an official character in the transaction, whatever may have been the appellee's view of his alleged official duties and powers: and, therefore, we think that the courts of the United States have in the present state of our legislation no jurisdiction whatever in the premises, and that the appellee should have been remanded to the custody of the sheriff....

The Attorney General of the United States has appeared in this case for the appellee.... He maintains that "The Constitution provides that before the President enters upon the execution of his office he shall take an oath — I do solemnly swear that I will faithfully execute the office of President of the United States, and will to the best of my ability *preserve, protect and defend* the Constitution of the United States." And he asks: "Has this clause no significance? Does it not, by necessary implication, invest the President with self-executing powers; that is, powers independent of statute?"

In reply to these propositions, we have this to say: We recognize that the Powers of the government, "within its sphere," as defined by the Constitution, and interpreted by the well-settled principles which have resulted from a century of wise and patriotic analysis, are supreme; that these supreme powers extend to the protection of itself and all of its agencies, as well as to the preservation and the perpetuation of its usefulness; and that these powers may be found not only in the express authorities conferred by the Constitution, but also in necessary and proper implications. But while that is all true, it is also true that the powers must be exercised, not only by the organs, but also in conformity with the modes, prescribed by the Constitution itself. These great federal powers, whose existence in all their plenitude and energy is incontestable, are not autocratic and lawless; they are organized powers, committed by the people to the hands of their servants for their own government, and distributed among the legislative, executive, and judicial departments; they are not *extra* to the Constitution, for, in and by that Constitution, and by it alone, the United States, as a great democratic federal republic, was called into existence and finds its continued existence possible....

The President is sworn to "preserve, protect and defend the Constitution." That oath *has* great significance.... But one very prominent feature of the Constitution which he is sworn to preserve, and which the whole body of the judiciary are bound to enforce, is the closing paragraph of sec. 8, Art. 1, in which it is declared that "the Congress shall have power ... to make all laws which shall be necessary and proper for carrying into execution the foregoing powers, and all other powers vested by this Constitution in the government of the United States, or in any department or officer thereof."

While it is the President's duty to take care that the laws be faithfully executed, it is not his duty to *make* laws or a law of the United States. The laws he is to see executed are manifestly those contained in the Constitution, and those enacted by Congress, whose duty it is to make all laws necessary and proper for carrying into execution the powers of those tribunals. In fact, for the President to have undertaken to make any law of the United States pertinent to this matter would have been to invade the domain of power expressly committed by the Constitution exclusively to Congress. That body was perfectly able to pass such laws as it should deem expedient in reference to such matter....

The gravamen of this case is in the assertion that Neagle slew Terry in pursuance of *a law* of the United States. He who claims to have committed a homicide by authority must show the authority. If he claims the authority of law, then *what* law? And if a law, how came it to be a law? Somehow and somewhere it must have had an origin. Is it a law because of the existence of a special and private authority issued from one of the executive departments? So in almost these words it is claimed in this case. Is it a law because of some constitutional investiture of sovereignty in the persons of judges who carry that sovereignty with them wherever they may go? Because of some power inherent in the judiciary to create for others a rule or law of conduct outside of legislation, which shall extend to the death penalty? So, also, in this case, in *totidem verbis* [in so many words], it is claimed. We dissent from both these claims. There can be no such law from either of those sources. The right claimed must be traced to legislation of Congress; else it cannot exist.... The common law never existed in our federal system....

It is claimed that such a law is found in section 787 of the Revised Statutes, which is as follows: "It shall be the duty of the marshal of each district to attend the district and circuit courts when sitting therein, and to execute, throughout the district, all lawful precepts directed to him, and issued under the authority of the United States; and he shall have power to command all necessary assistance in the execution of his duty."

It is contended that the duty imposed upon the marshal of each district by this section is not satisfied by a mere formal attendance upon the judges while on the bench; but that it extends to the whole term of the courts while in session, and can fairly be construed as requiring him to attend the judge while on his way from one court to another, to perform his duty. It is manifest that the statute will bear no such construction. In the first place, the judge is not the court; the person does not embody the tribunal, nor does the tribunal follow him in his journeys. In the second place the direction that he shall attend the court confers no authority or power on him of any character; it is merely a requirement that he shall be present, in person, at the court when sitting, in order to receive the lawful commands of the tribunal, and to discharge the duties elsewhere imposed upon him.

It is claimed that the law needed for appellee's case can be found in section 788 of the Revised Statutes. That section is as follows: "The marshals and their deputies shall have, in each State, the same powers, in executing the laws of the United States, as the sheriffs and their deputies in such State may have, by law, in executing the laws thereof."

It is then argued that by the Code of California the sheriff has extensive powers as a conservator of the peace, the statutes to that effect being quoted *in extenso*; that he also has certain additional common law powers and obligations to protect the judges and to personally attend them on their visits to that State; that, therefore, no statutory authority of the United States for the attendance on Mr. Justice Field by Neagle, and for Neagle's personal presence on the scene was necessary; and that that statute constituted Neagle a peace officer to keep the peace of the United States. This line of argument seems to us wholly untenable.

By way of preliminary remark it may be well to say, that so far as the simple fact of Neagle's attendance on Mr. Justice Field, and the fact of his personal presence, are concerned, no authority, statutory or otherwise, was needed. He had a right to be there; and being there, no matter how or why, if it became necessary to discharge an official duty, he would be just as much entitled to the protection of section 753 of the Revised Statutes as if he had been discharging an official duty in going there. The fallacy in the use made of section 788, in the argument just outlined, is this: That section gives to the officers named the same measure of powers when in the discharge of their duties as those possessed by the sheriffs, it is true; but it does not alter the duties themselves. It does not empower them to enlarge the scope of their labors and responsibilities, but only adds to their efficiency within that scope. They are still, by the very terms of the statute itself, limited to the execution of "the laws of the United States;" and are not in any way by adoption, mediate or immediate, from the code or the common law, authorized to execute the laws of California.... Murder is not an offence against the United States, except when committed on the high seas or in some port or harbor without the jurisdiction of the State, or in the District of Columbia, or in the Territories, or at other places where the national government has exclusive jurisdiction. It is well settled that such crime must be defined by statute, and no such statute has yet been pointed out. The United States government being thus powerless to try and punish a man charged with murder, we are not prepared to affirm that it is omnipotent to discharge from trial and give immunity from any liability to trial where he is accused of murder, unless an express statute of Congress is produced permitting such discharge.

For these reasons, as briefly stated as possible, we think the judgment of the court below should be reversed and the prisoner remanded to the custody of the sheriff of San Joaquin County, California; and we are the less reluctant to express this conclusion, because we cannot permit ourselves to doubt that the authorities of the State of California are competent and willing to do justice; and that even if the appellee had been indicted, and had gone to trial upon this record, God and his country would have given him a good deliverance.

MR. JUSTICE FIELD did not sit at the hearing of this case, and took no part in its decision.

Notes and Questions

1. *Source of the power.* Did the Court in *Neagle* hold that the Constitution authorizes the president to appoint bodyguards to protect Supreme Court justices in response to direct threats to their lives? Was it federal crime in 1899 to murder a Supreme Court justice? If not, what law was the marshal enforcing? The common law? Did the federal government adopt the British and colonial common law as its law in 1789 or earlier? Which governments passed legislation or constitutional provisions "receiving" the common law into their general laws—the national government or the states? Was Neagle enforcing the laws of California when he shot Terry to protect Field? Was he enforcing federal laws that defined the duties of federal judges and marshals?

2. *Inherent powers.* The *Neagle* case is often cited as the source of inherent presidential powers. See, for example, Chief Justice Vinson's dissent in *Youngstown Sheet & Tube Co. v. Sawyer, infra,* this chapter, and the 1971 testimony of William H. Rehnquist, then assistant attorney general and head of the Office of Legal Counsel, in which he invoked the *Neagle* decision as authority for the Army's use of 1,500 plainclothes agents to spy on lawful civilian political activity throughout the United States. *Federal Data Banks, Computers and the Bill of Rights,* Hearings before the Subcommittee on Constitutional Rights, Committee on the Judiciary, U.S. Senate, 92d Cong., 1st Sess. (1971), Part I at 598. Does the existence of this potential peace-keeping function mean that the military has the authority to compile potential round-up lists of "persons active in civil disorders"?

Where, according to the Court in *Neagle,* did the marshal get his authority to keep the "peace of the United States"—from the common law, from the Constitution, or from Congress? If the power came from Congress, is *Neagle* an "inherent powers" case?

In re Debs

158 U.S. 564 (1895)

In this case the Supreme Court upheld the constitutionality of an injunction obtained by President Grover Cleveland against Eugene V. Debs and other organizers of the great

In 1894 a wildcat strike against the Pullman Car Co. and its company town outside Chicago led 125,000 workers to walk off the job and crippled the nation's rail lines. President Grover Cleveland obtained a sweeping injunction against the strike's leaders and, over Governor John P. Altgeld's objections, dispatched 12,000 troops to put down the protest. Thirteen strikers were killed, 57 wounded.

Pullman Strike of 1894. The injunctive power upheld in that case set back the efforts of organized labor by more than thirty years. Following his release from prison, the charismatic Debs ran for president on the Socialist Party ticket and received 900,672 votes. He was later sentenced to ten years in prison for speaking out against American involvement in World War I.

MR. JUSTICE BREWER, after stating the case, delivered the opinion of the court.

The case presented by the bill is this: The United States, finding that the interstate transportation of persons and property, as well as the carriage of the mails, is forcibly obstructed, and that a combination and conspiracy exists to subject the control of such transportation to the will of the conspirators, applied to one of their courts, sitting as a court of equity, for an injunction to restrain such obstruction and prevent carrying into effect such conspiracy. Two questions of importance are presented: First. Are the relations of the general government to interstate commerce and the transportation of the mails such as authorize a direct interference to prevent a forcible obstruction thereof? Second. If authority exists, as authority in governmental affairs implies both power and duty, has a court of equity jurisdiction to issue an injunction in aid of the performance of such duty?

First. What are the relations of the general government to interstate commerce and the transportation of the mails? They are those of direct supervision, control, and management. While under the dual system which prevails with us the powers of government are distributed between the State and the Nation, and while the latter is properly styled a government of enumerated powers, yet within the limits of such enumeration it has all the attributes of sovereignty, and, in the exercise of those enumerated powers, acts directly upon the citizen, and not through the intermediate agency of the State.

"The government of the Union, then, is, emphatically and truly, a government of the people. In form and in substance it emanates from them. Its powers are granted by them, and are to be exercised directly on them, and for their benefit."

"No trace is to be found in the Constitution of an intention to create a dependence of the government of the Union on those of the States, for the execution of the great powers assigned to it. Its means are adequate to its ends: and on those means alone was it expected to rely for the accomplishment of its ends. To impose on it the necessity of resorting to means which it cannot control, which another government may furnish or withhold, would render its course precarious, the result of its measures uncertain, and create a dependence on other governments, which might disappoint its most important designs, and is incompatible with the language of the Constitution." Chief Justice Marshall in *McCulloch v. Maryland*, 4 Wheat. 316, 405, 424.

"Both the States and the United States existed before the Constitution. The people, through that instrument, established a more perfect union by substituting a national government, acting, with ample power, directly upon the citizens, instead of the confederate government, which acted with powers, greatly restricted, only upon the States." Chief Justice Chase in *Lane County v. Oregon*, 7 Wall. 71, 76, [stated]:

"We hold it to be an incontrovertible principle, that the government of the United States may, by means of physical force, exercised through its official agents, execute on every foot of American soil the powers and functions that belong to it. This necessarily involves the power to command obedience to its laws, and hence the power to keep the peace to that extent...." [citing *Neagle*]

Among the powers expressly given to the national government are the control of interstate commerce and the creation and management of a post office system for the nation. Article I, section 8, of the Constitution provides that "the Congress shall have power.... Third, to regulate commerce with foreign nations and among the several States, and with the Indian tribes.... Seventh, to establish post offices and post roads."

Congress has exercised the power granted in respect to interstate commerce in a variety of legislative acts....

Under the power vested in Congress to establish post offices and post roads, Congress has, by a mass of legislation, established the great post office system of the country, with all its detail of organization, its machinery for the transaction of business, defining what shall be carried and what not, and the prices of carriage, and also prescribing penalties for all offences against it....

As, under the Constitution, power over interstate commerce and the transportation of the mails is vested in the national government, and Congress by virtue of such grant has assumed actual and direct control, it follows that the national government may prevent any unlawful and forcible interference therewith. But how shall this be accomplished? Doubtless, it is within the competency of Congress to prescribe by legislation that any interference with these matters shall be offences against the United States, and prosecuted and punished by indictment in the proper courts. But is that the only remedy? Have the vast interests of the nation in interstate commerce, and in the transportation of the mails, no other protection than lies in the possible punishment of those who interfere with it? To ask the question is to answer it. By article 3, section 2, clause 3, of the Federal Constitution it is provided: "The trial of all crimes except in cases of impeachment shall be by jury; and such trial shall be held in the State where the said crime shall have been committed." If all the inhabitants of a State, or even a great body of them, should combine to obstruct interstate commerce or the transportation of the mails, prosecutions for such offences had in such a community would be doomed in advance to failure. And if the certainty of such failure was known, and the national government had no other way to enforce the freedom of interstate commerce and the transportation of the mails than by prosecution and punishment for interference therewith, the whole interests of the nation in these respects would be at the absolute mercy of a portion of the inhabitants of that single State.

But there is no such impotency in the national government. The entire strength of the nation may be used to enforce in any part of the land the full and free exercise of all national powers and the security of all rights entrusted by the Constitution to its care. The strong arm of the national government may be put forth to brush away all obstructions to the freedom of interstate commerce or the transportation of the mails. If the emergency arises, the army of the Nation, and all its militia, are at the service of the Nation to compel obedience to its laws.

But passing to the second question, is there no other alternative than the use of force on the part of the executive authorities whenever obstructions arise to the freedom of interstate commerce or the transportation of the mails? Is the army the only instrument by which rights of the public can be enforced and the peace of the nation preserved? Grant that any public nuisance may be forcibly abated either at the instance of the authorities, or by any individual suffering private damage there from, the existence of this right of forcible abatement is not inconsistent with nor does it destroy the right of appeal in an orderly way to the courts for a judicial determination, and an exercise of their powers by writ of injunction and otherwise to accomplish the same result....

So, in the case before us, the right to use force does not exclude the right of appeal to the courts for a judicial determination and for the exercise of all their powers of prevention. Indeed, it is more to the praise than to the blame of the government, that, instead of determining for itself questions of right and wrong on the part of these petitioners and their associates and enforcing that determination by the club of the policeman and the bayonet of the soldier, it submitted all those questions to the peaceful determination of judicial tribunals, and invoked their consideration and judgment as to the measure of its rights and powers and the correlative obligations of those against whom it made complaint. And it is equally to the credit of the latter that the judgment of those tribunals was by the great body of them respected, and the troubles which threatened so much disaster terminated.

Neither can it be doubted that the government has such an interest in the subject matter as enables it to appear as party plaintiff in this suit. It is said that equity only interferes for the protection of property, and that the government has no property interest. A sufficient reply is that the United States have a property in the mails, the protection of which was one of the purposes of this bill....

We do not care to place our decision upon this ground alone. Every government, entrusted, by the very terms of its being, with powers and duties to be exercised and discharged for the general welfare, has a right to apply to its own courts for any proper assistance in the exercise of the one and the discharge of the other, and it is no sufficient answer to its appeal to one of those courts that it has no pecuniary interest in the matter. The obligations which it is under to promote the interest of all, and to prevent the wrongdoing of one resulting in injury to the general welfare, is often of itself sufficient to give it a standing in court....

The petition for a writ of *habeas corpus* is *denied.*

Notes and Questions

1. *Source of the power.* What is the source of the authority of lower federal courts to decide cases? Does it come directly from Article III of the Constitution, or must Congress pass jurisdictional legislation first? In *Debs*, where did the court get the authority to enjoin a labor strike? Did any statute give the president the authority to go into court to obtain an injunction and an order sending the strikers back to work? In the absence of a statute specifically prescribing how the federal government should deal with strikes, from what source would the president get the authority to suppress strike-related violence with military force? When, in the ordinary course of mass violence, may the federal government step in to restore order? See 10 U.S.C. Secs. 331–34. Did the state ask for federal assistance? If not, where did the president get the authority to seek, and the court the authority to grant, the injunction? Does the existence of a congressional power to legislate give the president power to do what Congress might authorize, but hasn't? If so, what would that do to the system of checks and balances?

2. *Scope of the power.* Is it reasonable to infer, perhaps by analogy to *Neagle,* that the president has an "inherent power" to prevent interferences with federal government functions, such as the delivery of the mail? If so, should it make any difference whether he posts U.S. marshals to guard mailbags or direct them, and the army, to attack strikers who are preventing trains from running?

Debs is often cited as authority for inherent executive powers, including authority to wiretap and bug for national security purposes without a judicial warrant. Does the *Debs* decision support such a claim? Does *Debs* grant an inherent power to the executive alone? Does it authorize secret action, like spying, infiltration, or wiretapping of citizens by the military, at the president's command? Is *Debs* a *routine* powers case or an *emergency* powers case? Should that make a difference in how it is applied in the future?

3. *Power of Congress.* In the Chicago Seven case, the Justice Department defended its warrantless wiretapping of protest leaders at the 1968 Democratic National Convention on the grounds that Congress could not restrain the president in the use of "his" surveillance forces (Gov't Answer to Def.'s Motion for Disclosure of Electronic Surveillance, *United States v. Dellinger,* No. 69 Cr. 180 [ND. Ill., Feb. 20,1970]). Does either *Neagle* or *Debs* support that assertion?

4. *A "peace of the United States."* In both *Neagle* and *Debs,* the court assumed that there was a "peace of the United States" that the president might "keep" in certain circumstances. Which level of government—the nation or the states—inherited the general governmental duty to "keep the peace"? Compare the federal riot acts (now 10 U.S.C. Secs. 331–34), by which the first Congress authorized the use of troops as a backup force only.

5. *Aggregate powers.* In *Neagle* and *Debs*, the Court followed the Hamilton-Lincoln approach of postulating certain general, aggregate powers of the United States and then, in the absence of specific legislation to the contrary, attributing those aggregate powers to the presidency. Is this approach consistent with the idea of separated institutions sharing powers according to the theory of checks and balances?

United States v. Midwest Oil Co.
236 U.S. 459 (1915)

In the following opinion, the Supreme Court considered the question of how much weight, if any, should be given to historical practices, as opposed to judicial precedents. The case involved the relevance of administrative practices to understanding the meaning of a statute, but it has come to be cited for the proposition that executive practices can, over time, set "precedents" that add a "gloss" to the meaning of the Constitution.

MR. JUSTICE LAMAR delivered the opinion of the court.

All public lands containing petroleum or other mineral oils and chiefly valuable therefore, have been declared by Congress to be "free and open to occupation, exploration and purchase by citizens of the United States ... under regulations prescribed by law." Act of February 11, 1897, c. 216, 29 Stat. 526; R. S. 2319, 2329.

As these regulations permitted exploration and location without the payment of any sum, and as title could be obtained for a merely nominal amount, many persons availed themselves of the provisions of the statute. Large areas in California were explored; and petroleum having been found, locations were made, not only by the discoverer but by others on adjoining land. And, as the flow through the well on one lot might exhaust the oil under the adjacent land, the interest of each operator was to extract the oil as soon as possible so as to share what would otherwise be taken by the owners of nearby wells.

The result was that oil was so rapidly extracted that on September 17, 1909, the Director of the Geological Survey made a report to the Secretary of the Interior which, with enclosures, called attention to the fact that, while there was a limited supply of coal on the Pacific coast and the value of oil as a fuel had been fully demonstrated, yet at the rate at which oil lands in California were being patented by private parties it would "be impossible for the people of the United States to continue ownership of oil lands for more than a few months. After that the Government will be obliged to repurchase the very oil that it has practically given away...." "In view of the increasing use of fuel by the American Navy there would appear to be an immediate necessity for assuring the conservation of a proper supply of petroleum for the Government's own use ..." and "pending the enactment of adequate legislation on this subject, the filing of claims to oil lands in the State of California should be suspended."

This recommendation was approved by the Secretary of the Interior. Shortly afterwards he brought the matter to the attention of the President [Taft], who, on September 27, 1909, issued the following Proclamation:

"Temporary Petroleum Withdrawal No. 5"

"In aid of proposed legislation affecting the use and disposition of the petroleum deposits on the public domain, all public lands in the accompanying lists are hereby temporarily withdrawn from all forms of location, settlement, selection, filing, entry, or disposal under the mineral or non-mineral public land laws. All locations or claims existing and valid on this date may proceed to entry in the usual manner after field investigation and examination." The list attached described an area aggregating 3,041,000 acres in California and Wyoming — though, of course, the order only applied to the public lands therein, the acreage of which is not shown.

On March 27, 1910, six months after the publication of the Proclamation, William T. Henshaw and others entered upon a quarter section of this public land in Wyoming so withdrawn. They made explorations, bored a well, discovered oil and thereafter assigned their interest to the Appellees, who took possession and extracted large quantities of oil. On May 4, 1910, they filed a location certificate.

As the explorations by the original claimants, and the subsequent operation of the well, were both long after the date of the President's Proclamation, the Government filed, in the District Court of the United States for the District of Wyoming, a Bill in Equity against the Midwest Oil Company and the other Appellees, seeking to recover the land and to obtain an accounting for 50,000 barrels of oil alleged to have been illegally extracted. The court sustained the defendant's demurrer and dismissed the bill. Thereupon the Government took the case to the Circuit Court of Appeals of the Eighth Circuit which rendered no decision but certified certain questions to this court, where an order was subsequently passed directing the entire record to be sent up for consideration.

... On the part of the Government it is urged that the President, as Commander-in-Chief of the Army and Navy, had power to make the order for the purpose of retaining and preserving a source of supply of fuel for the Navy, instead of allowing the oil land to be taken up for a nominal sum, the Government being then obliged to purchase at a great cost what it had previously owned. It is argued that the President, charged with the care of the public domain, could, by virtue of the executive power vested in him by the Constitution (Art. 2, § 1), and also in conformity with the tacit consent of Congress, withdraw, in the public interest, any public land from entry or location by private parties.

The Appellees, on the other hand, insist that there is no dispensing power in the Executive and that he could not suspend a statute or withdraw from entry or location any land which Congress had affirmatively declared should be free and open to acquisition by citizens of the United States. They further insist that the withdrawal order is absolutely void since it appears on its face to be a mere attempt to suspend a statute — supposed to be unwise, — in order to allow Congress to pass another more in accordance with what the Executive thought to be in the public interest.

1. We need not consider whether, as an original question, the President could have withdrawn from private acquisition what Congress had made free and open to occupation and purchase. The case can be determined on other grounds and in the light of the legal consequences flowing from a long continued practice to make orders like the one here involved. For the President's proclamation of September 27, 1909, is by no means the first instance in which the Executive, by a special order, has withdrawn land which Congress, by general statute, had thrown open to acquisition by citizens. And while it is not known when the first of these orders was made, it is certain that "the practice dates from an early period in the

history of the government." *Grisar v. McDowell*, 6 Wall. 381. Scores and hundreds of these orders have been made; and treating them as they must be *(Wolsey v. Chapman*, 101 U.S. 769), as the act of the President, an examination of official publications will show that (excluding those made by virtue of special congressional action, *Donnelly v. United States*, 228 U.S. 255) he has during the past 80 years, without express statutory authority—but under the claim of power so to do—made a multitude of Executive Orders which operated to withdraw public land that would otherwise have been open to private acquisition. They affected every kind of land—mineral and non-mineral. The size of the tracts varied from a few square rods to many square miles and the amount withdrawn has aggregated millions of acres. The number of such instances cannot, of course, be accurately given, but the extent of the practice can best be appreciated by a consideration of what is believed to be a correct enumeration of such Executive Orders mentioned in public documents.

They show that prior to the year 1910 there had been issued

99 Executive Orders establishing or enlarging Indian Reservations;

109 Executive Orders establishing or enlarging Military Reservations and setting apart land for water, timber, fuel, hay, signal stations, target ranges and rights of way for use in connection with Military Reservations;

44 Executive Orders establishing Bird Reserves.

In the sense that these lands may have been intended for public use, they were reserved for a public purpose. But they were not reserved in pursuance of law or by virtue of any general or special statutory authority. For, it is to be specially noted that there was no act of Congress providing for Bird Reserves or for these Indian Reservations. There was no law for the establishment of these Military Reservations or defining their size or location. There was no statute empowering the President to withdraw any of these lands from settlement or to reserve them for any of the purposes indicated.

But when it appeared that the public interest would be served by withdrawing or reserving parts of the public domain, nothing was more natural than to retain what the Government already owned. And in making such orders, which were thus useful to the public, no private interest was injured. For prior to the initiation of some right given by law the citizen had no enforceable interest in the public statute and no private right in land which was the property of the people. The President was in a position to know when the public interest required particular portions of the people's lands to be withdrawn from entry or location; his action inflicted no wrong upon any private citizen, and being subject to disaffirmance by Congress, could occasion no harm to the interest of the public at large. Congress did not repudiate the power claimed or the withdrawal orders made. On the contrary it uniformly and repeatedly acquiesced in the practice and, as shown by these records, there had been, prior to 1910, at least 252 Executive Orders making reservations for useful, though non-statutory purposes.

This right of the President to make reservations,—and thus withdraw land from private acquisition,—was expressly recognized in *Grisar v. McDowell*, 6 Wall. 364 (1869), 381, where it was said that "from an early period in the history of the Government it has been the practice of the President to order, from time to time, as the exigencies of the public service required, parcels of land belonging to the United States to be reserved from sale and set apart for public uses."

But notwithstanding this decision and the continuity of this practice, the absence of express statutory authority was the occasion of doubt being expressed as to the power of the President to make these orders. The matter was therefore several times referred to the law officers of the Government for an opinion on the subject. One of them stated (19 Op. 370 [1889]) that the validity of such orders rested on "a long-established and long-recognized power in the President to withhold from sale or settlement, at discretion, portions of the public domain." Another reported that "the power of the President was recognized by Congress and that such recognition was equivalent to a grant" (17 Op. 163) (1881). Again, when the claim was made that the power to withdraw did not extend to mineral land, the Attorney General gave the opinion that the power "must be regarded as extending to any lands which belong to the public domain, and capable of being exercised with respect to such lands so long as they remain unappropriated" (17 Op. 232) [1881]).

Similar views were expressed by officers in the Land Department. Indeed, one of the strongest assertions of the existence of the power is the frequently quoted statement of Secretary Teller made in 1881:

"That the power resides in the Executive from an early period in the history of the country to make reservations has never been denied either legislatively or judicially, but on the contrary has been recognized. It constitutes in fact a part of the Land office law, exists *ex necessitati rei* [necessarily], is indispensable to the public weal and in that light, by different laws enacted as herein indicated, has been referred to as an existing undisputed power too well settled ever to be disputed." 1 L. D., 338 (1881–3).

2. It may be argued that while these facts and rulings prove a usage they do not establish its validity. But government is a practical affair intended for practical men. Both officers, law-makers and citizens naturally adjust themselves to any long continued action of the Executive Department — on the presumption that unauthorized acts would not have been allowed to be so often repeated as to crystallize into a regular practice. That presumption is not reasoning in a circle but the basis of a wise and quieting rule that in determining the meaning of a statute or the existence of a power, weight shall be given to the usage itself — even when the validity of the practice is the subject of investigation....

Reversed.

Notes and Questions

1. *Theory of presidential powers.* Which theory of presidential powers is implicit in the Court's decision: inherent, implied, of inferred constitutional authority, incidental powers pursuant to a constitutional authorization, incidental powers pursuant to a congressional delegation, or residual powers, in the sense that Article II is read to grant the president discretion to take actions "necessary and proper" to the carrying out of a congressional delegation? Compare this action by President Taft with the writings of Professor Taft in 1913 (*supra,* this chapter).

2. *Power by accretion.* Does the Court's decision in *Midwest Oil* stand for the proposition that the president may obtain some of his powers by the accumulation of uncontested political precedents, much as a landowner may destroy an easement across his land by uncontested adverse occupation for more than twenty years? Should the repeated fail-

ure of Congress to resist presidential assertions of authority be read by the courts as "precedents" that alter the meaning of the Constitution? Can the president and Congress together alter the meaning of the Constitution simply by agreeing to a particular distribution of political power?

3. *Political questions.* May congressional acquiescence in an executive practice over an extended period render impossible (nonjusticiable) a legal challenge to the assertion of the presidential authority implicit in the practice, on the ground that the passage of time has transformed a legal question into a mere "political question"? This was the view of district court judge Augustus Hand (brother of the more famous Learned Hand) in *United States v. Western Union Telegraph Co.*, 272 Fed. 311 (1921). At issue was whether the president had the authority, in the absence of congressional legislation, to prevent the operation of submarine cables to foreign countries in a manner that contravened his policies. The Constitution authorizes Congress to regulate commerce with foreign nations, and clearly Congress could have established policy to govern the operation of such cables if it wished. But could the president do so on his own initiative, in time of peace? The Justice Department argued that the president had done so on a number of instances in the past and Congress had neither objected or acted to preempt his policies. Hand was sympathetic to the argument that the president and Congress had concurrent authority in the matter, but avoided making a decision by declaring the issue to be a non-justiciable political question. Do you agree? For more on political questions, see *National Treasury Employees Union v. Nixon*, 492 F. 2d 587 (D.C.Cir. 1973).

4. *Contrary views.* Consider the following statements. Mr. Justice Frankfurter: "Illegality cannot attain legitimacy through practice" [*Inland Waterways Corp. v. Young*, 309 U.S. 517, 524 (1940)]. Chief Justice Warren: "That an unconstitutional action has been taken before surely does not render that action any less unconstitutional at a later date" [*Powell v. McCormack*, 395 U.S. 486, 546 (1969)].

5. *Secret action.* William Rehnquist, testifying on behalf of the Nixon administration, cited *Midwest Oil* for the proposition that a long-established practice of secret intelligence agencies not challenged by Congress could, in effect, enlarge presidential authority to spy on law-abiding political protesters. Does that follow?

Military Control of Civilian Populations

The ultimate executive prerogative is the power to control civilian populations through the application of military force.

The history of civil liberty in Britain and America has, since the seventeenth century, been a history of resistance to this prerogative. The use of military tribunals to punish civilian crimes and the quartering of troops in private homes during the early Stuart monarchies led to the historic Petition of Right (1628) and, ultimately, to the Puritan Revolution (1641–1651).[10] When Cromwell's republic degenerated into a military dictatorship, English and American Whigs came to realize that legislatures could be as much a source of arbitrary rule as kings. In 1679 the Restoration Parliament adopted the second Habeas Corpus Act in an effort to prevent future arbitrary arrests by the executive, but no legal constraint on legislatures was created until the Americans invented judicial review in the early nineteenth century. When the royal governor of Massachusetts authorized the military oc-

---

10. 3 Chas. I, c.1; Henry Hallam, *The Constitutional History of England*, 4 (2d ed., 1846), 531–33.

cupation of Boston in 1776, the war for American independence was born. One of the grievances listed in the Declaration of Independence was that the king had endeavored to render the military superior to the civil power.

The Constitution of 1789 did not expressly provide for the separation of civil and military functions. Like the right to vote, the separation probably was presumed. The prevailing view was probably best expressed by Governor Bowdoin of Massachusetts in his instructions to the militia charged with putting down Shays' Rebellion. The troops were to "protect the judicial courts, ... to assist the civil magistrates in executing the laws...," and to "aide them in apprehending the disturbers of the public peace." The commander was to regard himself "constantly as under the direction of the civil officer, saving where any armed force shall appear and oppose [his] marching to execute these orders."[11] President Washington's directives to the troops sent into western Pennsylvania to end the Whiskey Rebellion of 1794 were similar.[12]

In 1795, Congress passed the Insurrection Acts that codified this practice and assigned to federal troops the function of backing up civilian authorities in times of riot or insurrection, not supplanting them.[13] The theory of these acts was very clear. It was the duty of municipal authorities to deal with acts of lawlessness. If they could not handle it, then state authorities, including the state militia, would assist them, and if the militia could not handle the violence, then the federal government would help out, either by sending in militia from other states called into federal service by the president, or by committing federal troops. The core concept was military assistance to civil authorities, not military rule, unless the civil authorities, including the state and federal courts, could no longer function.

During the 1850s, the federal government triggered immense resentment by using federal troops as a militia to track down fugitive slaves in the northern states. After the Civil War, the enforcement of civil rights on behalf of newly freed blacks by Union troops alienated southern whites, and in 1878, Congress passed the Posse Comitatus Act. It made it a crime for federal soldiers to ride in civilian posses or otherwise execute civilian laws.[14] Similarly, legislation governing disaster relief charges the military with assisting, not supplanting, civil authorities.[15]

In times of war, and particularly in times of rebellion or feared invasion, military control of civilian populations is reasserted. The reassertion can take a variety of forms. In *Ex parte Milligan* (1866) and *Ex parte Quirin* (1942) the issue was the constitutionality of the trial of civilians by military tribunals. In *Ex parte McCardle* (1869), the issue of military rule of Southern states during Reconstruction was never reached. Of the following three cases that arose during World War II, *Hirabayashi* (1943) involved military curfews enforced by civilian courts. *Korematsu* (1944) involved military detention camps for citizens and aliens, while *Duncan* (1946) involved military prosecution of civilian offenses in military tribunals under martial law after the emergency has passed. These cases, even more than those arising out of the Civil War, demonstrate the extent to which fear of invasion can lead to military control of civilians.

---

11. *Federal Aid in Domestic Disturbances*, Sen. Doc. No. 263, 69th Cong., 2d Sess., 10.
12. Id., 31–32.
13. Now codified at 10 U.S.C. Sec. 331–34.
14. Now 18 U.S.C. Sec. 1385.
15. 42 U.S.C. Sec. 1855.

It is no exaggeration to say that during World War II President Roosevelt exercised near-dictatorial powers.[16] World War II was precisely the kind of emergency that John Locke had in mind when he advocated an emergency prerogative for republican executives.[17] Niccolò Machiavelli agreed: "those republics which in time of danger cannot resort to a dictatorship, or some similar authority, will generally be ruined when grave occasions occur." At the same time, Machiavelli wrote: "in a well-ordered republic it should never be necessary to resort to extra-constitutional measures; for although they may for the time be beneficial, yet the precedent is pernicious, for if the practice is once established of disregarding the laws for good objects, they will in a little while be disregarded under that pretext for evil purposes." (Machiavelli, in this respect, may have been a better whig than Locke.) Machiavelli also came to a whiggish conclusion: "no republic will ever be perfect if she has not by law provided for everything, having a remedy for every emergency, and fixed rules for applying it."[18]

Following Machiavelli, American political scientists and politicians since World War II have tried to specify in advance when, how, to what extent, and for how long the executive branch may exercise near-dictatorial powers. Their efforts, and those of the Supreme Court in *Youngstown Sheet and Tube Co. v. Sawyer* (1952), also follow.

Ex parte Quirin
317 U.S. 1 (1942)

On the evening of June 13, 1942, four German marines under orders to sabotage American war industries paddled ashore from a submarine at Amagansett Beach, Long Island. After bribing a Coast Guardsman who challenged them, they changed into civilian clothes, buried their uniforms and explosives, and headed for New York City. Four days later, another quartet under similar orders landed at Ponte Vedra Beach in Florida. The leader of the New York group soon defected to the FBI, and all of the marines were quickly rounded up. Following a closed trial before a military commission specially appointed by President Roosevelt under a broad claim of emergency war powers, six were sentenced to death and two were given long prison terms.

In their appeal to the Supreme Court, seven of the alleged "Nazi saboteurs" claimed that they should have been tried in civilian courts, under civilian law, because they were arrested by civilian authorities while in civilian clothes. The Supreme Court rejected their argument and the sentences were carried out.

MR. JUSTICE STONE delivered the opinion of the Court....

The question for decision is whether the detention of petitioners by respondent for trial by Military Commission, appointed by Order of the President of July 2, 1942, on charges preferred against them purporting to set out their violations of the law of war and of the Articles of War, is in conformity to the laws and Constitution of the United States....

The President, as President and Commander in Chief of the Army and Navy, by Order of July 2, 1942, appointed a Military Commission and directed it to try petitioners for offenses against the law of war and the Articles of War, and

16. E.g., see Clinton Rossiter, *Constitutional Dictatorship* (1948).
17. See "Of Prerogative" earlier in this chapter.
18. *The Prince and the Discourses* (1513; Lerner ed., 1950), ch. 34, 201–4.

prescribed regulations for the procedure on the trial and for review of the record of the trial and of any judgment or sentence of the Commission. On the same day, by Proclamation, the President declared that "all persons who are subjects, citizens or residents of any nation at war with the United States or who give obedience to or act under the direction of any such nation, and who during time of war enter or attempt to enter the United States ... through coastal or boundary defenses, and are charged with committing or attempting or preparing to commit sabotage, espionage, hostile or warlike acts, or violations of the law of war, shall be subject to the law of war and to the jurisdiction of military tribunals."

The Proclamation also stated in terms that all such persons were denied access to the courts.

The Commission met on July 8, 1942, and proceeded with the trial, which continued in progress while the causes were pending in this Court.... It is conceded that ever since petitioners' arrest the state and federal courts in Florida, New York, and the District of Columbia, and in the states in which each of the petitioners was arrested or detained, have been open and functioning normally....

Petitioners' main contention is that the President is without any statutory or constitutional authority to order the petitioners to be tried by military tribunal for offenses with which they are charged; that in consequence they are entitled to be tried in the civil courts with the safeguards, including trial by jury, which the Fifth and Sixth Amendments guarantee to all persons charged in such courts with criminal offenses. In any case it is urged that the President's Order, in prescribing the procedure of the Commission and the method for review of its findings and sentence, and the proceedings of the Commission under the Order, conflict with Articles of War adopted by Congress—particularly Articles 38, 43, 46, 50½ and 70—and are illegal and void.

The Government challenges each of these propositions. But regardless of their merits, it also insists that petitioners must be denied access to the courts, both because they are enemy aliens or have entered our territory as enemy belligerents, and because the President's Proclamation undertakes in terms to deny such access to the class of persons defined by the Proclamation, which aptly describes the character and conduct of petitioners. It is urged that if they are enemy aliens or if the Proclamation has force, no court may afford the petitioners a hearing. But there is certainly nothing in the Proclamation to preclude access to the courts for determining its applicability to the particular case. And neither the Proclamation nor the fact that they are enemy aliens forecloses consideration by the courts of petitioners' contentions that the Constitution and laws of the United States constitutionally enacted forbid their trial by military commission....

Congress and the President, like the courts, possess no power not derived from the Constitution. But one of the objects of the Constitution, as declared by its preamble, is to "provide for the common defence." As a means to that end, the Constitution gives to Congress the power to "provide for the common Defence," Art I, §8, cl. 1....

By the Articles of War ... Congress has provided ... the "military commission" appointed by military command as an appropriate tribunal for the trial and punishment of offenses against the law of war not ordinarily tried by court martial. See Arts. 12, 15. Articles 38 and 46 authorize the President, with certain limitations, to prescribe the procedure for military commissions. Articles 81 and 82 authorize trial, either by court martial or military commission, of those charged with relieving, harboring or corresponding with the enemy and those charged with spying. And Article 15 declares that "the provisions of these articles conferring jurisdiction upon courts martial shall not be construed as depriving military commissions ... or other military tribunals of concurrent jurisdiction in respect of offenders or offenses that by statute or by the law of war may be triable by such military commissions or other military tribunals." Article 2 includes among those persons subject to military law the personnel of our own military establishment. But this, as Article 12 provides, does not exclude from that class "any other person who by the law of war is subject to trial by military tribunals" and who under Article 12 may be tried by court martial or under Article 15 by military commission.

From the very beginning of its history this Court has recognized and applied the law of war as including that part of the law of nations which prescribes, for the conduct of war, the status, rights and duties of enemy nations as well as of enemy individuals....

It is no objection that Congress in providing for the trial of such offenses has not itself undertaken to codify that branch of international law or to mark its precise boundaries, or to enumerate or define by statute all the acts which that law condemns.... By universal agreement and practice, the law of war draws a distinction between the armed forces and the peaceful populations of belligerent nations and also between those who are lawful and unlawful combatants.... The spy who secretly and without uniform passes the military lines of a belligerent in time of war, seeking to gather military information and communicate it to the enemy, or an enemy combatant who without uniform comes secretly through the lines for the purpose of waging war by destruction of life or property, are familiar examples of belligerents who are generally deemed not to be entitled to the status of prisoners of war, but to be offenders against the law of war subject to trial and punishment by military tribunals.

Such was the practice of our own military authorities before the adoption of the Constitution, and during the Mexican and Civil Wars....

Citizenship in the United States of an enemy belligerent does not relieve him from the consequences of a belligerency which is unlawful because in violation of the law of war. Citizens who associate themselves with the military arm of the enemy government, and with its aid, guidance and direction enter this country bent on hostile acts, are enemy belligerents within the meaning of the Hague Convention and the law of war.... It is as an enemy belligerent that petitioner Haupt is charged with entering the United States, and unlawful belligerency is the gravamen of the offense of which he is accused....

But petitioners insist that, even if the offenses with which they are charged are offenses against the law of war, their trial is subject to the requirement of the Fifth Amendment that no person shall be held to answer for a capital or otherwise infamous crime unless on a presentment or indictment of a grand jury, and that such trials by Article III, § 2, and the Sixth Amendment must be by jury in a civil court. Before the Amendments, § 2 of Article III, the Judiciary Article, had provided, "The Trial of all Crimes, except in Cases of Impeachment, shall be by jury," and had directed that "such Trial shall be held in the State where the said Crimes shall have been committed."

Presentment by a grand jury and trial by a jury of the vicinage where the crime was committed were at the time of the adoption of the Constitution familiar parts of the machinery for criminal trials in the civil courts. But they were procedures unknown to military tribunals, which are not courts in the sense of the Judiciary Article.... As this Court has often recognized, it was not the purpose or effect of § 2 of Article III, read in the light of the common law, to enlarge the then existing right to a jury trial. The object was to preserve unimpaired trial by jury in all those cases in which it had been recognized by the common law and in all cases of a like nature as they might arise in the future, ... but not to bring within the sweep of the guaranty those cases in which it was then well understood that a jury trial could not be demanded as of right....

Since the Amendments, like § 2 of Article III, do not preclude all trials of offenses against the law of war by military commission without a jury when the offenders are aliens not members of our Armed Forces, it is plain that they present no greater obstacle to the trial in like manner of citizen enemies who have violated the law of war applicable to enemies. Under the original statute authorizing trial of alien spies by military tribunals, the offenders were outside the constitutional guaranty of trial by jury, not because they were aliens but only because they had violated the law of war by committing offenses constitutionally triable by military tribunal.

We cannot say that Congress in preparing the Fifth and Sixth Amendments intended to extend trial by jury to the cases of alien or citizen offenders against the law of war otherwise triable by military commission, while withholding it from members of our own armed forces charged with infractions of the Articles of War punishable by death. It is equally inadmissible to construe the Amendments—whose primary purpose was to continue unimpaired presentment by grand jury and trial by petit jury in all those cases in which they had been customary—as either abolishing all trials by military tribunals, save those of the personnel of our own armed forces, or, what in effect comes to the same thing, as imposing on all such tribunals the necessity of proceeding against unlawful enemy belligerents only on presentment and trial by jury. We conclude that the Fifth and Sixth Amendments did not restrict whatever authority was conferred by the Constitution to try offenses against the law of war by military commission, and that petitioners, charged with such an offense not required to be tried by jury at common law, were lawfully placed on trial by the Commission without a jury.

Petitioners, and especially petitioner Haupt, stress the pronouncement of this Court in the *Milligan* case, ... that the law of war "can never be applied to citizens in states which have upheld the authority of the government, and where the courts are open and their process unobstructed." Elsewhere in its opinion, ... the Court was at pains to point out that Milligan, a citizen twenty years resident in Indiana, who had never been a resident of any of the states in rebellion, was not an enemy belligerent either entitled to the status of a prisoner of war or subject to the penalties imposed upon unlawful belligerents. We construe the Court's statement as to the inapplicability of the law of war to Milligan's case as having particular reference to the facts before it. From them the Court concluded that Milligan, not being a part of or associated with the armed forces of the enemy, was a non-belligerent, not subject to the law of war save as—in circumstances found not there to be present, and not involved here—martial law might be constitutionally established.

The Court's opinion is inapplicable to the case presented by the present record. We have no occasion now to define with meticulous care the ultimate boundaries of the jurisdiction of military tribunals to try persons according to the law of war. It is enough that the petitioners here, upon the conceded facts, were plainly within those boundaries, and were held in good faith for trial by military commission, charged with being enemies who, with the purpose of destroying war materials and utilities, entered, and after entry remained in, our territory without uniform—an offense against the law of war. We hold only that those particular acts constitute an offense against the law of war which the Constitution authorizes to be tried by military commission....

MR. JUSTICE MURPHY took no part in the consideration or decision of these cases.

Notes and Questions

1. *Source of the authority.* According to the Court, where did the President's authority to create the military commission come from: the President's powers under Article II, Congress' authority under Article III, Congress' authority to create tribunals under Article I, international laws of war recognized by Congress, Congressionally enacted articles of war, or the "common law" of military commanders predating and post dating the Constitution? If his authority derived from an act of Congress, may the *Quirin* case be cited as a precedent for claims of inherent presidential power to create military commissions in times of emergency?

2. *Congressional authority.* Did the majority in *Ex parte Milligan* deny that Congress could authorize creation of a special military court to try civilians or enemy aliens in times of public danger? If Congress has such a power, from what provision of the Constitution is it derived? May Congress create emergency tribunals that are independent of, and not subject to, Supreme Court review or constitutionally guaranteed rights?

3. *A valid precedent?* Is the force of a legal precedent diminished if the means by which it was obtained were questionable, if not corrupt? Which, if any, of the following criticisms of the *Quirin* decision would justify ignoring it as a precedent? That the Supreme Court rushed to judgment, holding oral argument in a special summertime session, without reading the briefs beforehand and without taking sufficient time afterwards to read them carefully (less than 24 hours in which to read 180 pages)? That the Court rejected the legal challenge within 24 hours of oral argument, with virtually no collective deliberation, and without preparing an opinion? That Justice Felix Frankfurter secretly advised the Roosevelt administration how to structure the military commission to avoid a successful legal challenge by the defendants? That Justice James Byrne was simultaneously working as a lobbyist for the administration in Congress when he cast his vote? That Attorney General Nicholas Biddle secretly informed the justices that President Roosevelt would execute the defendants no matter what the Court decided, and that Justice Owen Roberts, for one, believed him? That Chief Justice Stone, while writing the opinion over the three months following the defendants' execution, confided in his clerk that "The President's order probably conflicts with the Articles of War," but then ignored this conclusion in his opinion? (The presidential order departed from the Articles of War by permitting the admission of hearsay evidence, reducing the number of votes required to

support a sentence of death, and changing the review procedure in death-penalty cases.) That the defendants' counsel, Col. Kenneth C. Royall, was ordered by President Roosevelt not to challenge the legality of the proceedings (an order Royall chose to violate)? That Justice Frankfurter shared with his colleagues a fictitious colloquy between himself and the defendants in which he denounced them for having a "hellava cheek" to raise the legal challenge, damned them for sowing "the seeds of a bitter conflict" between the branches of government, and concluded that "for you there are no procedural rights"? See Brief of Legal Scholars and Historians as *Amici Curiae* in Support of Petitioner, *Hamdan v. Rumsfeld*, No. 03-184, U.S. Supreme Court, 2005, and works cited therein.

4. *Judicial review.* While upholding the president's authority to establish a military tribunal, albeit on thin evidence of Congressional authorization, the Court also recognized the right of the defendants to appeal to the civilian courts. In an early draft of his opinion, Chief Justice Stone grounded this right in the Constitution, but in his final opinion, he simply acknowledged that "nothing" in the president's proclamation had precluded appellate review. In November 2001, Justice Department lawyer John Yoo and Vice President Cheney interpreted that change as allowing President George W. Bush to declare himself the exclusive and final reviewer of his military tribunals' decisions.

5. *What kind of Congressional authorization is necessary to create a new court system?* According to the Court in *Quirin,* the Congress in the Articles of War authorized "the President, with certain limitations, to prescribe the procedure for military commissions." Assuming that is what Congress intended by some vague and scattered references to commissions buried among rules governing courts-martial, may Congress' Article I power to create a new system of criminal courts be delegated to the president? Or should the Supreme Court require that any new court system be established by Congress, pursuant to a comprehensive statute like the Uniform Code of Military Justice (UCMJ), which, consistent with Articles I and III, makes courts martial inferior to the Supreme Court?

6. *Equal protection?* Can such a system satisfy the constitutional requirement of equal protection of the laws if it is not, like the UCMJ, grounded in a system of legal precedent administered by an independent judiciary? May such a Congressionally authorized system be used to try civilians, of U.S. or foreign citizenship, without violating the criminal justice guarantees of the Fourth, Fifth, and Sixth Amendments to the federal Constitution?

7. *The Articles of War superseded?* Given that the Articles of War, which embraced the use of tribunals from the Civil War through World War II, were replaced by the UCMJ, could a court today conclude that whatever common law power once justified the dispensation of summary justice through military tribunals has been superseded by the UCMJ statute? See *Hamdan v. Rumsfeld, infra,* chapter 5.

8. *The law of necessity.* In the late eighteenth and early nineteenth centuries, the practice of military tribunals dispensing summary justice was considered a necessary expedient, given the long periods in which armies and warships were out of touch with the War Department or U.S. courts. Today legal services can be supplied to military units in foreign lands; defendants can be transported to the United States for trial, all under an established military legal system with its own precedents, lawyers, and judges. Under these circumstances, does it still make sense to read vague legislation as giving presidents the authority to invent ad hoc tribunals, staffed by non-lawyers and ungrounded in legal precedents, as a "convenient alternative" to formal, professional legal systems authorized by comprehensive legislation?

9. *Secret trials.* Given that the Nazi saboteurs had all confessed, was it militarily necessary to try them in secret? The only "secret" was that their capture was due not to supersleuthing by the FBI, but to the voluntary surrender by one of the German marines, who had a hard time persuading the FBI that his story should be taken seriously. This fact was not only kept from the public, but also from the tribunal. It did not know that the German marine who turned the group in (and another who cooperated) had been promised leniency by the FBI and sentenced both to death.

According to the Justice Department, at least nine federal cases have been conducted in total secrecy since September 11, 2001. Are secret trials or executions necessary? Of enemy spies and saboteurs? Terrorists? War criminals? Can those necessities, if any, be met adequately by trial delays, POW detention, or trials pursuant to federal laws which regulate the handling of classified information at trial? According to the Justice Department, secret prosecutions are needed to persuade terrorists or their associates to work undercover for the United States. Are the risks posed by secret trials, and especially military trials without appeals to an independent judiciary, likely to outweigh whatever benefits secrecy may offer? In any case, does the Constitution permit secret trials and secret executions?

9. *Individual rights in war and peace* In *Milligan* the majority declared that the "Constitution ... is a law for rulers and people, equally in war and in peace, and covers with the shield of its protection all classes of men, at all times, and under all circumstances." Is the decision in *Quirin* consistent with this view? In *All the Laws but One: Civil Liberties in Wartime* 224–25 (1998), Chief Justice Rehnquist concluded: "It is neither desirable nor is it remotely likely that civil liberty will occupy as favored a position in wartime as it does in peacetime. But it is both desirable and likely that more careful attention will be paid by the court on the basis for the government's claims of necessity for curtailing civil liberties." Is it clear, from this statement, what degree of scrutiny Rehnquist considered appropriate when reviewing the constitutionality of military tribunals or mass detentions?

Hirabayashi v. United States
320 U.S. 81 (1943)

During World War II, President Roosevelt issued Executive Order 9066, dated February 19, 1942, which provided that the secretary of war and military commanders could prescribe military areas from which any or all persons could be excluded. The secretary of war was authorized to provide excluded residents with transportation, food, shelter, and other accommodations. On March 21, 1942, Congress made it a crime to violate military orders issued pursuant to this executive order. Three days later, General John L. DeWitt, military commander of the Western Defense Command, encompassing the State of Washington, issued a curfew order. Later, more than 112,000 persons of Japanese ancestry, more than 70,000 of whom were American citizens (and some Aluit indians), were uprooted and placed in detention centers (i.e., concentration camps) for the duration of the hostilities.

Gordon Hirabayashi was an American citizen of Japanese ancestry, born and raised in the United States. He had never visited Japan and was personally not suspected of any disloyalty to the United States. At the time of his arrest he was a senior at the University of Washington. He was convicted by a federal district court of two crimes: failing to register with other Japanese-Americans for evacuation to a military detention camp, and failing to obey a military curfew for persons of his race in the State of Washington. In

A Japanese-American family awaiting transportation from Los Angeles to an internment center in Owens Valley, California. Inset: General John L. DeWitt, who commanded the internment, assured Congress that the detentions were militarily necessary because "a Jap's a Jap."

this case the Supreme Court dealt only with the curfew issue, postponing until the *Korematsu* case in 1944 the constitutionality of the detention program.

MR. CHIEF JUSTICE STONE delivered the opinion of the Court....

The conclusion is inescapable that Congress, by the Act of March 21, 1942, ratified and confirmed Executive Order No. 9066.... And so far as it lawfully could, Congress authorized and implemented such curfew orders as the commanding officer should promulgate pursuant to the Executive Order of the President. The question then is not one of Congressional power to delegate to the President the promulgation of the Executive Order, but whether, acting in cooperation, Congress and the Executive have constitutional authority to impose the curfew restriction here complained of. We must consider also whether, acting together, Congress and the Executive could leave it to the designated military commander to appraise the relevant conditions and on the basis of that appraisal to say whether, under the circumstances, the time and place were appropriate for the promulgation of the curfew order and whether the order itself was an appropriate means of carrying out the Executive Order for the "protection against espionage and against sabotage" to national defense materials, premises and utilities. For reasons presently to be stated, we conclude that it was within the con-

stitutional power of Congress and the executive arm of the Government to prescribe this curfew order for the period under consideration and that its promulgation by the military commander involved no unlawful delegation of
legislative power.

Executive Order No. 9066, promulgated in time of war for the declared purpose of prosecuting the war by protecting national defense resources from sabotage and espionage, and the Act of March 21, 1942, ratifying and confirming
the Executive Order, were each an exercise of the power to wage war conferred
on the Congress and on the President, as Commander in Chief of the armed
forces, by Articles I and II of the Constitution. See *Ex parte Quirin*, 317 U.S. 1,
25–26. We have no occasion to consider whether the President, acting alone,
could lawfully have made the curfew order in question, or have authorized others to make it. For the President's action has the support of the Act of Congress,
and we are immediately concerned with the question whether it is within the
constitutional power of the national government, through the joint action of
Congress and the Executive, to impose this restriction as an emergency war measure. The exercise of that power here involves no question of martial law or trial
by military tribunal. Cf. *Ex parte Milligan*, 4 Wall. 2; *Ex parte Quirin*. Appellant
has been tried and convicted in the civil courts and has been subjected to penalties prescribed by Congress for the acts committed.

The war power of the national government is "the power to wage war successfully." See Charles Evans Hughes, "War Powers Under the Constitution," 42
A.B.A. Rep. 232, 238. It extends to every matter and activity so related to war as
substantially to affect its conduct and progress. The power is not restricted to
the winning of victories in the field and the repulse of enemy forces. It embraces
every phase of the national defense, including the protection of war materials
and the members of the armed forces from injury and from the dangers which
attend the rise, prosecution and progress of war.... Since the Constitution commits to the Executive and to Congress the exercise of the war power in all the vi-
cissitudes and conditions of warfare, it has necessarily given them wide scope
for the exercise of judgment and discretion in determining the nature and extent
of the threatened injury or danger and in the selection of the means for resisting it.... Where, as they did here, the conditions call for the exercise of judgment and discretion and for the choice of means by those branches of the
Government on which the Constitution has placed the responsibility of war-
making, it is not for any court to sit in review of the wisdom of their action or
substitute its judgment for theirs.

The actions taken must be appraised in the light of the conditions with which
the President and Congress were confronted in the early months of 1942, many
of which, since disclosed, were then peculiarly within the knowledge of the military authorities....

The challenged orders were defense measures for the avowed purpose of
safeguarding the military area in question, at a time of threatened air raids and
invasion by the Japanese forces, from the danger of sabotage and espionage.
As the curfew was made applicable to citizens residing in the area only if they
were of Japanese ancestry, our inquiry must be whether in the light of all the
facts and circumstances there was any substantial basis for the conclusion, in
which Congress and the military commander united, that the curfew as applied was a protective measure necessary to meet the threat of sabotage and es-

pionage which would substantially affect the war effort and which might reasonably be expected to aid a threatened enemy invasion. The alternative which appellant insists must be accepted is for the military authorities to impose the curfew on all citizens within the military area, or on none. In a case of threatened danger requiring prompt action, it is a choice between inflicting obviously needless hardship on the many, or sitting passive and unresisting in the presence of the threat. We think that constitutional government, in time of war, is not so powerless and does not compel so hard a choice if those charged with the responsibility of our national defense have reasonable ground for believing that the threat is real.

When the orders were promulgated there was a vast concentration, within Military Areas Nos. 1 and 2, of installations and facilities for the production of military equipment, especially ships and airplanes. Important Army and Navy bases were located in California and Washington....

In the critical days of March 1942, the danger to our war production by sabotage and espionage in this area seemed obvious. The German invasion of the Western European countries had given ample warning to the world of the menace of the "fifth column." Espionage by persons in sympathy with the Japanese Government had been found to have been particularly effective in the surprise attack on Pearl Harbor. At a time of threatened Japanese attack upon this country, the nature of our inhabitants' attachments to the Japanese enemy was consequently a matter of grave concern. Of the 126,000 persons of Japanese descent in the United States, citizens and non-citizens, approximately 112,000 resided in California, Oregon and Washington at the time of the adoption of the military regulations. Of these approximately two-thirds are citizens because born in the United States. Not only did the great majority of such persons reside within the Pacific Coast states but they were concentrated in or near three of the large cities, Seattle, Portland and Los Angeles, all in Military Area No. 1.

There is support for the view that social, economic and political conditions which have prevailed since the close of the last century, when the Japanese began to come to this country in substantial numbers, have intensified their solidarity and have in large measure prevented their assimilation as an integral part of the white population. In addition, large numbers of children of Japanese parentage are sent to Japanese language schools outside the regular hours of public schools in the locality. Some of these schools are generally believed to be sources of Japanese nationalistic propaganda, cultivating allegiance to Japan. Considerable numbers, estimated to be approximately 10,000, of American-born children of Japanese parentage have been sent to Japan for all or a part of their education.

Congress and the Executive, including the military commander, could have attributed special significance, in its bearing on the loyalties of persons of Japanese descent, to the maintenance by Japan of its system of dual citizenship. Children born in the United States of Japanese alien parents, and especially those children born before December 1, 1924, are under many circumstances deemed, by Japanese law, to be citizens of Japan. No official census of those whom Japan regards as having thus retained Japanese citizenship is available, but there is ground for the belief that the number is large.

The large number of resident alien Japanese, approximately one-third of all Japanese inhabitants of the country, are of mature years and occupy positions of influence in Japanese communities. The association of influential Japanese residents with Japanese Consulates has been deemed a ready means for the dissemination of propaganda and for the maintenance of the influence of the Japanese Government with the Japanese population in this country.

As a result of all these conditions affecting the life of the Japanese, both aliens and citizens, in the Pacific Coast area, there has been relatively little social intercourse between them and the white population. The restrictions, both practical and legal, affecting the privileges and opportunities afforded to persons of Japanese extraction residing in the United States, have been sources of irritation and may well have tended to increase their isolation, and in many instances their attachments to Japan and its institutions.

Viewing these data in all their aspects, Congress and the Executive could reasonably have concluded that these conditions have encouraged the continued attachment of members of this group to Japan and Japanese institutions. These are only some of the many considerations which those charged with the responsibility for the national defense could take into account in determining the nature and extent of the danger of espionage and sabotage, in the event of invasion or air raid attack. The extent of that danger could be definitely known only after the event and after it was too late to meet it. Whatever views we may entertain regarding the loyalty to this country of the citizens of Japanese ancestry, we cannot reject as unfounded the judgment of the military authorities and of Congress that there were disloyal members of that population, whose number and strength could not be precisely and quickly ascertained. We cannot say that the war-making branches of the Government did not have ground for believing that in a critical hour such persons could not readily be isolated and separately dealt with, and constituted a menace to the national defense and safety, which demanded that prompt and adequate measures be taken to guard against it.

Appellant does not deny that, given the danger, a curfew was an appropriate measure against sabotage. It is an obvious protection against the perpetration of sabotage most readily committed during the hours of darkness. It was an appropriate exercise of the war power and its validity is not impaired because it has restricted the citizen's liberty. Like every military control of the population of a dangerous zone in wartime, it necessarily involves some infringement of individual liberty, just as does the police establishment of fire lines during a fire, or the confinement of people to their houses during an air raid alarm — neither of which could be thought to be an infringement of constitutional right. Like them, the validity of the restraints of the curfew order depends on all the conditions which obtain at the time the curfew is imposed and which support the order imposing it.

It is true that the Act does not in terms establish a particular standard to which orders of the military commander are to conform, or require findings to be made as a prerequisite to any order. But the Executive Order, the Proclamations and the statute are not to be read in isolation from each other. They were parts of a single program and must be judged as such....

The military commander's appraisal of facts in the light of the authorized standard, and the inferences which he drew from those facts, involved the exercise of his informed judgment. But as we have seen, those facts, and the inferences which could be rationally drawn from them, support the judgment of the military commander, that the danger of espionage and sabotage to our military resources was imminent, and that the curfew order was an appropriate measure to meet it.…

The Constitution as a continuously operating charter of government does not demand the impossible or the impractical. The essentials of the legislative function are preserved when Congress authorizes a statutory command to become operative, upon ascertainment of a basic conclusion of fact by a designated representative of the Government.

Affirmed.

[JUSTICES DOUGLAS, MURPHY, and RUTLEDGE concurred, making the decision unanimous.]

Notes and Questions

1. *The commander-in-chief power.* In Executive Order 9066, President Roosevelt invoked the Commander-in-Chief Clause of Article II as authority for the exclusions and evacuations. Does the Commander-in-Chief Clause authorize the president to abrogate the liberties of citizens and aliens protected by the Bill of Rights and the habeas corpus clause? Did the Supreme Court accept Roosevelt's assertion that it did? Did the Court uphold the order as an exercise of an inherent or exclusive executive power?

2. *Congressional ratification.* May Congress pass a criminal law that says in effect that violations of military orders issued pursuant to an executive order are, *ipso facto*, criminal? May Congress constitutionally delegate to the president or military commanders the power to define what behavior constitutes a federal crime? Does such a delegation satisfy the Fifth Amendment's guarantee of due process of law, or should it be declared void for vagueness?

3. *Equal protection.* The curfew was not applied to persons of German or Italian ancestry. Does that omission constitute a violation of equal protection of the laws? Does it, or the fact that 158,000 persons of Japanese ancestry living in the Hawaiian Islands were not detained, cast doubt upon the administration's claims of military necessity?

4. *Judicial deference.* In times of crisis, like 1942 or 2001, should the courts grant more or less deference to an administration's claims to emergency powers? Should judges take judicial notice of the fact that politicians and voters usually over estimate national security threats following surprise attacks, like those that occurred in 1807, 1898, 1941, and 2001? Should the courts grant greater deference to such claims when they are made by both the president and Congress? When they invoke national security or international relations as grounds for curbing civil liberties? Or should the Court require that Congress hold hearings, make specific findings of fact, and set deadlines for reconsideration before holding that any emergency powers law is constitutional? See the discussion of the anti-delegation doctrine in Chapter 4 and the discussion of deference to the executive in *United States v. Curtiss-Wright* in Chapter 3.

Korematsu v. United States
323 U.S. 214 (1944)

Fred Korematsu, like Gordon Hirabayashi, was an American citizen who had never traveled outside of the United States. He grew up in Oakland, California, and was a shipyard welder until the Japanese attacked Pearl Harbor and the Boilermakers' Union expelled him. In love with a Caucasian girl, Korematsu wanted to avoid evacuation, have plastic surgery to alter his nose, marry, and stay in Oakland, but the FBI tracked him down. He was found guilty of violating the exclusion order, given a suspended sentence, and released on probation. Although Korematsu was set free by a court, which found his loyalty unquestionable, the army seized him anyway and his girlfriend jilted him. At issue was his right, and the right of all 112,000 detained persons, to habeas corpus and individualized justice.

MR. JUSTICE BLACK delivered the opinion of the Court....

In the light of the principles we announced in the *Hirabayashi* case, we are unable to conclude that it was beyond the war power of Congress and the Executive to exclude those of Japanese ancestry from the West Coast war area at the time they did. True, exclusion from the area in which one's home is located is a far greater deprivation than constant confinement to the home from 8 p.m. to 6 a.m. Nothing short of apprehension by the proper military authorities of the gravest imminent danger to the public safety can constitutionally justify either. But exclusion from a threatened area, no less than curfew, has a definite and close relationship to the prevention of espionage and sabotage....

Like curfew, exclusion of those of Japanese origin was deemed necessary because of the presence of an unascertained number of disloyal members of the group, most of whom we have no doubt were loyal to this country. It was because we could not reject the finding of the military authorities that it was impossible to bring about an immediate segregation of the disloyal from the loyal that we sustained the validity of the curfew order as applying to the whole group. In the instant case, temporary exclusion of the entire group was rested by the military on the same ground. The judgment that exclusion of the whole group was for the same reason a military imperative answers the contention that the exclusion was in the nature of group punishment based on antagonism to those of Japanese origin. That there were members of the group who retained loyalties to Japan has been confirmed by investigations made subsequent to the exclusion. Approximately five thousand American citizens of Japanese ancestry refused to swear unqualified allegiance to the United States and to renounce allegiance to the Japanese Emperor, and several thousand evacuees requested repatriation to Japan.[19]

We uphold the exclusion order as of the time it was made and when the petitioner violated it.... In doing so, we are not unmindful of the hardships imposed by it upon a large group of American citizens.... But hardships are part of war, and war is an aggregation of hardships. All citizens alike, both in and out of uniform, feel the impact of war in greater or lesser measure. Citizenship has its responsibilities as well as its privileges, and in time of war the burden is always heavier. Compulsory exclusion of large groups of citizens from their homes, except under circumstances of direst emergency and peril, is inconsistent with our basic governmental institutions. But when under conditions of modern warfare our shores are threatened by hostile forces, the power to protect must be commensurate with the threatened danger....

19. Hearings before the subcommittee on the National War Agencies Appropriation Bill for 1945, Part II, 608–726; Final Report, Japanese Evacuation from the West Coast, 1942, 309–327; Hearings before the Committee on Immigration and Naturalization, House of Representatives, 78th Cong., 2d Sess., on H. R. 2701 and other bills to expatriate certain nationals of the United States, pp. 37–42, 49–58.

It is said that we are dealing here with the case of imprisonment of a citizen in a concentration camp solely because of his ancestry, without evidence or inquiry concerning his loyalty and good disposition towards the United States. Our task would be simple, our duty clear, were this a case involving the imprisonment of a loyal citizen in a concentration camp because of racial prejudice. Regardless of the true nature of the assembly and relocation centers — and we deem it unjustifiable to call them concentration camps with all the ugly connotations that term implies — we are dealing specifically with nothing but an exclusion order. To cast this case into outlines of racial prejudice, without reference to the real military dangers which were presented, merely confuses the issue. Korematsu was not excluded from the Military Area because of hostility to him or his race. He was excluded because we are at war with the Japanese Empire, because the properly constituted military authorities feared an invasion of our West Coast and felt constrained to take proper security measures, because they decided that the military urgency of the situation demanded that all citizens of Japanese ancestry be segregated from the West Coast temporarily, and finally, because Congress, reposing its confidence in this time of war in our military leaders — as inevitably it must — determined that they should have the power to do just this. There was evidence of disloyalty on the part of some, the military authorities considered that the need for action was great, and time was short. We cannot — by availing ourselves of the calm perspective of hindsight — now say that at that time these actions were unjustified.

Affirmed.

MR. JUSTICE JACKSON, dissenting....

It would be impracticable and dangerous idealism to expect or insist that each specific military command in an area of probable operations will conform to conventional tests of constitutionality. When an area is so beset that it must be put under military control at all, the paramount consideration is that its measures be successful, rather than legal. The armed services must protect a society, not merely its Constitution. The very essence of the military job is to marshal physical force, to remove every obstacle to its effectiveness, to give it every strategic advantage. Defense measures will not, and often should not, be held within the limits that bind civil authority in peace. No court can require such a commander in such circumstances to act as a reasonable man; he may be unreasonably cautious and exacting. Perhaps he should be. But a commander in temporarily focusing the life of a community on defense is carrying out a military program; he is not making law in the sense the courts know the term. He issues orders, and they may have a certain authority as military commands, although they may be very bad as constitutional law.

But if we cannot confine military expedients by the Constitution, neither would I distort the Constitution to approve all that the military may deem expedient. That is what the Court appears to be doing, whether consciously or not. I cannot say, from any evidence before me, that the orders of General DeWitt were not reasonably expedient military precautions, nor could I say that they were. But even if they were permissible military procedures, I deny that it follows that they are constitutional. If, as the Court holds, it does follow, then we may as well say that any military order will be constitutional and have done with it....

Much is said of the danger to liberty from the Army program for deporting and detaining these citizens of Japanese extraction. But a judicial construction of the due process clause that will sustain this order is a far more subtle blow to liberty than the promulgation of the order itself. A military order, however unconstitutional, is not apt to last longer than the military emergency. Even during that period a succeeding commander may revoke it all. But once a judicial opinion rationalizes such an order to show that it conforms to the Constitution, or rather rationalizes the Constitution to show that the Constitution sanctions such an order, the Court for all time has validated the principle of racial discrimination in criminal procedure and of transplanting American citizens. The principle then lies about like a loaded weapon ready for the hand of any authority that can bring forward a plausible claim of an urgent need. Every repetition imbeds that principle more deeply in our law and thinking and expands it to new purposes.... A military commander may overstep the bounds of constitutionality, and it is an incident. But if we review and approve, that passing incident becomes the doctrine of the Constitution. There it has a generative power of its own, and all that it creates will be in its own image. Nothing better illustrates this danger than does the Court's opinion in this case ... The Court is now saying that in *Hirabayashi* we did decide the very things we there said we were not deciding. Because we said that these citizens could be made to stay in their homes during the hours of dark, it is said we must require them to leave home entirely; and if that, we are told they may also be taken into custody for deportation; and if that, it is argued they may also be held for some undetermined time in detention camps. How far the principle of this case would be extended before plausible reasons would play out, I do not know.

I should hold that a civil court cannot be made to enforce an order which violates constitutional limitations even if it is a reasonable exercise of military authority. The courts can exercise only the judicial power, can apply only law, and must abide by the Constitution, or they cease to be civil courts and become instruments of military policy....

I would reverse the judgment and discharge the prisoner.

[JUSTICE FRANKFURTER concurred, and JUSTICES ROBERTS, and MURPHY dissented, each in separate opinions.]

Notes and Questions

1. *Nature of the power.* Did the *Korematsu* case involve a unilateral executive action unauthorized by Congress? What kind of power was recognized here? Does the *Korematsu* decision stand as a precedent for legislation authorizing routine electronic surveillance by the National Security Agency, an arm of the military, contrary to the requirements of the Fourth Amendment?

2. *Ex parte Endo.* The exclusion and evacuation of Japanese-Americans were upheld under a theory of emergency powers. Should individual detentions be upheld once it becomes clear that the detained persons pose no threat to the nation's security? This question was presented in the case of *Ex parte Endo*, 323 U.S. 283 (1944), announced the same day as *Korematsu*. Mitsuye Endo was an American citizen who was evacuated to a relocation center. In July 1942, she filed a habeas petition, arguing that she was unlawfully detained

and confined under armed guard and against her will. In 1944, more than a year after the tide of war had turned in the Pacific, the Supreme Court ruled that she should be released. A unanimous Court held that the exclusion and relocation orders were constitutional, but that the continuing detention of manifestly loyal Americans exceeded the military's authority under the legislation and executive orders authorizing the exclusions. Left open was the question whether the president had the constitutional authority, at that point in the war, to order the continued detention of one who could not be shown to pose a security risk. Roosevelt did not claim the authority, and within forty-eight hours the mass exclusion and detention orders were revoked by military authorities.

3. *Individualized hearings?* Fred Korematsu was freed by a court, which found that he posed no threat to national security, but the military locked him up anyway. Did that make sense? Persons of German and Italian ancestry received individualized hearings to determine whether they posed a threat—hearings run by law firms. Should the courts have waited until the *Endo* case to hold that persons of Japanese ancestry were entitled to such hearings too?

4. *Aliens and the Constitution.* To understand the power recognized here, is it relevant that the persons interned appeared to be aliens, even though most of them were actually citizens? Would the Court have been likely to acknowledge a similar power in the national government if all of the internees had been *Mayflower* descendants? If not, should the *Korematsu* decision be granted any precedential respect at all?

5. *In retrospect.* No Japanese-American was convicted of a disloyal act during World War II. No Japanese-American spy rings were ever uncovered. The military was able to govern the Hawaiian Islands throughout the war without interning the 157,905 persons of Japanese ancestry (32.5 percent of the population) who lived there. Jacobus tenBroek, Edward N. Barnhart, and Floyd W. Matson, *Prejudice, War and the Constitution* (1954), 363, n. 186.

Meanwhile, the 442d Regimental Combat Team, a segregated Japanese-American fighting unit in Italy, became one of the most decorated units in American military history. Not one of its members ever deserted, although the unit suffered casualties amounting to 314 percent of the unit's original strength. Alan R. Bosworth, *America's Concentration Camps* (1968), 3–6. However, the parents of the fallen were not permitted to go to the docks to receive their sons' caskets.

In 1983, the Commission on Wartime Relocation and Internment of Civilians, created by Congress to study the mass internments of World War II, concluded: "The promulgation of Executive Order 9066 was not justified by military necessity, and the decisions that followed from it … were not driven by analysis of military conditions. The broad historical causes which shaped the decisions were race prejudice, war hysteria and a failure of political leadership."[20] Forty years after the detentions, Congress paid the remaining survivors approximately $20,000 each in compensation, and an education fund was set up to assure that nothing like the internment would happen again. In 1998, President Bill Clinton awarded the nation's highest civilian award, the Medal of Freedom, to Fred Korematsu.

6. *Fraud upon the court.* In January 1983, Gordon Hirabayashi, Fred Korematsu, and Minoru Yasui filed suits in separate federal courts to have their wartime convictions overturned on the ground that the military's claims of an emergency were based on intentional fabrications and falsehoods and constituted a fraud upon the courts. There simply

---

20. *Personal Justice Denied* (1982), 18.

was no credible evidence that persons of Japanese ancestry posed any threat to the nation's security, and never had been. The Justice Department agreed that Korematsu's conviction should be set aside, but refused to respond to his charges. Ruling that the Department's refusal was "tantamount to a confession of error," the court set aside Korematsu's conviction (*New York Times*, Nov. 11, 1983, B7). However, it did not overturn the holdings that upheld the legality of the detentions.

7. *Precedent?* Following the attacks of September 11, 2001, the administration of George W. Bush detained approximately 5,000 immigrants from the Middle East, ostensibly because they were "out of status" with the immigration service, but actually to keep them behind bars until the FBI could "clear" each of ties to terrorism. The Justice Department also refused to disclose their identities or why, specifically, each was being held, claiming that to do so would give terrorists a "roadmap" to its investigations. This secrecy was upheld in *Center for National Security Studies v. Department of Justice*, 331 F.3d 918 (D.C. Cir. 2003). On January 11, 2004, the Supreme Court refused to review the holding.

Duncan v. Kahanamoku, Sheriff
327 U.S. 304 (1946)

On December 7, 1941, immediately after the surprise attack on Pearl Harbor, the governor of the territory of Hawaii issued a proclamation suspending the privilege of the writ of habeas corpus and declaring "martial law." Section 67 of the Hawaiian Organic Act, passed by Congress when Hawaii became part of the United States, allowed him to take this action. President Roosevelt ratified the governor's actions two days later, and martial law remained in effect in Hawaii throughout the war.

Under martial law, military tribunals replaced civilian courts and were empowered to try all offenses, not just those which might impair the war effort. These tribunals could punish violators of orders issued by the military government with fines, imprisonment, or execution. The constitutionality of convictions issued by these tribunals and the persistence of martial rule long after the Japanese had ceased to pose a military threat to the islands was at issue in *Duncan*.

Lloyd Duncan was a civilian ship fitter convicted by a military court in 1944 of assaulting two Navy Yard sentries. By then the civilian courts had been reopened, and military tribunals were limited to trying civilians for violating military orders. Unfortunately for Duncan, assaulting sentries was a violation of military orders as well as a crime under civilian law. Harry White, whose case was joined with Duncan's for argument in the Supreme Court, was a civilian stockbroker convicted by a military tribunal of embezzling stock.

The Supreme Court did not decide these two cases until six months after the Japanese surrendered. At the time the two men were convicted it was generally assumed that the Japanese navy no longer threatened the Hawaiian Islands.

MR. JUSTICE BLACK delivered the opinion of the Court.

Did the Organic Act during the period of martial law give the armed forces power to supplant all civilian laws and to substitute military for judicial trials under the conditions that existed in Hawaii at the time these petitioners were tried?

… We note first that at the time the alleged offenses were committed the dangers apprehended by the military were not sufficiently imminent to cause them to require civilians to evacuate the area or even to evacuate any of the buildings necessary to carry on the business of the courts. In fact, the buildings had long been open and actually in use for certain kinds of trials. Our question does not involve the well-established power of the military to exercise jurisdiction over members of the armed forces, those directly connected with such forces, or enemy belligerents, prisoners of war, or others charged with violating the laws of war. We are not concerned with the recognized power of the military to try civilians in tribunals established as a part of a temporary military government over occupied enemy territory or territory regained from an enemy where civilian government cannot and does not function. For Hawaii since annexation has been held by and loyal to the United States. Nor need we here consider the power of the military simply to arrest and detain civilians interfering with a necessary military function at a time of turbulence and danger from insurrection or war. And finally, there was no specialized effort of the military, here, to enforce orders which related only to military functions, such as, for illustration, curfew rules or blackouts. For these petitioners were tried before tribunals set up under a military program which took over all government and superseded all civil laws and courts. If the Organic Act, properly interpreted, did not give the armed forces this awesome power, both petitioners are entitled to their freedom.

In interpreting the Act we must first look to its language. Section 67 makes it plain that Congress did intend the Governor of Hawaii, with the approval of the President, to invoke military aid under certain circumstances. But Congress did not specifically state to what extent the army could be used or what power it could exercise. It certainly did not explicitly declare that the Governor in conjunction with the military could for days, months or years close all the courts and supplant them with military tribunals.... If a power thus to obliterate the judicial system of Hawaii can be found at all in the Organic Act, it must be inferred from §67's provision for placing the Territory under "martial law." But the term "martial law" carries no precise meaning. The Constitution does not refer to "martial law" at all and no Act of Congress has defined the term. It has been employed in various ways by different people and at different times. By some it has been identified as "military law" limited to members of, and those connected with, the armed forces. Others have said that the term does not imply a system of established rules but denotes simply some kind of day to day expression of a general's will dictated by what he considers the imperious necessity of the moment.... In 1857 the confusion as to the meaning of the phrase was so great that the Attorney General in an official opinion had this to say about it: "The common law authorities and commentators afford no clue to what martial law, as understood in England, really is.... In this country it is still worse." 8 Op. Atty. Gen. 365, 367, 368. What was true in 1857 remains true today. The language of §67 thus fails to define adequately the scope of the power given to the military and to show whether the Organic Act provides that courts of law be supplanted by military tribunals.

Since the Act's language does not provide a satisfactory answer, we look to the legislative history for possible further aid in interpreting the term "martial law" as used in the statute. The Government contends that [w]hen Congress passed the Organic Act it simply enacted the applicable language of the Hawaiian Constitution and with it the interpretation of that language by the Hawaiian supreme court [authorizing broad martial law powers].

[M]ilitary trials of civilians charged with crime, especially when not made subject to judicial review, are so obviously contrary to our political traditions and our institution of jury trials in courts of law, that the tenuous circumstance offered by the Government can hardly suffice to persuade us that Congress was willing to enact a Hawaiian supreme court decision permitting such a radical departure from our steadfast beliefs.

Partly in order to meet this objection the Government further contends that Congress ... not only authorized military trials of civilians in Hawaii, but also could and intended to provide that "martial law" in Hawaii should not be limited by the United States Constitution or by established Constitutional practice. But when the Organic Act is read as a whole and in the light of its legislative history it becomes clear that Congress did not intend the Constitution to have a limited application to Hawaii. Along with §67 Congress enacted §5 of the Organic Act which provides "that the Constitution ... shall have the same force and effect within the said Territory as elsewhere in the United States...." 31 Stat. 141....

It follows that civilians in Hawaii are entitled to the constitutional guarantee of a fair trial to the same extent as those who live in any other part of our country. We are aware that conditions peculiar to Hawaii might imperatively demand extraordinarily speedy and effective measures in the event of actual or threatened invasion. But this also holds true for other parts of the United States....

... Our system of government clearly is the antithesis of total military rule and the founders of this country are not likely to have contemplated complete military dominance within the limits of a territory made part of this country and not recently taken from an enemy. They were opposed to governments that placed in the hands of one man the power to make, interpret and enforce the laws. Their philosophy has been the people's throughout our history. For that reason we have maintained legislatures chosen by citizens or their representatives and courts and juries to try those who violate legislative enactments. We have always been especially concerned about the potential evils of summary criminal trials and have guarded against them by provisions embodied in the Constitution itself. See *Ex parte Milligan*, 4 Wall. 2; *Chambers v. Florida*, 309 U.S. 227. Legislatures and courts are not merely cherished American institutions; they are indispensable to our Government.

Military tribunals have no such standing. For as this Court has said before: "... the military should always be kept in subjection to the laws of the country to which it belongs, and that he is no friend to the Republic who advocates the contrary. The established principle of every free people is that the law shall alone govern; and to it the military must always yield." *Dow v. Johnson*, 100 U.S. 158, 169. Congress prior to the time of the enactment of the Organic Act had only once authorized the supplanting of the courts by military tribunals. Legislation to that effect was enacted immediately after the South's unsuccessful attempt to secede from the Union. Insofar as that legislation applied to the Southern States after the war was at an end it was challenged by a series of Presidential vetoes as vigorous as any in the country's history. And in order to prevent this Court from passing on the constitutionality of this legislation Congress found it necessary to curtail our appellate jurisdiction. Indeed, prior to the Organic Act, the only time this Court had ever discussed the supplanting of courts by military tribunals in a situation other than that involving the establishment of a military government over recently occupied enemy territory, it had emphatically declared that "civil liberty and this kind of martial law cannot endure together; the antagonism is irreconcilable; and, in the conflict, one or the other must perish." [*Ex parte Milligan*]

We believe that when Congress passed the Hawaiian Organic Act and authorized the establishment of "martial law" it had in mind and did not wish to exceed the boundaries between military and civilian power, in which our people have always believed, which responsible military and executive officers had heeded, and which had become part of our political philosophy and institutions prior to the time Congress passed the Organic Act. The phrase "martial law" as employed in that Act, therefore, while intended to authorize the military to act vigorously for the maintenance of an orderly civil government and for the defense of the Islands against actual or threatened rebellion or invasion, was not intended to authorize the supplanting of courts by military tribunals. Yet the Government seeks to justify the punishment of both White and Duncan on the ground of such supposed congressional authorization. We hold that both petitioners are now entitled to be released from custody.

Reversed.

[MR. JUSTICE JACKSON took no part in the consideration or decision of these cases. JUSTICE MURPHY concurred.]

Notes and Questions

1. *Implicit assumptions.* Does the Court's decision in *Duncan* share the same premises about the degree of wartime necessity required for martial rule that the Court employed in *Ex parte Milligan?* If not, of what validity is the *Milligan* precedent?

2. *Wartime necessity.* By the standard of wartime necessity laid down in *Milligan,* how long should the military rule in Hawaii have lasted? If *Milligan* is the ruling precedent, was it necessary that the military prosecute a ship fitter for assault and a stockbroker for embezzlement? Did the military's failure to subject Japanese citizens and Japanese-Americans on the islands to internment render facially absurd the military's claims that both military rule on the islands and internment on the mainland were necessary?

3. *Judicial timing.* Like *Milligan* and *Endo, Duncan* was not announced until all danger of executive defiance had passed. Should these delays be deemed statesmanlike exercises of judicial self-restraint calculated to preserve the independence and integrity of the courts, or are they examples of judicial hypocrisy? Would courts today be more skeptical of claims of military necessity? Would they be quicker to challenge obvious breaches of constitutional limitations or constitutionally guaranteed rights?

Youngstown Sheet & Tube Co. v. Sawyer
343 U.S. 579 (1952)

At the height of the Korean War, labor negotiations in the steel industry reached an impasse, and the union threatened to go out on strike. President Truman, rather than alienate his political supporters in the labor movement, deliberately chose not to invoke his powers under the Taft-Hartley Act (which labor hated) and order an eighty-day cooling-off period. Instead he cajoled ninety-nine days out of the union by referring the issues of prices and wages to separate federal boards. When these failed to propose what Truman regarded as a settlement fair to labor, he ordered his secretary of commerce, Charles W. Sawyer, to seize the mills. Truman's strategy was to use the seizure to force concessions out of management and, failing that, settle the strike at terms favorable to labor, and then return control of the companies to their managers. The Republican-dominated Congress had sufficient opportunity to ratify the seizure and keep the steel mills open, but it chose to do nothing, and to allow the courts to resolve the issue.

MR. JUSTICE BLACK delivered the opinion of the Court.

We are asked to decide whether the President [Truman] was acting within his constitutional power when he issued an order directing the Secretary of Commerce to take possession of and operate most of the Nation's steel mills. The mill owners argue that the President's order amounts to lawmaking, a legislative function which the Constitution has expressly confided to the Congress and not to the President. The Government's position is that the order was made on findings of the President that his action was necessary to avert a national catastrophe which would inevitably result from a stoppage of steel production, and that in meeting this grave emergency the President was acting within the aggregate of his constitutional powers as the Nation's Chief Executive and the Commander in Chief of the Armed Forces of the United States. . . .

The President's power, if any, to issue the order must stem either from an act of Congress or from the Constitution itself. There is no statute that expressly authorizes the President to take possession of property as he did here. Nor is there any act of Congress to which our attention has been directed from which such a power can fairly be implied. Indeed, we do not understand the Government to rely on statutory authorization for this seizure. There are two statutes which do authorize the President to take both personal and real property under certain conditions. However, the Government admits that these conditions were not met and that the President's order was not rooted in either of the statutes. The Government refers to the seizure provisions of one of these statutes (§ 201 (b) of the Defense Production Act) as "much too cumbersome, involved, and time-consuming for the crisis which was at hand."

Moreover, the use of the seizure technique to solve labor disputes in order to prevent work stoppages was not only unauthorized by any congressional enactment; prior to this controversy, Congress had refused to adopt that method of settling labor disputes. When the Taft-Hartley Act was under consideration in 1947, Congress rejected an amendment which would have authorized such governmental seizures in cases of emergency. . . . Instead, the plan sought to bring about settlements by use of the customary devices of mediation, conciliation, investigation by boards of inquiry, and public reports. In some instances temporary injunctions were authorized to provide cooling-off periods. All this failing, unions were left free to strike [and the president was required to report to Congress on the emergency].

It is clear that if the President had authority to issue the order he did, it must be found in some provision of the Constitution. And it is not claimed that express constitutional language grants this power to the President. The contention is that presidential power should be implied from the aggregate of his powers under the Constitution. Particular reliance is placed on provisions in Article II which say that "The executive Power shall be vested in a President. . . ."; that "he shall take Care that the Laws be faithfully executed"; and that he "shall be Commander in Chief of the Army and Navy of the United States."

The order cannot properly be sustained as an exercise of the President's military power as Commander in Chief of the Armed Forces. The Government attempts to do so by citing a number of cases upholding broad powers in military commanders engaged in day-to-day fighting in a theater of war. Such cases need not concern us here. Even though "theater of war" be an expanding concept, we cannot with faithfulness to our constitutional system hold that the Commander in Chief of the Armed Forces has the ultimate power as such to take possession of private property in order to keep labor disputes from stopping production. This is a job for the Nation's lawmakers, not for its military authorities.

Nor can the seizure order be sustained because of the several constitutional provisions that grant executive power to the President. In the framework of our Constitution, the President's power to see that the laws are faithfully executed refutes the idea that he is to be a lawmaker. The Constitution limits his functions in the lawmaking process to the recommending of laws he thinks wise and the vetoing of laws he thinks bad. And the Constitution is neither silent nor equivocal about who shall make laws which the President is to execute [quoting Art. I, Sec. 1, and Art. I, Sec. 8, cl. 18].

The President's order does not direct that a congressional policy be executed in a manner prescribed by Congress—it directs that a presidential policy be executed in a manner prescribed by the President. The preamble of the order itself, like that of many statutes, sets out reasons why the President believes certain policies should be adopted, proclaims these policies as rules of conduct to be followed, and again, like a statute, authorizes a government official to promulgate additional rules and regulations consistent with the policy proclaimed and needed to carry that policy into execution. The power of Congress to adopt such public policies as those proclaimed by the order is beyond question. It can authorize the taking of private property for public use. It can make laws regulating the relationships between employers and employees, prescribing rules designed to settle labor disputes, and fixing wages and working conditions in certain fields of our economy. The Constitution does not subject this lawmaking power of Congress to presidential or military supervision or control.

It is said that other Presidents without congressional authority have taken possession of private business enterprises in order to settle labor disputes. But even if this be true, Congress has not thereby lost its exclusive constitutional authority to make laws necessary and proper to carry out the powers vested by the Constitution "in the Government of the United States, or any Department or Officer thereof."

The Founders of this Nation entrusted the lawmaking power to the Congress alone in both good and bad times. It would do no good to recall the historical events, the fears of power and the hopes for freedom that lay behind their choice. Such a review would but confirm our holding that this seizure order cannot stand.

The judgment of the District Court is

Affirmed.

MR. JUSTICE FRANKFURTER, concurring.

It cannot be contended that the president would have had power to issue this order had Congress explicitly negated such authority in formal legislation. Congress has expressed its will to withhold this power from the President as though it had said so in so many words.

By the Labor Management Relations Act of 1947, Congress said to the President, "You may not seize. Please report to us and ask for seizure power if you think it is needed in a specific situation."...

Apart from his vast share of responsibility for the conduct of our foreign relations, the embracing function of the President is that "he shall take Care that the Laws be faithfully executed...." Art. II, Sec. 3. The nature of that authority has for me been comprehensively indicated by Mr. Justice Holmes. "The duty of the President to see that the laws be executed is a duty that does not go beyond the laws or require him to achieve more than Congress sees fit to leave within his power" [*Myers v. United States*, 272 U.S. 52 (1926)]. The powers of the President are not as particularized as are those of Congress. But unenumerated powers do not mean undefined powers. The separation of powers built into our Constitution gives essential content to undefined provisions in the frame of our government.

To be sure, the content of the three authorities of government is not to be derived from an abstract analysis. The areas are partly interacting, not wholly disjointed. The Constitution is a framework for government. Therefore the way the framework has consistently operated fairly establishes that it has operated according to its true nature. Deeply embedded traditional ways of conducting government cannot supplant the Constitution or legislation, but they give meaning to the words of a text or supply them. It is an inadmissibly narrow conception of American constitutional law to confine it to the words of the Constitution and to disregard the gloss which life has written upon them. In short, a systematic, unbroken, executive practice, long pursued to the knowledge of the Congress and never before questioned, engaged in by Presidents who have also sworn to uphold the Constitution, making as it were such exercise of power part of the structure of our government, may be treated as a gloss on "executive Power" vested in the President by Sec. 1 of Art. II. [Citing, as an example, the land-management practices at issue in *Midwest Oil Co.,* Justice Frankfurter then carefully reviewed the historical record for instances that might provide precedent for Truman's seizure of the steel mills.]

Down to the World War II period, the record is barren of instances comparable to the one before us.... The list of executive assertions of the power of seizure in circumstances comparable to the present reduces to three in the six-month period from June to December of 1941. We need not split hairs in comparing those actions to the one before us, though much might be said by way of differentiation. Without passing on their validity, ... these three isolated instances do not add up, either in number, scope, duration of contemporaneous legal justification, to the kind of executive construction of the Constitution revealed in the *Midwest Oil* case. Nor do they come to us sanctioned by long-continued acquiescence of Congress giving decisive weight to a construction by the Executive of its powers....

MR. JUSTICE DOUGLAS, concurring.

The legislative nature of the action taken by the President seems to me to be clear. When the United States takes over an industrial plant to settle a labor controversy, it is condemning property. The seizure of the plant is a taking in the constitutional sense....

The power of the Federal Government to condemn property is well established.... It can condemn for any public purpose; and I have no doubt but that condemnation of a plant, factory, or industry in order to promote industrial peace would be constitutional. But there is a duty to pay for all property taken by the Government. The command of the Fifth Amendment is that no "private property be taken for public use, without just compensation."...

The president has no power to raise revenues. That power is in the Congress by Article I, Section 8 of the Constitution. The President might seize and the Congress by subsequent action might ratify the seizure. But until and unless Congress acted, no condemnation would be lawful....

If we sanctioned the present exercise of power by the President, we would be expanding Article II of the Constitution and rewriting it to suit the political conveniences of the present emergency....

We pay a price for our system of checks and balances, for the distribution of power among the three branches of government. It is a price that today may seem exorbitant to many. Today a kindly President uses the seizure power to effect a wage increase and to keep the steel furnaces in production. Yet tomorrow another President might use the same power to prevent a wage increase, to curb trade-unionists, to regiment labor as oppressively as industry thinks it has been regimented by this seizure.

MR. JUSTICE JACKSON, concurring in the judgment and opinion of the Court....

A judge, like an executive adviser, may be surprised at the poverty of really useful and unambiguous authority applicable to concrete problems of executive power as they actually present themselves. Just what our forefathers did envision, or would have envisioned had they foreseen modern conditions, must be divined from materials almost as enigmatic as the dreams Joseph was called upon to interpret for Pharaoh. A century and a half of partisan debate and scholarly speculation yields no net result but only supplies more or less apt quotations from respected sources on each side of any question. They largely cancel each other.[21] And court decisions are indecisive because of the judicial practice of dealing with the largest questions in the most narrow way.

The actual art of governing under our Constitution does not and cannot conform to judicial definitions of the power of any of its branches based on isolated clauses or even single Articles torn from context. While the Constitution diffuses power the better to secure liberty, it also contemplates that practice will integrate the dispersed powers into a workable government. It enjoins upon its branches separateness but interdependence, autonomy but reciprocity. Presidential powers are not fixed but fluctuate, depending upon their disjunction or conjunction with those of Congress. We may well begin by a somewhat over-simplified grouping of practical situations in which a President may doubt, or others may challenge, his powers, and by distinguishing roughly the legal consequences of this factor of relativity.

1. When the President acts pursuant to an express or implied authorization of Congress, his authority is at its maximum, for it includes all that he possesses

---

21. A Hamilton may be matched against a Madison. 7 *The Works of Alexander Hamilton*, 76–117; 1 Madison, *Letters and Other Writings*, 611–654. Professor Taft is counterbalanced by Theodore Roosevelt. Taft, *Our Chief Magistrate and His Powers*, 539–140; Theodore Roosevelt, *Autobiography*. 388–389. It even seems that President Taft cancels out Professor Taft. Compare his "Temporary Petroleum Withdrawal No. 5" of September 27, 1909, *United States v. Midwest Oil Co.*, 236 U.S. 459, 467, 468, with his appraisal of executive power in *Our Chief Magistrate and His Powers*, 139–140. [Footnote by Justice Jackson.]

in his own right plus all that Congress can delegate.[22] In these circumstances, and in these only, may he be said (for what it may be worth) to personify the federal sovereignty. If his act is held unconstitutional under these circumstances, it usually means that the Federal Government as an undivided whole lacks power. A seizure executed by the President pursuant to an Act of Congress would be supported by the strongest of presumptions and the widest latitude of judicial interpretation, and the burden of persuasion would rest heavily upon any who might attack it.

2. When the President acts in absence of either a congressional grant or denial of authority, he can only rely upon his own independent powers, but there is a zone of twilight in which he and Congress may have concurrent authority, or in which its distribution is uncertain. Therefore, congressional inertia, indifference or quiescence may sometimes, at least as a practical matter, enable, if not invite, measures on independent presidential responsibility. In this area, any actual test of power is likely to depend on the imperatives of events and contemporary imponderables rather than on abstract theories of law.[23]

3. When the President takes measures incompatible with the expressed or implied will of Congress, his power is at its lowest ebb, for then he can rely only upon his own constitutional powers minus any constitutional powers of Congress over the matter. Courts can sustain exclusive presidential control in such a case only by disabling the Congress from acting upon the subject.[24] Presidential claim to a power at once so conclusive and preclusive must be scrutinized with caution, for what is at stake is the equilibrium established by our constitutional system.

Into which of these classifications does this executive seizure of the steel industry fit? It is eliminated from the first by admission, for it is conceded that no congressional authorization exists for this seizure....

Can it then be defended under flexible tests available to the second category? It seems clearly eliminated from that class because Congress has not left seizure

---

22. It is in this class of cases that we find the broadest recent statements of presidential power, including those relied on here. *United States v. Curtiss-Wright Corp.*, 299 U.S. 304, involved, not the question of the President's power to act without congressional authority, but the question of his right to act under and in accord with an Act of Congress. The constitutionality of the Act under which the President had proceeded was assailed on the ground that it delegated legislative powers to the President. Much of the Court's opinion is *dictum*....

That case does not solve the present controversy. It recognized internal and external affairs as being in separate categories, and held that the strict limitation upon congressional delegations of power to the President over internal affairs does not apply with respect to delegations of power in external affairs. It was intimated that the President might act in external affairs without congressional authority, but not that he might act contrary to an Act of Congress. [Footnote by Justice Jackson.]

23. Since the Constitution implies that the writ of habeas corpus may be suspended in certain circumstances but does not say by whom, President Lincoln asserted and maintained it as an executive function in the face of judicial challenge and doubt. *Ex parte Merryman*, 17 Fed. Cas. 144; *Ex parte Milligan*, 4 Wall. 2. 125. Congress eventually ratified his action. [Footnote by Justice Jackson.]

24. President Roosevelt's effort to remove a Federal Trade Commissioner was found to be contrary to the policy of Congress and impinging upon an area of congressional control, and so his removal power was cut down accordingly. *Humphrey's Executor v. United States*, 295 U.S. 602. However, his exclusive power of removal in executive agencies, affirmed in *Myers v. United States*, 272 U.S. 52, continued to be asserted and maintained. *Morgan v. Tennessee Valley Authority*, 115 F. 2d 990, cert. denied. 312 U.S. 701; *In re Power to Remove Members of the Tennessee Valley Authority*, 39 Op. Atty. Gen, 145; President Roosevelt's Message to Congress of March 23, 1938, *The Public Papers and Addresses of Franklin D. Roosevelt*, 1938 (Rosenman), 151. [Footnote by Justice Jackson.]

of private property an open field but has covered it by three statutory policies inconsistent with this seizure....

This leaves the current seizure to be justified only by the severe tests under the third grouping, where it can be supported only by any remainder of executive power after subtraction of such powers as Congress may have over the subject. In short, we can sustain the President only by holding that seizure of such strike-bound industries is within his domain and beyond control by Congress.

... I did not suppose, and I am not persuaded, that history leaves it open to question, at least in the courts, that the executive branch, like the Federal Government as a whole, possesses only delegated powers. The purpose of the Constitution was not only to grant power, but to keep it from getting out of hand. However, because the President does not enjoy unmentioned powers does not mean that the mentioned ones should be narrowed by a niggardly construction. Some clauses could be made almost unworkable, as well as immutable, by refusal to indulge some latitude of interpretation for changing times. I have heretofore, and do now, give to the enumerated powers the scope and elasticity afforded by what seem to be reasonable, practical implications instead of the rigidity dictated by a doctrinaire textualism.

The Solicitor General seeks the power of seizure in three clauses of the Executive Article, the first reading, "The executive Power shall be vested in a President of the United States of America." Lest I be thought to exaggerate, I quote the interpretation which his brief puts upon it: "In our view, this clause constitutes a grant of all the executive powers of which the Government is capable." If that be true, it is difficult to see why the forefathers bothered to add several specific items, including some trifling ones.

The example of such unlimited executive power that must have most impressed the forefathers was the prerogative exercised by George III, and the description of its evils in the Declaration of Independence leads me to doubt that they were creating their new Executive in his image. Continental European examples were no more appealing. And if we seek instruction from our own times, we can match it only from the executive powers in those governments we disparagingly describe as totalitarian. I cannot accept the view that this clause is a grant in bulk of all conceivable executive power but regard it as an allocation to the presidential office of the generic powers thereafter stated.

The clause on which the Government next relies is that "The President shall be Commander in Chief of the Army and Navy of the United States...."... This loose appellation is sometimes advanced as support for any presidential action, internal or external, involving use of force, the idea being that it vests power to do anything, anywhere, that can be done with an army or navy.

That seems to be the logic of an argument tendered at our bar—that the President having, on his own responsibility, sent American troops abroad derives from that act "affirmative power" to seize the means of producing a supply of steel for them. To quote, "Perhaps the most forceful illustration of the scope of Presidential power in this connection is the fact that American troops in Korea, whose safety and effectiveness are so directly involved here, were sent to the field by an exercise of the President's constitutional powers." Thus, it is said, he has invested himself with "war powers."

... No doctrine that the Court could promulgate would seem to me more sinister and alarming than that a President whose conduct of foreign affairs is so largely uncontrolled, and often even is unknown, can vastly enlarge his mastery over the internal affairs of the country by his own commitment of the Nation's armed forces to some foreign venture. I do not, however, find it necessary or appropriate to consider the legal status of the Korean enterprise to discountenance argument based on it.

Assuming that we are in a war *de facto*, whether it is or is not a war *de jure*, does that empower the Commander in Chief to seize industries he thinks necessary to supply our army? The Constitution expressly places in Congress power "to raise and *support* Armies" and "to *provide* and *maintain* a Navy." (Emphasis supplied.) This certainly lays upon Congress primary responsibility for supplying the armed forces. Congress alone controls the raising of revenues and their appropriation and may determine in what manner and by what means they shall be spent for military and naval procurement. I suppose no one would doubt that Congress can take over war supply as a Government enterprise....

That military powers of the Commander in Chief were not to supersede representative government of internal affairs seems obvious from the Constitution and from elementary American history.

We should not use this occasion to circumscribe, much less to contract, the lawful role of the president as Commander in Chief. I should indulge the widest latitude of interpretation to sustain his exclusive function to command the instruments of national force, at least when turned against the outside world for the security of our society. But, when it is turned inward, not because of rebellion but because of a lawful economic struggle between industry and labor, it should have no such indulgence....

... What the power of command may include I do not try to envision, but I think it is not a military prerogative, without support of law, to seize persons or property because they are important or even essential for the military and naval establishment.

The third clause in which the Solicitor General finds seizure powers is that "he shall take Care that the Laws be faithfully executed...." That authority must be matched against words of the Fifth Amendment that "No person shall be ... deprived of life, liberty or property, without due process of law...." One gives a governmental authority that reaches so far as there is law, the other gives a private right that authority shall go no farther. These signify about all there is of the principle that ours is a government of laws, not of men, and that we submit ourselves to rulers only if under rules.

The Solicitor General lastly grounds support of the seizure upon nebulous, inherent powers never expressly granted but said to have accrued to the office from the customs and claims of preceding administrations. The plea is for a resulting power to deal with a crisis or an emergency according to the necessities of the case, the unarticulated assumption being that necessity knows no law.

Loose and irresponsible use of adjectives colors all nonlegal and much legal discussion of presidential powers. "Inherent" powers, "implied" powers, "incidental" powers, "plenary" powers, "war" powers and "emergency" powers are used, often interchangeably and without fixed or ascertainable meanings.

The vagueness and generality of the clauses that set forth presidential powers afford a plausible basis for pressures within and without an administration for presidential action beyond that supported by those whose responsibility it is to defend his actions in court. The claim of inherent and unrestricted presidential powers has long been a persuasive dialectical weapon in political controversy. While it is not surprising that counsel should grasp support from such unadjudicated claims of power, a judge cannot accept self-serving press statements of the attorney for one of the interested parties as authority in answering a constitutional question, even if the advocate was himself.* But prudence has counseled that actual reliance on such nebulous claims stop short of provoking a judicial test.... Many modern nations have forthrightly recognized that war and economic crises may upset the normal balance between liberty and authority. Their experience with emergency powers may not be irrelevant to the argument here that we should say that the Executive, of his own volition, can invest himself with undefined emergency powers.

Germany, after the First World War, framed the Weimar Constitution, designed to secure her liberties in the Western tradition. However, the President of the Republic, without concurrence of the Reichstag, was empowered temporarily to suspend any or all individual rights if public safety and order were seriously disturbed or endangered. This proved a temptation to every government, whatever its shade of opinion, and in 13 years suspension of rights was invoked on more than 250 occasions. Finally, Hitler persuaded President Von Hindenberg to suspend all such rights, and they were never restored.

The French Republic provided for a very different kind of emergency government known as the "state of siege." It differed from the German emergency dictatorship, particularly in that emergency powers could not be assumed at will by the Executive but could only be granted as a parliamentary measure. And it did not, as in Germany, result in a suspension or abrogation of law but was a legal institution governed by special legal rules and terminable by parliamentary authority.

Great Britain also has fought both World Wars under a sort of temporary dictatorship created by legislation. As Parliament is not bound by written constitutional limitations, it established a crisis government simply by delegation to its Ministers of a larger measure than usual of its own unlimited power, which is exercised under its supervision by Ministers whom it may dismiss. This has been called the "high-water mark in the voluntary surrender of liberty," but, as Churchill put it, "Parliament stands custodian of these surrendered liberties, and its most sacred duty will be to restore them in their fullness when victory has crowned our exertions and our perseverance." Thus, parliamentary control made emergency powers compatible with freedom.

This contemporary foreign experience maybe inconclusive as to the wisdom of lodging emergency powers somewhere in a modern government. But it suggests that emergency powers are consistent with free government only when their control is lodged elsewhere than in the Executive who exercises them. That is the safeguard that would be nullified by our adoption of the "inherent powers" formula....

---

* As Franklin Roosevelt's attorney general, Jackson argued that the president possessed broad inherent powers to seize factories to prevent strikes from crippling war production. [Editors' note.]

In the practical working of our Government we already have evolved a technique within the framework of the Constitution by which normal executive powers may be considerably expanded to meet an emergency. Congress may and has granted extraordinary authorities which lie dormant in normal times but may be called into play by the Executive in war or upon proclamation of a national emergency. In 1939, upon congressional request, the Attorney General listed ninety-nine such separate statutory grants by Congress of emergency or wartime executive powers. They were invoked from time to time as need appeared. Under this procedure we retain Government by law—special, temporary law, perhaps, but law nonetheless. The public may know the extent and limitations of the powers that can be asserted, and persons affected may be informed from the statute of their rights and duties.

In view of the ease, expedition and safety with which Congress can grant and has granted large emergency powers, certainly ample to embrace this crisis, I am quite unimpressed with the argument that we should affirm possession of them without statute. Such power either has no beginning or it has no end. If it exists, it need submit to no legal restraint. I am not alarmed that it would plunge us straightway into dictatorship, but it is at least a step in that wrong direction.

As to whether there is imperative necessity for such powers, it is relevant to note the gap that exists between the President's paper powers and his real powers. The Constitution does not disclose the measure of the actual controls wielded by the modern presidential office. That instrument must be understood as an Eighteenth Century sketch of a government hoped for, not as a blueprint of the Government that is. Vast accretions of federal power, eroded from that reserved by the States, have magnified the scope of presidential activity. Subtle shifts take place in the centers of real power that do not show on the face of the Constitution.

Executive power has the advantage of concentration in a single head in whose choice the whole Nation has a part, making him the focus of public hopes and expectations. In drama, magnitude and finality his decisions so far overshadow any others that almost alone he fills the public eye and ear. No other personality in public life can begin to compete with him in access to the public mind through modern methods of communications. By his prestige as head of state and his influence upon public opinion he exerts a leverage upon those who are supposed to check and balance his power which often cancels their effectiveness.

Moreover, rise of the party system has made a significant extraconstitutional supplement to real executive power. No appraisal of his necessities is realistic which overlooks that he heads a political system as well as a legal system. Party loyalties and interests, sometimes more binding than law, extend his effective control into branches of government other than his own and he often may win, as a political leader, what he cannot command under the Constitution. Indeed, Woodrow Wilson, commenting on the President as leader both of his party and of the Nation, observed, "If he rightly interpret the national thought and boldly insist upon it, he is irresistible.... His office is anything he has the sagacity and force to make it." I cannot ... believe that this country will suffer if the Court refuses further to aggrandize the presidential office, already so potent and so relatively immune from judicial review, at the expense of Congress.

But I have no illusion that any decision by this Court can keep power in the hands of Congress if it is not wise and timely in meeting its problems. A crisis that challenges the President equally, or perhaps primarily, challenges Congress. If not good law, there was worldly wisdom in the maxim attributed to Napoleon that "The tools belong to the man who can use them." We may say that power to legislate for emergencies belongs in the hands of Congress, but only Congress itself can prevent power from slipping through its fingers.... With all its defects, delays and inconveniences, men have discovered no technique for long preserving free government except that the Executive be under the law, and that the law be made by parliamentary deliberations.

Such institutions maybe destined to pass away. But it is the duty of the Court to be last, not first, to give them up.

MR. JUSTICE BURTON, concurring in both the opinion and judgment of the Court....

The President ... chose not to use the Taft-Hartley procedure. He chose another course, also authorized by Congress. He referred the controversy to the Wage Stabilization Board. If that course had led to a settlement of the labor dispute, it would have avoided the need for other action. It, however, did not do so.

Now it is contended that although the President did not follow the procedure authorized by the Taft-Hartley Act, his substituted procedure served the same purpose and must be accepted as its equivalent. Without appraising that equivalence, it is enough to point out that neither procedure carried statutory authority for the seizure of private industries in the manner now at issue. The exhaustion of both procedures fails to cloud the clarity of the congressional reservation of seizure for its own consideration.

The foregoing circumstances distinguish this emergency from one in which Congress takes no action and outlines no governmental policy....

This brings us to a further crucial question. Does the President, in such a situation, have inherent constitutional power to seize private property which makes congressional action in relation thereto unnecessary? We find no such power available to him under the present circumstances. The present situation is not comparable to that of an imminent invasion or threatened attack. We do not face the issue of what might be the President's constitutional power to meet such catastrophic situations. Nor is it claimed that the current seizure is in the nature of a military command addressed by the President, as Commander-in-Chief, to a mobilized nation waging, or imminently threatened with, total war.

MR. JUSTICE CLARK, concurring in the judgment of the Court.

In my view the Constitution does grant to the President extensive authority in times of grave and imperative national emergency.... As Lincoln aptly said, "[is] it possible to lose the nation and yet preserve the Constitution?" In describing this authority I care not whether one calls it "residual," "inherent," "moral," "implied," "aggregate," "emergency," or otherwise. I am of the conviction that those who have had the gratifying experience of being the President's lawyer have used one or more of these adjectives only with the utmost of sincerity and the highest of purpose.

I conclude that where Congress has laid down specific procedures to deal with the type of crisis confronting the President, he must follow those procedures in meeting the crisis; but that in the absence of such action by Congress, the President's independent power to act depends upon the gravity of the situation confronting the nation. I cannot sustain the seizure in question because here ... Congress had prescribed methods to be followed by the President in meeting the emergency at hand.

MR. CHIEF JUSTICE VINSON, with whom MR. JUSTICE REED and MR. JUSTICE MINTON join, dissenting.

We are not called upon today to expand the Constitution to meet a new situation. For, in this case, we need only look to history and time-honored principles of constitutional law—principles that have been applied consistently by all branches of the Government throughout our history. It is those who assert the invalidity of the Executive Order who seek to amend the Constitution in this case.

A review of executive action demonstrates that our Presidents have on many occasions exhibited the leadership contemplated by the Framers when they made the President Commander in Chief, and imposed upon him the trust to "take Care that the Laws be faithfully executed." With or without explicit statutory authorization, Presidents have at such times dealt with national emergencies by acting promptly and resolutely to enforce legislative programs, at least to save those programs until Congress could act. Congress and the courts have responded to such executive initiative with consistent approval. [The chief justice reviewed a number of historical instances, including the following.]

Beginning with the Bank Holiday Proclamation and continuing through World War II, executive leadership and initiative were characteristic of President Franklin D. Roosevelt's administration....

Some six months before Pearl Harbor, a dispute at a single aviation plant at Inglewood, California, interrupted a segment of the production of military aircraft. In spite of the comparative insignificance of this work stoppage to total defense production as contrasted with the complete paralysis now threatened by a shutdown of the entire basic steel industry, and even though our armed forces were not then engaged in combat, President Roosevelt ordered the seizure of the plant "pursuant to the powers vested in [him] by the Constitution and laws of the United States, as President of the United States of America and Commander in Chief of the Army and Navy of the United States." The Attorney General [Jackson] vigorously proclaimed that the President had the moral duty to keep this Nation's defense effort a "going concern." His ringing moral justification was coupled with a legal justification equally well stated: The Presidential proclamation rests upon the aggregate of the Presidential powers derived from the Constitution itself and from statutes enacted by the Congress....

This is but a cursory summary of executive leadership. But it amply demonstrates that Presidents have taken prompt action to enforce the laws and protect the country whether or not Congress happened to provide in advance for the particular method of execution.

The fact that Congress and the courts have consistently recognized and given their support to such executive action indicates that such a power of seizure has been accepted throughout our history....

Much of the argument in this case has been directed at straw men. We do not now have before us the case of a President acting solely on the basis of his own notions of the public welfare. Nor is there any question of unlimited executive power in this case. The President himself closed the door to any such claim when he sent his Message to Congress stating his purpose to abide by any action of Congress, whether approving or disapproving his seizure action. Here, the President immediately made sure that Congress was fully informed of the temporary action he had taken only to preserve the legislative programs from destruction until Congress could act.

The absence of a specific statute authorizing seizure of the steel mills as a mode of executing the laws — both the military procurement program and the anti-inflation program — has not until today been thought to prevent the President from executing the laws. Unlike an administrative commission confined to the enforcement of the statute under which it was created, or the head of a department when administering a particular statute, the President is a constitutional officer charged with taking care that a "mass of legislation" be executed. Flexibility as to mode of execution to meet critical situations is a matter of practical necessity. This practical construction of the "Take Care" clause, advocated by John Marshall, was adopted by this Court in *In re Neagle, In re Debs* and other cases.... See also *Ex parte Quirin*.... Although more restrictive views of executive power, advocated in dissenting opinions of Justices Holmes, McReynolds and Brandeis, were emphatically rejected by this Court in *Myers v. United States* ... members of today's majority treat these dissenting views as authoritative.

In *United States v. Midwest Oil* Co.... this Court approved executive action where, as here, the President acted to preserve an important matter until Congress could act — even though his action in that case was contrary to an express statute. In this case, there is no statute prohibiting the action taken by the President in a matter not merely important but threatening the very safety of the Nation. Executive inaction in such a situation, courting national disaster, is foreign to the concept of energy and initiative in the Executive as created by the Founding Fathers....

The broad executive power granted by Article II to an officer on duty 365 days a year cannot, it is said, be invoked to avert disaster. Instead, the President must confine himself to sending a message to Congress recommending action. Under this messenger-boy concept of the Office, the President cannot even act to preserve legislative programs from destruction so that Congress will have something left to act upon....

Notes and Questions

1. *Dicta and holding.* What, precisely, is the holding in *Youngstown*? Suppose that Congress had not enacted the Taft-Hartley Act or any other emergency legislation and had never voted against giving the president the powers he assumed. Would the outcome have been the same? Does *Youngstown* stand for, or against, a theory of inherent executive powers to seize war production industries in times of war?

2. *Inherent powers claims.* Consider the following exchange that occurred in the district court between Judge Pine and Assistant Attorney General Baldridge:

Judge Pine: So [the Constitution] limited the powers of Congress and limited the powers of the judiciary, but did not limit the powers of the executive. Is that what you say?

Mr. Baldridge: That is the way we read Article II of the Constitution.

Judge Pine: I see....[25]

A few days later, the president issued a disclaimer: "The powers of the President are derived from the Constitution, and they are limited, of course, by the provisions of the Constitution." But, in his memoirs, Truman insisted: "Whatever the six justices of the Supreme Court meant by their differing opinions, [the president] must always act in a national emergency."[26]

3. *Glosses on the Constitution.* How persuasive is Justice Frankfurter's view that unquestioned and continuous "executive practice" "may be treated as a gloss on 'Executive power'" granted by Article II? Are there likely to be many uncontested practices of the sort that occasioned this litigation? How persuasive was the historical record?

4. *The twilight zone.* What is the source of the executive power in Justice Jackson's "twilight zone" of concurrent power to initiate policy in an emergency?

5. *Jackson's third category.* Are there any situations in the realm of domestic affairs that are likely to fall within Justice Jackson's third category: a presidential power to act even in the face of contrary congressional directions? Are any such powers granted by Article II? For example, may the president refuse to spend (i.e. impound) funds specifically appropriated by Congress for a weapons system or other program that he does not want? May he issue a "signing statement" that instructs the executive branch not to enforce a measure that he has just signed into law? Were Ronald Reagan's subordinates acting within the president's authority when they secretly sold arms to Iran, then considered a terrorist nation, and used the profits to fund a covert war by Nicaraguan *contra*—a war for which Congress had expressly denied funds? Or, when Congress forbids funding for such a conflict, may the president or his men obtain private funds to finance the operation, and hire "off the shelf" mercenaries to carry it out, like retired General Richard Secord during the Iran-Contra affair, or the military contractor Blackwater during the wars in Iraq and Afghanistan?

6. *The forage power and "political questions."* Under the common law, military commanders may, in times of war, seize civilian goods for military purposes, but the government is supposed to pay compensation for them after the emergency has passed. Would this "forage power" supply an adequate basis for the power asserted by President Truman in the steel seizure case?

To the extent that there is such a power to seize civilian property for military purposes, may the government avoid paying just compensation by asserting that the decision to take the property was a non-justiciable "political question" assigned solely to the executive, or to the executive and Congress, to decide? See *Ramirez de Arelano v. Weinberger,* 745 F.2d 1500 (D.C. Cir. 1984) (en banc), *vacated,* 471 U.S. 1113 (1985), *on remand,* 788 F.2d 762 (1986) (rejecting the political question defense where the Defense Department had built a training facility on a ranch owned by Americans in Honduras and then refused to compensate the owners for their losses).

E. Emergency Powers: Can Standards Be Specified?

Looking back over this history of emergency powers assertions, what is to be learned? Has the legititmacy of a "constitutional dictatorship" in times of insurrection, threat-

---

25. Westin, *The Anatomy of a Constitutional Law Case* (1958), 64.
26. *Years of Trial and Hope* (1956), II, 475–78.

ened invasion, or foreign attack ever been upheld by the courts? Can such a case be made? If so, what circumstances would have to exist? What kinds of evidence of the threat would be required to prove the case? To whom? When and how often would the justification have to be made? Is there a case to be made for an indefinite or perpetual dictatorship, under circumstances, say, like President George W. Bush's "global war on terrorism"? Few, if any, dictators are total dictators. They are simply unlimited and unchallenged in some issue areas. Would you consider an American president to be a dictator, if he is able to deploy military, para-military, covert, or law enforcement agents secretly, without authorization from the Constitution or Congress, and without Congressional or judicial accountability, especially in ways that violate individual rights?

Presidents rarely act alone in alleged emergencies. Typically Congress gives them some powers, or acquiesces to their broad claims to power, while the courts find excuses for not deciding legal challenges to their actions until after the alleged crisis has passed. How, if at all, should presidential abuses of emergency powers be dealt with? Should courts insist that the authority be granted by Congress in advance, through a broad or narrow set of authorizations, perhaps with time limits? Should administration officials be prosecuted or impeached afterwards, or should Congress ratify the assertions or grant amnesty to the law-breakers? Should the courts delay legal challenges to illegitimate assertions of power during the alleged emergency, and then bless or punish them afterwards?

Academic Efforts at Specification

Specifying the conditions under which emergency powers might legitimately be exercised is a favorite exercise of academic students of the presidency. Consider the following three lists. Are they adequate? Would they be helpful to you if you were, say, a member of Congress or an assistant U.S. attorney general, during the Civil War, World War II, or the "war on terrorism"? Would you want to break the lists down further, for example, to deal separately with assertions of emergency powers to prosecute saboteurs, deal with large groups of potentially disloyal people ("copperheads," aliens, ethnic Americans), assure war production, silence dissent, or to prevent suicide attacks?

Clinton Rossiter,
Constitutional Dictatorship
(1948)

A free people should certainly be educated and encouraged to demand that the use of emergency powers in their defense conform to these standards. In general, they may be separated into three categories: those criteria by which the initial resort to constitutional dictatorship is to be judged, those by which its continuance is to be judged, and those to be employed at the termination of the crisis for which it was instituted. In the first category may be considered the following:

1. *No general regime or particular institution of constitutional dictatorship should be initiated unless it is necessary or even indispensable to the preservation of the state and its constitutional order.* This is the first and great commandment of constitutional dictatorship. As far as may be feasible, the salvation of a constitu-

tional democracy in crisis should be worked out through its regular methods of government. Only when the benefits to be assured by a resort to constitutional dictatorship clearly outweigh the dangers to be expected should emergency powers be called into action....

2. A criterion which suggests itself from Roman practice is this: *the decision to institute a constitutional dictatorship should never be in the hands of the man or men who will constitute the dictator.* In other words, no [American] dictator should be self-appointed. That this criterion has not been uniformly observed in modern experiences with emergency powers is obvious. The greatest of constitutional dictators was self-appointed, but Mr. Lincoln had no alternative. Few Americans seem to realize that almost all of the President's lengthy catalogue of emergency powers go into operation upon the declaration of an emergency ascertained and proclaimed by himself alone. This unquestionably leads to an increased frequency in the use of these powers....

3. *No government should initiate a constitutional dictatorship without making specific provision for its termination.* As the American people know only too well, it is far more difficult to end a period of national emergency than it is to declare one....

4. A criterion of cardinal importance both before and during a period of constitutional dictatorship is: *all uses of emergency powers and all readjustments in the organization of the government should be effected in pursuit of constitutional or legal requirements.* In short, constitutional dictatorship should be *legitimate.* It is an axiom of constitutional government that no official action should ever be taken without a certain minimum of constitutional or legal sanction. This is a principle no less valid in time of crisis than under normal conditions. The constitutional dictatorship should be instituted, as was the Roman dictatorship, according to precise constitutional forms; it should be continued in no less a spirit of devotion to constitutional provisions and principles. Give a government whatever power it may need to defend the state from its enemies, but ground that power in the constitution or the laws and make the dictatorship lawful—this is a fundamental requirement of constitutional dictatorship....

5. The first and most important of three criteria to be observed during the prosecution of a constitutional dictatorship is: *no dictatorial institution should be adopted, no right invaded, no regular procedure altered any more than is absolutely necessary for the conquest of the particular crisis....*

6. *The measures adopted in the prosecution of a constitutional dictatorship should never be permanent in character or effect.* Emergency powers are strictly conditioned by their purpose, and this purpose is the restoration of normal conditions. The actions directed to this end should therefore be provisional. For example, measures of a legislative nature which work a lasting change in the structure of the state or constitute permanent derogations from existing law should not be adopted under an emergency enabling act, at least not without the positively registered approval of the legislature. Permanent laws, whether adopted in regular or irregular times, are for parliaments to enact. By this same token, the decisions and sentences of extraordinary courts should be reviewed by the regular courts after the termination of the crisis....

7. *The dictatorship should be carried on by persons representative of every part of the citizenry interested in the defense of the existing constitutional order.* This is

the criterion which motivates the persistent demand that crisis government should be coalition government....

8. *Ultimate responsibility should be maintained for every action taken under a constitutional dictatorship.* This criterion is directed against one of the chief dangers of constitutional dictatorship: the transient abuses wrought and the needless dictatorial steps adopted by persons charged with extraordinary powers in time of crisis. It is manifestly impossible and even detrimental to demand that an official entrusted with some unusual duty under martial rule be made to answer in the heat of the crisis for actions taken in pursuit of that duty. It is imperative that he be held responsible for them after its termination. The knowledge of a future reckoning may make him overcautious in his emergency actions, and it is often unfair to judge the measures adopted in the turmoil of a grave national danger by the standards of official conduct which prevail in the period of popular reaction to strong government which usually follows the end of an emergency. Nevertheless, it would seem to be a categorical principle of constitutional democracy that every public act must be a responsible one and have a public explanation. The plea of necessity for any dictatorial action will almost always be honored by the courts, the legislature, and the people. Officials who abuse authority in a constitutional dictatorship—in other words, men who were charged with defending democracy but instead profaned it—should be ferreted out and severely punished....

9. *The decision to terminate a constitutional dictatorship, like the decision to institute one, should never be in the hands of the man or men who constitute the dictator.* This is a direct corollary of the second and third criteria. Congress, not the President, Parliament, not the Crown, ought to declare the beginning and end of all emergencies in which the executive is to be given abnormal powers, so far as is practicable and possible. It is in this respect that the permanent statutes delegating emergency powers to the American President are to be most heavily criticized....

10. *No constitutional dictatorship should extend beyond the termination of the crisis for which it was instituted.* It is the crisis alone which makes the dictatorship constitutional; the end of the crisis makes its continued existence unconstitutional. If the purpose of constitutional dictatorship is to defend constitutional democracy in time of peril, then it follows that an extension of the dictatorship beyond the cessation of the peril is directed to another purpose and becomes a dangerous display of unwonted power. The story of Cincinnatus should be required reading for all officials active in modern crisis government. This is one lesson of the Roman dictatorship which remains eternally valid.

11. Finally, *the termination of the crisis must be followed by as complete a return as possible to the political and governmental conditions existing prior to the initiation of the constitutional dictatorship.*

Constitutional Dictatorship (1948), 297–306.

Notes and Questions

1. *Usefulness.* Can you imagine Presidents Franklin Roosevelt, Harry Truman, or George W. Bush reading, let alone heeding, Professor Rossiter's list? If you were trying to curb excessive assertions of emergency powers, to whom would you turn: political scientists like Rossiter, or lawyers?

Arthur M. Schlesinger, Jr.,
The Imperial Presidency
(1974)

1. There must be a clear, present and uncontestable danger to the life of the nation;

2. the President must define and explain to Congress and the people the nature of this threat;

3. the perception of the emergency, the judgment that the life of the nation is truly at stake, must be broadly shared by Congress and by the people;

4. time must be of the essence; waiting for normal legislative action must constitute an unacceptable risk;

5. existing statutory authorizations must be inadequate, and Congress must be unwilling or unable to prescribe a national course;

6. the problem must be one that can be met in no other way than by presidential action beyond the laws and the Constitution;

7. the President must report what he has done to Congress, which will serve as the judge of his action;

8. none of the presidential acts can be directed against the political process itself.

The Imperial Presidency (1974), 450–51.

Richard M. Pious,
The American Presidency
(1979)

1. The exercise of power should not involve personal or partisan advantage, nor should it interfere with the constitutional processes of election or succession to office.

2. The powers must be exercised in a national emergency, when the continued existence of the Union and the physical safety of the people is at stake, when delay might prove fatal, and when traditional constitutional procedures would involve such delay.

3. The powers are exercised when no statute or precedent provides a viable alternative procedure, and nothing in the Constitution or laws of the land expressly prohibit the actions.

4. Use of prerogative powers should be preceded by the widest possible consultation within the government, including senior officials in the departments, and when possible, leaders of Congress. The president should try to create a consensus that emergency government must be instituted.

5. The president should make available to Congress and the judiciary a full record involving his actions as soon as practicable during or after the emergency. Courts should make the final determination if he claims executive privilege.

6. Once the emergency has passed Congress should legislate to routinize procedures, placing powers on a statutory basis, and should provide for legislative and judicial review if appropriate.

7. The checks and balances system must function throughout the emergency, permitting possible resolutions of censure or an impeachment proceeding.

The American Presidency (1979), 84.

Notes and Questions

1. *Criteria.* Are these criteria meant to be legally enforceable, or just political guidance as to when Americans might tolerate a presidential dictatorship? Could they be converted into statutory criteria that could be legally enforceable? Would some of these standards be of use in defining what should constitute an impeachable offense? For an analysis of Schlesinger's proposed standards, see Bessette and Tulis, eds., *The Presidency in the Constitutional Order* (1981), chap. 1. With the benefit of hindsight and this academic advice, how would you have advised presidents Lincoln and Roosevelt to deal with the risks of espionage, sabotage, and potentially disloyal populations that faced them?

Legislative Efforts at Specification

Congress has enacted many emergency powers laws. Ironically, one of the most restrictive of these laws was also one of the most threatening to political freedom: the Emergency Detention Act of 1950.

The Emergency Detention Act of 1950

FINDINGS OF FACT AND DECLARATION OF PURPOSE

SEC. 101. As a result of evidence adduced before various committees of the Senate and the House of Representatives, the Congress hereby finds that—

(1) There exists a world Communist movement which in its origins, its development, and its present practice, is a world-wide revolutionary movement whose purpose it is, by treachery, deceit, infiltration into other groups (governmental and otherwise), espionage, sabotage, terrorism, and any other means deemed necessary, to establish a Communist totalitarian dictatorship in all the countries of the world through the medium of a world-wide Communist organization....

(7) In the United States those individuals who knowingly and willfully participate in the world Communist movement, when they so participate, in effect repudiate their allegiance to the United States and in effect transfer their allegiance to the foreign country in which is vested the direction and control of the world Communist movement; and, in countries other than the United States, those individuals who knowingly and willfully participate in such Communist movement similarly repudiate their allegiance to the countries of which they are nationals in favor of such foreign Communist country....

(13) The recent successes of Communist methods in other countries and the nature and control of the world Communist movement itself present a clear and present danger to the security of the United States and to the existence of free American institutions, and make it necessary that Congress, in order to provide for the

common defense, to preserve the sovereignty of the United States as an independent nation, and to guarantee to each State a republican form of government, enact appropriate legislation recognizing the existence of such world-wide conspiracy and designed to prevent it from accomplishing its purpose in the United States.

(14) The detention of persons who there is reasonable ground to believe probably will commit or conspire with others to commit espionage or sabotage is, in a time of internal security emergency, essential to the common defense and to the safety and security of the territory, the people and the Constitution of the United States.

(15) It is also essential that such detention in an emergency involving the internal security of the Nation shall be so authorized, executed, restricted and reviewed as to prevent any interference with the constitutional rights and privileges of any persons and at the same time shall be sufficiently effective to permit the performance by the Congress and the President of their constitutional duties to provide for the common defense, to wage war, and to preserve, protect and defend the Constitution, the Government and the people of the United States.

DECLARATION OF "INTERNAL SECURITY EMERGENCY"

SEC. 102. (a) In the event of any one of the following:

(1) Invasion of the territory of the United States or its possessions,

(2) Declaration of war by Congress, or

(3) Insurrection within the United States in aid of a foreign enemy, and if, upon the occurrence of one or more of the above, the President shall find that the proclamation of an emergency pursuant to this section is essential to the preservation, protection and defense of the Constitution, and to the common defense and safety of the territory and people of the United States, the President is authorized to make public proclamation of the existence of an "Internal Security Emergency."

(b) A state of "Internal Security Emergency" (hereinafter referred to as the "emergency") so declared shall continue in existence until terminated by proclamation of the President or by concurrent resolution of the Congress.

DETENTION DURING EMERGENCY

SEC. 103. (a) Whenever there shall be in existence such an emergency, the President, acting through the Attorney General, is hereby authorized to apprehend and by order detain, pursuant to the provisions of this title, each person as to whom there is reasonable ground to believe that such person probably will engage in, or probably will conspire with others to engage in, acts of espionage or of sabotage.

(b) Any person detained hereunder (hereinafter referred to as "the detainee") shall be released from such emergency detention upon—

(1) the termination of such emergency by proclamation of the President or by concurrent resolution of the Congress;

(2) an order of release issued by the Attorney General;

(3) a final order of release after hearing by the Board of Detention Review, hereinafter established;

(4) a final order of release by a United States court, after review of the action of the Board of Detention Review, or upon a writ of habeas corpus.

PROCEDURE FOR APPREHENSION AND DETENTION

SEC. 104. (a) The Attorney General, or such officer or officers of the Department of justice as he may from time to time designate, are authorized during such emergency to execute in writing and to issue—

(1) a warrant for the apprehension of each person as to whom there is reasonable ground to believe that such person probably will engage in, or probably will conspire with others to engage in, acts of espionage or sabotage; and

(2) an application for an order to be issued pursuant to subsection (d) of this section for the detention of such person for the duration of such emergency. Each such warrant shall issue only upon probable cause, supported by oath or affirmation, and shall particularly describe the person to be apprehended or detained.

(b) Warrants for the apprehension of persons under this title shall be served and apprehension of such persons shall be made only by such duly authorized officers of the Department of Justice as the Attorney General may designate. A copy of the warrant for apprehension shall be furnished to any person apprehended under this title.

(c) Persons apprehended or detained under this title shall be confined in such places of detention as may be prescribed by the Attorney General. The Attorney General shall provide for all detainees such transportation, food, shelter, and other accommodation and supervision as in his judgment may be necessary to accomplish the purpose of this title....

DETENTION REVIEW BOARD

Sec. 105. (a) The President is hereby authorized to establish a Detention Review Board (referred to in this title as the "Board") which shall consist of nine members, not more than five of whom shall be members of the same political party, appointed by the President by and with the advice and consent of the Senate....

Sec. 109. (a) Any Board created under this title is empowered—

(1) to review upon petition of any detainee any order of detention ... ;

(2) to determine whether there is reasonable ground to believe that such detainee probably will engage in, or conspire with others to engage in, espionage or sabotage;

(3) to issue orders confirming, modifying, or revoking any such order of detention; and

(4) to hear and determine any claim made pursuant to this paragraph by any person who shall have been detained pursuant to this title and shall have been released from such detention, for loss of income by such person resulting from such detention if without reasonable grounds. Upon the issuance of any final order for indemnification pursuant to this paragraph, the Attorney General is authorized and directed to make payment of such indemnity to the person entitled thereto from such funds as may be appropriated to him for such purpose.

JUDICIAL REVIEW

SEC. 111. (a) Any petitioner aggrieved by an order of the Board denying in whole or in part the relief sought by him, or by the failure or refusal of the Attorney General to obey such order, shall be entitled to the judicial review or judicial enforcement....

P.L. 81-831, 64 Stat. 1019; repealed, P.L. 92-128; 85 Stat. 348 (1971).

Notes and Questions

1. *Criteria for emergency powers legislation?* Does the Emergency Detention Act of 1950 satisfy your criteria for emergency powers legislation? If not, why not? Was it any more protective of individual rights than the laws and practices of past wars?

2. *Executive detention program.* Unknown to the members of Congress who passed this legislation at the height of the cold war, the executive branch had its own secret program for emergency detention. That program would have made use of the internment camps that the legislation directed the Bureau of Prisons to keep in readiness, but would have ignored the act's provision for appeals to a review board and the courts. The executive branch also had no intention of respecting writs of habeas corpus, even though Congress had refused to authorize executive suspension of that privilege. The FBI was authorized to continue to compile its security index of "potentially dangerous" persons, but no effort was made by the Justice Department to make sure that the list met the statutory criteria of a predisposition to espionage or sabotage. As a result the Security Index and ancillary round up lists came to include more than 20,000 named individuals, including professors, teachers, and educators; labor union organizers and leaders; writers, lecturers, newsmen, and others in the mass media field; lawyers, doctors, and scientists; other potentially influential persons on a local or national level, and individuals who could potentially furnish financial or material aid.

See *Intelligence Activities and the Rights of Americans*, Book II, Final Report of the Select Committee to Study Governmental Operations with respect to Intelligence Activities, U.S. Senate, 94th Cong., 2d Sess. (1976), 54–55. See also Athan Theoharis, *Spying on Americans* (1978), chap. 2, "Emergency Detention Programs," 40–64.

The Emergency Detention Act was repealed in 1971, largely at the behest of Japanese-Americans and their congressmen. In repealing the act, Congress also declared that "no citizen shall be imprisoned or otherwise detained by the United States except pursuant to an act of Congress" (P.L. 92-128). The roundup lists were not destroyed until their existence and general contents were made public in the mid-1970s.

Ronald Goldfarb,
The Permanent State of Emergency
(1974)

A few years ago, when the Pentagon was faced with a congressional cutoff of Vietnam war funds, it found a unique way to provide money for U.S. troops in Southeast Asia. It revived an emergency statute dating back to the Civil War—a law originally intended to allow cavalry troops on the Western frontier to provide feed and forage for their horses—and used it to justify the continued flow of funds for our Vietnam forces.

This is only one way in which the government has exploited outdated emergency powers that have never been repealed. In fact, though it may be news to most Americans, we have been living for at least 40 years under a state of emergency rule, a condition which has vastly expanded the powers of the executive branch.

Under one emergency statute still on the books, for example, the Securities and Exchange Commission, with the permission of the President, may summarily seize all stock exchanges. Another old emergency law gives the President power to use the militia or armed forces to "take such measures as he considers necessary" to suppress domestic violence or conspiracies if state or federal laws are hindered thus creating the possibility of martial law. Still another dated statute gives the Federal Communications Commission power to grant permits and licenses as it sees fit, unrestrained by ordinary requirements of the law, and it allows the President to suspend or amend FCC rules and regulations, close stations and remove equipment.

As the Senate's Special Committee on the Termination of the National Emergency recently put it, four presidential proclamations and 470 separate laws have created a situation under which the President today may "seize property; organize and control the means of production; seize commodities; assign military forces abroad; institute martial law; seize and control all transportation and communication; regulate the operation of private enterprise; restrict travel; and, in a plethora of particular ways, control the lives of all American citizens.... For 40 years, freedoms and governmental procedures guaranteed by the Constitution have, in various degrees, been abridged by laws brought into force by states of national emergency."

The existence of even the theoretical possibility for using such emergency powers today is frightening. But, even without Watergate's lessons about the lengths to which the White House may go to get its way, the concern is not merely theoretical; the fear of such powers being abused is not paranoid. For the powers have been misused on numerous occasions, for purposes that are likely to disturb people of all ideologies.

In 1957, for example, President Eisenhower used emergency provisions dating from World War II to justify sending troops into Little Rock, Ark., to quell the conflict over desegregating Central High School there. Emergency powers to use military reserves were revived by President Kennedy in the Berlin crisis and by President Nixon in the recent Middle East flare-up.

A favorite old statute that has been put to mischievous uses through the years is the Trading with the Enemy Act. Passed in 1917, this World War I law was designed to allow the government to gain control over U.S. property owned by foreign (enemy) nationals or countries. But later amendments included regulations controlling the foreign investments of American citizens, and in 1968 President Johnson issued an executive order applying the act to U.S. companies investing in Switzerland.

Under this authority, the government recently prosecuted a Kentucky businessman for failing to report his investment in real property abroad, as required by Commerce Department regulations issued pursuant to the LBJ order. No foreign government owned any of the property in question, and lawyers for the defendant argued that the effect of the prosecution was "to stand the purpose of the statute on its head." U.S. District Court Judge George Hart dismissed the indictment, stating at a hearing that Congress "couldn't conceive of America sinking to this level" in passing the legislation in question.

A. Ernest Fitzgerald, the Defense Department gadfly, reports about another emergency power perversity in his book *The High Priests of Waste*. Fitzgerald's case involves P.L. 85-804, which allows the President and 11 other executive heads to declare a corporation essential to the national defense and thus give it public money not otherwise available.

Fitzgerald asked General Accounting Office officials how they rationalized using this emergency power to provide the Lockheed Corporation in 1971 with what he terms a billion-dollar "bail out" from its contract to produce the C-5A. He was told, correctly, that the state of emergency declared by President Truman on Dec. 16, 1950, when the Chinese entered the Korean War was the justification. One GAO lawyer told Fitzgerald that under P.L. 85-804, an agency head may declare a company essential to the national defense and give it contracts, modify existing contracts and provide funds without getting anything in return, without justification, and without challenge.

There is no denying, of course, that the problem raised by the legitimate needs of the executive for special powers in times of national emergency are fundamental and historic....

The problem is that while the emergency situations themselves have ended, the officially proclaimed states of emergency have not. Not only the 1950 Korean War emergency, but the 1933 emergency declared by President Franklin Delano Roosevelt, the 1970 postal strike emergency declared by President Nixon and the 1971 economic emergency proclaimed by President Nixon to impose import surcharges are all technically still in effect. It is these unending states of emergency that allow 470 other laws to be used for exotic purposes today.

As a result of this governmental phenomenon, in the Senate committee's words, "The extensive use of delegated powers exercised under an aura of crisis has become a dominant aspect of the presidency."

These presidential powers have gone relatively unchecked by the courts and by Congress. In fact, Congress has perfunctorily approved almost all presidential requests for emergency powers despite its constitutional charter to "make all laws."

The special Senate committee, while recognizing the need for special executive powers in emergencies, called for new procedures to enact future emergency powers, to assure effective legislative oversight over such powers, and to provide for termination of such grants of powers after the emergency subsides. Hopefully, its efforts will lead to the repeal of many obsolete delegations of emergency powers.

There are also other hopeful signs. When President Nixon recently sent to Congress his National Emergency Petroleum Act (the energy bill), the measure contained no termination date. Quietly, Sen. Frank Church (D-Idaho), co-chairman of the special Senate committee and also a member of the Senate Interior Committee, persuaded Interior Committee chairman Henry Jackson (D-Wash.) to add a provision ending the bill's powers a year after its enactment. Reporting requirements and oversight procedures also were adopted.

This incident did not attract wide attention, but it reflected the beginning of a legislative initiative in an area where historic congressional negligence and expanding presidential claims for special powers have produced an astounding phenomenon of unlimited executive power.

New legislation has also been drafted by Sens. Church and Charles McC. Mathias (R-Md.), the other co-chairman of the special committee. Likely provisions in the measure include:

• A requirement that all presidentially declared national emergencies end 90 days after they are declared unless Congress terminates them earlier or agrees to their extension.

• A stipulation that no such emergency powers shall continue after 180 days without another presidential or congressional declaration of emergency.

• A requirement that all proclamations of national emergencies by the President be disclosed to Congress.

• A stipulation that the President maintain and provide Congress with records of all executive orders and other exercises of emergency powers....

Washington Post, Jan. 6, 1974, B1.

Notes and Questions

1. *National Emergencies Act of 1976.* In 1976, at an historic low point in presidential power, Congress was able to pass legislation that placed the process of declaring, implementing, and ending a state of emergency on a statutory foundation. The National Emergencies Act, P.L. 94-412, 90 Stat. 1255, 50 U.S.C. 1601, terminated four existing states of emergency, abolished most existing emergency statutes, and created new procedures for delegating emergency powers to the president. Under this legislation the president can still use standing emergency legislation to declare a state of emergency, but his authority to act can only remain in effect for one year. The president is required to report to Congress his reasons for declaring the emergency, and must indicate in his report the constitutional and statutory bases for all emergency actions. He must also report to Congress every six months while the state of emergency remains in effect. Congress is required to vote at six-month intervals on whether to continue the state of emergency. At the end of the year, the president may ask Congress to renew the state of emergency for another year term. The law also provides that the House and Senate can end the state of emergency by a concurrent resolution not subject to presidential veto. (See *Immigration and Naturalization Service v. Chada,* 462 U.S. 979 [1983], regarding the constitutionality of these provisions.)

2. *Must presidents follow emergency powers legislation?* In the materials that follow, especially in Chapters 4 and 5, consider whether it is necessary for the executive to adhere to emergency powers legislation in order to 1) detain American citizens, resident aliens, or foreign citizen indefinitely without trial under brutal conditions; 2) deny them access to the writ of habeas corpus; their rights to counsel, a speedy trial, jury trial, and due process of law; 3) torture them, or subject them to cruel, inhuman and degrading treatment; 4) deliver them to foreign intelligence agencies for interrogation under torture; 5) hide them away in secret CIA prisons abroad; 6) assassinate suspected terrorists, including Americans, or 7) intercept electronic communications of millions of Americans without a court order?

Chapter Three

Foreign Affairs Powers

"The President is the sole organ of the nation in its external relations, and its sole representative with foreign nations."

—John Marshall,
10 *Annals of Congress* 613 (1800)

"The Constitution ... is an invitation to struggle for the privilege of directing American foreign policy."

—Edward S. Corwin, *The President:
Office and Powers* (1957)

A. Introduction

The Constitution contains relatively few provisions dealing with foreign affairs, and in the aggregate they do not add up to a comprehensive grant of authority or a clear allocation of that authority among the separated institutions of national government.

Thus the text of the Constitution has to be interpreted in light of the political theory that provides its context. Is the authority of the United States in foreign affairs plenary? May the United States do anything in foreign affairs that any foreign nation may do? Does the president have the same discretion as any dictator, or are there implied limitations on the purposes and methods of the United States and its president in the international arena—limitations that derive from a sense that the United States is not like other nations or, more precisely, that certain assertions of power by any government cannot be deemed legitimate and when asserted by the United States government must be deemed unconstitutional?

During the eighteenth and nineteenth centuries, the idea of implied limitations on the means and ends of American foreign policy enjoyed substantial support. Among the natural-rights doctrines that inspired many of the founders was the principle of national self-determination. From the revolution, through the Napoleonic Wars and the Latin American revolutions, to the anti-imperialism movement of the late-nineteenth century, there was a widespread belief that the United States was different from other nations and that this difference might have constitutional dimensions. The Supreme Court recognized this theory in 1850 when it ruled in *Fleming v. Page* (See Chapter 4), that "the genius and character of our institutions are peaceful, and the power to declare war was not conferred upon Congress for the purposes of aggression or aggrandizement...."

For the most part, however, the courts have abstained from invoking this theory of implied limitations on government, particularly in the realm of foreign affairs. They have done so chiefly by treating such issues as non-justiciable "political questions" exclusively committed to the discretion of the so-called political branches of government.

Legal positivists—persons who believe that the legality of any action is to be ascertained by reference to formal texts or to a "realistic" assessment of who holds effective political power—have interpreted judicial abstentions as acknowledgments of authority. The silences of the Constitution and the courts, they claim, amount to an affirmation that the United States may legitimately and constitutionally do anything that any foreign government may do. The acquisition of colonies, the support of brutal regimes that violate human rights, the use of military force and covert actions to advance the interests of American corporations, are all regarded by positivists as matters of mere policy, devoid of constitutional significance.

Most presidents, diplomats, and presidential lawyers have been legal positivists.

They have not only insisted that the authority of the United States in international relations is plenary, but that this authority has been constitutionally allocated to the president as "sole organ" in the realm of foreign affairs. When pressed, they have conceded that Article I of the Constitution grants some authority to Congress. However, they have hastened to add that these grants to Congress are not exclusive and, in the absence of legislation to the contrary, may be exercised by the president. By this theory of concurrent powers, and a broad interpretation of the Executive Powers Clause of Article II, they have claimed for the president virtually unlimited authority to take initiatives in foreign relations and to persist in those initiatives until restrained by Congress. Of course, for a congressional restraint to be binding, these presidentialists insist that it be passed over the president's veto and that its language be so unambiguous as to permit no evasions.

Most members of Congress and most scholars of the foreign affairs powers during the twentieth century have been legal positivists and have shared the presidential perspective. They have justified this approach by assuming that all the Constitution requires is that the plenary powers of the United States be exercised according to the precepts of "democracy," which they define in procedural terms. In their view, a country can be "democratic" so long as it makes decisions through freely elected representatives and through the competition, coalitions, and compromises of interest group politics. They consider these decisions "democratic" even if they are made in great secrecy. Thus, in their judgment, the United States can behave like the worst of the authoritarian regimes that the founders despised and still not violate its Constitution. Like Woodrow Wilson (see Chapter 1), the positivists assume that "the Constitution contains no theories" about either the means or the ends of foreign policy.

The positivist view has had significant consequences for the debate set forth in the materials which follow. First, it has reduced that debate to little more than a squabble over the allocation of decision-making authority—a squabble that most participants view cynically and consider beyond theoretical resolution. As a result, there has been virtually no discussion of the possibility that the CIA might lack constitutional authority to conduct covert bombing missions in Indonesia and Guatemala, plot the assassination of foreign leaders in Latin America and Africa, subvert the democratic political processes of Chile in favor of a military coup, fund a 10,000 man guerrilla force to invade Nicaragua, or kidnap people from the United States for delivery to a foreign intelligence agency that will torture them.

Second, the positivist view has culminated in the rather revolutionary assumption for the United States—that one person may legitimately create alliances, commit U.S. forces, trigger military conflict, and authorize lethal clandestine operations until and unless overwhelming political opposition can be mounted against him in Congress.

The following materials should be read in light of these alternative assumptions about the legitimacy of law.

B. The President as "Sole Organ"?

United States v. Curtiss-Wright Export Corp.
299 U.S. 304 (1936)

In 1932, landlocked Bolivia attempted to seize the northern Chaco to gain access to the Atlantic Ocean via the Paraguay River. Paraguay resisted, and American arms manufacturers secretly sought to supply both sides. As Clarence K. Webster of the Curtiss-Wright Export Corporation wrote to his agent in Bolivia: "National pride and stubbornness will not permit these countries to quit until they blow up through absolute bankruptcy, and while the show is going on, it is our job as distributors of munitions to get our share. If we don't, someone else will."[1] In an effort to cool down this war, which destroyed 100,000 lives and endangered the peace of all South America, Congress empowered the president to forbid the sale of munitions by American manufacturers to these countries with such limitations and exceptions as he should determine. The president then issued a proclamation imposing an embargo on arms sales, which the Curtiss-Wright Export Corporation proceeded to circumvent by labeling bombers destined for Bolivia passenger planes. The shipment of arms and planes sparked an investigation, and the Curtiss-Wright Export Corporation and its executives were eventually prosecuted for conspiring to smuggle machine guns for the planes in violation of the embargo. The Corporation argued in its defense that Congress's joint resolution was an unconstitutional delegation of legislative power to the president.

MR. JUSTICE SUTHERLAND delivered the opinion of the Court....

Whether, if the Joint Resolution had related solely to internal affairs it would be open to the challenge that it constituted an unlawful delegation of legislative power to the Executive, we find it unnecessary to determine. The whole aim of the resolution is to affect a situation entirely external to the United States, and falling within the category of foreign affairs. The determination which we are called to make, therefore, is whether the Joint Resolution, as applied to that situation, is vulnerable to attack under the rule that forbids a delegation of the law-making power. In other words, assuming (but not deciding) that the challenged delegation, if it were confined to internal affairs, would be invalid, may it nevertheless be sustained on the ground that its exclusive aim is to afford a remedy for a hurtful condition within foreign territory?

It will contribute to the elucidation of the question if we first consider the differences between the powers of the federal government in respect of foreign or external affairs and those in respect of domestic or internal affairs. That there are differences between them, and that these differences are fundamental, may not be doubted.

The two classes of powers are different, both in respect of their origin and their nature. The broad statement that the federal government can exercise no

---

1. Robert A. Divine, "The Case of the Smuggled Bombers," in John A. Garraty, ed., *Quarrels That Have Shaped the Constitution* (1962), 210, 212–13.

The Curtiss-Wright Corporation tried to smuggle B-2 Condor bombers (shown here), fighters, and machine guns to Bolivia during the Gran Chaco War in violation of President Herbert Hoover's neutrality policy. Eventually the company and two of its executives pleaded guilty and were fined for breaking the embargo.

powers except those specifically enumerated in the Constitution, and such implied powers as are necessary and proper to carry into effect the enumerated powers, is categorically true only in respect of our internal affairs. In that field, the primary purpose of the Constitution was to carve from the general mass of legislative powers *then possessed by the states* such portions as it was thought desirable to vest in the federal government, leaving those not included in the enumeration still in the states.... That this doctrine applies only to powers which the states had, is self evident. And since the states severally never possessed international powers, such powers could not have been carved from the mass of state powers but obviously were transmitted to the United States from some other source. During the colonial period, those powers were possessed exclusively by and were entirely under the control of the Crown. By the Declaration of Independence, "the Representatives of the United States of America" declared the United [not the several] Colonies to be free and independent states, and as such to have "full Power to levy War, conclude Peace, contract Alliances, establish Commerce and to do all other Acts and Things which Independent States may of right do."

As a result of the separation from Great Britain by the colonies acting as a unit, the powers of external sovereignty passed from the Crown not to the colonies severally, but to the colonies in their collective and corporate capacity as the United States of America. Even before the Declaration, the colonies were a unit in foreign affairs, acting through a common agency—namely the Continental Congress, composed of delegates from the thirteen colonies. That agency exercised the powers of war and peace, raised an army, created a navy, and finally adopted the Declaration of Independence. Rulers come and go; governments end and forms of government change; but sovereignty survives. A political society cannot endure without a supreme will somewhere. Sovereignty is never held in suspense. When, therefore, the external sovereignty of Great Britain in respect of the colonies ceased, it immediately passed to the Union.... That fact was given practical application almost at once. The treaty of peace, made on September 23, 1783, was concluded between his Brittanic Majesty and the "United States of America."

The Union existed before the Constitution, which was ordained and established among other things to form "a more perfect Union." Prior to that event, it is clear that the Union, declared by the Articles of Confederation to be "perpetual," was the sole possessor of external sovereignty and in the Union it remained without change save in so far as the Constitution in express terms qualified its exercise. The Framers' Convention was called and exerted its powers upon the irrefutable postulate that though the states were several their people in respect of foreign affairs were one....

It results that the investment of the federal government with the powers of external sovereignty did not depend upon the affirmative grants of the Constitution. The powers to declare and wage war, to conclude peace, to make treaties, to maintain diplomatic relations with other sovereignties, if they had never been mentioned in the Constitution, would have vested in the federal government as necessary concomitants of nationality.... As a member of the family of nations, the right and power of the United States in that field are equal to the right and power of the other members of the international family. Otherwise, the United States is not completely sovereign. The power to acquire territory by discovery and occupation.... The power to expel undesirable aliens.... the power to make such international agreements as do not constitute treaties in the constitutional sense.... none of which is expressly affirmed by the Constitution, nevertheless exist as inherently inseparable from the conception of nationality....

Not only, as we have shown, is the federal power over external affairs in origin and essential character different from that over internal affairs, but participation in the exercise of the power is significantly limited. In this vast external realm, with its important, complicated, delicate and manifold problems, the President alone has the power to speak or listen as a representative of the nation. He *makes* treaties with the advice and consent of the Senate; but he alone negotiates. Into the field of negotiation the Senate cannot intrude; and Congress itself is powerless to invade it. As Marshall said in his great argument of March 7, 1800, in the House of Representatives, "The President is the sole organ of the nation in its external relations, and its sole representative with foreign nations."...

"The President is the constitutional representative of the United States with regard to foreign nations. He manages our concerns with foreign nations and must necessarily be most competent to determine when, how, and upon what subjects negotiation may be urged with the greatest prospect of success. For his conduct he is responsible to the Constitution. The committee considers this responsibility the surest pledge for the faithful discharge of his duty. They think the interference of the Senate in the direction of foreign negotiations calculated to diminish that responsibility and thereby to impair the best security for the national safety. The nature of transactions with foreign nations, moreover, requires caution and unity of design, and their success frequently depends on secrecy and dispatch."…

It is important to bear in mind that we are here dealing not alone with an authority vested in the President by an exertion of legislative power, but with such an authority plus the very delicate, plenary and exclusive power of the President as the sole organ of the federal government in the field of international relations—a power which does not require as a basis for its exercise an act of Congress, but which, of course, like every other governmental power, must be exercised in subordination to the applicable provisions of the Constitution. It is quite apparent that if, in the maintenance of our international relations, embarrassment—perhaps serious embarrassment—is to be avoided and success for our aims achieved, congressional legislation which is to be made effective through negotiation and inquiry within the international field must often accord to the President a degree of discretion and freedom from statutory restriction which would not be admissible were domestic affairs alone involved. Moreover, he, not Congress, has the better opportunity of knowing the conditions which prevail in foreign countries, and especially is this true in time of war. He has his confidential sources of information. He has his agents in the form of diplomatic, consular and other officials. Secrecy in respect of information gathered by them may be highly necessary, and the premature disclosure of it productive of harmful results.…

When the President is to be authorized by legislation to act in respect of a matter intended to affect a situation in foreign territory, the legislator properly bears in mind the important consideration that the form of the President's action—or, indeed, whether he shall act at all—may well depend, among other things, upon the nature of the confidential information which he has or may thereafter receive, or upon the effect which his action may have upon our foreign relations. This consideration in connection with what we have already said on the subject, discloses the un-wisdom of requiring Congress in this field of governmental power to lay down narrowly definite standards by which the President is to be governed.…

In the light of the foregoing observations, it is evident that this court should not be in haste to apply a general rule which will have the effect of condemning legislation like that under review as constituting an unlawful delegation of legislative power.…

Notes and Questions

1. *Holding or dicta?* What, precisely, did the Court hold? Is this a case of exclusive presidential prerogatives, or is it a case of the Congress and the president exercising the sovereign powers of the United States?

2. *Sources of the foreign affairs power.* According to Justice Sutherland, a former chairman of the Senate Committee on Foreign Relations, from what source or sources do the foreign affairs powers come? Can there be an extraconstitutional source of governmental powers under the federal Constitution? Which theory of the origins of government is implicit in Sutherland's opinion: the social contract, the constitutional compact theory of the founders, or the nation-state theory of nineteenth and twentieth-century nationalism? Does it make any difference whether the foreign affairs power is deemed to be implicit in various constitutional provisions, a power inherited from the British Crown, or

a concomitant of nationality? Compare Sutherland's theory of the foreign affairs power to John Locke's theory of the federative power (see Chapter 1). Would Locke have disputed Sutherland on the source of the foreign affairs power?

3. *The limitability of presidential powers by Congress.* If the foreign affairs powers come from extraconstitutional sources, are they limitable by Congress? Does Justice Sutherland view the sovereign powers of the United States as presidential powers, or as national powers subject to the constitutional allocation of powers among the branches? Is there any provision of the Constitution that might be read as evincing an intent on the part of the framers to authorize Congress to limit the powers granted to the president by Article II? Recall Justice Jackson's opinion in *Youngstown Sheet & Tube Co. v. Sawyer* (see Chapter 2), in which he noted that, though *Curtiss-Wright* "intimated that the President might act in external affairs without Congressional authority," it did not state "that he might act contrary to an Act of Congress."

4. *The limitability of presidential powers by the courts.* If the president's foreign affairs powers are deemed to derive from extraconstitutional sources, are they limitable by the courts? Consider the following statement by Justice Jackson in *Chicago & Southern Airlines, Inc. v. Waterman Steamship Corp.,* 333 U.S. 103, 111 (1948):

> The very nature of executive decisions as to foreign policy is political, not judicial. Such decisions are wholly confided by our Constitution in the political departments of the government, Executive and Legislative. They are delicate, complex, and involve large elements of prophecy. They are and should be undertaken only by those directly responsible to the people whose welfare they advance or imperil. They are decisions of a kind for which the judiciary has neither aptitude, facilities, nor responsibility and which has long been held to belong in the domain of political power not subject to judicial intrusion or inquiry.

Can such a sharp distinction be drawn between political and judicial matters? What does Justice Jackson mean by "political" matters? Are these decisions allocated to the president and Congress on the basis of "aptitude"? Note that in *Valentine v. United States ex rel. Neidecker,* 299 U.S. 5 (1936), the Court, in an opinion by Justice Sutherland, ruled that the president did not have the authority to extradite an American citizen when not required to do so by a treaty or statute. Under international law, the power to extradite is not considered a concomitant of nationality, but is a power that can only come into existence by treaty.

5. *Justice Sutherland's history.* Is it true that the powers of external sovereignty have always been vested, unambiguously, in one national government? Did the Declaration of Independence clearly state an intention to create one sovereign entity? After independence, did any of the states consider themselves, for any period of time or for any purposes, sovereign, independent states capable of carrying on international relations? Did the Articles of Confederation portray the United States as one sovereign entity, or a band of sovereign entities that created a Congress and chose to act through it? For critical examinations of Sutherland's history, see David M. Levitan, "The Foreign Relations Power: An Analysis of Mr. Justice Sutherland's Theory," 55 *Yale L. J.* 467 (1946), and Charles A. Lofgren, "*United States v. Curtiss-Wright Export Corporation*: An Historical Reassessment," 83 *Yale L. J.* 1 (1973). For materials supporting Sutherland's view, see Professor Richard B. Morris' testimony before a master in *United States v. Maine,* No. 35 Original, U.S. Supreme Court (1972). Morris concludes that most of the delegates to the Constitutional Convention and most of the early justices of the Supreme Court took a nationalist view of the locus of sovereignty. Does the text of the Constitution offer any guidance? Consider the following passage from the Court's opinion in *Perez v. Brownell,* 356 U.S. 44, 57 (1958).

> Although there is in the Constitution no specific grant to Congress of power to enact legislation for the effective regulation of foreign affairs, there can be no doubt of the existence of this power in the law-making organ of the Nation [citing *Curtiss-Wright*]. The States that joined together to form a single Nation and to create, through the Constitution, a Federal Government to conduct the affairs of that Nation must be held to have granted that Government the powers indispensable to its functioning effectively in the company of sovereign nations.

Does the *Perez* approach avoid the problems raised by Sutherland's historiography? Is it more consistent with the shift in thinking from legislative sovereignty prevalent in the 1770s to the idea of popular sovereignty that came of age in the late 1780s?

6. *Justice Sutherland's constitutional theory.* Was Justice Sutherland a better theorist than historian? Consider Prof. Louis Henkin's restatement of Sutherland's theory:

> Even if it were assumed [that] the States were each independently sovereign up to (or even during) the Articles of Confederation, the crux of Sutherland's theory might yet stand: the States irrevocably gave up external sovereignty, and the United States became one sovereign nation, upon, or by, adopting the Constitution, but tacitly, by implication, outside the framework of the Constitution and its scheme of enumerated delegations. The Constitution, Sutherland might point out, does not explicitly terminate the sovereignty of the States or declare or recognize the United States as a nation, does not confer upon the federal government the powers of national sovereignty generally, or specify many of the powers implied in sovereignty. It is reasonable to conclude, he might say, that the Framers intended to deal in full only with the governance of domestic affairs where the distribution between nations and States was new and critical, where the States retained most of the powers and the new central government was to have only what was given it; but with a few explicable exceptions, they did not deal with, enumerate, allocate powers in foreign affairs where the federal government was to have all. (*Foreign Affairs and the Constitution* [1972], 24.)

7. *External versus internal sovereignty.* Can external and internal sovereignty be divided as Professor Henkin, a former legal adviser to the State Department, suggests without violating the theory that all sovereignty belongs to the people and that whatever powers government officials possess come to them via the Constitution? Consider Justice Black's statement in *Reid v. Covert,* 354 U.S. 1, 5–6 (1957): "The United States is entirely a creature of the Constitution. Its power and authority have no other source. It can only act in accordance with all the limitations imposed by the Constitution."

8. *The Supremacy Clause.* Article 6, paragraph 2, of the Constitution speaks of treaties made "under the authority of the United States" and laws made "in pursuance to" the Constitution. Does this distinction support the theory of an external sovereignty different from an internal sovereignty? What was the framers' intent in so phrasing the Supremacy Clause?

9. *Constitutional sources: are they adequate?* If we reject Justice Sutherland's inheritance theory of sovereign powers and the historiography that goes with it, and we read the "concomitants of nationality" into Articles I and II to give them a grounding in the Constitution and the consent of the governed, does that solve the problem of which branch of government may initiate what, and when, in the realm of foreign affairs policy? Can all of the president's foreign affairs powers be deduced from the power to receive ambassadors, or do at least some of them have to be deduced from the opening sentence of Article II, thereby making that statement a grant of "executive powers"? If

that statement has independent potency, and is not merely descriptive, is there any end to what the president may initiate in the absence of a statutory or constitutional provision?

10. *Domestic intelligence.* In the Chicago Seven case, the prosecution of organizers of antiwar protests at the 1968 Democratic National Convention, it was disclosed that the government had wiretapped the defendants without the warrants presumably required by the Fourth Amendment. The Nixon administration defended this warrantless surveillance on the ground that the president had an inherent constitutional power to ignore the warrant requirement where the purpose of the wiretapping was to collect "national security" intelligence. It was further suggested that even Congress could not constrain the president in the use of "his" surveillance forces (Gov't Answer of Def.'s Motion for Disclosure of Electronic Surveillance, *United States v. Dellinger,* No. 68 Cr. 180 (N.D. Ill. 1969). Does Justice Sutherland's opinion in *Curtiss-Wright* support either of these assertions? When a similar case, involving a domestic group charged with bombing a CIA office, reached the Supreme Court, the Nixon administration abandoned its claim of an inherent power to ignore congressional legislation defining acceptable investigative techniques, but it continued to claim an inherent presidential power to ignore the Fourth Amendment warrant requirement and the associated principle of probable cause to suspect that a crime has been, or is about to be, committed. The Court rejected the broad inherent powers claim, but observed in *dicta* that the probable cause and warrant requirement might be different, i.e., less stringent, in national security cases (*United States v. U.S. District Court,* 407 U.S. 297 [1972]). Does not a judicially declared exception to traditional warrant requirements constitute at least a partial recognition of a presidential prerogative in this area?

11. *Foreign intelligence.* In *United States v. U.S. District Court,* the Court was careful to limit its opinion to "the domestic aspects of national security," and expressed no opinion on "the issues which may be involved with respect to activities of foreign powers or their agents." In *United States v. Brown,* 484 F. 2d 418 (5th Cir. 1973), a court of appeals upheld the warrantless wiretapping of H. Rap Brown, a domestic black protest leader who engaged in occasional communications with persons in other countries: "because of the President's constitutional duty to act for the United States [in] the field of foreign relations, and his inherent power to protect national security in the context of foreign affairs, we reaffirm [that] the President may constitutionally authorize warrantless wiretaps for the purpose of gathering foreign intelligence." The term "foreign intelligence" was not defined by the court; nor was the warrantless wiretapping confined to suspected agents of a foreign espionage agency. The Supreme Court denied certiorari, 415 U.S. 960 (1974), and before this proposition could be tested in that Court, Congress passed the Foreign Intelligence Surveillance Act of 1978, 92 Stat. 1783, 50 U.S.C. 1801. Is that statute, which purports to limit the president's power to engage in foreign intelligence activity (such as the wiretapping of foreign embassies and trade missions), constitutional? President Carter supported passage of the act and promised to abide by it, but he refused to concede that he lacked constitutional authority to ignore it. Both Presidents Carter and Reagan asserted an inherent prerogative to order surreptitious entries (burglaries) to obtain foreign intelligence, despite the existence of a statute (18 U.S.C. Sec. 2236) that makes it a misdemeanor for any federal officer engaged in the enforcement of any law to search any private dwelling without a warrant. After the attacks of September 11, 2001, President George W. Bush secretly authorized massive warrantless wiretapping of millions of communications in total disregard of the Fourth Amendment and the Foreign Intelligence Surveillance Act. The practice, conducted by the National Security Agency, continued under the Obama administration.

C. The Treaty Power

Under Article II of the Constitution, the president has "the power, by and with the advice and consent of the Senate, to make treaties, provided that two thirds of the Senators present concur...." The president's authority to "make" treaties has come to mean the power to negotiate them, to submit them to the Senate, and, if the Senate consents, to make the final decision whether to ratify them on behalf of the United States. Thus to speak of senatorial "ratification," as many senators do, is imprecise.

According to Article VI of the Constitution, "treaties made, or which shall be made, under the authority of the United States, shall be the supreme law of the land." The reference to "treaties made.... under the authority of the United States" was made to preserve in force treaties negotiated prior to the ratification of the Constitution in 1789. There is no evidence that the framers intended to give the president the authority to "make" treaties, with the Senate's consent, with complete abandon, as if the rest of the Constitution did not exist. Still, the plain text is open to that interpretation.

The ambiguity of the treaty provisions of Articles II and VI (and Article III) makes possible vigorous debate over several very important questions. For example, may the president and two-thirds of the Senate, by an agreement with a foreign country, authorize the federal government to do something that the Constitution does not authorize it to do by legislation? Are treaties self-executing (i.e., do they automatically become law), or must all or some of them be implemented by legislation? May both houses of Congress implement the terms of a treaty by legislation when Congress could not constitutionally enact those terms by legislation alone? Or, conversely, is the authority of the president and Senate to effectuate treaties limited to those subjects on which Congress can legislate in the absence of a treaty? May the president and the Senate, by treaty, authorize restrictions on individual liberty that Congress could not enact without violating the Bill of Rights or other constitutional guarantees?

As the following materials demonstrate, these are not abstract questions, but go to the very heart of the Constitution's system for allocating authority within the national government, between the nation and the states, and between the national government and all individuals (citizens and aliens) protected by the Constitution.

Missouri v. Holland
252 U.S. 416 (1920)

MR. JUSTICE HOLMES delivered the opinion of the Court.

This is a bill in equity brought by the State of Missouri to prevent a game warden of the United States from attempting to enforce the Migratory Bird Treaty Act of July 3, 1918, [on the ground] that the statute is an unconstitutional interference with the rights reserved to the States by the Tenth Amendment....

On December 8, 1916, a treaty between the United States and Great Britain was proclaimed by the President. It recited that many species of birds in their annual migrations traversed many parts of the United States and of Canada, that they were of great value as a source of food and in destroying insects injurious to vegetation, but were in danger of extermination through lack of adequate protection. It therefore provided for specified closed seasons and protection in other forms, and agreed that the two powers would take or propose to their lawmaking bodies the necessary measures for carrying the treaty out....

To answer this question it is not enough to refer to the Tenth Amendment ... because by Article 2, Section 2, the power to make treaties is delegated expressly, and by Article 6 treaties made under the authority of the United States, along with the Constitution and laws of the United States made in pursuance thereof, are declared the supreme law of the land. If the treaty is valid there can be no dispute about the validity of the statute under Article 1, Section 8, as a necessary and proper means to execute the powers of the Government....

It is said that a treaty cannot be valid if it infringes the Constitution, that there are limits, therefore, to the treaty-making power, and that one such limit is that what an act of Congress could not do unaided, in derogation of the powers reserved to the States, a treaty cannot do.

... Acts of Congress are the supreme law of the land only when made in pursuance of the Constitution, while treaties are declared to be so when made under the authority of the United States. It is open to question whether the authority of the United States means more than the formal acts prescribed to make the convention. We do not mean to imply that there are no qualifications to the treaty-making power; but they must be ascertained in a different way. It is obvious that there may be matters of the sharpest exigency for the national well being that an act of Congress could not deal with but that a treaty followed by such an act could, and it is not lightly to be assumed that, in matters requiring national action, "a power which must belong to and somewhere reside in every civilized government" is not to be found....

... The treaty in question does not contravene any prohibitory words to be found in the Constitution. The only question is whether it is forbidden by some invisible radiation from the general terms of the Tenth Amendment. We must consider what this country has become in deciding what that amendment has reserved.

... The whole foundation of the State's rights is the presence within their jurisdiction of birds that yesterday had not arrived, tomorrow may be in another State and in a week a thousand miles away. If we are to be accurate we cannot put the case of the State upon higher ground than that the treaty deals with creatures that for the moment are within the state borders, that it must be carried out by officers of the United States within the same territory, and that but for the treaty the State would be free to regulate this subject itself....

Here a national interest of very nearly the first magnitude is involved. It can be protected only by national action in concert with that of another power. The subject matter is only transitorily within the State and has no permanent habitat therein. But for the treaty and the statute there soon might be no birds for any powers to deal with.

Notes and Questions

1. *Limitations on the treaty power.* Is the treaty power broader than, or limited to, the enumerated powers of Congress? In other words, can the president and the Senate accomplish through treaties ends which the president and both Houses of Congress could not accomplish by legislation alone? If so, is there any limit to the capacity of the president and Senate to expand the regulatory powers of the national government by entering into treaties? Consider the following efforts to define limits to the treaty power. Are they helpful?

Justice Story:

> Though the [treaty] power is … general and unrestricted, it is not to be so construed as to destroy the fundamental laws of the State. A power given by the Constitution cannot be construed to authorize a destruction of other powers given in the same instrument. It must be construed, therefore, in subordination to it and cannot supersede or interfere with any other of its fundamental provisions. (*Commentaries on the Constitution of the United States* (1833; 3d ed.; 1858), Sec. 1508.)

Justice Field:

> [The treaty power] extends to all proper subjects of negotiation between our government and the governments of other nations…. [It] is in terms unlimited except by those restraints which are found in [the Constitution] against the action of the government or of its departments, and those arising from the nature of the government itself and of that of the States. It would not be contended that it extends so far as to authorize what the Constitution forbids, or a change in the character of the government or in that of one of the States, or a cession of any portion of the territory of the latter, without its consent. (*Geofroy v. Riggs*, 133 U.S. 258, 266–67 [1890]).

American Law Institute, *Restatement (Second) Foreign Relations Law of the United States*, Sec. 40 (1965):

> An international agreement of the United States must relate to the external concerns of the nation as distinguished from matters of purely internal nature.

Would a treaty expanding the political rights of persons to vote be "a proper subject of negotiation" or a matter of "external concern" to the United States? If so, who should decide? Should the judiciary second-guess the president and Senate on such matters? If not, who could?

2. *The Bricker Amendment controversy.* Between 1952 and 1957, the conservative wing of the Republican Party attempted unsuccessfully to persuade Congress to approve a constitutional amendment that would have included the House of Representatives in the making of all treaty law. Section 2 of the version recommended by the Senate Judiciary Committee in 1953 provided: "A treaty shall become effective as internal law in the United States only through legislation which would be valid in the absence of treaty." Thus, the proposed amendment sought to prevent the enlargement of legislative powers through treaties, as in *Missouri v. Holland*, and repeal the doctrine, accepted since *Ware v. Hylton*, 3 U.S. (3 Dall.) 199 (1796), that treaty provisions not requiring appropriations are self-executing.

The proponents of the Bricker Amendment were isolationists who believed that American national and state sovereignty were threatened by the United Nations and a "new school of internationalists" who dominated postwar foreign policy. They were particularly opposed to the United Nations Economic and Social Council, which Frank E. Holman, a past president of the American Bar Association, described as "the organ … through which the socialists and communists and 'do-gooders' proposed to … remake the world along the lines of so-called social and economic equality…."[2] Much of the conservatives' effort was directed against the Council's Convention on Human Rights, not only because it declared that people had (moral) rights to jobs, housing, and leisure, but because its political and civil rights provisions were seen as a backdoor way of enacting President Truman's civil rights program.

---

2. Frank E. Holman, *Story of the "Bricker" Amendment* (1954), 2, 5, and passim.

If the internationalists were not checked, Holman warned, they would use treaty obligations as an excuse for triggering the kinds of sweeping emergency powers that President Truman had claimed in the Steel Seizure case. Internationalists, he added, would also involve the United States "in IndoChina with the prospect of having another Korea on our hands; meddling everywhere throughout the world in the affairs of other people and meanwhile, in the UN, letting all other people meddle in our affairs."

The conservatives viewed the treaty power as undemocratic, in that it placed law made by the president, foreigners, and two-thirds of the Senate on an equal footing with legislation passed by both houses of Congress. They saw mutual assistance treaties like the SEATO pact as a way in which Congress' power to declare war could be transferred to foreign governments or to the president alone, and they viewed human rights covenants both as watered-down substitutes for American constitutional rights and as encroachments on the authority of state governments to pass laws forbidding racial marriages and limiting the property holdings of aliens.[3] Wall Street attorney John Foster Dulles, before he became Eisenhower's Secretary of State, went so far as to declare that treaties are "more supreme than ordinary law. [They] can override the Constitution...."[4]

The Bricker Amendment failed by one vote, but is there merit to any of the arguments advanced on its behalf? What is the rationale for vesting the treaty power in the president and two-thirds of the Senate? In *The Federalist* No. 64, John Jay argued that decisions on treaties should be entrusted to senators because they were to be chosen by the "select assemblies" of state legislatures and thus would presumably have better judgment than popularly elected members of the House. Is any validity left to this argument now that the Seventeenth Amendment (1913) provides for the direct election of senators? Can it be argued that the advice and consent of the Senate is more valuable than the views of the House because senators represent larger constituencies and thus may be more cosmopolitan in their outlook? Is it democratic to permit one-third plus one of the Senate's membership to veto treaties? Does this procedure institutionalize an internationalist or a parochial outlook on the part of the Senate? Or does this procedure simply reflect a belief on the part of the framers that treaties should not be entered into lightly lest the United States become entangled in too many discomforting alliances? Is there any theory that can guarantee that only the wisest heads will prevail in the making of international agreements?

3. *The growth of legislative powers.* Consider Louis Henkin:

> The [Bricker] amendment's proponents did not recognize however, that *Holland* had already lost its importance: its principal point, that there were 'matters of the sharpest exigency for the national well being that an act of Congress could not deal with but that a treaty followed by such an act could,' ceased to be true in fact, for [in light of the explosion of congressional powers which had taken place since 1920] there were virtually no matters of any exigency—including human rights legislation—that Congress could not deal with even in the absence of treaty. Since the Bricker controversy, further extensions of the powers of Congress to enact human rights legislation, by new readings of the Thirteenth and Fourteenth Amendments, render it even clearer that the Bricker Amendment would not have effectively barred adherence to the treaties at which it aimed. (*Foreign Affairs and the Constitution* [1972], 147).

---

3. Ibid.
4. TIME Magazine, "The Bricker Amendment," July 13, 1953.

Is Henkin correct, or has he overstated the extent to which congressional power to legislate on behalf of human rights has grown? Is the "state action" doctrine, which has historically barred the federal government from imposing human rights legislation (such as a general system of criminal law) on the relations among private persons, dead or dying? Assuming, *arguendo,* that Henkin is right about the growth of legislative power, would the Bricker Amendment be superfluous, or would it still effect a redistribution of political power? Can the consequences of such a redistribution be predicted, in the long run, on all issues that might arise through exercise of the treaty power?

4. *A reassurance from the Supreme Court.* Section 1 of the Bricker Amendment would have provided that "a provision of a treaty which conflicts with this Constitution shall not be of any force or effect." Was this provision necessary? Justice Black, writing for the Supreme Court in *Reid v. Covert,* 354 U.S. 1, 16–17 (1957), emphasized that

> no agreement with a foreign nation can confer power on the Congress, or on any other branch of Government, which is free from the restraints of the Constitution....
>
> There is nothing in [the Supremacy Clause] which intimates that treaties and laws enacted pursuant to them do not have to comply with the provisions of the Constitution. Nor is there anything in the debates which accompanied the drafting and ratification of the Constitution which even suggests such a result. These debates as well as the history that surrounds the adoption of the treaty provision in Article VI make it clear that the reason treaties were not limited to those made in "pursuance" of the Constitution was so that agreements made by the United States under the Articles of Confederation, including the important peace treaties which concluded the Revolutionary War, would remain in effect. It would be manifestly contrary to the objectives of those who created the Constitution, as well as those who were responsible for the Bill of Rights—let alone alien to our entire constitutional history and tradition—to construe Article VI as permitting the United States to exercise power under an international agreement without observing constitutional prohibitions. In effect, such construction would permit amendment of that document in a manner not sanctioned by Article V. The prohibitions of the Constitution were designed to apply to all branches of the National Government and they cannot be nullified by the Executive or by the Executive and the Senate combined.

Justice Black's comments did much to quell the apprehensions of conservatives like John Foster Dulles. Efforts to reassert the role of the House of Representatives in the making of international agreements did not revive until the 1970s and 1980s.

5. *Power of Congress to pass legislation inconsistent with prior treaties.* While the president and the Senate may make treaty law that is legally binding in the United States, is there anything to prevent subsequent Congresses and presidents from enacting legislation that, in effect, nullifies the treaty and puts the United States in default? In 1888 Congress passed a law prohibiting Chinese laborers from entering the United States, even though the law violated the rights of Chinese nationals under earlier treaties between the United States and China. The Supreme Court upheld the legislation on the theory that treaties and acts of Congress are of equal dignity, and that "the last expression of the sovereign will must control." (Citing *Chae Chan Ping v. United States* [*The Chinese Exclusion Case*], 130 U.S. 581 [1889]). See also *Whitney v. Robinson,* 124 U.S. 190 [1880].) Must treaties and federal statutes be of equal dignity? Is it not equally persuasive to argue that statutes should always prevail because they represent a broader base in the electorate, or that treaties

should always prevail on the grounds that the only proper way to abrogate a treaty is by the procedure that led to its adoption? Why do you suppose that the Supreme Court in *Reid* chose to rule in favor of the subsequent legislation? Would it have been wiser to declare the matter a nonjusticiable "political question" and refuse to rule on it? Is it "anomalous," as Professor Henkin has argued, "to accord [subsequent Congresses and presidents] power to disregard a treaty obligation, compel its violation, and put the United States in default?"[5] Compare this method of abrogation of treaties with others discussed in the next section, "The Abrogation of Treaties." If two-thirds of each house wish to pass a law over a president's veto in order to abrogate a treaty, should they be allowed by the courts to do so? Or must abrogation always have the president's concurrence?

6. *When treaties are not self-executing: the House of Representatives and the Panama Canal treaties.* In 1964, anti-American riots in Panama launched a decade of negotiations directed at turning over control of the canal to the Panamanian government. Conservatives in the House of Representatives watched these negotiations with rising apprehension. Their constitutional concern was twofold: the treaties would arguably involve the cession of sovereign territory to a foreign government, a decision that Article IV, Section 3, Clause 2, of the Constitution allocates to Congress, and they would require implementing appropriations. In the minds of the conservatives there was no doubt; the Canal Zone was American soil. Before the negotiations were completed, the House adopted an amendment to an appropriations bill that would have prohibited the use of any funds "for the purpose of negotiating the surrender or relinquishment of any U.S. rights in the Panama Canal Zone." The Senate refused to agree. The negotiations went forward, but House members continued to insist that a treaty with Panama involving either the transfer of American property or the payment of money would have to be approved by both houses of Congress.

In 1979, after a fractious nationwide debate, the Senate gave its consent to treaties negotiated by the Carter administration, and the president ratified them, thereby making the treaties law. The House of Representatives, however, took the view that it was not bound by the executive branch's interpretation of the treaty, and in an implementing bill added its "understanding" that payments to Panama would cease if that government were found to be interfering in the internal affairs of another nation. Another House proviso would have diverted the first $10 million of canal profits from Panama to the United States to defray the cost of maintaining a U.S. presence in Panama. A third provision would have subordinated the new binational Panama Canal Commission to the U.S. secretary of defense, while another would have granted control of the canal back to the United States in event of war. Finally, the House bill would have required that each transfer of American property to Panama be approved by subsequent statutory enactments.[6]

Was the legislation which the House proposed unconstitutional? Was the legislation likely to become law if two-thirds of the Senate and the president supported the treaties? What would have happened if deadlock had resulted between the House and Senate, or between the House and the president? Did the Senate and the president need House concurrence to abrogate earlier treaties, and thus give Panama immediate control if the House did not concur? See *Cong. Rec.*, June 21, 1979, H4844-45 (Mr. Levitas). Professor Henkin has argued that Congress "probably has a constitutional obligation to implement the

---

5. *Foreign Affairs and the Constitution* (1972), 164.
6. *Cong. Rec.*, June 26, 1975, H6226-36; July 26, 1979, S10646-47; June 20, 1979, H790-91; June 21, 1979, H4844-45.

treaties which the President and Senate make...."[7] Is that true? If the House has an obligation to follow the lead of the Senate and president, do the Senate and president have a similar obligation to follow prior House resolutions stating what kinds of non-self-executing treaties the House will approve? What kinds of "constitutional obligation" is professor Henkin invoking: a legal obligation or a moral one?

Does the Constitution require that the president obtain House approval before transferring properties pursuant to a treaty? In *Edwards v. Carter,* 580 F. 2d 1055 (D.C. Cir. 1978), *cert. denied,* 436 U.S. 907 (1978), the court of appeals held that the president and Senate had the authority to dispose of U.S. property in the Canal Zone without passage of implementing legislation. The appeals court also rejected the argument that the zone itself was part of the sovereign territory of the United States.

7. *Conditional consent by the Senate.* Article II, Section 2, of the Constitution provides that the president "shall have Power, by and with the Advice and Consent of the Senate, to make Treaties, provided two thirds of the Senators present concur." Technically, this means that presidents remain free, even after the Senate gives its advice and consent, to refuse to ratify and thus give effect to a treaty. Since the provision provides for the Senate's "advice and consent," is there any reason why that body should not give conditional consent, and thereby send the president back to the negotiating table to win foreign acceptance for new provisions or interpretations?

8. *Senate modification of treaties.* The Panama Canal treaties were unclear on several points, including the right of the United States to ensure the Canal's neutrality in time of war, or to use force to prevent interference with U.S. shipping through it. The Senate, by majority vote, amended the treaties and attached reservations to them before consenting to their ratification and sending them to the president. The president then had to win Panamanian acceptance of these changes. If consent requires a two-thirds vote of the Senate, must modifications voted on prior to the final consent vote also be passed by a two-thirds majority?

9. *States rights and the treaty power.* Are there some states' rights that may not be abridged by treaties? For example, could the president and Senate make a valid treaty that would cede the territory of an American state to a foreign country? Modify the internal form of government within a state so that it is no longer "republican"? Abolish the state militia as part of a general treaty of disarmament? Provide for international inspection of state facilities as part of a treaty of disarmament?

D. The Abrogation of Treaties

The Constitution prescribes how treaties shall be made, but says nothing about how they shall be terminated. May the president abrogate a treaty without the advice and consent of the Senate, or of the House where the treaty was implemented by legislation?

Presidents have claimed the power to recognize a breach by a foreign signatory and to respond immediately on behalf of the United States. Thus President Theodore Roosevelt decided that the United States had no obligation to extradite persons to Greece after Greece refused to return a celebrated stock manipulator. *Charlton v. Kelly,* 229 U.S. 447

---

7. *Foreign Affairs and the Constitution* (1972), 164.

(1913). Similarly, Franklin Roosevelt denounced the Treaty of Commerce, Friendship and Navigation with Japan when that country's imperial ambitions became clear in 1939.

However, does the president have authority to abrogate a treaty when the foreign signatory is not in default? This issue arose in the late 1970s after President Carter recognized the People's Republic of China (on the mainland) and withdrew recognition of the Republic of China (on Taiwan). Pursuant to this change in executive policy, the president announced that the mutual defense treaty with the Nationalist Chinese on Taiwan would terminate on January 1, 1980, in accordance with a treaty provision that permitted either "party" to terminate the agreement on one year's notice. The debate over that unilateral assertion of presidential authority follows.

Barry Goldwater,
Treaty Termination Is a Shared Power

[By unilaterally abrogating the 1955 Mutual Defense Treaty] President Carter has not only usurped powers conferred on the Congress, but has attempted to exercise a function the Supreme Court has said is clearly reserved to the judicial branch, the power "to say what the law is." *United States v. Nixon,* 418 U.S. 683 (1974).

The question is not whether any past precedents justify the president's assertion of independent power, although I believe the weight of historical evidence proves that treaties are normally terminated only with legislative approval. The true question is whether his action represents the original intent of the people who drafted the Constitution.

[C]ontemporary materials and the text of the Constitution show that the termination of a treaty, involving as it does the sacred honor of the country and serious policy interests, is a decision of such major importance that the framers required the joint participation of both political departments, the executive and legislative, in making that decision. If left unchallenged, the president's unilateral action will set a dangerous precedent that would enable him or a future president to terminate any defense treaty at will. In fact, the precedent could be used for the presidential termination of any treaty to which the United States may now be a party or become a party in the future—for instance, with Israel. This unchecked concentration of power is totally inimical to our democratic, representative form of government.

The Constitution is silent as to how a treaty shall be terminated. It is also silent on how a statute or any other law shall be cancelled. Yet no one makes the argument that the president alone can repeal a statute. In fact, in *The Confiscation Cases,* 20 Wall. 92 (1874), the Supreme Court expressly said that "no power was ever vested in the president to repeal an act of Congress."

It is my belief that by placing treaties among "the supreme Law of the Land" in Article VI, Clause 2, and by requiring in Article II, Section 3, that the president "shall take care that the Laws be faithfully executed," the framers meant, and expected without saying more, that the president would carry out a treaty in good faith. This is exactly the opposite of giving him an implied authority to cancel any treaty at will. It is also well known that the framers were concerned with restoring dependability to treaties made by the United States. They were anxious to gain the respect and confidence of foreign nations by keeping our treaty commitments....

Would the framers, who regarded violation of "the sacred faith of treaties" as "wicked," "dishonorable," and contrary to the best interests of the country in acquiring respect in the community of nations, have contradicted these purposes by making it as easy under the new Constitution for a single officer of the government to repeal a treaty as it had been for individual states to nullify a treaty under the Articles of Confederation? ...

Without any supporting textual evidence to show it, it is inconceivable that the framers assigned to one person power to denounce a commercial treaty that would be highly beneficial to the interests of a particular geographic region or a peace treaty that had formally concluded a war and whose faithful adherence would presumably avert the chance of resumption of hostilities, however slight that chance may be. As the language of the Constitution does not distinguish commercial and peace treaties from other treaties, such as a security pact, it is obvious that all treaties share the same protective armor....

The early authorities, including some among the Founding Fathers, saw the repeal of a treaty in the same light as they saw the repeal of a statute. It would have been strange to hear anyone argue that the president, by his sole authority, could terminate whatever treaty he wished, whenever he wished. James Madison, for one, believed that "the same authority, precisely," would be "exercised in annulling as in making a treaty." Thomas Jefferson, when he was Washington's first secretary of state, wrote a report in which he reasoned that the same authority who possessed the power of making treaties consequently had the power of declaring them dissolved. And, when he was vice president, Jefferson compiled the first manual of rules of the Senate, in which he wrote: "Treaties being declared equally with the laws of the United States, to be the supreme law of the land, it is understood that an act of the legislature alone can declare them infringed and rescinded."

Further evidence that the framers linked the repeal of treaties to the repeal of statutes appears in John Jay's brief analogy in *The Federalist*, Number 64: "They who make laws may, without doubt, amend or repeal them, and it will not be disputed that they who make treaties may alter or cancel them...."

Another authority who believed the legislature must act before a treaty is terminated is James Buchanan. In writing about the anticipated cancellation of a commercial treaty with Denmark considered damaging to our exports, then Secretary of State Buchanan wrote that "an act must first pass Congress to enable the president to give the required notice...."

When the United States finally cancelled the treaty with Denmark, it was accomplished by a Senate resolution of March 3, 1855, passed unanimously, which advised and consented to authorizing President Pierce to give notice of its termination. The president had requested the authority, thereby giving some indication of his belief that the decision-making authority was jointly possessed by him and the legislature, or at least one branch of it, and was not vested in him alone.

The incident led to an authoritative report by the Senate Foreign Relations Committee in 1856. In response to public discussion over whether the Senate had acted properly in authorizing presidential action without the concurrence of the House of Representatives, the committee concluded that the Senate and president jointly possessed competence to terminate a treaty "without the aid or in-

3 · FOREIGN AFFAIRS POWERS

tervention of legislation" by the other house. Speaking precisely to the same issue presented by Article X of the Republic of China defense treaty, the committee decided that "where the right to terminate a treaty at discretion is reserved in the treaty itself, such discretion resides in President and Senate."

The committee explained: "The whole power to bind the government by treaty is vested in the president and Senate, two thirds of the senators present concurring. The treaty in question was created by the will of the treaty-making power, and it contained a reservation by which that will should be revoked or its exercise cease on a stipulated notice. It is thus the will of the treaty-making power which is the subject of revocation, and it follows that the revocation is incident to the will." Thus, the committee clearly took a position at odds with the novel theory asserted by President Carter today.

Henry Cabot Lodge, when he was chairman of the Senate Foreign Relations Committee in 1911, also believed the power of treaty termination was jointly possessed by the president and legislature. In response to a question in the Senate whether notice, given Russia by President Taft to terminate a commercial treaty because of Soviet violations, would be legal in the absence of congressional ratification, he replied, "Of course, Congress can disapprove his action; and then, I take it, the notice fails...." Senator Lodge added his opinion that the power to terminate that treaty by notice, as authorized in an article thereof, was vested in the Senate and president together "because in making such a treaty the Senate and the president represent the high contracting party."...

The only remaining question is whether, although the president normally cannot terminate a treaty without further legislative action, the Senate has consented to his action in the case of this treaty by having approved language in it that allows termination by notice. The answer is clear that no authority of this type can be inferred from the treaty or legislative history.

First, it should be noted that the provision does not authorize termination after notice by "the president" or "executive" of either country. The treaty uses the term "party." This obviously means the sovereign authority of the state giving notice. In determining who represents the sovereign authority, it is necessary to consult the constitutional processes of the state in order to find what power makes the decision to give notice and, after that decision has been made, what power shall actually transmit the notice. Under our Constitution, it is clear that whoever communicates notice, the power of making the initial decision belongs jointly to the president and Senate or Congress.

Although it is generally accepted that the president is "the sole organ of the nation in its external relations, and its sole representative with foreign nations" (229 U.S. 304, 319–20), this proves no more than that it is the president who shall act as the official representative of the nation in communicating with the foreign government. His capacity as a diplomatic organ in no way need imply a power of making the critical policy decision required before delivery of the notice....

The Senate, together with the president and often with the House of Representatives, had participated in the termination of nearly 40 treaties by 1955, virtually all of which contained duration provisions similar to Article X of the R.O.C. defense treaty. From this, if any understanding could be attributed to the Senate when the treaty was ratified, it was that the term "party" meant the president and Senate jointly.

But the State Department would not only attribute a meaning to the R.O.C. defense treaty of which it never informed the Senate. It would put the same meaning on dozens of other major treaties that contain similar provisions. For example, the North Atlantic Treaty Alliance and our security pacts with South Korea, Japan, and the Philippines include articles allowing either "party" to withdraw after one year's notice....

When it suddenly suits the needs of expediency for its policy of the moment, the State Department unveils a doctrine it has hidden from public discussion. After having exploited the use of executive agreements to the point where the president can make virtually any treaty he wants by calling it a mere executive agreement, now the State Department is ready to usurp the power of unmaking treaties as well.

65 Am.Bar.Assn. J. 198–200 (1979).

Edward M. Kennedy,
Treaty Termination Is Not a Shared Power
(1979)

Although the Constitution requires the President to obtain the advice and consent of the Senate prior to concluding a treaty, it sets forth no such requirement for terminating a treaty. Of course, in approving the 1954 defense treaty with the Republic of China, the Senate might have required the President to obtain the approval of the Senate or Congress prior to terminating the treaty, but it chose not to do so. The treaty simply provides for termination with one year's notice; in the light of twentieth-century practice, this plainly confers upon the President the power to terminate the treaty at his own sole discretion....

Presidents have given notice of treaty termination independent of the Senate or Congress on fourteen separate occasions in our nation's history—and eleven of these instances have occurred in the past fifty years....

Since 1920, only Presidents Hoover and Nixon have not terminated treaties pursuant to a notice provision. All other modern Presidents, from Wilson through Carter, have exerted their valid constitutional authority by terminating treaties without formal advice and consent. And their actions have been accepted by the Congress and unchallenged in the courts....

... The issue of treaty termination is often intimately related to the question of recognition of a foreign sovereign and establishment of diplomatic relations, as indeed it is in the case of China, and both questions have been regarded as requiring political judgments that are within the President's authority....

Sound historical and policy reasons sustain this conclusion. The Framers of our Constitution feared "entangling alliances" and therefore required the President to obtain the advice and consent of two-thirds of the Senate prior to concluding a treaty. The Framers manifested no similar concern with the President's exercise of discretion to disentangle the nation from alliances, and the Constitution thus imposed no requirement of Senate participation in treaty termination.

In the absence of specific constitutional, treaty or statutory language restraining the President, it has been understood that he is responsible for determining how to deal with treaties once concluded. For example, in referring to the 1793 Neutrality Proclamation by President Washington and its relation to American treaties with France, Alexander Hamilton wrote that "treaties can only be made by the president and senate jointly; but their activity maybe continued or suspended by the president alone."...

Despite the fact that the President's independent power to terminate treaties is today well established, supported decisively by modern practice and accepted by the Congress and most scholars, Senator Goldwater now seeks to challenge it. Because the President has occasionally, especially in the nineteenth century, terminated a treaty with prior or subsequent Senate or congressional participation, he argues that the President must always obtain legislative approval except "that history indicates the President may, if Congress raised no objection, determine whether or not a treaty (1) has been superseded by a later law or treaty inconsistent with or clearly intended to revise an earlier one, (2) has already been abrogated because of its violation by the other party, or (3) cannot be carried out because conditions essential to its continued effectiveness no longer exist and the change is not the result of our own action." He thus seeks to dismiss the many instances of independent Presidential treaty termination as "exceptions" to the supposed general rule requiring legislative approval.

Senator Goldwater's analysis is seriously flawed, however. When carefully examined, the instances of independent Presidential termination do not fall into the three categories of so-called "exceptions" that he suggests. Rather, they demonstrate that the President has been free to terminate treaties in a variety of situations in which the common denominator is that in each case it was no longer wise for the United States to adhere to the treaty in question. Indeed, contrary to Senator Goldwater's assertion, most instances of independent Presidential termination have occurred in circumstances in which there was no inconsistent law or treaty superseding the treaty in question, in which there was no violation by the other party and in which there was no impossibility of performing treaty obligations....

The treaty power is not the only one in which the Constitution requires the approval of the Senate before the President takes certain action but does not require similar approval when he undoes the action. For example, the Senate's consent is necessary for the reappointment of Cabinet officers, but not for their removal.

In seeking to bolster his position, Senator Goldwater relies on a quotation from Thomas Jefferson and another from James Madison—uttered before the nation had any experience with treaty termination—to the effect that legislative consent is legally required. Yet, in the same discussion Jefferson conceded that there were disagreements about the treaty power, and in 1815 Madison became the first President to terminate a treaty without legislative consent. Subsequent Presidential practice—until now unchallenged by Senator Goldwater and other Members of Congress—has plainly repudiated the early view of Jefferson and Madison and confirmed that of Hamilton and the later Madison.

Nor is there substance to Goldwater's general argument that, apart from the many "exceptions," when the President terminates a treaty without legislative consent he violates his constitutional duty to "take care that the laws be faithfully executed," because the Constitution makes a treaty "the supreme law of the land." This misses the point of the very case at issue. Article 10 of the treaty in question provided for its termination. In giving notice of an intent to terminate the treaty pursuant to that provision, the President was not violating the treaty but acting according to its terms — terms that were approved by the Senate when it consented to the treaty....

This suggests the proper course for senators who are troubled by the President's independent authority to terminate a particular treaty or category of treaties. At the time that each such treaty is made and submitted for their advice and consent, they should seek to condition Senate approval upon acceptance of the Senate's participation in its termination.

"Normal Relations with China: Good Law, Good Policy," *Policy Review* 7 (1979), 125–32.

Goldwater v. Carter
481 F. Supp. 949, 617 F. 2d 697, 444 U.S. 996 (1979)

Unable to win their argument in the Senate, Senator Goldwater and other members of the Senate and the House went to court and asked for declaratory and injunctive relief against the abrogation notice. The district court found that they had standing to sue the president and that the issue they raised was justiciable. Judge Oliver Gasch then ruled that the president's abrogation of the treaty was unconstitutional.

... The prime question confronting the Court in this case is what governmental action is required by the Constitution to terminate the 1954 Mutual Defense Treaty with Taiwan. Because that treaty contains a termination clause stating that notice of termination may be given by either party, the narrower issue becomes whether the President of the United States is a "party" for purposes of this clause and thus able to take unilateral action with respect to the notice of termination.

Unlike its careful allocation of the power to enter into treaties, the Constitution contains no specific reference to the manner in which treaties are to be terminated. Nor is there any definitive evidence of the intentions of the Framers. No court has ever addressed the precise issue here presented of the President's authority to effect termination of a validly binding treaty, let alone a mutual defense treaty, without legislative participation. A wide range of legal opinion has been presented by scholars and commentators who are unable to agree concerning which branch of the federal government has authority to represent the United States in treaty terminations.[8]

Since the first treaty to which the United States was a party was terminated in 1798 by an act of Congress, a variety of means have been used to terminate treaties: by statute directing the President to deliver notice of termination; by the President acting pursuant to a joint resolution of Congress or otherwise acting with the concurrence of both houses of Congress; by the President acting

---

8. See, e. g., L. Henkin, *Foreign Affairs and the Constitution* 167–71 (1972); Scheffer, "The Law of Treaty Termination as Applied to United States De-recognition of the Republic of China," 19 *Harv. Int'l L.J.* 931 (1978); Nelson, "The Termination of Treaties and Executive Agreements by the United States: Theory and Practice," 42 *Minn.L.Rev.* 879 (1958); Riesenfeld, "The Power of Congress and the President in International Relations: Three Recent Supreme Court Decisions," 25 *Calif.L.Rev.* 643, 658–664 (1937); M. Reisman & M. McDougal, "Who Can Terminate Mutual Defense Treaties?," *The National Law Journal*, May 21, 1979, at 19. See generally *Resolution Concerning Mutual Defense Treaties: Hearings on S. Res. 15 Before the Committee on Foreign Relations*, 96th Cong., 1st Sess. (1979).

with senatorial consent; and by the President acting alone. The final method of termination is of particular relevance here, but the precedents involving unilateral executive action are of only marginal utility. None of these examples involves a mutual defense treaty, nor any treaty whose national and international significance approaches that of the 1954 Mutual Defense Treaty.[9] Virtually all of them, moreover, can be readily distinguished on the basis of some triggering factor not present here.[10]

The great majority of the historical precedents involve some form of mutual action, whereby the President's notice of termination receives the affirmative approval of the Senate or the entire Congress. Taken as a whole, the historical precedents support rather than detract from the position that the power to terminate treaties is a power shared by the political branches of this government.

Defendants' argument that the President has authority to terminate unilaterally the Mutual Defense Treaty is premised on the executive power over foreign affairs. This authority derives from the enumerated Article II powers, including those that authorize the President to make treaties with the advice and consent of the Senate and to receive representatives of foreign nations.

Because the President has been termed "the sole organ of the federal government in the field of international relations," defendants argue that construing the Constitution to require that the Senate or the Congress also has a right to participate in treaty termination would be inconsistent with the President's constitutional authority over foreign affairs. They further urge that the Senate's role of advising and consenting in the making of treaties is not an independent source of legislative power, but only a limitation upon the treaty-making power of the President. Such limitations, they conclude, must be strictly construed and not extended by implication. (See *Myers v. United States*, 272 U.S. 52, 164 [1926].)

An attempt to justify a unilateral presidential power to terminate treaties by analogy to the Supreme Court's treatment of the removal power in *Myers* is unpersuasive. The power to remove executive personnel cannot be compared with the power to terminate an important international treaty. The removal power is restricted in its exercise to "purely executive officers" charged with a duty unrelated to the legislative or judicial power. It concerns the President's administrative control over his subordinates and flows from the President's obligations to see that the laws are faithfully executed. By contrast, treaty termination impacts upon the substantial role of Congress in foreign affairs — especially in the context of a mutual defense pact involving the potential exercise of congressional war powers — and is a contradiction rather than a corollary of the Executive's enforcement obligation. The same separation of powers principles that dictate presidential independence and control within the executive establishment pre-

---

9. Most of the terminations by the President alone involved commercial situations where the need for the treaty, or the efficacy of it, was no longer apparent.

10. Unilateral executive action in terminating a treaty would presumably be permissible, as both parties recognize, when the treaty is superseded by an inconsistent law or treaty; when the treaty becomes impossible to perform or is otherwise rendered inoperative; when the treaty is violated or denounced by the other party; or when there has been a fundamental change in circumstances affecting the treaty. In such cases, the President may determine that the continuing validity of the treaty has been destroyed, either because under principles of international law the United States could justifiably withdraw from the treaty or because the treaty is in conflict with more recent legislation....

clude the President from exerting an overriding influence in the sphere of constitutional powers that is shared with the legislative branch. A power to terminate treaties that are made "by and with the Advice and Consent of the Senate" simply does not fall within the limited scope of the *Myers* rationale.

Nor, for reasons more fully set forth below, can the President's status as the nation's spokesman and representative in foreign affairs serve as the basis for exclusive executive power over the entire process of treaty termination. While the President may be the sole organ of communication with foreign governments, he is clearly not the sole maker of foreign policy. In short, the conduct of foreign relations is not a plenary executive power.

Defendants also suggest that the recognition power of the President is directly implicated in the present situation because termination of the 1954 Mutual Defense Treaty was generally viewed as a prerequisite to normalization of relations between the United States and the People's Republic of China. As a result, defendants urge that the President's notice of termination is supported by his exclusive "[p]ower to remove ... obstacles to ... recognition," a power that has been acknowledged by the Supreme Court. [*United States v. Pink, United States v. Belmont*; see next section of this chapter.]

Defendants' argument lacks merit. The power to terminate a Mutual Defense Treaty cannot similarly be described as a "modest implied power of the President." A holding that the recognition power incidentally confers the power to make an executive agreement settling property claims and that such agreement has supremacy over conflicting state law does not justify an incidental power to terminate treaties without congressional approval. The argument that any executive action becomes constitutional if it is ancillary to an act of recognition is without merit. If limitations imposed by other constitutional provisions exist, the recognition power cannot be used as a "bootstrap" to support the President's unilateral action in terminating the Mutual Defense Treaty with Taiwan.

The termination of a treaty is not a single act entrusted by the Constitution to one or the other of our political branches. Like treaty formation, treaty termination is comprised of a series of acts that seek to maintain a constitutional balance. Initially, a policy determination must be made concerning whether the treaty should be terminated and the appropriate negotiations to effect termination undertaken. Such actions are clearly within the competency of the executive branch. Similarly, the communication of the message terminating a treaty, as here by delivery of formal notice to the other party pursuant to the terms of the agreement, is committed to the President as the sole representative of our country in foreign affairs.

But these purely executive functions are not the only elements involved in treaty termination. Termination of a treaty also involves a repeal of the "law of the land" established by the agreement. It is in this area that congressional participation is required under the present circumstances. The mere fact that the President has the authority to make an initial policy determination regarding the exercise of an option to terminate, and to notify the foreign state of termination, does not vest him with the unilateral power to complete the termination process and thereby effect the abrogation of the treaty. As two scholars have recently noted, "[i]t is inherently inconceivable that ... a constitutional policy requiring joint action for external agreement and internal legislation could allow that agreement and law to be terminated by the president alone, against the intentions of the legislature." ...

Article II, section three of the Constitution requires that the President "shall take care that the Laws be faithfully executed." This constitutional responsibility clearly extends to all laws of the land, including in this instance the Mutual Defense Treaty. The President cannot faithfully execute that treaty by abrogating it any more than he can faithfully execute by failing to administer. He alone cannot effect the repeal of a law of the land which was formed by joint action of the executive and legislative branches, whether that law be a statute or a treaty. The limits upon his authority are in no way altered by the inclusion of a termination provision in Article X of the Mutual Defense Treaty, allowing either party to terminate upon one year notice. The President's powers of administering the Treaty do not include the power to terminate in accordance with the provisions of Article X. The "party" to which the termination provision refers is the United States, not the President alone, and such termination can only be effectuated in accordance with United States constitutional processes.

The requirements imposed by the Supremacy Clause and the President's responsibility to faithfully execute the laws are further supported by the doctrine of separation of powers and its corollary concept of checks and balances, which lies at the heart of our constitutional system. In the treaty formation process, the Constitution expressly limits the Executive's role by requiring the advice and consent of two-thirds of the Senate. This constitutional requirement reflects the concern of the Founding Fathers that neither political branch possess unchecked power.

A judicial determination that the President enjoys unilateral authority to terminate treaties would raise the same fears and present the same possibility of abuse. It would be incompatible with our system of checks and balances if the executive power in the area of foreign affairs were construed to encompass a unilateral power to terminate treaties. It is undisputed that the President is without power to amend the terms of a treaty. Any such amendment must be submitted to the Senate for its advice and consent. If the lesser power to amend treaties is denied the President, a *fortiori*, the greater power to annul should also be denied. ...

The predominant United States' practice in terminating treaties, including those containing notice provisions, has involved mutual action by the executive and legislative branches. In most instances, the President's notice of termination has received the affirmative approval of either the Senate or the entire Congress. Although no one constitutional interpretation has been accepted, nor has a definitive procedure emerged, the weight of historical precedent clearly supports the view that some form of congressional concurrence is required. Support can be found for requiring either of two alternatives: 1) the approval of a majority of both houses of Congress, or 2) the consent of two-thirds of the Senate. The latter is of course the most analogous to the treaty-making power, while the former is based primarily on congressional authority to repeal a law of the land.

When faced with an apparent gap in the Constitutional allocation of powers, the Court must refer to the fundamental design of the entire document and determine how its purposes would be best served in the gap area. The Court believes that either of these two alternative procedures for congressional participation is a constitutionally sound means of terminating treaties. The important point is that treaty termination generally is a shared power, which cannot be exercised by the President acting alone. Neither the executive nor legislative branch has exclusive power to terminate treaties. At least under the circumstances of this case—involving a significant mutual defense treaty with a faithful ally, who has not violated the terms of the agreement, and the validity of which has not otherwise been destroyed—any decision of the United States to terminate that treaty, must be made with the advice and consent of the Senate or the approval of both houses of Congress. That decision cannot be made by the President alone....

The Court of Appeals for the District of Columbia Circuit agreed with Judge Gasch that the members of Congress had standing to sue the president and that the case did not involve a nonjusticiable "political question." However, the court of appeals disagreed with Judge Gasch on the merits.

We turn first to the argument, embraced by the District Court [which] is that, since the President clearly cannot enter into a treaty without the consent of the Senate, the inference is inescapable that he must in all circumstances seek the same senatorial consent to terminate that treaty....

Expansion of the language of the Constitution by sequential linguistic projection is a tricky business at best. Virtually all constitutional principles have unique elements and can be distinguished from one another. As the Supreme Court has recognized with respect to the clause in question, it is not abstract logic or sterile symmetry that controls, but a sensible and realistic ascertainment of the meaning of the Constitution in the context of the specific action taken.

The District Court's declaration, in the alternative, that the necessary authority in this instance may be granted by a majority of each house of Congress presumably has its source in the Supremacy Clause of Article VI. The argument is that a treaty, being a part of the "supreme Law of the Land," can only be terminated at the least by a subsequent federal statute.

The central purpose of the Supremacy Clause has been accepted to be that of causing each of the designated supreme laws—Constitution, statute, and treaty—to prevail, for purposes of domestic law, over state law in any form. Article VI speaks explicitly to the judges to assure that this is so. But these three types of supreme law are not necessarily the same in their other characteristics, any more than are the circumstances and terms of their creation the same. Certainly the Constitution is silent on the matter of treaty termination. And the fact that it speaks to the common characteristic of supremacy over state law does not provide any basis for concluding that a treaty must be unmade either by (1) the same process by which it was made, or (2) the alternative means by which a statute is made or terminated.

The constitutional institution of advice and consent of the Senate, provided two-thirds of the Senators concur, is a special and extraordinary condition of the exercise by the President of certain specified powers under Article II. It is not lightly to be extended in instances not set forth in the Constitution. Such an extension by implication is not proper unless that implication is unmistakably clear.

The District Court's absolutist extension of this limitation to termination of treaties, irrespective of the particular circumstances involved, is not sound. The making of a treaty has the consequences of an entangling alliance for the nation.

Similarly, the amending of a treaty merely continues such entangling alliances, changing only their character, and therefore also requires the advice and consent of the Senate. It does not follow, however, that a constitutional provision for a special concurrence (two-thirds of the Senators) prior to entry into an entangling alliance necessarily applies to its termination in accordance with its terms.

The Constitution specifically confers no power of treaty termination on either the Congress or the Executive. We note, however, that the powers conferred upon Congress in Article I of the Constitution are specific, detailed, and limited, while the powers conferred upon the President by Article II are generalized in a manner that bespeaks no such limitation upon foreign affairs powers.[11] ...

... In general, the powers of the federal government arise out of specific grants of authority delegated by the states — hence the enumerated powers of Congress in Article I, Section 8. The foreign affairs powers, however, proceed directly from the sovereignty of the Union. "[I]f they had never been mentioned in the Constitution, [they] would have vested in the federal government as necessary concomitants of nationality." [*United States v. Curtiss-Wright Export Corp.*]

The President is the constitutional representative of the United States with respect to external affairs. It is significant that the treaty power appears in Article II of the Constitution, relating to the executive branch, and not in Article I, setting forth the powers of the legislative branch. It is the President as Chief Executive who is given the constitutional authority to enter into a treaty; and even after he has obtained the consent of the Senate it is for him to decide whether to ratify a treaty and put it into effect. Senatorial confirmation of a treaty concededly does not obligate the President to go forward with a treaty if he concludes that it is not in the public interest to do so.

Thus, in contrast to the lawmaking power, the constitutional initiative in the treaty-making field is in the President, not Congress. It would take an unprecedented feat of judicial construction to read into the Constitution an absolute condition precedent of congressional or Senate approval for termination of all treaties, similar to the specific one relating to initial approval. And it would unalterably affect the balance of power between the two Branches laid down in Articles I and II....

The recognized powers of Congress to implement (or fail to implement) a treaty by an appropriation or other law essential to its effectuation, or to supersede for all practical purposes the effect of a treaty on domestic law, are legislative powers, not treaty-making or treaty termination powers. The issue here, however, is not Congress' legislative powers to supersede or affect the domestic impact of a treaty; the issue is whether the Senate (or Congress) must in this case give its prior consent to discontinue a treaty which the President thinks it desirable to terminate in the national interest and pursuant to a provision in the treaty itself. The existence, in practical terms, of one power does not imply the existence, in constitutional terms, of the other.

If we were to hold that under the Constitution a treaty could only be terminated by exactly the same process by which it was made, we would be locking the United States into all of its international obligations, even if the President and

---

11. Contrastingly, Article I, Section 1, provides: "All legislative Powers *herein granted* shall be vested in a Congress of the United States ..." [emphasis supplied].

two-thirds of the Senate minus one firmly believed that the proper course for the United States was to terminate a treaty. Many of our treaties in force, such as mutual defense treaties, carry potentially dangerous obligations. These obligations are terminable under international law upon breach by the other party or change in circumstances that frustrates the purpose of the treaty. In many of these situations the President must take immediate action. The creation of a constitutionally obligatory role in all cases for a two-thirds consent by the Senate would give to one-third plus one of the Senate the power to deny the President the authority necessary to conduct our foreign policy in a rational and effective manner....

The District Court concluded that the diversity of historical precedents left an inconclusive basis on which to decide the issue of whether the President's power to terminate a treaty must always be "shared" in some way by the Senate or Congress. We agree. Yet we think it is not without significance that out of all the historical precedents brought to our attention, in no situation has a treaty been continued in force over the opposition of the President.

There is on the other hand widespread agreement that the President has the power as Chief Executive under many circumstances to exercise functions regarding treaties which have the effect of either terminating or continuing their vitality.[12] Prominent among these is the authority of the President as Chief Executive (1) to determine whether a treaty has terminated because of a breach, *Charlton v. Kelly*, 229 U.S. 447, 473–476 (1913); and (2) to determine whether a treaty is at an end due to changed circumstances.

How the vital functions of the President in implementing treaties and in deciding on their viability in response to changing events can or should interact with Congress' legitimate concerns and powers in relating to foreign affairs is

---

12. The Senate Committee on Foreign Relations, after careful consideration of the matter, came to the conclusion that there were 14 different bases on which the President could terminate a treaty in the course of his executive function. The grounds identified are the following:

(1) in conformity with the provisions of the treaty;

(2) by consent of all the parties after consultation with the other contracting states;

(3) where it is established that the parties intended to admit the possibility of denunciation or withdrawal;

(4) where a right of denunciation or withdrawal may be implied by the nature of the treaty;

(5) where it appears from a later treaty to the same subject matter that the matter should be governed by that treaty;

(6) where the provisions of the later treaty are so far incompatible with those of the earlier one that the two treaties are not capable of being applied at the same time;

(7) where there has been a material breach by another party;

(8) where the treaty has become impossible to perform;

(9) where there has been a fundamental change of circumstances;

(10) where there has been a severance of diplomatic or consular relations and such relations are indispensable for the application of the treaty;

(11) where a new peremptory norm in international law emerges which is in conflict with the treaty;

(12) where an error was made regarding a fact or situation which was assumed by that state to exist at the time when the treaty was concluded and formed an essential basis of its consent to be bound;

(13) where a state has been induced to conclude a treaty by the fraudulent conduct of another state; and

(14) where a state's consent to be bound has been procured by the corruption or coercion of its representatives by the threat or use of force.

an area into which we should not and do not prematurely intrude. History shows us that there are too many variables to lay down any hard and fast constitutional rules.

We cannot find an implied role in the Constitution for the Senate in treaty termination for some but not all treaties in terms of their relative importance. There is no judicially ascertainable and manageable method of making any distinction among treaties on the basis of their substance, the magnitude of the risk involved, the degree of controversy which their termination would engender, or by any other standards. We know of no standards to apply in making such distinctions. The facts on which such distinctions might be drawn may be difficult of ascertainment; and the resolution of such inevitable disputes between the two Branches would be an improper and unnecessary role for the courts. To decide whether there was a breach or changed circumstances, for example, would involve a court in making fundamental decisions of foreign policy and would create insuperable problems of evidentiary proof. This is beyond the acceptable judicial role. All we decide today is that two-thirds Senate consent or majority consent in both houses is not necessary to terminate this treaty in the circumstances before us now.…

[Judge MACKINNON dissented on the merits and presented an extensive historical review of past exercises of the power to terminate treaties.]

The Supreme Court, without hearing argument, ordered that the complaint be dismissed. However, the justices could not agree why the suit was not appropriate for judicial resolution. Justice Marshall concurred in the result, without opinion. Justice Powell thought that the case was not ripe. Justices Rehnquist, Burger, Stewart, and Stevens took the position that the case was "political," and therefore not justiciable. Only Justice Brennan reached the merits, and he took the view that "abrogation of the defense treaty with Taiwan was a necessary incident to Executive recognition of the Peking government.…"

Notes and Questions

1. *Criteria of analysis.* What are the appropriate criteria for resolving this question of authority? The intent of the framers? If so, which framers? Past executive practice? Can past practice place a "gloss" upon the Constitution, as Justice Frankfurter contended in *Youngstown*, citing the rationale of *Midwest Oil* (see Chapter 2)? Was Judge Gasch correct to reason by extension? Does it follow that the means for abrogating treaties should be the same as those for making or implementing them? In all cases? Is that practical? Are the procedures for entering the Union the same as for leaving it? Can a state withdraw its assent to a constitutional amendment in the same way that it assented? Must the Senate consent to the firing of an executive official whose appointment it approved?

2. *Treaty-making powers.* Does the power to make treaties belong exclusively to the president, subject only to the advice and consent of the Senate? Or is it a joint power, permitting the Senate to influence the negotiations and to put conditions on its provisions as the price for its consent? As a matter of international law, who actually ratifies a treaty—the last step in making it law? In the *Prize Cases* (see Chapter 4), the Supreme Court held that the president had the constitutional authority to recognize that a state of war existed and to respond accordingly without waiting for Congress to

act. Should he not have comparable authority, at least in some instances, to recognize when a treaty has been violated by another party or no longer serves American interests? If so, should he be able to abrogate the treaty with finality, or simply suspend American adherence until the Senate or Congress formally consents to its renunciation? How does the appeals court justify its answer? Are its grounds practical rather than constitutional, or are they both?

3. *Democratic values.* Is democratic theory relevant to the resolution of this issue? Is it democratic to allow one-third plus one of the senators to veto the renunciation of a treaty? Is that not the kind of factional power that Madison claimed (in *The Federalist* No. 51) that the Constitution was designed to avoid? Is it democratic to leave the power of abrogation wholly in the hands of the president? Is there anything in the Constitution that suggests an intent, where treaties are concerned, to invest the president with an exclusive prerogative? What does the court of appeals mean when it refers to the "sterile" reasoning of the district court? Which court do you think is more sterile in its reasoning?

4. *Some comparisons.* Compare the reasoning used by the two courts with the Pacificus-Helvidius debates (in Chapter 2). Have the positions changed much? Compare the reasoning of the appeals court in *Goldwater* with Justice Jackson's concurring opinion in *Youngstown* (Chapter 2). How does the "zenith" of authority referred to by Judge Gasch differ from Jackson's three criteria? Is the court of appeals willing to permit the president to exercise authority that Congress might not grant him, and might even deny him, by legislation?

5. *Political questions.* When the case reached the Supreme Court, Justice Rehnquist, joined by Justices Burger, Stewart, and Stevens, argued that the dispute was "political" because "it involves the authority of the president in the conduct of our foreign relations." That argument did not attract a majority, and thus has no precedential value, but does it persuade you? Rehnquist claimed that the controversy "should be left for resolution by the Executive and Legislative branches" because the Constitution "is silent as to [the Senate's] participation in the abrogation of a Treaty." Should the courts refuse to decide cases whenever the solution is not dictated by the plain language of the relevant laws? Finally, Rehnquist argued that the question "must surely be controlled by political standards" because this was "a dispute between coequal branches of our government, each of which has resources available to protect and assert its interests. . . ." If so, should the Court have decided *Youngstown* (the steel seizure case) or *United States v. Nixon* (the Watergate tapes case)? Should the courts refuse to adjudicate cases simply because a minority of either house can prevent that house from asserting its institutional interests? Suppose that the treaty had created legal rights in a powerful corporation? Would abrogation still be a "political question"? The Justice Department argued that self-executing treaties involving external relations and not creating private rights should be treated as "political" and not as the "law of the land." Do you agree?

6. *Resolution of the issue.* Did the Supreme Court affirm the decision of either lower court? If not, what was the practical effect of its ruling? What is the appropriate way to resolve this issue? By judicial interpretation, as the lower courts attempted? By judicial abstention, as the Supreme Court did? By constitutional amendment? By inserting provisions for abrogation in every treaty to which the Senate consents? Could the Senate condition its consent to a treaty on the requirement that the president obtain Senate or congressional consent when he decides that a treaty should be terminated? If so, may the House incorporate a similar condition in any implementing legislation it votes to enact? How might the two situations differ?

7. *Are treaties "self-executing"*? Article VI, para. 2, of the Constitution says that "all Treaties made ... under the Authority of the United States, shall be the supreme Law of the Land." But do they become law following the Senate's consent and the president's ratification, or do they become law only if Congress passes implementing legislation? According to Prof. John Yoo, who wrote pro-torture memoranda for the administration of President George W. Bush when he served in the Justice Department, there should be a presumption against judicial enforcement of any treaty unless Congress, in separate legislation, clearly provides otherwise. *The Powers of War and Peace: The Constitution and Foreign Affairs After 9/11* (2005), ch. 7. Do you agree? Would such a presumption be consistent with Article VI of the Constitution? At the Convention of 1787, the framers voted unanimously to omit treaty enforcement from Congress' powers, "as being superfluous since treaties were to be laws." Farrand, *The Records of the Federal Convention of 1787*, vol. 2, 389–90. Is this evidence of framers' intent dispositive?

8. *Presidential powers of interpretation.* Yoo also argues that the president, as the chief organ of government in foreign affairs, has exclusive constitutional authority to interpret, reinterpret, and terminate treaties and, for example, declare the Geneva Conventions inapplicable to al Qaeda and Taliban captives. Memorandum to William J. Haynes, General Counsel, Department of Defense, Re: Application of Treaties and Laws to al Qaeda and Taliban Detainees, in *The Torture Papers* (Greenburg and Dratel, eds., 2005), 38. Were the president to have that power, would treaties be "law," or would they be more like international political promises, breakable at will by the current occupant of the White House? See, generally, Carlos Manuel Vazquez, "Laughing at Treaties," 99 *Colum. L. Rev.* 2145 (1999). In *Hamdan v. Rumsfeld*, 548 U.S. 557 (2006) the Supreme Court rejected the political promise theory of treaties, holding, without comment, that the Geneva Conventions are law, binding on Presidents.

9. *Delegating an exclusive power to interpret treaties to the President.* May Congress, by legislation, delegate to the President exclusive authority to interpret the meaning of a human rights treaty, thereby stripping courts of the authority to say what a war crime is in a given case? Congress purported to do this in the Military Commissions Act passed in September 2006. Rather than abrogate Common Article 3 of the Geneva Conventions, as some Bush administration officials advocated, Congress delegated to the President exclusive authority to decide what that article means when it bans the "cruel, inhuman, and degrading treatment" of prisoners. May Congress delegate to the President exclusive authority to say what is, or is not, a crime under American law?

E. Executive Agreements

United States v. Belmont

301 U.S. 324 (1937)

Outraged at the triumph of totalitarian communism in Russia, the United States waited until 1933 to recognize the Soviet government. As part of the recognition agreements, the Soviet government agreed not to sue American banks for funds deposited by Russian companies prior to the Russian Revolution. Instead, the Soviet government assigned its claims to those funds, obtained through uncompensated expropriations, to the United States government, which then sought to recover them from American bankers. The executors of one of those bankers, August Belmont II, resisted on the ground that it was against the public policy of the State of New York, where the funds of the Petrograd Metal Works had been deposited with Belmont, to recognize the legality of a foreign act of expropriation. Had the expropriation and assignments been recognized by a treaty, there would have been no doubt about the validity of the U.S. government's claim to the deposits. But here the assignment was accomplished by an exchange of diplomatic correspondence with Maxim Litvinov, the Soviet foreign minister, to which the Senate had not given its consent.

MR. JUSTICE SUTHERLAND delivered the opinion of the Court....

We take judicial notice of the fact that coincident with the assignment set forth in the complaint, the President recognized the Soviet Government, and normal diplomatic relations were established between that government and the Government of the United States, followed by an exchange of ambassadors. The effect of this was to validate, so far as this country is concerned, all acts of the Soviet Government here involved from the commencement of its existence. The recognition, establishment of diplomatic relations, the assignment, and agreements with respect thereto, were all parts of one transaction resulting in an international compact between the two governments. That the negotiations, acceptance of the assignment and agreements and understandings in respect thereof were within the competence of the President may not be doubted. Governmental power over internal affairs is distributed between the national government and the several states. Governmental power over external affairs is not distributed, but is vested exclusively in the national government. And in respect of what was done here, the Executive had authority to speak as the sole organ of that government. The assignment and the agreements in connection therewith did not, as in the case of treaties, as that term is used in the treaty making clause of the Constitution (Art. II, Sec. 2), require the advice and consent of the Senate.

A treaty signifies "a compact made between two or more independent nations with a view to the public welfare."... But an international compact, as this was, is not always a treaty which requires the participation of the Senate. There are many such compacts, of which a protocol, a modus vivendi, a postal convention, and agreements like that now under consideration are illustrations. See 5 Moore, *Int'l. Law Digest*, 210–221.

Plainly, the external powers of the United States are to be exercised without regard to state laws or policies. And while the supremacy of a treaty in this respect is established by the express language of cl. 2, Art. VI, of the Constitution, the same rule would result in the case of all international compacts and agreements from the very fact that complete power over international affairs is in the national government and is not and cannot be subject to any curtailment or interference on the part of the several states. [*United States v. Curtiss-Wright Export Corp.*] ... In respect of all international negotiations and compacts, and in respect of our foreign relations generally, state lines disappear. As to such purposes the State of New York does not exist....

The public policy of the United States relied upon as a bar to the action is that declared by the Constitution, namely, that private property shall not be taken without just compensation. But the answer is that our Constitution, laws and policies have no extraterritorial operation, unless in respect of our own citizens.... What another country has done in the way of taking over property of its nationals, and especially of its corporations, is not a matter for judicial consideration here. Such nationals must look to their own government for any redress to which they may be entitled. So far as the record shows, only the rights of the Russian corporation have been affected by what has been done; and it will be time enough to consider the rights of our nationals when, if ever, by proper judicial proceeding, it shall be made to appear that they are so affected as to entitle them to judicial relief. The substantive right to the moneys, as now disclosed, became vested in the Soviet Government as the successor to the corporation; and this right that government has passed to the United States. It does not appear that respondents have any interest in the matter beyond that of a custodian. Thus ... no question under the Fifth Amendment is involved....

Notes and Questions

1. *A "modest power"?* In *United States v. Pink*, 315 U.S. 203 (1942), the United States went into a New York court to recover the assets of a nationalized Russian insurance company, arguing that its claim should prevail over the claims of foreign creditors because the Litvinov Assignment was supreme over state policy. The state courts rejected the argument but the Supreme Court reversed in an opinion by Justice Douglas.

> If the priority [over the claims of foreign creditors] had been accorded American claims by treaty with Russia, there would be no doubt as to its validity.... The same result obtains here. The powers of the President in the conduct of foreign relations included the power, without consent of the Senate, to determine the public policy of the United States with respect to the Russian nationalization decrees.... Power to remove such obstacles to full recognition as settlement of claims of our nationals ... certainly is a modest implied power of the President who is the "sole organ of the federal government in the field of international relations." [*United States v. Curtiss-Wright Corp.*] Effectiveness in handling the delicate problems of foreign relations requires no less. Unless such a power exists, the power of recognition might be thwarted or seriously diluted. No such obstacle can be placed in the way of rehabilitation of relations between this country and another nation, unless the historic conception of the powers and responsibilities of the President in the conduct of foreign affairs.... is to be drastically revised. It was the judgment of the political department that full recognition of the Soviet Government required the settlement of all outstanding problems including the claims of our nationals. Recognition and the Litvinov Assignment were interdependent. We would usurp the executive function if we held that that decision was not final and conclusive in the courts.
>
> "All constitutional acts of power, whether in the executive or in the judicial department, have as much legal validity and obligation as if they proceeded from the legislature...." *The Federalist*, No. 64. A treaty is a "Law of the Land" under the supremacy clause (Art. VI, Para. 2) of the Constitution. Such international compacts and agreements as the Litvinov Assignment have a similar dignity. [*United States v. Belmont.*]

Is the power claimed in *Belmont* and *Pink* a "modest power?" When President Carter unilaterally abrogated the Mutual Defense Treaty with Taiwan in order to clear away an "obstacle" to the recognition of mainland China, was he exercising a "modest power"? Suppose that under the Litvinov agreements the president had not obtained priority for American claims to the assets, but had traded away those American claims as a price of recognition. Would such an action run afoul of the Fifth Amendment's due process and just compensation clauses? Or would the United States have to pay those claims out of its treasury? Could such payments be made without authorizing legislation? Suppose that Congress refused to enact such legislation?

2. *Scope of the rulings.* Is the authority for the kind of executive agreement upheld in *Belmont* and *Pink* to be derived only from the president's "specific and exclusive" powers (e.g., his powers of recognition and as commander in chief), or may it be derived from the "executive power" referred to in the opening sentence of Article II? See Henkin, *Foreign Affairs and the Constitution* (1972), 178–79.

3. *Sources of authority.* Do *Belmont* and *Pink,* particularly when read in light of *Curtiss-Wright,* support a broad and independent presidential authority to enter into executive agreements, or is it important to distinguish among the sources of presidential authority, much as Justice Jackson did in *Youngstown*? Most executive orders, including those cited in *Carter, Belmont,* and *Pink,* fall into Jackson's first category: power to make them was delegated to the president by legislation. In which of Jackson's categories should the Litvinov Assignment be placed? If power to negotiate it is derived from the power of recognition only, does Congress possess any authority to interfere with the power's exercise? Could Congress enact guidelines for the making of executive agreements pursuant to its powers under the Necessary and Proper Clause?

4. *Executive agreements versus prior congressional legislation.* The *Belmont* and *Pink* decisions upheld an executive agreement against prior state law. May an executive agreement effectively "repeal" or nullify prior congressional legislation? In *United States v. Capps,* 204 F. 2d 655 (4th Cir. 1953), a court of appeals ruled that an agreement with Canada regulating the importation of potatoes was invalid because it conflicted with a prior act of Congress passed pursuant to its power to regulate foreign commerce *(aff'd on other grounds,* 348 U.S. 296 [1955]). The Court of Appeals held: "while the President has certain inherent powers under the Constitution such as the power pertaining to his position as Commander in Chief … and the power necessary to see that the laws are faithfully executed, the power to regulate interstate and foreign commerce is not among the powers incident to the Presidential office, but is expressly vested by the Constitution in Congress" [204 F. 2d 659]. Does it follow that because certain powers are expressly granted to Congress by Article I that concurrent authority is implicitly denied to the president by Article II, even though Congress has not yet spoken and the matter is of grave international significance?

5. *Roosevelt's "destroyers for bases" agreement.* In September 1940, President Roosevelt announced conclusion of an executive agreement with Great Britain by which he turned over fifty U.S. destroyers in return for the right to use certain British naval bases in the Caribbean. Roosevelt did not submit the agreement to either the Senate or the Congress for approval. His attorney general, Robert H. Jackson, argued that the president had authority as commander in chief to alienate U.S. title to the ships and had authority under the foreign affairs power to obtain use of the bases. Since the exchange did not require the appropriation of any money or formally commit the United States to any specific course of action, Jackson argued, congressional or senatorial consent was not required (39 Ops. Atty. Gen. 484 [1940]). Do you agree? Where does the president get the authority to trade away U.S. military property? Would the attorney general have been on stronger ground if he had simply asserted a presidential power to lend the ships to Great Britain, rather than a power to alienate title to them utterly?

6. *Conditional consent.* After he had won reelection in November 1940, President Roosevelt submitted the policy of aid to Great Britain—a policy that risked immedi-

The "over-aged" destroyers transferred to Great Britain by President Roosevelt before U.S. entry into World War II were slow and unwieldy, and emitted black smoke that could be seen for miles. But they were still U.S. government property, which the president did not really lend, but transferred outright by an executive agreement.

ate war with Nazi Germany—to full congressional approval. In March 1941, Congress enacted a lend-lease bill, thereby ratifying the president's policy. In light of this ratification, should lend-lease be seen as an example of what Justice Jackson would later call a "Category 2" exercise of power? Attached to the Lend-Lease Act (and to the First War Powers Act, the Emergency Price Control Act, the Stabilization Act, and the War Labor Disputes Act) was a provision that Congress could repeal the measure and reclaim its powers by the passage of a concurrent resolution, which, unlike a joint resolution, could not be vetoed by the president. Roosevelt signed the bills, but attacked the provisos as unconstitutional. Do you agree? (See *Immigration and Naturalization Service v. Chadha*, 462 U.S. 919 [1983][the legislative veto case]). Which is a more "democratic" method of congressional consent: a concurrent resolution, or a joint resolution which must be passed by a two-thirds vote of both houses if it is to surmount a presidential veto?

7. *An historian's justification.* Consider the following analysis of the destroyer deal by historian Arthur Schlesinger, Jr.:

> When Roosevelt announced the destroyer deal, he said, "Preparation for defense is an inalienable prerogative of a sovereign state. Under present circumstances this exercise of sovereign right is essential to the maintenance of our peace and safety."... Professor Edward S. Corwin ... called the deal "an endorsement of unrestrained autocracy in the field of our foreign relations," adding that "no such dangerous opinion was ever before penned by an Attorney General of the United States." But was Corwin right?...
>
> The destroyer deal was compelled by a threat to the nation surpassed only by the emergency which led Lincoln to take his actions after Sumter. In working it out, Roosevelt paid due respect to the written checks of the Constitution and displayed an unusual concern for the unwritten checks on presidential initiative. Though the transaction was unilateral in form, it was accompanied by extensive and vigilant consultation—within the executive branch, between the executive and legislative branches, among leaders of both parties and with the press. To have tried to get destroyers to Britain by the treaty route was an alternative only for those who did not want Britain to get destroyers at all. Congress soon gave the

deal its implicit sanction. The public reception, despite dissonant notes, was predominantly favorable.... In retrospect, this seems less a flagrant exercise in presidential usurpation than a rather circumspect application of the Locke-Jefferson-Lincoln doctrine. (*The Imperial Presidency* [1973], 108–9.)

Do you agree? Does Schlesinger offer a political or a legal justification? Was supplying warships to a belligerent nation "circumspect," or did Roosevelt unilaterally expose the United States to the risk of attack by signing this non-treaty? Is there a Locke-Jefferson-Lincoln doctrine?

8. *The difference between executive agreements and treaties.* What is the difference between executive agreements and treaties? Section 3 of the Bricker Amendment sought to abolish the difference by making all agreements with foreign powers subject to congressional consent. Senator Walter George's substitute for the Bricker Amendment, which came within one vote of winning a two-thirds vote of the Senate, attempted to preserve the distinction by permitting treaties to be approved by the traditional vote of the Senate, but providing that "an international agreement other than a treaty shall become effective as internal law ... only by an act of the Congress." The amendment might well have passed had its proponents been able to explain which agreements would go to the Senate for a two-thirds vote and which would go to the full Congress for majority votes by both houses.

In response to the Bricker Amendment campaign, the State Department tried to distinguish between agreements and treaties. John B. Stevenson, legal adviser to the Department of State, summarized these guidelines for the Senate Subcommittee on Separation of Powers in 1972:

> With respect to the decision whether an agreement should be concluded as an executive agreement or as a treaty, the Department's guidelines provide as follows:
>
> Executive agreements should not be used when the subject matter should be covered by a treaty. The executive agreement form should be used only for agreements which fall into one or more of the following categories:
>
> (a) agreements which are made pursuant to or in accordance with existing legislation or a treaty; (b) agreements which are made subject to congressional approval or implementation; or (c) agreements which are made under and in accordance with the President's constitutional power.
>
> ... We have taken the view that the treaty form should be used in five circumstances—
>
> (a) when the subject matter has traditionally been dealt with by treaty; (b) when the subject matter is not wholly within the delegated powers of the Congress and not within the independent constitutional authority of the President; (c) when the agreement itself is to have the force of law without legislative action by the Congress, and the action contemplated is not within the President's independent constitutional authority; (d) when the agreement involves important commitments affecting the nation as a whole, such as our defense commitments; or (e) when it is decided to give utmost formality to the commitment. (*Congressional Oversight of Executive Agreements*, Hearings before the Subcommittee on Separation of Powers, Committee on the Judiciary, U.S. Senate, 92d Cong., 2d Sess. [1972], 250.)

Senator Clifford Case, speaking at the same hearings, offered an alternative set of distinctions:

The executive agreement should only be used if the matter under discussion with a foreign country is relatively unimportant. If the United States seeks to increase the size of its embassy in a particular country or arrange an exchange of scholars, there is no need for a treaty to be concluded. In fact, if treaties were used in those minor matters, the whole business of conducting the nation's foreign affairs would be hampered. . . .

There is no question that a mutual defense agreement with another country should be a treaty. I believe the Executive Branch would agree with me on this, although even here there seems to be some dispute. I am thinking of the so-called Thai contingency plan which may or may not have committed the United States to take certain actions to defend Thailand in the event of certain contingencies. While this issue was clouded by Executive secrecy, my view is that this contingency plan legally had no effect without the advice and consent of the Senate, but I am not sure the Thai ever understood this. As a practical matter, an executive agreement can take on a life of its own in the eyes of foreign countries, the American public, and even our own government officials.

Agreements closely related to our country's national security should also be treaties, and I shall list three types which have lately been dealt with, incorrectly I believe, as executive agreements. These are: (1) agreements providing for U.S. military bases abroad; (2) agreements revising or extending arrangements for these military bases; and (3) agreements providing for the storage of nuclear weapons overseas.

There are other important matters such as taxation, extradition, and consular relations which at times should be included in treaties, but my primary concern is with questions that touch on our national security, and my list should not be regarded as all inclusive.

The stationing of American troops abroad can lead to a commitment to the host country and ultimately to war. It is simply too important a question, from both a Constitutional and a practical standpoint, to be left to ratification by the stroke of a diplomat's pen.[13]

In *United States v. Capps* (see note 4, *supra*), the court of appeals suggested that executive agreements were, in effect, those international agreements that 1)were based on the president's specific powers as commander in chief and recognizer of foreign governments; 2) did not infringe on the enumerated powers of Congress; and 3) the president chose not to submit to the Senate for its consent. This view was expanded upon by the Nixon administration's Justice Department at the 1972 hearings when Ralph Erickson of the Office of Legal Counsel added to that familiar list of specific powers the more general "executive power" of the first sentence of Article II. Others have suggested that a treaty is supposed to express a continuing obligation undertaken between nations, whereas an executive agreement is only supposed to facilitate a particular arrangement during a limited time between governments.[14]

9. *The use of executive agreements.* In practice, none of these textbook distinctions have withstood the demands of political expediency. Between 1789 and 1939, more than 1,300 agreements were concluded with foreign countries without the consent of the Senate.[15] Be-

---

13. *Congressional Oversight of Executive Agreements,* 106.
14. Pious, *The American Presidency* (1979), 340.
15. Corwin, *The President: Office and Powers* (1957), 442, n. 123.

tween 1946 and 1971, the United States entered into 361 treaties and more than 5,559 executive agreements. Of the 4,359 agreements in force in 1972, the vast majority involved some collaboration with Congress, either through prior authorizations or subsequent approval or implementing legislation. Three percent of these agreements were negotiated and implemented without congressional participation.[16] About 400 of these involved major commitments and de facto alliances with other nations.[17] Executive agreements have dealt with grave issues of national importance. For example, the Rush-Bagot Agreement of 1817 disarmed the Great Lakes. The Root-Takahira and Lansing-Ishii agreements established American policy toward the Far East for decades, while the "Gentleman's Agreement" of 1907 limited Japanese immigration into the United States. In 1905, Theodore Roosevelt negotiated the Dillingham-Sanchez Protocol, which put the bankrupt customs houses of Santo Domingo under American supervision. Senate pressure forced Roosevelt to submit the protocol as a treaty, but when Senate Democrats attempted to block its consideration, Roosevelt declared that he would implement it until such time as the Senate gave its consent. McKinley contributed troops to protect Western legations in China from the Boxer Rebellion. In addition to the destroyers for bases agreement, Roosevelt made executive agreements with Churchill and Stalin that helped to reshape world politics after the Second World War. Truman followed suit. The agreements at Tehran, Potsdam, and Yalta led proponents of the Bricker Amendment to try, unsuccessfully, to bring executive agreements under the same procedure of legislative consent as treaties.

10. *National commitments.* In the 1950s, it was the conservative Republicans who feared that executive agreements would involve the United States in entangling alliances. In the late 1960s and early 1970s, it was the liberals and moderates of both parties who feared executive agreements and sought to reassert the principle of checks and balances. The first product of their labors was a "National Commitments" resolution sponsored by Senator J. William Fulbright (D-Ark.), and passed by the Senate in June 1969. It declared "the sense of the Senate" to be that the United States could not make a binding national commitment to use military force or financial resources on behalf of another country, either immediately or on the happening of certain events, unless the commitment was accomplished "by means of a treaty, statute, or concurrent resolution of both Houses of Congress specifically providing for such a commitment" (115 *Cong. Rec.* 17245 [1969]). The Nixon administration ignored the resolution since it lacked the force of law and in 1970 concluded a military base agreement with Spain that contained various security guarantees. The Senate countered with another resolution declaring that the agreement was not a national commitment, notwithstanding anything the executive branch might have told the Spanish government (S. Res. 469, 92d Cong., 1st Sess. [1971]).

The following year the Nixon administration exchanged notes with Portugal and Bahrain regarding American rights to use certain military bases and in those notes agreed to make payments and extend credits totaling more than $369 million to Portugal, and hundreds of thousands of dollars to Bahrain. The Senate tried to cut off funds for the facilities, but the House supported the administration, and the effort failed. The Senate then passed a resolution requiring the administration to submit the two agreements to the Senate as treaties, but Nixon refused (S. Res. 214, 92d Cong., 2nd Sess. [1972]). In hearings before Senator Sam J. Ervin's Subcommittee on Separation of Powers, J. Fred Buzhardt, general counsel to the Department of Defense, argued that Congress would infringe the

16. John B. Rehm, "Making Foreign Policy through International Agreement," in Wilcox and Franck, eds., *The Constitution and the Conduct of Foreign Policy* (1976), 127.
17. Raoul Berger, "The Presidential Monopoly of Foreign Relations," 71 *Mich. L. Rev.* 1, 34 (1972).

president's constitutional power to negotiate international agreements if it were to provide that any agreement which required subsequent congressional implementation be placed in the form of a treaty and submitted to the Senate for consent [*Congressional Oversight of Executive Agreements*, Hearings before the Subcommittee on Separation of Powers, Committee on the Judiciary, U.S. Senate, 92d Cong., 2d Sess. (1972), 342–45]. Ralph Erickson, representing the Justice Department, argued that Congress may not, by subsequent concurrent resolution, strip an executive order of its legally binding effect. He further argued that Congress lacked constitutional authority to legislate in advance as to which international agreements must be made by treaty and which may be made by executive agreement. The president's "independent powers" under the Executive Power, Commander in Chief, and Recognition Clauses, he argued, could not be curbed by Congress in exercising its powers under the Necessary and Proper Clause.

Reread the Necessary and Proper Clause (Article I, Section 8, Clause 18). Does it limit Congress' legislative powers to effectuating its own enumerated powers? Or may Congress legislate with regard to "all other powers" conferred by the Constitution, including powers granted by Article II? Where executive agreements are concerned, may Congress nullify them by concurrent resolutions (not requiring a presidential signature), or must they enact a joint resolution over the president's veto? Erickson conceded that Congress could refuse to appropriate implementing funds but denied that it could do anything in advance, or subsequently, that would "in any way interfere with the President's exercise of his independent powers as Commander in Chief or as Chief Executive." Thus, the only way in which Congress could disapprove a presidential promise of millions of dollars in aid to a foreign power would be to refuse to appropriate the money, by a bill subject to the president's veto. Do you agree?

The moderate and liberal opponents of the Nixon administration were no more successful than the conservative proponents of the Bricker Amendment in bringing Congress into the making of executive agreements. However, they did score two minor victories. In 1971 a military appropriations bill providing money for military and economic assistance to Cambodia contained a disclaimer of any commitment to the defense of Cambodia [P.L. 91-652], and in 1972 a statute provided that "the text of any international agreement, other than a treaty, [be submitted to the Congress] as soon as is practicable after such agreement has entered into force with respect to the United States but in no event later than sixty days thereafter" [P.L. 92-403, 86 Stat. 619, 1 USC Sec. 112 (b)]. However, the statute, which thereby acknowledged the legitimacy of executive agreements, permitted the president to classify certain agreements as secret, and give them only to the foreign relations committees of both houses, where they could not be made public without "due notice to the president." The Nixon and Ford administrations refused to consider mere "accords" with foreign nations to be executive agreements and failed to transmit them to Congress.

Dames & Moore v. Regan
452 U.S. 654 (1981)

President Carter's decision to admit the deposed Shah of Iran to the United States for medical treatment in 1979 was followed by the seizure of American diplomatic and military personnel by Iranian militants in Tehran. The Iranian government facilitated the seizure, creating a crisis between Iran and the United States that lasted until an agreement was reached to release the hostages.

That agreement took the form of an executive agreement. The United States pledged "that it is and from now on will be the policy of the United States not to intervene, directly or indirectly, politically or militarily, in Iran's internal affairs." The American government undertook to transfer billions of dollars in frozen Iranian assets to the Bank of England for later transfer to Iran.

This agreement had constitutional implications, because it affected the rights of American citizens. One provision terminated all lawsuits in the United States courts by private claimants against the government of Iran, and nullified all court orders and judgments against frozen Iranian assets. Another prohibited future litigation by Americans and American-owned companies against Iran. Claims would be settled by international arbitration. At the time of the agreement, more than three hundred claims had already been filed (totaling more than $3 billion), and an estimated two thousand claims remained to be filed. Can an American president overturn judicial orders attaching and freezing assets of another nation? Can such an agreement deprive Americans of access to the courts of the United States?

Although the Reagan administration was unhappy with the agreement, it strongly defended these presidential prerogatives in court. The Justice Department argued that the Constitution provided the president with "plenary power to enter into agreements for the settlement of claims with foreign nations" and added that "such agreements are binding upon the courts."

These issues were raised in a case brought by a Los Angeles engineering firm, Dames and Moore, which had won a $3.8 million attachment against Iranian assets in federal court prior to the presidential order transferring these assets. On the last day of the 1981 term, only seventeen days before more than $2 billion in Iranian assets were due to be transferred, the Supreme Court handed down its decision.

MR. JUSTICE REHNQUIST delivered the opinion of the Court.

In nullifying post-November 14, 1979, attachments and directing those persons holding blocked Iranian funds and securities to transfer them to the Federal Reserve Bank of New York for ultimate transfer to Iran, President Carter cited five sources of express or inherent power. The Government, however, has principally relied on Sec. 1702 of the IEEPA [International Emergency Economic Powers Act] as authorization for these actions. Section 1702 (a) (1) provides in part [that the president may]:

(B) investigate, regulate, direct and compel, nullify, void, prevent or prohibit, any acquisition, holding, withholding, use, transfer, withdrawal, transportation, importation or exportation of, or dealing in, or exercising any right, power or privilege with respect to, or transactions involving, any property in which any foreign country or a national thereof has any interest; by any person, or with respect to any property, subject to the jurisdiction of the United States.

The Government contends that the acts of "nullifying" the attachments and ordering the "transfer" of the frozen assets are specifically authorized by the plain language of the above statute. The two Courts of Appeals that have considered the issue agreed with this contention....

Petitioner contends that we should ignore the plain language of this statute because an examination of its legislative history as well as the history of Sec. 5(b) of the Trading With the Enemy Act (hereinafter "TWEA"), 50 U.S.C. App. Sec. 5 (b), from which the pertinent language of § 1702 is directly drawn, reveals that the statute was not intended to give the President such extensive power over the assets of a foreign state during times of national emergency. According to petitioner, once the President instituted the November 14, 1979, blocking order, Sec. 1702 authorized him "only to continue the freeze or to discontinue controls." Brief for Petitioner, at 32.

We do not agree and refuse to read out of Sec. 1702 all meaning to the words "transfer," "compel," or "nullify." Nothing in the legislative history of either Sec. 1702 or Sec. 5(b) of the TWEA requires such a result. To the contrary, we think both the legislative history and cases interpreting the TWEA fully sustain the broad authority of the Executive when acting under this congressional grant of power....

This Court has previously recognized that the congressional purpose in authorizing blocking orders is "to put control of foreign assets in the hands of the President...." Such orders permit the President to maintain the foreign assets at his disposal for use in negotiating the resolution of a declared national emergency. The frozen assets serve as a "bargaining chip" to be used by the President when dealing with a hostile country.

Because the President's action in nullifying the attachments and ordering the transfer of the assets was taken pursuant to specific congressional authorization, it is "supported by the strongest of presumptions and the widest latitude of judicial interpretation, and the burden of persuasion would rest heavily upon any who might attack it." [*Youngstown,* Jackson, J., concurring.] Under the circumstances of this case, we cannot say that petitioner has sustained that heavy burden. A contrary ruling would mean that the Federal Government as a whole lacked the power exercised by the President, and that we are not prepared to say....

Although we have concluded that the IEEPA constitutes specific congressional authorization to the President to nullify the attachments and order the transfer of Iranian assets, there remains the question of the President's authority to suspend claims pending in American courts.

... The claims of American citizens against Iran are not in themselves transactions involving Iranian property or efforts to exercise any rights with respect to such property. An *in personam* lawsuit, although it might eventually be reduced to judgment and that judgment might be executed upon, is an effort to establish liability and fix damages and does not focus on any particular property within the jurisdiction. The terms of the IEEPA therefore do not authorize the President to suspend claims in American courts.

Although we have declined to conclude that the IEEPA or the Hostage Act directly authorizes the President's suspension of claims..., we cannot ignore the general tenor of Congress' legislation in this area in trying to determine whether the President is acting alone or at least with the acceptance of Congress. As we have noted, Congress cannot anticipate and legislate with regard to every possible action the President may find it necessary to take or every possible situation in which he might act. Such failure of Congress specifically to delegate authority does not, "especially ... in the areas of foreign policy and national security," imply "congressional disapproval" of action taken by the Executive. *Haig v. Agee*, [453 U.S. 280], 101 S.Ct. 2766, 2774, (1981). On the contrary, the enactment of legislation closely related to the question of the President's authority in a particular case which evinces legislative intent to accord the President broad discretion may be considered to "invite" "measures on independent presidential responsibility." [*Youngstown,* Jackson, J., concurring.] At least this is so where there is no contrary indication of legislative intent and when, as here, there is a history of congressional acquiescence in conduct of the sort engaged in by the President. It is to that history which we now turn.

Not infrequently in affairs between nations, outstanding claims by nationals of one country against the government of another country are "sources of friction" between the two sovereigns.

To resolve these difficulties, nations have often entered into agreements settling the claims of their respective nationals.

... The United States has repeatedly exercised its sovereign authority to settle the claims of its nationals against foreign countries. Though those settlements have sometimes been made by treaty, there has also been a longstanding practice of settling such claims by executive agreement without the advice and consent of the Senate. Under such agreements, the president has agreed to renounce or extinguish claims of United States nationals against foreign governments in return for lump sum payments or the establishment of arbitration procedures. To be sure, many of these settlements were encouraged by the United States claimants themselves, since a claimant's only hope of obtaining any payment at all might lie in having his government negotiate a diplomatic settlement on his behalf. But it is also undisputed that the "United States has sometimes disposed of the claims of citizens without their consent, or even without consultation with them, usually without exclusive regard for their interests, as distinguished from those of the nation as a whole."... It is clear that the practice of settling claims continues today. Since 1952, the President has entered into at least 10 binding settlements with foreign nations, including an $80 million settlement with the People's Republic of China.

Crucial to our decision today is the conclusion that Congress has implicitly approved the practice of claim settlement by executive agreement. This is best demonstrated by Congress' enactment of the International Claims Settlement Act of 1949, 22 U.S.C. Sec. 1621 *et seq.*, as amended (1980).

Over the years Congress has frequently amended the International Claims Settlement Act to provide for particular problems arising out of settlement agreements, thus demonstrating Congress' continuing acceptance of the President's claim settlement authority. With respect to the Executive Agreement with the People's Republic of China, for example, Congress established an allocation formula for distribution of the funds received pursuant to the Agreement. As with legislation involving other executive agreements, Congress did not question the fact of the settlement or the power of the President to have concluded it....

Finally, the legislative history of the IEEPA further reveals that Congress has accepted the authority of the Executive to enter into settlement agreements. Though the IEEPA was enacted to provide some limitation on the President's emergency powers, Congress stressed that "nothing in this Act is intended to interfere with the authority of the President to [block assets], or to impede the settlement of claims of United States citizens against foreign countries." S. Rep. No. 95-466, 95th Cong., 2d Sess., 6 (1977)....

In addition to congressional acquiescence in the President's power to settle claims, prior cases of this Court have also recognized that the President does have some measure of power to enter into executive agreements without obtaining the advice and consent of the Senate. In *United States v. Pink*, ... for example, the Court upheld the validity of the Litvinov Assignment, which was part of an Executive Agreement whereby the Soviet Union assigned to the United States amounts owed to it by

American nationals so that outstanding claims of other American nationals could be paid. The Court explained that the resolution of such claims was integrally connected with normalizing United States' relations with a foreign state....

[W]e do not believe that the President has attempted to divest the federal courts of jurisdiction. Executive Order No. 12294 purports only to "suspend" the claims, not divest the federal court of "jurisdiction." As we read the Executive Order, those claims not within the jurisdiction of the Claims Tribunal will "revive" and become judicially enforceable in United States courts. This case, in short, illustrates the difference between modifying federal court jurisdiction and directing the courts to apply a different rule of law.... The President has exercised the power, acquiesced in by Congress, to settle claims and, as such, has simply effected a change in the substantive law governing the lawsuit....

In light of all of the foregoing, ... we conclude that the President was authorized to suspend pending claims pursuant to Executive Order No. 12294. As Justice Frankfurter pointed out in *Youngstown*, ... "a systematic, unbroken executive practice long pursued to the knowledge of Congress and never before questioned may be treated as a gloss on 'Executive Power' vested in the President by Sec. 1 of Art. II." Past practice does not, by itself, create power, but "long continued practice, known to and acquiesced in by Congress, would raise a presumption that the [action] has been [taken] in pursuance of its consent...." [*United States v. Midwest Oil Co.*]

... Such practice is present here and such a presumption is also appropriate. In light of the fact that Congress may be considered to have consented to the President's action in suspending claims, we cannot say that action exceeded the President's powers....

Just as importantly, Congress has not disapproved of the action taken here. Though Congress has held hearings on the Iranian Agreement itself, Congress has not enacted legislation, or even passed a resolution, indicating its displeasure with the Agreement. Quite the contrary, the relevant Senate Committee has stated that the establishment of the Tribunal is "of vital importance to the United States." S. Rep. No. 97-71, 97th Cong., 1st Sess., 5 (1981). We are thus clearly not confronted with a situation in which Congress has in some way resisted the exercise of presidential authority.

Finally, we reemphasize the narrowness of our decision. We do not decide that the President possesses plenary power to settle claims, even as against foreign governmental entities.... But where, as here, the settlement of claims has been determined to be a necessary incident to the resolution of a major foreign policy dispute between our country and another, and where, as here, we can conclude that Congress acquiesced in the President's action, we are not prepared to say that the President lacks the power to settle such claims.

Notes and Questions

1. *Source of the power.* The Justice Department's argument in this case relied in part on the constitutional authority of the president to settle claims with foreign nations. Does the Court accept the argument, or does it rely solely on statutory authority?

2. *Power by invitation.* Justice Rehnquist conceded that the statute under which the president nullified the court attachments cannot be read as authorizing the president to

suspend claims pending in American courts. Yet Rehnquist argued that the president possessed this power because Congress had, by giving him broad discretion in related areas, "invited" its assertion. Until this case, had the Supreme Court ever endorsed a theory of presidential power by invitation? Did Justice Jackson, whose concurring opinion in *Youngstown* Rehnquist cited as authority for this theory, actually propound it? Or did Jackson simply describe what was likely to happen when law is vague and an emergency seems to exist?

4. *Power by acquiescence.* Rehnquist argued that there is a history of congressional acquiescence in the settlement of international claims by the executive. Is his evidence convincing? Or is it more accurate to state that Rehnquist found contemporary acquiescence? Can mere contemporary acquiescence put a "gloss" upon the laws? Is this what the Court held in *Midwest Oil* (see Chapter 2)? If so, what does this theory of contemporary acquiescence do to the constitutional schemes for express delegation of authority by legislation? As a practical matter, how can a Court which has great difficulty discerning legislative intent with a full record of hearings, committee reports, and floor debate, ascertain contemporary acquiescence where the full legislative process has not played itself out?

5. *Private property as a "bargaining chip."* By what authority may the president by executive agreement (the president and Senate by treaty, or the president and both houses of Congress by legislation) transform private property into a species of public property— "a bargaining chip" to win the release of hostages? Note that Justice Rehnquist's opinion ignores a contrary ruling by the Court of Claims in *Seery v. United* States, 127 F. Supp. 601 (Ct. Cl. 1955), cert. denied, 359 U.S. 943 (1959).

6. *A political decision?* Consider the following observation by Professor Arthur H. Miller: "To understand the Supreme Court's decision in *Dames & Moore v. Regan,* one should perceive at the outset that it is basically a compromise between harsh international reality and abstract constitutional norms. Although crafted in familiar lawyers' language, Justice William H. Rehnquist's opinion for the Court reeks with the odor of compromise forced by necessity. Principle, as usual, gave way to *realpolitik.* The Justices had, in the last analysis, no choice save to sustain the validity of President Carter's hurried deal for the release of the hostages."[18] Do you agree?

7. *Role of the court in the political process.* Do decisions like *Curtiss-Wright, Belmont, Pink,* and *Dames & Moore* support the assertion by Professor Martin Shapiro that "To the extent that courts make law, judges will be incorporated into the governing coalition, the ruling elite, the responsible representatives of the people, or however else the political regime may be expressed"?[19] To what extent can it be said that the United States has, in the realm of foreign affairs, an independent judiciary enforcing the rule of Law?

F. Projecting Power

The foreign affairs power of the United States is deeply influenced, if not dominated, by the accumulation of military garrisons around the world. According to Chalmers Johnson, this "vast network of American bases on every continent except Antarctica ... con-

---

18. *"Dames & Moore v. Regan*: A Political Decision by a Political Court," 29 *U.C.L.A. L. Rev.* 1104 (1982).

19. *Courts: A Comparative and Political Analysis* (1981), 34.

stitutes a new form of empire" which has the potential of "undermining our constitutional order."[20]

In 2008, the Pentagon acknowledged 865 overseas bases, not counting approximately 100 in Iraq and more than 80 in Afghanistan. Many are legacies of past wars, including 268 in Germany, 124 in Japan, and 87 in South Korea. Still others have recently been acquired in countries like Uzbekistan, Kyrgyzstan, Qatar, Bahrain, Oman, Kuwait, and the United Arab Emirates. American bases with the capacity to affect foreign relations can be found in approximately 130 foreign countries.

The American Enterprise Institute, a neo-conservative think tank, envisions units assigned to these bases as a sort of "a global cavalry," ready to ride out from "frontier stockades" to engage "bad guys," much as the French Foreign Legion once maintained the French Empire. According to Brig. Gen. Mastin Robeson, who commanded 1,800 U.S. marines at an old Foreign Legion base in Djibouti, the United States needs a "global presence" in order to engage in "preventive war" (discussed in Chapter 4). American military operations against suspected terrorists in Kenya and pirates in Somalia are run out of Djibouti, which is at the mouth of the Persian Gulf.[21] In November 2002, an unmanned Predator drone launched by the CIA from that country fired a missile that killed six suspected terrorists, including an American citizen from Detroit, as they were driving across a desert in Yemen.

These "stockades" include not only large airbases like Ramstein, Germany, and Diego Garcia in the Indian Ocean, but nuclear aircraft carriers and their supporting fleets. Smaller garrisons can be found throughout the Caribbean and Latin America where American troops and law enforcement agencies help the governments of Colombia and Ecuador fight drug lords and, indirectly, protect oil supplies from seizure by rebel forces. During the first administration of President George W. Bush, the Central Intelligence Agency operated secret prisons in Thailand, Poland, Bulgaria, Lithuania, Afghanistan, and Iraq, and sent suspected terrorists to Morocco, Libya, Egypt, Jordan, and Uzbekistan for interrogation by torture.

The agreements establishing these overseas bases were usually negotiated by executive agreements rather than treaties, even though their existence might expose American troops to attack or draw the U.S. into regional conflicts. Some of these agreements contain leases; others limit who has access to the American bases or knows what goes on there, such as the storage of nuclear weapons or the use of torture. Status of Forces Agreements (SOFAs) typically shield U.S. troops and private contractors (including interrogators and guards) from being prosecuted by the local government for crimes allegedly committed while on duty.

In 2002, the Bush administration found a new use for executive agreements when it threatened more than 100 foreign countries with loss of American foreign aid if they did not agree to shield American war criminals from extradition to the new International Criminal Court.

---

20. "America's Empire of Bases," Jan. 15, 2004, http://commondreams.org/views04/0115-08.html.
21. Ibid.

Chapter Four

Military Force, Paramilitary Force, and Covert Action

"As long as it remains national policy [to combat Communism internationally], another important requirement is an aggressive covert psychological, political and paramilitary organization more effective, more unique, and if necessary, more ruthless than that employed by the enemy. No one should be permitted to stand in the way of the prompt, efficient, and secure accomplishment of this mission.

It is now clear that we are facing an implacable enemy whose avowed objective is world domination by whatever means and at whatever cost. There are no rules in such a game. Hitherto acceptable norms of human conduct do not apply. If the U.S. is to survive, longstanding American concepts of "fair play" must be reconsidered. We must develop effective espionage and counterespionage services and must learn to subvert sabotage, and destroy our enemies by more clever, more sophisticated and more effective methods than those used against us. It may become necessary that the American people be made acquainted with, understand and support this fundamentally repugnant philosophy."

—Top secret report on CIA activities prepared in connection with the second Hoover Commission (1954)

A. Introduction

It is convenient, but imprecise, to speak of the "war power" or the "war powers." The larger issue is the control, deployment, and use of military force for a variety of purposes, only some of which may result in war.

The Constitution does not establish a "war power." It allocates control over the armed forces between the president and Congress and, because it is law, makes that allocation subject to judicial review. Congress (and therefore the president) has the authority by legislation to "raise and support Armies," "provide and maintain a Navy," and "make Rules for the Government and Regulation of the land and naval Forces." Congress is granted authority to "declare" war, but the president has de facto power to "make" war by the way in which he conducts foreign relations, deploys the armed forces as their commander in chief, and uses the clandestine services as chief executive.

The distinction between declaring and making war was quite deliberate. When it was proposed at the Constitutional Convention that Congress be authorized to "make war," Charles Pinckney protested that legislative proceedings "were too slow." Rufus King objected that "make war" might be misconstrued to mean "conduct war," which should be an executive function. James Madison and Elbridge Gerry then moved to substitute "declare" for "make," thereby "leaving to the Executive the power to repel sudden attacks." The motion carried.[1]

Authority to conduct military actions short of war was touched upon only briefly when the power to issue letters of marque and reprisal (authorizing privateers and warships to seize foreign shipping) was granted to Congress. This was the common way in which maritime nations engaged in limited hostilities in the eighteenth century. It is also likely that the founders anticipated the use of military force in nondeclared warfare intended to protect American lives and property, to protect border settlements, and to advance territorial claims. In their time, as in ours, nondeclared wars were more common than declared wars.

Curiously, the term "war" has no fixed meaning, either in U.S. law or in the law of nations. When presidents assert their "war powers," they really mean the power to use military force, paramilitary force, or, in the case of George W. Bush, covert action. "War" has always meant more than formally declared military conflicts with foreign states, but how much more is difficult to say.

For example, was the American Civil War a "war?" The Confederates liked to think so, because that would have entitled their political union to international recognition, and with it, legal legitimacy. But the Union government refused to accept that characterization, and successfully prevented that rebellion from gaining the status of a war between nations.

To complicate matters further, what are we to make of the so-called "war" against the Barbary pirates, the Indian wars, or the suppression of Aguinaldo's rebellion in the Philippines? Did the U.S. invasions of Nicaragua, the Dominican Republic, Haiti, Grenada, and Panama constitute wars? And what are we to make of the "drug war," which has involved paramilitary operations in Latin American countries, or the "war against terrorism," which has involved kidnappings in Italy and Macedonia?

In war, the goal of victory (or survival) is assumed by most to justify degrees of arbitrariness and brutality not permitted in peacetime. Thus, if a president can order the U.S. military into armed conflict he can curb the liberties of Americans and evade legal or political accountability under the system of checks and balances. If courts choose to defer to his broad assertions of power, as they typically do in times of war, then he can, temporarily, at least, alter the meaning of the Constitution.

Scholars disagree as to whether the term "commander in chief" was meant to confer a title or grant authority. Strict constructionists delight in quoting Alexander Hamilton, the leading promoter of a strong presidency, who in *The Federalist* No. 69 predicted that the office "would amount to nothing more than the supreme command and direction of the military and naval forces, as first general and first admiral."[2] However, it is unlikely that General Washington's former aide-de-camp would have supported such a narrow interpretation in practice. Madison was probably closer to the consensus of his time when, as Helvidius, he wrote:[3]

> In no part of the constitution is more wisdom to be found, than in the clause which
> confides the question of war or peace to, the legislature, and not to the execu-

---

1. Max Farrand, ed., *The Records of the Federal Convention of 1787*, vol. II (1937), 318–19.
2. (Cooke ed., 1961), 495.
3. Madison had the opportunity to reconsider these observations in 1812 when the War Hawks in Congress demanded war with Great Britain.

tive department. Beside the objection to such a mixture to heterogeneous powers, the trust and the temptation would be too great for any one man; not such
as nature may offer as the prodigy of many centuries, but such as may be expected in the ordinary successions of magistracy. War is in fact the true nurse of
executive aggrandizement. In war, a physical force is to be created; and it is the
executive will, which is to direct it. In war, the public treasuries are to be un-
locked; and it is the executive hand which is to dispense them. In war, the hon-
ours and emoluments of office are to be multiplied; and it is the executive
patronage under which they are to be enjoyed. It is in war, finally, that laurels are
to be gathered; and it is the executive brow they are to encircle. The strongest pas-
sions and most dangerous weaknesses of the human breast: ambition, avarice,
vanity, the honourable or venial love of fame, are all in conspiracy against the
desire and duty of peace. [*Writings*, VI (Hunt ed., 1906), 174].

What not to do, in the judgment of virtually all of the founders, was to return to the
old British system of Crown prerogatives, which gave to the monarch not only the power
to declare and make war, but to raise fleets and armies and to demand funds to finance
them. As Jefferson boasted, "We have already given in example one effective check to the
Dog of war by transferring the power of letting him loose from the Executive to the Legislative body, from those who are to spend to those who are to pay."[4]

History provides little support for the effectiveness of the check that Jefferson applauded. Indeed, Jefferson as president personally loosed the Dog of War against the Barbary "pirates" through secret dispatches and then deceived Congress into confirming what
he had done.[5] Although military force has been used hundreds of times, only five wars have
been declared and in only one, the War of 1812, were the merits debated seriously in
Congress. Once into war, Congress has generally supported the president.

The greatest check on presidential war making prior to 1940 was the unwillingness of
Congress to support a large peacetime military force. Nothing has curbed the ambition
of presidents so much as the lack of an immediate military capability. So long as presidents were dependent upon the state militia for large armies, and so long as the need for
a large navy was obviated by the "wooden walls of England," an aggressive international
role for the United States was impossible.

Since World War II, no president has lacked the capacity to intervene militarily (or para-
militarily) in the affairs of lesser nations. Most have exercised this power, on their own initiative, without the formal concurrence of Congress, in situations that did not pose a direct
and immediate threat to the security of the United States. The list is long: Korea, the CIA
backed coup in Guatemala, the CIA-backed bombing in Indonesia, the CIA-backed invasion of Cuba, the Cuban missile crisis and blockade, the invasion of the Dominican Republic,
the Vietnam War, the secret war in Laos, the Cambodian incursion, the Cambodian bombing, the *Mayaguez* incident, and the CIA-backed attempts to overthrow the government
of Nicaragua. "By the early 1970s," Arthur Schlesinger, Jr., has written, "the American Presidency has become on issues of war and peace the most absolute monarch (with the possible exception of Mao Tse-tung of China) among the great powers of the world."[6]

Today the terms "cold war" and "national security" have blurred the distinction between war and peace, while the growth of clandestine services and covert operations have

---

4. *Papers*, XV (Boyd ed., 1958), 397.
5. Abraham D. Sofaer, *War, Foreign Affairs and Constitutional Power: The Origins* (1976), 208–27.
6. *The Imperial Presidency* (1973), ix.

made "military force" inadequate to describe the powers asserted by, or in the name of, the modern presidency. Since the early 1950s, the CIA has actively supported guerrilla movements or private armies in many countries, including Poland, Albania, Ukraine, Tibet, Burma, Guatemala, Kurdistan, and Nicaragua. By the late 1960s and early 1970s, the CIA had more than 35,000 foreign troops on its payroll (mostly in Laos) and a larger fleet of aircraft than Pan American World Airways.[7]

In the 1960s and 1970s, the CIA plotted the assassination of at least two foreign leaders, encouraged the abduction of another, and supplied arms to foreign dissidents with the knowledge that those dissidents intended to assassinate the head of their state.[8] Following the attacks of 2001, it set up secret prisons in at least eight foreign countries, where suspected terrorists were tortured, abused, or made to "disappear."

Over the years, executive assertions of authority to employ military and paramilitary force have fallen into certain recognizable patterns. One has been to claim that Congress somehow *delegated* authority for the actions to the president. Often the legislation cited is rather general in nature. A second technique has been to justify the action in terms of some *specific grant* of presidential power, such as the power to receive foreign ambassadors or the Commander-in-Chief Clause. Often these powers are said to grant the president some "independent power"—power independent of congressional efforts to limit it. Third, if the claim to a specific grant of authority seems unpersuasive, lawyers for the executive branch will often resort to the "executive power" mentioned in the first sentence of Article II. Like the commander-in-chief power, the executive power is not deemed to be mere description, but is said to constitute a positive grant of affirmative power that allows the president to do anything necessary and proper to achieve national security or to promote national interests.

In each of the foregoing instances, the focus has been on a particular provision of the Constitution, however vague and open-ended it might be. An alternative approach, first suggested by Alexander Hamilton in *The Federalist* No. 23, is to look upon the war power as an *aggregate* of all the powers granted to the Union by the Constitution, and all powers necessary and proper for carrying out the legitimate objects of that union.[9] Abraham Lincoln took this theory one step further when he conceived of the war power as an aggregation of constitutionally granted powers that, in times of wartime emergency, flowed to the president as commander in chief or chief executive without formal legislation.[10] Aggregation takes the focus off of *means* and puts it on *ends*, which can then be used to justify the means and break the bonds of strict construction.

The next stage of argumentation is to break free from the Constitution entirely. This approach was first advanced by the Supreme Court in *Penhallow v. Doane*, 3 U.S. (3 Dall.) 54 (1795), where the power to conduct war was characterized as a matter of *national sovereignty* and therefore not specifically dependent upon any of the affirmative provisions of the Constitution. Justice Sutherland developed this theory in *Curtiss-Wright* and, like many "strong" presidents, encouraged the assumption that because the president speaks for the United States in foreign affairs, he must be, de facto, the sovereign. Often the argument is that the power must be recognized in the president because other states grant it to their chief executives.

---

7. Morton H. Halperin et al., *The Lawless State* (1976), chap. 2, *passim*.
8. *Alleged Assassination Plots Involving Foreign Leaders*. An Interim Report of the Select Committee to Study Governmental Operations with Respect to Intelligence Activities, U.S. Senate, 94th Cong., 1st Sess. (1975) (the Church Committee).
9. (Cooke ed., 1961), 148–51.
10. See, e.g., Schlesinger, *The Imperial Presidency* (1973), 60–67.

Finally, there is the larger claim of an extraconstitutional prerogative power, which may be derived from George III, international law, or "the concomitants of nationality." This claim has taken many forms, from the absolute prerogatives of the Stuart kings (based on the law of God), to the Locke-Jefferson theory of emergency powers (based on the hope of popular acceptance), to the Nixon theory of inherent national security powers (rooted in secrecy). In each of these instances, the end is said to justify the means.

The broader claims of presidential power to use military force in times of emergency were discussed in Chapter 2. In this chapter we examine those claims in a nonemergency context and in situations in which the ends may not so happily excuse the means. Some of the questions to be explored are: When, if ever, is a congressional declaration of war necessary? If a declaration is not required, is any form of legislative approval necessary before the president takes the country into war? If so, what constitutes legislative approval? A resolution? Appropriations? Long-term acquiescence? What action may the president take in advance of legislative authority that may expose the United States to war? Provocative positioning of forces? Preventive strikes? May the president, on his own authority, authorize covert operations to subvert foreign governments? May Congress authorize him or his agencies to engage in such activities? Are there, or should there be, any limits to the kinds of covert actions the United States may employ?

B. Authority for Imperfect Wars

The Quasi-War with France

Does the grant of authority to Congress to declare war mean that the United States may not engage in limited hostilities with another country, in response to that country's hostile acts, without a formal declaration, particularly when a formal declaration may signify a greater commitment to war than is intended and will then require a formal treaty of peace?

This issue was raised by the undeclared naval war with France (1798–1800) and in *Bas v. Tingy*, 4 U.S. (4 Dall.) 37 (1800), the Supreme Court ruled that a formal declaration was not required. There was no opinion for the Court in those days, but the *seriatum* opinions are instructive. Justice William Paterson wrote:

> The United States and the French Republic are in a qualified state of hostility. An imperfect war, or a war, as to certain objects, and to a certain extent, exists between the two nations; and this modified warfare is authorized by the constitutional authority of our country. It is a war *quo ad hoc* [as regards this particular matter]. As far as Congress tolerated and authorized the war on our part, so far we may proceed in hostile operations. Ibid., 45.

Justice Bushrod Washington agreed: "Those who are authorized to commit hostilities, act under special authority, and can go no farther than to the extent of their commission" [ibid., 40]. Accord: *Talbot v. Seeman*, 5 U.S. (1 Cranch) 1 (1801).

Is there support in the text of the Constitution for the assertion that Congress, and only Congress, can go beyond a presidential repulsion of sudden attack and direct the conduct of an imperfect or limited war? In the absence of a standing navy, how were limited naval operations carried out in the eighteenth century? In the absence of a standing army, how were companies of soldiers formed? To which branch of government was allocated the power to grant letters of marque and reprisal authorizing the private arming

During the quasi-war with France (1798–1800), which was fought to protect American ship-ping from French raiders, the new 38-gun American frigate *Constellation* defeated the 40-gun French frigate *L'Insurgente* (right), the 54-gun *L'Vengeance*, and several French privateers, all without a formal declaration of war against the European superpower.

of ships to prey on enemy shipping and the private organizing of companies of soldiers to march under the state and national flags?

In *Little v. Barreme*, 6 U.S. (2 Cranch) 170 (1804), the question arose whether the seizure of a foreign merchant vessel by two navy warships during the quasi-war with France was legal when the seizure was pursuant to executive instructions but beyond the powers delegated to the executive by Congress. The Supreme Court said no. Congress' act authorizing the navy to seize ships sailing *to* French ports was read as denying authority to seize ships sailing *from* such ports.

In *United States v. Smith*, 27 F. Cas. 1192, 1230 (C.C. N.Y. 1806), the issue was whether the president could disregard the Neutrality Act of 1794. Supreme Court Justice William Paterson, writing for a circuit court, held that "The President of the United States can-not control the statute, nor dispense with its execution, and still less can he authorize a person to do what the law forbids.... If the United States were invaded, Paterson recog-nized, the president would be obliged to resist with force. But, he added, there is a "man-ifest distinction" between going to war with a nation at peace and responding to an actual invasion. "In the former case," the justice ruled, "it is the exclusive province of congress to change a state of peace into a state of war."

The Barbary Pirates

A more difficult question of authority involved the deployment of American warships between the Barbary "pirates" and the American merchant ships the pirates sought to

The U.S.S. *Enterprise*, left, attacking a Tripolitan cruiser in May 1801, under secret orders from President Jefferson, without a declaration of war from Congress.

loot. On May 20, 1801, President Thomas Jefferson issued secret orders to squadron commander Richard Dale providing that "if there should be any cause for apprehension from either [Algiers or Tripoli], you must place your ships in a situation to chastise them, in case of their declaring War or committing hostilities." If all of the Barbary powers should declare war on the United States, the President added, "you will then distribute your force in such manner ... so as best to protect our commerce and chastise their insolence — through sinking, burning or destroying their ships and vessels wherever you shall find them."[11]

When Dale and his squadron arrived in the Mediterranean, he learned that Tripoli had declared war on the United States. He promptly warned its pasha that he intended to capture Tripolitan ships and subjects at every opportunity, and issued orders to that effect. Shortly thereafter, the twelve-gun schooner *Enterprise* defeated a fourteen-gun Tripolitan cruiser, stripped it of masts and guns, and set it adrift. Had the *Enterprise* not been bound for Malta to obtain fresh water for the squadron, it would have been entitled, under Jefferson's orders, to keep the cruiser as a prize of war, making the attack an offensive operation. President Jefferson chose to conceal that fact from Congress, falsely portraying the battle as a defensive encounter.

> Unauthorized by the Constitution, without the sanction of Congress to go beyond the line of defense, the vessel, being disabled from committing further hostilities, was liberated with its crew. The Legislature will doubtless consider whether, by authorizing measures of offence also, they will place our force on equal footing with that of its adversaries. I communicate all material on this subject, that in the exercise of this important function confided by the Constitution to the Legislature exclusively, their judgment may form itself on a knowledge and consideration of every circumstance of weight. [James D. Richardson, *A Compilation of the Messages and Papers of the Presidents*, I, 315]

---

11. *Naval Documents Related to the United States War with the Barbary Powers* (1939), I, 465–67.

Most scholars have accepted this message as proof that Jefferson had a "defensive war" theory of presidential power. See, for example, Schlesinger, *The Imperial Presidency* (1973), 22. Is that true? If so, to which theory of "defensive war" did Jefferson subscribe?

Alexander Hamilton, who in 1798 had not been "ready to say that [the president] has any other power than merely to employ ships or convoys, with authority to repel *force* by *force* [but not to capture]," ridiculed Jefferson's apparent scruples. When a foreign power has declared war, he argued, then war exists, "and any declaration on the part of Congress is nugatory; it is at least unnecessary."[12] Do you agree? Congress considered the matter and decided that to declare war against "pirates" would be demeaning. However, it did pass a law authorizing the navy to wage a limited war against Tripoli.

In his 1798 statement, Hamilton argued that "anything beyond [the provision of convoy protection] must fall under the idea of *reprisals*, and require the sanction of that department which is to declare or make war."[13] If Hamilton's original view is correct, should a foreign declaration of war have the effect of transferring the reprisal power, recognized under international law, from the Congress to the president? Must an offensive defense necessarily constitute a "reprisal"? Was it realistic to think that navy frigates could be kept on a short congressional leash in the early nineteenth century? Is it any more realistic to think that a short leash would be practical under the condition of twentieth-century communications? Does the answer depend on the kind of leash Congress and the president employ?

The primary purpose of the undeclared hostilities with the Barbary powers was to protect American lives and property. Military action by a nation to protect the lives and property of its nationals is deemed legitimate under international law, provided that it is proportionate to the threat. But while protection of American lives and property thus may be deemed a "concomitant of nationality," the Constitution is silent as to which branch may authorize military action for this purpose. When the Constitution is silent and Congress has not delegated authority to the president in advance, may the president commit military force on his own initiative? What degree of military force, if any, may he employ? This issue will be discussed at greater length in connection with the Greytown incident, discussed below in section C.

Avenging the Chesapeake

During the early days of the republic, one of the greatest sources of potential warfare for the United States involved the seizure (impressment) of alleged British sailors by the British navy from the crews of American ships. There were many to be found; British warships during the Napoleonic wars were virtual hellholes, and their crews deserted whenever possible to the U.S. Navy and merchant marine. In 1807, for example, the crew of the U.S.S. *Constitution* had 149 avowed British subjects out of a total complement of 419. That same year the British man-of-war *Leopard* flagged down the American frigate *Chesapeake*, ostensibly to deliver a letter to the captain. The letter demanded permission to search for deserters, and when the American commander refused, the British warship opened fire, killing three Americans and wounding eighteen others, including the captain.

---

12. Quoted in Schlesinger, Jr., *The Imperial Presidency* (1973), 425.
13. Ibid., 425.

The American frigate was forced to strike its colors and submit to a search. Four seamen were removed, three of whom later turned out to be American citizens.

The *Chesapeake* affair was a great humiliation to the United States, and in 1811 the U.S.S. *President* attacked the H.M.S. *Little Belt*, believing, wrongly, that it had recently impressed an American seaman. The British vessel, which was severely damaged, suffered nine dead and twenty-three wounded. According to historian Albert Z. Carr, "few on board the *President* doubted that this would be their chance to avenge the *Chesapeake*."[14]

Does the president have the authority, by what he orders or tolerates from his military commanders, to use military force to avenge an offense against the United States, particularly by a powerful nation capable of making devastating war on the United States? If so, from what source does this authority come? May he delegate that power—the power to trigger a war—to naval commanders? Does the Constitution's grant to Congress of authority to issue letters of marque and reprisal preclude executive initiatives of this sort?

Andrew Jackson in Florida

President Madison obtained authority from Congress for limited hostilities against Algeria in 1815, but President Monroe initiated covert military operations in Florida in 1817–1818 without congressional knowledge or consent. The domestic purpose of these operations was to defeat Seminole Indian raiding parties that used Florida as a refuge; the international objective was to persuade the Spanish government that it could no longer expect to hold Florida if the Americans decided to take it by force. The excuse for sending troops into Florida was that the Spanish authorities there had failed to live up to the provisions of a treaty that obliged them to keep the Seminoles peaceful. One reason the Seminoles were not peaceful was that Americans attacked them when they declined an "invitation" to parley.[15]

The first general in charge of dealing with the Seminoles was authorized to attack them within Spanish Florida, if necessary, but not if they should avail themselves of the protection of a Spanish fort. A copy of his instructions was sent to Andrew Jackson in Tennessee, who promptly replied with a confidential letter to the president suggesting that the United States should seize all of East Florida "as an indemnity for the outrages of Spain upon the property of our Citizens.... This can be done," Jackson assured Monroe, "without implicating the Government; let it be signified to me through any channel (say Mr. J. Rhea) that the possession of the Floridas, would be desirable to the United States and in sixty days it will he accomplished."[16]

Before Jackson's proposal reached the president, orders were issued placing Jackson in charge of the Florida operation. Those orders did not mention the earlier directive that the indians were not to be attacked if they were under the shelter of a Spanish fort, but that directive was not revoked either. There is no evidence that the president or Secretary of War John C. Calhoun ever instructed Jackson that conquering Florida was not what they had in mind. The entire matter was left vague. Jackson raised troops, invaded Florida, seized Spanish posts, and even hanged two Englishmen who had traded with the indians.

14. *The Coming of War* (1960), 290.
15. Our account of these controversial and complicated events is taken primarily from Sofaer, *War, Foreign Affairs and Constitutional Power* (1976), 341–65.
16. Ibid., 343.

When the Spanish protested, Monroe was free to claim that he had not ordered the attacks on its Florida forts. In modern parlance, this would be called a "plausible denial." He was also free to exploit the lesson that Jackson's operation had taught the Spanish who, with Latin America in revolt, were in no position to reinforce their Florida garrisons.

Before Spain capitulated, however, there were some stormy debates over the constitutional significance of what Jackson had done. At the beginning of the cabinet meeting of July 15, 1818, President James Monroe, Treasury Secretary William H. Crawford, Secretary of War John C. Calhoun, and Attorney General William Wirt all agreed "that Jackson acted not only without, but against, his instructions; that he has committed war upon Spain, which cannot be justified, and in which, if not disavowed by the Administration, ... will be abandoned by the country."[17]

Only John Quincy Adams, Monroe's secretary of state, defended Jackson's actions. The warfare, he argued, was not against Spain, but against the indians. Where the president got the authority to attack the Indians on Spanish territory, Adams did not say; presumably they were analogous to criminals, pirates, or what we would today call "terrorists." "Even ... the order for taking the Fort of Barrancas by storm," Adams argued, "was incidental, deriving its character from the object, which was not hostility to Spain, but the termination of the indian war."

Is Adams' theory of defensive war persuasive? May the defeat of the Spanish garrisons be justified as a "reprisal"' for Spain's failure to control the indians? If so, may a president today undertake a reprisal against a foreign country, like Somalia or Afghanistan, that fails to restrain pirates or terrorists operating from their soil? Compare Adams' theory of defensive war to President Nixon's defense of the Cambodian incursion of 1970 (see chapter 4, *infra*).

Adams' argument was ingenious, but it did not convince Monroe and his cabinet, perhaps because they knew that it would not persuade Congress. Monroe disavowed any presidential power to seize the Spanish forts, but defended the constitutionality of the secret orders directing the incursion. By refusing to punish Jackson for exceeding his authority and waging war against a foreign power, Monroe encouraged similar risk taking by military commanders in the future. Indeed, he seemed to argue that commanders in the field could take actions that the president himself could not constitutionally authorize.

Congress refused to repudiate anything that Jackson did. Ignorant of the secret correspondence with Jackson and eager not to impede the effort to acquire Florida by a combination of threats and negotiations, the House defeated resolutions that would have declared the seizure of the forts and the execution of British subjects unconstitutional. It also refused to consider a bill that would have required prior congressional permission for future border crossings by army troops, unless those troops were in "fresh pursuit" of a "defeated enemy."[18] Spain got the message and ended the constitutional dispute by ceding Florida to the United States in 1819.

Should congressional votes rejecting a resolution embodying a particular theory regarding the allocation of powers be considered "precedent" for a cumulative "consensus" regarding the proper allocation of those powers? Can constitutional powers grow by the gradual accumulation of unrebuffed practices, or are the issues forever fresh, on the theory that the only precedents that matter are judicial holdings?

---

17. Ibid., 349.
18. Ibid., 359–63.

John Quincy Adams believed that it was an "error in our Constitution which confers upon the legislative assemblies the power of declaring war, which, in the theory of government, according to Montesquieu and Rousseau, is strictly an Executive Act." It was an error, he asserted, because "whenever secrecy is necessary for an operation of the Executive, involving the question of peace and war, Congress must pass a secret law to give the President the power."[19] Does Adams have a point? Is secret legislation practical, or even possible, especially given the size of the modern Congress? What did Adams implicitly assume about the relationship between military force and diplomacy? Did the founders share his assumption? Where did their assumptions come from? Are they valid today?

The Monroe Doctrine

From the beginning of the Republic there has been little doubt about the authority of the president to *speak* for the country in foreign relations. However there has always been doubt about his authority to declare *national commitments* without the concurrence of Congress, particularly where the commitment could involve a promise to use force. Such was the issue raised by the Monroe Doctrine of 1823. In that now famous pronouncement President Monroe unilaterally declared that the United States was opposed to all future efforts by European powers to recolonize the Americas, that the United States had no intention of meddling in "the politics or wars of European powers relating to themselves," and that the United States would regard "the effort of any European power to interfere with the political system of the American continents, or to acquire any new territory on these continents" as "the manifestation of an unfriendly disposition" towards the United States.[20]

Presidents have been declaring similar doctrines and making similar warnings to foreign powers ever since, but no "doctrine" has ever gained more popular acceptance than Monroe's. By the early twentieth century, many Americans had come to regard it as part of the organic law of the land, equal in dignity with the Constitution. But is it law? To what extent, if at all, can the president declare a national commitment to defend other nations from attack? When Colombia asked the Monroe administration what it intended to do if a European power intervened militarily in Latin America, Secretary of State Adams replied that the president would recommend to Congress "the adoption of the measures exclusively of their resort."[21] A few years later, Adams' Secretary of State Henry Clay gave the same answer to the Argentines: "Congress alone ... is competent by our Constitution, to decide that question."[22]

Jackson's Request for Reprisal Power

As president, Andrew Jackson was more cautious with the use of military force against foreign powers than he had been as a general. In 1834, when France showed no signs of paying for the damage done to American shipping during the Napoleonic Wars, Jackson asked Congress for legislation "authorizing reprisals upon French property, in case pro-

---

19. J.Q. Adams, *Memoirs* (C. F. Adams ed., 1977), IV, 32.
20. Richardson, *Messages*, vol. 2, 218.
21. R. J. Bartlett, ed., *The Record of American Diplomacy* (1947), 185–86.
22. Samuel Flagg Bemis, *The Latin American Policy of the United States* (1943), 70.

vision shall not be made for the payment of the debt."[23] Opponents of the measure denounced it as a request that Congress delegate its power to declare war to the president, and the request was denied.

Contingent Authority to Defend the Maine Border

In 1839, when it seemed that the United States and Great Britain might come to blows over several thousand acres of potato land on the border between Maine and Canada, Congress passed a measure giving President Martin Van Buren contingent authority to repel any invasion that might occur.[24] Is this authorization distinguishable from the one denied to Jackson?

Tyler Protects Texas

In 1844, when it appeared that Mexico might reconquer the independent state of Texas rather than permit its annexation by the United States, President John Tyler sent a naval force into the Gulf of Mexico and secretly sent U.S troops deep into Texas to serve as a potential blocking force while treaty negotiations were underway. The emissaries from Texas, well aware that Congress held the power to declare war, demanded a formal assurance from the American Secretary of State, John C. Calhoun, that the American forces would be concentrated to meet any emergency "during the pendency of the treaty."[25] Calhoun, a strict constructionist on most constitutional matters, agreed, on the theory that if war broke out, it would be defensive in nature, and thus within the power of the president to authorize. Does Calhoun's theory of defensive war comport with the framers' theory? Is it legitimate for the president to place troops deep within a foreign country, where they may be attacked by another foreign country, in order to protect his diplomatic objectives?

Polk Provokes War with Mexico

Tyler's deployment of troops did not provoke war, and Texas was peacefully annexed by a joint resolution of Congress in 1845. However, war did break out when Tyler's successor sent troops into disputed border territory in 1846. Polk's maneuvers were similar to Monroe's. By deploying troops near the disputed border and the positioning of reinforced naval units in the Pacific where they would be able to seize the Mexican province of Upper California, including San Francisco, Polk sought to make the Mexicans feel militarily insecure. Secret agents encouraged American settlers in the coveted provinces to revolt, while at the same time diplomats offered to purchase California for as much as $40 million. Congress tried to restrain Polk by refusing funds for the purchase, and the opposition Whig Party denied Polk's claim to the territory between the Nueces and Rio Grande Rivers.

Nevertheless, Polk ordered General Zachary Taylor into the disputed territory. Taylor's troops occupied the high ground above the Mexican village of Matamoros and trained

---

23. Richardson, *Messages*, III, 106.
24. 5 Stat. 355 (March 3, 1839).
25. Bemis, *A Short History of American Foreign Policy and Diplomacy* (1959), 124.

In 1846, President Polk ordered U.S. troops into disputed territory between the Rio Grande and Nueces Rivers, provoking the Mexicans to attack. Here the two forces are shelling each other, as seen from the American side.

their artillery on the town square. Mexico declared "defensive war" and some American troops were killed in an engagement. Polk had already decided to ask for a congressional declaration of war when news of the incident enabled him to claim, falsely, that Mexico had invaded Texas. Congress then voted to recognize the existence of a state of war and to reinforce General Taylor's forces.

Two years later, as the war dragged on and Congress learned more about its origins, the House of Representatives passed a resolution declaring that the war had been "unnecessarily and unconstitutionally begun by the President."[26] Do you agree? Was it beyond the authority of the president to position military forces in such a manner that a foreign government might be "persuaded" that it had no choice but to accept the president's diplomatic offers? Was it beyond Polk's authority, as chief executive, chief diplomat, and commander in chief, to send troops into territory that he believed belonged to the United States, even though he knew that the action might provoke Mexico, already enraged by the annexation of Texas, to view the troops as invaders and attack them? Does the answer depend less on a theory of shared powers than on the strength of the American claim and the military weakness of Mexico? Was Polk under any constitutional obligation to keep Congress fully and fairly informed of the facts, so that Congress could disavow his actions if it wished?

Among the Whigs who denounced Polk's deceptions was Abraham Lincoln, a first-term congressman from the backwoods of Illinois. Lincoln also took issue with Polk's theory of defensive warfare. In a letter to William H. Herndon, his law partner back home, the future president wrote:

> ... Let me first state what I understand to be your position. It is, that if it shall become *necessary to repel invasion,* the President may, without violation of the Constitution, cross the line, and *invade* the territory of another country; and that whether such *necessity* exists in any given case, the President is to be the *sole* judge.

26. *Cong. Globe*, 30th Cong., 1st Sess. (Jan. 3, 1848), 95.

… Allow the President to invade a neighboring nation, whenever *he* shall deem it necessary to repel an invasion, and you allow him to do so, *whenever he may choose to say* he deems it necessary for such purpose—and you allow him to make war at pleasure. Study to see if you can fix *any limit* to his power in this respect, after you have given him so much as you propose. If, today, he should choose to say he thinks it necessary to invade Canada, to prevent the British from invading us, how could you stop him?…

The provision of the Constitution giving the war-making power to Congress was dictated, as I understand it, by the following reasons. Kings had always been involving and impoverishing their people in wars, pretending generally, if not always, that the good of the People was the object. This our Convention understood to be the most oppressive of all Kingly oppressions; and they resolved to frame the Constitution that *no one man* should hold the power of bringing this oppression upon us. But your view destroys the whole matter, and places our President where kings have always stood. [Lincoln, *Collected Works*, I (Basler ed., 1953), 451–52.]

Arthur Schlesinger, Jr., has written: "Lincoln's doctrine of 'no one man'—an unconscious restatement of James Wilson's view that it should not be in the power of 'a single man' to bring the country into war—unquestionably expressed the original intent."[27] Is that true? If so, did Polk's consultations with executive branch officials bestow legitimacy on his actions?

Inherent Limitations on the Purposes for Which War May Be Fought?

During the nineteenth and early-twentieth centuries it was widely assumed that there were certain inherent limitations on what a government could do. These were derived from a vision of political morality in both domestic and international relations. The objectives of the United States, and hence the scope of its governmental powers, were supposed to be different from the objectives of those corrupt European regimes that abused their people at home and engaged in bloody conquests abroad. Occasionally this theory of moral limitations on government found expression in the opinions of the Supreme Court. One example is *Fleming v. Page*, 50 U.S. (9 How.) 603 (1850), in which the owners of the schooner *Catharine* sought to reclaim duties which they had been forced to pay on cargo shipped out of the Mexican port of Tampico while that port was occupied by the United States during the Mexican War. The U.S. tax collector argued that the conquest of Mexico pursuant to a congressional declaration (acknowledgment) of war made Tampico an American port within the meaning of the tax laws. The Supreme Court, in an opinion by Chief Justice Taney, disagreed:

The port of Tampico, at which the goods were shipped, and the Mexican State of Tamaulipas, in which it is situated, were undoubtedly at the time of the shipment subject to the sovereignty and dominion of the United States. The Mexican authorities had been driven out, or had submitted to our army and navy; and the country was in the exclusive and firm possession of the United States, and governed by its military authorities, acting under the orders of the Presi-

----
27. *The Imperial Presidency* (1973), 43.

dent. But it does not follow that it was a part of the United States, or that it ceased to be a foreign country, in the sense in which these words are used in the acts of Congress.

The country in question had been conquered in war. But the genius and character of our institutions are peaceful, and the power to declare war was not conferred upon Congress for the purposes of aggression or aggrandizement, but to enable the general government to vindicate by arms, if it should become necessary, its own rights and the rights of its citizens.

A war, therefore, declared by Congress, can never be presumed to be waged for the purpose of conquest or the acquisition of territory; nor does the law declaring the war imply an authority to the President to enlarge the limit of the United States by subjugating the enemy's country. The United States, it is true, may extend its boundaries by conquest or treaty, and may demand the cession of territory as the condition of peace in order to indemnify its citizens for the injuries they have suffered, or to reimburse the government for the expenses of the war. But this can be done only by the treaty-making power or the legislative authority, and is not a part of the power conferred upon the President by the declaration of war. His duty and his power are purely military. As commander-in-chief, he is authorized to direct the movements of the naval and military forces placed by law at his command, and to employ them, in the manner he may deem most effectual to harass and conquer and subdue the enemy. He may invade the hostile country, and subject it to the sovereignty and authority of the United States. But his conquests do not enlarge the boundaries of this Union, nor extend the operation of our institutions and laws beyond the limits before assigned to them by the legislative power.

Does the Court clearly rule that an aggressive war, ordered by Congress solely for purposes of territorial aggrandizement, would be unconstitutional? Would you rely upon such a ruling if it did? What, precisely, does the Court hold? Should the war powers of the United States be defined wholly in terms of international law and practice, or should they be held to a moral theory of why the government of the United States was established? As a strictly political matter, is it realistic to expect the Supreme Court to enforce such a standard against a Congress, a president, and a people convinced that their nation's "manifest destiny" lies in the conquest of foreign lands? Does the decision in *Fleming v. Page* support the proposition that an American writ of habeas corpus could not be used to free a person incarcerated by American forces in a foreign nation?

C. Protection of American Lives and Property

We have seen how early presidents threatened, risked, provoked, and waged war without formal congressional authority. In each instance, the foreign power toward which the American armed forces took a belligerent stance was capable of attacking United States territory on a scale sufficient to be deemed war.

Now we turn to the president's use of military force to protect American lives and property in circumstances that posed no serious risk of war with a major military power or a bordering state. Only one of these confrontations, the Koszta affair, involved a direct challenge to a major European power.

In each instance, the military's role was regarded by the U.S. government and people largely in humanitarian terms. The United States did not, like the European powers, seek an empire of colonies. Its military force was used sparingly (and there wasn't much to spare) against pirates, primitive peoples, lawless mobs, and Far Eastern isolationists who sought to expel European and American traders by force. It was also used to protect American legations and traders from attack during foreign insurrections. This is not to say that the protection of American lives and property did not also advance American economic interests. Clearly it did, but during the nineteenth century the military tended to follow, rather than lead, the forces of commerce. "Gunboat diplomacy" is more common to the twentieth than to the nineteenth century, and will be examined more closely in Section D, *infra*.

The Koszta Affair

In what Arthur Schlesinger, Jr., has aptly called "the spread-eagle mood" of the early 1850s, the American people thrilled to accounts of national assertiveness, and no account thrilled them more than the rescue of Martin Koszta in 1853. Koszta, a Hungarian who was in the process of becoming an American citizen, was seized during a visit to Turkey and clapped in irons on board the Austrian brig-of-war *Hussar*. Learning of Koszta's status and plight, the captain of an American sloop-of-war *St. Louis* trained his guns on the Austrian warship and compelled it to deliver the prisoner into the neutral hands of the French consul general. Diplomatic negotiations eventually won Koszta's freedom. Despite the fact that the military action violated the sovereignty of two nations, President Franklin Pierce accepted responsibility for the captain's actions and Congress voted the captain a medal.

In 1890, the Supreme Court cited this "attractive historical incident" as a precedent for the president's unilateral appointment of a bodyguard to protect Justice Field [*In re Neagle*, 135 U.S. 64 (1890), in a passage not reproduced in Chap. 2.] Where does the president get the authority to authorize the military to protect the lives and property of Americans (or incipient Americans) with warships in foreign harbors, absent congressional legislation?

Recall the *Chesapeake* affair of 1807. Was the United States justified in regarding that attack on one of its warships as an act of war? If so, by what authority did President Pierce endorse an act of war against Austria? Or was it an "act of war"? Did Austria have any reason to believe that the United States intended a more extensive confrontation? Was it likely, given her military resources, the unrest in Hungary, and the British control of the Atlantic, that Austria would go to war with the United States over Martin Koszta or the more general American enthusiasm for the Hungarian Revolution? Is the term "act of war" susceptible to a legal definition? If not, is the president's use of military force susceptible to constitutional constraints?

Greytown

While Americans thrilled at their nation's new assertiveness, others came to resent it. Resentment was particularly strong in Nicaragua, where the descendants of Jamaican slaves and Mosquito indians watched Cornelius Vanderbilt and New York bankers make millions by providing what was, in the early 1850s, the fastest, cheapest passage from the

East Coast of the United States to the gold fields of California. At Greytown (San Juan del Norte), the eastern terminus of the trans-Nicaragua route, the city council and Vanderbilt's Accessory Transit Company got into repeated squabbles which the city council (or persons claiming to act under its authority) attempted to resolve by burning company buildings and arresting company employees. During one of these conflicts, the U.S. minister to Central America was mobbed and struck with a bottle, and a boatload of Americans who tried to come to his aid was fired upon.

Angered by what it saw as the lawless harassment of an influential American company and the affront to an American diplomat, the Pierce administration dispatched the U.S.S. *Cyane* to obtain reparations for the company and apologies for the United States. Captain Hollins was instructed that the people of Greytown "should be taught that the United States will not tolerate these outrages...."[28]

Arriving at Greytown, Hollins informed the residents that they had twenty-four hours to meet the U.S. demands or he would bombard the town. The commander of a British war schooner protested: "The inhabitants of this city, as well as the houses and property, are entirely defenseless and at your mercy. I do, therefore, notify you that such an act will be without precedent among civilized nations; and I beg to call your attention to the fact that a large amount of property of British subjects, as well as others, ... will be destroyed...."[29] Hollins was unmoved, despite the fact that Greytown was at least nominally under a British protectorate. His was the more powerful ship.

The residents of Greytown did not comply with the ultimatum, and at nine a.m., July 13, 1854, the shelling commenced. It continued at intervals until four p.m., when a landing party was put ashore to complete the destruction with torches. No lives were lost, but every building (except those belonging to the Accessory Transit Company, located on the other side of the harbor) was destroyed. President Pierce, in his second annual message to Congress, responded to charges that his administration had usurped the warmaking power of Congress by characterizing Greytown as "a pretended community, a heterogeneous assemblage gathered from various countries, and composed for the most part of blacks and persons of mixed blood [who] did not profess to belong to any regular government, ... a marauding establishment too dangerous to be disregarded and too guilty to pass unpunished...." So viewed, the destruction of Greytown could be analogized to the destruction of "a piratical resort of outlaws or a camp of savages...."[30]

The analogy to pirates or savages was important, because there was widespread recognition under international law for military police actions against such groups. Operating under this theory of international law, the American military had occupied Amelia Island off Georgia in 1817,[31] burned pirate settlements in Cuba in 1822, 1823, and 1825, destroyed three forts and most of a town in Sumatra in 1832 (killing approximately 150 local residents), burned three towns and killed fifty-seven natives in the Fiji Islands in 1840, burned one town and killed twelve "savages" on Drummond Island in 1841, destroyed one town and two villages in the Fiji Islands in 1855, destroyed three forts and killed approximately four hundred Chinese near Canton in 1856, and destroyed 100 huts and killed fourteen natives in the Fiji Islands in l858.[32] In each instance, the purpose of the mil-

---

28. John Bassett Moore, *Digest of International Law* (1906), VII, 351.

29. Ibid.

30. Richardson, *Messages*, VI, 2815.

31. Sofaer, War, *Foreign Affairs and Constitutional Power* (1976), 337.

32. Milton Offutt, "The Protection of Citizens Abroad by the Armed Forces of the United Stares," *Johns Hopkins University Studies in Historical and Political Science*, Series 46, no. 4 (1928), passim.

itary action was to teach the pirates or natives not to attack American shipping or molest shipwrecked American seamen.

By analogizing the attack on Greytown to these police actions, Pierce sought to avoid the charge that he had usurped the reprisal power from Congress. Such a reprisal against a "civilized" nation would have been, as Jefferson had written in 1793, "an act of war ... expressly lodged with [Congress] by the Constitution, and not with the Executive."[33]

Several years later, Captain Hollins was sued by an American citizen named Durand for destroying Durand's property at Greytown. Justice Nelson of the Supreme Court, sitting as a circuit judge in New York, denied the claim for compensation: "Whether it was the duty of the president to interpose for the protection of the [American] citizens at Greytown against an irresponsible and marauding community, was a public political question, in which the government, as well as the citizens whose interests were involved, was concerned, and which belonged to the executive to determine; and his decision is final and conclusive.... (*Durand v. Hollins*, 8 Fed. Cas. 111 (No. 4186 [1860]). Do you agree? Whose property did Hollins act to protect? Was that his only purpose? If not, did Durand have a valid claim for compensation against the United States under the Taking Clause of the Fifth Amendment? If *Durand* is a valid precedent, would President Carter have been within his constitutional powers to bomb the U.S. embassy in Tehran after the hostages had been released? *Durand* is frequently cited by State Department lawyers as authority for unilateral presidential military action against sovereign states. Should it be? Is there still a political questions doctrine? See Henkin, "Is There a 'Political Question' Doctrine?," 85 *Yale L. J.* 597 (1976).

D. Military Action to Achieve Diplomatic and Economic Objectives

As the bombardment of Greytown demonstrates, it is often difficult to separate the protection of American lives and property, a static concept, from the active use of military force, or the threat of force, to achieve diplomatic and economic objectives on behalf of influential American businessmen like Cornelius Vanderbilt.

During the late-eighteenth and early-nineteenth centuries, most Americans exulted in their isolation from the rest of the world and their freedom from the expense of supporting a military establishment of imperial proportions. Even so, the eagerness of Yankee shipowners to trade with both sides during the Napoleonic Wars drew the United States into its first two wars. By the 1830s, the growth of the American merchant marine was drawing the U.S. Navy into minor conflicts in some of the more remote regions of the world. American shipowners did not entice their government to join in the race for foreign colonies, but they did demand vigorous diplomatic and military efforts to extend and protect foreign markets and sources of raw material. Until the rise of Nazi Germany and the Great Depression in the 1930s, the U.S. navy's chief mission was to defend "free trade."

---

33. Quoted in Moore, *Digest*, VII, 123. Commodore David Porter had been court-martialed in 1825 for conducting a similar reprisal against the Spanish authorities in Puerto Rico. Offutt, 15.

The Falkland Islands

The search for whales, seals, and fish drew American sailing ships as far south as the Falkland (Malvinas) Islands, a frozen, windswept archipelago 250 miles east of the Straits of Magellan to which both Great Britain and Argentina (then the United Provinces of South America) laid claim. In 1831, Argentinians in temporary control of the islands seized three American ships on the grounds that they had violated fishing regulations. When word of the seizures reached Captain Silas Duncan of the U.S.S. *Lexington* at Montevideo, he sailed immediately to Buenos Aires, where he gave the new revolutionary government less than three days to disavow the seizure. When that government did not act before his deadline, Duncan sailed to the Falklands, entered Port Soledad under a French flag, seized the settlement, destroyed all of the guns at its fort, and carried its leaders back to Montevideo in chains. The raid effectively destroyed the fledgling colony and, in the view of the Argentinians, cleared the way for the British occupation of the islands in 1833.

In destroying the Argentinian colony, Captain Duncan acted under general instructions for the protection of American commerce and fisheries. President Jackson later endorsed his actions. Indeed, as soon as he learned of the seizures, but before he knew of Duncan's initiative, the president dispatched a warship to the scene. Treating the seizures as an act of piracy, the secretary of the navy instructed the commander of the warship to ascertain whether the government of Buenos Aires had authorized the seizures and, if it had, to retake the vessels and prevent further captures.[34] Jackson then informed Congress that he had dispatched the warship and requested contingent authority to take military action, if necessary. The authority was never granted and, after news of Duncan's raid reached Washington, was no longer needed.

As a result of Duncan's raid, diplomatic relations between the United States and Argentina ceased for more than a decade. For many years thereafter the Argentinian government sought indemnity for the raid from the United States, but was always refused on the grounds that Argentina's sovereignty over the islands was in doubt. Argentinians have never ceased to interpret the raid, and the U.S. government's refusal to pay indemnities, as proof that the United States sought to assist Great Britain in its claim to the islands.

In 1853, the tables were turned when the British government notified the United States of its intention to send a military force to the Falklands to prevent further depredations by the crews of American vessels who, hungry for fresh meat, were stealing livestock on the islands. The U.S.S. *Germantown* was immediately dispatched to defend American interests, but before it arrived, a British man-of-war seized the U.S. whaler *Hudson* and charged her captain with the nautical equivalent of cattle rustling. The *Germantown* prepared to retake the *Hudson* by force, but after lengthy negotiations the ship was released.[35]

Under international law, an attack on the forts or warships of a foreign nation is an act of war. May a president, by a standing order directing naval commanders to protect American commerce, authorize one of his commanders to attack an Argentinian fort on an island to which the United States has no territorial claim? May the president legitimately ratify such action afterward? May he order the commander of another warship to recapture an American vessel seized by a foreign nation for violation of its laws? As a matter

---

34. Dickens, "The Falkland Islands Dispute," *Hispanic American Historical Review*, 9 (1929), 471, 474–80.
35. V. F. Boyson, *The Falkland Islands* (1924), 123, 124, 132.

of law, should it make a difference which government has seized the American ship? If so, when should it make a difference and why? Was authorization (by ratification) by Congress necessary to legitimate Duncan's raid, a minor incident in American naval history, but an injury that Argentinians have never forgotten or forgiven?

The Opening of Japan to American Trade

In 1844, Caleb Cushing, the first U.S. minister to China, negotiated a treaty which gave American ships and merchants limited access to certain Chinese seaports. Opening feudal Japan to American trade was more difficult and required some "gunboat diplomacy." The gunboat diplomat assigned the task was Commodore Matthew C. Perry, son of Oliver Hazard Perry, hero of the Battle of Lake Erie in 1813. Commodore Perry's principal instruction was to negotiate a treaty to protect stranded American seamen, a serious problem since Japan refused to allow foreign ships into port to collect their seamen or deliver Japanese sailors wrecked abroad. Perry also was authorized to obtain a coaling station for the Navy's new steam-driven warships, and ostensibly as an afterthought, articles of trade similar to those recently negotiated with Siam, Muscat, and China providing for "friendly commercial intercourse and nothing more."[36]

Perry was given a squadron of five steamers and six sailing ships as an "imposing persuader." His instructions regarding the use, or threat, of force were suitably ambiguous. "If, after having exhausted every argument and means of persuasion, the commodore should fail to obtain from the government any relaxation of their system of exclusion, or even any assurance of humane treatment of our ship-wrecked seamen, he will then change his tone, and inform them ... that if any acts of cruelty should hereafter be practiced upon citizens of this country, whether by the government or the inhabitants of Japan, they will be severely chastised." The instructions cautioned that "he will bear in mind that as the President has no power to declare war his mission is necessarily of a pacific character, and will not resort to violence unless in self-defense."[37] Self-defense was defined not only as the protection of his ships and crews, but as the resentment of any acts of personal violence to himself or one of his officers. The latter provision was included because a failure to resent a personal affront during Cushing's previous diplomatic effort was deemed a cause of its failure.

On July 8, 1853, Perry's squadron, smaller than originally planned, anchored in the mouth of Tokyo Bay, its decks cleared for action. Perry refused to comply with a Japanese order to retire immediately to Nagasaki, but presented a letter from the president to two high princes and then departed, promising to return in the spring with a larger squadron. If by then the president's letter had not been received by the emperor and properly replied to, he "would not hold himself responsible for the consequences."[38] When Perry returned, the Japanese were more conciliatory. A treaty was negotiated that provided for shipwrecked seamen and gave American ships limited trading rights, which would be expanded as Japan gradually became acquainted with the vast range of goods Americans and Europeans had to offer.

Is this sort of "gunboat diplomacy" a legitimate exercise of presidential power? Does its legitimacy depend on which of its several purposes was primary? If its principal pur-

---

36. Bemis, *A Short History of American Foreign Policy and Diplomacy* (1959), 186.
37. S. E. Morison, *"Old Bruin": Commodore Mathew C. Perry* (1967), 282, 290, 416; Bartlett, *The Record of American Diplomacy* (1948), 269–70; Bemis, *Short History*, 185–88.
38. Bemis, *Short History*, 187.

Japanese images of what the Americans of Commodore Perry's party and his warship looked like. For years afterwards, Japanese mothers would tell their children to behave, or the Americans would come after them.

pose was to promote foreign trade, should Congress have authorized the mission in advance? Or does the president, as chief diplomat, have a concurrent power to promote trade with threats of force? Does the office of commander in chief mean, as the Court suggested in *Fleming v. Page*, that the president's "duty and power are purely military," or does it vest him with the authority to back his diplomacy with the threat of war? Congress, delighted with the outcome of Perry's mission, voted him thanks and a $20,000 bonus.

The Hawaiian Islands

As American ships spread out across the Pacific, the Hawaiian (Sandwich) Islands took on increased commercial and military significance. President Pierce, flushed with the success of Perry's mission, sought to annex them in 1854, but the treaty fell through when the islands' monarch died and the British made known their opposition. Thereafter, until annexation in 1898, the United States sought to prevent the islands from becoming a colony of any other world power, and to support American economic interests there. This policy was achieved, in large part, by timely demonstrations of American military strength. In 1889 a show of force by seventy marines and the loan of 10,000 rounds of ammunition to a pro-American faction helped to squelch an insurrection, and in 1893, another landing of 154 marines, ostensibly to protect American lives and property, had the intended effect of deterring royalist forces from regaining control during a pro-American revolt. In neither instance did the marines use force, but in both their mere presence (not authorized by Congress or the president) proved decisive. President Grover Cleveland believed that the 1893 intervention was morally wrong, but he did not appear to doubt the military's constitutional authority to intervene at the behest of the U.S. minister to Hawaii. Annexation finally came at the Hawaiians' initiative when the Japanese began demonstrating their military strength and the Spanish-American War reminded the United States of the islands' military value. Unable to muster two-thirds of the Senate to support annexation by treaty, President McKinley accomplished the same result by a joint resolution of Congress. Had that measure proved impractical, he was prepared at one point to annex the islands by executive decree as a war measure.[39] Would such an assertion of presidential authority as commander in chief have been constitutional?

The Shimonoseki Affair

The expansion of European and American trade in the Far East was not universally welcomed, and the United States occasionally resorted to military force, not just to protect American lives and property from immediate harm, but also to defeat the opponents of westernization. In 1863, when the warships of the isolationist Japanese Prince of Nagato attacked the American steamer *Pembroke*, the U.S.S. *Wyoming* retaliated by destroying one of the prince's steamers and badly damaging two of his sailing ships. A year later the United States contributed a hospital ship to an international naval expedition that defeated the prince, cleared the way for more trade and lower tariffs, and helped unleash the forces that were to modernize Japan in one generation.

The Boxer Rebellion

In 1900, joint military action was again necessary, not just to protect lives and property, but to keep the door open to American trade with China. In June of that year, members of the militantly antiforeign Society of Harmonious Fists, known in the West as the Boxers, overran Peking and laid siege to the foreign legations there. When it appeared that the Chinese government would not break the siege, and was actually giving covert support to the Boxers, an international relief expedition was formed and more than 15,000 U.S. troops were ordered to China. Between 5,000 and 6,000 arrived before the capture of Peking, but only about 2,500 saw combat. The purpose of this heavy commitment was not only to save lives, but to give the McKinley administration the leverage it needed to prevent Japan and the European powers from partitioning China. China declared war on the United States, but the United States did not reciprocate. Even so, one federal court ruled that a state of war had existed [*Hamilton v. McLaughry*, 136 Fed. 445 (1905)]. Congress was not in session when the fighting began, but it did not reject the president's action afterward. Nor did it doubt the president's authority to maintain garrisons in China as part of the settlement.

Panama

Insurrections everywhere posed a threat to American lives and property, but on the Isthmus of Panama, commercial and strategic interests also were involved. In an 1848

---

39. Alexander De Conde, *A History of American Foreign Policy*, I (1978), 302.

This *Harper's Monthly* cartoon from 1900 depicts McKinley and Uncle Sam battling fanatical Chinese Boxers, ostensibly to relieve foreign legations under siege, but mainly to assure U.S. businesses that they would not be excluded from China's markets.

treaty, the government of Colombia (then New Granada) granted the United States a right-of-way across the isthmus in return for guarantees of free transit from sea to sea and of "the rights of sovereignty and of property which New Granada has and possesses over the said territory."[40]

During the next fifty years, the state of Panama was torn by fifty-three outbreaks, revolutions, and violent disturbances. On no less than ten of these occasions, usually by invitation, U.S. forces were landed to protect both the lives and property of Americans and the "right of free transit." In all but one instance, involving the recapture of a steamboat from revolutionaries, the American forces managed to avoid hostilities.[41]

In 1903, when still another revolution was anticipated, American forces were deployed to protect the railroad and port facilities. This time, however, the Americans physically blocked Colombian forces from using the railroad, thereby assuring the success of the revolution. The revolutionaries then declared Panama independent of Colombia and negotiated a treaty whereby the United States obtained canal rights at a price far below that which the Colombians had been asking. In return, the United States agreed to guarantee the independence of Panama.

The United States did not make the Panamanian revolution; nor did it "take" the isthmus, as President Roosevelt would later boast.[42] But, as in Hawaii, the positioning of a

---

40. Quoted in Bemis, *Short History*, 158.

41. Offutt, passim.

42. There is a story that President Roosevelt turned to his secretary of state, Elihu Root, during a Cabinet meeting about his actions regarding Panama and asked, "Well, have I answered the charges?

military blocking force made possible the success of a pro-American revolution. By so doing, Roosevelt not only used the military as an extension of his diplomacy; he abrogated the 1848 treaty by which the United States had promised to guarantee Colombia's sovereignty and property in the isthmus. In 1914, the Wilson administration negotiated a treaty with Colombia, ratified in 1921, by which the United States expressed "sincere regret that anything should have occurred to interrupt or mar the relations of cordial friendship that had so long subsisted between the two governments," and agreed to pay an indemnity of $25 million.[43]

The Roosevelt Corollary to the Monroe Doctrine

Theodore Roosevelt justified his speedy recognition of the Panamanian revolutionaries as "an act justified by the interests of collective civilization."[44] He advanced a similar justification for military interventions in the affairs of Caribbean countries that could not maintain order or pay their bills to European and American creditors:

> All that this country desires is to see the neighboring countries stable, orderly, and prosperous. Any country whose people conduct themselves well can count upon our hearty friendship. If a nation shows that it knows how to act with reasonable efficiency and decency in social and political matters, if it keeps order and pays its obligations, it need fear no interference from the United States. Chronic wrongdoing, or an impotence which results in a general loosening of the ties of civilized society, may in America, as elsewhere, ultimately require intervention by some civilized nation, and in the Western Hemisphere the adherence of the United States to the Monroe Doctrine may force the United States, however reluctantly, in flagrant cases of such wrongdoing or impotence, to the exercise of an international police power....
>
> Our interests and those of our southern neighbors are in reality identical. They have great natural riches, and if within their borders the reign of law and justice obtains, prosperity is sure to come to them. While they thus obey the primary laws of civilized society they may rest assured that they will be treated by us in a spirit of cordial and helpful sympathy. We would interfere with them only in the last resort, and then only if it became evident that their inability or unwillingness to do justice at home and abroad had violated the rights of the United States or had invited foreign aggression to the detriment of the entire body of American nations. It is a mere truism to say that every nation, whether in America or anywhere else, which desires to maintain its freedom, its independence, must ultimately realize that the right of such independence can not be separated from the responsibility of making good use of it. [Richardson, *Messages*, XIV, 6923.]

Politically, Roosevelt had little choice. Either the United States "policed" the impecunious Caribbean states or European powers would do it. In fact, they had done so in 1902 when the Venezuelan dictator, Cipriano Castro, defaulted on some foreign debts. Britain and

---

Have I defended myself?" "You certainly have," Root replied. "You have shown that you were accused of seduction and you have conclusively proved that you were guilty of rape." Quoted in Jessup, *Elihu Root*, I (1938), 404–05.

43. Bemis, *Short History*, 307. The discovery of oil in Colombia helped to encourage this contrition.

44. De Conde, *A History of American Foreign Policy*, I, 348.

Germany captured four Venezuelan gunboats, Britain landed troops at La Guayra and bombarded forts at Puerto Cabello, while British, German, and Italian ships blockaded Venezuela's major ports. Roosevelt shared the Europeans' contempt for the black and racially mixed societies of Latin America, but he also recognized that if the United States did not bring some stability to the finances and politics of Caribbean nations, foreign intervention to protect foreign creditors could end up threatening the security of the Panamanian isthmus. The result was Roosevelt's theory of "preventive intervention" by the president as commander in chief and chief diplomat exercising what he called an "international police power."

Between 1901 and 1917, the United States instituted a system of "protectorates" in the Caribbean to forestall European intervention. The chief recipients of this "protection," which came in the form of military occupations, were Cuba, Panama, Nicaragua, and Haiti.

Are these interventions valid historical precedents for President George W. Bush's invasion of Iraq in 2003?

Nicaragua

Nicaragua, with its alternative canal route, was of continuing interest to the United States, even while the Panama Canal was being dug. As part of its search for stability in the Caribbean, the United States chose to break diplomatic relations with Nicaragua in 1909 when its dictator approved the execution of two Americans for joining a revolutionary army. In 1910, 100 marines were sent into Bluefields, Nicaragua, ostensibly to protect American lives and property, but also to free revolutionary forces from having to garrison the town. The revolutionary forces then defeated a government force and a new government, more sympathetic to the United States, was established. This new government, led by Adolfo Díaz, negotiated a treaty that provided for American control of the customs service and an American loan. When the Senate refused to ratify the treaty, its provisions were carried out by executive action.

In 1912, 2,350 sailors and marines were sent into Nicaragua to rescue Díaz's reform administration from another uprising. The American forces occupied the capital, seized the towns of León and Chinandega, defeated a rebel force holding the railroad between Managua and Granada, and generally assured the survival of the Díaz regime. For thirteen years thereafter, the United States maintained a large marine contingent in Managua as a deterrent to future uprisings. As a result of this intervention, the United States secured a perpetual monopoly over the Nicaraguan canal route and the option of setting up naval bases, should they be needed, at either end of the route.

Haiti

The Negro state of Haiti, unlike most Caribbean countries, had maintained its independence from foreign domination since 1804. It was better at paying its foreign debts than its neighbors, but it, too, was wracked by frequent revolutions and corrupt tyrannies. Financial and political instability, large German investments, and the outbreak of World War I caused the Wilson administration to fear for the security of the new Panama Canal should Haiti be occupied by Imperial Germany.

During a revolution in 1914, both Germany and the United States landed forces at Port-au-Prince to protect their interests. Thereafter, President Wilson pressed for an American customs receivership like one that had been successfully imposed on the Dominican Republic. The Haitians resisted until the brutal regime of Guillaume Sam dissolved in an orgy of political murders. Then the United States sent in 2,000 marines, restored order and imposed an American military government that, for all practical purposes, ruled Haiti until 1934.

The Dominican Republic

The American navy also policed the Dominican Republic. In 1912, President Taft sent in a U.S. commission, backed by 750 marines, to end revolutionary interference with five U.S.-run customs houses and to redefine the Haiti-Dominican Republic border. The commissioners also forced the corrupt Dominican president to resign by cutting off his revenues from the customs service. In July 1914, during another revolution, the U.S.S. *Machais* opened fire on Dominican government artillery batteries in order to end their bombardment of Puerto Plata, and forced that government to recognize the city as a neutral zone. In 1916, when another revolution broke out, the Wilson administration sent two warships and nearly 1,000 sailors and marines who, after several military engagements, forced the revolutionaries to lay down their arms and accept a provisional government. Subsequently, when it appeared likely that the Dominicans would elect the revolutionary leader president, Wilson authorized a proclamation decreeing U.S. military rule. The American navy governed the Dominican Republic until 1924.

Veracruz

While the smaller states of the Caribbean could be "policed" with a few warships and several battalions of marines, Mexico was not so easily dominated. In 1911, Francisco I. Madero overthrew the aged dictator, Porfirio Díaz. He also instituted a democratic government and land reforms that inspired American liberals but alienated American business interests, which owned over forty percent of Mexico's property. During the Taft administration, the U.S. ambassador encouraged Victoriano Huerta, a leading general, to overthrow the Madero regime and institute a government more hospitable to American business interests. However, when Huerta followed his successful coup by having Madero shot, President Wilson refused to recognize Huerta's government and sought to topple him from power. Wilson did not consider the protection of American lives and property in Mexico to be his job, but he did recognize an obligation to oppose dictators. He began by lifting the embargo on arms shipments to Mexico so that Huerta's foes could be resupplied. He also exaggerated several insignificant affronts to the U.S. flag, unavoidable in any civil war, in order to justify a military intervention. At first an intervention was planned at the oil-rich port of Tampico, but when news came that Huerta was expecting a shipment of arms at Veracruz, the marines were sent ashore there instead. Like Theodore Roosevelt, Wilson acted out of a duty to "civilization," but unlike Roosevelt, he naively expected that the Mexican people would welcome an invasion. They did not. Hundreds of Mexicans and nineteen Americans died in the fighting for Veracruz. Wilson ordered the invasion, which was clearly an act of war, on his own authority, but with the all but certain knowledge that Congress would ratify his action, which it did the very next day. Besieged by three Mex-

A contingent of U.S. sailors from the battleship *Utah*, led by a Mexican brass band, marches through Veracruz, Mexico, 1914.

ican armies and cut off from Veracruz, Huerta resigned, but the civil war among contending factions continued, and Veracruz remained occupied for seven months.

Reprisal. May the president use military force against another nation in order to "enforce respect" for the government and people of the United States? This is a theme that runs through many uses of military force, from the punishment of pirates, to the chastisement of Japanese warlords, to the occupation of Veracruz. The "right" of nations to conduct limited and proportional acts of reprisal against those who affront them is "recognized" in international law and practice, and the law of nations is generally regarded as a source of national authority. However, may the president, on his own, order military reprisals against foreign nations, revolutionaries, or mobs? If so, when? If not, why not?

The Pershing Expedition

In 1915, after withdrawing from Veracruz and watching developments within Mexico, President Wilson chose to recognize the government of General Venustiano Carranza and to embargo arms shipments to his opponents, including General Francisco ("Pancho") Villa. Infuriated by this action, Villa hoped to precipitate a Mexican-American war by attacking "the barbarians of the North." On January 10, 1916, he stopped a train in northern Mexico, ordered seventeen young American engineers out, and had sixteen shot on the spot. Two months later he sent 400 of his men across the border into Columbus, New Mexico, where they shot everyone in sight and set fire to the town. Nineteen Americans and sixty-seven Mexicans died in the raid, and Wilson sent General John ("Black Jack") Pershing and a force of 7,000 soldiers into Mexico in pursuit of Villa. They did not capture him, but fought with forces of the recognized government instead. Wilson ordered the National Guard into federal service, and for a moment it appeared that the two nations would go to war, just as Villa had planned. But then the Germans sank the *Lusitania*, and Pershing's troops were withdrawn in anticipation of U.S. entry into World War I.

Hot pursuit. Wilson sought to justify the Pershing expedition in terms of the idea of "hot pursuit." At common law, the "hot pursuit" doctrine permits police officers to invade the sanctity of private homes when they are in "hot pursuit" of felons. At international law, the doctrine of "hot pursuit" permits coastal states to invade the sanctity of the high seas in order to capture ships that have violated their territorial waters. Are either of these analogies persuasive justifications for the Pershing expedition? Did Villa's murderous raid

General "Black Jack" Pershing's troops invaded Mexico in 1916 in a failed attempt to capture "Pancho" Villa, a border raider.

on Columbus, New Mexico, justify Wilson's decision to invade Mexico from the north without first obtaining Congress's permission? Did Pershing's expedition constitute an "act of war" or was Mexico, at that moment, a "failed state?"

Nicaragua

In 1926, President Coolidge ordered the military to occupy Nicaragua again to end civil war and reestablish order. The intervention was supported by several political factions, but opposed by one of the Liberal generals, and he and his supporters waged guerrilla warfare against the U.S. troops for several years. The U.S. forces in or en route to Nicaragua grew to 5,000 at one point, and remained until 1933. Like his predecessors, Coolidge undertook this "police action" on his own initiative. The Senate Committee on Foreign Relations supported retention of the troops but took no position on the constitutionality of Coolidge's decision to deploy them.

The "Police Power" Reviewed

What conclusions can be drawn from this brief review of the use of American military force in the Far East, Caribbean, and Mexico during the late-nineteenth and early-twentieth centuries? Does the absence of effective congressional resistance to these presidential initiatives put a "gloss" upon the Constitution that adds to the president's powers and makes similar military actions in the future constitutionally legitimate? Can distinctions of constitutional significance be drawn among the various deployments according to their announced or actual purposes? Was the primary purpose of most of these "police actions," like the invasion of China in 1900, really to promote law, order, and civilization? Which, if any, may be so characterized? Should a constitutional distinction be drawn between "police actions" to stamp out piracy and slavery, or to rescue U.S. nationals (or other "innocent" persons), and actions calculated to change the distribution of political power or the structure of legal authority within a foreign land? Or is it the function of the president, acting alone, to use the armed forces to "make the world safe" for, and even hospitable to, American economic interests? Does the fear that a hostile great power like Germany (or the Soviet Union) might gain military bases in the Caribbean through its assertion of an international "police power" justify the forceable occupation of Caribbean countries by the United States? If so, on whose authority? The president's alone, or the president and Congress, perhaps by joint resolution?

The "Act of War" Doctrine

Should congressional involvement turn on the likely threat of war from the country to be "policed" or its allies, with the result that presidents may unilaterally intervene militarily in the affairs of small, weak nations, or large nations torn by civil war, because they are, at the moment, incapable of effective retaliation? This is the theory of the *act of war" doctrine* popular during the nineteenth century. Robert William Russell has described the doctrine:

> It is not a simple matter to arrive at conclusions concerning [the 19th century] in which the constitutional interpretation was far from consistent, where Grant's extreme view is sandwiched between the conservative views of Buchanan and Cleveland. But there was one opinion that enjoyed wide acceptance: the President could constitutionally employ American military force outside the nation as long as he did not use it to commit "acts of war." While the term was never precisely defined, an "act of war" in this context usually meant *the use of military force against a sovereign nation* without that nation's *consent* and without that nation's having declared war upon or used force against the United States. To perform acts of war, the President needed the authorization of Congress. ["The United States Congress and the Power to Use Military Force Abroad," Ph.D. thesis, Fletcher School of Law and Diplomacy, 1967.]

Does the "act of war" doctrine provide a sound conceptual basis on which to build a constitutional policy governing when the president may, or may not, use military force on his own authority? Was the "act of war" doctrine followed by Presidents McKinley, Roosevelt, Taft, and Wilson in their "policing" of the Caribbean?

Interposition and Intervention

One justification offered for the presidential use of military force to protect American lives and property was that the president was not committing an "act of war," but merely *interposing* U.S. forces between disorganized governments, revolutionary forces, or mobs and American interests. In using the term, presidents sought to convey the impression, not always true, that the United States was essentially indifferent toward the outcome of the violence. The theory wore thin, of course, when occupation followed interposition. Then it became known as the doctrine of *intervention*, which was alleged to be temporary in nature and as much for the good of the foreign country as it was for the United States. The doctrines of interposition and intervention helped to distinguish American foreign policy from that of the colonial superpowers. They were invoked anew in 1965 when President Johnson ordered the military to occupy the Dominican Republic. More recent terms for intervention are "regime change" and "nation building."

The Dominican Republic

When Franklin Roosevelt assumed the presidency, he pledged an end to gunboat diplomacy and the beginning of a "good neighbor" policy toward Latin America. In 1947, President Truman joined with other members of the Organization of American States (OAS) to foreswear unilateral intervention. This policy persisted until the early 1960s, when rising Soviet influence in Cuba again subordinated the sovereignty of Caribbean nations to the security concerns of the United States.

When the United States Navy withdrew from the Dominican Republic in 1924, it left behind a centralized Dominican army under the control of Rafael Trujillo, Sr. Trujillo's avidly pro-American foreign and economic policies encouraged successive presidents to overlook the fact that he had also established one of the most murderous feudal dictatorships in modern Caribbean history. U.S. support for his regime began to falter only when it became clear that support for moderate, or somewhat left-of-center, governments might be the only way to prevent export of the Communist revolution in Cuba. Then the CIA began to provide arms to dissident Dominicans bent on assassinating Trujillo.[45]

On May 31, 1961, Trujillo was assassinated, and the Dominican Republic was plunged into a long period of political chaos. Within days of the assassination, the U.S. Navy's Caribbean "ready force" of three aircraft carriers, five support ships, and a contingent of five thousand marines entered Dominican waters on what was called a "routine training exercise." President Kennedy stated his objectives succinctly: "There are three possibilities …: a decent democratic regime, a continuation of the Trujillo regime or a Castro regime. We ought to aim at the first but we really can't renounce the second until we are sure we can avoid the third."[46] Kennedy got the second with promises of eventual liberalization. To enforce these promises, he obtained OAS support for economic sanctions and maintained a "ready squadron" of one carrier, several amphibious vessels, and 1,200 marines off the Dominican coast. When the Trujillo family was permitted to return from exile, the force was augmented, moved up into plain sight of Santo Domingo, and directed to send its jet fighters streaking up and down the Dominican coast. Meanwhile, the Trujillos and their retainers were told bluntly that U.S. military force would be used, if necessary, to force the creation of a provisional government that did not support the Trujillos. The threats succeeded, and the Trujillo faction abandoned its effort to regain control.

When Juan Bosch was elected to the Dominican presidency in 1962, there were high hopes within the Kennedy administration that progress had been made toward the establishment of democracy. However, when Bosch initiated programs calculated to bring about a substantial redistribution of wealth, and then refused to suppress radical groups, American support was withdrawn and Bosch was overthrown by a pro-business, right-

---

45. *Alleged Assassination Plots Involving Foreign Leaders.* An Interim Report of the Select Committee to Study Government Operations With Respect to Intelligence Activities, U.S. Senate, 94th Cong., 1st Sess. (1975), 5, 191–216.

46. Schlesinger, Jr., *A Thousand Days: John F. Kennedy in the White House* (1965), 769.

of-center military coup. The Kennedy administration did not want this coup, but rejected Ambassador Martin's request for an aircraft carrier to dramatize American opposition. The new regime, headed by Donald Reid Cabral, a wealthy businessman, promised new elections, but severe economic difficulties and his efforts to stamp out military corruption gradually eroded his support. When it became clear that Reid intended either to cancel the elections or rig them in his favor, a small group of colonels who favored the return of Juan Bosch attempted a coup.

By 1965, the U.S. State Department had come to view the return of Bosch as a major step toward a Communist takeover in the Dominican Republic. When it became uncertain that the right-of-center military faction could prevail over Bosch's supporters, President Johnson decided to intervene militarily. On April 28, when the first American troops went ashore, Johnson justified the landing solely in terms of accomplishing the safe evacuation of American and foreign nationals. Two days later, the president spoke ominously of "people trained outside the Dominican Republic ... seeking to gain control," and on May 2, after the evacuation of American residents was largely complete, he sent in two thousand more marines and announced, for the first time, that "Our goal, in keeping with the principles of the inter-American system, is to prevent another Communist state in this hemisphere."[47] In fact, the invasion made a mockery of the first principle of the inter-American system, expressed in OAS agreement of 1948, which was that no member nation should engage in unilateral military action against another.

By May 9, there were 23,000 American troops in the country (with tanks) and another 3,300 marines on board a 35-ship task force waiting offshore. The U.S. troops kept the contending factions apart, skirmished with pro-Bosch Constitutionalists (leaving sixty-seven dead), and kept other factions from defeating the Constitutionalists. Eventually a peace commission from the OAS, backed by an Inter-American Peace Force, negotiated a provisional government and free elections. In those elections Joaquín Balaguer, Trujillo's retainer and president until the Bosch election, was reelected by a wide margin over Bosch, very possibly because a vote for Balaguer was seen by many as a vote for stability and respite from military coups and foreign interventions. After the elections, U.S. forces were withdrawn, along with the OAS peace commission.

President Johnson ordered the Dominican intervention on his own authority. According to a leading scholar of the event, no prior objection was raised by any of the government officials, including those members of Congress who knew about it in advance.[48] Several resolutions in support of the move were offered in Congress, and one, which endorsed the use of force individually or collectively by any country in the Western hemisphere to prevent a Communist takeover, passed the House by a vote of 312 to 52.[49] The Senate took no action.

Grenada

On October 25, 1983, President Reagan ordered 1,900 army and marine troops to invade the Island of Grenada. The invasion took place during an attempted coup by radical pro-Cuban Marxists against moderate pro-Cuban Marxists. The purpose of the invasion,

---

47. *Dept. of State Bull.* 52, No. 1351 (May 17, 1965).
48. Abraham F. Lowenthal, *The Dominican Intervention* (1972), 151.
49. *Background Information on the Use of U.S. Armed Forces in Foreign Countries*, 1975 Revision, U.S. Library of Congress (1975), 54.

the president said, was not only to "protect our own citizens" (of whom there were about one thousand on the island), but also to "help in the restoration of democratic institutions in Grenada" where, he said, "a brutal group of leftist thugs violently seized power."

Secretary of State George Shultz, when asked to reconcile the invasion with Articles 15 and 17 of the OAS charter forbidding member states to use armed force against each other, said that the United States had invaded Grenada at the urgent request of neighboring island countries and that those countries had acted pursuant to the treaty which established the Organization of Eastern Caribbean States (OECS).[50]

The United States was not a party to that treaty but, with Grenada, had signed the OAS treaty. The United States was also a party, with Grenada, to the Charter of the United Nations. That treaty forbids the United States to use "the threat or use of force" in international affairs except for individual or collective self-defense against "armed attack." (Articles 4 and 51.)

There had been no armed attack by Grenada on any country. However, Grenada was, with Cuban, Soviet, and British assistance, building a ten thousand foot-long runway capable of supporting military attacks on oil tankers, depots, and refineries in nearby Venezuela. Secretary Shultz denied that the invasion had any other purpose than to protect Americans and restore "law and order," but he offered no evidence that Americans in Grenada were endangered by the coup, or that many Americans on the island were seeking to depart. The invasion had, in fact, been planned for several years as a means for deposing the moderate Marxist regime.

By what authority, then, did the president authorize this invasion? Does the president have inherent authority to order "police actions" whenever he wishes if his purpose is to restore "democratic institutions," or was the invasion an "act of war" requiring a congressional declaration of war? Can foreign invitations to organize and lead a multinational invasion force confer war-making authority on the president? Does the president have the authority unilaterally to abrogate the charters of the United Nations and the Organization of American States?

Persian Gulf War

> *"I didn't have to get permission from some old goat in the United States Congress kick Saddam Hussein out of Kuwait."*
>
> — George H. W. Bush[51]

After Iraq invaded Kuwait in August 1990, President George H. W. Bush deployed U.S. forces to the region on his own initiative. The deployment was allegedly to deter further aggression, especially against Saudi Arabia, but in November Bush doubled the size of U.S. forces, claiming the need for an "adequate offensive military option." At this point the issue arose: May a president take the nation from a defensive to offensive posture without first obtaining permission from Congress?

Secretary of Defense Dick Cheney insisted that President Bush did not require "any additional authority from the Congress" before attacking Iraq.[52] Fifty-four members of Con-

---

50. *New York Times*, Oct. 26, 1983, A19, A18.
51. Remarks before the Texas State Republican Convention, Dallas, Texas, June 20, 1992.
52. "Crisis in the Persian Gulf Region," Hearings before the Senate Committee on Armed Services, 101st Cong., 2d Sess. 701 (1990).

gress challenged this view in federal district court. Judge Harold H. Greene ruled that they had standing to sue, but dismissed their case as not ripe for adjudication. *Dellums v. Bush,* 752 F. Supp. 1141 (D.D.C. 1990). At what point in a military build-up may courts properly hold that the executive must seek authority from Congress before attacking another country? If the courts refuse to decide these cases, haven't they, in effect, allowed the executive to usurp authority clearly granted by the Constitution to Congress?

Suppose both Houses of Congress were to pass concurrent resolutions forbidding offensive military action by the President. Would that be sufficient to make a lawsuit by members of Congress ripe for adjudication?

While Judge Greene dismissed the *Dellums* case as premature, he rejected the Justice Department's claim that the president might label offensive military action as something short of "war." He also denied that the Constitution commits decisions regarding offensive military operations to the political branches of government only.

On January 12, 1991, Congress bowed to the inevitability of war and passed a joint resolution "supporting" the president's policy in the Persian Gulf.[53] Is a resolution "supporting" a general policy sufficient to grant the President authority to attack another nation? Two days later, President Bush stated that "my signing this resolution does not constitute any change in the long-standing positions of the executive branch on either the president's constitutional authority to use the Armed Forces to defend vital U.S. interests or on the constitutionality of the War Powers Resolution."[54]

Previously, on November 29, the United Nations Security Council had issued a resolution which "authorized" member states to take all necessary steps to enforce Security Council resolutions condemning Iraq's invasion. Is this the same as directing the United States to invade Iraq, rather than just authorizing it to expel Iraqi forces from Kuwait? May the UN order any nation to invade another country? May it override Congress' authority to "declare war"?

An American invasion force drove Iraqi troops from Kuwait, but stopped short of occupying Iraq.

Missile Attacks on Baghdad

In 1993, the Kuwaiti government charged sixteen suspects, including two Iraqi nationals, of attempting to assassinate former President Bush. Without waiting for the Kuwaiti court to render a verdict, President Bill Clinton ordered a missile attack on the Iraqi capital of Baghdad. Twenty-three cruise missiles struck the city, damaging the Iraqi intelligence services headquarters and destroying nearby homes, killing eight people and wounding at least twelve others. The President did not seek Congress' permission for this attack, but claimed constitutional authority under his commander-in-chief and foreign-affairs powers. Is this persuasive? The attack was "essential to protect our sovereignty," he said, and to "send a message to those who engage in state sponsored terrorism...."[55] Does the Constitution grant the president authority to bomb foreign cities to send diplomatic messages? Does it give him the authority to use missile attacks as a reprisal against assassination attempts on former U.S. officials?

53. 105 Stat. 3 (1991).
54. 27 Weekly Comp. Pres. Doc. 48 (1991).
55. 29 Weekly Com. Pres. Doc. 1181.

Relevance of Framers' Intent

Consider the following passage by John Bassett Moore, the leading American authority on international law during the late nineteenth and early-twentieth centuries. "There can hardly be room for doubt that the framers of the Constitution, when they vested in Congress the power to declare war, never imagined that they were leaving it to the executive to use the military and naval forces of the United States all over the world for the purpose of actually coercing other nations, occupying their territory, and killing their soldiers and citizens, all according to his notion of the fitness of things, as long as he refrained from calling his action war or persisted in calling it peace."[56] If this is true, is it still relevant, given the history of presidentially ordered military interventions tolerated by Congress and unquestioned by the courts? Should the founders' intent continue to set constitutional standards when the circumstances of world order and American economic and strategic concerns have been so radically altered by technology, secrecy, a huge standing military force, and a substantial capability for paramilitary and covert operations?

Relevance of Congressional Attitudes

When the framers wrote the Constitution, they anticipated a relatively small Congress, and an even smaller Senate, with whom the president might consult with relative ease, provided that they were in session. Today Congress is almost always in session, or can be quickly recalled, but it has grown so large as to make meaningful consultations (or secrecy) nearly impossible. Moreover, as the Steel Seizure case and most of the foregoing incidents suggest, members of Congress are hesitant to oppose limited military actions at the outset. Like most Americans, they admire decisiveness and are patriotic in times of crisis, and are willing to presume that the president is well informed and knows what he is doing. Those with misgivings often choose to remain silent, either because they are not confident of their own sources of information or because they fear embarrassment or political reprisals. Finally, some members of Congress, particularly of the opposing party, may be reluctant to share responsibility for a potentially unpopular action. By resisting the joint role that the founders appear to have prescribed, members of Congress remain in the politically safe position of being able to call for decisive action (without specifying what that action should be), supporting "our boys" (but not necessarily the president) when the shooting starts, and then criticizing the president (but not "our boys") when the mission ends in failure.

If this is an accurate characterization of congressional attitudes—and these attitudes reflect a shrewd assessment of electoral realities in the age of electronic communications and well-organized interest groups—does it make sense to insist upon a return to the framers' intent? If Congress were more involved in these decisions, would the quality of decision making improve? Would the frequency of military actions decrease? Would significant opportunities be lost? Would lives be saved? Would American foreign policy become more consistent? Would the process be more "democratic"?

---

56. Moore, *Collected Papers*, V (1944), 195–96.

Dignity

Consider the following statement by Senator Paul Douglas (D-Ill.) during the early days of the Korean War.

> There is indeed good reason, besides the need for speed, why the President should have been permitted to use force in these cases without a formal declaration of war by Congress. That is because international situations frequently call for the retail use of force in localized situations which are not sufficiently serious to justify the wholesale and widespread use of force which a formal declaration of war would require.
>
> In other words, it may be desirable to create a situation which is half-way between complete peace, or the absence of all force, and outright war marked by the exercise of tremendous force on a wholesale scale. This is most notably the case when big powers deal with small countries, and in situations where only a relatively temporary application of force is needed to restore order and to remove the threat of aggression. It would be below the dignity of the United States to declare war on a pigmy state, but it might be necessary to apply force in such a case in order to prevent attacks on American lives and property. [96 *Cong. Rec.* 9648, July 5, 1950]

Do you agree? Did North Korea, supported by China and the Soviet Union, turn out to be a "pigmy state"? Did the wars in Vietnam, Afghanistan, and Iraq turn out to involve "relatively temporary applications of force"?

E. Authority to Wage and Risk Modern Warfare

In many respects, the American Civil War (1861–1865) was the first war of the industrial age. It was the first war of mass conscript armies equipped with mass-produced weapons, transported by trains and steamships, and controlled by electronic communications. The scale of its carnage and the speed of its devastation made the "imperfect wars" of the previous century seem child's play by comparison.

The Industrial Revolution transformed the concept of warfare, the requisites of national security, and the range of purposes for which military force could be applied. It gave industrialized nations the capacity to maintain or quickly mobilize large military forces and to deploy them swiftly, and thereby increased the opportunities, temptations, and risks of warfare. It also created huge arms industries with a stake in military solutions to international problems, and gave the industrial nations an impetus to compete in the sale of arms to less developed countries.

Neutrality and isolationism no longer guaranteed freedom from foreign military entanglements. Nineteenth-century Americans could think of national security largely in terms of continental defense; twentieth-century Americans had to consider the balance of powers, alliances, and collective security. The lines between foreign and domestic affairs blurred as the nation mobilized for total war, and as national security concerns spawned intelligence agencies focused on domestic politics as well as international relations. Concern for the maintenance of favorable balances of power also led to the increased use of paramilitary and covert action to attack, undermine, and destabilize foreign governments and foreign economies.

In this section we examine the president's authority to wage and risk warfare in the light of these developments.

Presidential Recognition That a "State of War" Exists

When the framers chose to give Congress the power to "declare" rather than "make" war, they thought that they were giving the president the power to repel sudden attacks. They did not pause to consider whether the president could, in the course of responding to an attack, declare the existence of a *"state of war"* and thereby alter the legal rights and obligations of citizens and foreigners alike. Nor did they discuss the possibility that a president, like Polk, might provoke an attack, and then recognize the existence of a state of war in the legal, as well as military, sense.

The Constitution does not define all hostile military actions against U.S. interests as acts of war that necessarily create a state of war with all of its adverse legal consequences to the liberty and property of the belligerents and those who do business with them. The text speaks of war, rebellion, and invasion, and implicitly acknowledges imperfect war by the clause governing letters of marque and reprisal. Thus, there is no textual impediment to treating each of these circumstances differently as a matter of constitutional law.

On the other hand, if one thinks of the *war power* in monolithic terms, it is not difficult to accept the thesis that in times of dire emergency all of the accouterments of that power must be entrusted to the president as commander in chief. By talking of a single, comprehensive war power, one also shifts the definitional referents from the Constitution and its allocation of powers, to international law and its lack of concern for constitutional theories regarding the locus of sovereignty. This was the view of Abraham Lincoln as president. "I think the Constitution invests its commander-in-chief clause with the law of war, in time of war," he wrote in 1863, implicitly contradicting the position he had taken against Polk during the Mexican War.[57] In his message to Congress on July 8, 1861, Lincoln announced that he had taken it upon himself "to call out the war power of the Government and to resist force employed for its destruction...."[58] Later he asserted that "As commander-in-chief ... I have a right to take any measure which may best subdue the enemy,"[59] including, he told another correspondent, "things ... which cannot constitutionally be done by Congress."[60]

When the southern states declared independence from the United States in April 1861, Lincoln refused to treat them as a nation that other nations might recognize and supply. Nor could he treat them as a mere criminal conspiracy or minor uprising, which would require him to respect their property rights even as he used the military to suppress their violence. So he chose to treat them as nongovernmental belligerents, in the nature of, but not technically, foreign states. Pursuant to this concept, Lincoln violated laws and constitutional provisions by assembling the militia, enlarging the army and navy beyond

---

57. Letter to J. G. Conkling, Aug. 26, 1863, *Works*, VI, 406.
58. Richardson, *Messages*, IV, 23.
59. Letter to a Chicago church committee, Sept. 13, 1862, *Works*, V, 421.
60. Letter to S. P. Chase, Sept. 2, 1863, *Works*, VI, 428. But see *Fleming v. Page*, 50 U.S. (9 How.) 603 (1850), in which the Supreme Court took the position that the Commander-in-Chief Clause did not "extend the operation of our institutions beyond the limits assigned to them by the legislative power." See also Lincoln's message (footnote 2 of this section), in which he claimed that nothing he had done exceeded the powers of Congress.

their authorized strengths, calling for volunteers for three years' service, spending public money without congressional appropriations, suspending the privilege of the writ of habeas corpus, arresting people on mere suspicion of disloyalty, and instituting a naval blockade of the Confederacy. All of these actions, he later told Congress, "whether strictly legal or not, were ventured upon under what appeared to be a popular demand and a public necessity; trusting then as now that Congress would readily ratify them."[61]

The Prize Cases
67 U.S. (2 Black) 635 (1863)

Congress did not ratify Lincoln's blockade until July 1861. In the interim, a number of southern and foreign ships were seized by Union warships and put up for sale. The owners of four of these ships argued in court that the president had no authority to order the blockade or the seizure and sale of blockade runners and their cargoes. Counsel for the owners of the Mexican schooner *Brilliante* noted that the power "to declare war, grant letters of marque and reprisal, and make rules concerning captures on land and water" was vested by the Constitution in Congress, not the president. He added:

> The principle of self-defense is asserted; and all power is claimed for the President. This is to assert that the Constitution contemplated and tacitly provided that the President should be dictator, and all Constitutional Government be at an end, whenever he should think that 'the life of the nation' is in danger....
>
> It comes to the plea of necessity. The Constitution knows no such word. (67 U.S. [2 Black], 648).

The Court, in a 5–4 decision, upheld Lincoln's actions without accepting (or rejecting) his theory of wartime necessity.

MR. JUSTICE GRIER....

War has been well defined to be "That state in which a nation prosecutes its right by force."

The parties belligerent in a public war are independent nations. But it is not necessary to constitute war that both parties should be acknowledged as independent nations or sovereign States. A war may exist where one of the belligerents claims sovereign rights as against the other.

---

61. Richardson, *Messages*, IV, 23.

… When the party in rebellion occupy and hold in a hostile manner a certain portion of territory; have declared their independence; have case off their allegiance; have organized armies; have commenced hostilities against their former sovereign, the world acknowledges them as belligerents, and the contest *a war*. …

As a civil war is never publicly proclaimed, *eo nomine* [by that name], against insurgents, its actual existence is a fact in our domestic history which the Court is bound to notice and to know.

The true test of its existence, as found in the writings of the sages of the common law, may be thus summarily stated: "'When the regular course of justice is interrupted by revolt, rebellion, or insurrection, so that the Courts of Justice cannot be kept open, *civil war exists* and hostilities may be prosecuted on the same footing as if those opposing the Government were foreign enemies invading the land."

By the Constitution, Congress alone has the power to declare a national or foreign war. It cannot declare war against a State, or any number of States, by virtue of any clause in the Constitution. The Constitution confers on the president the whole Executive power. He is bound to take care that the laws be faithfully executed. He is Commander-in-chief of the Army and Navy of the United States, and of the militia of the several States when called into the actual service of the United States. He has no power to initiate or declare a war either against a foreign nation or a domestic State. But by the Acts of Congress of February 28th, 1795, and 3d of March, 1807, he is authorized to call out the militia and use the military and naval forces of the United States in case of invasion by foreign nations, and to suppress insurrection against the government of a State or of the United States.

If a war be made by invasion of a foreign nation, the President is not only authorized but bound to resist force by force. He does not initiate the war, but is bound to accept the challenge without waiting for any special legislative authority. And whether the hostile party be a foreign invader, or States organized in rebellion, it is none the less a war, although the declaration of it be *"unilateral."* …

This greatest of civil wars was not gradually developed by popular commotion, tumultuous assemblies, or local unorganized insurrections. However long may have been its previous conception, it nevertheless sprung forth suddenly from the parent brain, a Minerva in the full panoply of *war*. The President was bound to meet it in the shape it presented itself, without waiting for Congress to baptize it with a name; and no name given to it by him or them could change the fact.

It is not the less a civil war, with belligerent parties in hostile array, because it may be called an "insurrection" by one side, and the insurgents be considered as rebels or traitors. It is not necessary that the independence of the revolted province or State be acknowledged in order to constitute it a party belligerent in a war according to the law of nations. Foreign nations acknowledge it as war by a declaration of neutrality. …

After such an official recognition by the sovereign, a citizen of a foreign State is estopped to deny the existence of a war with all its consequences as regards neutrals. They cannot ask a Court to affect a technical ignorance of the existence of a war, which all the world acknowledges to be the greatest civil war known in the history of the human race, and thus cripple the arm of the Government and paralyze its power by subtle definitions and ingenious sophisms....

Whether the President in fulfilling his duties, as Commander-in-chief, in suppressing an insurrection, has met with such armed hostile resistance, and a civil war of such alarming proportions as will compel him to accord to them the character of belligerents, is a question to be decided *by him*, and this Court must be governed by the decisions and acts of the political department of the Government to which this power was entrusted. "He must determine what degree of force the crisis demands." The proclamation of blockade is itself official and conclusive evidence to the Court that a state of war existed which demanded and authorized a recourse to such a measure, under the circumstances peculiar to the case....

If it were necessary to the technical existence of a war, that it should have a legislative sanction, we find it in almost every act passed at the extraordinary session of the Legislature of 1861, which was wholly employed in enacting laws to enable the Government to prosecute the war with vigor and efficiency. And finally, in 1861, we find Congress *"ex major cautela"* [with the most careful consideration] and in anticipation of such astute objections, passing an act "approving, legalizing, and making valid all the acts, proclamations, and orders of the President, &c., as if they had been *issued and done under the previous express authority* and direction of the Congress of the United States."...

Without admitting that such an act was necessary under the circumstances, it is plain that if the President had in any manner assumed powers which it was necessary should have the authority or sanction of Congress, ... this ratification has operated to perfectly cure the defect.

The objection made to this act of ratification, that it is *ex post facto*, and therefore unconstitutional and void, might possibly have some weight on the trial of an indictment in a criminal Court. But precedents from that source cannot be received as authoritative in a tribunal administering public and international law.

... Therefore we are of the opinion that the president had a right, *jure belli* [under the laws of war], to institute a blockade of ports in possession of the States in rebellion, which neutrals are bound to regard....

MR. JUSTICE NELSON, dissenting.

Now, in one sense, no doubt this is war, and may be a war of the most extensive and threatening dimensions and effects, but it is a statement simply of its existence in a material sense, and has no relevancy or weight when the question is what constitutes war in a legal sense, in the sense of the law of nations, and of the Constitution of the United States. For it must be a war in this sense to attach to it all the consequences that belong to belligerent rights. Instead, therefore, of inquiring after armies and navies, and victories lost and won, or organized rebellion against the general Government, the inquiry should be into the law of nations and into the municipal fundamental laws of the Government. For we find there that to constitute a civil war in the sense in which we are speaking, before it can exist, in contemplation of law, it must be recognized or declared by the sovereign power of the State, and which sovereign power by our Constitution is lodged in the Congress of the United States—civil war, therefore, under our system of government, can exist only by an act of Congress, which requires the assent of two of the great departments of the Government, the Executive and Legislative....

… The laws of war, whether the war be civil or *inter gentes* [between members of the family of nations], as we have seen, convert every citizen of the hostile State into a public enemy, and treat him accordingly, whatever may have been his previous conduct. This great power over the business and property of the citizen is reserved to the legislative department by the express words of the Constitution. It cannot be delegated or surrendered to the Executive. Congress alone can determine whether war exists or should be declared; and until they have acted, no citizen of the State can be punished in his person or property, unless he has committed some offence against a law of Congress passed before the act was committed, which made it a crime, and defined the punishment. The penalty of confiscation for the acts of others with which he had no concern cannot lawfully be inflicted.…

CHIEF JUSTICE TANEY, JUSTICE CATRON and JUSTICE CLIFFORD, concurred in the dissenting opinion of JUSTICE NELSON.

Notes and Questions

1. *Holding or dicta?* The majority ultimately concluded that the blockade was ratified by Congress. Does this concession render the portion of its opinion dealing with the presidential power *obiter dicta* (statements unnecessary to the holding of the case, and therefore not precedent)? In *Freeborn v. "The Protector,"* 79 U.S. (12 Wall.) 700 (1872), the Court was required to ascertain the exact date the war began. It chose the day on which the president proclaimed the blockade.

2. *Scope of the precedent.* How broad is the precedent in the *Prize Cases*? Does it apply only to full-blown secessionist insurrections and foreign invasions, or does it authorize future presidents to "declare war" whenever foreign or domestic "acts of war" create what the president chooses to regard as a "state of war" requiring the full commitment of military resources and the triggering of wartime regulations governing the liberty and property of aliens and citizens? In the eighteenth century, immediate action by the president was probably required only in cases of direct attacks on the United States within its own territory. In the twentieth century, national security has become more collective, and a Soviet attack upon an important ally, such as West Germany, would have been regarded as the equivalent of a Soviet attack on the United States. Do the *Prize Cases* provide any guidance to a president faced with such a circumstance?

In 1962, the Soviet Union placed missiles in Cuba, and President Kennedy seriously contemplated ordering a "surgical air strike" to destroy them before they became operational. Do the *Prize Cases* provide any guidance to a president considering that kind of preemptive military action?

3. *Scope of the opinion.* Did the majority have to go as far as it did in the *Prize Cases*? For example, could the Court have upheld the blockade as a necessary defensive measure, but denied the president authority to have the ships and cargoes sold for prize money? Instead, they could have been impounded for the duration of the war, or until Congress could meet and decide what should become of them. Such a decision would have enabled the president to do what the framers expected him to do, and would have preserved for Congress the right and duty to baptize Lincoln's actions with both retroactive and prospective legal authority.

4. *The legal effect of a foreign attack on U.S. forces.* Must every attack upon the U.S. military forces necessarily create a "state of war" in American law and thereby make it le-

gitimate for the president to invoke the full range of his war-making power? In 1801, President Jefferson told Congress that Tripoli's attacks on American ships, including a naval schooner, did not automatically vest him with the authority to launch offensive action against the Algerians. (In fact, Jefferson had authorized offensive naval action in secret including the action that led to the attack on the naval schooner.) [See Section B, "Barbary Pirates," in this chapter.] Jefferson sought congressional authority for offensive action against Tripoli on the theory that his own warmaking powers were essentially defensive in nature. Was that request necessary? Would it have been legitimate for the president to declare the existence of a "state of war" or launch full-scale offensive military operations in response to the following incidents: the mysterious explosion of the battleship *Maine* in 1898, the Japanese bombing of the U.S. gunboat *Panay* in 1937, the North Vietnamese attack on U.S. destroyers in the Gulf of Tonkin in 1964, the Israeli bombing of the spy ship *Liberty* in 1967, the North Korean seizure of the spy ship *Pueblo* in 1969, the Cambodian seizure of the merchant ship *Mayaguez* in 1976, the Libyan attack on planes from the carrier *Nimitz* in 1981, or the Iraqi attack on the destroyer *Stark* in 1987? If the president does not have unilateral authority to declare "a state of war" in instances of this sort, how should the Court's decision in the *Prize Cases* be read?

5. *Effect of foreign declarations of war.* According to Alexander Hamilton, Tripoli's formal declaration of war against the United States made Jefferson's request for congressional authority to go beyond defensive action unnecessary.[62] Do you agree? May the president ignore a foreign declaration of war? Bulgaria, Romania, and Hungary declared war upon the United States on December 13, 1941, but President Roosevelt ignored the declarations until June 1942, when at the behest of the Soviet Union, he asked Congress to recognize that the United States was at war with those countries (88 Cong. Rec. 4787 [1942]).

6. *Ending wars.* If a president may recognize the existence of a state of war, and thereby deprive citizens and aliens of certain legal rights, may he continue to deprive them of those rights by declaring that the state of war continues even after hostilities have come to an end? In *Freeborn v. The "Protector"* (see note 1, *supra*), the Court decided that the Civil War ended when the president said that it had ended, but in that instance his proclamation coincided with the end of hostilities. In cases arising out of World War I and World War II, the Court has consistently treated this question as "political" and beyond its jurisdiction, but in every case the president's "war measures" in the postwar interim between the end of hostilities and the signing of peace treaties were carried out pursuant to a legislative authorization and were not clearly contrary to the legislature's will. See, for example, *Woods v. Miller Co.*, 333 U.S. 138 (1948), upholding a postwar rent control statute passed to deal with the lack of housing caused by demobilization, and *Ludecke v. Watkins*, 335 U.S. 160 (1948), upholding the deportation of a German national in 1946 pursuant to a statute that gave the president that power in time of "declared war."

Weighted Neutrality in the North Atlantic

Perfect neutrality in the midst of a foreign war is probably impossible. Neutrality that favors trade with both sides ends up helping one side more than the other. Neutrality that tries to avoid contact with either side ends up advantaging the stronger of the belligerents. To a nation that sees its security dependent upon a balance of military power in favor of its friends, a policy of neutrality must always be selective.

---

62. C. A. Berdahl, *War Powers of the Executive in the United States* (1921), 64.

During the 1930s, however, isolationist sentiment blinded most Americans to this obvious fact. According to one Gallup poll, 71 percent of all Americans believed that their country had been tricked into World War I. The Veterans of Foreign Wars campaigned for twenty-five million signatures to convince Congress that stricter neutrality legislation was needed,[63] and in 1937 Gallup found that three-quarters of the country favored a constitutional amendment that would have provided that, except in the case of an invasion, "the authority of Congress to declare war shall not become effective until confirmed by a majority of all votes cast in a Nation-wide referendum."[64]

Franklin Roosevelt did not share this sentiment. He saw the war clouds rising, and he sought Senate approval of a resolution permitting him to embargo arms shipments to aggressor nations. The Senate Foreign Relations Committee, however, amended the resolution to compel the president to stop arms shipments to *all* nations involved in war, thus advantaging the more heavily armed aggressors.[65] In 1940, after the British had been driven into the sea at Dunkirk and Winston Churchill had sent out his plea for "the loan of forty or fifty of your older destroyers" so that the Royal Navy could hold the English Channel, the Senate amended the naval appropriations bill to forbid the president to send military material to a foreign country unless the chief of staff of the army or the chief of naval operations certified that it was "not essential" to the defense of the United States.[66] Consider the constitutionality of each of these limitations on the president's authority to conduct foreign relations and carry out his responsibilities as commander in chief.

For several months, Roosevelt shared the general view that he could not supply Britain with the destroyers without congressional approval, which Congress was not about to grant. As Britain's plight became even more desperate, however, the president decided to act without Congress' permission and signed an executive agreement transferring the warships outright to Great Britain in return for leases permitting the U.S. to use British bases in the Caribbean. For Attorney General Jackson's legal defense of this "destroyers for bases" agreement, and subsequent comment on it, see notes 5–7 following *United States v. Belmont* in Chapter 3. Do you agree with Jackson that the exchange did not commit the United States to any specific course of action? In 1967, at the height of the war in Vietnam, the Senate Committee on Foreign Relations concluded that "the exchange of over-aged American destroyers for British bases in the Western Hemisphere was accomplished by executive agreement, in violation of the Senate's treaty power, and was also a violation of the international law of neutrality, giving Germany legal cause, had she chosen to take it, to declare war on the United States. The transaction was an *emergency* use of Presidential power, taken in the belief that it might be essential to save Great Britain from invasion."[67] Do you agree? Should one-third of the senators plus one have veto power over such a decision, on the ground that it could lead the nation into war?

In March 1941, eight months before the attack on Pearl Harbor, Congress ratified Roosevelt's lend-lease agreement. At this point, was the president alone in risking an attack upon the United States? Attached to the Lend-Lease Act was a two-house veto provision, allowing Congress to repeal the law and reclaim its powers by a mere concurrent resolution (not requiring the president's signature). Roosevelt regarded this congressional veto

63. William Manchester, *The Glory and the Dream* (1973), 126.
64. Schlesinger, Jr., *The Imperial Presidency* (1973), 98.
65. Ibid., 96.
66. Id., 105–106.
67. *National Commitments*, S. Rep. No. 797, 90th Cong., 1st Sess. (1967), 13.

An American destroyer attacks a German U-boat with depth charges. In 1941, President Roosevelt waged a secret war in the North Atlantic. Although the United States was supposed to be neutral towards the war then raging in Europe and in Asia, it was neutral on behalf of Great Britain, providing armed escorts to her supply ships from Canada most of the way across the Atlantic prior to Congress's declaration of war on December 8, 1941.

unconstitutional and, had it been exercised, was resolved to defy it. However, like Jefferson and the Louisiana Purchase, he signed the act and kept his reservations secret.

In May, Roosevelt revealed that American warships "are helping now to insure the delivery of the needed supplies to Britain,"[68] and in July signed another executive agreement which stationed U.S. troops in Iceland.[69] Senator Robert A. Taft (R-Ohio) protested that the president had "no legal or constitutional right to send American troops to Iceland" without Congress' permission. A decision of that sort, he said, risked war and was therefore a matter for Congress to decide. Do you agree? Is it significant that only one senator supported Taft's protest?

Was Roosevelt acting within his constitutional powers as commander in chief when he ordered the navy to escort British supply ships in the western Atlantic? Was it within his powers to authorize American ships to help the British locate German U-boats in the vicinity of the convoys? When the U.S. destroyer *Greer* was fired upon by a German submarine after radioing the submarine's location to the British, who sent planes to attack it, Roosevelt announced that American warships would thereafter shoot on sight any German or Italian warships west of the twenty-sixth meridian. The Fulbright Committee concluded that "by the time Germany and Italy declared war on the United States, in the wake of the Japanese attack on Pearl Harbor, the United States had already been committed by its President, acting on his own authority, to an undeclared naval war in the Atlantic."[70]

Does the legitimacy of the president's war in the North Atlantic turn on the extent to which there was informed support for it in Congress? In the electorate? Does the secrecy that Roosevelt maintained about actual naval operations in the North Atlantic undermine the legitimacy of his policies, or does Congress' acquiescence in the destroyer deal provide legislative blessing for a policy of weighted neutrality, the details of which could be filled in by the president as commander in chief or chief diplomat? Could Roosevelt have maintained the policy of weighted neutrality if he had made public the true nature of U.S. naval operations, or would that publicity have forced the Germans and Italians to

---

68. Gloria J. Barron, *Leadership in Crisis* (1973), 96.
69. Bruce N. Russett, *No Clear and Present Danger* (1972), 26.
70. S. Rept. No.129, 91st Cong. 1st Sess. 8 (1969), 13.

declare war sooner? Did Congress really have a policy of weighted neutrality, or was it simply indecisive, willing to let the president take the lead so long as he took the political heat? When Congress is indecisive, or sharply divided and unable to agree upon a policy, does the legitimacy of presidential initiatives turn on an assessment of the wisdom of his policies?

Arthur Schlesinger, Jr., an admirer of Roosevelt's policies, has written:

> [It cannot be said] that Roosevelt made much effort to offer Congress a real, as contrasted to a symbolic, role, or that he even told it fully and candidly what was going on in the North Atlantic. Still even a symbolic concern for Congress expressed a lurking sensitivity to constitutional issues. Though the threat to the United States from Nazi Germany could be persuasively deemed somewhat greater than that emanating thirty years later from North Vietnamese troops in Cambodia, and though his commitment of American forces to combat was far more conditional, Roosevelt made no general claims to inherent presidential power. In particular, he did not assert in the later royal manner that there was no need to consider Congress because his role as Commander in Chief gave him all the authority he needed. Indeed, the pre-Pearl Harbor documents are notable for the singular lack of reference to the office of Commander in Chief. Jackson's opinion on the destroyer deal showed how undeveloped Commander in Chief theory was in 1940; and in 83 press conferences in 1941 up to Pearl Harbor, Roosevelt never once alleged special powers in foreign affairs as Commander in Chief. When the title was mentioned in his speeches and messages, it generally signified only the narrow and traditional view of the Commander in Chief as the one who gave orders to the armed forces.
>
> Nevertheless, 1941 marked a significant change in Roosevelt's approach to presidential power. "There is Presidential initiative *and* Presidential initiative," E. S. Corwin wrote after the war, "— that type which, recognizing that Congress has powers — great powers — in the premises, seeks to win collaboration; and that type which, invoking the 'Commander-in-Chief' clause or some even vaguer theory of 'executive power,' proceeds to stake out Congress's course by a series of *faits accomplis*." Roosevelt, in Corwin's view, had generally employed the first type in constructing his New Deal. But, after the enactment of Lend-Lease, he shifted to the second, "a course that must in the end have produced a serious constitutional crisis had not the Japanese obligingly come to the rescue." (*The Imperial Presidency* [1973], 113.)

Collective Security, International Obligations, and Korea

As a result of World War II, collective security replaced isolationism as the organizing theory of American foreign policy. The United States replaced Great Britain and France as the chief guardian of Western interests against the Communist regimes of Eastern Europe, the Soviet Union, and mainland China. Containment of Communist regimes became a primary objective of both Democrats and Republicans.

When the North Korean army marched into South Korea on June 24, 1950, the collective security system was threatened. On June 25, the U.N. Security Council condemned the invasion as "a breach of the peace," called upon North Korea to withdraw, and directed its member states "to render every assistance" to the U.N. in the execution of this resolution. That evening, after consulting with executive branch officials only, President Truman ordered American forces stationed in Japan to aid in the defense of South Korea. Truman did so even though no American forces or citizens had been attacked, no mutual defense treaty with South Korea existed, no request for troops had been received from South Korea, no American commitment to defend South Korea had been made, and no call for military intervention had been received from the U.N. Not until June 27 did Truman meet with congressional leaders, at which time he simply explained his decision and obtained their support. That evening, at the behest of the United States and in the absence of the Soviet Union, the U.N. Security Council approved a resolution that "the members of the United Nations furnish such assistance to the Republic of Korea as may be necessary to repel the armed attack and to restore international peace and security in the area."[71]

On June 28, Senator Taft announced that although he supported the decision, there was "no legal authority" for what the president had done. Do you agree? Senator William Knowland of California, another conservative Republican, took the position that the president had all the authority he required under the U.N. Charter and the Commander-in-Chief Clause. What do you think?

Article 55 of the U.N. Charter, which is a treaty ratified by the Senate, requires the United States to cooperate with the organization in maintaining international peace and security. Did the Security Council resolution of June 27 authorize and require the president to commit U.S. forces to the defense of South Korea? May a treaty delegate to an international organization authority to order American troops into war? Can such an alteration in the sovereign powers of the people be achieved by that means?

May Congress legislate limits on how the president shall carry out a treaty? Section 6 of the United Nations Participation Act provides that the president may negotiate agreements with the Security Council to make American forces available for peace-keeping purposes, but specifies that the agreements are subject to the approval of Congress by act or by joint resolution.[72]

Truman did not seek a congressional declaration of war or any other express resolution or act supporting his decision. Instead, he took the advice of Secretary of State Dean Acheson and invoked his constitutional powers as chief executive and commander in chief. On July 3, the State Department turned out a memorandum listing eighty-seven instances in which previous presidents had used military force without the express consent of Congress.[73] None differed from the kinds of uses summarized in sections B through E of this chapter. Do those instances, from the quasi-war with France to the occupation of Caribbean countries, furnish persuasive historical analogies for the power the president claimed in Korea?

When Senator Paul H. Douglas' defended President Truman's unilateral war making, he argued that using American forces to drive the North Koreans back to their own borders "was not an act of war, but, instead, merely the exercise of police power under international sanction."[74] Is this the same sort of "police power" that previous presidents invoked to protect American lives and property and to police the Caribbean countries that risked European occupation through their financial mismanagement? (See Section D, *supra,* this chapter: "The 'Police Power' Reviewed.")

---

71. S/1505/Rev.
72. 22 U.S.C. Sess. 287a, 287d.
73. *Dept. of State Bull.* 23, No. 578 (July 31, 1950), 173–79.
74. 96 Cong. Rec. 9649 (July 5, 1950).

Although Truman initiated the Korean War, Congress financed it, enacted selective service legislation, and passed laws to facilitate mobilization of the domestic economy.

Did these measures create the functional equivalent of a declaration of war?

Provocative or Entangling Force Deployments

Provocative force deployments by American presidents are not new. From Jefferson's decision to station warships off Malta in 1803 to Reagan's decision to protect Kuwaiti oil tankers, presidents have risked war by the manner in which they have positioned forces under their command.

During the nineteenth century, the scale and frequency of provocative force deployments were limited, not only by a policy of avoiding "entangling alliances," but by a lack of sufficient forces. Presidents could order the marines to guard U.S. embassies and the navy to show the flag, but the positioning of army garrisons abroad was out of the question. The tiny U.S. army had all it could do to man the coast artillery, guard the borders, corral Indians, and suppress Philippine nationalists. However, when post-World War II power vacuums around the globe forced the United States to maintain large military forces at the ready, the opportunities for provocative and entangling force deployments burgeoned.

As presidents took some of these opportunities, two constitutional questions arose. First, does the Constitution give them the discretion to position forces wherever they want, whatever the risks of warfare? And second, are such force deployments by the president beyond congressional limitation?

NATO. In 1950, President Truman sparked conservative protests when he ordered four more army divisions to reinforce troops already in Europe. By positioning the troops in West Germany, Truman effectively committed the United States to that nation's defense against its Communist neighbors. Protesting this unilateral decision, Senator Frederic R. Coudert Jr., (R-N.Y.) introduced a sense-of-the-Congress resolution declaring that "no additional military forces" could be sent abroad "without the prior authorization of the Congress in each instance."[75]

In the debate that followed, Senator Robert A. Taft (R-Ohio) asserted that it was "a complete usurpation by the President of authority to use the Armed Forces of this country" when he sent troops to Korea, and he was now doing the same thing by sending troops to Europe.[76] Do you agree? Are the deployments comparable?

The Truman administration could scarcely conceal its contempt for those who raised the constitutional question. As Secretary of State Acheson remarked: "We are in a position in the world today where the argument as to who has the power to do this, that, or the other thing, is not exactly what is called for from America in this very critical hour."[77]

When the debate was over, the Senate approved Truman's deployment of the four divisions but declared that no additional troops should be stationed in Western Europe "without further congressional approval."[78] In Acheson's opinion, the resolution was

---

75. Quoted in Schlesinger, Jr., *The Imperial Presidency* (1973), 135–36.
76. 96 *Cong. Rec.*, 9323 (June 28, 1950).
77. Quoted in *National Commitments*, S. Rep. 797, 90th Cong., 1st Sess. (1967), 17.
78. Frank W. Heller, *The Korean War* (1977), 64.

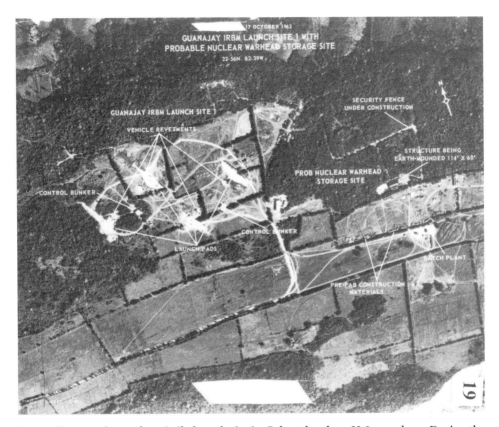

An intelligence photo of a missile launch site in Cuba taken by a U-2 spy plane. During the Cuban missile crisis, President Kennedy blockaded the island of Cuba with 180 American warships and put America's entire nuclear strike force on highest alert. Unknown to the generals who urged the president to attack Soviet bases in Cuba, some of the nuclear missiles they sought to neutralize with a "surgical air strike" were already operational.

"without the force of law."[79] Do you agree? In what ways, if any, may Congress constitutionally limit the authority of the commander in chief to deploy military forces?

The Blockade of Cuba, 1962. In some instances, the diplomatic utility of force deployments will be lost if the government does not move quickly. The Cuban missile crisis of 1962 may have been such an instance. On October 14, 1962, an American U-2 reconnaissance plane furnished photographic proof that the Soviet Union was installing intermediate-range ballistic missiles on the island of Cuba. When operational, these missiles would not substantially diminish America's overall military superiority, but they would make cities as far away as New York vulnerable to Soviet attack earlier than expected. More importantly, in the judgment of the president and his advisers, the balance of power would have been "altered in appearance; and in matters of national will and world leadership, ... such appearances contribute to reality."[80] Having failed to remove Castro and his Communism by a CIA-sponsored invasion in 1961, Kennedy felt a special need to demonstrate his determination to stand up to the Russians, not just to deter similar So-

---

79. *Present at the Creation* (1969), 496.
80. Theodore Sorensen, *Kennedy* (1965), 678.

viet gambles in the future, but to reassure the American electorate that the Democrats were at least as "tough" as the Republicans. Numerous alternatives were discussed within the Executive Committee of the National Security Council, including a full-scale invasion, a "surgical" air strike, a naval blockade, and diplomatic negotiations. Ultimately, the president decided to employ a naval blockade. Congress was not consulted in the making of this decision, although it confronted a major world power with nuclear weapons. On October 22, as Kennedy announced his decision on nationwide television, 180 American warships encircled Cuba, and B-52 bombers armed with nuclear bombs took to the skies. Then the world held its breath to see what the Russians ships steaming toward Cuba would do.

The Soviet ships stopped. The Russians agreed to remove the missiles in return for an American promise not to invade Cuba again. American missiles in Turkey also were removed. The crisis was averted.

The Cuban missile crisis represented an enormous gamble with the lives of millions of people. Robert Kennedy, a participant in the White House deliberations, later commented that while his brother had unusually competent advisers, "if six of them had been President..., I think that the world might have blown up."[81] "We were in luck," John Kenneth Galbraith later observed, "but success in a lottery is no argument for lotteries."[82]

What, if anything, can the Cuban missile crisis tell us about the proper allocation of decision-making authority between the president and Congress? According to Theodore Sorensen, Kennedy's White House Counsel, the president acted "by Executive Order, Presidential proclamation and inherent powers, not under any resolution or act of Congress."[83] Do presidents have an "inherent power" to take risks of this magnitude without authority from Congress? If so, under what kinds of circumstances? Is it true, as political scientist Richard Neustadt told a Senate committee in 1963, that "when it comes to action risking war, technology has modified the Constitution"?[84] Under what circumstances, if any, should the president be denied constitutional authority to use the threat of military force as an element of international negotiations? Would the participation of members of Congress in the White House deliberations have made Kennedy's ultimate decision any more legitimate? Is there any method of consultation with, or authorization from, Congress that would have added legitimacy to the decision and still preserved the secrecy and dispatch deemed essential to success? Would congressional participation have contributed to a wiser decision? For what kinds of decisions, if any, is the Cuban missile crisis a persuasive precedent for unilateral risk-taking by the president?

Deliberate Violations of the Neutrality of Other Nations

Just as neutral nations are rarely neutral in all respects, so belligerent nations are rarely fastidious in their respect for the neutrality of others. If military necessity seems to require

---

81. Quoted in Ronald Steel, "Endgame," *New York Review of Books*, March 13, 1969, 22.
82. "The Plain Lessons of a Bad Decade," *Foreign Policy*, Vol. 5 (Winter 1971–72), 32.
83. *Kennedy* (1965), 702.
84. *Administration of National Security*. Hearings before the Subcommittee on National Security, Staffing and Operations, Committee on Government Operations, U.S. Senate, 88th Cong., 1st Sess. (1963), 77.

Between 1918–1920, President Wilson sent 7,950 U.S. troops into Vladivostok (shown here) to rescue 40,000 Czechoslovakian troops and deter Japanese ambitions. He sent another 5,000 troops to Archangel, where they fought Bolsheviks and aided the White Russian opposition. Although the American troops saw combat, Wilson did not ask Congress to authorize their deployment.

the violation of a neutral nation's territory, then international law is unlikely to prevent it. *Inter arma silent leges*—in time of war the laws are silent.[85]

Wilson's invasion of Russia, 1918–1920. In 1917, Congress declared war on Imperial Germany, then fighting on two fronts. In March 1918, however, the new revolutionary government of Russia signed a treaty of peace with the Germans and pulled out of the war. From the Bolsheviks' point of view, the withdrawal was the only alternative left to their exhausted and divided nation; from the Allied perspective, it was a betrayal, possibly motivated by pro-German sympathies on Lenin's part. Pro-German or not, the anti-capitalist, pro-revolutionary Bolsheviks were viewed as a substantial threat to the postwar settlement.

The question of what to do about the Bolsheviks was the cause of much frustration to President Wilson, but in June 1918 he decided to send troops into Russia. Exactly why he sent the troops has been the subject of much debate. Those that entered Siberia by way of Vladivostok on the Pacific coast were supposed to relieve Czechoslovakian troops struggling to defeat German prisoners of war allegedly trying to fight their way home. More likely the American troops were landed to discourage a much larger contingent of Japanese troops from establishing an imperial foothold in eastern Russia. Another contingent of American troops, accompanying a larger British force, entered Russia from the north, supposedly to guard military stores from possible seizure and use by the Germans, but also to allow the Russians who did not support the peace treaty to reorganize. Both American contingents were instructed not to involve themselves in the internal affairs of Russia, then in a full-fledged civil war between the Bolsheviks and the moderates and czarists

---

85. A legal maxim derived from Cicero, *Pro Milone*, IV, ii.

they sought to crush. In fact, the American intervention favored the anti-Bolsheviks, particularly in the North, where the British set military policy. An intent to accomplish more than the defeat of Germany may be inferred from the fact that U.S. troops remained in Russia until early 1920, and funneled money and supplies to anti-Bolshevik White Russian forces long after the armistice had been declared.[86]

In the midst of the war, when emotions against the Germans and the Bolsheviks ran high, little attention was paid to the constitutional question of where President Wilson got the authority to (1) extend the war against Germany into the newly neutral Russia, and (2) use the intervening forces to assist one side in the Russian civil war. Does Wilson's intervention in Russia establish any sort of precedent for the proposition that a president possesses inherent authority, as commander in chief, to extend a declared war into the territory of, and against the government of, a declared neutral? Does a declaration of war against one country carry with it an implicit delegation of authority to invade other countries without supplemental authorization?

The Cambodian Incursion, 1970. The president's authority to extend the boundaries of an established, if undeclared, war was more vigorously questioned in 1970 when President Nixon ordered American troops operating in South Vietnam to invade neighboring Cambodia. Under Prince Norodom Sihanouk, Cambodia had attempted to maintain a policy of neutrality during the early years of the Vietnam War, but lacked the military forces to prevent violations of its long, unmarked, sparsely populated jungle borders. Publicly, the Johnson and Nixon administrations professed respect for Cambodia's neutrality; covertly (by secret military operations and false denials), the United States violated Cambodian neutrality repeatedly to bomb suspected North Vietnamese forces, defoliate suspected sanctuaries (including huge rubber plantations), and assassinate suspected Vietcong agents. Politically, the best Sihanouk could do was tolerate his neighbors' intrusions and hope that the devastation they brought would remain confined in area and limited in scale.

However, in March 1970 Sihanouk was overthrown by a military coup d'état. The extent of American involvement in this coup remains a matter of controversy, but on April 30, 1970, President Nixon ordered U.S. troops to join South Vietnamese forces in an invasion of Cambodian territory for the purpose of locating and destroying alleged North Vietnamese sanctuaries. When Nixon first announced the invasion, he claimed that it was by invitation, but the new Cambodian regime promptly denied that claim.[87] Suppose the claim were true. As a matter of constitutional (as opposed to international) law, may a president extend the scope of a war by invitation?

In his legal defense of the Cambodian invasion, then Assistant Attorney General William H. Rehnquist argued that "the President's determination to authorize incursion into these Cambodian border areas is precisely the sort of tactical decision confided to the Commander-in-Chief in armed conflict."[88] Do you agree? If such decisions are "tactical," are there any decisions that are "strategic" and hence for Congress to decide? Would it have been legitimate for President Truman to have ordered an invasion of China in order to achieve a tactical advantage in Korea?

---

86. See generally George F. Kennan, *Soviet American Relations, 1917–1920: The Decision to Intervene* (1958).

87. 6 Weekly Comp. Pres. Doc. No. 18, 597 (1970); *Congress, the President and the War Powers,* Hearings before the Subcommittee on National Security and Scientific Developments, Committee on Foreign Relations, U.S. House of Representatives, 91st Cong., 2d Sess. (1970), 546, n. 8. Assistant Attorney General Rehnquist later argued that Cambodia's protest was "perfunctory" and thus really not an objection at all. Id., 544.

88. "The Constitutional Issues-Administration Position," 45 *N.Y.U.L. Rev.* 628, 638, (1970).

Remains of some of the 2.4 million Cambodians killed in the genocide that followed President Nixon's unilateral decision in 1970 to expand the war against North Vietnam into Cambodia.

Rehnquist also cited *Durand v. Hollins* (See "Greytown," Section C, this chapter) and the *Prize Cases* (discussed earlier in this section) as authority for the president's Cambodian "incursion." Are these valid precedents?

Suppose that Cambodia had not been neutral or that the president decided that its failure to prevent belligerents from using its soil constituted a breach of its duties under international law. Would either of these findings authorize the president to invade Cambodia?

As a matter of constitutional authority, should it matter that the invasion was meant to be temporary and was directed at non-Cambodian forces within Cambodia? As a result of Nixon's unilateral decision, made without consideration of the long-term consequences, the Khmer Rouge came to power and executed approximately 2.4 million Cambodians. Another 1.5 million remain unaccounted for.

Contingent Authority

In a number of instances presidents have sought and Congresses have granted resolutions authorizing the president to take military action at his initiative should certain contingencies come to pass.[89] On other occasions Congress has passed resolutions "acknowledging" the president's constitutional authority to initiate hostilities should cer-

---

89. Recall, for example, President Andrew Jackson's unsuccessful request for reprisal powers and the 1839 resolution authorizing President Van Buren to go to war with Great Britain, if necessary, to defend U.S. claims to land on the border between Maine and Canada (see Section B of this chapter).

tain circumstances occur. Some of these resolutions have been specific; others have been remarkably open-ended. Together they raise serious questions about the way in which the United States has risked, and even gone to, war.

The Formosa Resolution, 1955. When the Nationalist forces of Chiang Kai-shek were driven off the mainland of China in 1948, they retreated to Formosa (Taiwan) and the Pescadore Islands. In 1955, when the Chinese Communists threatened to seize Quemoy, Matsu, and several other Nationalist-held islands close to the mainland, Congress passed a joint resolution that read in part:

> *Resolved* ... That the President is authorized to employ the Armed Forces of the United States as he deems necessary for the specific purpose of securing and protecting Formosa and the Pescadores against armed attack, this authority to include the securing and protection of such related positions and territories of the area now in friendly hands and the taking of such other measures as he judges to be required or appropriate in assuring the defense of Formosa and the Pescadores.
>
> This resolution shall expire when the President shall determine that the peace and security of the area is reasonably assured by international conditions created by action of the United Nations or otherwise, and shall so report to Congress. (P.L. 84-4, 69 Stat. 7; repealed, P.L. 93-475, 88 Stat. 1439 [1974].)

Is this a well-drafted grant of authority? If not, why not? Is it a constitutional delegation of Congress' authority to declare war? What, in your opinion, would constitute a well-drafted, responsible delegation of contingent authority to initiate military operations? For a critique of the Formosa Resolution, see Schlesinger, Jr., *The Imperial Presidency* (1973), 160.

The Middle East Resolution, 1957. In 1957, Congress passed another joint resolution, which provided in part:

> The President is authorized to undertake, in the general area of the Middle East, military assistance programs with any nation or group of nations of that area desiring such assistance. Furthermore, the United States regards as vital to the national interest and world peace the preservation of the independence and integrity of the nations of the Middle East. To this end, if the President determines the necessity thereof, the United States is prepared to use armed forces to assist any such nation or group of such nations requesting assistance against armed aggression from any country controlled by international communism.... (P.L. 85-7, 71 Stat. 5.)

Does this resolution constitute a formal delegation of war-making authority to the president?[90] If not, what is it? In 1958, when President Eisenhower sent fourteen thousand troops to Lebanon to bolster a pro-Western government battling rebels supported by the then pro-Communist but highly nationalistic United Arab Republic (of Egypt and Syria), he chose not to invoke the Middle East Resolution, but asserted his own powers to protect American lives and property. Did Eisenhower have authority to deploy military forces in Lebanon at the request of that country's government?

The Gulf of Tonkin Resolution, 1964. In early August 1964, several North Vietnamese torpedo boats made unsuccessful attacks (or passes) at two U.S. destroyers in the Gulf of Tonkin, apparently in the belief that the warships were providing offshore support for

---

90. A similarly phrased joint resolution was passed by Congress regarding Cuban efforts to extend Communism in the Western Hemisphere. P.L. 87-733, 76 Stat. 697 (1962).

South Vietnamese raids (sponsored in great secrecy by the CIA) on the North Vietnamese coast. Much mystery surrounds these incidents. North Vietnam admitted one of the attacks and denied the other. The skipper of one of the destroyers later admitted that a second attack might not have taken place. It was nighttime, and the sonar men on the destroyer might have mistaken the sound of their ship's own propellers against a turning rudder for the sound of attacking torpedo boats.

No harm was done to the American ships, but President Johnson had been looking for an incident that would justify an expansion of the United States' role in Vietnam's war. Surrounding the ships and their crews in secrecy, he used his own version of the attacks to rush a pro-war resolution through Congress. This resolution read in part:

> … That the Congress approves and supports the determination of the President, as Commander in Chief, to take all necessary measures to repel any armed attack against the forces of the United States and to prevent further aggression [in Southeast Asia].

> … The United States is prepared, as the President determines, to take all necessary steps, including the use of armed force, to assist any member or protocol state of the Southeast Asia Collective Defense Treaty requesting assistance in defense of its freedom.

> This resolution shall expire when the President shall determine that the peace and security of the area is reasonably assured by international conditions created by action of the United Nations or otherwise, except that it may be terminated earlier by concurrent resolutions of Congress. (P.L. 88-108, 78 Stat. 384 [1964].)

The resolution passed the House unanimously; only Wayne L. Morse (D-Ore.) and Ernest H. Gruening (D-Alaska) voted against it in the Senate. By 1967, the war in Vietnam had become the third largest in the history of American foreign wars, in terms of both troops committed and casualties suffered.

But was it constitutional? The answer to this question depends, in large part, upon the significance of the Gulf of Tonkin Resolution. In 1967, Undersecretary of State Nicholas Katzenbach told the Senate Foreign Relations Committee that, in his judgment and that of the Johnson administration, the Gulf of Tonkin Resolution was "the functional equivalent" of a declaration of war.[91] Do you agree? Does the resolution expressly delegate any authority to the president? If not, what does it do? Does it do anything more than acknowledge the authority of the president, as commander in chief, to repel armed attacks against U.S. forces?

Unlike his undersecretary of state, President Johnson attached no legal significance to the Gulf of Tonkin Resolution. "We stated then," he told congressional leaders in 1967, "and we repeat now, we did not think the resolution was necessary to what we did and what we're doing."[92]

Repeal of the Gulf of Tonkin Resolution, 1971. In 1971, the Senate and the House repealed the Gulf of Tonkin Resolution by a cryptic, one-sentence amendment to the Foreign Military Sales Act.[93] What is the legal significance of such a repeal? Is it to be read as an end-the-war resolution, or as simply a return to whatever inherent war-making powers the president may have? If the latter, how much authority did that leave President Nixon?

---

91. *U.S. Commitments to Foreign Powers*, Hearings before the Committee on Foreign Relations, U.S. Senate, 90th Cong., 1st Sess. (1967), 82.

92. *New York Times*, Aug. 19, 1967.

93. 84 Stat. 2055 (Jan. 12, 1971).

Does a president who inherits a war that his predecessor had no authority to initiate suddenly gain authority to fight that war to a successful conclusion, no matter the cost?

The Beirut Resolution, 1983. Worried that President Reagan was expanding U.S. military involvement in Lebanon from peacekeeping in the wake of the Israeli withdrawal to actively assisting Christians against the Syrian-backed Moslems, Congress agreed to a joint resolution in October 1983 that purported to both authorize and limit that presidentially initiated use of military force. The resolution expressly authorized U.S. participation in the multinational peacekeeping force but limited that participation to eighteen months. In return for this endorsement of his use of force in Lebanon, the president accepted a provision that limited the American military role to the purposes set forth in the diplomatic correspondence establishing the multinational force. The president insisted upon and obtained another provision (sec. 3) allowing him to take "such protective measures as may be necessary to insure the safety of the Multinational Force in Lebanon." Does this latter provision render the former meaningless? (Recall that the Cambodian invasion was justified as a troop protection measure.) Section 7(a) of the resolution added: "[n]othing in this joint resolution shall preclude the Congress by joint resolution from directing … a withdrawal." (*Cong. Rec.*, Sept. 29, 1983, S13 168.) Does this section mean that Congress acknowledges that the only way that it can direct a withdrawal is by a joint resolution subject to the president's veto? Would a concurrent resolution forbidding further warfare in Lebanon and ordering an immediate withdrawal of all U.S. forces be unconstitutional? Under what constitutional provisions might such a concurrent resolution be constitutional?

The President signed the resolution in order to obtain congressional approval for the marine presence for eighteen months. Did that mean that Reagan accepted the constitutionality of the War Powers Resolution itself? Or that he would abide by a joint resolution passed by Congress directing him to withdraw the troops? Did Reagan at any time explicitly acknowledge the constitutionality of the Resolution? If not, must the courts accept his signature as presumptive acknowledgment of his acceptance of the constitutionality of the Act? Compare with arguments in *Chadha v. INS*, 462 U.S. 919 (1983), in which the Court assumed that sometimes presidents accept acts of Congress in order to obtain authority they need, even without accepting the constitutionality of all provisions.

The Beirut Resolution, which started the War Powers "clock," was passed by Congress and sent to the President for approval. It was a piece of ordinary legislation. Did the War Powers Act contemplate that the "clock" would start only after a legislative act initiated it? Or could the "clock" be set by Congress without any approval from the President? If so, which branch has extended its authority in this instance? Which has gained a check on the other?

While the "clock" was ticking, a suicide bomber drove a truckload of explosives into the Marines' barracks, killing 241 servicemen and forcing withdrawal of the international peacekeeping force. A few days later, President Reagan diverted attention from this debacle by invading Grenada.

Treaties as a Source of War-Making Authority

In addition to the Gulf of Tonkin Resolution, lawyers for the Johnson and Nixon administrations cited the SEATO treaty[94] as authority for American involvement in the war

---

94. 6 U.S.T. 81 (1955).

In 1983, a Marine stands guard in front of his barracks in Beirut, Lebanon, after 241 of his comrades were killed by a suicide truck bombing. According to the Reagan administration, the deployment of these soldiers on a peace-keeping mission did not place them in imminent danger of hostilities within the meaning of the War Powers Resolution.

in Vietnam.[95] In so doing, they followed in the tradition of Theodore Roosevelt, who invoked the "Platt Amendment" to the 1903 treaty with Cuba to justify his decision to occupy that country militarily from 1906 to 1909. Roosevelt also interpreted an 1846 treaty with New Granada (later Colombia) guaranteeing "perfect neutrality" to that country's Isthmus of Panama, as justifying the American military intervention that prevented Colombia's armed forces from quelling the Panamanian revolution. President Truman invoked the UN Charter as authority for his intervention in Korea. In each instance, a treaty was cited as authority for unilateral military action by the president.

Most analyses of these claims to presidential authority focus on the precise language of the treaties, and most scholars agree that the treaties do not, by their terms, confer the powers that presidents and their lawyers have claimed to find in them.[96] Suppose, however, that a treaty did expressly confer upon the president—rather than the United States—the obligation to use military force on a scale and for purposes that cannot be called anything but war. Would the treaty be constitutional? To be more precise, may the president,

---

95. Meeker, "The Legality of United States Participation in the Defense of Vietnam." 54 *Dep't State Bull.* 474 (1966).

96. See, for example, Wormuth, "The Nixon Theory of the War Power: A Critique," 60 *Calif. L. Rev.* 623 (1972); Bickel, "Congress, the President, and the Power to Wage War," 48 *Chi.-Kent L. Rev.* 131 (1971); and Van Alstyne, "Congress, the President, and the Power to Declare War: A Requiem for Vietnam," 121 *U. Pa. L. Rev.* 1 (1972).

with the advice and consent of two-thirds of the Senate, confer upon himself authority to use military forces not just to repel invasions and sudden attacks and to protect American lives and property, but to involve the United States in large-scale hostilities against foreign military forces at some time in the indefinite future, under circumstances not known at the time the treaty is ratified? Can a treaty of this sort be the "functional equivalent" of a declaration of war?

In section 8(2) of the War Powers Resolution, *infra,* this chapter, Congress expressly declared that treaties may not, by their terms alone, authorize the president to introduce military forces "into hostilities, or situations where involvement in hostilities is clearly indicated by the circumstances." Section 8(1) of that act further provides that no law, including an appropriations act, may be cited as authority for president to introduce military forces into such circumstances, unless the legislation *specifically* authorizes the action. Are these provisions meant to be judicially enforceable?

The Antidelegation Doctrine and the War Powers

What, if anything, may be considered the "functional equivalent" of a declaration of war?

Professor Alexander Bickel of the Yale Law School took the position that Congress may delegate the "war power" to the president, but not "without standards." "Delegation without standards," he wrote, "short-circuits the lines of responsibility that make the political process meaningful."[97] If you were to invoke the antidelegation doctrine against a treaty or a joint resolution granting contingent warmaking authority to the president, what standards would you insist upon?

Professor William Van Alstyne of the Duke Law School has taken the position that "the exclusive responsibility of Congress to resolve the necessity and appropriateness of war as an instrument of national policy at any given time is uniquely not delegable at all."[98] In support of this view, Van Alstyne focused exclusively on the opinions of anti-Federalists and President Adams at the time that Adams was trying to resist pressure from Hamilton to go to war with France.[99] Is it appropriate to hold closely to the framers' intent when the technology of warfare and the proliferation of arms have so altered international relations?

As a matter of wise political theory, however, does it make sense to hold Congress responsible for the making of war policy? Van Alstyne believed that it does.

> ... I believe that the declaration of war clause disallows any delegation at all, *i.e.,* that Congress not only lacks power to relieve itself of that responsibility by shifting it generally to the President, but that it may not do so even fortified with the strictest and most unequivocal guidelines "merely" enabling the President to direct the sustained use of armed force when, in *his* judgment specific conditions have arisen to trigger a prior authorization by Congress. Consider it as one will, the requirement that Congress shall declare war if and when war is to be declared at all leaves no room for contingent declarations where the determination of the contingency is sought to be dislocated from Congress subject only to

---

97. Bickel, 48 *Chi.-Kent L. Rev.* 131, 137 (1971).
98. Van Alstyne, 121 *U. Pa. L. Rev.* 16 (1972).
99. Ibid., 18–19.

a power to reclaim it too late to serve the function of the clause. The congressional responsibility may not be thus diluted, no matter how eagerly Congress itself might wish to be quit of it, nor will it do at all to argue that Congress might always reclaim its authority and thereupon vote *against* the pursuit of war if in disagreement with the President's assessment that led him to trigger the use of armed force pursuant to the congressional delegation. For again, the function of the clause was to force a momentary pause upon Congress even on the brink of hostilities, that there could be no slipping into war where the slippage itself ought well transfigure what would otherwise have been a congressional decision not to become engaged. (121 *U. Pa. L. Rev.* 22.)

Are modern Congresses capable of shouldering the responsibility that Van Alstyne believes is their constitutional burden? If not, is the answer to expect less of them and more of the president, or to press for congressional reform? What changes in the way members of Congress are chosen might be necessary to produce wiser legislative deliberation on matters of war and peace?

According to Arthur Schlesinger, Jr., the chief defect of the joint resolutions of the 1950s and 1960s was that they were adopted without meaningful consultation with Congress.[100] Is "meaningful consultation" an adequate substitute for carefully drawn instructions to the president — whether they are called "delegations" or "directions"? If the antidelegation doctrine were applied to such instructions, would more meaningful consultation have to occur?

Like Bickel, Van Alstyne accepted the view, first propounded by Justice Chase in *Bas v. Tingy*, 4 U.S. (4 Dall.) 37, 43 (1800), that "Congress may wage a limited war; limited in place, in objects, in time" without the benefit of a formal declaration of war. However,

[E]ven assuming a limited power in Congress to shift the determination to embark upon war to the President, under specified conditions expressed in clear and definite guidelines, the transfer of such authority cannot be accomplished by *treaty*. The House of Representatives' prerequisite consent to this nation's involvement in war was most deliberately required by the declaration of war clause after consideration of several alternatives, including the specific proposed alternative of vesting the power jointly in the Senate and President alone which was itself rejected. As the House does not consent to treaties, manifestly a treaty cannot be among the possible means of delegating its authority. To imply that the constitutional draftsmen could possibly have formulated a document so specific in its precautions against involvements of war while simultaneously creating an enormous loophole of exclusive Senate power to give it away by simple treaty ratification is wholly without logic or evidence. (121 *U. Pa. L. Rev.* 22.)

F. Inferred Ratification

A strong case can be made for the proposition that Congress never authorized the war in Vietnam in the sense of issuing the "functional equivalent" of a declaration of war. An equally strong case can be made that Congress did not formally ratify the war in the sense

---

100. *The Imperial Presidency* (1973), 159–76.

that Congress ratified Lincoln's emergency actions following the attack on Fort Sumter. However, as Arthur Schlesinger, Jr., has asked, did there not "come a point where legislative acquiescence in presidential war became so systematic, pervasive and comprehensive that it amounted in every practical sense to ratification?"[101]

The Mutual Participation Test

Senator Barry Goldwater clearly thought so. In a speech to the Senate in 1971, Goldwater cited twenty-four statutes that Congress had passed to facilitate the war, including appropriations bills and selective service laws. "The fact is," he told his colleagues, "Congress has been involved up to its ears in the war in Southeast Asia.... No one can now claim innocence of what he was voting about."[102]

Several courts agreed. In two cases decided in 1970, *Orlando v. Laird* and *Berk v. Laird*, district court judges John Dooling and Orrin Judd decided independently that proof of "joint action" or "mutual participation" in the policy of escalation might, over time, constitute, *in toto*, the functional equivalent of ratification.[103] What Congress refused to do expressly, it might be held to have done indirectly and *sub silentio*. In 1971, a three-judge panel of the U.S. Court of Appeals for the First Circuit accepted this test in *Massachusetts v. Laird*, the case that follows.

Massachusetts v. Laird
451 F. 2d 26 (1971)

COFFIN, Circuit Judge.

The question sought to be raised in this action is whether the United States involvement in Vietnam is unconstitutional, a war not having been declared or ratified by the Congress. Plaintiffs seek a declaration of unconstitutionality and an injunction against the Secretary of Defense barring further orders to duty in Southeast Asia of Massachusetts inhabitants if within ninety days of a decree the Congress has not declared war or otherwise authorized United States participation....

The Commonwealth of Massachusetts is a plaintiff pursuant to an act of its legislature proscribing military service by its inhabitants in the conduct of extraterritorial non-emergency armed hostilities in the absence of a Congressional declaration of war and directing its Attorney General to bring an action in the Supreme Court or, in the event of a final determination that such action is not one of which that Court has original jurisdiction, an action in an inferior federal court to defend the rights of its inhabitants and of the Commonwealth....

... The complaint repeatedly alleges the absence of a Congressional declaration of war or ratification. The Commonwealth alleges damage both as a sovereign state and as *parens patriae*, citing the deaths and injuries of its inhabitants, consequential loss of their prospective civic and tax contributions, increased claims of dependents, additional burdens on its economy, disadvantage to its

---

101. Ibid., 292.
102. 117 *Cong. Rec.* S12446, 12448 (July 29, 1971).
103. *Orlando v. Laird*, 317 F. Supp. 1013 (1970); *Berk v. Laird*, 317 F. Supp. 715 (E.D.N.Y. 1970).

absentee voters, mass demonstrations, and damage to its public's morale. It also asserts its interest in "maintaining the integrity of the Constitution" which is allegedly impaired in that "one branch, the executive, has exercised war-making powers, which the Commonwealth and its sister states had agreed would be exercised only by Congress."

The Massachusetts statute, pursuant to which plaintiffs bring this action, is based on the simple proposition that participation by the United States in hostilities other than an emergency is unconstitutional unless "initially authorized or subsequently ratified by a congressional declaration of war according to the constitutionally established procedures in Article I, Section 8 [Clause 11th], of the Constitution." M.G.L.A. c. 33 app., Sec. 26-1. The complaint expands this theory by recognizing that constitutionality could be achieved by a "constitutional equivalent" for a declaration of war or by specific ratification of executive actions.

In any event, despite some language charging the executive with exercising the "war-making powers" of Congress, the thrust of the complaint is not that the executive has usurped a power—the power to declare war—given to Congress. There is no claim that the executive has made any declaration. The charge is, rather, that since hostilities have long since transcended a response to an emergency, both Congress and the executive have acted unconstitutionally in sustaining the hostilities without a Congressional declaration of war. In effect the relief sought by the complaint is to order the executive to "get out or get a declaration from Congress."...

... The complaint at one point alleges that the executive has usurped the war-making power of Congress but more generally alleges that the executive errs only in proceeding to make war without Congressional declaration or ratification. This very ambiguity underscores the fact that the war power of the country is an amalgam of powers, some distinct and others less sharply limned. In certain respects, the executive and the Congress may act independently. The Congress may without executive cooperation declare war, thus triggering treaty obligations and domestic emergency powers. The executive may without Congressional participation repel attack, perhaps catapulting the country into a major conflict. But beyond these independent powers, each of which has its own rationale, the Constitutional scheme envisages the joint participation of the Congress and the executive in determining the scale and duration of hostilities....

While the fact of shared war-making powers is clearly established by the Constitution, however, and some of its elements are indicated, a number of relevant specifics are missing. The Constitution does not contain an explicit provision to indicate whether these interdependent powers can properly be employed to sustain hostilities in the absence of a Congressional declaration of war. Hence this case.

The brief debate of the Founding Fathers sheds no light on this. All we can observe, after almost two centuries, is that the extreme supporters of each branch lost; Congress did not receive the power to "make war"; the executive was given the power to repel attacks and conduct operations; the Congress was given the power to "declare" war—and nothing was said about undeclared hostilities....

[W]e note that the Congressional power to declare war implies a negative: no one else has that power. But is the more general negative implied—that Congress has no power to support a state of belligerency beyond repelling attack and short of a declared war? The drafters of the Constitution, who were not inept, did not say, "power to commence war." Nor did they say, "No war shall be engaged in without a declaration by Congress unless the country is 'actually invaded, or in such imminent Danger as will not admit of delay.'" (Language from Article I, Section 10, proscribing states from engaging in war.) Nor did they resort to other uses of the negative as they so often did elsewhere....

Finally, we give some significance to the fact that in the same "power to declare war clause," Article I, Section 8, Clause 11th, there is the power to grant letters of marque and reprisal. Were this a power attendant to and dependent upon a declared war, there would be no reason to specify it separately. Indeed, it was first broached by Gerry as a matter not included in the "declare" power. [2 Farrand 326.] Nevertheless, this is a power to be invoked only against an enemy. It is clear that there can be an "enemy," even though our country is not in a declared war. [*Bas v. Tingy.*] The hostilities against France in 1799 were obviously not confined to repelling attack. This was an authorized but undeclared state of warfare. [See also *Prize Cases.*]

As to the power to conduct undeclared hostilities beyond emergency defense, then, we are inclined to believe that the Constitution, in giving some essential powers to Congress and others to the executive, committed the matter to both branches, whose joint concord precludes the judiciary from measuring a specific executive action against any specific clause in isolation....

We need not go so far as to say that in a situation of shared powers, the executive acting and the Congress silent, no constitutional issue arises. Here the complaint itself alleges the escalation of expenditures supporting United States efforts in Vietnam from $1.7 billion in 1965 to over $30 billion annually today, and a total expenditure over the past decade of $110 billion. Whether or not such appropriating and other actions of the Congress during the past six years can be said to amount to an "equivalent" of a declaration, or express or implied ratification is an issue we do not reach. At the very least, the complaint reveals a prolonged period of Congressional support of executive activities....

... All we hold here is that in a situation of prolonged but undeclared hostilities, where the executive continues to act not only in the absence of any conflicting Congressional claim of authority but with steady Congressional support, the Constitution has not been breached. The war in Vietnam is a product of the jointly supportive actions of the two branches to whom the congeries of the war powers have been committed. Because the branches are not in opposition, there is no necessity of determining boundaries. Should either branch be opposed to the continuance of hostilities, however, and present the issue in clear terms, a court might well take a different view. This question we do not face.

Notes and Questions

1. *Orlando v. Laird.* The same test was accepted by the Court of Appeals for the Second Circuit in *Orlando v. Laird,* 443 F.2d 1039, 1042–43 (2d Cir. 1971):

The Congress and the Executive have taken mutual and joint action in the prosecution and support of military actions in Southeast Asia.... The Tonkin Gulf Resolution ... was passed at the request of President Johnson.... Congress has ratified the executive's initiative by appropriating billions of dollars to carry out military operations in Southeast Asia and by extending the Military Selective Service Act with full knowledge that persons conscripted under that act had been, and would continue to be sent to Vietnam....

There is, therefore, no lack of clear evidence to support a conclusion that there was an abundance of continuing mutual participation in the prosecuting of the war. Both branches collaborated in the endeavor, and neither could long maintain such a war without the concurrence and cooperation of the other.

2. *Authorizations versus appropriations.* Congress authorizes programs on the advice of its substantive committees. Then it appropriates money to carry out those authorizations, based on a separate set of recommendations from appropriations committees. Given this two-step procedure, should an appropriation for the Department of Defense or the CIA be deemed to authorize a specific program of military or paramilitary operations?

3. *Fixing the date.* By 1971, most realists would have to admit that, in retrospect, Congress and the public had acquiesced in the escalation policies of Presidents Johnson and Nixon. Indeed, acquiescence is too mild a term for the support that most Democrats gave to the war prior to the stunning Tet Offensive of 1968, and that most Republicans gave to the war until Nixon's invasion of Cambodia in 1970. But how is a court to go about fixing the date at which Congress ratified the policy of escalation absent unambiguous votes of each house? If the date of ratification cannot be ascertained with some precision, then how are rights and obligations to be fixed with any certainty? Consider, for example, the plight of the young man who has received a draft notice which he would not otherwise have received, but for the Vietnam buildup. He believes the war to be unconstitutional on the theory that the president's escalation of the conflict has far exceeded his authority to repel attacks on U.S. troops or citizens. What is the young man to do?

4. *Accumulation.* In both *Massachusetts v. Laird* and *Orlando v. Laird*, the courts seem to concede that none of the supportive legislation actually constituted a formal ratification or authorization of the president's war policies, in and of itself. Rather, ratification is discerned from an examination of all these laws, taken *in toto*. Is that logical? Can nothing and nothing and more nothings add up to something?

5. *The effects of ratification.* If the non explicit support that Congress gave to the war constitutes the functional equivalent of an express ratification, what exactly does that support ratify? Everything the president had done to date, including the secret war in Laos, assassination missions across the Cambodian border, secret B-52 raids on Cambodia prior to formal violation of Cambodia's neutrality, and secret bombing raids on North Vietnam (hidden from Congress by the deliberate falsification of records)? Once ratification is inferred, does it simply legitimize all that has occurred, or does it constitute authorization for anything the president chooses to do thereafter?

6. *Purpose of the Declaration-of-War Clause.* According to William Van Alstyne, neither the Tonkin Gulf Resolution, the SEATO treaty, nor the various "supportive" pieces of legislation enacted to support the armed forces generally "can ... repair the omission of a declaration of war required *before* hostilities had been allowed to proceed in a manner making it impossible to say how far they had trammeled the congressional choice. In short, the Declaration-of-War Clause provides no means by which Congress can reduce its responsibility to a different task than that assigned to it, *i.e.*, the qualitatively different task, rejected as an inadequate constitutional safeguard, to check the dog of war *after* it had already been released by executive action."[104] Do you agree?

---

104. Van Alstyne, 121 *U. Pa. L. Rev.* 23 (1972).

Mitchell v. Laird
488 F. 2d 611 (D.C. Cir. 1973)

Not all cases decided in the federal courts followed this line of reasoning. In *Mitchell v. Laird* the Court of Appeals for the District of Columbia considered how the intent of Congress could be determined by the judiciary. In the absence of a declaration of war, what actions by Congress could be considered its equivalent, or some sort of ratification of a president's initiative?

WYZANSKI, Senior District Judge:

[On] April 7, 1971 thirteen members of the United States House of Representatives, as plaintiffs, filed in the District Court a complaint against the president of the United States, the Secretaries of State, Defense, Army, Navy, and Air Force, and the United States of America. Plaintiffs alleged that for seven years the United States, by the named individual defendants and their predecessors, has been engaged in a war in Indo-China without obtaining "either a declaration of war or an explicit, intentional and discrete authorization of war" and thereby "unlawfully impair and defeat plaintiffs' Constitutional right, as members of the Congress of the United States, to decide whether the United States should fight a war." Plaintiffs prayed for first, an order that defendants be enjoined from prosecuting the war in Indo-China unless, within 60 days from the date of such order, the Congress shall have explicitly, intentionally and discretely authorized a continuation of the war, and, second, "a declaratory judgment that defendants are carrying on a war in violation of Article I, Section 8, Clause 11 of the United States Constitution."...

[This lawsuit] invites inquiry as to whether Congress has given, in a Constitutionally satisfactory form, the approval requisite for a war of considerable duration and magnitude. Originally Congress gave what may be argued to have been its approval by the passage of the Gulf of Tonkin Resolution, 78 Stat. 384 (1964). [See *Orlando v. Laird*.] However, that resolution cannot serve as justification for the *indefinite* continuance of war since it was repealed by subsequent Congressional action, 84 Stat. 2055 (1971). Apparently recognizing that point, the Government contends that Congressional approval has been given by appropriation acts, by extension of the Selective Service and Training Act, and by other measures.

We are unanimously agreed that it is constitutionally permissible for Congress to use another means than a formal declaration of war to give its approval to a war such as is involved in the protracted and substantial hostilities in Indo-China.... That conclusion, however, leaves unanswered the further question whether the particular forms which the Government counsel at our bar refer to as having been used by Congress in the Indo-China war are themselves of that character which makes them *in toto*, if not separately, a constitutionally permissible form of assent.

The overwhelming weight of authority, including some earlier opinions by the present writer, holds that the appropriation, draft extension, and cognate laws enacted with direct or indirect reference to the Indo-China war ... did constitute a constitutionally permissible form of assent.... But Chief Judge Bazelon and I now regard that body of authority as unsound. It is, of course, elementary that in many areas of the law appropriations by Congress have been construed by the courts as involving Congressional assent to, or ratification of, prior or continuing executive action originally undertaken without Congressional legislative approval. Without a pause to cite or to examine in detail the vast body of cases involving such construction, it is more relevant to emphasize the special problem which is presented when one seeks to spell out from military appropriation acts, extensions of selective service laws, and cognate legislation the purported Congressional approval or ratification of war already being waged at the direction of the President alone. This court cannot be unmindful of what every schoolboy knows: that in voting to appropriate money or to draft men a Congressman is not necessarily approving of the continuation of a war no matter how specifically the appropriation or draft act refers to that war. A Congressman wholly opposed to the war's commencement and continuation might vote for the military appropriations and for the draft measures because he was unwilling to abandon without support men already fighting. An honorable, decent, compassionate act of aiding those already in peril is no proof of consent to the actions that placed and continued them in that dangerous posture. We should not construe votes cast in pity and piety as though they were votes freely given to express consent. Hence, Chief Judge Bazelon and I believe that none of the legislation drawn to the court's attention may serve as a valid assent to the Vietnam war.

Notes and Questions

1. *Congressional intent.* In determining Congressional intent, must the Court restrict itself simply to taking note of the presence or absence of statutory and budgetary authority to wage war?

2. *Congressional dilemmas.* What problem does Congress face when it votes on war measures requested by the president? Why might "yes" votes on such measures not be construed by the courts as a constitutionally permissible form of congressional assent to presidential war making? Do you think the courts can judge the true motives of legislators as they cast their votes? Can such motivations become part of the factual record in a case?

3. *Holding or dicta?* The appeals court did not decide this case in favor of the plaintiffs. Instead, it determined that the case involved a "political question." What is the practical effect of such a ruling? Does it matter that congressional action is not to be taken as support of congressional war making? Or is it simply dicta?

G. Denials of Authority

If ratification of a president's military operations is to be inferred from patterns of legislative acquiescence, how are laws purporting to restrict presidential initiatives to be read? If they must be explicit and precise, should not expressions of support be read the same way?

The Selective Service Act of 1940

On September 16, 1940, following Germany's occupation of France and just before Japan's occupation of Indochina, Congress passed its first peacetime conscription act by a one-vote margin. To obtain support for the measure, President Roosevelt had to accept the following provision: "Persons inducted into the land forces of the United States under this Act shall not be employed beyond the limits of the Western Hemisphere except in the Territories and Possessions of the United States, including the Philippine Islands."[105] How should Roosevelt have read this provision? Did it deny him authority to station troops in Iceland in 1941 to prevent seizure of that strategic island by Germany? Did it prevent the navy from convoying British merchant ships east of the Greenwich meridian? Did it prevent the president from deploying army and marine units composed entirely of volunteers wherever he wished?

After the Japanese attack on Pearl Harbor, restrictions of this sort went out of fashion. A chagrined Congress accepted the concept of collective security and largely deferred to the military judgments of successive presidents. Not until the Vietcong's Tet Offensive of 1968 did support for similar legislation revive.

Limits on the Use of Appropriated Funds

The first explicit denial of war-making authority to the president was included in the Defense Appropriations Act of 1970, passed on December 22, 1969. Passed following discovery of a secret war in northern Laos involving a 25,000-man force covertly supported by the CIA, this law provided: "In line with the expressed intention of the President..., none of the funds appropriated by this Act shall be used to finance the introduction of American ground combat troops into Laos or Thailand."[106] Was President Nixon incorrect to read this law as not prohibiting the continued use of army helicopter pilots and "advisers" inside Laos? Did it forbid continued operations by the U.S. Air Force inside Thailand, or covert operations by the CIA? Did it prohibit the invasion of Cambodia? What significance, if any, is to be deduced from Congress' failure to close these obvious loopholes in the provision?

The Cooper-Church Amendment

The conjunction of the invasion of Cambodia and the slaying of antiwar protesters at Kent State University in late April and early May of 1970 produced an enormous outpouring of opposition to the war in Southeast Asia. Instead of winding down the war, the president seemed to be expanding it, not unlike President Barack Obama in Afghanistan. Numerous proposals to limit the president's war-making authority were introduced in Congress, but attention gradually came to focus on the Cooper-Church Amendment sponsored by the Senate Committee on Foreign Relations. It provided:

> Sec. 47. Prohibition of assistance to Cambodia. — In order to avoid involvement of the United States in a wider war in Indochina and to expedite the withdrawal of American forces from Vietnam, it is hereby provided that, unless specifically authorized by law hereafter enacted, no funds authorized or appropriated pursuant to this Act or any other law may be expended for the purpose of
>
> (1) retaining United States forces in Cambodia;

---

105. P.L. 76-783, 54 Stat. 885.
106. P.L. 91-171, 83 Stat. 487 (Dec. 29, 1969). The same prohibition was enacted the following year.

(2) paying the compensation or allowance of, or otherwise supporting, directly or indirectly, any United States personnel in Cambodia who furnish military instruction to Cambodian forces or engage in any combat activity in support of Cambodian forces;

(3) entering into or carrying out any contract or agreement to provide military instruction in Cambodia or to provide persons to engage in any combat activity in support of Cambodian forces; or

(4) conducting any combat activity in the air above Cambodia in support of Cambodian forces. [S. Rep. No. 90-865, 91st Cong., 2d Sess. (1970), 15]

The Cooper-Church Amendment was allowed to pass the Senate only after all U.S. forces had departed from Cambodia, and never came to a formal vote in the House. Instead, the House voted to table a motion that would have instructed House conferees to accept the Senate's amendment to the Foreign Military Sales Act. The motion to table was passed with full knowledge that the conferees would not accept the amendment unless formally instructed to do so. In avoiding a clear, on-the-record vote, the House again manifested what many of its members cynically referred to as the "hawk-on-the-floor, dove-on-the-hustings" syndrome.[107]

Six months later, Congress and the president agreed to the following amendment to the Supplemental Foreign Assistance Authorization of 1971: "In line with the expressed intention of the President..., none of the funds authorized or appropriated pursuant to this or any other Act may be used to finance the introduction of United States ground combat troops into Cambodia, or to provide United States advisers to or for Cambodian military forces in Cambodia."[108] What significance should a court or a citizen accord to Congress' failure to enact some of the restrictions proposed in the Cooper-Church Amendment, including restrictions on combat activity in the air above Cambodia?

The Mansfield Amendment

In 1971, Congress also repealed the Tonkin Gulf Resolution and enacted the Mansfield Amendment to the Defense Procurement Authorization Act of 1972. The amendment declared it "to be the policy of the United States to terminate at the earliest practicable date all military operations of the United States in Indochina, and to provide for the prompt and orderly withdrawal of all United States military forces at a date certain, subject to the release of all American prisoners of war held by the Government of North Vietnam and forces allied with such Government and an accounting for Americans missing in action who have been held by or known to such Government or such forces."[109] President Nixon signed the bill, but issued a "signing statement" declaring that the bill did "not represent the policies of the Administration" and was "without binding force or effect."[110] As a matter of law, was he correct?[111] As a practical matter, did the Mansfield Amendment constrain him in any way?

---

107. Mikva and Lundy, "The 91st Congress and the Constitution," 38 *Chi. L. Rev.* 449, 493 (1971).
108. P.L. 91-652, 85 Stat. 1942 (Jan. 5, 1971).
109. P.L. 92-156, 85 Stat. 423–430 (Nov. 17, 1971).
110. *Public Papers of the President* (1971), 1114.
111. See *DaCosta v. Nixon*, 55 F.R.D. 145 (1972).

The Eagleton "End-the-War" Amendment

In January 1973, the United States and North Vietnam signed a cease-fire agreement, and by the end of March the last U.S. troop units were withdrawn from the country. On July 1, 1973, Congress enacted the following "end-the-war" amendment to the Supplemental Appropriations Bill of that year: "Notwithstanding any other provision of law, on or after August 15, 1973, no funds herein or heretofore appropriated may be obligated or expended to finance directly or indirectly combat activities by United States military forces in and over or from off the shores of North Vietnam, South Vietnam, Laos or Cambodia."[112] Whether the courts would enforce this provision was the subject of the following court of appeals decision:

Holtzman v. Schlesinger
484 F.2d 1307 (1973)

MULLIGAN, Circuit Judge:

This is an appeal from a judgment of the United States District Court, Eastern District of New York, Hon. Orrin G. Judd, District Judge, dated July 25, 1973, 361 F. Supp. 553, granting plaintiffs' motion for summary judgment and providing both declaratory and injunctive relief. The judgment declared that "there is no existing Congressional authority to order military forces into combat in Cambodia or to release bombs over Cambodia, and that military activities in Cambodia by American armed forces are unauthorized and unlawful...."

... At the outset, as the parties [have] agreed, ... we ... are not deciding the wisdom, the propriety, or the morality of the war in Indo-China and particularly the on-going bombing in Cambodia. This is the responsibility of the Executive and the Legislative branches of the government. The role of the Judiciary is to determine the legality of the challenged action and the threshold question is whether under the "political question" doctrine we should decline even to do that....

The most recent holding of this court now pertinent is Da Costa v. Laird, 471 F. 2d 1146 (1973) where an inductee urged that the President's unilateral decision to mine the harbors of North Vietnam and to bomb targets in that country constituted an escalation of the war, which was illegal in the absence of additional Congressional authorization. Judge Kaufman found that this was a political question which was non-justiciable, recognizing that the court was incapable of assessing the facts. He stated in part:

Judges, deficient in military knowledge, lacking vital information upon which to assess the nature of battlefield decisions, and sitting thousands of miles from the field of action, cannot reasonably or appropriately determine whether a specific military operation constitutes an escalation of the war or is merely a new tactical approach within a continuing strategic plan. What if, for example, the war "de-escalates" so that it is waged as it was prior to the mining of North Vietnam's harbors, and then "escalates" again? Are the courts required to oversee the conduct of the war on a daily basis, away from the scene of action? In this instance, it was the President's view that the mining

---

112. P.L. 93-52, 87 Stat. 130 (July 1, 1973).

of North Vietnam's harbors was necessary to preserve the lives of American soldiers (*sic*) in South Vietnam and to bring the war to a close. History will tell whether or not that assessment was correct, but without the benefit of such extended hindsight we are powerless to know.

We fail to see how the present challenge involving the bombing in Cambodia is in any significant manner distinguishable from the situation discussed by Judge Kaufman in Da Costa *v.* Laird. Judge Judd found that the continuing bombing of Cambodia, after the removal of American forces and prisoners of war from Vietnam, represents "a basic change in the situation, which must be considered in determining the duration of prior Congressional authorization." He further found such action a tactical decision not traditionally confided to the Commander-in-Chief. These are precisely the questions of fact involving military and diplomatic expertise not vested in the judiciary, which make the issue political and thus beyond the competence of that court or this court to determine. We are not privy to the information supplied to the Executive by his professional military and diplomatic advisers and even if we were, we are hardly competent to evaluate it. If we were incompetent to judge the significance of the mining and bombing of North Vietnam's harbors and territories, we fail to see our competence to determine that the bombing of Cambodia is a "basic change" in the situation and that it is not a "tactical decision" within the competence of the President....

Since the argument that continuing Congressional approval was necessary, was predicated upon a determination that the Cambodian bombing constituted a basic change in the war not within the tactical discretion of the President and since that is a determination we have found to be a political question, we have not found it necessary to dwell at length upon Congressional participation.

... We cannot resist, however, commenting that the most recent expression of Congressional approval by appropriation, the Joint Resolution Continuing Appropriations for Fiscal 1974 (P.L. 93-52), enacted into law July 1, 1973, contains the following provision:

"Sec. 108. Notwithstanding any other provision of law, on or after August 15, 1973, no funds herein or heretofore appropriated may be obligated or expended to finance directly or indirectly combat activities by United States military forces in or over or from off the shores of North Vietnam, South Vietnam, Laos or Cambodia."

Assuming arguendo that the military and diplomatic issues were manageable and that we were obliged to find some participation by Congress, we cannot see how this provision does not support the proposition that the Congress has approved the Cambodian bombing. The statute is facially clear but its applicability is contested by plaintiffs on several grounds which were essentially adopted by the court below. The argument is made that the Congress didn't really mean what it said because it was coerced by the President who had vetoed Congressional bills which would have immediately cut off Cambodian funds. Not being able to muster sufficient strength to overcome the veto, the argument runs, the Congress was forced willy nilly to enact the appropriation legislation. Resort is made to the floor debate which it is argued bolsters the view that individual legislators expressed personal disapproval of the bombing and did not interpret the appropriation as an approval to bomb but simply a recognition that it gave the

President the power to bomb. It is further urged that since the Constitution entrusts the power to declare war to a majority of the Congress, the veto exercised makes it possible for the President to thwart the will of Congress by holding one-third plus one of the members of either House. We find none of these arguments persuasive....

... A fair reading on the Congressional Record for June 29, 1973 establishes this proposition. Member of Congress Drinan and the plaintiff Holtzman here, for example, both voted against the measure because it would authorize the bombing until August 15, 1973.

While the court below relied on the colloquy between Senators Eagleton and Fulbright, it inadvertently omitted the following:

"Mr. Eagleton. In the light of the legislative history, meaning the statement of former Secretary of Defense Richardson that we will continue the bombing unless the funds are cut off, will we with the adoption of this resolution permit the bombing of Cambodia for the next 45 days? This is the question I pose to the Senator from Arkansas.

"Mr. Fulbright. *Until August 15....*"

We cannot agree that the Congress was "coerced" by the President's veto. There was unquestionably a Congressional impasse resulting from the desire of a majority of Congress to stop bombing immediately and the desire of the President that his discretion be unfettered by an arbitrarily selected date. Instead of an acute constitutional confrontation, as Senator Javits noted, an "agreement" was reached.

OAKES, Circuit Judge (dissenting):

... The Defense Department is continuing to bomb in Cambodia despite the cease-fire in Vietnam and despite the return of our prisoners of war from North Vietnam. The justiciable question then is whether there is any Constitutional authorization for the employment of United States armed forces over Cambodia, now that the war in Vietnam has come to an end....

Has Congress ratified or authorized the bombing in Cambodia by appropriations acts or otherwise? Congress can confer power on the Executive by way of an appropriations act.

... But for authorization on the part of Congress by way of an appropriation to be effective, the congressional action must be based on a knowledge of the facts.

... I am aware of only one instance in which it has previously been argued that a war was illegal as a result of Congress being misinformed as to the underlying facts surrounding American participation in that war. While the argument was unique and unsuccessful to boot, however, time has vindicated it, I believe. Furthermore, it was advanced by one whose views are worth consideration, even if they were expressed in "dissent," so to speak. I refer of course to Abraham Lincoln and his argument as a lone Congressman on January 12, 1848, in opposition to our "incursion" into Mexico and what later was called the Mexican War....

And here, incredibly enough, it appears that neither the American people nor the Congress, at the time it was voting appropriations in aid of the war in Vietnam, were given the facts pertaining to our bombing in Cambodia. Recent disclosures have indicated that Air Force B-52 bombers were secretly attacking Cambodia in 1969, 1970 and even later while the United States was publicly proclaiming respect for Cambodian neutrality.

The government argues that these secret bombings occurred in 1969 and 1970, and ended when our activities in Cambodia became open subsequently. But the Congress whose ratification by way of appropriations acts is contended for here did not become aware of these covert bombings until July of 1973. And meanwhile the Congress had declared, in the so-called Mansfield Amendment, that it was "the policy of the United States to terminate at the earliest practicable date all military operations of the United States in Indochina...." Appropriations Authorization-Military Procurement Act of 1972, Pub. L. No, 92-156, Sec. 601, 85 Stat. 423 (92nd Cong., 1st Sess. 1971).

The combination of concealment of the facts from Congress together with the enactment of a policy of "earliest practicable" withdrawal do not amount in my mind to an appropriations carte blanche to the military to carry on bombing in Cambodia after the cease-fire, withdrawal of our troops from Vietnam, and return of our prisoners of war from North Vietnam.

We come then to the effect of the legislation, following upon a presidential veto of an immediate prohibition against the use of funds to bomb in Cambodia, adopted as a compromise this July 1st: the Continuing Appropriations Act for Fiscal Year 1974, Pub. L. No. 93-52, 93rd Cong. 2nd Sess. (July 1, 1973) which expressly provided that "... on or after August 15, 1973, no funds herein or heretofore appropriated may be obligated or expended to finance directly or indirectly combat activities by United States military forces in or over or from off the shores of North Vietnam, South Vietnam, Laos or Cambodia." Sec. 108. In colloquy between Senators Eagleton and Fulbright, inadvertently omitted in the briefs of appellees and the opinion of the lower court, the former inquired whether "the adoption of this resolution [would] permit the bombing of Cambodia" and Senator Fulbright replied, "Until August 15". 119 Cong. Rec. S 12562 (daily ed. June 29, 1973). Again, in the same colloquy Senator Fulbright, conceding "'Presidential power," said that "The President has the power to do a lot of things of which I do not approve," after being asked by Senator Eagleton whether under the resolution the President's "power to bomb in Indochina ... will now be sanctioned by our action." *Id.* In neither case, however, is there recognition of *legality* or *past authorization.* Senator Fulbright had previously stated, as Judge Judd recognized, that "The acceptance of an August 15 cut off date should in no way be interpreted as recognition by the committee of the President's authority to engage U.S. forces in hostilities until that date. The view of most members of the committee has been and continues to be that the President does not have such authority in the absence of specific congressional approval." 119 Cong. Rec. S 12560 (daily ed. June 29, 1973).

It can be argued that Congress could, if it had desired, cut off the funds for bombing Cambodia immediately by overriding the Presidential veto. This was indeed championed by those voting against the ultimate compromise Resolution. But it does not follow that those who voted in favor of the Resolution were thereby putting the Congressional stamp of approval on the bombing continuation. While the Resolution constituted a recognition that Executive *power* was being exercised, it did not constitute a concession that such exercise was rightful, lawful or constitutional....

... I cannot find any express congressional authorization for such a continuation of the Cambodian bombing, nor do I think that authorization can be implied from prior appropriation acts. This being true, affirmative action on the part of Congress was not necessary as a matter of constitutional law. An agreement by the Executive to some cut off date was essential, however, because the *legality* of bombing continuation might not be tested or testable for months to come, by the very nature of the judicial process. Therefore, Congress as I see it, took the only practical way out. It acknowledged the reality of the Executive's exercise of power even while it disputed the Executive's authority for that exercise. It agreed to a final cut-off date as the best practical result but never conceded the legality or constitutionality of interim exercise.

Thus the Resolution of July 1, 1973, cannot be the basis for legalization of otherwise unlawful Executive action. We are talking here about the separate branches of government, and in doing so we must distinguish between the exercise of power on the one hand and authorization for such exercise on the other. That the Executive Branch had the power to bomb in Cambodia, there can be no doubt; it did so, and indeed is continuing to do so. Whether it had the constitutional authority for its action is another question.

Notes and Questions

1. *Political questions.* What does the "political questions" doctrine mean? Does it mean that while the Constitution is *law*, it contains law that the courts may not apply, or does it mean that there are legal requirements in the Constitution that may be violated without giving rise to correlative rights that courts may remedy? If it means the latter, what is to be made of the right to life guaranteed by the Fifth Amendment's Due Process Clause? If the president is under no enforceable legal obligation to follow "due process" in the use of the military, say, in detaining and interrogating suspected terrorists, then does he not have the equivalent of an absolute royal prerogative to send citizens to their death in military operations of his own choosing? Is the political questions doctrine an example of an area of jurisprudence in which courts still do not "take rights seriously"?

2. *Judicial prudence.* Would it be too candid to say that the political questions doctrine is an unprincipled device whereby judges avoid confrontations with elected officials on fundamental issues freighted with such political passion that the judges are likely to be ignored? Or, if they are not ignored, will their decisions require policy reversals too massive in scale, cost, or embarrassment to be ordered by unelected officials?

3. *Pregnant negatives.* According to the majority, Congress's negation of funds for further combat in Southeast Asia on or after August 15, 1973, was pregnant with an implicit authorization of any and all military operations up until that date. Do you agree? Should the intent of Congress be inferred from a literal interpretation of the text (in which case a back-handed authorization must be found), from a study of the congressional debates (which may prove inconclusive), or from a constitutional rule that says, in effect, that the Declaration-of-War Clause means that decisions authorizing combat are too serious to be inferred?

H. Extrication Authority

Assume that a president finds himself in the position of superintending a war for which he lacks constitutional or other authority. (Perhaps he inherited the war from his predecessor, or Congress expressly denied him authority to continue the war, or the courts declared the war unconstitutional.) What authority, if any, does he have as commander in chief or chief diplomat beyond extricating American forces with as few casualties as possible?

To Win a "Just Peace"

President Nixon took the position that the repeal of the Tonkin Gulf Resolution did not alter his authority to do what he was doing, and that his constitutional authority included not only the power to protect U.S. troops then in Vietnam, but "at the same time to win a just peace. Now, by winning a just peace," he explained, "what I mean is not victory over North Vietnam…, but … simply the right of the people of South Vietnam to determine their own future without having us impose our will upon them, or the North Vietnamese, or anybody else outside impose their will upon them."[113] Do you agree?

In pursuit of a "just peace," President Nixon ordered massive B-52 bombings of Cambodia and North Vietnam from 1969 to 1973. In tonnage alone, more bombs were dropped in Southeast Asia under the Nixon administration than in all theaters of war during World War II. Dissatisfied with the cease-fire terms offered by the North Vietnamese at the Paris talks in November 1972, Nixon ordered the carpet bombing of Hanoi over the Christmas holidays. The use of that bombing wholly for diplomatic ends, and the heavy civilian casualties it caused, brought worldwide condemnations of the United States. The bombing also failed to achieve its objectives. The cease-fire signed in January 1973 was virtually identical to the terms offered two months earlier.

Nixon continued to bomb Cambodia throughout the spring and early summer of 1973, despite the cease-fire (which the North was violating), North Vietnam's return of American prisoners of war (a condition of the accord), and the removal of the last American ground combat units in March. The legality of this bombing in support of the South Vietnamese military, when no tactical or protective function could be claimed, was the subject of some *dicta* in *Holtzman v. Schlesinger* (*supra*, Section G).

Mitchell v. Laird

In *Mitchell v. Laird* (*see* Section F), a three-judge panel of the Court of Appeals for the District of Columbia Circuit rejected contentions that Congress had inferentially ratified the war in Vietnam, but expressed sympathy for President Nixon's "peace with honor" theory of extrication authority:

> … When on January 20, 1969, President Nixon took office, and when on the same or even later dates the other individual defendants took their present offices, they were faced with a belligerent situation not of their creation. Obviously, the President could not properly execute the duties of his office or his responsibility as Commander-in-Chief by ordering hostilities to cease on the very day he took office. Even if his predecessors had exceeded their constitutional authority, President Nixon's duty did not go beyond trying, in good faith and to the best of his ability, to bring the war to an end as promptly as was con-

---

113. *Public Papers of the President*, July 1, 1970, 546–47.

sistent with the safety of those fighting and with a profound concern for the durable interests of the nation—its defense, its honor, its morality.

Whether President Nixon did so proceed is a question which at this stage in history a court is incompetent to answer. A court cannot procure the relevant evidence: some is in the hands of foreign governments, some is privileged. Even if the necessary facts were to be laid before it, a court would not substitute its judgment for that of the President, who has an unusually wide measure of discretion in this area, and who should not be judicially condemned except in a case of clear abuse amounting to bad faith. Otherwise a court would be ignoring the delicacies of diplomatic negotiation, the inevitable bargaining for the best solution of an international conflict, and the scope which in foreign affairs must be allowed to the President if this country is to play a responsible role in the council of the nations.

In short, we are faced with what has traditionally been called a "political question" which is beyond the judicial power conferred by Article III of the United States Constitution. And on that ground the complaint was properly dismissed by the District Court. (488 F.2d 612).

I. The War Powers Resolution

On November 7, 1973, Congress passed the War Powers Resolution over President Nixon's veto.[114] As you read the following excerpts, consider these questions: Does Congress, by this resolution, accept the contention that presidents have "inherent" authority (from Article II or elsewhere) to use military forces in certain circumstances and that this inherent authority may not be constrained by Congress in any way? Does the resolution purport to withdraw any of the president's constitutional authority from him? Does it delegate to the president any of Congress' authority to "declare war"? What power, if any, does the resolution grant to, or recognize in, the president? Does the resolution "fulfill the intent of the framers of the Constitution," as its Preamble promises?[115] How might it be strengthened, if more prior restraints upon the president's use of military force were deemed wise?

Purpose and Policy

Sec. 2 (a) It is the purpose of this joint resolution to fulfill the intent of the framers of the Constitution of the United States and insure that the collective judgment of both the Congress and the President will apply to the introduction of United States Armed Forces into hostilities, or into situations where imminent involvement in hostilities is clearly indicated by the circumstances, and to the continued use of such forces in hostilities or in such situations.

(b) Under article I, section 8, of the Constitution, it is specifically provided that the Congress shall have the power to make all laws necessary and proper for carrying into execution, not only its own powers but also all other powers vested by the Constitution in the Government of the United States, or in any department or officer thereof.

---

114. P.L. 93-148, 87 Stat. 555, 50 U.S.C. Sec. 1541–48.
115. 50 U.S.C. Sec. 1541 (a).

(c) The constitutional powers of the President as Commander-in-Chief to introduce United States Armed Forces into hostilities, or into situations where imminent involvement in hostilities is clearly indicated by the circumstances, are exercised only pursuant to (1) a declaration of war, (2) specific statutory authorization, or (3) a national emergency created by attack upon the United States, its territories or possessions, or its armed forces.

Consultation

Sec. 3. The President in every possible instance shall consult with Congress before introducing United States Armed Forces into hostilities or into situations where imminent involvement in hostilities is clearly indicated by the circumstances, and after every such introduction shall consult regularly with the Congress until United States Armed Forces are no longer engaged in hostilities or have been removed from such situations.

Reporting

Sec. 4 (a). In the absence of a declaration of war, in any case in which United States Armed Forces are introduced—

(1) into hostilities or into situations where imminent involvement in hostilities is clearly indicated by the circumstances;

(2) into the territory, airspace or waters of a foreign nation, while equipped for combat, except for deployments which relate solely to supply, replacement, repair, or training of such forces; or

(3) in numbers which substantially enlarge United States Armed Forces equipped for combat already located in a foreign nation;

the President shall submit within 48 hours to the Speaker of the House of Representatives and to the President pro tempore of the Senate a report, in writing [setting forth "the circumstances necessitating the introduction of armed forces," "the constitutional and legislative authority" under which it occurred, "the estimated scope and duration of the hostilities," and "such other information as the Congress may request."]

Congressional Action ...

Sec 5. ... (b) Within sixty calendar days after a report is submitted or is required to be submitted pursuant to section 4(a) (1), whichever is earlier, the President shall terminate any use of United States Armed Forces with respect to which such report was submitted (or required to be submitted), unless the Congress (1) has declined or has enacted a specific authorization for such use of United States Armed Forces, (2) has extended by law such sixty-day period, or (3) is physically unable to meet as a result of an armed attack upon the United States. Such sixty-day period shall be extended for not more than an additional thirty days if the President determines and certifies to the Congress in writing that unavoidable military necessity respecting the safety of United States Armed Forces requires the continued use of such armed forces in the course of bringing about a prompt removal of such forces.

(c) Notwithstanding subsection (b), at any time that United States Armed Forces are engaged in hostilities outside the territory of the United States, its possessions and territories without a declaration of war or specific statutory authorization, such forces shall be removed by the President if the Congress so directs by concurrent resolution....

Interpretation of Joint Resolution

See. 8. (a) Authority to introduce United States Armed Forces into hostilities or into situations wherein involvement in hostilities is clearly indicated by the circumstances shall not be inferred (1) from any provision of law (whether or not in effect before the date of the enactment of this joint resolution), including any provision contained in any appropriation Act, unless such provision specifically authorizes the introduction of United States Armed Forces into hostilities or into such situations and stating that it is intended to constitute specific statutory authorization within the meaning of this joint resolution; or

(2) from any treaty heretofore or hereafter ratified unless such treaty is implemented by legislation specifically authorizing the introduction of United States Armed Forces into hostilities or into such situations and stating that it is intended to constitute specific statutory authorization within the meaning of this joint resolution.

(b) Nothing in this joint resolution shall be construed to require any further specific statutory authorization to permit members of United States Armed Forces to participate jointly with members of the armed forces of one or more foreign countries in the headquarters operations of high-level military commands which were established prior to the date of enactment of this joint resolution and pursuant to the United Nations Charter or any treaty ratified by the United States prior to such date.

(c) For purposes of this joint resolution, the term "introduction of United States Armed Forces" includes the assignment of members of such armed forces to command, coordinate, participate in the movement of, or accompany the regular or irregular military forces of any foreign country or government when such military forces are engaged, or there exists an imminent threat that such forces will become engaged, in hostilities.

(d) Nothing in this joint resolution

(1) is intended to alter the constitutional authority of the Congress or of the President, or the provisions of existing treaties; or

(2) shall be construed as granting any authority to the President with respect to the introduction of United States Armed Forces into hostilities or into situations wherein involvement in hostilities is clearly indicated by the circumstances which authority he would not have had in the absence of this joint resolution....

Notes and Questions

1. *Defining the president's powers.* What is the legal significance of the "Purpose and Policy" section of the resolution? Is it to provide an authoritative definition of "the constitutional powers of the President as Commander-in-chief"? May Congress impose on the president a legally binding definition of his *constitutional* powers? What is the purpose of the reminder in subsection (b) that Congress has the power under Article I not only to make all laws necessary and proper for carrying into execution its enumerated

powers, but also to legislate with regard to "*all other powers* vested by the Constitution in the Government of the United States, or in any ... officer thereof"? Can subsections (b) and (c) be read together as saying, in effect, that while Article II makes the president commander in chief, Congress may define the powers of that office, and herewith has chosen to limit the authority of the officer to introduce armed forces into hostilities, or the imminent danger of hostilities, only under certain enumerated circumstances? Would such a limitation, if that is what Congress intended, be beyond the power of Congress under the All-Other-Powers Clause of Article 1, Sec. 8, Clause 18? Under the appropriations power? Has the Supreme Court ever ruled that the president has any powers, inherent or specific, that could not be constrained by Congress, if it so chose?

2. *Prior restraints.* Does the War Powers Resolution expressly impose any restraints upon the president's use of military force? Should such an intent be inferred by reading subsections (b) and (c) of Section 2 together? Does the brevity of the list in Section 2(c) suggest an intent by Congress to be comprehensive and specific? A much longer list proposed by the Senate (discussed in note 3 below) was rejected. In addition, the conference committee that patched the resolution together reported that "subsequent sections of the joint resolution are not dependent upon the language of this subsection...."[116] The labeling of Section 2 "Purpose and Policy" also had the effect of making it a preamble, which, under the normal rules of legislative interpretation, is not legally binding. For this reason one of the chief sponsors of the resolution in the Senate voted against passage of the final draft. See Eagleton, *War and Presidential Power* (1974), chap. 12.

3. *Twilight zone power.* Assume that Congress has not spoken. What authority does the president have as commander in chief to introduce armed forces into hostilities, or into situations where hostilities are likely? Is the list in Section 2(c) adequate? The original Senate bill would have allowed the commander in chief to introduce the armed forces into hostilities only:

(1) to repel an armed attack upon the United States, its territories and possessions; to take necessary and appropriate retaliatory actions in the event of such an attack; and to forestall the direct and imminent threat of such an attack;

(2) to repel an armed attack against the Armed Forces of the United States located outside of the United States, its territories and possessions, and to forestall the direct and imminent threat of such an attack;

(3) to protect while evacuating citizens and nationals of the United States, as rapidly as possible, from (A) any situation on the high seas involving a direct and imminent threat to the lives of such citizens and nationals, or (B) any country in which such citizens and nationals are present with the express or tacit consent of the government of such country and are being subjected to a direct and imminent threat to their lives, either sponsored by such government or beyond the power of such government to control; but the President shall make every effort to terminate such a threat without using the Armed Forces of the United States to protect citizens and nationals of the United States being evacuated from such country; or

(4) pursuant to specific statutory authorization.... (S. 440, 93d Cong., 1st Sess. [1973], Sec. 3.)

---

116. *The War Powers Resolution: Relevant Documents, Correspondence, Reports*, Subcommittee on International Security and Scientific Affairs, Committee on International Relations, U.S. House of Representatives, 94th Cong., 1st Sess. (Comm. Print, 1975), 13, 14.

Test this list against past presidential uses of the military in hostile contexts and against your own imagination. Is it adequate to define those situations in which the president should be deemed to have constitutional authority to act on his own initiative, without waiting for special congressional authority?

Monroe Leigh, legal adviser to the State Department, offered an alternative list:

> Besides the three situations listed in subsection 2(c) of the War Powers Resolution, it appears that the President has the constitutional authority to use the Armed Forces to rescue American citizens abroad, to rescue foreign nationals where such action directly facilitates the rescue of U.S. citizens abroad, to protect U.S. Embassies and Legations abroad, to suppress civil insurrection, to implement and administer the terms of an armistice or ceasefire designed to terminate hostilities involving the United States, and to carry out the terms of security commitments contained in treaties. We do not, however, believe that any single definitional statement can clearly encompass every conceivable situation in which the President's Commander in Chief authority can be exercised. (*Compliance with the War Powers Resolution*, Hearings before the Subcommittee on International Security And Scientific Affairs, Committee on International Relations, U.S. House of Representatives, 94th. Cong., 1st Sess. [1975], 90–91.)

What kind of initiatives would Leigh legitimize that the original Senate bill would not?

4. *Backhanded authorization.* Representative Elizabeth Holtzman (D-N.Y.), who learned about pregnant negatives in *Holtzman v. Schlesinger* (see section G), voted against the War Powers Resolution on the ground that "it does not prevent the commencement of an illegal war, but allows one to continue for from 60 to 90 days."[117] Senators Gaylord Nelson (D-Wisc.) and Thomas Eagleton (D-Mo.), cosponsors of the Senate bill, voted against the resolution for the same reason. Were they correct? If the president had constitutional authority to initiate hostilities in the circumstances listed in note 3, above, can the Congress limit that initiative to a set number of days? If so, then is not the resolution a limitation on presidential authority? Under what clause of Article I might the Congress legitimately curb authority allocated to the president under Article II?

5. *Congressionally ordered withdrawals.* In Section 5(c), Congress claims the authority to order the president to withdraw his forces "if the Congress so directs by concurrent resolution." If the president is acting pursuant to his *constitutional* powers, can Congress limit those powers by a *concurrent* resolution? Is the concurrent resolution procedure in the War Powers Resolution a condition placed upon the delegation of war-making authority to the president? Or could it be a legislative veto, barred by *Immigration and Naturalization Service v. Chadha,* 462 U.S. 919 (1983)?

6. *Declaration of "no war."* Could the concurrent resolution be deemed a declaration of "no war" issued pursuant to Congress's power to declare war, in which case it would not require the president's signature and be subject to his veto? How might the Supreme Court respond to such an assertion of Congressional authority? Would it be likely to decide the constitutional question, or would it retreat behind the political questions doctrine?

7. *The legal significance of Congressional inaction.* Reread Section 5 of the resolution. Suppose that the sixty (or ninety) days pass and Congress is unable to agree on a course of action. Must the president withdraw the troops? If Congress has the authority, e.g., under the All-Other-Powers Clause, to impose a time limit on the president's exercise of

---

117. 119 *Cong. Rec.* 33872 (1973).

his Article II powers, would the courts be likely to enforce this authority against the president? Or would they again retreat behind the political question doctrine? See *Lowery v. Reagan, infra.*

8. *Funding restrictions.* If there is doubt regarding the potency of the All-Other-Powers Clause, is there any doubt about the potency of the appropriations power or the power to prohibit specific expenditures of appropriated funds? See Glennon, "Strengthening the War Powers Resolution: The Case for Purse-Strings Restriction," 60 *Minn. L. Rev.* 1(1975).

9. *Legislative vetoes and the power of the purse.* If congressional vetoes of any kind are no longer constitutional under *Immigration and Naturalization Service v. Chadha,* what happens to Congress' power of the purse? As a practical matter, is there any way in which Congress can oversee and prevent the president from reprogramming funds appropriated for, say, military training, to an ostensibly similar, but substantively different purpose, such as military maneuvers to threaten a nation with invasion?

10. *The evacuations of South Vietnam and Cambodia.* By early April 1975, it had become clear that both South Vietnam and Cambodia were about to fall to Communist forces. On April 4, President Ford reported to Congress that he had ordered naval vessels carrying some seven hundred marines equipped for combat into the territorial waters of South Vietnam to "assist in the evacuation [of "refugees and U.S. nationals"], including the maintenance of order on board the vessels engaged in that task."[118] On April 10, Ford went before a joint session of Congress to ask it to "clarify immediately its restrictions on the use of U.S. military forces in Southeast Asia for the limited purposes" of evacuating Americans and South Vietnamese. The statutory restrictions to which he referred were undoubtedly funding limitations, since it was unlikely that the evacuation would take longer than sixty days. Two days later, the president reported that the Khmer Rouge had reached the outskirts of Phnom Penh and that he had directed the U.S. military, on his own authority, to proceed with the planned evacuation of that capital. Eighty-two Americans, 159 Cambodians, and 35 persons from other countries were evacuated in four hours, and, although the last helicopters were fired upon, no casualties were suffered. On April 14, Senate majority whip Robert Byrd (D-W.Va.) introduced a bill that would have lifted the funding restrictions by *authorizing* the evacuation of American citizens from Vietnam. The Ford administration proposed an alternative bill that would have permitted a "humanitarian evacuation" of South Vietnamese and others by construing the funding limitations as no obstacle to the use of military force for that purpose. On April 29, when it appeared that the Senate bill's language might triumph, President Ford went ahead and ordered the evacuation of Saigon and Danang on his own authority. Later that day South Vietnam surrendered. In the course of the evacuation, U.S. fighter aircraft "suppressed" anti-aircraft fire, and U.S. ground forces occasionally returned enemy rifle fire. Four members of the armed forces were killed in the course of the nineteen-hour operation and, as in Cambodia, more foreign nationals than Americans were evacuated. Many of these were South Vietnamese officials who had collaborated with the United States and faced certain death at the hands of the Vietcong, spouses of American personnel, and children fathered by Americans. For reasons that remain unclear, Speaker Carl Albert (D-Okla.) then removed the proposed authorization from the House calendar, rather than allow it to be passed as a ratification.

---

118. 121 Cong. Rec. 5820 (daily ed., Apr. 7, 1975).

These 23 servicemen died en route to rescue the crew of the merchant vessel *Mayaguez* when their helicopter malfunctioned and crashed. The rescue operation was ordered by President Ford despite the fact that funding for military action in or over Cambodia had been denied by Congress.

Were these two evacuations beyond the president's powers? If so, what would you have done in his place?

11. *The Mayaguez incident.* The funding restriction and War Powers Resolution were still in effect on May 12, 1975, when a Cambodian naval patrol boat seized the S.S. *Mayaguez*, an American containership, about 2.2 miles off of the Poulo Wai islands. Although sovereignty over the islands was in dispute, they were known to be occupied by the Khmer Rouge forces of Cambodia. The *Mayaguez* was flying no flag at the time of her capture and was outside of internationally recognized shipping lanes. Under international law, therefore, she was subject to detention and search by coastal authorities. Presumably unknown to the Cambodians, the *Mayaguez* had left Saigon nine days earlier, just before that city's fall to the Communists, with seventy-seven containers of military goods and several containers of still undisclosed cargo from the U.S. embassy in Saigon. Fearing another incident like that involving the spy ship *Pueblo*, and smarting from the fall of Saigon, President Ford claimed that the *Mayaguez* had been seized in international waters and directed the U.S. military to rescue both the ship and her crew. Ignoring the funding constraints on military operations within or over Cambodia, Ford ordered a series of operations that included the sinking of Cambodian gunboats, a disastrous marine assault on an island where the crew of the *Mayaguez* was believed to be held, recapture of the unoccupied ship, the bombing of a Cambodian military airfield, and the bombing of a Cambodian oil depot. The forty crewmen were released at the cost of forty-one U.S. military personnel dead and seventy-one injured. The operation was popular until the casualties became known, and then attention focused more on military than legal judgments. Indeed, members of Congress who had fought for the funding restrictions and the War Powers Resolution found it politically impossible to criticize the president in this instance for ignoring both.

12. *Consultation.* Section 3 of the War Powers Resolution states that "the President in every possible instance shall consult with Congress before introducing United States

Armed Forces into hostilities or into situations where imminent involvement in hostilities is clearly indicated by the circumstances, and after every such introduction shall consult regularly with the Congress until United States Armed Forces are no longer engaged in hostilities or have been removed from such situations." President Ford gave members of Congress notice of his decisions to evacuate Phnom Penh, Danang, and Saigon, and his decision to try to rescue the crew of the *Mayaguez*, but he did not consult with them in any way that might be called collaborative. His decision to use U.S. forces to evacuate Americans from Lebanon in 1976 was also made without collaboration. To the extent that Ford communicated to members of Congress during these crises, he did so by "taking note of" rather than "acting pursuant to" the War Powers Resolution. Thus he refused to acknowledge that the resolution limited his constitutional authority in any way. Similarly, President Carter did not involve members of Congress in the planning of his unsuccessful military attempt to rescue American embassy personnel held hostage in Iran in 1980. Four Americans died in that operation.

13. *Reporting.* On September 29, 1982, shortly after introducing marines into Beirut, Lebanon, as part of a multinational peacekeeping force, President Reagan sent the speaker of the House and the president pro tem of the Senate a rather disingenuous letter stating that "there is no intention or expectation that U.S. armed forces will become involved in hostilities." Following the example set by Presidents Ford and Carter, Reagan did not specify which, if any, section of the War Powers Resolution he was following in making this report. On the contrary, he declared that the deployment "is being undertaken pursuant to the President's constitutional authority with respect to the conduct of foreign relations and as Commander in Chief...." Similarly, in informing Congress that he had ordered the invasion of Grenada on October 25, 1983, Reagan refused to report that troops had been introduced "into hostilities," even though they were clearly engaged in combat and had taken casualties. In short, he refused to do anything that might trigger the sixty-day clock. If presidents will not start the war powers clock voluntarily, how is it to be started?

14. *Military operations during the Iraq-Iran War.* The War Powers Resolution did not prevent American forces from being placed in harm's way during the Iraq-Iran War of the 1980s. In the 1980s President Reagan went further and, without consulting Congress, authorized Kuwaiti tankers to fly the American flag, so that an attack on them could be considered an attack upon the United States. He claimed that the War Powers Resolution did not require consultation with Congress because his intent in flagging the foreign tankers was not to put U.S. forces in harm's way, but to deter military action by the warring parties. Reagan held to this position even after an Iraqi missile devastated the destroyer U.S.S *Stark,* killing thirty-seven sailors, and after he ordered U.S. warships in the Gulf to shoot at Iraqi or Iranian aircraft that appeared to be threatening them. As a result of this attack, a super-alert U.S.S. *Vincennes* accidentally shot down an Iranian airbus, flying in Iranian airspace, killing all 290 people on board, including 66 children.

Fearing that these provocative deployments would lead the United States into war, 110 members of Congress sought an injunction to force the president to comply with the War Powers Resolution's reporting and consulting requirements. Their suit was promptly dismissed for raising a nonjusticiable "political question." *Lowery v. Reagan,* 676 F. Supp. 333 (D.D.C. 1987).

Once it became clear to President Reagan that his supporters in the Senate could block any action against his Persian Gulf policy, he permitted limited consultation with the Congress. He also reported to Congress after the U.S. Navy, on his orders, attacked three Iranian warships and two Iranian oil platforms. However, Reagan made it clear that his report was not "pursuant to the War Powers Resolution," but only "consistent with" it.

U.S.S. *Stark* lists after being hit by an Iraqi missile in May 1987, during the Iran-Iraq War. Thirty-seven sailors died; 21 were injured in the attack. To avoid application of the War Powers Resolution, President Reagan denied that he was placing the ship in harm's way by dispatching it to the Persian Gulf to protect Kuwaiti tankers flying the American flag.

According to Richard M. Pious, "the WPR has been a failure. Presidents have ignored its requirements with impunity, confident that its provisions would never stand up in court. Members of Congress have used it as a convenient way to distance themselves from the administration—unless it turns out that the operations are successful, in which case they drop their objections and ignore the WPR. Congress has not insisted that the administration adhere to the terms of the WPR, and there is no reason to think it will be anything more than a dead letter in the future."[119]

Crockett v. Reagan
558 F.Supp. 893 (D.D.C. 1982), *aff'd* 720 F.2d 1355, *cert. denied*, 467 U.S. 1251 (1984)

In the following case, twenty-nine members of Congress sued President Reagan for failing to file a report that would start the clock running in his use of U.S. military advisers in the civil war in El Salvador in the early 1980s. The plaintiffs sought a declaratory judgment that the president had violated the resolution and a court order directing the withdrawal of U.S. forces and other aid.

District court judge Joyce Green began her opinion by ruling that the case was not yet ripe for adjudication because there was no evidence, "except through inadmissible newspaper articles," that U.S. military advisers had been introduced into hostilities. Judge

---

119. From "Presidential War Powers, the War Powers Resolution, and the Persian Gulf," in Martin Fausold and Alan Shank, eds., *The Constitution and the American Presidency* (1991).

Green also declined to hold a hearing to ascertain those facts (at which newspaper reporters could have been called to testify). She ruled that such a hearing would probe a "political question" beyond the competence of the courts.

GREEN, District Judge:

[I]n order to determine the application of the 60-day provision, the Court would be required to decide at exactly what point in time U.S. forces had been introduced into hostilities or imminent hostilities, and whether that situation continues to exist. This inquiry would be even more inappropriate for the judiciary.

In *Baker v. Carr*, 369 U.S. 186 (1962), Justice Brennan identified several categories of "political questions." The question here belongs to the category characterized by a lack of judicially discoverable and manageable standards for resolution. The Court disagrees with defendants that this is the type of political question which involves potential judicial interference with executive discretion in the foreign affairs field. Plaintiffs do not seek relief that would dictate foreign policy, but rather to enforce existing law concerning the procedures for decision-making. Moreover, the issue here is not a political question simply because it involves the apportionment of power between the executive and legislative branches. The duty of courts to decide such questions has been repeatedly reaffirmed by the Supreme Court.

However, the question presented does require judicial inquiry into sensitive military matters. Even if the plaintiffs could introduce admissible evidence concerning the state of hostilities in various geographical areas in El Salvador where U.S. forces are stationed and the exact nature of U.S. participation in the conflict (and this information may well be unavailable except through inadmissible newspaper articles), the Court no doubt would be presented conflicting evidence on those issues by defendants. The Court lacks the resources and expertise (which are accessible to the Congress) to resolve disputed questions of fact concerning the military situation in El Salvador.

... The subtleties of fact finding in this situation should be left to the political branches. If Congress doubts or disagrees with the Executive's determination that U.S. forces in El Salvador have not been introduced into hostilities or imminent hostilities, it has the resources to investigate the matter and assert its wishes. The Court need not decide here what type of congressional statement or action would constitute an official congressional stance that our involvement in El Salvador is subject to the WPR, because Congress has taken absolutely no action that could be interpreted to have that effect. Certainly, were Congress to pass a resolution to the effect that a report was required under the WPR, or to the effect that the forces should be withdrawn, and the President disregarded it, a constitutional impasse appropriate for judicial resolution would be presented.

Even if the factfinding here did not require resolution of a political question, this Court would not order withdrawal of U.S. forces at this juncture. At most, it could order that a report be filed. This conclusion is based upon the structure and legislative history of the WPR....

Plaintiffs contend that the Resolution is fully self-executing, designed as it is to prevent involvement in military actions without positive action by Congress. When U.S. forces are introduced into hostilities or a situation of imminent hostilities, the reporting requirement automatically comes into play, and the President violates the law if he does not make the mandated report. Further, whether or not he makes the report, the 60-day period begins to run from the time the report should have been submitted.

... Plaintiffs contend that a court may find the facts as to whether the situation into which American forces have been introduced constitutes hostilities or imminent hostilities, and if it so finds, it may order the President to make the report or to withdraw the forces.

Defendants do not dispute the interpretation of the basic purpose of the WPR presented here and emphasized by plaintiffs. However, they deny that it is self-executing in a situation where a report has not been submitted. They argue that the decision as to whether a situation warrants a report under the WPR is left to the President's discretion in the first instance. In their view, his failure to submit a report does not justify a court action, and the 60-day period does not begin to run from the time he assertedly should have filed the report. Rather, in instances of disagreement between the President and Congress as to whether a report is required, a "second trigger" is needed to bring the WPR into play. Congress must either take action to express its view that the WPR is applicable to the situation and that a report is required, or, if it desires immediate withdrawal of forces, pass a concurrent resolution directing removal of the forces....

The Court finds that the legislative scheme did not contemplate court-ordered withdrawal when no report has been filed, but rather, it leaves open the possibility for a court to order that a report be filed or, alternatively, withdrawal 60 days after a report was filed or required to be filed by a court or Congress.... If plaintiffs' position is correct, total congressional inaction (which perhaps could signify general agreement with the President's appraisal that no report is required) could result in mandatory withdrawal of U.S. forces if a court adjudged that they had been introduced into hostilities or imminent hostilities more than 60 days previously. In all of the extensive debate on the mandatory withdrawal provision, this possibility was never entertained.

[I]n a situation where no report has been filed, and the priority procedures would not be invoked, the majority of Congress might not be of the opinion that a specific authorization is necessary for continued involvement and take no action, unaware that this course would result in mandatory withdrawal. In that instance court-ordered withdrawal could thwart the will of the majority of Congress. Therefore, when a report has not been filed, it is consistent with the purposes and structure of the WPR to require further congressional action before the automatic termination provision operates.

The requirement to file a report, however, is a different matter. The mere filing of a report cannot thwart congressional will, but can only supply information to aid congressional decisionmaking. Although the Court need not reach the question because the nature of the factfinding in these circumstances precludes judicial inquiry, it does not foreclose the possibility of a court determination that a report is required under the WPR. If, hypothetically, a court did order a report under the WPR, Congress would then have 60 days to give the matter its full consideration in accordance with the priority procedures of the Resolution before withdrawal would be automatically required. Likewise, if Congress itself requires a report, the 60 days for consideration of whether or not to authorize the action would begin at that point. Of course, Congress can always order immediate withdrawal if it so chooses.

The arguments discussed above convince the Court that the case must be dismissed. Therefore, it is unnecessary to reach the other asserted bases for dismissal, which include standing, equitable discretion and lack of a private right of action. As already stated, the Court does not decide that all disputes under the War Powers Resolution would be inappropriate for judicial resolution.

Notes and Questions

1. *Political questions.* Do you agree with Judge Green that a court is not capable of determining whether U.S. forces have been introduced into foreign hostilities? Is Congress more capable than the courts of ascertaining such facts? Who within Congress is "capable" of issuing an authoritative finding of fact: a committee, one house, or both houses? Suppose that one or both houses had authorized this suit. Would that authorization amount to a finding by Congress that U.S. forces had, in fact, been introduced into hostilities?

2. *Nature of the remedy.* Suppose that one or both houses of Congress did ask the court to remedy a presidential violation of the reporting requirement of the War Powers Resolution. What is the appropriate remedy: an order that the president file a report and start the clock, or an order directing the withdrawal of all forces? Does the resolution clearly establish a two-trigger procedure: the first being a congressionally requested court order to start the clock and the second a court order sixty days later requiring withdrawal? What effect does Judge Green's opinion have on the sixty-day timetable?

3. *Hostilities.* On February 4, 1983, according to inadmissible newspaper reports, an unarmed American military adviser to El Salvador was wounded by sniper fire as his helicopter swooped low over a rebel position. The Defense Department insisted that the mission on which the adviser was flying was solely for the purpose of repairing a communications line, and therefore did not involve the introduction of U.S. forces "into hostilities or into situations where imminent hostilities are clearly indicated by the circumstances." No report was filed under the War Powers Resolution. Nor was any report filed when a marine was killed by a land mine in Beirut and a marine captain confronted an Israeli tank commander with a loaded weapon. Should reports have been filed in these circumstances? Should President Carter have filed reports when he sent a carrier task force into the Persian Gulf in 1980 during the Iran-Iraq War or when he dispatched four AWAC aircraft to Saudi Arabia to monitor that war by radar? In September 1983, President Reagan denied the existence of "imminent hostilities" in Lebanon even though marines had been killed by artillery and U.S. warships had shelled artillery positions. As public fear of another Vietnam mounted, many members of Congress began asserting that the 60-day clock of the War Powers Resolution had begun running on August 29, when the marines in Beirut had first come under hostile fire. Do you agree? Would it be legitimate for a court, or Congress, to so rule months later in order to justify an order of immediate withdrawal? Or should courts or Congress always start the clock running from the time they decide that it should be running? That is what Congress decided to do in October 1983, when it agreed to authorize U.S. participation in the international peacekeeping force in Lebanon for eighteen months—past the November 1984 presidential and congressional elections. [For more on the Beirut resolution, see the discussion of "Contingent authority" in section E, *supra*.]

4. *A better war powers resolution?* Professor John Hart Ely of the Stanford Law School proposed an alternative war powers resolution to overcome Congress' reluctance to take responsibility for military action. His first objective was to eliminate the "loss of author-

ity clock" and therefore any implication that Congress has, or may, give the president 60 (or 90) "free days to fight any war he likes."

Instead, Ely suggested that an "appropriations clock" might be substituted for a "loss-of-authority clock." Presidential lawyers can always argue that Congress may not constitutionally encroach upon the president's powers as commander in chief, but they cannot easily challenge Congress' power over the purse strings. Thus, a clock provision requiring that express appropriations must be obtained after a specified number of days might drive the president to seek legislative approval, regardless of whether he had constitutional authority to initiate the operation.

Second, Ely would have had the act grant standing to members of Congress to persuade a court to declare that the appropriations clock is not only running, but is about to run out, unless Congress acts to appropriate funds. In other words, the court would not be required to declare that the president's use of military power was unconstitutional; only that the time is approaching for him to obtain authority from Congress before his authority to spend money on it ends. The court could specify that appropriations authority will run out in a specified number of days from the issuance of its order, remanding the question of authority for the operation to Congress. This process-oriented approach would minimize quibbles over when the operation actually began, or whether the president had authority to begin it, and focus attention instead on his obligation to seek, and the full Congress to grant or deny, the necessary funds to allow the operation to continue.

Third, Ely questioned the efficacy of Congress listing the occasions on which the president might legitimately initiate military action on his own without granting him excessive excuses to initiate combat without consulting Congress or obtaining its permission. Most scholars concede that if section 2(c) were to be removed from the preamble and made binding, it would have to be broadened, at least to grant the president some discretion to protect or rescue American citizens in dire straits. But then the executive would wish to add other powers, including authority to protect U.S. embassies abroad, suppress civil insurrection at home, enforce cease-fire agreements, or carry out the security commitments contained in treaties. Each of these powers is plausible, but each is a double-edged sword. It may grant the president more authority than he needs, give Congress too much of an excuse to sit back and do nothing, or possibly encourage a rare court to attempt to stop the president's action with a specific injunction, when what is really needed is a full and public debate.

Instead of again becoming mired in the listing process, Congress might state a general principle, much as Senator Joseph Biden (D-Del.) tried to do in a proposed "Use of Force Act":

> In the absence of a declaration of war or statutory authorization for a specific use of force, the President is authorized to use force abroad ... to respond to a foreign military threat that severely and directly jeopardizes the supreme national interests of the United States under extraordinary emergency circumstances that do not permit sufficient time for Congress to consider statutory authorization.[120]

If this were law, would President Reagan have been able to invade Grenada without prior congressional approval? Would President George H. W. Bush have been able to invade Panama to abduct General Noriega? Could President Clinton have ordered U.S. bombing in Kosovo or Serbia? Could he have lawfully fired cruise missiles at Al Qaeda train-

---

120. Quoted in Michael Glennon, *Constitutional Diplomacy,* 332 (1990).

ing camps in Afghanistan or at a suspected poison-gas factory in Sudan in reprisal for Al Qaeda's attacks on U.S. embassies in East Africa? Does Senator Biden's proposal provide courts with "judicially manageable standards" for issuing injunctions to protect military personnel endangered by such operations?

Fourth, Ely proposed to abolish section 8(d), which disclaims any Congressional intent to alter the constitutional authority of either Congress or the president. That disclaimer, he believed, would give White House lawyers too much opportunity to quibble over whether the resolution recognizes the president's independent authority (whatever that might be) or unconstitutionally encroaches on that authority (e.g. by reporting requirements).

Fifth, Ely believed that genuine consultation with Congress could be improved if Congress were to specify more clearly who should be consulted and, thus, who could best initiate resolutions of approval or disapproval. Congress did this in the late 1970s when it required the CIA to consult with the intelligence committees (which have appropriations powers) before undertaking covert operations, but crippled the process by allowing the CIA to silence the committees with secrecy requirements.

J. Political Questions?

1. *Dellums v. Bush.* On August 2, 1990, Iraq invaded and occupied Kuwait. Reagan's successor, George H. W. Bush, blockaded Iraq and prepared for war, sending more than 230,000 troops the Persian Gulf. Fifty-four members of the House and one senator went to court, seeking an injunction, arguing that for the president to order warfare without first obtaining Congress' permission would, in effect, strip them of their constitutional right to debate and vote on a declaration of war. Judge Harold Greene rejected the Justice Department's argument that the issue was a "political question" beyond the competence of courts to decide. He also ruled that the legislators had standing to sue, but decided that their case was not yet ripe for judicial review. 752 F. Supp. 1141 (D.D.C. 1990).

2. *Ange v. Bush.* About the same time, Judge Royce Lamberth of the same district court, rejected an army sergeant's request that the president be enjoined from ordering him into war with Iraq without first complying with the Declaration-of-War Clause and the War Powers Resolution. The sergeant's motion, Lamberth ruled, raised a nonjusticiable "political question" because, in part, the Constitution explicitly entrusted the decision to initiate war to the Congress and president together, and to them alone. *Ange v. Bush,* 752 F. Supp. 509 (D.D.C. 1990). Do you agree?

3. *Judicially manageable standards?* In *Dellums,* the Justice Department argued that the "simultaneous existence" of war powers in Articles I and II makes it impossible for judges to isolate the war-declaring power. In other words, there are no "judicially manageable standards" by which a judge could decide that the president is exceeding his "war-making" powers and violating Congress' authority to "declare war." Is that true? Should the same lack-of-manageable standards argument be applied to the Constitution's guarantees of free expression or due process of law, which are also not very explicit? In *Ange,* Judge Lamberth declared that courts should draw back from invitations to undertake a "structural analysis of the political branches' respective roles." 752 F. Supp. 509, n. 4. Why? Should the Supreme Court have drawn back from deciding *Youngstown,* the steel seizure case (*supra,* chapter 2), because it too required a structural analysis of the respective roles of the political branches?

4. *Campbell v. Clinton.* In 1999, thirty-one House members sought a judicial ruling that President Clinton had violated both the Constitution and the War Powers Resolution by conducting air strikes in Yugoslavia without prior Congressional authorization. On appeal, judges Silberman and Tatel could not agree. Silberman insisted that "no one" could legally challenge the bombing because of the absence of "judicially manageable standards" for resolving what was essentially a "political question." Judge Tatel concluded that "[w]hether the military activity in Yugoslavia amounted to 'war' within the meaning of the Declare War Clause . . . is no more standardless than any other question regarding the constitutionality of government action." 203 F.2d 19, 24–25 (D.C. Cir. 2000). Is it necessary for the courts to promulgate an all-purpose definition of "war" before holding that continuation of military action should have the express concurrence of Congress?

K. "Peacekeeping" and "Mission Creep"

During the Cold War, Congressional and voter tolerance of presidential war-making was relatively high. As the Cold War diminished, Congress' deference to the president's secret knowledge declined. The fall of the Berlin Wall in 1989, the dissolution of the Soviet Union, and the emergence of the United States as the world's only superpower, left many local and regional conflicts without the great power rivalry that had helped fuel them, ushering in a new era of U.N. or multinational peacekeeping operations. These developments have drawn the United States into a variety of multinational coalitions that are meant to 1) maintain peace among warring ethnic groups within or between nations, 2) create conditions for something vaguely like democracy, and 3) provide humanitarian relief to the victims of internal convulsions without escalating into "war."

Somalia and Famine Relief

In 1991, the Somali government collapsed and rival clans resumed their struggle for power. By 1993, an estimated three hundred thousand Somalis had died of famine and civil strife. More than one million crowded into refugee camps where international relief workers were frequently attacked and robbed.

The United Nations dispatched a small force of Pakistani troops to protect the workers and keep relief supplies flowing. In April 1992, Congress passed the Horn of Africa Recovery and Food Security Act committing "the United States to [support] all aspects of relief operations in the Horn of Africa and to work in support of [the] United Nations . . . in breaking the barriers currently threatening the lives of millions of refugees."[121] Later that year, after Somali warlords interfered with the flow of relief supplies brought in by a U.S. military airlift, Congress declared that international peacekeeping could take many forms, but chose not include within its list military action to protect relief workers.[122] Even so, President George H. W. Bush ordered U.S. military forces to secure the airfield and port facilities at Mogadishu. Within a month, twenty-eight thousand U.S. soldiers and sailors were stationed in Somalia or off its shores. Was the president within his authority to pro-

---

121. Pub. L. No. 102-274, 106 Stat. 115.
122. Pub. L. No. 102-484, Sec. 1342 (a) (2), 106 Stat. 2315.

vide security for U.S. troops, ships, and planes, and to protect international relief workers? Did the U.N. Security Council's resolution calling on member states to provide troops to protect its relief workers impose any legal obligation on the president to do so?

On June 5, 1993, forces loyal to one of the Somali warlords, General Mohammed Aidid, ambushed a U.N. convoy, killing twenty-four Pakistani soldiers and wounding three American soldiers. The U.S. Quick Reaction Force responded with air strikes and ground attacks against Aidid's headquarters in Mogadishu, hoping to capture him. On October 3, 1993, a firefight with Aidid's troops broke out, during which seventeen American soldiers were killed and eighty-four wounded. The body of one dead American soldier was dragged through the streets, a humiliation dramatized by the film *Blackhawk Down*.

Members of Congress and the press soon began criticizing the Clinton administration for not adequately arming American troops and for crossing the line (later known as the "Mogadishu line") between peacekeeping and peacemaking. U.S. enthusiasm for humanitarian relief efforts plummeted and Clinton ordered American troops withdrawn from this U.N. mission.

If U.S. forces were properly assigned to assist in the U.N.'s relief efforts in Somalia, did the president need separate permission from Congress before joining the U.N.'s effort to suppress Aidid? Would it be practical or reasonable for presidents to have to return to Congress for authority to take aggressive action in the hope of enhancing security for a peacekeeping or humanitarian effort that Congress had expressly funded?

Suppose that Congress had not authorized the relief effort. Should the president, as commander in chief (and chief diplomat), have had the authority not just to rescue American relief workers from General Aidid's attacks, but to provide long-term military security for their relief operation, or for that of the United Nations? If the president may order U.S. forces to rescue American relief workers, may he also order them to rescue foreign relief workers?

As U.S. casualties mounted, opposition to "nation building" in Somalia increased and Congress pressured the president to withdraw. A compromise provision in the defense appropriations bill cut off funds for U.S. forces in Somalia after March 31, 1994, and limited the use of funds in the meantime to protecting diplomatic facilities and American citizens. The amendment also made it clear that U.S. forces in Somalia were not to be under U.N. control.[123]

Kosovo and Ethnic Cleansing

In 1992, President George H. W. Bush warned Yugoslavia's Serbian president Slobodan Milosevic that any military action against the Albanian majority in Kosovo would result in U.S. military action. In 1998, President Clinton renewed that threat, claiming that he could conduct air strikes against Serbian forces as a leader of NATO without first obtaining permission from Congress, NATO, or the United Nations. The threat worked for a few months, during which the U.N. Security Council was persuaded to enact a resolution which, while it did not urge military action, did deplore the "excessive and indiscriminate use of force by Serbian security forces and the Yugoslav army." On January 30, 1999, NATO endorsed the U.S. warning and reserved the right to take whatever steps might be necessary to avert a "humanitarian catastrophe." In February thirty-eight mem-

---

123. 107 Stat. 1475–77, sec. 8151 (1993).

bers of Congress objected to the administration's "go-it-alone" strategy, but Undersecretary of State Thomas Pickering argued that the exercise of Congress' war powers was not necessary in any situation short of an attack upon the United States—the very sort of situation that the *Prize Cases* allowed the president to repel without waiting for Congress' permission. Eventually, both Houses of Congress passed separately worded resolutions approving U.S. participation in a NATO peacekeeping force.[124] However, when the air strikes began, Clinton ignored those resolutions, insisting that "I have taken these actions pursuant to my constitutional authority to conduct U.S. foreign relations and as Commander in Chief and Chief Executive."[125]

Haiti and the Restoration of Social Order

In 1994, the Clinton administration threatened to invade Haiti in order to oust a military junta and restore the democratically elected government that the junta had overthrown. One of Clinton's purposes was to promote democracy and restore peace and economic stability to a desperately poor Caribbean people long plundered by brutal regimes. Another was to create social order, and thereby stem waves of illegal immigration to the United States by thousands of uneducated, non-English-speaking blacks.

The use of American military force to drive the junta of General Raoul Cedras from power and reinstate President Jean-Bertrand Aristide had the support of the United Nations[126] and a coalition of small Caribbean countries. On July 31, the U.N. Security Council passed a resolution "inviting" all states, including those in the region, to use "all necessary means" to remove the military regime. Would it have been legitimate for President Clinton to accept the U.N. "invitation" as sole authority to invade the island?

On August 3, a Republican-led Senate unanimously resolved that the U.N.'s invitation "does not constitute authorization for the deployment of United States Armed Forces in Haiti under the Constitution of the United States or pursuant to the War Powers Resolution." President Clinton promptly declared that "Like my predecessors of both parties, I have not agreed that I was constitutionally mandated" to obtain the support of Congress.

His administration also argued that the planned invasion would "not be 'war' in the constitutional sense [because] the planned deployment [had] the full consent of the legitimate government, and did not involve the risk of major or prolonged hostilities or serious casualties to either the United States or Haiti."[127] Should consent and an allegedly low risk obviate the need for Congressional permission when there is time to seek it? Did Congress, in its War Powers Resolution, define "war" as narrowly as the Clinton administration subsequently did?

The threat of a U.S. invasion had the desired effect. The junta leaders accepted safe passage out of the country and the American forces entered unopposed. Aristide's government was restored, but the larger goals of stability, prosperity, and democracy could not be attained in the six months that Senate Republicans gave the administration to complete the operation.

---

124. *Congressional Record* (March 11, 1999), H1249; (March 23, 1999), S3110.
125. *Public Papers of the Presidents* (March 24, 1999), 451–53.
126. Security Council Resolution 940 (1994) expressly authorized member states "to form a multinational force ... to use all necessary means to [restore] democracy in Haiti."
127. Letter of Walter Dellinger, Assistant Attorney General, Office of Legal Counsel, to Senator Robert Dole, Sept. 27, 1994.

L. New Forms of Military Action

Panama: Extradition by Invasion

As the Cold War wound down, the demand for military assistance to civilian law enforcement, particularly in the war on illegal drugs, grew. A prime target for prosecution was General Manuel Noriega, Panama's de facto head of state who, in the early 1980s, had become involved in the laundering of drug money. The U.S. government had known about Noriega's role in the drug trade, but had tolerated it, in part, because he had helped the Drug Enforcement Agency capture rival drug smugglers and supported the Reagan administration's secret war against the Nicaraguan Sandanistas. (Noreiga was actually a paid CIA "asset.") After the Iran-Contra scandal broke, only the DEA wanted the general's services, and even its protection ended when U.S. attorneys in Miami, driven by Congressional critics, obtained indictments against him.

Several alternatives for dealing with Noriega were considered. Assassination, either directly or by proxy, was rejected; President Ford's executive order (No. 12,333) seemed to forbid it. In October 1989, after a second coup attempt failed, Senator Jesse Helms (R-N.C.) sponsored a bill that would have authorized the army to kidnap the general (a forerunner of "extraordinary rendition" under George W. Bush), but President George H. W. Bush did not wait. On December 20, 1989, he ordered more than twenty-four thousand U.S. troops to invade Panama to seize its dictator. Twenty-six Americans and more than seven hundred Panamanians, mostly civilians, died in the conflict. Property damage exceeded $1.5 billion.

What constitutional provision, if any, authorizes the president to invade a foreign country in order to serve an arrest warrant? The Posse Comitatus Act of 1878 makes it a crime to use the military to enforce civilian laws.[128] Should that prohibition be read as only applying within the United States?

In 1841, President Tyler declared that "This Government can never concede to any foreign government the power, except in a case of the most urgent and extreme necessity, of invading [United States] territory, either to arrest the persons or destroy the property of those who may have violated the municipal laws of such foreign government, or have disregarded their obligations arising under the law of nations."[129] By this standard, did the first President Bush violate international law to capture Noriega?

Regime change. The Panama invasion can also be seen as an invasion to achieve a regime change. The United Nations Charter requires the United States to "refrain ... from the ... use of force against the territorial integrity or political independence of any State."[130] The Charter of the Organization of American States, which the United States also ratified, declares "the territorial integrity of a State is inviolable."[131] Did the United States have a sufficient justification for violating either of these charter provisions? The federal judge who tried and sentenced Noriega to prison ruled that how the general was brought before the court was none of his business.[132]

---

128. 18 U.S.C. Sec. 1385.
129. J. Richardson, ed., *A Compilation of the Messages and Papers of the Presidents*, Vol. III, 1929.
130. Art. 2, para. 5.
131. 2 U.S.T. 2394, T.I.A.S. no. 2361, art. 17.
132. *United States v. Noriega*, 746 U.S. 1506, 1529 (S.D. Fla. 1991).

The War on Terrorism: When the Enemy Is Not a State

On September 11, 2001, suicide squads hijacked four U.S. civilian airliners, crashing two into the twin towers of the World Trade Center in New York, one into the Pentagon, and a fourth into a field in western Pennsylvania. Nearly three-thousand innocent people died. The attacks were quickly traced to the al Qaeda organization of Osama bin Laden, a wealthy Saudi Arabian whose operatives had previously bombed the World Trade Center, two U.S. embassies in Africa, and the U.S. destroyer *Cole.*

The AUMF. On September 18, 2001, Congress passed a joint resolution called the Authorization to Use Military Force (AUMF). It authorized the president "to use all necessary and appropriate force against those nations, organizations, or persons he determines planned, authorized, committed, or aided the terrorist attacks that occurred on September 11, 2001, or harbored such organization or persons, in order to prevent any future acts of international terrorism against the United States by such nations, organizations or persons."[133]

The GWOT. As an attack on al Qaeda's bases in Afghanistan, and on the Taliban regime that sheltered al Qaeda's operatives (for large subsidies), the military action that Congress authorized looked reasonably conventional — at least as conventional as American military operations against the "Tripoli pirates" during Jefferson's administration. But George W. Bush insisted that this "war" on terrorism was not confined to Afghanistan. It was a "global war on terrorism," unlimited in scope and with no clear end. To this end, the president claimed that he had the authority to send covert operatives into any country on earth to capture suspected terrorists and deliver them to secret CIA prisons, military prisons in Afghanistan and Cuba, or to foreign intelligence agencies known for their use of torture. Do you agree?

The Bush administration also claimed that the existence of this war against global terrorism, whether authorized by Congress or not, allowed it to detain indefinitely terrorists of any political stripe as "enemy combatants," from al Qaeda to the IRA. Can there be a "war" against an "ism," a tactic, or a private criminal syndicate? Is that clear from the face of the AUMF? Does this resolution, or the president's duty to protect the nation from attack, permit him to detain indefinitely alleged terrorists not captured in active combat in 1) military prisons, or 2) CIA prisons, or 3) federal prisons?

Does the president's power to use military commissions depend on whether Congress' resolution authorizing the president to respond to al Qaeda's attacks was an exercise of 1) its power to declare war, or 2) its power to authorize reprisals? Can members of groups as large as al Qaeda and the Irish Republican Army, or as small as Timothy McVeigh and Terry Nichols, legally be tried as "war criminals"? If not, then is the "war against terrorism" a "war" for the purpose of defining the scope of the president's powers, or the rights of persons under the protection of the Constitution?

If, as the administration claimed, captured Taliban soldiers and al Qaeda operatives were not entitled to prisoners-of-war status under the Geneva Conventions, then should it be able to label the conflict against them "war"? On the other hand, if the war against terrorism is not a war in the constitutional sense, does that mean that the president has more (or less) authority to wage it, or to wage it free of constitutional or legal restraints"?

---

133. Authorization for Use of Military Force, Pub. L. No. 107-40, 115 Stat. 224 (2001). The U.N. Security Council also adopted a resolution condemning the attacks and reaffirming "the inherent right of individual or collective self-defense" in accordance with the Charter. U.N. Doc. S/RES/1368 (2002). See also U.N. Doc. S/RES/1373 (2001).

Remote-controlled Predator drones have been used by armchair pilots of the CIA to kill suspected terrorists from hundreds of miles away, in Yemen as well as Afghanistan and Pakistan.
(The pilots shown here are U.S. military personnel.)

Is the CIA a military agency? On November 3, 2002, a remote-controlled CIA drone
flying over Yemen fired a rocket that destroyed an automobile carrying six suspected al
Qaeda members, including Kamel Derwish, an American citizen from Lackawana, N.Y.
May the president lawfully authorize such strikes 1) on his own authority, or 2) pursuant
to Congress' resolution, 3) with (or without) the foreign nation's permission?

Should it make a difference which government agency carries out the killing? Is the
CIA part of the armed forces of the United States? If that agency's operatives may go
around the world assassinating suspected enemies with drones, or kidnapping them out
of Italy, Sweden, or the United States, should that be specified in the authorization for the
use of military force or some other law?

Scope of the "war." Most Congressional authorizations specify or presume a restricted
theater of military operations, so that an extension of the war to neutral neighboring nations ought to require separate authority from Congress. Of course, both Wilson and
Nixon disregarded this assumption when they extended their wars to Russia and Cambodia,
respectively. Does the 2001 AUMF against those responsible for 9/11 permit the president to use military or paramilitary tactics, such as assassination drones or kidnap squads,
by civilian as well as military agencies, anywhere on earth? If it does not, should the courts
hold that the president lacks authority to extend the "war" wherever he wishes, or should
they continue to duck the issue by invoking the political questions doctrine?

Preventive War against Iraq

During the summer of 2002, President George W. Bush insisted that he possessed all
the authority he needed to initiate war against Saddam Hussein's Iraq in order to 1) deprive him of weapons of mass destruction before they could be used against the United
States, 2) to effect a "regime change" so that such weapons would not be developed in
the future, and 3) to turn Iraq into a "democracy" ("nation building," thereby transforming the politics of the region)? Are these the kind of executive uses of military power
that the framers of the Constitution or the Congress that passed the War Powers Resolution had in mind?

Like many presidents, Bush was imprecise about the sources of his legal authority. More
often than not, his legal claims were made by unnamed officials, in what appeared to be
deliberate attempts to confuse. Thus, White House lawyers claimed that while the presi-

dent might consult with Congress, he had all the authority he needed to invade Iraq, either from 1) his authority as commander in chief to defend the United States from future threats, or 2) the 1991 Congressional resolution authorizing Bush's father to oust Iraqi forces from Kuwait pursuant to resolutions of the United Nation's Security Council.

Those U.N. resolutions were the basis for the cease-fire agreement of April 4, 1991, in which Iraq agreed not to possess weapons of mass destruction, and to allow U.N. inspectors to verify the elimination of those weapons. To prevent Iraqi warplanes from attacking Kurds in the north and threatening Iraqi's neighbors to the east and south, the coalition (but not the U.N. Security Council) imposed "no-fly zones" over both northern and southern Iraq—areas in which Iraqi planes and helicopters could not fly without being shot down.

Iraqi ground forces fired on coalition aircraft, prompting frequent bombings of Iraq's radar stations and airstrips by U.S. and British war planes. Military action to enforce the terms of the Gulf War cease-fire was more or less continuous from 1991 to 2002, and involved more than 250,000 sorties by U.S. and coalition warplanes.

U.N. inspectors were able to identify and dispose of some chemical and biological weapons, but Iraqi forces interfered with their work and they withdrew in 1998. The inspectors also withdrew, in part, to avoid being hit by a four-day barrage of cruise missiles fired on President Clinton's orders in reprisal for an Iraqi plot against the life of his predecessor, George H. W. Bush. Should such a reprisal be authorized by Congress, or can it be considered within the president's authority to carry out the Congressional resolution authorizing him to enforce U.N. policy?

Preventive warfare. While George W. Bush could have claimed that a U.S. attack on Iraq in 2003 would be no more than a continuation of military operations authorized by Congress and the United Nations in 1991, he chose to rely on what his aides called "preemptive warfare" or "anticipatory self defense." He argued that the United States needed to invade Iraq, overthrow Hussein, and install a less threatening regime before Hussein acquired nuclear weapons, or perfected an alleged arsenal of chemical and biological weapons and used them against the United States.[134]

Reasonable people have differed as to whether the installation of nuclear missiles in Cuba sufficiently changed the balance of power so as to justify preemptive action by President Kennedy, acting alone. Even so, the sense of threat from the Cuban missiles was immediate, compared to the threat posed by the possibility that Iraq possessed chemical and biological weapons, or was attempting to acquire nuclear weapons. Under such circumstances, is there less justification for President George W. Bush's claim that he could launch a preventive war against Iraq without obtaining further authorization from Congress or the United Nations? Does a military operation, projected to involve more than two-hundred thousand soldiers and sailors, which could require the United States to occupy all or parts of Iraq for many years, and which could destabilize the Middle East and prompt more terrorist attacks, require special authorization from 1) Congress, or 2) from Congress and the United Nations together?

May the president, when necessary to defend the country from an imminent threat of attack, launch a preemptive strike, like the one that President Kennedy contemplated,

---

134. On September 20, 2002, the administration published a lengthy paper on "The National Security Strategy of the United States," in which it declared: "The greater the threat, the greater is the risk of inaction—and the more compelling the case for taking anticipatory action to defend ourselves, even if uncertainty remains as to the time and place of the enemy's attack. To forestall or prevent such hostile acts by our adversaries, the United States will, if necessary, act preemptively." Quoted by Anthony Lewis, "Bush and Iraq," *The New York Review of Books,* Nov. 7, 2002, 4.

but did not use, after discovering that the Soviet Union was in the process of placing nuclear missiles on the island of Cuba? May it be argued that Kennedy's naval blockade of Cuba was a preventive "act of war"? If so, should it have required prior Congressional authorization?

In 1962, President Kennedy hesitated to launch a preemptive strike against Soviet missiles in Cuba in part because he did not want such an attack equated with the Japanese attack on Pearl Harbor in 1941. Was the Japanese attack a preemptive strike against a country poised to attack it, like Israel's preemptive strike in 1967 against Egyptian forces massing for an immediate attack? Or was it more analogous to Israel's bombing of Iraq's Osirak nuclear facility in 1981?

Are there any past military actions by American presidents that could be classified as historic precedents for preventive war against Iraq? For example, was President Reagan's conquest of Grenada in 1983, which effected a regime change and deprived the Soviet Union of the use of an airstrip its Cuban proxies were helping to build within striking distance of the Panama Canal, an act of preventive warfare? If so, when might future presidents be justified in launching similar attacks on their own authority?

J. Q. Adams on aggressive war. In 1821, Secretary of State John Quincy Adams opposed the sending of warships to evict Spain from Venezuela and Peru. "America," he said, "goes not abroad in search of monsters to destroy." To do so would involve the U.S. "beyond the power of extrication, in all wars of interests and intrigue, of individual avarice, envy, and ambition, which assumes the colors and usurps the standards of freedom. The fundamental maxims of her policy would insensibly change from *liberty* to *force*.... She might become the dictatress of the world. She would no longer be the ruler of her own spirit."[135]

Webster's test. In 1837, a small British force crossed the Niagara River into the United States and destroyed the steamboat *Caroline,* in order to prevent it from running more guns to Canadian rebels. Secretary of State Daniel Webster protested, calling this act of preventive warfare unjustified under international law because the British government could not show "a necessity of self-defense, instant, overwhelming, leaving no choice of means, no moment for deliberation." The British government defended the attack, claiming that it was compelled to act because neither New York nor federal authorities had done enough to stop the gun-running.

Webster also argued that the attack was disproportionate to the threat—the British force did not need to attack at night, when its volunteers could not discriminate between gun runners and innocent persons. Nor did it need to set fire to the ship and send her out into the river, to be destroyed on rocks above the falls, when innocent people might still be sleeping on board.[136]

Magnitude of the potential harm test. According to the Bush administration, Webster's criteria should set the standard for justifiable self-defense under international law, but with one addition.[137] Factored into the analysis should be the *magnitude of the harm* that could result from waiting too long. Thus, the United States did not need to wait until it had clear evidence that Saddam Hussein intended to use his weapons of mass destruction

135. Quoted by Lewis H. Lapham in *Gag Rule* (2004), 140.

136. *The Works of Daniel Webster,* Vol. 4, 261. Erroneous reports claimed that sleeping persons had been left on board the steamboat.

137. Speech by John Bellinger III, to a national security conference of the American Bar Association, Nov. 22, 2002.

against the United States or any other country. It was enough that he had such weapons and had launched gas attacks in the past. Is this persuasive? Is it relevant that the United States has used nuclear weapons in the past?

As previously noted, President Bush argued that he did not need authority from either Congress or the United Nations to conduct a preventive attack against Iraq, not just to destroy its weapons but to install a new regime that would be less likely to reconstitute them. Is this a power that the framers would have intentionally granted to the executive alone? Given the nature of modern weaponry, and the government's capacity for clandestine operations, is this a power that should be denied to the president?

Compare Bush's *magnitude of the potential harm* test to the "gravity of the evil discounted by its probability" test advanced as grounds for silencing freedom of speech and association in the Cold War case of *Dennis v. United States,* 341 U.S. 494 (1951) (abandoned in *Brandenburg v. Ohio,* 395 U.S. 444 [1969]). Under Bush's test, would there be anything in the Constitution to prevent a president from attacking on his own any foreign country, much as Israel attacked Iraq's nuclear facility in 1981, to destroy its capacity to produce or launch weapons of mass destruction?

Does the *magnitude of the potential harm test* effectively nullify Webster's other criteria for a justifiable preventive action—the presence of an instant, overwhelming threat, a lack of alternatives, and no time for deliberation? Conversely, should the United States have to wait until a threat of attack is so imminent that there is no time for deliberations or the pursuit of alternatives?

In 1967, Israel detected Egyptian troops massing for an attack. Rather than wait, Israel struck first and, by so doing, probably reduced its casualties significantly. It also deliberately bombed the American spy ship *Liberty*, killing more than seventy Americans, in order to prevent the communications it was seeking to intercept from being used against Israel's interests in the Six-Day War with Egypt. But, is the reduction of potential casualties a significant justification for striking at a growing, but not immediate threat, such as the stockpiling of weapons? Would the United States be justified in destroying North Korea's nuclear stockpiles, much as Israel destroyed Iraq's nuclear facility, rather than wait for that "rogue state" to acquire atomic weapons?

The American spy ship *Liberty* was disabled and nearly sunk after being attacked by Israeli planes and gunboats to prevent it from aiding Egypt during the Six-Day War in 1967. More than 70 American sailors lost their lives in this attack, the purpose of which was concealed by the Johnson administration.

Terrorists, of course, do not mass troops, but the Bush administration also feared that Iraq (or some other "rogue state") might use al Qaeda's play book to plant a nuclear device (poison gas or anthrax) in an American city. When might such a present fear of future harm become sufficient to permit the president (or Congress and the president) to authorize a preventive strike?

Iraq resolution. On October 11, 2002, Congress enacted a joint resolution authorizing the president to use military force against Iraq. Section 3 of that resolution provides:

(A) AUTHORIZATION

The president is authorized to use the armed forces of the United States as he determines to be necessary and appropriate in order to:

(1) defend the national security of the United States against the continuing threat posed by Iraq; and

(2) enforce all relevant United Nations Security Council resolutions regarding Iraq. (P.L. No. 107-243, 116 Stat. 1498, 50 U.S.C. 1541.)

Under this resolution, was the president limited to defending the United States against an imminent or actual attack by Iraqi forces? Did Congress, by granting the president authority to "defend the national security" of the United States against Iraq, authorize offensive action to 1) destroy Iraq's weapons of mass destruction, 2) effect a regime change, or 3) establish a "democracy" in Iraq?

Interventions and the United Nations. When the United States helped to create the United Nations, it did not cede "sovereignty" to the world body. Neither did member countries. The UN was founded on the assumption that the national borders of all member states were inviolable. Over time, this principle has provided considerable protection for dictators, who have since World War II slaughtered more of their own citizens than have died in all international wars during the same period. This has led to calls for the United States, with or without the United Nations or NATO, to intervene, on humanitarian grounds, to end civil wars, ethnic massacres, "ethnic cleansing," and coups d'état.[138] The U.S. intervention in the former Yugoslavia in the 1990s, as head of a NATO force, is one example of humanitarian intervention. George W. Bush's brief deployment of U.S. marines in Liberia in 2003 could be considered another.

According to Professor Michael Ignatieff, "there are five clear cases when [a more representative] United Nations [Security Council] could authorize [the United States or any other member state] to intervene: when, as in Rwanda or Bosnia, ethnic cleansing and mass killing threaten large numbers of civilians and a state is unwilling or unable to stop it; when, as in Haiti, democracy is overthrown and people inside a state call for help to restore a freely elected government; when, as in Iraq, North Korea and possibly Iran, a state violates the nonproliferation protocols regarding the acquisition of chemical, nuclear or biological weapons; when, as in Afghanistan, states fail to stop terrorists on their soil from launching attacks on other states; and finally, when, as in Kuwait, states are victims of aggression and call for help." "A Mess of Intervention," *New York Times Sunday Magazine*, Sept. 7, 2003, 85.

Ignatieff called each of these interventions "humanitarian," but is there any real limit to this justification, conceptually or practically, for military intervention in the internal affairs of other nations? When the framers of the Constitution allocated authority over the use of American military forces, did they anticipate humanitarian interventions of the sort Ignatieff has advocated?

---

138. See, e.g., John H. F. Shattuck, *Freedom on Fire* (2003).

Professor Ignatieff also recommended that the United States seek to reorganize the United Nations so that its Security Council may direct member states to intervene militarily in the internal affairs of historically sovereign states for essentially humanitarian reasons. If so, may this change in authority be accomplished simply by revising the UN Charter (an American treaty), or would the cession of sovereignty involved in such a move require a constitutional amendment? Should interventions to stabilize the price of oil on the world market, or reconfigure the nature of politics in the Middle East, count as "humanitarian justifications" for military intervention? Do nations typically go to war for purely altruistic, or purely self-defense, reasons?

M. Paramilitary and Covert Action

Alexis de Tocqueville warned his readers that "foreign politics demand scarcely any of those qualities which are peculiar to a democracy.... [A democracy] cannot combine its measures with secrecy or await their consequences with patience." These qualities, Tocqueville observed, "more especially belong to an individual or an aristocracy,"[139] or, he might have added, a bureaucracy.

Prior to World War II, the United States lacked both the capacity and desire to influence the internal affairs of foreign states through paramilitary or covert action. Following World War II, the United States acquired not only a permanent military establishment, but a host of clandestine services, including the Central Intelligence Agency (1947), the National Security Agency (1952), and the Defense Intelligence Agency (1961). It also expanded the intelligence services of the army, navy, and air force, and the counterintelligence and domestic intelligence capabilities of the Federal Bureau of Investigation. With the advent of the Cold War, the United States also pursued an interventionist foreign policy, much of it carried out by the CIA and military intelligence agencies. Moreover, the techniques of covert action developed for use abroad were turned inward against dissent within the United States, as the investigations of congressional committees during the Watergate era demonstrated most dramatically.

Covert Action: An Inventory

Before we consider the legitimacy of covert action, a brief review of the kinds of activities it has involved may help to focus the analysis. As you review the following inventory, consider the constitutional, legal, ethical, and policy issues that these clandestine activities may raise for a society that believes in open government, civil liberties, and the rule of law.

Covert Collection. Intelligence agents are attached to the staffs of most U.S. embassies abroad. They pretend to work for the State Department, often as legal and political officers, but their intelligence function is known (or suspected) by host country officials and other attentive elites. In some countries, the CIA station chief is more pretentious than the U.S. ambassador, but in most countries he maintains a low profile. Like the military

---

139. Quoted in Robert Borosage, "Para-Legal Authority and Its Perils," 40 *L. & Contemp. Prob.* 166, 167 (1976).

attachés (who work for the Defense Intelligence Agency), these CIA officers are known as "legal spies" in the sense that their presence on the embassy staff is tolerated as a matter of reciprocity. Like diplomats, intelligence officers develop contacts within the host country, particularly with military personnel whose support is essential to maintaining (or overthrowing) the regime currently in power.

Unlike diplomats, intelligence officers use bribery and blackmail to recruit informants or turn them into "agents of influence." Contrary to the image these agencies like to convey, there is no easy way to separate covert collection from covert action.

Advice and persuasion. Like diplomats, intelligence officers are used to persuade host country politicians and military men to pursue policies favorable to the United States. Much of the advice is informal and direct; at other times it is given through persons not known to be speaking for the United States. Since World War II, most of this advice has been calculated to persuade host countries to oppose international Communism, provide a hospitable climate for American investment, and maintain domestic stability. As former National Security staff member Roger Morris has observed, "One searches in vain for any evidence that the [CIA] has intervened anywhere in two decades on behalf of human rights."[140]

Internal security assistance. Much American foreign aid since World War II has been used to help authoritarian regimes combat left-wing and pro-Communist uprisings. The CIA has been instrumental in training and equipping some of the most brutal secret police agencies, including South Korea's KCIA, Iran's SAVAK, and Chile's DINA. In South Vietnam, American advisers witnessed, tolerated, and sometimes participated in acts of torture, and American aid funds helped to pay for the infamous "tiger cages" in which suspected Vietcong were penned in such cramped positions that their legs withered and became useless.

Foreign secret police agencies assisted by the CIA have sometimes repaid the favor by exporting their covert operations to the United States. Agents from South Korea, Taiwan, South Africa, the Philippines, and Iran have spied on, harassed, and intimidated dissident nationals studying and working in the United States, while assassins employed by Chile and Libya have murdered or attempted to murder critics of their regimes living in the U.S. and other countries.

Financial assistance and bribery. Through the CIA and its dummy corporations, the United States has covertly funneled millions of dollars in financial assistance and bribes to foreign political figures, organizations, newspapers, political parties, and governments. Covert assistance to the Christian Democratic Party in Italy is frequently credited with preventing a Communist electoral victory there in 1948. Between 1948 and 1968, the CIA spent over $65 million on secret activities in Italy, and as recently as 1976, President Ford personally approved $6 million in secret subsidies to anti-Communist groups there for election expenses. Foreign leaders who have received covert financial assistance from the United States since World War II include the former Shah of Iran, Willy Brandt of West Germany, and Indira Gandhi of India. When the former Belgian Congo (now the Democratic Republic of the Congo) won its independence in the mid-1960s, the United States was one of several nations that attempted to bribe enough politicians there to control its new legislature.

Propaganda and disinformation. Much covert financial assistance has been used for propaganda purposes, or for the spreading of "disinformation"—false or misleading in-

---

140. "CIA's Covert Operations and Human Rights," Center for National Security Studies (1978), 6.

formation—designed to manipulate foreign political opinion and disrupt alliances among groups and individuals hostile to American interests. For example, the CIA spent $8 million in Chile between 1963 and 1973 to influence elections through subsidies to newspapers, television stations, and radio stations, through assistance to reporters, and through the financing of wall posters, leaflets, and other street activities. For many years "Radio Free Europe" was a CIA proprietary operation, beaming unrealistic encouragement to Central Europeans who dreamed of Western liberation from Communism. The agency also subsidized a number of scholarly journals, professors, and student groups, and helped to finance more than 1,250 books without disclosing its role.

Aggressive collection. American intelligence agencies sometimes collect information by highly aggressive and provocative means. The use of high-flying reconnaissance aircraft like the U-2 to penetrate deep into foreign airspace is well known. Less well known, and perhaps more risky, was the use of warplanes to fly at the borders of Communist countries at high speeds and low altitudes, in order to force military units there to activate their communications networks which American spy ships and planes could then record, pinpoint, and analyze.

These ships and planes, like the U.S.S. *Liberty* and Russian "trawlers," skirted dangerously close to hostile shores. In 1969, North Korea captured the U.S. spy ship *Pueblo* and subjected its crew to brutal incarceration. American submarines also entered Soviet harbors, sometimes bumping into the undersides of Soviet ships. In 1983, the Soviet Union shot down a Korean Airlines passenger jet, killing all 269 persons on board. The airliner, which had flown over Soviet military installations on Sakhalin Island, was either mistaken for an American reconnaissance aircraft it had passed earlier in the night, or was itself suspected of electronic intelligence gathering for the United States.

Economic destabilization. Some countries are so dependent upon U.S. trade, investment, and loans that loss of American support can pave the way for a coup d'état. Such was the case in 1970, when Chile elected Salvador Allende president. Equating Allende's Marxism with Soviet-style Communism, President Nixon resolved, as CIA Director Richard Helms noted at the time, to "make the economy scream."[141] American companies were warned not to invest in Chile, and loans from private and international banks influenced by the United States were cut to a minimum. The effect on Chile's foreign exchange was devastating. Shortages of food and spare parts quickly developed, and a major financial panic ensued. Conditions were thus created that favored a CIA-backed coup by right-wing generals.

Covert support for coups and revolutions. The CIA-backed coup that took place in Chile in 1973 was only one of many that the United States has clandestinely supported since World War II. During the 1950s, the CIA supplied guerrilla movements in Albania, Poland, and the Soviet Ukraine with agents, equipment, and gold. American agents were sent into Communist China in an effort to support remnants of Nationalist resistance there. All attempts to overthrow Communist regimes ended in failure, and in the imprisonment, torture, and deaths of many of the foreign nationals that the CIA supported. However, similar operations were successful in preventing the rise of leftist regimes elsewhere.

The pattern was set in the mid-1950s, when CIA assistance made possible the overthrow of Mohammed Mossadegh in Iran and Jacobo Arbenz in Guatemala. Thereafter, in Latin

---

141. "Covert Action in Chile, 1963–1973," Staff Report reprinted in *Covert Action*, Hearings before the Select Committee to Study Governmental Operations with Respect to Intelligence Activities, 94th Cong., 1st Sess. (1976), vol. 7, 180 (Staff Report, 33).

America, Africa, and the Middle East, the United States clandestinely supported author-itarian capitalists against leftist and pro-Communist regimes. Opposition to "Communism" and prevention of the expropriation of American corporate assets appear to have been the primary objectives, while the short-term stability offered by military regimes was pre-ferred over the more risky alternative of democratic socialism.

At times, American objectives have been more difficult to ascertain. During the early 1970s, for example, the Nixon administration assisted the Shah of Iran in his border dis-pute with Iraq by covertly supplying an armed Kurdish revolt within Iraq. However, as soon as Iraq and Iran settled that dispute, the CIA withdrew its support and the Iraqi army swept down upon the Kurds, killing thousands and driving more than 200,000 into exile. Secretary of State Kissinger refused humanitarian assistance to these refugees, ex-plaining that "covert action should not be confused with missionary work."[142]

Guerrilla raids and invasions. Covert support for coups and revolutions has led, in a num-ber of occasions, to direct CIA involvement in military and paramilitary operations. In 1954, for example, when the CIA-backed invasion of Guatemala faltered, the Agency pro-vided additional supplies, intercepted government communications, and transmitted false and misleading replies. Several American pilots associated with the CIA flew bomb-ing and strafing runs for the invasion force, and when one crashed into the sea, he was rescued by the U.S. Navy. In 1958, at least one CIA pilot flew bombing runs in support of a futile revolution against President Sukarno of Indonesia.

The largest covert operation prior to the war in Southeast Asia was the Bay of Pigs in-vasion of Cuba in 1961. For this operation, the CIA recruited, trained, and equipped an army of more than 1,400 Cuban exiles, supplied them with ships and planes, and even flew air cover for them over the beaches. The invasion failed, and the United States was forced to ransom the captured force with nearly $53 million in medical supplies. In 1962, when President Kennedy was presented with the flag of the ransomed brigade at an emo-tional welcome-back ceremony in Miami's Orange Bowl, he promised that "this flag will be returned to this Brigade in a free Havana."[143]

Kennedy's pledge was well publicized, but what few Americans knew at the time was that he had already decided to continue the clandestine war against Cuba on a smaller scale. For the next five years, more than two thousand opponents of the Castro regime, supervised and assisted by more than six hundred CIA officers, launched hundreds of raids against the island of Cuba from the Florida coast, burning fields of sugar cane, sab-otaging industrial facilities, and contaminating food shipments.

Operation MONGOOSE, as this war was called, was terminated by the Johnson ad-ministration in 1967, but the CIA's Cuban protégés did not all leave the underworld of covert operations. Several joined the White House "plumbers unit" along with former CIA employees James McCord and E. Howard Hunt and were captured in the Watergate burglary of 1972. Others assisted in the 1976 assassination of Orlando Letelier in Wash-ington, D.C., on contract with the DINA, Chile's secret police. Still others have contin-ued the war against Cuba without CIA support, bombing diplomatic and airline facilities in the United States and abroad, and destroying a Cuban airliner with seventy-three pas-sengers on board. Former members of the Cuban Brigade have also been credited with scores of bombings and killings within Miami's exile community.

---

142. Quoted in Halperin et al., *The Lawless State* (1976), 41.
143. Quoted in the transcript of "CBS Reports: The CIA's Secret Army," CBS-TV, June 10, 1977, p. 10.

In the early years of the war in Vietnam, the CIA organized a series of clandestine raids against the coast of North Vietnam by South Vietnamese commandos operating out of heavily armed, high-speed patrol boats. Raids by these forces may have triggered the Tonkin Gulf incident in 1964—the attack on U.S. destroyers used by President Johnson to gain congressional endorsement for expanded military operations in the area. After studying operations like these, Senator Church's Select Committee on Intelligence concluded that "paramilitary operations have a great potential for escalating into major military commitments."[144]

However, fears of escalating involvement did not stop the Reagan administration from covertly funding a force of more than ten thousand guerillas determined to overthrow the Marxist government of Nicaragua.

Assassination. Assassination was still another covert technique employed by the United States during the 1960s and 1970s. Unsuccessful plots to kill Patrice Lumumba of the Congo and Fidel Castro of Cuba were undertaken by the CIA during the early 1960s, and American officials encouraged, supplied, or were privy to the plots that resulted in the assassination of President Rafael Trujillo of the Dominican Republic in 1961, President Ngo Dinh Diem of South Vietnam in 1964, and General Rene Schneider of Chile in 1973. There is additional evidence that the CIA may have been involved in plots to assassinate President Sukarno of Indonesia, "Papa Doc" Duvalier of Haiti, and General Abdul Karim Kassem of Iraq.

The most elaborate efforts to kill a foreign leader were directed against Fidel Castro between 1960 and 1965. At least eight plots were developed, involving such exotic items as explosive seashells, a deadly fountain pen, poison pills, and a skin-diving suit dusted with a chronic skin fungus called madura foot and tubercle bacilli. In two instances, the task of killing Castro was subcontracted to members of the Mafia.

The largest program of assassination was the PHOENIX Program for "neutralizing" the Vietcong infrastructure in Vietnam. Ideally, neutralization was to be achieved by arrest, interrogation, prosecution, and imprisonment; in fact the paramilitary teams of South Vietnamese supervised by the CIA employed the same sort of terrorist tactics used by the Vietcong, often killing innocent people. William Colby, who headed the program before becoming director of the CIA, credited the PHOENIX Program with killing, or at least recording the deaths of, 20,587 Vietcong during its first two-and-a-half years of operations.

The line between reprisals and assassinations is a fine one. In April 1986, President Reagan ordered an air strike on Tripoli in reprisal for Libya's involvement in the terrorist bombing of a discotheque in Berlin that killed and wounded American servicemen. The administration denied any intent to kill the Libyan leader, Mohamar Qadhaffi, but the bombs struck his compound, killing one of his daughters.

Similarly, after Al Qaeda operatives bombed two U.S. embassies in East Africa in 1998, President Clinton launched a cruise missile attack on Al Qaeda training camps in Afghanistan, timing it to strike during a meeting of the organization's top leadership. He also ordered a four-day air strike on Baghdad, after learning of an Iraqi plot to kill former President George H. W. Bush.

On November 3, 2002, President George W. Bush authorized the CIA to kill six Al Qaeda operatives traveling by car across a desert in Yemen. The killings, accomplished by

144. *Foreign and Military Intelligence*, Final Report of the Select Committee to Study Governmental Operations with Respect to Intelligence Activities, U.S. Senate, 94th Cong., 2d Sess. (1976), Book I, 154.

10

firing a rocket from a remote-controlled CIA drone flying above the car, apparently had the approval of Yemeni officials. One of the passengers turned out to be an American citizen.

In December 2002, the *New York Times* reported that the Bush administration had prepared a list of terrorist leaders that the CIA was authorized to kill, if capture was impractical and civilian casualties could be minimized. This "high-value target" list, as it is called, was authorized by a secret presidential "finding" on September 17, 2001, and was issued without revoking the existing executive order banning assassinations.[145] According to the *Times*, "the president is not legally required to approve each name added to the list, nor is the C.I.A. required to obtain presidential approval for specific attacks." The list was to be revised periodically through consultations with other agencies, but the criteria for marking a person for assassination were not specified.[146]

When Barack Obama assumed the presidency in 2009 he continued the assassination policy. As his director of national intelligence Dennis Blair explained to the House intelligence committee on February 4, 2010, the CIA would have to obtain special permission from a high level committee to assassinate an American thought to have joined al Qaeda, but there is no geographic limit on where these killings could take place. During the administration of George W. Bush, the CIA reportedly spent more than a million dollars training agents for these operations, but later claimed that the assassination program was never put into effect. At least one CIA team was sent to assassinate a suspected terrorist in Germany, but the mission was aborted. In 2001, a CIA drone flying over Yemen launched a Hellfire missile that killed six al Qaeda suspects, one of whom was an American from Detroit. From what source does the president get the authority to authorize assassinations?

If the president can order assassinations, is there anything to prevent him from ordering kidnappings or torture? Did the framers intended to give the president these powers, which were royal prerogatives during the seventeenth century?

Extraordinary rendition. We now know that the CIA has kidnapped suspected terrorists from a number of foreign countries, including Sweden, Italy, Macedonia, and the United States and delivered them to foreign intelligence agencies for interrogation under torture. The agency also operated at least eight detention centers in foreign countries, including Poland, Romania, and Thailand, where some prisoners were subjected to waterboarding—controlled drowning. One prisoner was waterboarded 83 times; another was waterboarded 183 times, with permission granted in each instance by officials at the CIA's headquarters who watched the torture via an Internet connection.

Secret bombing. Americans are accustomed to thinking of the CIA as an agency that devotes most of its resources to the collection and analysis of information. By 1970, however, the scale of its paramilitary operations had transformed it into a smaller version of the Defense Department, complete with its own armies of mercenaries and an air force that, until 1973, flew more aircraft than Pan American World Airways.

But the CIA is not the only agency that has conducted undisclosed military operations. The air force conducted extensive bombing raids in Laos, Cambodia, and North Vietnam despite State Department denials. These raids were concealed from Congress and the press through a deliberate program of "back-channel" communications and falsified records, so that the Nixon administration could claim that it was honoring the neutral-

145. Executive Order No. 12,333, 46 Fed. Reg. 59,941 (1981).
146. James Risen and David Johnson, "Bush Has Widened Authority of C.I.A. to Kill Terrorists," *New York Times,* Dec. 16, 2002, A1.

ity of Laos and Cambodia and confining the war to South Vietnam when it was actually pounding all three countries with high explosives.

The scale of this undisclosed warfare was substantial. According to a Cornell University study, the United States dropped six million tons of bombs and other munitions in Indochina, three times the total tonnage—and many more times the explosive power—of all the bombs dropped by the United States during World War II. Figures released by the Pentagon indicate that more bombs—nearly three million tons—were dropped in Indochina during Nixon's first three years in office than during Johnson's last three years. Discounting for the overlap in these figures and taking account of the secret bombing of Cambodia that continued after the American invasion of 1970 ended, it is still possible to get some sense of the enormous destructive power of undisclosed presidential warfare.

Secret wars. The most ambitious of all covert military operations took place in Laos, beginning in the late 1950s when the United States sought to counter the influence of the Communist Pathet Lao, North Vietnam, China, and the Soviet Union through covert military assistance to anti-Communist factions. During the late 1950s and early 1960s, the United States spent close to a half-billion dollars trying to turn Laos into a bastion of anti-Communism. Under the Johnson administration this policy changed, or appeared to change, into support for a neutral Laos under international guarantees. In fact, however, the United States covertly followed North Vietnam's lead in militarizing the area. Starting in 1962, the CIA armed and trained Meo tribesmen both to resist the Pathet Lao and to harass North Vietnamese troops moving south along the Ho Chi Minh Trail. Later, after Thailand became a base for undisclosed air strikes against North Vietnam, the Meos were used to defend air force navigation beacons and NSA listening posts located on Laotian mountaintops. The CIA's army of Meo tribesmen gradually grew from a few small guerrilla units to a thirty-thousand-man force capable of battalion-sized operations. Involvement in the war, however, eventually destroyed the Meos as a tribe. Of perhaps two hundred and fifty thousand Meos living in 1962, only about ten thousand escaped to Thailand in 1975.

Virtually nothing about the war in Laos appeared in the American press or the debates of Congress until antiwar sentiment led members of Congress to "discover" it. In fact, members of the Senate Foreign Relations Committee had been briefed on CIA operations there as early as 1966, and Senator Symington, a member of the committee, had visited Laos in 1967 and stayed with the CIA station chief in Vientiane. The station chief was invited to testify before the committee in secret and following his testimony was praised for the sensible and cost-efficient way his agency was fighting that war.

The CIA entered a similarly "secret" war in Angola in 1975, when President Ford authorized the covert expenditure of more than $31 million in military hardware, transportation, and cash for two of the three factions fighting in that country's civil war. While members of several congressional committees were given sketchy and misleading briefings about CIA operations in Angola, they honored administration demands for secrecy until press coverage made it impossible for them to ignore the war any longer. Then, as an apparent atonement for letting covert action in Southeast Asia get out of hand, they passed the Clark Amendment forbidding the expenditure of funds for military or paramilitary operations in Angola.

Funding secret wars: the Iran-Contra affair. In 1985 and 1986, White House staff members, working with the director of Central Intelligence, secretly sold U.S. arms to Iran, then considered a terrorist state, and secretly used the profits to support efforts by Nicaraguan "contras" based in Honduras to invade and overthrow the Nicaraguan government. The secret arms sales were undertaken because Congress refused to finance the contras. Indeed, successive appropriations bills enacted between 1982 and 1986 contained "Boland amendments" (after Representative Edward Boland (D-Mass.) barring "any agency or entity of the United States involved in intelligence activities" from spending appropriated funds "to support military or paramilitary operations in Nicaragua."[147]

May the president, or executive officials, secretly sell government property and use the proceeds for a secret war that Congress has not authorized, or has expressly denied funding?

Covert War against Iraq

In February or March 2002, a year before the U.S. invasion, President George W. Bush signed a secret order (called a "presidential finding") authorizing the CIA to recruit and train a paramilitary group of Iraqis, code-named the Scorpions, to enter Iraq, encourage rebellion, conduct light sabotage, identify targets, and create the impression of a popular rebellion. Many of the Scorpions were exiled Kurds, trained at two secret bases in Jordan, and surreptitiously sent into Iraq before Congress authorized the president to invade that country in 2003.[148]

Do such operations constitute acts of war and, if so, where does the president get the authority to begin a war in advance of a Congressional authorization?

Legal Justifications

It would be naive to assume that constitutional or legal justifications were foremost in the minds of the officials who ordered, planned, or conducted the paramilitary and covert operations of the past thirty-five years. The clandestine services expect to function outside of foreign law, and sometimes American law. Intelligence operatives tend to believe either that the laws are not meant to apply to them or that the law is no different from Victorian morality—a hypocritical system of rules that permits society to espouse Christian principles and still "get the job done."

On those rare occasions in which the CIA has found it necessary to offer legal justification for its paramilitary and covert operations, it has advanced three familiar doctrines: inherent executive power, Congressional delegation of authority, and Congressional ratification. It is to these justifications that we now turn.

Inherent executive power. The Supreme Court has never squarely considered the question of whether the president may order an agency of the government to conduct paramilitary or covert operations in a foreign country. The argument that he may is normally presented in four stages.

Stage one consists of broad assertions like that of John Marshall, who said, "The President is sole organ of the nation in its external relations...."[149] Stage two claims that "these

---

147. For the text of these amendments see 133 *Cong. Rec.* H14982-87 (daily ed., June 15, 1987).

148. Dana Priest and Josh White, "Before the War, CIA Purportedly Trained a Team of Iraqis to Aid US," *Washington Post,* Aug. 3, 2005.

149. Statement of Mitchell Rogovin, Special Counsel to the CIA, before the House Select Committee on Intelligence, Dec. 9, 1975, p. 3, citing 10 *Annals of Congress* 613 (1800). This statement is hereinafter cited as the Rogovin memorandum.

powers do not depend upon the affirmative grants of the Constitution," but are "necessary concomitants of nationality,"[150] and stage three denies that these powers must come to the president first from legislation.[151] For obvious reasons, the CIA prefers to rest its constitutional theory on Justice Sutherland's broad *dicta* in *Curtiss-Wright* and to ignore the narrower conceptions of authority by Locke, Jefferson, Lincoln, and Robert Jackson.

Stage four is the familiar theory of accretion, that long-term practice establishes an inherent power to act, perhaps even over the opposition of a subsequent Congress. The accretion argument consists of two kinds of historical precedents. The first is CIA special counsel Mitchell Rogovin's list of one hundred and twenty-five assorted incidents in history in which the president employed military force without the express permission of Congress.[152]

Although Rogovin claimed that "early examples of covert action performed by these agents are legion," only three are cited: an attempt by an agent of President Tyler to influence public and official opinion in Great Britain by private discussions, the secret dispatch of an agent to California by President Polk to try to prevent Mexico from ceding that province to Great Britain, and the deployment by President Grant of an agent to western Canada in an attempt to foment sentiment for separation from Canada and union with the United States. Another CIA memorandum prepared in 1962 cites an additional example: the Lewis and Clark Expedition of 1803.[153]

The second list cites more than four hundred instances in which presidents employed special executive agents to deal with special problems in American foreign policy during the eighteenth and nineteenth centuries. Drawn largely from Henry Merritt Wriston's seminal book, *Executive Agents in American Foreign Relations*, this list is somewhat disingenuous.[154] The vast majority of the executive agents it cites were not covert operatives in the modern sense. Many had secret instructions, as most diplomats do, but virtually all of them were given assignments that would in no way violate the law of the host country. Most attended international conferences, appeared at ceremonial occasions, spoke for the president personally, or dealt with technical matters requiring substantial expertise. A few were charged with making contact with unrecognized governments.[155]

Are these examples persuasive precedent for the sorts of paramilitary and covert actions engaged in by the United States since World War II? Are they indicative of the framers' intent? Has the Supreme Court ever accepted the theory that history can place a "gloss" upon the Constitution? Would the Court be likely to accept the theory that covert assertions of authority can alter the meaning of the Constitution?

Congressional delegation. The CIA's 1962 memorandum , prepared by general counsel Lawrence Houston, conceded that "there is no specific statutory authorization to any agency to conduct covert cold war activities."[156] The National Security Act of 1947,[157]

---

150. Secret Memorandum prepared for Lawrence Houston, General Counsel of the CIA, Jan. 1962, reprinted in Orman, *Presidential Secrecy and Deception* (1980), 211. Hereinafter cited as the Houston memorandum.
151. Ibid., 212.
152. Rogovin memorandum, 6.
153. In Orman, *Presidential Secrecy and Deception*, 214.
154. (1929; reprinted, 1967). Cited in the Rogovin memorandum, 8–9.
155. Borosage, "Para-Legal Authority and Its Perils," 40 *Law & Contemp. Prob.* 166, 173 (1976).
156. Ibid., 215.
157. P.L. 80-253, 61 Stat. 495 (codified at scattered sections of 5, 10, 31 and 50 U.S.C., including 50 U.S.C. Sec. 403).

which created the CIA, charged the agency with the coordination, development, and analysis of intelligence, but it contains no explicit authority for either the covert collection of intelligence or the covert intervention of spies, mercenaries, or special military units in the internal affairs of foreign states. Whatever authority the CIA may lawfully derive from its statutory charter for covert operations must come from the "other functions" clause of Section 102(d)(5). It authorized the agency "to perform such other functions and duties related to intelligence affecting the national security as the National Security Council may from time to time direct."

May the text of this provision be interpreted, on its face, to authorize the covert collection of intelligence or covert, and sometimes paramilitary, intervention in foreign lands? Can the phrase "related to intelligence" be reasonably stretched to encompass any activities that "may involve use of the same or similar contacts, operatives and methods [as clandestine collection activities] and may yield important intelligence results"?[158]

If textual analysis alone is not sufficient, may a larger legislative purpose to authorize covert action be inferred from the understandings of those who enacted the statute? If so, how much evidence of Congressional comprehension would be sufficient to convert the "other functions" clause into a charter for covert action? The CIA has been unable to find anything in the public record to support its theory of Congressional purpose. The Rogovin memorandum did cite two colloquies from hearings held in executive session, but these are difficult to assess because the full exchanges remain classified.[159] Suppose that it could be established that the committees that approved this legislation fully understood that the words "related to intelligence" were code words for covert collection and covert intervention. If this understanding was not communicated to the Congress as a whole, and there is no evidence that it was, should it be considered part of the legislature's purpose? In a democracy, can legislation ever have a secret purpose? Is the CIA's theory of legislative purpose consistent with the anti-delegation doctrine as you understand it? Is this an instance in which that doctrine should be revived?

Congressional ratification. Today it is no secret that the CIA and military agencies engage in covert intelligence collection and covert interventions in foreign countries. Does awareness of this well-documented fact mean that Congress has, by its inaction or by its appropriation of undisclosed sums of money for the CIA and other agencies, ratified each and every one of their covert operations, retrospectively and prospectively?

The leading Supreme Court decision on ratifications is *Brooks v. Dewar*, 313 U.S. 354 (1941), and both the Houston and Rogovin memorandums relied upon it heavily. In *Brooks*, the Court upheld a program for licensing ranchers who wished to graze cattle on federal lands, even though Congress had not specifically authorized the program in advance. The Court found that the program had gone on for years, that information about it within Congress was plentiful, and that repeated appropriations turning over the proceeds to the federal treasury constituted a ratification.

Does *Brooks v. Dewar* provide a valid precedent for the sort of ratification that the CIA advocates? Is there a difference between the ratification of a single, discrete program, the full ramifications of which are known, and the ratification of a method of operation that may be employed in hundreds of secret programs, some of which could lead to war? How specific must a ratification be?

---

158. Houston memorandum in Orman, 216.
159. Borosage, "Para-Legal Authority," 176.

Backhanded authorization. During the fall of 1974, several attempts were made in Congress to limit the CIA's power to conduct covert action. In the House, Representative Elizabeth Holtzman (D-N.Y.) tried unsuccessfully to forbid the use of any CIA funds for "the purpose of undermining or destabilizing the government of any foreign country."[160] In the Senate, Senator James Abourezk (D-S.D.) failed to win approval of a measure that would have forbidden the use of any funds by an agency of the United States to "carry out any activity within any foreign country which violates, or is intended to encourage the violation of, the laws of the United States or of such country."[161] Does the defeat of these proposals by vote of their respective houses constitute legislative authorization of the conduct they sought to forbid?

In December 1974, Congress chose instead to pass the Hughes-Ryan Amendment to the Foreign Assistance Act. It provided that "no funds appropriated under ... this or any other Act may be expended by or on behalf of the Central Intelligence Agency for operations in foreign countries, other than activities intended solely for obtaining necessary intelligence, unless and until the President finds that each such operation is important to the national security of the United States and reports, in a timely fashion, a description ... to the appropriate committees of Congress...."[162] A report of the Association of the Bar of the City of New York has concluded that this provision constitutes "clear Congressional authorization for the CIA to conduct covert activities...."[163] Do you agree? Recall the debate over the War Powers Resolution (see section I, *supra,* this chapter).

In 1975, the CIA secretly spent more than $31 million to back two of the three contending factions in the Angolan civil war and recruited mercenaries to fight there. When the Senate Committee on Foreign Relations came to suspect this involvement, the Ford administration agreed to explain the operation in executive session, provided that the members of the committee promised not to reveal what they were told. Thus silenced, the committee was briefed, incompletely, inaccurately, and probably falsely.[164]

Senator Dick Clark (D-Iowa), bound by his oath not to reveal his secret knowledge that the CIA's public denials of involvement were false, joined with Senators John Tunney (D-CA) and Alan Cranston (D-Calif.) to sponsor what has come to be known as the Clark Amendment to the International Security Assistance and Arms Export Control Act of 1976. It expressly denied funds for military and paramilitary operations in Angola, "unless and until ... Congress enacts a joint resolution approving the furnishing of such assistance."[165]

Does the Clark Amendment, by prohibiting military and paramilitary operations in one country, necessarily imply that authority exists for the conduct of similar operations elsewhere?

Ambiguous prohibitions. How explicit must a prohibition on covert action be? In December 1982, Congress attached a restriction on covert action, sponsored by House Intelligence Committee chairman Edward P. Boland (D-Mass.), to a stop-gap defense appropriations bill. The Boland amendment provided that "none of the funds provided in this Act may be used by the Central Intelligence Agency or the Department of Defense to furnish military equipment, military training or advice, or other support for military

---

160. Rogovin memorandum, 19.
161. Ibid.
162. Foreign Assistance Act of 1961, Section 663, 22 U.S.C. Sec. 2242 (1970).
163. The Central Intelligence Agency: Oversight and Accountability (1975), 15.
164. Orman, *Presidential Secrecy and Deception*, 152–55.
165. P.L. 94-329, 90 Stat. 757 (1976).

activities, to any group or individual, not part of a country's armed forces, for the purpose of overthrowing the Government of Nicaragua or provoking a military exchange between Nicaragua and Honduras."[166] The prohibition was scheduled to expire with the appropriations on September 30, 1983. If you were counsel for the CIA, how many loopholes could you find in this prohibition?

In July 1983, as covert support for guerrilla operations against Nicaragua escalated and President Reagan threatened U.S. military maneuvers in the region, the House of Representatives endorsed another restriction. The Boland-Zablocki amendment, had it passed both houses, would have provided that "none of the funds appropriated for FY 1983 or FY 1984 for the CIA or any other department, agency, or entity of the United States involved in intelligence activity may be obligated or expended for the purpose of which would have the effect of supporting, directly or indirectly, military or paramilitary operations in Nicaragua by any nation, group, organization, movement, or individual."

Had more general language of this sort been passed by both Houses over the president's almost certain veto, would it be sufficient to end the covert action?

The criminal law. Nearly all of the public debate over the lawfulness of paramilitary and covert operations has occurred at a high level of generalization, as if there was no legal difference between undisclosed efforts to influence foreign political opinion and clandestine efforts to foment coups, plot assassinations, conduct guerrilla raids, organize invasions, and sponsor mercenary armies. There is a substantial moral difference, of course, and it is to be found in the criminal laws of the federal and state governments of the United States.

Under federal neutrality legislation, it is a crime for anyone within the United States to assist in any military action against a nation with which the United States is at peace. Section 960 of Title 18 of the federal criminal code provides that "whoever, within the United States, knowingly begins or sets on foot or provides or prepares a means for or furnishes the money for, or takes part in, any military or naval expedition or enterprise to be carried on from thence against the territory or dominion of any foreign prince or state, or of any colony, district, or people with whom the United States is at peace, shall be fined not more than $3,000 or imprisoned not more than three years or both." First enacted in 1794, this law expresses the intent of the framers to keep the United States out of the internal affairs of other countries. Under this law, an American ship captain was convicted of transporting Cuban rebels from New Jersey to Cuba,[167] an Arizona gun dealer was convicted of selling arms to Indians planning a revolt against Mexico,[168] and as recently as 1971, a group of civilians was convicted under its provisions for conspiring to overthrow the government of Haiti.[169]

Under the laws of every state and the District of Columbia, it is a crime to conspire to commit murder, riot, insurrection, bribery, forgery, arson, and assault. Like the neutrality law, these statutes make no exception for government officials.

Can the general language of the National Security Act of 1947 or the Hughes-Ryan Act of 1974 be read to exempt CIA operatives from these criminal laws? May Congress constitutionally exempt CIA operatives from these laws in circumstances short of war? May the president, on his own authority, grant licenses to commit crimes? Is such a power

---

166. P.L. 97-377, Sec. 793 (Dec. 21, 1982).
167. *United States v. Hughes*, 75 Fed. 267 (1896).
168. *Gandara v. United States*, 33 F. 2d 394 (1929).
169. *United States v. Leon*, 441 F. 2d 175 (1971).

part of his authority to grant pardons? May pardons be granted prospectively? In any case, may the president make exceptions to the criminal laws of the states?

International law. According to Article VI of the Constitution, treaties made under the authority of the United States are the supreme law of the land. In its effort to become a "good neighbor," the United States has signed several treaties pledging to respect the territorial integrity and internal sovereignty of Latin American countries.[170] Under the Charter of the Organization of American States, for example, the United States has promised not to "use or encourage the use of coercive measures of an economic or political character in order to force the sovereign will of another [member] State and obtain from it advantages of any kind."[171]

May the president unilaterally abrogate these treaties by such means as fomenting a coup in Guatemala, backing an invasion and secret war against Nicaragua, encouraging a coup and destabilizing the economy in Chile, or threatening a naval quarantine of Nicaragua? Recall the discussion of the power to abrogate treaties in Chapter 3, Section C.

Prosecutorial discretion. When a federal agency has reason to believe that any of its employees may be engaged in illegal activities, it has an obligation to refer the matter to the Department of Justice for investigation and possible prosecution. Between 1954 and 1975, however, the CIA was under instructions from the Justice Department to conduct its own investigations and, if it found that prosecution might disclose sensitive operations or methods, not to refer the case for prosecution.[172] May the Department of Justice delegate its prosecutorial discretion to any other agency of government or, for that matter, to the president?

During this period, the CIA engaged in a number of illegal activities, including the surreptitious opening of hundreds of thousands of pieces of first-class mail in direct violation of the Fourth Amendment[173] and three federal statutes.[174] When this illegality was made public, the Justice Department studied the matter for almost two years and, when the statute of limitations was just about to run out, announced that it would not prosecute any of the officials involved. The department conceded that these activities "would be unlawful if undertaken today," but argued that they were not unlawful when taken, despite clear statutory and judicial prohibitions, because they were based on the conviction that "the president's constitutional power to authorize collection of intelligence was of extremely broad scope."[175] The department reached this conclusion despite a documentary and testimonial record that clearly demonstrated that agency officials fully understood that the mail opening was illegal and that it was for this reason that presidential authority (or even a legal opinion from the CIA's general counsel) was not sought.[176]

170. E.g., Protocol of Relative Non-Intervention (1963), 51 Stat. 41–47 (1938); Convention on the Rights and Duties of States [1935], 49 Stat. 3101 (1936); Inter-American Treaty of Reciprocal Assistance (Rio Pact) [1949], 62 Stat. 1700 (1949); and Charter of the Organization of American States [1952], 2 U.S.T. 2419 (1952).
171. OAS Charter, 2 U.S.T. 2420 (1952).
172. *Report to the President by the Commission on CIA Activities within the United States* (Rockefeller Commission) (1975), 75.
173. *Ex parte Jackson*, 96 U.S. 727, 733 (1878).
174. 18 U.S.C. Secs. 1701–1703.
175. *Justice Department Internal Investigation Policies*, Hearings before the Subcommittee on Government Information and Individual Rights, Committee on Government Operations, U.S. House of Representatives, 94th Cong., 1st Sess. (1975), 137–38, 162–63.
176. See, for example, Supplementary Detailed Staff Reports on Intelligence Activities and the Rights of Americans, Book III of the Final Report of the Select Committee to Study Governmental Operations with Respect to intelligence Activities, U.S. Senate, 94th Cong., 2d Sess. (1976), 559–678.

The pardon power. The only governmental officials to be convicted for the commission of illegal covert operations as a result of all of the disclosures of the 1970s were two former FBI officials, W. Mark Felt and Edward S. Miller. They were convicted of ordering the burglary by FBI agents of the homes of persons suspected of associating with fugitives suspected of engaging in terrorist bombings. President Reagan pardoned both men, stating that "the record demonstrates that [they] acted not with criminal intent, but in the belief that they had grants of authority reaching to the highest level of government."[177] In fact, Miller and Felt had claimed only that they had received general authority from their immediate superior, L. Patrick Gray, then director of the FBI. Gray denied authorizing the burglaries, and the jury found no evidence to contradict the denial or to establish that the burglaries had been authorized by anyone in a higher position of authority.

The Eichmann defense. By concluding that the officials lacked criminal intent, President Reagan seemed to say that the same burglaries could be committed today and not violate the criminal law. In other words, so long as the covert operative believes that he has the authority of someone at the highest levels of government, he can violate constitutional rights. Some critics call this the Eichmann defense, after Adolf Eichmann, who defended his participation in the mass execution of Jews in Nazi Germany by claiming that he was only following orders. In fact, however, the Justice Department's version was somewhat broader, because it did not require proof of the existence of any orders. According to proponents of this defense, the operative need only believe that he was acting with authority—a subsequent ratification might even suffice. This was the defense of good motives raised by Nixon aide John Ehrlichman at his trial for ordering the burglary of a psychiatrist's office by the Watergate "plumbers" team. It was not accepted by the court.[178]

A variant of the Eichmann defense is "My lawyer said I could do it." The administrations of George W. Bush and Barack Obama have both accepted this assertion as sufficient grounds for refusing to prosecute alleged torturers who claimed to rely, "in good faith," on secret Justice Department legal memoranda declaring that what they proposed to do was not really torture. See, *inter alia,* Christopher H. Pyle, *Getting Away with Torture* (Potomac, 2009).

Administrative law restraints. The instinctive response of most American lawyers to the problem of unauthorized bureaucratic activity has been to tie the agencies down with rules that require them to get their orders in writing, establish their legal authority before they act, and report regularly and fully to their overseers in the executive branch and Congress. This was the theory behind the unsuccessful attempt by the Senate Select Committee to draft a comprehensive "charter" for the CIA in the late 1970s.

Other reformers lack confidence in the capacity of procedural limitations to constrain a profession that employs deceit as a primary mode of operation. They point out that the covert actions of the Cold War era were not the product of low-level initiatives or "rogue elephants" in the bureaucracy, but were the result of policies and directives initiated by the president, his national security adviser, and a committee of the National Security Council (commonly known as the "Forty Committee") which authorized most major covert operations. Accordingly, these critics argue, the abuses of the Cold War era will not be ended until the United States adopts a less interventionist foreign policy.[179] Do you agree?

---

177. *New York Times,* Apr. 10, 1981.

178. *United States v. Ehrlichman,* 376 F. Supp. 39 (D.D.C. 1974), *aff'd* 546 F. 2d 910 (1976), *cert. denied,* 429 U.S. 1120 (1977).

179. See, for example, Borosage, "Para-Legal Authority, 166.

Paralegal authority. Robert Borosage, among others, has argued that the function of legal memoranda like those produced by CIA and Justice Department counsel is not so much to establish the agency's authority to engage in covert action as it is to paint such assertions of authority with a patina of legality. This patina is necessary so that covert operatives can claim that they acted pursuant to the law as explained to them by competent counsel, and the president, Congress, and the agencies can all pretend that covert operations are permissible because it is not perfectly clear that they are illegal. Borosage made this observation in 1976, 25 years before it was used by the Justice Department and White House of George W. Bush to create a patina of legality for their program of torture.

Covert action and constitutional democracy. Is covert action consistent with the principles of a constitutional democracy? Is the political theory implicit in the Constitution and laws of the United States adequate to the challenges of participation in an international environment largely populated by authoritarian nations that regularly use paramilitary and covert action as instruments of their foreign relations?

Chapter Five

Secret Government Versus the Rule of Law

"[T]he war against terrorism is a new kind of war ... which places a high premium on ... the ability to quickly obtain information from captured terrorists and their sponsors in order to avoid further atrocities against American civilians.... In my judgment, this new paradigm renders obsolete Geneva's strict limitations on questioning of enemy prisoners and renders quaint some of its provisions....."

—White House Counsel Alberto Gonzales (2002)[1]

The Geneva Conventions are the "outmoded relic of a chivalrous notion of warfare" and inappropriate to the "struggle to the death for the destruction of Bolshevik terrorism."

—Wilhelm Keitel, Hitler's de facto minster of war,
hanged at Nuremberg as a war criminal[2]

A. Introduction

According to President George W. Bush, the attacks of September 11, 2001, were not just crimes, but a new kind of global "war" between the United States and an amorphous, non-governmental enemy called al Qaeda (the base) and whichever Muslims chose to join its jihad (struggle). In this conflict, the president's lawyers said, the laws of war and the constitutionally based rules of criminal justice simply did not apply.

The rationale for this new kind of war was contained in a series of legal memoranda prepared in secret by Justice Department lawyers selected by Vice President Dick Cheney and his attorney David Addington. Chief among the legal draftsmen was John Yoo, a young law professor on leave from the University of California at Berkeley who had previously served as a law clerk to Supreme Court Justice Clarence Thomas.

According to Yoo, treaties, such as the Geneva Conventions forbidding torture and cruelty, did not protect suspected enemies in this kind of warfare, or could in any case be secretly abrogated by the president. The Constitution, he advised, did not limit what government agents could do to their prisoners outside U.S. territory. Indeed, he told the

---

1. Memorandum to President George W. Bush, Jan. 25, 2002, Memo 7 in Greenberg and Dratel, *The Torture Papers* (2005), 118.
2. Quoted by Scott Horton in Greenberg, ed., *The Torture Debate* (2006), 140,146, n. 7 (German text).

303

The Pentagon in the aftermath of the terrorist attack of September 11, 2001.

general counsel of the navy, that prisoners at Guantánamo and scores of other U.S. detention facilities in foreign lands, could be tortured, if necessary, because American law did not reach them. According to Yoo and Vice President Cheney, the U.S. Army could even be used to wage "war" on terrorists within the United States, arresting individual conspirators and holding them indefinitely, denying them access to judicial review. Indeed, the president's authority as commander in chief trumps both the First Amendment's guarantee of free expression and the Fourth Amendment's protection against warrantless wiretaps and otherwise unreasonable searches and seizures. No administration, at least not since Charles I occupied the throne of England, had ever gone this far.

B. Torture as U.S. Policy[3]

The full significance of what these claims to power meant did not become widely appreciated until April 28, 2004. That morning, during oral argument over the detention of alleged terrorists at Guantánamo Bay, Supreme Court Justice Ruth Bader Ginsburg asked a government lawyer: "Suppose the executive says, 'Mild torture, we think, will help get this information.' Some systems do that to get information."

"Well, our executive doesn't," Deputy Solicitor General Paul Clement replied.

Eight hours later the first photographs of prisoner abuse at the Abu Ghraib prison in Iraq appeared on national television. In less than a year, more than 251 American sol-

---

3. Sources for this information can be found in Christopher H. Pyle, *Getting Away with Torture: Secret Government, War Crimes, and the Rule of Law* (2009) and Richard M. Pious, *The War on Terrorism and the Rule of Law* (2006).

Army specialist Sabrina Harman poses over the corpse of Manadel al-Jamadi, who was severely beaten by Navy SEALS before he was brought to Abu Ghraib where, after further interrogation, his wrists were chained to a window frame behind his back. He died about an hour later. His death was ruled a homicide, but the CIA agent and army colonel responsible were never prosecuted.

diers had been tried at courts-martial or given administrative reprimands for abusing prisoners. As of February 2006, ninety-eight prisoners had died in U.S. custody. Of them, thirty-four were suspected or confirmed homicides.

Contrary to what administration officials said when the Abu Ghraib scandal broke, the widespread torture and abuse of suspected terrorists was not the work of a few misguided prison guards on the night shift. It was an administration policy that involved the highest officials in the land, including the president, vice president, attorney general, secretary of defense, CIA director, and numerous attorneys besides John Yoo.

The torture policy began on September 13, 2001, when President Bush assured Prince Bandar, the Saudi ambassador, that "if captured terrorists don't cooperate with us, we'll send them to you." Four days later Bush secretly ordered the CIA to engage in "extraordinary rendition"—the kidnapping of suspected terrorists for interrogation by foreign regimes that practice torture.

On November 13, 2001, the President authorized the creation of special military commissions to try alleged terrorists as war criminals. There was only one reason to create these irregular courts, and that was to evade the ordinary rules of evidence, including those that banned the use of hearsay and coerced statements. Otherwise, regular military or civilian courts would have sufficed.

Internal documents reveal that the administration intended from the start to use torture as an interrogation tool.[4] That is why its lawyers persuaded the president to suspend application of the Geneva Conventions. They did not want interrogators or their superiors to be vulnerable to prosecution as war criminals. Alberto Gonzales, then White House counsel, and John Ashcroft, then attorney general, admitted this purpose in separate memoranda to President Bush in early 2002.

By then the policy of torture and abuse had already been put into effect. One of its first victims was John Walker Lindh, the so-called American Taliban, who was captured in late November 2001. Torture was not necessary to get him to talk. He spoke willingly to a reporter. The abuses inflicted on Lindh, including a 14-day delay in attending to his gunshot wound, appear to have been gratuitous revenge for 9/11.

---

4. See, for example, *The Torture Papers* (Greenberg & Dratel, eds., 2005).

Lindh's suffering was not just the work of soldiers in the field. His interrogation was monitored daily from the Pentagon. According to documents turned over to defense counsel, the harsh treatment was approved by the Defense Department's general counsel, Jim Haynes. If so, he acted in direct violation of the Geneva Conventions, which had not then been suspended. The Lindh case set a widespread pattern of cruel and degrading treatment of prisoners in Afghanistan, Iraq, Guantánamo, and in secret CIA prisons in at least eight foreign countries.

Legal justification for abusing prisoners was provided by John Yoo, who began by claiming unlimited—and illimitable—presidential powers in time of war. Interestingly, Yoo's early memoranda did not cite the well-known case of *Youngstown Sheet and Tube Co. v. Sawyer* in which the Supreme Court had rejected similarly sweeping claims by President Harry S. Truman.

On November 13, 2001, President Bush ordered the creation of military commissions and authorized them to try suspected terrorists in secret, without having to obey prohibitions on the use of evidence obtained by torture, and without fully granting them the right to legal counsel or the right to confront the witnesses against them. Indeed, the president secretly authorized both the military and Central Intelligence Agency to create prisons in foreign countries where American law, including the privilege of writ of habeas corpus, would presumably not apply.

In January 2002, Yoo advised the president that he could suspend the operation of any treaty he wished, including the Geneva Conventions, which defined what war crimes may be prosecuted under the War Crimes Act of 1996. On June 29, 2006, the Supreme Court rejected this assertion in *Hamdan v. Rumsfeld, infra.*

Amnesty for War Crimes

The *Hamdan* decision threw the Bush administration into a panic, because it exposed every official involved in the torture policy to criminal prosecution for war crimes. The president, vice president, secretary of defense, attorney general, and their politically appointed lawyers were all implicated. And so the President did something unprecedented in American history. He personally went to Capitol Hill to plead with fellow Republicans to pass a law granting administration officials amnesty for their policy of torture and abuse.

That was the main purpose of the Military Commissions Act that President George W. Bush signed into law on October 17, 2006.[5] It didn't grant amnesty to *military* interrogators or guards; they could still be prosecuted under the Uniform Code of Military Justice. But it did grant amnesty to CIA agents, private contractors, and administration officials for all war crimes committed in the previous seven years.

The law also permitted the executive to conceal its commission of war crimes by denying the victims of torture and abuse the right to sue their torturers in civilian courts. Whether this provision is constitutional remains to be seen. Article I, Section 9, of the Constitution provides that the privilege of the writ of habeas corpus may only be suspended in times of invasion or rebellion, and then only when the public safety requires it.

By this new law, Congress expressly authorized military commissions to try alleged terrorists for "war crimes" even though they, or the witnesses against them, may have

---

5. P.L. 109-336, 120 Stat. 2600.

been tortured. On its face, the act seems to bar evidence obtained by torture, but it still permits the government to hide how incriminating statements were obtained by 1) classifying documents describing sources and methods, and 2) offering hearsay testimony by witnesses who remember the statements but claim to know nothing about how they were obtained.

It is possible that the Supreme Court will reject these commissions too, on the same ground that it struck down the earlier tribunals in *Hamdan*—that no military necessity justifies evading the regularly constituted courts envisioned by the Geneva Conventions.

President Obama has promised not to allow the military or CIA to torture prisoners in the future, but still plans to prosecute some of them before military commissions.

Legalizing Torture and Cruelty

The Military Commissions Act did not repeal Common Article 3 of the four Geneva Conventions, as the administration requested. Instead, it repealed portions of the War Crimes Act of 1996, which had been passed to enforce the war crimes provisions of Article 3. Then it permitted the president to authorize the CIA to use any interrogation practices he believes do not constitute "cruel, inhuman, and degrading treatment" banned by Article 3, even though international legal interpretations may disagree with him. In other words, Congress delegated to the president the power to define what constitutes a war crime under Article 3.

Other provisions of the Military Commissions Act granted the president authority to designate any person, citizen or foreigner, an "enemy combatant" and imprison him indefinitely. Victims of torture may not sue their interrogators for what federal courts may consider "cruel, inhuman, or degrading treatment." The act also granted interrogators and their superiors immunity from civil suits by the victims of torture.

Since passage of this law, administration lawyers have argued that judges should not permit al Qaeda suspects to tell their lawyers or explain in open court which "alternative interrogation methods" were used to obtain their alleged confessions. The Bush administration argued that torture itself constitutes a state secret that cannot, under any circumstance, be disclosed in court.

Relying on Yoo's legal advice, the military and Central Intelligence Agency used so-called enhanced interrogation techniques against suspected terrorists, including sleep deprivation, extremes of heat or cold, stress positions, slamming into walls, and waterboarding (controlled drowning). Many prisoners were mentally unhinged by the mistreatment they experienced; several died.

Both the Bush and Obama administrations have refused to order criminal investigations of any of the officials who developed, justified, supervised, or concealed the torture policy. Democrats, who gained control of Congress in 2006, refused to impeach President Bush or Vice President Cheney, and have shown no interest in repealing the amnesty granted by the Military Commissions Act of 2006. Meanwhile, lower court judges, mostly appointed by Republican presidents, have repeatedly dismissed lawsuits brought by the victims of torture and kidnapping, usually on the ground that to hold trials in their cases would expose "state secrets." Again, see, generally, Christopher H. Pyle, *Getting Away with Torture* (2009) and works cited therein.

Essential to any torture regime is the ability to hold prisoners incommunicado—away from family, friends, lawyers, and inspectors from the International Committee of the

Red Cross. So the main focus of litigation against the Bush administration has involved petitions for habeas corpus against indefinite detention without trial or administrative hearings.

C. Presidential Detention of Citizens

Battlefield detentions under the war powers. Yaser Esam Hamdi, an American citizen, surrendered to Northern Alliance in Afghanistan, which turned him over to the U.S. Army. It transported him to the United States and held him, incommunicado, first in a floating Navy brig in Norfolk, Virginia, and later in a navy brig in South Carolina. Had the army kept Hamdi in Afghanistan, the legality of his detention might not have been open to challenge under *In re Territo*, 156 F. 2d 142 (9th Cir. 1946), which held that an American citizen who served in the Italian Army during World War II could be held as a prisoner of war for the duration of the war. Unlike Territo, however, Hamdi was not held as a prisoner of war, because President Bush had declared on February 7, 2002, that al Qaeda and Taliban soldiers were not entitled to the humanitarian protections that the Third Geneva Convention bestows on enemy soldiers captured in a regular war. They were to be held as "enemy combatants," a previously unheard of category, not POWs.

The Bush administration brought Hamdi to the United States, first thinking that as a citizen, he might be prosecuted for treason. Then, probably for lack of evidence, it decided to hold him in military custody as an "enemy combatant."

In defending Hamdi's detention, the Defense Department did not claim that he had committed any crime. It did not accuse him of engaging in combat against the United States, which would have constituted treason. Nor did it allege that he was a member of the Taliban or al Qaeda, had ever seen combat, or had been picked up on a battlefield. Its two-page affidavit simply claimed vaguely that he had been "affiliated with a Taliban unit and had received weapons training."

District Judge Robert Doumar, a Reagan appointee, did not challenge the military's authority to detain enemy combatants—even those with American citizenship, citing *Territo*. However, he found the affidavit factually insufficient. When the government refused to produce anything more, the judge concluded that "Without access to the screening criteria actually used by the government in [deciding that Hamdi was a combatant], this court is unable to determine whether the government has paid adequate consideration to [Hamdi's] due process rights…."[6]

On December 8, 2002, a three-judge panel of the U.S. Court of Appeals for the Fourth Circuit unanimously upheld Hamdi's detention, holding that

> "The factual averments in the affidavit, if accurate, are sufficient to confirm that Hamdi's detention conforms with a legitimate exercise of the war powers given to the executive…. Asking the executive to provide more detailed factual assertions would be to wade further into the conduct of war than we consider appropriate and is unnecessary to a meaningful judicial review of this question."[7]

---

6. *Hamdi v. Rumsfeld,* 243 F. Supp. 2d 527 (D. Va. 2002).
7. 296 F.3d 278 (4th Cir. 2002).

Do you agree? If the trial judge cannot ask for "more detailed factual assertions," how can he determine if they are "accurate," or otherwise exercise "meaningful judicial review"? What is the appropriate degree of judicial review of a decision to strip an American citizen of his constitutional right to be free from arbitrary detention? What degree of scrutiny should be exercised in such a case? What degree of scrutiny was employed here?

On July 9, 2003, the full Fourth Circuit Court affirmed the decision of its three-judge panel.[8] In her dissent, Circuit Judge Diana Gribbon Motz noted that the ruling "marks the first time in our history that a federal court has approved the elimination of protections afforded a citizen by the Constitution solely on the basis of the executive's designation of that citizen as an enemy combatant, without testing the accuracy of that designation." The case then went to the Supreme Court, which vacated the Fourth Circuit's ruling.

Hamdi v. Rumsfeld
542 U.S. 507 (2004)

JUSTICE O'CONNOR announced the judgment of the Court and delivered the following plurality opinion, joined by CHIEF JUSTICE REHNQUIST and JUSTICES KENNEDY and BREYER....

The threshold question before us is whether the Executive has the authority to detain citizens who qualify as "enemy combatants." [T]he Government has never provided any court with the full criteria that it uses in classifying individuals as such. It has made clear, however, for the purposes of this case, the "enemy combatant" that it is seeking to detain is an individual who, it alleges, was "part of or supporting forces hostile to the United States or coalition partners" in Afghanistan who "engaged in an armed conflict against the United States" there. We therefore answer only the narrow question before us: whether the detention of citizens falling within that definition is authorized.

The Government maintains that no explicit congressional authorization is required, because the Executive possesses plenary authority to detain pursuant to Article II of the Constitution. We do not reach [that] question..., however, because we agree with the Government's alternative position, that Congress has in fact authorized Hamdi's detention, through [its Authorization for Use of Military Force (the AUMF), 115 Stat. 224].

[Hamdi] posits that his detention is forbidden by 18 U.S.C. Sec. 4001 (a), [which] states that "[n]o citizen shall be imprisoned or otherwise detained by the United States except pursuant to an Act of Congress." [W]e conclude that the AUMF is explicit congressional authorization for the detention of individuals in the narrow category we describe (assuming, without deciding, that such authorization is required ... and assuming, without deciding, that Sec. 4001 (a) applies to military detentions).... The capture and detention of lawful combatants and the capture, detention, and trial of unlawful combatants, ... are "important incident[s] of war." [*Quirin.*]

There is no bar to this Nation's holding one of its own citizens as an enemy combatant.... [N]othing in *Quirin* suggests that Haupt's citizenship would have precluded his mere detention for the duration of the relevant hostilities....

---

8. 337 F.3d 335 (4th Cir. 2003).

In light of these principles, it is of no moment that the AUMF does not use specific language of detention.... Hamdi objects, nevertheless, that Congress has not authorized the *indefinite* detention to which he is now subject.... As the Government concedes, "given its unconventional nature, the current conflict is unlikely to end with a formal cease-fire agreement." [Thus] Hamdi's detention could last for the rest of his life....

Hamdi contends that the AUMF does not authorize indefinite or perpetual detention. Certainly, we agree that indefinite detention for the purpose of interrogation is not authorized.... [But i]f the record establishes that United States troops are still involved in active combat in Afghanistan, those detentions ... are authorized by the AUMF. *Ex parte Milligan* ... does not undermine our holding about the Government's authority to seize enemy combatants, as we define that term today.... Milligan was not a prisoner of war, but a resident of Indiana, arrested while at home there....

Even in cases in which the detention of enemy combatants is legally authorized, there remains the question of what process is constitutionally due to a citizen who disputes his enemy-combatant status.... All [parties] agree that, absent suspension, the writ of habeas corpus remains available to every individual detained within the United States.... All agree suspension of the writ has not occurred here. Thus, it is undisputed that Hamdi was properly before an Article III court to challenge his detention under [the habeas corpus statute].... Most notably, section 2243 [of that statute] provides that "the person detained may, under oath, deny any of the facts set forth in the return or allege any other material facts" and section 2246 allows the taking of evidence in habeas proceedings by deposition, affidavit, or interrogatories.

The simple outline of section 2241 makes clear that Congress envisions that habeas petitioners would have some opportunity to present and rebut facts and that courts in cases like this retain some ability to vary the ways in which they do so as mandated by due process. The Government recognizes the basic procedural protections required by the habeas statute, but asks us to hold that [the two-page affidavit submitted to the district court] completed the factual development....

This argument is easily rejected. [T]he circumstances surrounding Hamdi's seizure cannot in any way be characterized as "undisputed," ... because Hamdi has not been permitted to speak for himself or even through counsel as to those circumstances.... Further, the "facts" [alleged in the Government's affidavit] are insufficient to support Hamdi's detention.... An assertion that one *resided* in a country in which combat operations are taking place is not a concession that one was "*captured* in a zone of active combat operations in a foreign theater of war," and certainly not a concession that one was "part of or supporting forces hostile to the United States or coalition partners" and "engaged in an armed conflict against the United States....

Under the Government's most extreme rendition, ... "[r]espect for separation of powers and the limited institutional capabilities of the courts in matters of military decision-making in connection with an ongoing conflict" ought to eliminate entirely any individual process, restricting the courts to investigate only whether legal authorization exists for the broader detention scheme. At most, the Government argues, courts should review its determination that a citizen is an enemy combatant under a very deferential "some evidence" standard. ("Under the some evidence standard, the focus is exclusively on the factual basis supplied by the Executive to support its determination.") ... Under this review, a court would assume the accuracy of the Government's articulated basis for Hamdi's detention, as set forth in the [two-page affidavit]. ...

With due recognition of [competing concerns for personal liberty and national security], we believe that neither the process proposed by the Government nor the process apparently envisioned by the District Court below strikes the proper constitutional balance when a United States citizen is detained in the United States as an enemy combatant. ... We therefore hold that [as a matter of due process] a citizen-detainee seeking to challenge his classification as an enemy combatant must receive notice of the factual basis for his classification, and a fair opportunity to rebut the Government's factual assertions before a neutral decisionmaker. ...

At the same time, the exigencies of the circumstances may demand that, aside from these core elements, enemy combatant proceedings may be tailored to alleviate their uncommon potential for burdening the Executive at the time of ongoing military conflict. Hearsay, for example, may need to be accepted as the most reliable evidence from the Government in such a proceeding. Likewise, the Constitution would not be offended by a presumption in favor of the Government's evidence, so long as that presumption remained a rebuttable one and fair opportunity for rebuttal were provided. Thus, once the Government puts forward credible evidence that the habeas petitioner meets the enemy-combatant criteria, the onus would shift to the petitioner to rebut that evidence with more persuasive evidence that he falls outside the criteria. A burden-shifting scheme of this sort would meet the goal of ensuring that the errant tourist, embedded journalist, or local aid worker has a chance to prove military error while giving due regard to the Executive. ...[9]

We think it unlikely that this basic process will have the dire impact on the central functions of war making that the Government forecasts. The parties agree that initial captures on the battlefield need not receive the process we have discussed here; that process is due only when the determination is made to continue to hold those who have been seized. ... Any fact-finding imposition created by requiring a knowledgeable affiant to summarize [detention records] to an independent tribunal is a minimal one. Likewise, arguments that military officers ought not to have to wage war under the threat of litigation lose much of their steam when factual disputes at enemy combat hearings are limited to the alleged combatant's acts. [T]he threats to military operations posed by a basic system of independent review are not so weighty as to trump a citizen's core rights to challenge meaningfully the Government's case and to be heard by an impartial adjudicator.

In so holding, we necessarily reject the Government's assertion that separation of powers principles mandate ... that the courts must forgo any examination of the individual case and focus exclusively on the legality of the broader detention scheme ... as this approach serves only to condense power into a single branch of government. We have long made it clear that a state of war is

---

9. Because we hold that Hamdi is constitutionally entitled to the process described above, we need not address at this time whether any treaty guarantees him similar access to a tribunal for a determination of his status. (Footnote by Justice O'Connor.)

not a blank check for the President when it comes to the rights of the nation's citizens [citing *Youngstown*]. Whatever power the United States Constitution envisions for the Executive in its exchanges with other nations or with enemy organizations in times of conflict, it most assuredly envisions a role for all three branches when individual liberties are at stake.... Likewise, we have made clear that, unless Congress suspends it, the Great Writ of habeas corpus allows the judicial branch to play a necessary role in maintaining this delicate balance of governance, serving as an important judicial check on the Executive's discretion in the realm of detentions. "At its historical core, the writ of habeas corpus has served as a means of reviewing the legality of Executive detention, and it is in that context that its protections have been strongest." [citation omitted]. Thus, while we do not question that our due process assessment must pay keen attention to the particular burdens faced by the Executive in the context of military action, it would turn our system of checks and balances on its head to suggest that a citizen could not make his way to court with a challenge to the factual basis for his detention by his government, simply because the Executive opposes making available such a challenge. Absent suspension of the writ by Congress, a citizen detained as an enemy combatant is entitled to this process.

Because we conclude that due process demands some system for a citizen detainee to refute his classification, the proposed "some evidence" standard is inadequate. Any process in which the Executive's factual assertions go wholly unchallenged, or are simply presumed correct without any opportunity for the alleged combatant to demonstrate otherwise falls constitutionally short....

An interrogation by one's captor, however effective as an intelligence-gathering tool, hardly constitutes a constitutionally adequate fact-finding before a neutral decisionmaker.... Plainly, the "process" Hamdi has received is not that to which he is entitled under the Due Process Clause.

There remains the possibility that the standards we have articulated could be met by an appropriately authorized and properly constituted military tribunal. Indeed, it is notable that military regulations already provide for such process ... to determine the status of enemy detainees who assert prisoner-of-war status under the Geneva Convention.... In the absence of such process, however, a court that receives a petition for a writ of habeas corpus from an alleged enemy combatant must assure itself that the minimum requirements of due process are achieved.... As we have discussed, a habeas court in a case such as this may accept affidavit evidence like that contained in the [hearsay declaration submitted below by Defense official Michael Mobbs], so long as it also permits the alleged combatant to present his own factual case to rebut the Government's return....

Hamdi asks us to hold that the Fourth Circuit also erred by denying him immediate access to counsel upon his detention and by disposing of the case without permitting him to meet with an attorney. Since our grant of certiorari in this case, Hamdi has been appointed counsel, ... with whom he is now being granted unmonitored meetings. He unquestionably has the right to access to counsel in connection with this proceeding on remand. No further consideration of this issue is necessary at this stage of the case.

The judgment of the United States Court of Appeals for the Fourth Circuit is vacated, and the case is remanded for further proceedings.

JUSTICE SOUTER, with whom JUSTICE GINSBERG joins, concurring in part, dissenting in part, and concurring in the judgment....

The plurality ... accept the Government's position that if Hamdi's designation as an enemy combatant is correct, his detention (at least as to some period) is authorized by an Act of Congress [the Authorization for Use of Military Force, 115 Stat. 244] as required by the [non-detention without act of Congress statute, 28 U.S.C. Sec. 4001 (a).]

I disagree.... The Government has failed to demonstrate that the [Use of Force Resolution] authorizes [Hamdi's detention] even on the facts the Government claims. If the Government raises nothing further than the record now shows, the Non-Detention Act entitles Hamdi to be released....

The threshold question is how ... to read the Non-Detention Act, the tone of which is severe: "No citizen shall be imprisoned or otherwise detained by the United States except pursuant to an Act of Congress." ... The fact that Congress intended to guard against a repetition of the World War II internments when it repealed the 1950 [emergency detention] statute and gave us section 4001 (a) provides a powerful reason to think that section 4001 (a) was thought necessary to require clear congressional authorization before any citizen can be placed in a cell. To appreciate what is most significant, one must only recall that the internments of the 1940's were accomplished by Executive action. Although an Act of Congress ratified and confirmed an Executive order authorizing the military to exclude individuals from defined areas and accommodate those it might remove, ... the statute said nothing whatever about the detention of those who might be removed; internment camps were creatures of the Executive, and confinement in them rested on assertion of Executive authority.... In requiring that any Executive detention be "pursuant to an Act of Congress," then, Congress necessarily meant to require a congressional enactment that clearly authorized detention or imprisonment....

In a government of separated powers, deciding finally on what is a reasonable degree of guaranteed liberty whether in peace or war (or some condition in between) is not well entrusted to the Executive Branch of Government, whose particular responsibility is to maintain security.... A reasonable balance is more likely to be reached on the judgment of a different branch, just as Madison said [in *Federalist* No.51]:

> "the constant aim is to divide and arrange the several offices in such a manner as that each may be a check on the other...." Hence the need for an assessment by Congress before citizens are subject to lockup, and likewise the need for a clearly expressed congressional resolution of the competing claims....

Next, there is the Government's claim, accepted by the Court, that the terms of the Force Resolution are adequate to authorize detention of an enemy combatant under the circumstances described, ... but [the Force Resolution] never so much as uses the word detention, and there is no reason to think Congress might have perceived any need to augment Executive power to deal with dangerous citizens within the United States, given the well-stocked statutory arsenal of ... criminal offenses ... that a citizen sympathetic to terrorists might commit....

Because I find Hamdi's detention forbidden by [the Non-Detention Act] and unauthorized by the Force Resolution, I would not reach any questions of what process he may be due ... in a proceeding under the habeas statute or prior to the habeas inquiry itself.... Since this [view] does not command a majority of the Court, however, the need to give practical effect to the conclusions of eight members of the Court rejecting the Government's position calls for me to join with the plurality in ordering remand on the terms closest to what I would impose.... Although I think litigation of Hamdi's status as an enemy combatant is unnecessary, the terms of the plurality's remand will allow Hamdi to offer evidence that he is not an enemy combatant, and he should have the benefit of that opportunity.

It should go without saying that I do not adopt the plurality's resolution of constitutional issues that I would not reach. It is not that I could disagree with the plurality's determinations (given the plurality's view of the Force Resolution) that someone in Hamdi's position is entitled to a minimum of notice of the Government's claimed factual basis for holding him, and to a fair chance to rebut it before a neutral decision maker; nor, of course, could I disagree with the plurality's affirmation of Hamdi's right to counsel. On the other hand, I do not mean to imply agreement that the Government could claim an evidentiary presumption casting the burden of rebuttal on Hamdi, or that an opportunity to litigate before a military tribunal might obviate or truncate enquiry by a court on habeas.

Subject to these qualifications, I join with the plurality in a judgment of the Court vacating the Fourth Circuit's judgment and remanding the case.

JUSTICE SCALIA, with whom JUSTICE STEVENS joins, dissenting....

Where the Government accuses a citizen of waging war against it, our constitutional tradition has been to prosecute him in federal court for treason or some other crime. Where the exigencies of war prevent that, the Constitution's Suspension Clause, Article I, Sec. 9, cl. 2, allows Congress to relax the usual protections temporarily.

Absent suspension, however, the Executive's assertion of military exigency has not been thought sufficient to permit detention without charge. No one contends that [the Force Resolution] on which the government relies to justify its actions here, is an implementation of the Suspension Clause. Accordingly, I would reverse the decision below.

The very core of liberty secured by our Anglo-Saxon system of separation of powers has been freedom from indefinite imprisonment at the will of the Executive. Blackstone stated this principle clearly:

> "... To bereave a man of life, or by violence to confiscate his estate, without accusation or trial, would be so gross and notorious an act of despotism, as must at once convey the alarm of tyranny throughout the kingdom. But confinement of the person, by secretly hurrying him to gaol, where his sufferings are unknown or forgotten; is a less public, a less striking, and therefore a more dangerous engine of arbitrary government...."

The two ideas central to Blackstone's understanding—due process as the right secured, and habeas corpus as the instrument by which due process could be insisted upon by a citizen illegally imprisoned—found expression in the Constitution's Due Process and Suspension Clauses....

Justice O'Connor, writing for a plurality of this Court, asserts that captured enemy combatants (other than those suspected of war crimes) have traditionally been detained until the cessation of hostilities and then released. That is probably an accurate description of wartime practice with respect to enemy *aliens*. The tradition with respect to American citizens, however, has been quite different. Citizens aiding the enemy have been treated as traitors subject to the criminal process....

The Government justifies the imprisonment of Hamdi on principles of the law of war and admits that, absent the war, it would have no such authority. But if the law of war cannot be applied to citizens where courts are open, then Hamdi's imprisonment without criminal trial is no less unlawful than Milligan's trial by military tribunal....

The proposition that the Executive lacks indefinite wartime detention authority over citizens is consistent with the Founders' general mistrust of military power permanently at the Executive's disposal. In the Founders' view, the "blessings of liberty" were threatened by "those military establishments which must gradually poison its very foundation." *The Federalist 45* (Madison). No fewer than 10 issues of the Federalist were devoted in whole or in part to allying fears of oppression from standing armies in peacetime.... A view of the Constitution that gives the Executive authority to use military force rather than the force of law against citizens on American soil flies in the face of the mistrust that engendered these provisions [restraining military power].

The Government argues that [*Ex parte Quirin*] ratifies its indefinite imprisonment of a citizen [Hans Haupt] within the territorial jurisdiction of federal courts.... [That] case was not this Court's finest hour. The Court upheld the commission and denied relief ... the day after oral argument ... ; a week later the Government carried out the commission's death sentence upon six saboteurs, including Haupt. The Court eventually explained its reasoning ... several months later....

In *Quirin* it was uncontested that the petitioners were members of enemy forces. But where those jurisdictional facts are *not* conceded—where the petitioner insists that he is *not* a belligerent—*Quirin* left the pre-existing law in place: Absent suspension of the writ, a citizen held where the courts are open is entitled either to criminal trial or a judicial decree requiring his release.

It follows ... that Hamdi is entitled to a habeas decree requiring his release unless (1) criminal proceedings are promptly brought, or (2) Congress has suspended the writ of habeas corpus. A suspension of the writ could, of course, lay down conditions for continued detention, similar to those that today's opinion prescribes under the Due Process Clause. But there is a world of difference between the people's representatives determining the need for that suspension (and prescribing the conditions for it) and this Court's doing so.

The plurality finds justification for Hamdi's imprisonment in the [Force Resolution, but this] is not remotely a congressional suspension of the writ, and no one claims it is. Contrary to the plurality's view, I do not think this statute even authorizes the detention of a citizen with the clarity necessary to satisfy the interpretive canon that statutes should be construed so as to avoid grave constitutional concerns, ... or with the clarity necessary to overcome [the Non-Detention Act]. But, even if it did, I would not permit it to overcome Hamdi's entitlement to habeas corpus relief.... If the Suspension Clause does not guarantee the citizen that he will either be tried or released, unless the conditions for suspending the writ [of habeas corpus] exist and the grave action of suspending the writ has been taken; if it merely guarantees the citizen that he will not be detained unless Congress by ordinary legislation says he can be detained; it guarantees him very little indeed....

Having found a congressional authorization for detention of citizens where none clearly exists; and having discarded the categorical procedural protection of the Suspension Clause; the plurality then proceeds, under the guise of the Due Process Clause, to prescribe what procedural protections it thinks appropriate. It "weigh[s] the private interest ... against the Government's asserted interest" and—just as though writing a new Constitution—comes up with an unheard-of-system in which the citizen rather than the Government bears the burden of proof, testimony is by hearsay rather than live witnesses, and the presiding officer may well be a "neutral" military officer rather than a judge and jury....

Having distorted the Suspension Clause, the plurality finishes up by [directing] the District Court to "engag[e] in a fact finding process that is both prudent and incremental."... It is not the habeas court's function to make illegal detention legal by supplying a process that the Government could have provided, but chose not to. If Hamdi is being imprisoned in violation of the Constitution (because without due process of law) then his habeas petition should be granted; the Executive may then hand him over to the criminal authorities, whose detention for the purpose of prosecution will be lawful, or else it must release him. [This] approach ... reflects what might be called a Mr. Fix-it Mentality. The plurality seems to view ... its mission to Make Everything Come Out Right, rather than merely to decree the consequences, as far as individual rights are concerned, of the other two branches' actions and omissions. Has the Legislature failed to suspend the writ in the current dire emergency? Well, we will remedy that failure by prescribing the reasonable conditions that a suspension should have included. And has the Executive failed to live up to those reasonable conditions? Well, we will ourselves make that failure good, so that this dangerous fellow (if he is dangerous) need not be set free....

If the situation demands it, the Executive can ask Congress to authorize suspension of the writ—which can be made subject to whatever conditions Congress deems appropriate, including even the procedural novelties invented by the plurality today. To be sure, suspension is limited by the Constitution to cases of rebellion or invasion. But whether the attacks of September 11, 2001, constitute an "invasion," and whether those attacks still justify suspension several years later, are questions for Congress rather than this Court. If civil rights are to be curtailed during wartime, it must be done openly and democratically, as the Constitution requires, rather than by silent erosion through an opinion of this Court.

JUSTICE THOMAS, dissenting:

[Hamdi's] detention falls squarely within the Federal Government's war powers, and we lack the expertise and capacity to second-guess that decision. As such, petitioner's habeas challenge should fail, and there is no reason to remand the case.

The power to protect the nation "ought to exist without limitation [b]ecause it is impossible to foresee or define the extent and variety of national exigencies, or the correspondent extent and variety of the means which may be necessary to satisfy them. The circumstances that endanger the safety of nations are infinite; and for this reason no constitutional shackles can wisely be imposed on the power to which the care of it is committed." [*The Federalist No. 23,* Hamilton.] ...

I acknowledge that the question whether Hamdi's executive detention is lawful is a question properly resolved by the Judicial Branch, though the question comes to the Court with the strongest presumptions in favor of the Government. The plurality agrees that Hamdi's detention is lawful if he is an enemy combatant. But the question whether Hamdi is actually an enemy combatant is "of a kind for which the Judiciary has neither aptitude, facilities nor responsibility and which has long been held to belong in the domain of political power not subject to judicial intrusion or inquiry." ...

Notes and Questions

1. *Different approaches.* The plurality, led by Justice O'Connor, held that Congress, together with the President, had indirectly but "clearly" authorized the detention of "enemy combatants" of all nationalities by passing the use of force resolution, but reserved to the courts the power to develop constitutionally-mandated limitations on the exercise of this statutory power on behalf of both aliens and citizens. Justices Souter and Ginsberg, concurring, would have required Congress, presumably working with the president, to use their collective war powers to set up a detention scheme for aliens and citizens, and then have courts subject that scheme to judicial review under the due process clause. Justices Scalia and Stevens would have required Congress to exercise its power under Article I, Section 9, to enact a carefully tailored suspension of the writ of habeas corpus before detaining any American citizens. Which approach would you have taken, and why? Is Justice Scalia right to accuse the plurality of playing "Mr. Fix It"?

2. *Invasions or rebellions.* Do the attacks of September 11, or attacks on U.S. embassies and warships overseas, qualify as "invasions" or "rebellions" that might permit Congress to suspend the privilege of the writ of habeas corpus? If not, on what would you ground the military's power to detain persons suspected of attacking its forces in the field, or being part of the worldwide cabal of "enemy combatants"? Should the power to detain "enemy combatants" be deemed inherent in any congressional authorization for the use of military force, as Justice O'Connor claims? Or should Congress have to specify the nature and scope of the military's powers of detention each time military force is authorized, as Justice Souter contended?

3. *Due process requirements.* According to the plurality, and probably the two concurring justices, Congress may authorize battlefield detentions, but may not constitutionally strip *citizens* of their rights to know the grounds of their detention and rebut those claims before a "neutral" decision maker. Would you hold that a military officer or panel can be a truly neutral decision maker? Would you allow military officers to make the initial determination, say for a period of months, subject to subsequent review by civilian judges? Who should devise these due process standards, at least initially: a district court, Congress, or the Executive? Does anything in the Constitution or the opinions of the justices prevent Congress from enacting a special detention statute, or the Executive from issuing new regulations? Should the attacks of 9/11 be deemed satisfy the constitutional requirement of an "invasion" or "rebellion?" Which would be politically easier for Congress to pass: a wartime preventive detention law or a wartime suspension of habeas statute? Would the courts still be free, in appropriate cases, to impose due process limitations on the administration of such detention laws?

4. *Sources of the habeas right.* According to the plurality, did Hamdi's habeas rights derive from a statute or the Constitution? What difference would that make? Does Article 1, Section 9, create a constitutional right to challenge indefinite, incommunicado deten-

tions and torture? Or does it simply incorporate a statute, which Congress may amend at will? Would you presume that the framers intended to incorporate a statute into the Constitution? Would a federal habeas corpus statute have existed under the Articles of Confederation, when there were no federal courts? If no such law existed, then should we assume that the framers intended for Congress to define who might assert this historic, and crucial, right? Did the framers authorize Congress to amend by mere legislation any other rights secured by the Constitution, or would that have been contrary to the very idea of a Constitution?

5. *Military tribunals.* In his military order authorizing the creation of military commissions to try enemy combatants for war crimes and the like, President Bush purported to bar any judicial review of the tribunals' decisions. Does the Court's decision in *Hamdi* reject that claim? See also *Rasul v. Bush, infra.*

6. *The executive's reaction.* In response to the *Hamdi* decision, the Pentagon issued new regulations that (1) set up "combat status review tribunals" (CSRTs) to review the factual basis for each detainee's classification as an "enemy combatant," (2) informed all Guantánamo Bay detainees of their right to challenge the factual basis of their detention before these tribunals, (3) gave each detainee the right to a "personal representative" from the U.S. armed forces to make arguments for him before the panel, but (4) did not grant detainees the right to military or civilian legal representation. Should this satisfy a majority of the justices if the detainee is (a) an alien, or (b) a citizen? Does the answer depend on how long the military detains those prisoners found by its panel to be "enemy combatants"? Does the creation of such panels foreclose subsequent habeas challenges (presumably in the U.S. District Court for the District of Columbia)?

7. *Split decisions.* The adequacy of the new screening panels was challenged in separate sets of habeas petitions before Judges Joyce Green and Richard Leon in the District Court for the District of Columbia. Judge Green ruled that they were inadequate in *In re Guantánamo Detainee Cases,* 355 F. Supp. 2d 443 (2005); Judge Leon approved them in *Khalid v. Bush,* 355 F. Supp. 2d 311 (2005), and the court of appeals sided with Judge Leon. At first the Supreme Court refused to review the adequacy of the CSRTs, giving the executive more time to work with them, and to interrogate prisoners under harsh conditions. In 2006, however, it struck down the presidentially created commissions without reviewing the adequacy of their practices. *Hamdan v. Rumsfeld, infra.* Congress then reestablished military commissions, but as of 2010 the adequacy of their procedures remains in doubt.

8. *Hamdi released.* When the case against Hamdi was reviewed by a CSRT, it proved to be weaker than the Bush administration alleged, and he was subsequently released without trial, on condition that he voluntarily renounce his citizenship and move to Saudi Arabia. At the same time, another American citizen, John Walker Lindh, was serving a 20-year sentence for essentially the same actions — marching with a Taliban unit that was intending to engage troops of a rival warlord who became allied with the United States while they were on the march. May the U.S. government hold one of its citizens without trial for three years and then condition his release on his agreement to surrender his citizenship? Should such a renunciation, made under duress, be legally valid?

Non-Battlefield Detainees: Citizen Padilla

Military detention. Jose Padilla (pron. Puh-DILL-uh), an American citizen, was arrested at O'Hare International Airport in Chicago, as a material witness to a terrorist conspiracy to make and detonate a radioactive "dirty bomb." He had allegedly researched and discussed making such a weapon while visiting al Qaeda terrorists in Pakistan. Padilla was arrested on May 8, 2002, but his detention was not announced until June 10. Two days before the legality of that detention could be tested in federal district court in New York, President George W. Bush designated Padilla an "enemy combatant" and authorized his transfer from civilian detention in New York to a Navy brig in South Carolina. The transfer was done secretly, at night, so that his court-appointed counsel could not challenge the decision in court. Later, when she filed a petition for habeas corpus on Padilla's behalf in New York, as his court-appointed lawyer, the Justice Department claimed that the petition was not valid because it did not bear the prisoner's signature, which the Department had made impossible by holding him incommunicado. The Department also claimed that she should have brought the habeas action in South Carolina, where his immediate prison warden was based, rather than in New York, where his warden-in-chief, Defense Secretary Donald Rumsfeld, was subject to service of process. The district court judge in Manhattan rejected that argument, and rendered an opinion upholding Padilla's detention on a deferential "some evidence" standard. This opinion was upset by the U.S. Supreme Court's decision in *Hamdi*.

Scope of the battlefield. In oral argument before the U.S. Court of Appeals for the Second Circuit, Deputy Solicitor General Paul D. Clement argued that "al Qaeda made the battlefields the United States," so that Padilla was, in effect, a "battlefield detainee." *Boston Globe,* Nov. 18, 2003, A-3. Is that the kind of "war zone" the Court had in mind in *Milligan*? In *Korematsu*? Is the threat posed by al Qaeda comparable to the emergency that the Union faced from the armies of the Confederacy? (Note that Confederate raiders did occasionally attack the Union far from military battlefields, e.g.their raid on St. Albans, Vermont, from Canada, but that did not lead the Court in *Milligan* to accept the proposition that the entire country was a war zone.) If the attacks of September 11 are constitutionally sufficient to trigger "wartime" detentions of private American citizens by the military, then is there any limit to what occasions might trigger similar "wartime" detentions? For example, could the President have ordered similar detentions after the 1995 bombing of the Murrah Federal Office Building in Oklahoma City, when the identity of those bombers was not known, but Middle Eastern terrorists were suspected? Isn't this what the Posse Comitatus Act of 1878 was meant to prevent?

Detention by labeling. Jose Padilla was detained because the President chose to label him an "enemy combatant." Judge Michael B. Mukasey, later President Bush's third attorney general, chose to accept this designation as conclusive. *Padilla v. Rumsfeld,* 233 F. Supp. 2d 564 (S.D.N.Y. 2002), 243 F. Supp. 2d 42 (S.D.N.Y. 2003). Should he have, when it was clear from the record that Padilla, like Milligan, had never belonged to a combat unit, had never seen combat, and was not a member of the enemy organization? Nor was there any evidence that Padilla had ever tried to build a dirty bomb—only that he had discussed the possibility with al Qaeda members and done some research about radioactive materials on the Internet.

Fundamental rights. Judge Mukasey did not weigh Padilla's Fourth, Fifth, and Sixth Amendment rights against the government's claim of authority to detain him. Should he have? Does this refusal permit repetition of the executive detentions during the Red Scares of 1919 and 1920, or the detention of Japanese-Americans during World War II, either to question detainees about possible foreign ties or to hold them for the duration of what the president deems to be a national emergency?

The U.S. Court of Appeals for the Second Circuit overturned Judge Mukasey's decision, 352 F.3d 695 (2d. Cir. 2003), but the administration appealed. The Supreme Court avoided addressing the merits of Padilla's detention by ruling, 5–4, that his lawyer should not have filed her habeas petition on his behalf against Secretary Rumsfeld in New York, but should have filed it in South Carolina, where the military had taken him. *Rumsfeld v. Padilla,* 542 U.S. 426 (2004).

In the Fourth Circuit. In response to Padilla's second petition for habeas relief, Judge Henry F. Floyd of the U.S. District Court for South Carolina ruled that the president lacked the authority to detain Padilla. His detention violated the Constitution and laws of the United States, the judge ruled, and the government should either try or release him. To evade this ruling, the administration then dropped the criminal charges against Padilla and reclassified him an "enemy combatant," an action that was upheld by the court of appeals, even though Padilla had been arrested in Chicago and had never been part of a combat unit. Within the Fourth Circuit, at least, it was and remains lawful for the military to detain an American citizen indefinitely, simply by labeling him an "enemy combatant." This would be lawful even though the detainee had never belonged to a combat unit and had been seized at a Chicago airport, far from any battlefield. The rationale of *Ex parte Milligan* no longer applied; the basic premise of Bush's "global war on terrorism," first articulated by John Yoo's secret memoranda, had been judicially embraced. *Padilla v. Hanft,* 423 F.3d 386 (2005).

Knowing that this precedent was not likely to be upheld on appeal, but wanting to keep it on the books, the Justice Department changed tactics again. It withdrew its claim that Padilla was an enemy combatant and indicted him in Florida on charges of conspiring to aid al Qaeda prior to going to the Middle East.

Many observers condemned these switches as abuses of the legal process, and a denial of Padilla's constitutional right to a speedy trial, but the judge accepted jurisdiction anyway. When the jury convicted Padilla of conspiring to go to an al Qaeda training camp, she ignored evidence that he had been abused during years of incarceration and sentenced him to seventeen more years in prison.

D. Do Aliens Have Constitutional Rights?

When President George W. Bush ordered the creation of military tribunals on November 13, 2001, he promised that they would be used against aliens only. Aliens "who come into the United States illegally," his vice president declared, and "conduct a terrorist operation" do not "deserve the same guarantees that would be used for an American citizen going through the same process."[10] In *Hamdi,* Justice Scalia similarly assumed that the right to habeas corpus belongs only to citizens. Do you agree? Does the Bill of Rights reserve its guarantees against unreasonable detentions, unfair trials, and denial of legal counsel to citizens only?

Habeas corpus for enemy soldiers in declared wars. In both the *Quirin* case and the case of the Japanese general tried after World War II for alleged war crimes (*infra,* next case) the Supreme Court accepted, but denied, habeas challenges from foreign soldiers to the jurisdiction of the military tribunals which tried them. A majority also refused to consider whether the commissions had accorded the soldiers a fair trial. Two dissents from that reasoning follow.

---

10. Elizabeth Bumiller and Steven Lee Myers, "Senior Administration Officials Defend Military Tribunals for Terrorist Suspects," *New York Times,* Nov. 15, 2001, B6.

Japanese general Tomoyuki Yamashita was sentenced to death by a U.S. military commission following World War II for atrocities he did not order, but for which he was held responsible under the doctrine of command responsibility.

In re Yamashita
327 U.S. 1 (1946)

JUSTICE MURPHY, dissenting:

An American military commission has been established [in the Philippines] to try a fallen military commander of a conquered nation for an alleged war crime.... The grave issue ... is whether a military commission ... may disregard the procedural rights of an accused person as guaranteed by the Constitution, especially the due process clause of the Fifth Amendment. The answer is plain. The Fifth Amendment guarantee of due process of law applies to "any person" who is accused of a crime by the Federal Government or any of its agencies. No exception is made as to those who are accused of war crimes or as to those who possess the status of an enemy belligerent. Indeed, such an exception would be contrary to the whole philosophy of human rights which makes the Constitution the great living document it is. The immutable rights of the individual ... belong not alone to the members of those nations that excel on the battlefield or that subscribe to the democratic ideology. They belong to every person in the world, victor or vanquished, whatever may be his race, color or beliefs. They rise above any status of belligerency or outlawry. They survive any popular passion or frenzy of the moment. No court or legislature or executive, not even the mightiest army in the world, can ever destroy them. Such is the universal and indestructible nature of the rights which the due process clause of the Fifth Amendment recognizes and protects when life or liberty is threatened by virtue of the authority of the United States.

The existence of these rights, unfortunately, is not always respected. They are often trampled under by those who are motivated by hatred, aggression or fear. But in this nation individual rights are recognized and protected, at least in regard to governmental action. They cannot be ignored by any branch of the Government, even the military, except under the most extreme and urgent circumstances.

The failure of the military commission to obey the dictates of the due process [clause] is apparent in this case. The petitioner was the commander of an army totally destroyed by the superior power of this nation. While under heavy and destructive attack by our forces, his troops committed many brutal atrocities.... Hostilities ceased and he voluntarily surrendered [and thereby became] entitled, as an individual protected by the due process clause of the Fifth Amendment, to be treated fairly and justly....

A military commission was appointed [by General MacArthur] to try the petitioner for an alleged war crime. The trial was ordered [by the general] to be held in territory [the Philippines] over which the United States has complete sovereignty. No military necessity or other emergency demanded the suspension of the safeguards of due process. Yet petitioner was rushed to trial under an improper charge, given insufficient time to prepare an adequate defense, deprived of the benefits of some of the most elementary rules of evidence and summarily sentenced to be hanged. [T]here was no serious attempt to charge or to prove that he committed a recognized violation of the laws of war. He was not charged with personally participating in the acts of atrocity or with ordering or condoning their commission. Not even knowledge of these crimes was attributed to him.... This indictment in effect permitted the military commission to make the crime whatever it willed, dependent upon its biased view as to petitioner's duties and his disregard thereof....

In my opinion, such a procedure is unworthy of the traditions of our people.... The high feelings of the moment doubtless will be satisfied. But in the sober afterglow will come the realization of the boundless and dangerous implications of the procedure sanctioned today. No one in a position of command in an army, from sergeant to general, can escape its implications. Indeed the fate of some future President of the United States and his chiefs of staff and military advisers may well have been sealed by this decision.

Jurisdiction [has been properly asserted by this Court] to inquire "into the cause of restraint of liberty".... Thus the obnoxious doctrine asserted by the Government..., to the effect that restraints of liberty resulting from military trials of war criminals are political matters completely outside the arena of judicial review, has been rejected....

This does not mean, of course, that the foreign affairs and policies of the nation are proper subjects of judicial inquiry. But when the liberty of any person is restrained by reason of the authority of the United States the writ of habeas corpus is available to test the legality of that restraint, even though direct court review of the restraint is prohibited....

The ultimate nature and scope of the writ of habeas corpus are within the discretion of the judiciary unless validly circumscribed by Congress. Here we are confronted with a use of the writ under circumstances novel in the history of the Court. For my part, I do not feel that we should be confined by the traditional line of review drawn in connection with the use of the writ by ordinary criminals who have direct access to the judiciary in the first instance. Those held by the military lack any such access; consequently the judicial review available by habeas corpus must be wider than usual....

The Court, in my judgment, demonstrates conclusively that the military commission was lawfully created.... [H]owever, I find it impossible to agree that the charge against the petitioner stated a recognized violation of the laws of war....

At a time like this when emotions are understandably high it is difficult to adopt a dispassionate attitude toward a case of this nature. Yet now is precisely the time when that attitude is most essential.... We live under the Constitution [a]nd it is applicable in both war and peace. We must act accordingly. Indeed, an uncurbed spirit of revenge and retribution, masked in formal legal procedure for purposes of dealing with a fallen enemy commander, can do more lasting harm than all of the atrocities giving rise to that spirit. The people's faith in the fairness and objectiveness of the law can be seriously undercut by that spirit.

JUSTICE RUTLEDGE, dissenting:

We are technically still at war, because peace has not been negotiated finally or declared. But there is no longer the danger which always exists before surrender and armistice. Military necessity does not demand the same measures [as in *Ex parte Quirin*].

... Although it was ruled in [*Quirin*] that this Court had no function to review the evidence, it was not there or elsewhere determined that it could not ascertain whether conviction is founded upon evidence expressly excluded by Congress or treaty, nor does the Court purport to do so now.

Notes and Questions

1. *Source of the authority.* Does the majority in *Yamashita* derive any authority for the military tribunal from Article II of the Constitution? Does the authority of this particular tribunal, sitting in the Philippines, come from the president, or from the field commander?

2. *Common law military tribunals.* The military tribunal that sent Tomoyuki Yamashita to his death was not created by Congress, with a body of procedural law, like the Uniform Code of Military Justice, to assure that it provided both due process and equal protection. Rather, according to Chief Justice Stone, it was a "common law tribunal" which could do just about whatever its convening general told it to do, and the power of such convening generals to create such ad hoc tribunals was granted by Congress in Article 15 of the Articles of War. This "common law tribunal" was convened in the Philippines, then American territory, where the U.S. Constitution would presumably protect the rights of civilians to due process and equal protection of the laws. Interestingly, the Congress never passed a statute receiving the common law of Britain (military or civilian) into U.S. law. What Stone appears to be describing is some sort of "common law" built up by military commanders (perhaps by the sort of accretion recognized in *Midwest Oil, supra,* chapter 2). In *Erie Railroad v. Tompkins,* 304 U.S. 64 (1938), the Supreme Court held that "[t]here is no federal general common law," but left federal courts free to develop specialized areas of "common law" if so authorized by legislation or the Constitution. Nothing in *Erie* or federal law expressly authorizes military commanders, or the president, to create a court system. For more on the "common law" of military tribunals, see *Hamdan v. Rumsfeld, infra,* this chapter.

3. *Interpreting Article 15.* Compare the majority's opinion in *Yamashita* to the following admonition by Chief Justice John Marshall: "Where rights are infringed, where fundamental principles are overthrown, where the general system of laws is departed from, the legislative intent must be expressed with irresistible clearness to induce a court of justice to suppose a design to effect such objects." *United States v. Fisher,* 6 U.S. 358, 390 (1805). Did the Court's decisions regarding Congress' intent in passing Article 15 meet this test?

4. *Right of aliens to petition for habeas release.* The German marines in *Quirin* were in the United States when they persuaded the Supreme Court to hear their petition; Gen-

eral Yamashita was in the Philippines, then an American possession, when he obtained Supreme Court review. In 2002, the Bush administration sought to interrogate suspected terrorists captured in Afghanistan and other locations overseas in ways that might not withstand judicial review. At first it considered jailing them on the island of Guam, an American possession, until it was pointed out that Guam had a federal district court, served by an independent prosecutor. So the administration moved the prisoners to the U.S. naval base at Guantánamo Bay, Cuba, where there was no federal court or federal prosecutor. When several British, Australian, and Kuwaiti prisoners of the Afghan war challenged the legality of their detentions at that base, the Justice Department argued that the writ of habeas corpus can only be sought within the jurisdiction of a federal district court, and Cuba was outside the jurisdiction of any civilian court. Although the petitioners argued that they were not soldiers or spies for al Qaeda or the Taliban, but mere humanitarian aid workers wrongly accused by bounty-hunting Afghan warlords, the Court of Appeals for the District of Columbia ruled that they had no right, as aliens held outside U.S. territory, to have the legality of their detention by the military reviewed in civilian court. Although the United States navy maintained total jurisdiction and control over the base, the appellate court accepted the administration's argument that it was not really U.S. territory, for purposes of habeas review, because the Cuban government had, by the lease agreement, retained ultimate sovereignty. Therefore, the indefinite detention of prisoners, and their alleged mistreatment while in detention, was beyond federal court review. *Al Odah v. United States*, 321 F. 3d 1134 (2003). The prisoners asked the Supreme Court to overturn this decision in *Rasul v. Bush*.

Rasul v. Bush
542 U.S. 466 (2004)

JUSTICE STEVENS delivered the opinion of the Court:

As Justice Jackson wrote in an opinion respecting the availability of habeas corpus to aliens held in U.S. custody:

> "Executive imprisonment has been considered oppressive and lawless since John, at Runnymede, pledged [in Magna Carta] that no free man should be imprisoned, dispossessed, outlawed, or exiled save by the judgment of his peers and the law of the land. The judges of England developed the writ of habeas corpus largely to preserve these immunities from executive restraint." ...

Consistent with the historical purpose of this writ, this Court has recognized the federal courts' power to review applications for habeas relief in a wide variety of cases involving Executive detention, in wartime as well as in times of peace. [Citing *Milligan, Quirin,* and *Yamashita.*] The question now before us is whether the habeas statute [28 U.S.C. Sec. 2241] confers a right to judicial review of the legality of Executive detention of aliens in a territory over which the United States exercises plenary and exclusive jurisdiction [Guantánamo Bay], but not "ultimate sovereignty."

[The Executive argues] that the answer ... is controlled by our decision in [*Johnson v.*] *Eisentrager* [339 U.S. 763 (1950), in which the Supreme Court ruled that the district court] lacked authority to issue a writ of habeas corpus to 21 German citizens who had been captured by U.S. forces in China, tried and convicted of war crimes by an American military commission headquartered in Nanking, and incarcerated ... in occupied Germany.... [But the Guantanomo

Bay petitioners] differ from the *Eisentrager* detainees in important respects: They are not nationals of countries at war with the United States, and they deny that they have engaged in or plotted acts of aggression against the United States; they have never [unlike the Germans] been afforded access to any tribunal, much less charged with and convicted of wrongdoing, and for more than two years they have been imprisoned in territory over which the United States exercises exclusive jurisdiction and control.

Not only are petitioners differently situated from the *Eisentrager* detainees, but the Court in *Eisentrager* made quite clear that ... the facts critical to its disposition were relevant only to the question of the prisoner's *constitutional* entitlement to habeas corpus.

The Court had far less to say on the question of the petitioners' *statutory* entitlement to habeas review.... [S]ubsequent decisions of this Court have [made it unnecessary for] persons detained outside the territorial jurisdiction of any federal district court ... to rely [only] on the Constitution as the source of their right to federal habeas review....

[The administration contended that the habeas statute, 28 U.S.C. Sec. 2241, should not be presumed to have extraterritorial effect unless such intent by Congress is clearly manifested.] Whatever traction the presumption against [the extraterritorial application of U.S. laws] might have in other contexts, it certainly has no application ... with respect to persons detained within "the territorial jurisdiction of the United States."... By the express terms of its agreements with Cuba, the United States exercises "complete jurisdiction and control" over the Guantánamo Bay Naval Base, and may continue to exercise such control permanently if it so chooses.... Respondents themselves concede that the habeas statute would create federal-court jurisdiction over the claims of an American citizen held at the base. Considering that the statute draws no distinction between Americans and aliens held in federal custody, there is little reason to think that Congress intended the geographical coverage of the statute to depend on the detainee's citizenship. Aliens held at the base, no less than American citizens, are entitled to invoke the federal courts' authority under [the habeas statute].

JUSTICE KENNEDY, concurring in the judgment.

... While I reach the same conclusion [as the majority], my analysis follows a different course....

Eisentrager considered the scope of the right to petition for a writ of habeas corpus against the backdrop of the constitutional command of the separation of powers. The issue before the Court [in that case] was whether the Judiciary could exercise jurisdiction over the claims of German prisoners held in the Landsberg prison following the cessation of hostilities in Europe. The Court concluded that ... the petition was not within the proper realm of the judicial power. It concerned matters within the exclusive province of the Executive, or the Executive and Congress, to determine.

The Court began by noting "the ascending scale of rights" that courts have recognized for individuals depending on their connection to the United States. Citizenship provides a longstanding basis for jurisdiction, the Court noted, and among aliens physical presence within the United States also "gave the Judiciary power to act."... Physical presence in the United States "implied protection, whereas in *Eisentrager* "th[e] prisoners at no relevant time were within any territory over which the United States is sovereign."… Because the prisoners in *Eisentrager* were proven enemy aliens found and detained outside the United States, and because the existence of jurisdiction [in the courts] would have had a clear harmful effect on the Nation's military affairs, the matter was appropriately left to the Executive Branch.…

The facts here are distinguishable from those in *Eisentrager* in two critical ways, leading to the conclusion that a federal court may entertain the petitions. First, Guantánamo Bay is in every practical respect a United States territory, and it is one far removed from any hostilities.…

The second critical set of facts is that the detainees at Guantánamo Bay are being held indefinitely, and without benefit of any legal proceeding to determine their status. In *Eisentrager*, the prisoners were tried and convicted by a military commission of violating the laws of war and were sentenced to prison terms.… Indefinite detention without trial or other proceeding presents altogether different considerations. It allows friends and foes alike to remain in detention. It suggests a weaker case of military necessity and much greater alignment with the traditional function of habeas corpus. Perhaps, where detainees are taken from a zone of hostilities, detention without proceedings or trial would be justified by military necessity for a matter of weeks; but as the period of detention stretches from months to years, the case for continued detention to meet military exigencies becomes weaker.

In light of the status of Guantánamo Bay and the indefinite pretrial detention of the detainees, I would hold that federal-court jurisdiction is permitted in these cases. This approach would avoid creating automatic statutory authority to adjudicate the claims of persons located outside the United States.…

JUSTICE SCALIA, with whom THE CHIEF JUSTICE and JUSTICE THOMAS join, dissenting.…

As we have repeatedly said: "Federal courts are courts of limited jurisdiction. They possess only that power authorized by Constitution and statute, which is not to be expanded by judicial decree."… Even a cursory reading of the habeas statute shows that it presupposes a federal district court with territorial jurisdiction over the detainee. Section 2241 (a) states:

> "Writs of habeas corpus may be granted by the Supreme Court, any justice thereof, the district courts and any circuit judge *within their respective jurisdictions.*" (Emphasis added).

… No matter to whom the writ is directed, custodian or detainee, the statute could not be clearer that a necessary requirement for issuing the writ is that *some* federal district court have territorial jurisdiction over the detainee. Here, as the Court allows, the Guantánamo Bay detainees are not located within the territorial jurisdiction of any federal district court. One would think that is the end of this case.…

[Subsequent to its decision in *Eisentrager*, Justice Scalia conceded, the Court had broadly interpreted the habeas statute in *Braden v. 30th Judicial District Court of Ky.*, 410 U.S. 484 (1973), to permit American citizens confined overseas to file habeas petitions in federal district courts, even though they were not within the territorial bounds of that judicial district. But he and the other dissenters refused to extend that exception to non-citizens held by U.S. authorities overseas.]

The reality is this: Today's opinion ... overrules *Eisentrager* ... and ... extends the habeas statute ... to aliens beyond the sovereign territory of the United States and beyond the territorial jurisdiction of its courts. No reasons are given for this result; no acknowledgement of its consequences made.... Today, the Court springs a trap on the Executive, subjecting Guantánamo Bay to the oversight of the federal courts ... and thus making it a foolish place to have housed alien wartime detainees.

In abandoning the venerable statutory line drawn in *Eisentrager,* the Court boldly extends the scope of the habeas statute to the four corners of the earth.... Today's carefree Court disregards ... the dire warning of a more circumspect Court in *Eisentrager*:

"To grant the writ to these prisoners [then millions of foreign POWs] might mean that our army must transport them across the seas for a hearing.... It might also require transportation for whatever witnesses the prisoners desire to call as well as transportation for those necessary to defend legality of the sentence. The writ, since it held as a matter of right, would be equally available to enemies during active hostilities as in the present twilight between war and peace. Such trials would hamper the war effort and bring aid and comfort to the enemy."...

Notes and Questions

1. *Basis of the ruling.* May Congress and the president, if they wish, change the habeas statute to strip noncitizens of the statutory right recognized by the Court in *Rasul*? If the right to habeas is grounded in the Constitution, may legislation alter it? See *Hamdan v. Rumsfeld, infra.*

2. *Territorial reach.* By a secret "finding" issued on September 17, 2001, President George W. Bush authorized the CIA and Defense Department to set up secret interrogation centers in at least eight foreign countries, including Afghanistan, Pakistan, Iraq, Qatar, and Thailand. Does the decision in *Rasul* grant detainees in such centers statutory access to the privilege of the writ of habeas corpus, assuming they can contact lawyers? If not, what is to prevent the Executive from transferring prisoners at Guantánamo Bay to these secret prisons, even while their petitions for habeas corpus are pending? Does Justice Kennedy's concurring opinion signal his belief that the Executive may, as a practical matter, detain and torture alleged terrorists indefinitely, so long as it does so outside U.S. territory?

3. *Reasons.* Justice Scalia complained that the majority did not give adequate reasons for extending the habeas jurisdiction of federal courts to aliens at the U.S. navy base at Guantánamo Bay. Did he have a point? What reasons might the majority have given?

4. *The Bybee memorandum on torture.* Following oral argument in *Rasul,* it was disclosed that Assistant Attorney General Jay Bybee, by then a judge on the Ninth Circuit Court of Appeals, had sent a secret memorandum to the White House on August 2, 2002, explaining how legal liability for authorizing torture could be evaded. Where the president's power to conduct war is concerned, Bybee asserted, the Justice Department "will not read a criminal statute as infringing on the President's ultimate authority.... We would require an express statement by Congress [in a criminal law] before assuming it intended the President's performance of his statutory duties to be reviewed [judicially] for abuse of discretion.... Congress may no more regulate the President's ability to detain and interrogate enemy combatants than it may regulate his ability to direct troop movements

on the battlefield." Memorandum for Alberto R. Gonzales, Counsel to the President, Re: Standards of Conduct for Interrogation, August 1, 2002, in *The Torture Papers,* 2005), 203. Do you agree? Does the Constitution separate powers to this extent, or does it give Congress and the courts power to limit presidential authority even in the conduct of war?

Should courts assume that a "wartime" president may detain anyone they label an "enemy combatant" unless Congress expressly passes a law over his veto denying him that power? Or should courts assume that the president has no such power unless and until Congress expressly grants it, consistent with the suspension of the Habeas Clause? Which assumption would be more consistent with the Constitution's plan and the Non-Detention Act of 1972, invoked by Justice Souter, concurring in *Hamdi*?

Johnson v. Eisentrager
339 U.S. 763 (1950)

JUSTICE BLACK, with whom JUSTICE DOUGLAS and JUSTICE BURTON concur, dissenting.

Does a prisoner's right to test legality of a sentence ... depend on where the Government chooses to imprison him? Certainly the *Quirin* and *Yamashita* opinions lend no support to that conclusion, for in upholding jurisdiction they place no reliance whatever on territorial location. The Court is fashioning wholly indefensible doctrine if it permits the executive branch, by deciding where its prisoners will be tried and imprisoned, to deprive all federal courts of their power to protect against a federal executive's illegal incarcerations.

[That] the Court is adopting a broad and dangerous principle ... is underlined by the argument of the Government brief that habeas corpus is not even available for American citizens convicted and imprisoned in Germany by American military tribunals. While the Court wisely disclaims any such necessary effect for its holding, rejection of the Government's argument is certainly made difficult by the logic of today's opinion. Conceivably a majority may hereafter find citizenship a sufficient substitute for territorial jurisdiction and thus permit courts to protect Americans from illegal sentences. But the Court's opinion inescapably denies courts power to afford the least bit of protection for any alien who is subject to our occupation government abroad, even if he is neither enemy nor belligerent and even after peace is officially declared. ...

The question here ... is whether the judiciary has power in habeas corpus proceedings to test the legality of criminal sentences imposed by the executive through military tribunals in a country which we have occupied for years. The extent of such a judicial test ..., as we have already held in the *Yamashita* case, is of most limited scope.

We ask only whether the military tribunal was legally constituted and whether it had jurisdiction to impose punishment for the conduct charged. Such a limited habeas corpus review is the right of every citizen of the United States. ... Any contention that a similarly limited use of habeas corpus for these prisoners would somehow give them a preferred position in the law cannot be taken seriously. ...

Perhaps, as some nations believe, there is merit in leaving the administration of criminal laws to executive and military agencies completely free from judicial scrutiny. Our Constitution has emphatically expressed a contrary policy.

As the Court points out, Paul was fortunate enough to be a Roman citizen when he was made the victim of prejudicial charges, but other martyred disciples were not so fortunate....

Conquest by the United States, unlike conquest by many other nations, does not mean tyranny.... Our nation proclaims a belief in the dignity of human beings as such, no matter what their nationality or where they happen to live. Habeas corpus, as an instrument to protect against illegal imprisonment, is written into the Constitution. Its use by courts cannot in my judgment be constitutionally abridged by Executive or by Congress. I would hold that our courts can exercise it whenever any United States official illegally imprisons any person in any land we govern. Courts should not for any reason abdicate this, the loftiest power with which the Constitution has endowed them.

Notes and Questions

1. *First principles.* In times of crisis "which try men's souls," Thomas Paine wrote, it is necessary to revert to "first principles." If so, which is the most relevant first principle? Limited government, via checks and balances and the Bill of Rights, or unlimited executive government resulting in arbitrary detentions, trials, and sentences? Can the principle of limited government be vindicated by a doctrine that denies standing to sue to the overseas victims of American power?

2. *Rights of aliens.* In determining the right of aliens to be free from arbitrary detention, which should take precedence: the broad wording of the Bill of Rights or the narrow wording of a Congressional statute? If we accept the proposition that Congress can provide for the detention of enemy aliens in times of declared war, does it necessarily follow that they can be stripped of all rights, as the dissenters in *Rasul* and the majority in *Eisentrager* appeared to believe? Those who would deny aliens these rights often reason from the idea of a social or political compact to which only citizens, or perhaps resident aliens, belong. Those who would give aliens a legally enforceable right to be free from arbitrary imprisonment by U.S. officials often invoke the principles of limited government, due process, international human rights, and concepts of mutuality (at least for resident aliens). Which approach would you take?

3. *Authority to torture aliens.* For example, could Congress authorize the president to torture enemy aliens in order to extract intelligence, provided, say, that the information obtained is not offered in evidence in a criminal trial in a civilian U.S. court? Could the president order the torture of aliens on his own authority? In the United States? At Guantánamo Bay, Cuba? In Afghanistan?

4. *Protecting Americans from punishment for torture.* The Bush administration negotiated agreements with thirty countries to immunize CIA and military personnel, and civilian contractors working for them, from local prosecution for abusing suspected terrorists on those countries' soil. It persuaded another ninety regimes to promise not to extradite American government personnel to the International Criminal Court to be tried for war crimes. These agreements were sought before the abuses at Abu Ghraib were made public.

5. *Territorial jurisdiction.* Do the dissenters in *Rasul* conflate a plaintiff's standing to sue with a court's territorial jurisdiction? The U.S. District Court for the District of Columbia presumably has territorial jurisdiction over officials who illegally order someone's detention overseas. If the detainee is an American citizen, he presumably has standing to

invoke that territorial jurisdiction. If so, then why shouldn't a noncitizen have standing, if the issue is the legality of the detention system?

6. *Habeas corpus.* The United States took its writ of habeas corpus from British law. The first habeas act of 1640 codified the basic common law privilege, but was evaded by the restoration monarchy of Charles II during the early 1660s. Edward Hyde, Earl of Clarendon and Lord High Chancellor, hid political prisoners away in remote places, including the Isle of Jersey, where they had no access to courts or counsel and where the servers of writs, should someone obtain one on their behalf, could not reach them and their jailors. The House of Commons undertook to impeach Clarendon for these and other abuses 1667 and in the second Habeas Corpus Act of 1679 tried to plug the loopholes before the autocratic James II succeeded to the throne. 31 Car. 2, c. 2. Consider the preamble to the 1679 Act: "An Act for the better securing of the Liberty of the Subject, and for Prevention of Imprisonment beyond the Seas." Section XII of the Act expressly made it an offense for the Crown officials to detain persons in places where the writ could not be served. Versions of the 1679 Act were adopted by the legislatures of all thirteen colonies. Are the history and wording of the 1679 Act and its colonial adaptations helpful to understanding the meaning of the Habeas Clause of the federal Constitution?

7. *Blackstone.* The framers of the U.S. Constitution knew the British habeas laws well. Their primary source would have been William Blackstone's *Commentaries on the Law of England* (1768). Blackstone described the writ of habeas corpus as "the great and efficacious writ in all manner of illegal confinement, … running into all parts of the king's dominions: for the king is at all times entitled to have an account [of] why the liberty of any of his subjects is restrained, wherever that restraint may be inflicted." 3 Blackstone's *Commentaries*, 131. In deciding what the framers meant by the Suspension (of habeas) Clause in Article I, Section 9, would you look to Blackstone, as you might look to the *Federalist Papers,* or would you confine yourself to British case law at the time, as Justice Scalia would do? Which is more indicative of the "original intent" of the framers?

7. *Rental property.* The district court in *Rasul* held that the naval base there was not analogous to the Philippines in 1946, because Guantánamo was a rental property over which Cuba, by the treaty of 1903, expressly retained "sovereignty." Is that a persuasive argument? Is it persuasive if we define sovereignty in the traditional, pragmatic sense of "that legal authority above and beyond which there is no authority?" Note that for many years the United States had a federal district court in the Panama Canal Zone, another area over which it exercised dominion and control but did not claim sovereignty. The United States also convened a district court in occupied Berlin in 1979, using German citizens as jurors. See Herbert J. Stern, *Judgment in Berlin* (1984), and the film by that name.

8. *Declared war.* Justice Jackson limited the scope of the Court's holding in *Eisentrager* to the detention of enemy soldiers who had been convicted of crimes stemming from a declared war. Do the conflict with al Qaeda, the "global war on terrorism," or the assistance given to the government of Afghanistan by U.S. forces qualify as declared wars, as understood by the Court in *Eisentrager*?

9. *What did Congress authorize?* On September 14, 2001, Congress authorized the president "to use all necessary and appropriate force against those nations, organizations, or persons he determines planned, authorized, or aided" the attacks of September 11 and recognized the president's "authority under the Constitution to take action to deter and prevent acts of international terrorism against the United States." 115 Stat. 224, 224 (2001). Does this resolution authorize an irregular, largely covert "war" on terrorists that knows no geographical boundaries? Does it authorize the use of military commissions to try

persons alleged to have ties to terrorists, but who, like Padilla, were not captured in what the *Milligan, Quirin,* or *Korematsu* decisions considered a "war zone"? If so, could military commissions be used to try organized criminals, including drug lords, Mafia dons, and pirates, whatever their citizenship, on the theory that wars against criminal syndicates are indistinguishable from wars against foreign nations? Or should terrorists, drug lords, Mafiosi, and pirates continue to be dealt with as a law enforcement problem?

9. *Wartime rationalizations?* Justice Jackson, dissenting in *Korematsu,* warned that "A military order, however unconstitutional, is not apt to last longer than the military emergency.... But once a judicial opinion ... rationalizes the Constitution to show that the Constitution sanctions such an order, the Court for all time has validated the principle [which] then lies about like a loaded weapon ready for the hand of any authority that can forward a plausible claim of an urgent need." Was Jackson's opinion in *Eisentrager* the kind of decision he warned against in *Korematsu?*

E. Military Tribunals Revisited

Hamdan v. Rumsfeld
548 U.S. 557 (2006)

Salim Ahmed Hamdan, one of Osama bin Laden's former drivers and bodyguards, filed a habeas corpus petition from Guantánamo Bay challenging the legality of the military commissions before which he was scheduled to be tried for one count of conspiracy "to commit ... offenses triable by military commission." The district court granted his request; a three-judge panel of the U.S. Court of Appeals for the District of Columbia (including then Judge John Roberts) denied it, upholding the legality of the commissions. The Supreme Court, in a 5–3 decision, ruled that the structures and procedures of the Bush administration's commissions violated both the Uniform Code of Military Justice (UCMJ) and the Geneva Conventions. It did not hold the commissions unconstitutional, but rather found that they did not meet the legal standard set by Congress back in 1916 in Article 15 of the Articles of War (now Article 21 of the UCMJ).

> JUSTICE STEVENS delivered the judgment of the Court and an opinion in which JUSTICES SOUTER, GINSBERG, and BREYER joined, and in which JUSTICE KENNEDY partially concurred, making an opinion of the Court.
>
> ... Whether ... the President may constitutionally convene military commissions "without the sanction of Congress" is a question this Court has not answered definitively, and need not answer today.... We [also] have no occasion to revisit *Quirin's* controversial characterization of Article of War 15 as congressional authorization for military commissions [because] even *Quirin* did not view [Article 15] as a sweeping mandate for the President to "invoke military commissions when he deems them necessary."... Rather, the *Quirin* Court recognized that Congress had simply preserved what power, under the Constitution and the common law of war, the President had had before 1916 to convene military commissions—with the express condition that the President and those under his command comply with the laws of war....
>
> The Government would have us dispense with the inquiry that the *Quirin* Court undertook and find in the AUMF [Authorization to Use Military Force] or the DTA [Detainee Treatment Act] specific, overriding authorization for [Ham-

Navy attorney Charles Swift, together with civilian co-counsel, persuaded the Supreme Court that his commander in chief, George W. Bush, had broken the law by authorizing a military commission to try Salim Hamdan, Osama bin Laden's driver. Two weeks later, the Navy denied Swift a promotion, effectively ending his military career.

dan's] commission. Neither of these congressional Acts, however, [expressly] expands the President's authority to convene military tribunals....

Together, the UCMJ, the AUMF, and the DTA at most acknowledge a general Presidential authority to convene military commissions in circumstances where justified under the "Constitution and laws," including the law of war. Absent a more specific congressional authorization, the task of this Court is, as it was in *Quirin*, to decide whether Hamdan's military commission is so justified....

Commissions historically have been used in three situations.... First, they have substituted for civilian courts at times and in places where martial law has been declared [citing *Milligan* and *Duncan*]. Second, commissions have been established to try civilians "as part of a temporary military government over occupied enemy territory or territory regained from an enemy where civilian government cannot and does not function [e.g. occupied Germany]. The third type of commission, convened as an "incident to the conduct of war" when there is a need "to seize and subject to disciplinary measures those enemies who in their attempt to thwart and impede our military effort have violated the law of war." *Quirin* has been described as "utterly different" from the other two.... Not only is its jurisdiction limited to offenses cognizable during time of war, but its role is primarily a factfinding one — to determine, typically on the battlefield itself, whether the defendant has violated the law of war [*Quirin* and *Yamashita*]....

Quirin is the model the Government invokes most frequently [which is] unsurprising [s]ince Guantanámo Bay is neither enemy occupied territory nor under martial law.... [N]o more robust model of executive power exists; *Quirin* represents the high-water mark of military power to try enemy combatants for war crimes.

[Under the common law of war, as summarized in Winthrop's treatise], at least four preconditions must exist for exercise of jurisdiction by a tribunal [like Hamdan's.] First, "[a] commission can legally assume jurisdiction ... in the "theatre of war." Second, the offense charged "must have been committed within the period of the war."... Third, a military commission not established pursuant to martial law or an occupation may try only "individuals of the enemy's army who have been guilty of illegitimate warfare or other offenses in violation of the laws of war".... Finally, a law-of-war commission has jurisdiction to try only two kinds of offense: "Violations of the laws and usages of war cognizable by military tribunals only," and "[b]reaches of military orders ... not legally triable by court-martial under the Articles of war."

All parties agree that Colonel Winthrop's treatise accurately describes the common law governing military commissions, and that the jurisdictional limitations he identifies were incorporated in Article of War 15 and, later Article 21 of the UCMJ.... The question is whether the preconditions designed to ensure that a military necessity exists to justify the use of this extraordinary tribunal have been satisfied here....

[I]nternational sources confirm that the crime charged here [conspiracy] is not a recognized violation of the law of war. [N]one of the major treaties [including the Geneva Conventions] governing the law of war identifies conspiracy as a violation thereof....

The charge's shortcomings are not merely formal, but are indicative of a broader inability on the Executive's part here to satisfy the most basic precondition—at least in the absence of specific congressional authorization—... military necessity. Hamdan's tribunal was not appointed by a military commander in the field of battle, but a retired major general stationed away from any active hostilities.... Hamdan is charged not with an overt act for which he was caught redhanded in a theater of war and which military efficiency demands he be tried expeditiously, but with an *agreement* the inception of which long predated the attacks of September 11, 2001 and the AUMF. That may well be a crime, but it is not an offense that "by the law of war may be tried by a military commissio[n]." None of the overt acts alleged to have been committed in furtherance of the agreement is itself a war crime, or even necessarily occurred during time of, or in a theater of, war. Any urgent need for imposition or execution of judgment is utterly belied by the record; Hamdan was arrested in November 2001 and he was not charged until mid-2004....

Whether or not the Government has charged Hamdan with an offense against the law of war cognizable by military commission, the commission lacks power to proceed.

The UCMJ conditions the President's use of military commissions on compliance not only with the American common law of war, but also with the rest of the UCMJ itself, insofar as applicable, and with the "rules and precepts of the law of nations."... The procedures that the Government has decreed will govern Hamdan's trial by commission violate these laws.

[For example, t]he accused and his civilian counsel may be excluded from, and precluded from ever learning what evidence was presented during any part of the proceeding that either the Appointing Authority or the presiding officer decides to "close." ... Another striking feature ... is that [the rules of evidence] permit the admission of *any* evidence that, in the opinion of the presiding officer, "would have probative value to a reasonable person." Under this test, not only is testimonial hearsay and evidence obtained through coercion fully admissible, but neither live testimony nor witnesses' written statements need be sworn.... Once all the evidence is in, ... [a] two-thirds vote will suffice for both a verdict of guilty and for imposition of any sentence not including death....

[T]he procedures governing trials by military commissions historically have been the same as those governing courts-martial.... There is a glaring historical exception ... [t]he procedures and evidentiary rules used to try General Yamashita.... At least partially in response to subsequent criticism of [his] trial, the UCMJ's codification of the Articles of War after World War II expanded the category of persons subject thereto to include defendants in Yamashita's (and Hamdan's) position,.... The most notorious exception to the principle of uniformity, then, has been stripped of its precedential value....

The president here has determined ... that it is impracticable to apply to rules and principles of law that govern "the trial of criminal cases in the United States district courts," [but he] has not ... made a similar official determination that it is impracticable to apply the rules for courts-martial. [T]he only reason offered [in support of these commissions] is the danger posed by international terrorism. Without for one moment underestimating that danger, it is not evident to us why it should require, in the case of Hamdan's trial, any variance from the rules that govern courts-martial....

The military commission was not born of a desire to dispense a more summary form of justice than is afforded by courts-martial; it developed, rather, as a tribunal of necessity to be employed when courts-martial lacked jurisdiction over either the accused or the subject matter. Exigency lent the commission its legitimacy, but did not further justify the wholesale jettisoning of procedural protections....

The procedures adopted to try Hamdan also violate the Geneva Conventions.... Common Article 3 [to the four Conventions] provides that [sentences may only be passed and executions carried out] by a regularly constituted court affording all the judicial guarantees which are recognized as indispensable by civilized peoples." ... Common Article 3 ... affords ... protection ... to individuals associated with neither a signatory nor even a nonsignatory "Power" who are involved in a conflict "in the territory of" a signatory.... Common Article 3, then, ... requires that Hamdan be tried by a "regularly constituted court affording all the judicial guarantees which are recognized as indispensable by civilized peoples." ... At a minimum, a military commission can be "regularly constituted" by the standards of our military justice system only if some practical need explains deviations from court-martial practice. [N]o such need has been demonstrated here....

It bears emphasizing that Hamdan does not challenge, and we do not today address, the Government's power to detain him for the duration of active hostilities in order to prevent such harm. But in undertaking to try Hamdan and subject him to criminal punishment, the Executive is bound to comply with the Rule of Law that prevails in this jurisdiction.

The judgment of the Court of Appeals is reversed....

The CHIEF JUSTICE took no part in the consideration or decision of this case. The concurring opinions of JUSTICES KENNEDY and BREYER, and the dissenting opinions of JUSTICES SCALIA AND THOMAS, both joined by JUSTICE ALITO, have been omitted.

Notes and Questions

1. *Political strategies.* Why do you suppose the majority did not rule that the president lacked constitutional authority to create any tribunals, and that creation of tribunals would require an act of Congress comparable, in detail, to the Uniform Code of Military Justice?

2. *Implications.* How does the ruling regarding Common Article 3 affect the Bush administration's policy of torturing and abusing prisoners? Are those responsible for that policy open to possible prosecution as war criminals?

3. *Rethinking Padilla.* Does the Supreme Court's effort to narrow when military commissions may be convened as a matter of military necessity affect thinking about the military's need to label Jose Padilla an "enemy combatant"? In light of the Court's decision in *Hamdan,* was it militarily necessary to remove Padilla from pretrial custody and subject him to indefinite detention as an "enemy combatant?" If Padilla can be classified an "enemy combatant," does the word "combatant" have any meaning? If it doesn't, then wasn't he detained as an alleged "enemy," a concept that could encompass just about anyone, including, as a Bush administration attorney once claimed in court, "a little old lady in Switzerland" who gives money to an Islamic charity with no knowledge that some of its funds were being diverted to terrorist activity?

F. Habeas as a Constitutional Right of Aliens

Boumediene v. Bush
553 U.S. 723; 128 S. Ct. 229 (2008)

In October 2001, Lakhdar Boumediene and five other Algerians living in Bosnia were seized by local authorities in response to U.S. allegations that they were plotting to bomb the U.S. embassy in Sarajevo. After a three-month investigation, the Bosnian Supreme Court found no evidence to support the charges and ordered the men released, but Bosnian authorities turned them over to American peacekeeping forces who labeled them "enemy combatants" and shipped them to Guantánamo Bay, Cuba, for indefinite detention. In 2006, after the Supreme Court ruled in *Hamdan* that prisoners there were entitled to challenge their detentions in federal civilians courts under the federal habeas corpus statute, the Congress passed the Military Commissions Act (MCA), taking away that *statutory* right and substituting a different procedure prescribed by the Detainee Treatment Act of 2005 (DTA).

The first issue before the Supreme Court in *Boumediene* was whether the Suspension Clause, Article 1, Section 9, of the Constitution grants these aliens (and by implication citizens) a *constitutional* right to habeas relief. Attorney General Alberto Gonzales had argued before Congress that it did not. The second was whether the substitute procedure—a hearing without counsel before a Combat Status Review Tribunal, followed by a limited appeal to the U.S. Court of Appeals for the District of Columbia—was an adequate alternative to the constitutional right.

After more than seven years, 120 interrogations, and extensive litigation, the Bush administration finally decided that Lakhdar Boumediene, a former Red Crescent aid worker, no longer posed a threat to the United States. When he deplaned in France after eight years in detention, neither he nor his children recognized each other.

JUSTICE KENNEDY delivered the opinion of the Court.

We hold these prisoners do have [a constitutional] right to habeas corpus and ... that [the DTA's] procedures are not an adequate and effective substitute.... Therefore, section 7 of the [MCA] operates as an unconstitutional suspension of the writ....

[W]e cannot ignore that the MCA was a direct response to *Hamdan's* holding that the DTA's jurisdiction-stripping provision had no application to pending cases.... [W]e agree with [the Court of Appeals] that the MCA deprives the federal courts of jurisdiction to entertain the habeas corpus actions now before us.

In deciding the constitutional questions ... we must determine whether petitioners are barred from seeking the writ or invoking the protections of the Suspension Clause either because [they have been] designated enemy combatants, or [because of] their physical location ... at Guantánamo Bay. The Government contends that non-citizens designated as enemy combatants and detained in territory outside our Nation's borders have no constitutional rights and no privilege of habeas corpus....

We begin with a brief account of the history and origins of the writ.... The Framers viewed freedom from unlawful restraint as a fundamental precept of liberty, and they understood the writ of habeas corpus as a vital instrument to secure that freedom. Experience taught, however, that the common-law writ all too often had been insufficient to guard against the abuse of monarchical power. That history counseled the necessity for specific language in the Constitution to secure the writ and ensure its place in our legal system.

Magna Carta decreed that no man would be imprisoned contrary to the law of the land.... Holdsworth tells us ... that gradually the writ of habeas corpus became the means by which the promise of Magna Carta was fulfilled. [A]t the outset it was used to protect not the rights of citizens but those of the King and his courts.... Over time it became clear that by issuing the writ of habeas corpus common law courts sought to enforce the King's prerogative to inquire into the authority of a jailer to hold a prisoner.

[According to Chief Justice Joseph Story of the U.S. Supreme Court,] the writ ran "into all parts of the king's dominions [because] the king is entitled, at all times, to have an account of why the liberty of any of his subjects is restrained."

Even so, ... it was understood that the King too was subject to the law.... And, by the 1600's, the writ was deemed less an instrument of the King's power and more a restraint upon it.... Still, the writ proved to be an imperfect check. [H]abeas relief often was denied by the courts or suspended by Parliament. Denial or suspension occurred in times of political unrest, to the anguish of the imprisoned and the outrage of those in sympathy with them.

A notable example ... was *Darnel's Case*, 3 How. St. Tr. 1 (K.B.1627).... [I]n a display of the Stuart penchant for authoritarian excess, Charles I demanded that Darnel and at least four others lend him money. Upon their refusal, they were imprisoned. The prisoners sought a writ of habeas corpus. [The king objected and the] court held this was a sufficient answer and justified the subject's continued imprisonment.

There was an immediate outcry of protest. The House of Commons promptly passed the Petition of Right, [*supra*, chapter 1] which condemned executive "imprison[ment] without any cause shown," and declared that "no freeman in any such manner [shall] be imprisoned or detained." Yet a full legislative response was long delayed. The ... Parliament was dissolved. When [it] reconvened in 1640, it sought to secure access to the writ by [the Habeas Corpus Act of 1640 which] expressly authorized use of the writ to test the legality of commitment by command or warrant of the King or the Privy Council. Civil strife followed ... and not until 1679 did Parliament try once more to secure the writ, this time through the Habeas Corpus Act of 1679, ... which ... was the model upon which the habeas statutes of the 13 American Colonies were based....

This history was known to the Framers.... The Framers' inherent distrust of governmental power ... is evident from the care taken to specify the limited grounds for [the writ's] suspension: "The Privilege of the Writ of Habeas Corpus shall not be suspended, unless in Cases of Rebellion or Invasion the Public Safety may require it."... The Clause ... ensures that, except during periods of formal suspension, the Judiciary will have a time-tested device, the writ, to maintain the "delicate balance of governance" that is itself the surest safeguard of liberty.... The separation-of-powers doctrine, and the history that influenced its design, therefore must inform the reach and purpose of the Suspension Clause.

The broad historical narrative of the writ and its function is central to our analysis ... The Court has been careful not to foreclose the possibility that the protections of the Suspension Clause have expanded along with post-1789 developments that define the present scope of the writ. But the analysis may begin with precedents as of 1789, for the Court has said that "at the absolute minimum" the Clause protects the writ as it existed when the Constitution was drafted and ratified.... The Government argues that the common-law writ ran only to those territories over which the Crown was sovereign. Petitioners argue that jurisdiction followed the King's officers. Diligent search by all parties reveals no certain conclusions. In none of the cases cited do we find that a common-law court would or would not have granted, or refused to hear for lack of jurisdiction, a petition for a writ of habeas corpus brought by a prisoner deemed an enemy combatant under a standard like the one the Department of Defense has used in these cases, and, when held in a territory, like Guantánamo, over which the Government has total military and civilian control.

We know that at common law a petitioner's status as an alien was not a categorical bar to habeas corpus relief. See, *e.g., Sommersett's Case,* 20 How. St. Tr. 1, 80–82 (1772) (ordering an African slave freed upon finding the custodian's return insufficient). We know as well that common-law courts entertained habeas petitions brought by enemy aliens detained in England.... See *Case of Three Spanish Sailors,* 2 Black. W. 1354, 96 Eng. Rep. 775 (C.P. 1779).

We find the evidence as to the geographical scope of the writ informative, but, again, not dispositive. Petitioners argue that the site of their detention is analogous to two territories outside of England to which the writ did run: the so-called "exempt jurisdictions" like the Channel Islands and (in former times) India. [The exempt jurisdictions], while not in theory part of the realm of England, were nonetheless under the Crown's control. And there is some indication that these jurisdictions were considered sovereign territory [which would make them not analogous to present-day Guantánamo]....

British courts in India granted writs of habeas corpus to non-citizens detained in territory over which the Moghul Emperor retained formal sovereignty,[but that it had the power to issue the writ [there] does not prove that common-law courts sitting in England had the same power....

The Government argues, in turn, that Guantánamo is more closely analogous to Scotland and Hanover [which had separate legal systems and where the English writ did not run].... The prudential barriers that may have prevented the English courts from issuing the writ to Scotland and Hanover [while issuing it to Ireland and later Canada] are not relevant here [because we] have no reason to believe an order from a federal court would be disobeyed at Guantánamo. No Cuban court has jurisdiction to hear these petitioners' claims, and no law other than the laws of the United States applies at the naval station.... This is reason enough for us to discount the relevance of the Government's analogy.

Each side in the present matter argues that the very lack of a precedent on point supports its position. The Government points out there is no evidence that a court sitting in England granted habeas relief to an enemy alien detained abroad; petitioners respond there is no evidence that a court refused to do so for lack of jurisdiction.

Both arguments are premised ... upon the assumption that the historical record is complete and that the common law, if properly understood, yields a definitive answer to the questions before us. There are reasons to doubt both assumptions. Recent scholarship [notes] that most reports of 18th century habeas proceedings were not printed. And given the unique status of Guantánamo Bay and the particular dangers of terrorism in the modern age, the common-law courts may not have confronted cases with close parallels to this one. We decline, therefore, to infer too much, one way or the other, from the lack of historical evidence on point....

Drawing upon its position that at common law the writ ran only to territories over which the Crown was sovereign, the Government says the Suspension Clause affords petitioners no rights because the United States does not claim sovereignty over the place of detention.... This was the Government's position well before the events of September 11, 2001. [E.g. it was the Clinton administration's position when trying to avoid judicial review of its detention of Haitian boat people at Guantánamo in the early 1990s, ed.] But this does not end the analysis.... As commentators have noted, "'[S]overeignty' is a term used in many senses and is much abused."...

The Court has discussed the issue of the Constitution's extraterritorial application on many occasions. These decisions undermine the Government's argument that, at least as applied to non-citizens, the Constitution necessarily stops where *de jure* [formal, legal] sovereignty ends.... In ... the *Insular Cases*, the Court addressed whether the Constitution, by its own force, applies in any territory that is not a State.... The Court held that the Constitution has independent force in these territories, not contingent upon acts of legislative grace.... As the Court later made clear, "the real issue in the *Insular Cases* was not whether the Constitution extended to the Philippines or Porto Rico ... but which of its provisions were applicable by way of limitation upon the exercise of executive and legislative power in dealing with new conditions and requirements."... [A]s early as *Balzac* [*v. Porto Rico,* 258 U.S. 298, 312] in 1922, the Court took it for granted that even in unincorporated Territories the Government of the United States was bound to provide to non-citizen inhabitants "guarantees of certain fundamental personal rights declared in the Constitution."...

The necessary implication of the [Government's] argument is that by surrendering formal sovereignty over any unincorporated territory to a third party, while at the same time entering into a lease that grants total control over the territory to United States, it would be possible for the political branches to govern without legal constraint. Our basic charter cannot be contracted away like this.... To hold the political branches have the power to switch the Constitution on or off at will ... would permit a striking anomaly in our tripartite system of government, leading to a regime in which Congress and the President, not this Court, say "what the law is."...

[W]e conclude that at least three factors are relevant in determining the reach of the Suspension Clause: (1) the citizenship and status of the detainee and the adequacy of the process through which that status determination is made, (2) the nature of the sites where apprehension and then detention took place, and (3) the practical obstacles inherent in resolving the prisoner's entitlement to the writ.

Applying this framework, we note at the onset that the status of these detainees is a matter of dispute. [They] deny they are enemy combatants, [and] the procedural protections afforded ... in the CSRT hearings are far more limited, and, we conclude, fall well short of the procedures and adversarial mechanisms that would eliminate the need for habeas corpus review. [In the CSRT proceedings] the detainee is allowed to present "reasonably available" evidence, but his ability ... is limited by the circumstance of his own confinement and his lack of counsel.... And although the detainee can seek review of his status determination in the Court of Appeals, that review process cannot cure all defects in the earlier proceedings....

Guantánamo Bay ... is no transient possession. In every practical sense, Guantánamo is not abroad; it is within the constant jurisdiction of the United States.

As to the third factor, we recognize ... that there are costs to holding the Suspension Clause applicable in a case of military detention abroad. Habeas corpus proceedings may require expenditure of funds ... and may divert the attention of military personnel from other pressing tasks. While we are sensitive to these concerns, we do not find them dispositive. The Government presents no credible arguments that the military mission at Guantánamo would be compromised if habeas corpus courts had jurisdiction to hear the detainees' claims.... We hold that Art. I, Sec. 9, cl. 2, of the Constitution has full effect at Guantánamo Bay.

In light of this holding the question becomes whether the statute stripping jurisdiction to issue the writ [provides] adequate substitute procedures for habeas corpus.... In the ordinary course we would remand to the Court of Appeals to consider this question in the first instance, [but] the fact that these detainees have been denied meaningful access to a judicial forum for a period of years render[s] these cases exceptional. [I]n all likelihood a remand simply would delay ultimate resolution of the issue by this Court....

To determine the necessary scope of habeas corpus review, therefore, we must assess the CSRT process, the mechanism through which petitioners' designation as enemy combatants became final.... The most relevant [deficiencies] for our purposes are the constraints upon the detainee's ability to rebut the factual basis for the Government's assertion that he is an enemy combatant. [At] the CSRT stage the detainee has limited means to find or present evidence to challenge to Government's case against him. He does not have the assistance of counsel and may not be aware of the most crucial allegations that the Government relied upon to order his detention.... [G]iven that there are in effect no limits on the admission of hearsay evidence, ... the detainee's opportunity to question witnesses is likely to be more theoretical than real....

The DTA does not explicitly empower the Court of Appeals to order the applicant ... released should the court find that the standards and procedures used at his CSRT hearing were insufficient to justify detention. [T]he "Scope of Review" provision [of the DTA] confines the Court of Appeals' role to reviewing whether the CSRT followed the "standards and procedures issued by the Department of Defense...." [It does not give the detainee an opportunity to] present relevant exculpatory evidence that was not made part of the record in the earlier proceedings.... Although we do not hold that an adequate substitute [for the constitutional right] must duplicate it in all respects, it suffices that the Government has not established that [Congress has enacted] an adequate substitute for the [constitutional] writ of habeas corpus. MCA Section 7 thus effects an unconstitutional suspension of the writ.

[T]he question remains whether there are prudential barriers to habeas corpus review under these circumstances.... In cases involving foreign citizens detained abroad ... it likely would be both ... impractical and unprecedented ... to assume that habeas corpus would be available at the moment the prisoner is taken into custody. [P]roper deference can be accorded to reasonable procedures for screening and initial detention under lawful and proper conditions of confinement and treatment for a reasonable period of time.... And there has been no showing that the Executive faces such onerous burdens that it cannot respond to habeas corpus actions.... While some delay in fashioning new procedures is unavoidable, the costs of delay can no longer be borne by those who are held in custody. The detainees in these cases are entitled to a prompt habeas corpus hearing....

Certain accommodations can be made to reduce the burden habeas corpus proceedings will place on the military without impermissibly diluting the protections of the writ [such as] channeling future cases to one district court.... We recognize ... that the Government has a legitimate interest in protecting sources and methods of intelligence gathering.... These and other remaining questions are within the expertise and competence of the District Court to address in the first instance....

JUSTICE SOUTER, with whom JUSTICE GINSBURG and JUSTICE BREYER join, concurring....

A ... fact insufficiently appreciated by the dissents is the length of the disputed imprisonments; some of the prisoners represented here today have been locked up for six years. Hence the hollow ring when the dissenters suggest that the Court is somehow precipitating the judiciary into reviewing claims that the military [and the Court of Appeals] could handle [under the DTA] in a reasonable period of time.... These suggestions of judicial haste are all the more out of place given the Court's realistic acknowledgement that in periods of exigency the tempo of any habeas review must reflect the immediate peril facing the country.

CHIEF JUSTICE ROBERTS, with whom JUSTICE SCALIA, JUSTICE THOMAS, and JUSTICE ALITO join, dissenting.

Today the Court strikes down as inadequate the most generous set of procedural protections ever afforded aliens detained by this country as enemy combatants. The political branches crafted these procedures amidst an ongoing military conflict, after much careful investigation and thorough debate. The Court rejects them today out of hand, without bothering to say what due process rights the detainees possess, without explaining how the statute fails to vindicate those rights, and before a single petitioner has even attempted to avail himself of the law's operation.... One cannot help but think, after surveying the modest practical results of the majority's ambitious opinion, that this decision is not really about the detainees at all, but about control of federal policy regarding enemy combatants....

JUSTICE SCALIA, with whom THE CHIEF JUSTICE, JUSTICE THOMAS, and JUSTICE ALITO join, dissenting....

The game of bait-and-switch that today's opinion plays upon the Nation's Commander in Chief will make the war harder on us. It will almost certainly cause more Americans to be killed.... In the short term ... the decision is devastating. At least 30 of those prisoners hitherto released from Guantánamo Bay have returned to the battlefield. Some have been captured or killed. But others have succeeded in carrying on their atrocities against innocent civilians.... These, mind you, were detainees whom *the military* had concluded were not enemy combatants.... Henceforth, ... how to handle enemy prisoners in this war will ultimately lie with the branch that knows the least about national security concerns that the subject entails....

It is nonsensical to interpret [the habeas clause] in light of some general "separation-of-powers principles" dreamed up by the Court. Rather they must be interpreted to mean what they were understood to mean when the people ratified them.

… "Manipulation" of the territorial reach of the writ by the Judiciary poses just as much threat to the proper separation of powers as "manipulation" by the Executive. [And] manipulation is what is afoot here.…

Notes and Questions

1. *Reconsideration.* Initially, Justices Kennedy and Stevens voted against granting certiorari in the *Boumediene* case, but changed their minds after receiving an affidavit from a former Army lawyer who described, on the basis of direct personal knowledge, how rigged the Combat Status Review Tribunals (CSRTs) were.

2. *Scope of the writ.* Historically, the writ of habeas corpus only exists to challenge the legality of an indefinite detention, not to question the mistreatment of a prisoner. Does the majority hint that the writ might someday be expanded to challenge torture and cruelty?

3. *How to read a constitution.* Do you agree with Justice Kennedy that a specific provision of the Constitution, like the Habeas Clause, must be read in light of history, precedent, and the broader constitutional scheme? Or do you agree with Justice Scalia, that the clause should be read only in light of the common law, as it was understood at the time the Constitution was ratified?

4. *No habeas for prisoners at Bagram.* On May 21, 2010, the Court of Appeals for the District of Columbia held that aliens seized in Pakistan and Thailand and imprisoned by the United States at Bagram Air Base in Afghanistan had no constitutional or statutory right to challenge the legality of their detention in federal court. Detention at Bagram differs from detention at Guantanamo, the court ruled, because it occurs in "an active theater of war" that is not under the *de facto* or *de jure* sovereignty of the United States. The judges added that "We do not ignore the arguments [that the executive] might be able 'to evade judicial review … by transferring detainees into active conflict zones [and] thereby … switch the Constitution on or off at will,'" but found no evidence that the government had done that. Are you persuaded? Wasn't Guantanamo chosen instead of Guam precisely to avoid habeas challenges? Should judges take judicial notice of such facts "notorious in the community" but not on the record of the case below? *Al Maqualeh, et al. v. Gates*, No. 09-5265 (D.C. Cir. 2010). The deputy attorney general who won this decision for the Obama administration was Neal Kumar Katyal, the same attorney who won the *Hamdan* decision for the prisoners in 2006.

The Constitution of the United States of America

We the People of the United States, in Order to form a more perfect Union, establish Justice, insure domestic Tranquility, provide for the common defence, promote the general Welfare, and secure the Blessings of Liberty to ourselves and our Posterity, do ordain and establish this Constitution for the United States of America.

Article I

Section 1. All legislative Powers herein granted shall be vested in a Congress of the United States, which shall consist of a Senate and House of Representatives.

Section 2. [1] The House of Representatives shall be composed of Members chosen every second Year by the People of the several States, and the Electors in each State shall have the Qualifications requisite for Electors of the most numerous Branch of the State Legislature.

[2] No Person shall be a Representative who shall not have attained to the Age of twenty five Years, and been seven Years a Citizen of the United States, and who shall not, when elected, be an Inhabitant of that State in which he shall be chosen.

[3] Representatives and direct Taxes shall be apportioned among the several States which may be included within this Union, according to their respective Numbers, which shall be determined by adding to the whole Number of free Persons, including those bound to Service for a Term of Years, and excluding Indians not taxed, three fifths of all other Persons. The actual Enumeration shall be made within three Years after the first Meeting of the Congress of the United States, and within every subsequent Term of ten Years, in such Manner as they shall by Law direct. The Number of Representatives shall not exceed one for every thirty Thousand, but each State shall have at Least one Representative; and until such enumeration shall be made, the State of New Hampshire shall be entitled to chuse three, Massachusetts eight, Rhode Island and Providence Plantations one, Connecticut five, New York six, New Jersey four, Pennsylvania eight, Delaware one, Maryland six, Virginia ten, North Carolina five, South Carolina five, and Georgia three.

[4] When vacancies happen in the Representation from any State, the Executive Authority thereof shall issue Writs of Election to fill such Vacancies.

[5] The House of Representatives shall chuse their Speaker and other Officers; and shall have the sole Power of Impeachment.

Section 3. [1] The Senate of the United States shall be composed of two Senators from each State, chosen by the Legislature thereof, for six Years; and each Senator shall have one Vote.

[2] Immediately after they shall be assembled in Consequence of the first Election, they shall be divided as equally as may be into three Classes. The Seats of the Senators of the first Class shall be vacated at the Expiration of the Second Year, of the second Class at the Expiration of the fourth Year, and of the third Class at the Expiration of the sixth Year, so that one third may be chosen every second Year; and if Vacancies happen by Resignation, or otherwise, during the Recess of the Legislature of any State, the Executive thereof may make temporary Appointments until the next Meeting of the Legislature, which shall then fill such Vacancies.

[3] No Person shall be a Senator who shall not have attained to the Age of thirty Years, and been nine Years a Citizen of the United States, and who shall not, when elected, be an Inhabitant of that State for which he shall be chosen.

[4] The Vice President of the United States shall be President of the Senate, but shall have no Vote, unless they be equally divided.

[5] The Senate shall chuse their other Officers, and also a President pro tempore, in the Absence of the Vice President, or when he shall exercise the Office of President of the United States.

[6] The Senate shall have the sole Power to try all Impeachments. When sitting for that Purpose, they shall be on Oath or Affirmation. When the President of the United States is tried, the Chief Justice shall preside: And no Person shall be convicted without the Concurrence of two thirds of the Members present.

[7] Judgment in Cases of Impeachment shall not extend further than to removal from Office, and disqualification to hold and enjoy any Office of honor, Trust, or Profit under the United States: but the Party convicted shall nevertheless be liable and subject to Indictment, Trial, Judgment, and Punishment, according to Law.

Section 4. [1] The Times, Places and Manner of holding Elections for Senators and Representatives, shall be prescribed in each State by the Legislature thereof; but the Congress may at any time by Law make or alter such Regulations, except as to the Places of chusing Senators.

[2] The Congress shall assemble at least once in every Year, and such Meeting shall be on the first Monday in December, unless they shall by Law appoint a different Day.

Section 5. [1] Each House shall be the Judge of the Elections, Returns, and Qualifications of its own Members, and a Majority of each shall constitute a Quorum to do Business; but a smaller Number may adjourn from day to day, and may be authorized to compel the Attendance of absent Members, in such Manner, and under such Penalties as each House may provide.

[2] Each House may determine the Rules of its Proceedings, punish its Members for disorderly Behaviour, and, with the Concurrence of two thirds, expel a Member.

[3] Each House shall keep a Journal of its Proceedings, and from time to time publish the same, excepting such Parts as may in their judgment require Secrecy; and the Yeas and Nays of the Members of either House on any question shall, at the Desire of one fifth of those Present, be entered on the Journal.

[4] Neither House, during the Session of Congress, shall, without the Consent of the other, adjourn for more than three days, nor to any other Place than that in which the two Houses shall be sitting.

Section 6. [1] The Senators and Representatives shall receive a Compensation for their Services, to be ascertained by Law, and paid out of the Treasury of the United States.

They shall in all Cases, except Treason, Felony and Breach of the Peace, be privileged from Arrest during their Attendance at the Session of their respective Houses, and in going to and returning from the same; and for any Speech or Debate in either House, they shall not be questioned in any other Place.

[2] No Senator or Representative shall, during the time for which he was elected, be appointed to any civil Office under the Authority of the United States, which shall have been created, or the Emoluments whereof shall have been increased during such time; and no Person holding any Office under the United States, shall be a Member of either House during his Continuance in Office.

Section 7. [1] All Bills for raising Revenue shall originate in the House of Representatives; but the Senate may propose or concur with Amendments as on other Bills.

[2] Every Bill which shall have passed the House of Representatives and the Senate, shall, before it become a Law, be presented to the President of the United States; If he approves he shall sign it, but if not he shall return it, with his Objections to that House in which it shall have originated, who shall enter the Objections at large on their Journal, and proceed to reconsider it. If after such Reconsideration two thirds of that House shall agree to pass the Bill, it shall be sent, together with the Objections, to the other House, by which it shall likewise be reconsidered, and if approved by two thirds of that House, it shall become a Law. But in all such cases the Votes of both Houses shall be determined by yeas and Nays, and the Names of the Persons voting for and against the Bill shall be entered an the Journal of each House respectively. If any Bill shall not be returned by the President within ten Days (Sundays excepted) after it shall have been presented to him, the Same shall be a Law, in like Manner as if he had signed it, unless the Congress by their Adjournment prevent its Return in which Case it shall not be a Law.

[3] Every Order, Resolution, or Vote, to Which the Concurrence of the Senate and House of Representatives may be necessary (except on a question of Adjournment) shall be presented to the President of the United States; and before the Same shall take Effect, shall be approved by him, or being disapproved by him, shall be repassed by two thirds of the Senate and House of Representatives, according to the Rules and Limitations prescribed in the Case of a Bill.

Section 8. [1] The Congress shall have Power To lay and collect Taxes, Duties, Imposts and Excises, to pay the Debts and provide for the common Defence and general Welfare of the United States; but all Duties, Imposts and Excises shall be uniform throughout the United States;

[2] To borrow Money on the credit of the United States:

[3] To regulate Commerce with foreign Nations, and among the several States and with the Indian Tribes;

[4] To establish an uniform Rule of Naturalization, and uniform Laws on the subject of Bankruptcies throughout the United States;

[5] To coin Money, regulate the Value thereof, and of foreign Coin, and fix the Standard of Weights and Measures;

[6] To provide for the Punishment of counterfeiting the Securities and current Coin of the United States;

[7] To Establish Post Offices and Post Roads;

[8] To Promote the Progress of Science and useful Arts, by securing for limited Times to Authors and Inventors the exclusive Right to their respective Writings and Discoveries;

[9] To constitute Tribunals inferior to the supreme Court;

[10] To define and punish Piracies and Felonies committed on the high Seas, and Offences against the Law of Nations:

[11] To declare War, grant Letters of Marque and Reprisal, and make Rules concerning Captures on Land and Water;

[12] To raise and support Armies, but no Appropriation of Money to that Use shall be for a longer Term than two Years;

[13] To provide and maintain a Navy;

[14] To make Rules for the Government and Regulation of the land and naval Forces;

[15] To provide for calling forth the Militia to execute the Laws of the Union, suppress Insurrections and repel Invasions;

[16] To provide for organizing, arming, and disciplining, the Militia, and for governing such Part of them as may be employed in the Service of the United States, reserving to the States respectively, the Appointment of the Officers, and the Authority of training the Militia according to the discipline prescribed by Congress;

[17] To exercise exclusive Legislation in all Cases whatsoever, over such District (not exceeding ten Miles square) as may, by Cession of particular States, and the Acceptance of Congress, become the Seat of the Government of the United States, and to exercise like Authority over all Places purchased by the Consent of the Legislature of the State in which the Same shall be, for the Erection of Forts, Magazines, Arsenals, dock-Yards, and other needful Buildings;—And

[18] To make all Laws which shall be necessary and proper for carrying into Execution the foregoing Powers, and all other Powers vested by this Constitution in the Government of the United States, or in any Department or Officer thereof.

Section 9. [1] The Migration or Importation of Such Persons as any of the States now existing shall think proper to admit, shall not be prohibited by the Congress prior to the Year one thousand eight hundred and eight, but a Tax or duty may be imposed on such Importation, not exceeding ten dollars for each Person.

[2] The Privilege of the Writ of Habeas Corpus shall not be suspended, unless when in Cases of Rebellion or Invasion the public Safety may require it.

[3] No Bill of Attainder or ex post facto Law shall be passed.

[4] No Capitation, or other direct, Tax shall be laid, unless in Proportion to the Census or Enumeration herein before directed to be taken.

[5] No Tax or Duty shall be laid on Articles exported from any State.

[6] No Preference shall be given by any Regulation of Commerce or Revenue to the Ports of one State over those of another: nor shall Vessels bound to, or from, one State be obliged to enter, clear, or pay Duties in another.

[7] No Money shall be drawn from the Treasury, but in Consequence of Appropriations made by Law: and a regular Statement and Account of the Receipts and Expenditures of all public Money shall be published from time to time.

[8] No Title of Nobility shall be granted by the United States; And no Person holding any Office of Profit or Trust under them, shall, without the Consent of the Congress, accept of any present, Emolument, Office, or Title, of any kind whatever, from any King, Prince, or foreign State.

Section 10. [1] No State shall enter into any Treaty, Alliance, or Confederation; grant Letters of Marque and Reprisal; coin Money; emit Bills of Credit; make any Thing but gold and silver Coin a Tender in Payment of Debts; pass any Bill of Attainder, ex post facto Law, or Law impairing the Obligation of Contracts, or grant any Title of Nobility.

[2] No State shall, without the Consent of the Congress, lay any Imposts or Duties on Imports or Exports, except what may be absolutely necessary for executing its inspection Laws; and the net Produce of all Duties and Imposts, laid by any State on Imports or Exports, shall be for the Use of the Treasury of the United States; and all such Laws shall be subject to the Revision and Controul of the Congress.

[3] No State shall, without the Consent of Congress, lay any Duty of Tonnage, keep Troops, or Ships of

War in time of Peace, enter into any Agreement or Compact with another State, or with a foreign Power, or engage in War, unless actually invaded, or in such imminent Danger as will not admit of delay.

Article II

Section 1. [1] The executive Power shall be vested in a President of the United States of America, He shall hold his office during the Term of four Years, and, together with the Vice president, chosen for the same Term, be elected, as follows:

[2] Each State shall appoint, in such Manner as the Legislature thereof may direct, a Number of Electors, equal to the whole Number of Senators and Representatives to which the State may be entitled in the Congress; but no Senator or Representative, or Person holding an Office of Trust or Profit under the United States, shall be appointed an Elector.

[3] The Electors shall meet in their respective States, and vote by Ballot for two Persons, of whom one at least shall not be an Inhabitant of the same State with themselves. And they shall make a List of all the Persons voted for, and of the Number of Votes for each; which List they shall sign and certify, and transmit sealed to the Seat of the Government of the United States, directed to the President of the Senate. The President of the Senate shall, in the Presence of the Senate and House of Representatives, open all the Certificates, and the Votes shall then be counted. The Person having the greatest Number of Votes shall be the President, if such Number be a Majority of the whole Number of Electors appointed; and if there be more than one who have such Majority, and have an equal Number of Votes, then the House of Representatives shall immediately chuse by Ballot one of them for President; and if no Person have a Majority, then from the five highest on the List the said House shall in like Manner chuse the President. But in chusing the President, the Votes shall be taken by States, the Representation from each State having one Vote; A quorum for this Purpose shall consist of a Member or Members from two thirds of the States, and a Majority of all the States shall be necessary to a Choice. In every Case, after the Choice of the President, the Person having the greater Number of Votes of the Electors shall be the Vice President. But if there should remain two or more who have equal Votes, the Senate shall chuse from them by Ballot the Vice President.

[4] The Congress may determine the Time of chusing the Electors, and the Day on which they shall give their Votes; which Day shall be the same throughout the United States.

[5] No person except a natural born Citizen, Or a Citizen of the United States, at the time of the Adoption of this Constitution, shall be eligible to the Office of President; nei-

ther shall any Person be eligible to that Office who shall not have attained to the Age of thirty five Years, and been fourteen Years a Resident within the United States.

[6] In case of the removal of the President from Office, or of his Death, Resignation or Inability to discharge the Powers and Duties of the said Office, the Same shall devolve on the Vice President, and the Congress may by Law provide for the case of Removal, Death, Resignation or Inability, both of the President and Vice President, declaring what Officer shall then act as President, and such Officer shall act accordingly, until the Disability be removed, or a President shall be elected.

[7] The President shall, at stated Times, receive for his Services, a Compensation, which shall neither be increased nor diminished during the Period for which he shall have been elected, and he shall not receive within that Period any other Emolument front the United States, or any of them.

[8] Before he enter on the Execution of his Office, he shall take the following Oath or Affirmation: "I do solemnly swear (or affirm) that I will faithfully execute the Office of President of the United States, and will to the best of my Ability, preserve, protect and defend the Constitution of the United States."

Section 2. [1] The President shall be Commander in Chief of the Army and Navy of the United States, and of the militia of the several States, when called into the actual Service of the United States; he may require the Opinion, in writing, of the principal Officer in each of the executive Departments, upon any Subject relating to the Duties of their respective Offices, and he shall have Power to grant Reprieves and Pardons for Offenses against the United States, except in Cases of Impeachment.

[2] He shall have Power, by and with the Advice and Consent of the Senate, to make Treaties, provided two thirds of the Senators present concur; and he shall nominate, and by and with the Advice and Consent of the Senate, shall appoint Ambassadors, other public Ministers and Consuls, Judges of the supreme Court, and all other Officers of the United States, whose Appointments are not herein otherwise provided for, and which shall be established by Law; but the Congress may by law vest the Appointment of such inferior Officers, as they think proper, in the President alone, in the Courts of law, or in the Heads of Departments.

[3] The President shall have Power to fill up all Vacancies that may happen during the Recess of the Senate, by granting Commissions which shall expire at the End of their next Session.

Section 3. He shall from time to time give to the Congress Information of the State of the Union, and recommend to their Consideration such Measures as he shall judge necessary and expedient; he may, on extraordinary Occasions, convene both Houses or either of them, and in Case of Disagreement between them, with Respect to the Time of Adjournment, he may adjourn them to such Time as he shall think proper; he shall receive Ambassadors and other public Ministers; he shall take Care that the laws be faithfully executed, and shall Commission all the Officers of the United States.

Section 4. The President, Vice President and all civil Officers of the United States, shall be removed from Office on Impeachment for, and Conviction of, Treason, Bribery, or other high Crimes and Misdemeanors.

Article III

Section 1. The judicial Power of the United States, shall be vested in one supreme Court, and in such inferior Courts as the Congress may from time to time ordain and establish. The Judges, both of the supreme and inferior Courts, shall hold their Offices during good Behaviour, and shall, at stated Times, receive for their Services a Compensation, which shall not be diminished during their Continuance in Office.

Section 2. [1] The judicial Power shall extend to all Cases, in Law and Equity, arising under this Constitution, the Laws of the United States, and Treaties made, or which shall be made, under their Authority;—to all Cases affecting Ambassadors, other public Ministers and Consuls;—to all Cases of admiralty and maritime Jurisdiction;—to Controversies to which the United States shall be a Party;—to Controversies between two or more States;—between a State and Citizens of another State;—between Citizens of different States;—between Citizens of the same State claiming Lands under the Grants of different States, and between State, or the Citizens thereof, and foreign States, Citizens or Subjects.

[2] In all Cases affecting Ambassadors, other public Ministers and Consuls, and those in which a State shall be a Party, the supreme Court shall have original Jurisdiction. In all other Cases before mentioned, the supreme Court shall have appellate Jurisdiction, both as to Law and Fact, with such Exceptions, and under such Regulations as the Congress shall make.

[3] The trial of all Crimes, except in Cases of Impeachment, shall be by Jury; and such Trial shall be held in the State where the said Crimes shall have been committed; but when not committed within any State, the Trial shall be at such Place or Places as the Congress may by Law have directed.

Section 3. [1] Treason against the United States, shall consist only in levying War against them, or, in adhering to their Enemies, giving them Aid and Comfort. No Person shall be convicted of Treason unless on the Testimony two Witnesses to the same overt Act, or on Confession in open Court.

[2] The Congress shall have Power to declare the Punishment of Treason, but no Attainder of Treason shall work Corruption of Blood, or Forfeiture except during the Life of the Person attainted.

Article IV

Section 1. Full Faith and Credit shall be given in each State to the public Acts, Records, and judicial Proceedings of every other State. And the Congress may by general laws prescribe the Manner in which such Acts, Records and Proceedings shall be proved, and the Effect thereof.

Section 2. [1] The Citizens of each State shall be entitled to all Privileges and Immunities of Citizens in the several States.

[2] A Person charged in any State with Treason, Felony, or other Crime, who shall flee from Justice, and be found in another State, shall on demand of the executive Authority of the State from which he fled, be delivered up, to be removed to the State having Jurisdiction of the Crime.

[3] No Person held to Service or Labour in one State, under the Laws thereof, escaping into another, shall, in Consequence of any Law or Regulation therein, be discharged from such Service or Labour, but shall be delivered up on Claim of the Party to whom such Service or Labour may be due.

Section 3. [1] New States may be admitted by the Congress into this Union; but no new State shall be formed or erected within the Jurisdiction of any other State; nor any State be formed by the Junction of two or more States, or parts of States, without the Consent of the Legislatures of the States concerned as well as of the Congress.

[2] The Congress shall have Power to dispose of and make all needful Rules and Regulations respecting the Territory or other Property belonging to the United States; and nothing in this Constitution shall be so construed as to Prejudice any Claims of the United States, or of any particular State.

Section 4. The United States shall guarantee to every State in this Union a Republican Form of Government, and shall protect each of them against Invasion; and on Application of the Legislature, or of the Executive (when the legislature cannot be convened) against domestic Violence.

Article V

The Congress, whenever two thirds of both Houses shall deem it necessary, shall propose Amendments to this Constitution, or, on the Application of the Legislatures of two thirds of the several States, shall call a Convention for proposing Amendments, which, in either Case, shall be valid to all Intents and Purposes, as part of this Constitution, when ratified by the Legislatures of three fourths of the several States, or by Conventions in three fourths thereof, as the one or the other Mode of Ratification may be proposed by the Congress: Provided that no Amendment which may be made prior to the Year One thousand eight hundred and eight shall in any Manner affect the first and fourth Clauses in the Ninth Section of the first Article; and that no State, without its consent, shall be deprived of its equal Suffrage in the Senate.

Article VI

[1] All Debts contracted and Engagements entered into, before the Adoption of this Constitution, shall be as valid against the United States under this Constitution, as under the Confederation.

[2] This Constitution, and the Laws of the United States which shall be made in Pursuance thereof; and all Treaties made, or which shall be made, under the Authority of the United States, shall be the supreme Law of the Land; and the Judges in every State shall be bound thereby, any Thing in the Constitution or Laws of any State to the Contrary notwithstanding.

[3] The Senators and Representatives before mentioned, and the Members of the several State Legislatures, and all executive and judicial Officers, both of the United States and of the several States, shall be bound by Oath or Affirmation, to support this Constitution; but no religious Test shall ever be required as a Qualification to any Office or public Trust under the United States.

Article VII

The Ratification of the Conventions of nine States shall be sufficient for the Establishment of this Constitution between the States so ratifying the Same.

Articles in Addition to, and Amendment of, the Constitution of The United States of America, Proposed by Congress and Ratified by the Legislatures of the Several States Pursuant to the Fifth Article of the Original Constitution:

Amendment I [1791]

Congress shall make no law respecting an establishment of religion, or prohibiting the free exercise thereof; or abridging the freedom of speech, or of the press; or the right of the people peaceably to assemble, and to petition the Government for a redress of grievances.

Amendment II [1791]

A well regulated Militia, being necessary to the security of a free State, the right of the people to keep and bear Arms, shall not be infringed.

Amendment III [1791]

No Soldier shall, in time of peace be quartered in any house, without the consent of the Owner, nor in time of war, but in a manner to be prescribed by law.

Amendment IV [1791]

The right of the people to be secure in their persons, houses, papers, and effects, against unreasonable searches and seizures, shall not be violated, and no Warrants shall issue, but upon probable cause, supported by Oath or affirmation, and particularly describing the place to be searched, and the persons or things to be seized.

Amendment V [1791]

No person shall be held to answer for a capital, or otherwise infamous crime, unless on a presentment or indictment of a Grand Jury, except in cases arising in the land or naval forces, or in the Militia, when in actual service in time of War or public danger; nor shall any person be subject for the same offence to be twice put in jeopardy of life or limb; or shall be compelled in any criminal case to be a witness against himself, nor be deprived of life, liberty, or property, without due process of law; nor shall private property be taken for public use without just compensation.

Amendment VI [1791]

In all criminal prosecutions, the accused shall enjoy the right to a speedy and public trial, by an impartial jury of the State and district wherein the crime shall have been committed, which district shall have been previously ascertained by law, and to be informed of the nature and cause of the accusation; to be confronted with the witnesses against him; to have compulsory process for obtaining witnesses in his favor, and to have the Assistance of Counsel for his defence.

Amendment VII [1791]

In Suits at common law, where the value in controversy shall exceed twenty dollars, the right of trial by jury shall be preserved, and no fact tried by jury, shall be otherwise re-examined in any Court of the United States, than according to the rules of the common law.

Amendment VIII [1791]

Excessive bail shall not be required, nor excessive fines imposed, nor cruel and unusual punishments inflicted.

Amendment IX [1791]

The enumeration in the Constitution, of certain rights, shall not be construed to deny or disparage others retained by the people.

Amendment X [1791]

The powers not delegated to the United States by the Constitution, nor prohibited by it to the States, are reserved to the States respectively, or to the people.

Amendment XI [1798]

The Judicial power of the United States shall not be construed to extend to any suit in law or equity, commenced or prosecuted against one of the United States by Citizens of another State, or by Citizens or Subjects of any Foreign State.

Amendment XII [1804]

The Electors shall meet to their respective states and vote by ballot for President and Vice-President, one of whom, at least, shall not be an inhabitant of the same state with themselves; they shall name in their ballots the person voted for as President, and in distinct ballots the person voted for as Vice-President, and they shall make distinct lists of all persons voted for as President, and of all persons voted for as Vice-President, and of the number of votes for each, which lists they shall sign and certify, and transmit sealed to the seat of the government of the United States, directed to the President of the Senate;—The President of the Senate shall, in the presence of the Senate and House of Representatives, open all the certificates and the votes shall then be counted;—The person having the greatest number of votes for President, shall be the President, if such number be a majority of the whole number of Electors appointed; and if no person have such majority, then from the persons having the highest numbers not exceeding three on the list of those voted for as President, the House of Representatives shall choose immediately, by ballot, the President. But in choosing the President, the votes shall be taken by states, the representation from each state having one vote; a quorum for this purpose shall consist of a member or members from two-thirds of the states, and a majority of all the states shall be necessary to a choice. And if the House of Representatives shall not choose a President whenever the right of choice shall devolve upon them before the fourth day of March next following, then the Vice-President shall act as President, as in the case of the death or other constitutional disability of the President.—The person having the greatest number of votes as Vice-President, shall be the Vice-President, if such number be a majority of the whole number of Electors appointed, and if no person have a majority, then from the two highest numbers on the list, the Senate shall choose the Vice-President; a quorum for the purpose shall consist of two-thirds of the whole number of Senators, and a majority of the whole number shall be necessary to a choice. But no person constitutionally ineligible to the office of President shall be eligible to that of Vice-President of the United States.

Amendment XIII [1865]

Section 1. Neither slavery nor involuntary servitude, except as a punishment for crime whereof the party shall have been duly convicted, shall exist within the United States, or any place subject to their jurisdiction.

Section 2. Congress shall have power to enforce this article by appropriate legislation.

Amendment XIV [1868]

Section 1. All persons born or naturalized in the United States, and subject to the jurisdiction thereof, are citizens of the United States and of the State wherein they reside. No State shall make or enforce any law which shall abridge the privileges or immunities of citizens of the United States; nor shall any State deprive any person of life, liberty, or property, without due process of law; nor deny to any person within its jurisdiction the equal protection of the laws.

Section 2. Representatives shall be apportioned among the several States according to their respective numbers, counting the whole somber of persons in each State, excluding

Indians not taxed. But when the right to vote at any election for the choice of electors for President and Vice President of the United States, Representatives in Congress, the Executive and Judicial officers of a State, or the members of the Legislature thereof, is denied to any of the male inhabitants of such State, being twenty-one years of age, and citizens of the United States, or in any way abridged, except for participation in rebellion, or other crime, the basis of representation therein shall be reduced in the proportion which the number of such male citizens shall bear to the whole number of male citizens twenty-one years of age in such State.

Section 3. No person shall be a Senator or Representative in Congress, or elector of President and Vice President, or hold any office, civil or military, under the United Stases, or under any State, who having previously taken an oath, as a member of Congress, or as an officer of the United States, or as a member of any State legislature, or as an executive or judicial officer of any State, to support the Constitution of the United States, shall have engaged in insurrection or rebellion against the same, or given aid or comfort to the enemies thereof. But Congress may by a vote of two-thirds of each House, remove such disability.

Section 4. The validity of she public debt of the United States, authorized by law, including debts incurred for payment of pensions and bounties for services in suppressing insurrection or rebellion, shall not be questioned. But neither the United States nor any State shall assume or pay any debt or obligation incurred in aid of in insurrection or rebellion against the United States, or any claim for the loss or emancipation of any slave; but all such debts, obligations and claims shall be held illegal and void.

Section 5. The Congress shall have power to enforce, by appropriate legislation, the provisions of this article.

Amendment XV [1870]

Section 1. The right of citizens of the United States to vote shall not be denied or abridged by the United States or by any State on account of race, color, or previous condition of servitude.

Section 2. The Congress shall have power to enforce this article by all appropriate legislation.

Amendment XVI [1913]

The Congress shall have power to lay and collect taxes on incomes, from whatever source derived, without apportionment among the several States, and without regard to any census or enumeration.

Amendment XVII [1913]

[1] The Senate of the United States shall be composed of two Senators from each State, elected by the people thereof, for six years; and each Senator shall have one vote. The Electors in each State shall have the qualifications requisite for electors of the most numerous branch of the State legislatures.

[2] When vacancies happen in the representation of any State to the Senate the executive authority of such State shall issue writs of election to fill such vacancies: *Provided*, That the legislature of any State may empower the executive thereof to make temporary appointments until the people fill the vacancies by election as the legislature may direct.

[3] This amendment shall not be so construed as to affect the election or term of any Senator chosen before it becomes valid as part of the Constitution.

Amendment XVIII [1919]

Section 1. After one year from the ratification of this article the manufacture, sale, or transportation of intoxicating liquors within, the importation thereof into, or the exportation thereof from the United States and all territory subject to the jurisdiction thereof for beverage purposes is hereby prohibited.

Section 2. The Congress and the several States shall have concurrent power to enforce this article by appropriate legislation.

Section 3. This article shall be inoperative unless it shall have been ratified as an amendment to the Constitution by the legislatures of the several States, as provided in the Constitution, within seven years from the date of the submission hereof to the States of the Congress.

Amendment XIX [1920]

[1] The right of citizens of the United States to vote shall not be denied or abridged by the United States or by an any State on account of sex.

[2] Congress shall have power to enforce this article by appropriate legislation.

Amendment XX [1933]

Section 1. The terms of the President and Vice president shall end at noon on the 20th day of January, and the terms of Senators and Representatives at noon on the 3d day of January, of the years is which such terms would have ended if this article had not been ratified; and the terms of their successors shall then begin.

Section 2. The Congress shall assemble at least once in every year, and such meeting shall begin at noon on the 3d day of January, unless they shall by law appointment a different day.

Section 3. If, at the time fixed for the beginning of the term of the President, the President elect shall have died, the Vice President elect shall become President. If the President shall not have been chosen before the time fixed for the beginning of his term, or if the President elect shall have failed to qualify, then the Vice President elect shall act as President until a President shall save qualified; and the Congress may by law provide for the case wherein neither a President elect nor a Vice President elect shall have qualified, declaring who shall then act as President, or the manner in which one who is to act shall be selected, and such person shall act accordingly until a President or Vice President shall have qualified.

Section 4. The Congress may by law provide for the case of the death of any of the persons from whom the House of Representatives may choose a President whenever the right of choice shall have devolved upon them, and for the case of the death of any of the persons from whom the Senate may choose a Vice President whenever the right of choice shall have devolved upon them.

Section 5. Sections 1 and 2 shall take effect on the 15th day of October following the ratification of this article.

Section 6. This article shall be inoperative unless it shall have been ratified as an amendment to the Constitution by the legislatures of three-fourths of the several States within seven years from the date of its submission.

Amendment XXI [1933]

Section 1. The eighteenth article of amendment to the Constitution of the United States is herein repealed.

Section 2. The transportation or importation into any State, Territory, or possession of the United States for delivery or use therein of intoxicating liquors, in violation of the laws thereof, is hereby prohibited.

Section 3. This article shall be inoperative unless it shall have been ratified as an amendment to the Constitution by Conventions in the several States, as provided in the Constitution, within seven years from the date of the submission hereof to the States by the Congress.

Amendment XXII [1951]

Section 1. No person shall be elected to the office of the President more than twice, and no person who has held the office of President, or acted as President, for more than two years of a term to which some other person was elected President shall be elected to the office of President more than once. But this Article shall not apply to any person holding the office of President when this Article was proposed by the Congress, and shall not prevent any person who may be holding the office of President, or acting as President, during the term within which this Article becomes operative from holding the office of President or acting as President during the remainder of such term.

Section 2. This article shall be inoperative unless it shall have been ratified as amendment to the Constitution by the legislatures of three-fourths of the several States within seven years from the date of its submission to the States by the Congress.

Amendment XXIII [1961]

Section 1. The District constituting the seat of Government of the United States shall appoint in such manner as the Congress may direct:

A number of electors of President and Vice President equal to the whole number of Senators and Representatives in Congress to which the District would be entitled if it were a State, but in no event more than the least populous state; they shall be in addition to those appointed by the states, but they shall be considered, for the purposes of the election of President and Vice President, to be electors appointed by a state; and they shall meet in the District and perform such duties as provided by the twelfth article of amendment.

Section 2. The Congress shall have power to enforce this article by appropriate legislation.

Amendment XXIV [1964]

Section 1. The right of citizens of the United States to vote in any primary or other election for President or Vice President, for electors for President or Vice President, or for Senator or Representative in Congress, shall not be denied or abridged by the United States or any State by reason of failure to pay any poll tax or other tax.

Section 2. The Congress shall have power to enforce this article by appropriate legislation.

Amendment XXV [1967]

Section 1. In case of the removal of the President from office or of his death or resignation, the Vice President shall become President.

Section 2. Whenever there is a vacancy in the office of the Vice President, the President shall nominate a Vice President who shall take office upon confirmation by a majority vote of both Houses of Congress.

Section 3. Whenever the President transmits to the President pro tempore of the Senate and the Speaker of the House of Representatives his written declaration that he is unable to discharge the powers and duties of his office, and until he transmits to them a written declaration to the contrary, such powers and duties shall be discharged by the Vice President as Acting President.

Section 4. Whenever the Vice President and a majority of either the principal officers of the executive departments or of such other body as Congress may by law provide, transmit to the President pro tempore of the Senate and the Speaker of the House of Representatives their written declaration that the President is unable to discharge the powers and duties of his office, the Vice President shall immediately assume the Powers and duties of the office as Acting President.

Thereafter, when the President transmits to the President pro tempore of the Senate and the Speaker of the House of Representatives his written declaration that no inability exists, he shall resume the powers and duties of his office unless the Vice President and a majority of either the principal officers of the executive department or of such other body as Congress may by law provide, transmit within four days to the President pro tempore of the Senate and the Speaker of the House of Representatives their written declaration that the President is unable to discharge the powers and duties of his office. Thereupon Congress shall decide the issue, assembling within forty-eight hours for that purpose if not in session. If the Congress, within twenty-one days after receipt of the latter written declaration, or, if Congress is not in session, within twenty-one days after Congress is required to assemble, determines by two-thirds vote of both Houses that the President is unable to discharge the powers and duties of his office, the Vice President shall continue to discharge the same as Acting President; otherwise, the President shall resume the powers and duties of his office.

Amendment XXVI [1971]

Section 1. The right of citizens of the United States, who are eighteen years of age or older, to vote shall not be denied or abridged by the United States or by any State on account of age.

Section 2. The Congress shall have power to enforce this article by appropriate legislation.

Amendment XXVII [1992]

No law, varying the compensation for the services of the Senators and Representatives, shall take effect until an election of Representatives shall have intervened.

Index of Cases

General Index

Page numbers in italics indicate illustrations.

commerce power, 42

common law: legitimacy of, 52; "state of war" in, 230

Confederates, as nongovernmental belligerents, 228

Congress: attitudes of regarding military interventions, 226; of 1861, enabling legislation enacted by, 231; increased powers of, 159–60; intent of, 255; lawmaking power of, 124; legal significance of inaction by, 268–69; powers of to approve military commissions, 83–84; reporting to, 271; in wartime, 40

conscription, 41

conspiracy, status of as violation, 333

Constitution: acts of war in, 228; ambiguity of treaty provisions in, 156; disputes about reinterpretation of, 4; external application of, 339; flexibility of, 126; function versus process in, 28–29; "gloss" on, 97, 125, 135; grants of presidential power in, 56, 57–59; interpretation of, xvii-xviii; lack of theory in, 34; literary theory of, 33, 34; mixed, 11; modes of analysis of, xvii, 21–22, 29. *See also* individual Articles

constitution, British, 13

Constitutional Convention, 25–26; on war power, 193–94

constitutional law, role of, xvi

Continental Congress, 150

Continuing Appropriations Act for Fiscal Year 1974, 261

contracts, international, 178

Convention on Human Rights, 158–59

Coolidge, Calvin, 220

Cooper-Church Amendment, 256–57

Corwin, Edward S., 35, 39–43, 147, 181, 236

Coudert, Frederic R., Jr., 238

counsel, right to, 306, 312, 320, 339

court stripping, in First Reconstruction Act of 1867, 86

covert action, 288–95; administrative law restraints on, 301; ambiguity of prohibitions of, 298–99; backhanded authorization for, 298, 302; Congres-

sional delegation as legal justification for, 296–97; and constitutional democracy, 302; criminal law and, 299–300; legal justifications for, 295–302

criminal procedure: legality of criminal sentences in, 328; racial discrimination in, 117

Cuba: Bay of Pigs invasion of, 291; blockade of, 239–240; missile launch site in, *239*

Cuban missile crisis: as preemptive action, 284–85; resolution of, 240

curfew, Japanese, 113–14

Debs, Eugene V., 92–93

Declaration of Rights of 1689, 6–7, 52

declaration-of-war clause: purpose of, 253; use of as requirement, 330

Defense Appropriations Act of 1970, 256

Defense Intelligence Agency, 288

Defense Procurement Authorization Act of 1972, 257, 261

deployment of forces: post-World War II, 238; provocative, 238–40

"destroyers-for-bases" executive agreement, 180–82, 234

Detainee Treatment Act of 2005 (DTA), 331–32, 335; procedures under, 335–36, 340–41; "scope of review" provision in, 340

detainee, territorial jurisdiction over, 326–27

detention: indefinite, 282, 310; secret executive program of, 143; standards for, 140–46

DeWitt, John L., 109, *110*

dicta, defined, 49

dictatorship, constitutional: legitimacy of, 137; right to terminate, 138; standards for, 136–38, 139–40

Diem, Ngo Dinh, 292

dignity, maintaining posture of, 227

dispensation power, 7

Dominican Republic, American military government in, 218

Douglas, Paul H., 227, 237

Douglas, William O., 125–26

Lewis, Sinclair, *It Can't Happen Here*, 47

limited government. *See* government

limited powers, implications of New Deal on, 39–40

Lincoln, Abraham, *64*, 69, 75, 78, 205–206; as constitutional dictator, 137, 140; on inherent power, 296; opposition of to Mexican War, 260; "The Preservation of the Union," 64–65; "On Suspension of the Writ of Habeas Corpus," 66–67; view of war powers of, 228–29; as wartime president, 40–41

Lindh, John Walker, 305–306, 318

Litvinov Assignment, 177–78, 179

Locke, John, *8*, 48, 64, 296; "Of Prerogative," 49–52; *The Separation of Powers*, 7–10

Lodge, Henry Cabot, 165

"loss of authority clock," 275–76

Louisiana Purchase: constitutionality of, 60–62; as unilateral presidential initiative, 61

Lowi, Theodore, 39

McCord, James, 291

Machiavelli, Niccolò, 103

McKinley, William, 184, 214, *215*, 221

Madison, James, 54, *58*, 164, 167, 176; *Federalist No. 45*, 315; *Federalist No. 51*, 3, 20–21, 313; *Helvidius, Letter No. 1*, 57–60, 194–95; at Constitutional convention, 25, 26, 27; on separation of powers, 11

Magna Carta, 4–5, *5*, 34, 324

magnitude of potential harm test, 285–86

Mansfield Amendment, to Defense Procurement Authorization Act, 257, 261

Mardian, Robert, 47

Marshall, John, xvii, xviii, 94, 134, 147, 151–52, 295–96, 323

martial law: and civil liberty, 80–83, 84–85; in Hawaii after Pearl Harbor, 119, 120–21; modified, 76; proper, 84, 85

Mathias, Charles McC., 146

Mayaguez Incident, 270, *270*

Merrick, William Matthew, 86

Mexican War, 204–206, *205*

Mexico: Pershing expedition to, 219, *220*; Veracruz expedition in, 218–19

Middle East Resolution, 1957, 244

military action, new forms of, 281–88

Military Commanders Act (MCA)

military commissions: in Articles of War, 104–105, 106, 107; in Civil War, 79; Congressional power to create, 107; creation of, 305, 306

Military Commissions Act, 306, 307

military force, uses of without approval of Congress, 296

military jurisdiction, types of, 84

military necessity, absence of, 333

military police actions: to achieve diplomatic and economic objectives, 210–27; Jefferson on, 210; against pirates or savages, 209–10

military tribunals, 328, 331–42; common law, 323; in Hawaii, 119, 121; historical use of, 332; preconditions for, 333; procedures governing, 333–34

Miller, Arthur S., "*The Rise of the Positive State*," 34–39

Miller, Arthur H., 190

"minimalists," judicial, xix

"mission creep," 278–80

Missouri Compromise, 65

Monroe, James, 41, 201, 202

Monroe Doctrine, 203; Roosevelt corollary to, 216–17; used as international police power, 216, 217

Montesquieu, Baron de, *The Spirit of the Laws*, 9–10, 14, 19–20, 26

Moore, John Bassett, on war and peace, 226

Morris, Gouverneur, 48

Morris, Robert, 24, 48

Mossadegh, Mohammed, overthrow of, 290

Mukasey, Michael B., 319–20

murder, state versus federal jurisdiction over, 91–92

Murphy, Frank, 321–33

mutual defense agreement, 183

Mutual Defense Treaty 1954, 168, 169

mutual participation test, 250–55

Photo Credits

Page Source

5 Cassell, *History of England* (1902)
8 Library of Congress, LC-USZ62-20180
12 Library of Congress, LC-USZ62-45327
15 Library of Congress, LC-USZ62-20180
31 Library of Congress, LC-USZ62-132907
53 Sir Edward Coke from the frontispiece of his *First Institutes*, 4th ed., 1639, courtesy of Daniel Coquillette. James I from Library of Congress, LC-USZ62-51173
55 Library of Congress, LC-USZ62-48610
58 Library of Congress, LC-USZ62-106865
61 Library of Congress, LC-USZ62-53985
64 Library of Congress, LC-USZ62-11896
68 Library of Congress, LC-USZ61-800
70 Library of Congress, LC-USZ62-105141
71 Library of Congress, LC-USZ62-87317
73 Library of Congress, LC-USZ62-13037
93 *Harper's Weekly*, 1894
110 Japanese family, Library of Congress, LC-USZ62-129841. Inset Department of Defense.
150 Department of Defense, USAF.
181 Department of Defense.
198 Department of the Navy.
199 Department of the Navy.
205 George Wilkins Kendall & Carl Nebel: *The War between the United States and Mexico Illustrated*, 1851. Lithograph by Adolphe Bayot after a drawing by Carl Nebel.
213 Library of Congress: left LC-USZC4-10386, right LC-USZC4-1274.
215 *Harper's Monthly*, 1900.
219 U.S. Naval Historical Center.
220 U.S. Army.
235 Department of Defense.
239 U.S. Air Force.
241 Department of Defense.
243 Photo by Adam Jones, adamjones.freeservers.com.
247 Department of Defense.
270 U.S. Air Force.
272 U.S. Navy.
283 Department of Defense.
286 U.S. Navy.

Page	Source
304	Department of Defense.
305	Department of Defense.
321	U.S. Archive, ARC Identifier: 292616
332	Associated Press, photo by Kevin P. Casey
336	ABC News.